John Foster Dulles

John Foster Dulles

The Road to Power

Ronald W. Pruessen

THE FREE PRESS
A Division of Macmillan Publishing Co., Inc.
NEW YORK

Collier Macmillan Publishers
LONDON

Copyright © 1982 by The Free Press
A Division of Macmillan Publishing Co., Inc.

The Free Press
A Division of Macmillan Publishing Co., Inc.
866 Third Avenue, New York, N. Y. 10022

Collier Macmillan Canada, Inc.

Library of Congress Catalog Card Number: 81–69264

Printed in the United States of America

printing number

1 2 3 4 5 6 7 8 9 10

Library of Congress Cataloging in Publication Data

Pruessen, Ronald W.
  John Foster Dulles: the road to power.

  Bibliography: p.
  Includes index.
  1. Dulles, John Foster, 1888–1959. 2. Statesmen--
United States--Biography. I. Title.
E748.D868P78   973.921′092′4 [B]   81–69264
ISBN 0–02–925460–4 (v. 1)   AACR2

Excerpts from the papers of John Foster Dulles are published with the permission of the Princeton
University Library and the John Foster Dulles Committee.

Pages 153–163 and 175: Excerpts from John Foster Dulles, "The Road to Peace," *Atlantic Monthly*, 156
(October 1935). Reprinted by permission of The Atlantic Monthly Company.

Pages 157, 159, 161–162, 171, and 175: Excerpts from John Foster Dulles, *War, Peace and Change*.
Copyright 1939 by Harper & Row, Publishers, Inc. Reprinted by permission of the publisher.

For Alice

Contents

Acknowledgments

I owe many debts of gratitude to those who offered help during the research and writing of this book; some of these I have already thanked personally. Some deserve special mention. My warm thanks:

To what seems like an endless number of librarians in many places, most particularly those in the Manuscripts Division of the Princeton University Library for years of help with the John Foster Dulles Papers;

To the John Foster Dulles Committee for permission to quote from materials in the John Foster Dulles Papers;

To the Canada Council and the Humanities and Social Sciences Research Committee at the University of Toronto, for the financial support needed to visit important manuscript collections;

To several historians who have made advice and assistance available so regularly: Thomas C. Cochran, whose kind concern for former graduate students goes on as long as his distinguished career; Walter LaFeber, whose interest and expertise he is so willing to have tapped; and, most of all, Gabriel Kolko, who has offered a model of a humane and engaged scholarly career to many who have worked with him;

· To my colleagues Bruce White, Claire La Vigna, Bill Berman and Ken McNaught, for creating a congenial, supportive, and stimulating environment at the University of Toronto: I have worked where those qualities did not exist and have deep appreciation for them now;

To Charlie Smith at The Free Press, for endless understanding; to Laura Wolff at the The Free Press, for valued suggestions;

To Sam Lieberstein, a friend whose great reservoirs of humor and ideas have meant so much for so long;

To Linda, Michael, and Caroline, for slowing me down, but keeping me going: a contradiction I would not have understood before you were all here, but which I love living with now;

And most of all to Alice, for the typing that was helpful . . . and for the patience and love that were essential.

Introduction

It's not just what we inherit from our fathers and mothers that lives on in us, but all kinds of old dead doctrines and opinions and beliefs. They're not alive in us, but they hang on all the same and we can't get rid of them. I only pick up a newspaper. It's as if I could see the ghosts slipping between the lines. They must be haunting the whole country. So many, thick, they're like grains of sand.

—Henrik Ibsen, *Ghosts*

Mrs. Alving's words seem appropriate as the mind jumps from the 1980s back to the days of John Foster Dulles. Born-again Jimmy Carter's emphasis on "morality" in foreign policy, so easily edging over into self-righteousness or so blandly ignored when other interests called; Ronald Reagan's strident, simplistic rhetoric about the Soviet menace, weighted down with the melodrama of B-westerns: they are not unlike ghosts slipping between the lines of recent newspapers. Dulles has long had a notorious reputation in some quarters as the Cold Warrior *par excellence*, as a strikingly clear embodiment of some of the worst characteristics of modern American diplomacy. Are we not seeing fresh, blatant reminders of the kind of thoughts and actions for which he is often remembered?

But the Dulles reputation presents a formidable problem to the historian or biographer: How much should its sharply etched components be allowed to predetermine evolving analysis? I should be frank and admit that when I began studying the man I thought I already knew him. I had heard or read both his defenders and critics and had long be-

fore found the latter more convincing. I was a faithful fan of Herblock car-
toons and relished moments of Mort Sahl one-liners. (Was it Sahl who
commented on the Secretary's love of traveling and pact-negotiating by
saying that "Dulles flies now and we pay later?") What I expected to accomplish in my research and writing was to fill in the details of a rough
sketch of Dulles as a rabid and unbalanced anticommunist, a megaloma-
niacal Presbyterian preacher, a viciously partisan Republican, and a Mc-
Carthyite pushover.

It has turned out differently in the end. What I found in Dulles as my
research progressed was a man who barely touched any of the bases I had
laid out for him, certainly not in the order I had laid them out. Nor did my
evolving understanding of Dulles coincide with the man described in
previous work by historians, political scientists, and journalists. Where
some have written about a Secretary of State who was intellectually narrow and pompously crude, I found and have written about a man who
combined certain narrow interests with considerable intelligence and
shrewdness. Where some have described an unbalanced idealist with his
head in the clouds, I have described a frequently devout pragmatist with a
fundamental concern for the condition of the American economy. Where
some have focused on deep religiosity, even fanaticism, I have pointed to a
selective Presbyterian piety that always involved cognizance of the
materialistic side of the Calvinist coin. Where some have condemned the
ideologue that Dulles could be, I have cited the Dulles who knew the uses
of ideology and melodramatic rhetoric. Where some have praised his anticommunist services to the nation, I have suggested that those services
were often built on simplistic assumptions and tended to feed an already
hyperactive sense of "manifest destiny" among his countrymen. The John
Foster Dulles who finally took form for me is a complex amalgam, many of
whose characteristics have not really been understood before. Some of
those characteristics may seem contradictory in their complexity, but I
hope to show the way in which they were all expressions of Dulles's ultimately human nature.

My altered portrait of John Foster Dulles emerges more than anything
else from a careful examination of his *entire* life. Other biographers and ap-
praisers have chosen to concentrate almost all of their attention on the
events of the 1950s, in which Dulles often played a dramatic role. While
those events do provide the ultimate measure of his significance in twenti-
eth-century international affairs, they do not seem to me to be the logical
point of departure. Dulles was, after all, sixty-four years old when Dwight
Eisenhower appointed him secretary of state. Sixty-four years old. He
would spend less than 10 percent of his life as the primary formulator of

American foreign policy—after having spent 90 percent of it in many other roles. It seems undeniable to me that the *patterns* of his personality, activity, and thought were set long before 1953. The way he saw the world, in particular—the kinds of problems he identified and the kinds of concerns that led him to identify them—had been shaped by a lifetime of experiences. To study those experiences promises both a deeper understanding of Dulles and a broader perspective on the 1950s that will not be predetermined by conventional approaches, which essentially ignore the man's own history.

This volume, therefore, follows the road Dulles traveled from 1888 to 1952. It focuses on the many things he did during his long life, the many things he thought, and the order of his doing and thinking. It delineates the process of Dulles's development over time, the way layer upon layer of experience produced the individual who became Secretary of State.

Among the elements of Dulles's life that helped shaped what he brought to foreign policy making after 1953, I have been most interested in examining the following:

1. His family background, early home life, and education
2. His career as a lawyer and businessman between 1911 and 1949
3. His early experiences with government and foreign policy during World War I
4. His formal political associations and activities
5. His religious traditions and activities
6. His role in foreign policy deliberations during the Truman administration

It deserves mention at the outset that Dulles's career as a lawyer was particularly important to me in providing insight into his evolving thoughts and actions. Diplomacy was an avocation for Dulles, I would argue now, whereas law was an almost lifelong vocation. Foreign policy making was something of great interest and attraction, but his extensive personal involvement came only late in life. Until well into his fifties, it was lawyer's work that filled the great majority of his days. Most significantly, Dulles was a lawyer of a particular sort—a member and long-time senior partner in the Wall Street firm of Sullivan & Cromwell, a specialist in corporate, banking, and government clients interested in the international economy. Day-to-day work for such clients, spread out over forty years, strongly affected his perspective on international affairs and helped shape the frame of reference from which he operated long before and while he was Secretary of State. It helped develop a particular interest in the commercial and financial facets of international relations and a particular attentiveness to what he thought were the economic imperatives of American foreign policy. A strong economic strain has not usually been associated with Dulles, but I think a study of his life as a whole necessitates placing it alongside images of ideological impulses, religious proclivities, and vigorous partisanship. Indeed, I hope to show that economic preoccupations were often a dominant and initiating force in his world view and thought.

The John Foster Dulles who reached the apex of his career and the end of his life in the 1950s seems to me now to be a figure of great significance for anyone interested in understanding modern American foreign policy —before, during, and after the "Cold War." In an obvious sense, he was a participant in important events at a number of stages in his life. He was involved in economic and reparations negotiations at the Paris Peace Conference of 1919; he was active in the major international expansion of American business and banking which took place during the 1920s; he was a key figure in Republican Party politics after 1940; he was an important foreign policy adviser for the Truman administration, an integral participant in deliberations on matters as diverse as the United Nations, the Marshall Plan, and the Japanese Peace Treaty; and he was, of course, Secretary of State from 1953 to 1959.

In another sense, Dulles's importance transcends particular events and policy developments. He is to me a quintessential figure in American foreign affairs. His life and career offer evidence in microcosm of many of the economic, political, ideological, psychological, and religious currents that have shaped the United States's relations with the rest of the world throughout this century. His reactions to those currents—the way he personally understood them, the way he ranked them as to priority, the way he integrated them into a complex of concerns and motivations—offer insights into the foreign policy making of both his predecessors and successors.

John Foster Dulles

1
Roots, 1888–1911

The end is the beginning.

—Samuel Beckett

DECEMBER 1952. Victorious Dwight Eisenhower had kept his campaign pledge to go to Korea and was on a leisurely journey home. At Wake Island, he boarded the U.S.S. *Helena* for a three-day cruise to Hawaii, in the company of some of the major figures of his embryonic administration. Secretary of Defense-designate Charles Wilson was among those in the group, as were George Humphrey, headed for the Treasury Department, and Admiral Arthur Radford, soon to be Chairman of the Joint Chiefs of Staff. John Foster Dulles was also on board.

Eisenhower's public relations team billed the cruise as a "mid-Pacific conference" on combatting communism. More to the point, it was designed to combat the President-Elect's relative ignorance of key men he would be working with so shortly. None of the appointees were old friends of Eisenhower's, and he was anxious to assess in his own mind the nature of the men who had been so frequently recommended to him.

In all cases but one, Eisenhower quickly developed friendly relationships on board the *Helena*. With Wilson, Humphrey, and Radford, camaradarie seemed to come easy. Hours were wiled away in leisurely talk

1

and drinking. But not with Foster Dulles. The man who would soon be Secretary of State proved to be something of a loner during the three days at sea. Witnesses claim he was ill at ease in the company of his future colleagues and particularly ill at ease with Eisenhower. He also talked too much—and too pedantically. One of those present has described the boredom evident in Eisenhower's "all-too-expressive face" as he listened to Dulles "expanding at philosophic length upon his estimate of the Communist challenge, or responding at legalistic length to a specific question. . . ." [1]

It was a strange beginning for the Dulles–Eisenhower working relationship. One wonders what the new President and the others thought of Dulles at that point. Just what kind of a man did they see when they looked at him? Did Eisenhower, perhaps, think he had made a mistake? If, as some have suggested, he had thought of other men for State before settling on Dulles, did he think of them again? Dulles's relationship with Eisenhower would improve greatly—becoming more solid than any of the others, in fact—but at that stage, the President-Elect must have been uncomfortably unsure as he tried to take the measure of the man.

Decades later, it is still not easy to take the measure of the man. It is simply not possible to jump to conclusions about John Foster Dulles, to take some characteristic blatantly obvious to the public, for example, and deduce the whole of his nature from it. Dulles, though hardly unique, had a complexity as a policy maker and as an individual that defies simple categorization. The patterns of his life and character were intricate ones. To those who worked with him, like Eisenhower, they became apparent and intelligible only slowly. To those who now wish to understand him, the patterns emerge no more swiftly.

One advantage available to the biographer of today, and not to the men who met Dulles on board the *Helena* or at other points during the 1950s, is that it is possible to begin at the beginning in trying to take the measure of the man. His early life experiences can be examined as the first stage in a life process that produced the Secretary of State of mid-century, that produced the thought and behavior patterns of that Secretary of State. A study of Dulles really makes sense, in fact, only if it does approach his life as a process—and only if it deals with that process in its sequential entirety, first step to last, root to branch.

I

Dulles's roots seem deceptively simple at first glance. Born on February 25, 1888, he was the first son of the Reverend Allen Macy Dulles and

Edith Foster Dulles of Watertown, New York. At the time of their son's birth, the Dulleses had just moved to their upstate New York home in order to assume pastoral duties at the First Presbyterian Church. They remained for seventeen years, until after their son had gone off to college.[2]

Thinking of a Watertown parsonage in the late nineteenth century conjures up strong images of what the lifestyle and environment might have been like for the young John Foster Dulles. Something of a combination of small-town, almost rural, experience and pervasive religiosity comes to mind—and there are enough snatches of information to suggest that such images are apt, at least in part.

There does seem to have been an old-fashioned charm to life in Watertown before the turn of the century. The Dulles family quickly grew into a large one, John Foster, or Foster as he was called, being followed by three sisters and a brother. Their home was a big white clapboard house, and it was always remembered as the center of a joyful childhood. In winter there was skating and snowhouses and tobogganing down the backyard slopes. Spring brought bicycle riding, boating, and fishing; fall, nutting and hiking and camping. During the summers, life became idyllic as the family moved to a house in nearby Henderson Harbor, on the shores of Lake Ontario.

Foster is said to have been a vigorous and adventurous boy who thrived in this environment. He loved to explore the area around Watertown and early took to extending his curiosity out into the waters of Lake Ontario, sailing along the coastline and stopping off on small islands. He became an expert fisher and swimmer. One of his favorite pastimes was adding to a prized collection of birds' eggs: a story that became a family staple recounted his assault on a nest high in a maple tree behind the house at Henderson harbor and his descent with a crow's egg in his mouth.[3]

Surrounding these childhood pleasures for the Dulles children was a compelling religious atmosphere. For generations their father's family had been involved in church service. Ancestors included a number of ministers and several missionaries to outposts such as India and Ceylon.[4] The Reverend Dulles of Watertown maintained earlier traditions, with the result that religion was taken very seriously as a part of everyday life in his household.

Foster himself never recorded memories of the religious facts of his childhood, but his sisters have. Margaret, for example, has recalled a typical Sunday in the Dulles home:

> Of course, we all went to church, we all went to Sunday School, and then we had my mother—my father was too busy on Sundays—and my

3

mother carried on Bible studies with us in the afternoons, so that we really knew our Bibles. . . .

Our Sundays were quite strict, but they were very happy days . . . every Sunday morning, as our family grew up, we five children led by my mother, walked sedately up the church aisle, and took our places in the next to the front pew. And each of us was equipped—this was my father's idea—each of us was equipped with pencil and notebook. We were to take notes on the sermon. . . . And then at Sunday dinner our notes were brought forth, and we discussed the sermon. . . .

On other days, the routine was not quite as rigorous, but similar. Weekdays always began with cold baths. The call to breakfast consisted of hymn playing on the piano by Mrs. Dulles; after prayers, everyone would eat. At Henderson Harbor, the family would gather on the porch at eight o'clock on most mornings to sing hymns and read from the Bible, using selections from a book compiled by Reverend Dulles's father and circulated among soldiers during the Civil War.[5]

In such a household, Foster Dulles felt the impact of religion at an early age. There are shreds of information in a brittle-paged album that Edith Dulles kept about her first son's early years. In its pages, she wrote of her two year old's concern for the "blessing" at meals and the morning prayers, the way he "always says Amen very heartily." She wrote too, of the four year old who was going to church and Sunday School regularly, and behaving so well; of the five year old who had such a "lovely devotional spirit"; of the seven year old who had learned seven psalms and a long list of hymns by heart.[6]

On the basis of recollections, at least, it deserves mention that the pervasive religiosity of childhood in Watertown does not seem to have been a strain on any of the Dulles children. As Margaret put it, Sundays were "strict" but "happy"—"I don't recall that I dreaded them." Eleanor, likewise, has described the religious atmosphere of home as "congenial and natural."[7]

But John Foster Dulles' life was not the simple tale of the upstate preacher's son who eventually went to the big city to make his career and fame. There was much more in his childhood and family than glimpses of idyllic adventures and religious routines would suggest, and the something more was of great importance to Dulles's evolution into adulthood.

Most important in contributing to the complexity of Dulles's childhood is the fact that Allen Macy Dulles was simply not a typical small-town parson and Edith Foster Dulles was not a typical small-town parson's wife. The Reverend Dulles came from a relatively comfortable old American family. There had been Dulleses involved in the early history of South Carolina and Dulleses who had fought in the Revolution. By the nineteenth century, there was enough money to provide Allen Macy Dulles with an education that included Princeton and postgraduate studies at Leipsig and Göttigen. His first meeting with his future wife, in fact, took place in Paris while he was returning to the United States from a trip to the Middle East. Education and early travels left a permanent mark. All through his years as a minister in Detroit and Watertown, Allen Dulles combined a considerable aptitude for languages and intellectual pursuits with normal pastoral duties. His expertise was demonstrated in a number of writings and eventually acknowledged by his peers. In 1904, the same year his eldest son went off to college, Reverend Dulles was invited to fill the Chair of Theism and Apologetics at the Theological Seminary in nearby Auburn, New York. While there, he wrote a widely read book entitled *The True Church,* which helped win him a reputation as a "liberal" within the Presbyterian establishment.[8]

In addition to these somewhat special characteristics of his father's, John Foster Dulles's mother also brought to the family environment something not completely in keeping with the Watertown atmosphere. She was the daughter of John Watson Foster, after whom she named her first son. During the child's early life, this grandfather lived in Washington, D.C., and although hundreds of miles from the Dulles home, his influence was in many ways as substantial as that of the parents.

When his grandson was born, John Watson Foster was only a few years away from becoming one of Benjamin Harrison's Secretaries of State. A newspaper editor in Indiana, Foster rose to prominence in the Republican Party after helping to swing his state behind General Grant in the election of 1872. The plum bestowed for his efforts was the post of United States Minister to Mexico, which he was to hold for seven years. It was the beginning of a long and highly successful diplomatic career. In 1880, he served briefly as Minister to Russia; in 1883, he was appointed Minister to Spain. After Harrison's election in 1888, Foster came to Washington to participate in negotiations on reciprocity treaties and replaced James Blaine as Secretary of State in early 1892. For Grover Cleveland, he went on to participate in negotiations over Canadian questions with Great Britain; for William McKinley, who wanted to appoint him Ambassador to Spain in 1897, he worked on Bering Sea problems; and for Theodore Roosevelt, he became a general adviser to the State Department on Canadian affairs and an expert on the Alaskan boundary dispute.[9]

Of particular interest when compared to his grandson's future, Foster also built another and simultaneous career for himself outside the world of international diplomacy. When Cleveland brought the Democrats victory in 1884, Foster feared that he would be forced to return to Indiana and pick up the threads of his earlier life. He hesitated and decided on a new course instead. He worked out a plan "of attempting to build up a practice in international law in the National Capital, making available the experience I had acquired and the acquaintance I had made abroad." Urged on by friends, he definitely decided to pursue this goal after a friend told him of a brief visit he had paid to his hometown in Indiana: "During the visit he went into the court, where he found some of his former associates at the bar earnestly engaged before the judge in contesting the ownership of a hog! He congratulated himself that when he retired from Congress he had located in Washington where large interests are involved in litigation and great questions discussed."

To such "large interests" Foster turned his attention. He built up a substantial law practice in Washington and managed to keep his diplomatic career afloat at the same time. He was counsel to both the Mexican and Chinese legations in the United States, and his ties with them remained close for many years. In 1894, after leaving the State Departments he was appointed by the Chinese government to assist in the negotiations of a peace treaty following the Sino-Japanese War. (Years later, his grandson would hang on a wall of his study a painting showing Foster with the Chinese and Japanese representatives who signed the Treaty of Shimonoseki.) Other clients over the years included the government of Chile and numerous American banks and corporations with interests abroad.[10]

It was from this background that John Foster Dulles's mother emerged. By the time Edith Foster met her future husband in Paris, she had had what one of her daughters casually referred to as "an international upbringing." In an autobiography printed for her family late in her life, Dulles's mother gave ample testimony to this fact. She had been ten years old when her father was appointed to his post in Mexico, and her adolescent years there left her with deep memories of an exotic lifestyle. At seventeen, her family's travels to Russia included a grand tour that took them across Europe. The new minister's daughter made her "debut" in St. Petersburg, and the glittering highlife of this capital impressed her enormously. Her autobiography speaks lovingly of ice-skating and troika parties and is replete with chatty details of Russian and foreign nobility. At one point, she recounts a party given by a Prince Oldenberg:

> It was said that three thousand invitations were issued, but however many there may have been, the palace was so large that there was no crowd. . . . The display of jewels was bewildering. The rooms seemed endless. Ices, teas and cakes were passed all the time. There was a buffet for

gentlemen and one for ladies, a dining room for members of the royal family, another for members of the diplomatic corps. It was a dazzling spectacle, uniforms, evening gowns, priceless jewels, all in a magnificent setting.[11]

When Edith Foster moved first to Detroit and then to Watertown with her young husband, she may have left a dazzling and elegant lifestyle behind, but its impress on her personality and outlook always remained. For the rest of her life, she brought to her family an intense interest in the world outside her small-town home and a great love of traveling. She significantly reinforced her husband's inclination to broaden their children's vistas, and between them they imparted truly worldly perspectives to Foster and his brother and sisters. They created in their parsonage what must have been a stimulating atmosphere. In addition to their religious instruction, for example, the children were encouraged to read widely in literature. (A favorite family tale tells of an elaborate production of *The Merchant of Venice* that the children put on in the dining room— young Foster played Shylock!) Some of the children, including Foster, attended a small private school in Watertown because the parents did not believe that the public schools alone offered enough intellectual excitement. Each of the children, including all three sisters, eventually attended college.[12]

Further, Allen and Edith Dulles took as many opportunities as availed themselves for family visits to Europe. Aside from what they viewed as the general benefits of travel experience, they both seemed anxious to pass on their own considerable language abilities. In 1903 and 1904, for example, Edith singlehandedly took Foster and Margaret off for a year on the Continent. After a tour of Italy, they settled down for a long stay in Lausanne—not in a hotel, but in residence with a Swiss painter and his wife in order that the children could develop some expertise in French. Allen Dulles joined them for a while at the end of this year's stay, and he and his eldest son went off alone on a mountain climbing expedition in Zermatt and a bicycle jaunt across southern France before stopovers in London and Paris.[13]

John Watson Foster further enriched his grandchildren's lives. If he had remained aloof in Washington, his influence on them would have been indirectly exercised through their mother. As it turned out, he never remained in the background. Edith Dulles's album about her son's childhood, for example, notes that he was born not in Watertown but in his grandfather's house on I Street in Washington. Edith had gone to her parents' home to await the birth of her first child; the baby arrived during the famous blizzard of '88, and mother and child did not travel home to upstate New York until three months later. This initial experience in

Washington is perfectly symbolic of many later ones, for during their early lives, the Dulles children were to spend months and seasons at a time in their grandparents' home. Foster's official and private work, with his resulting status and circle of friends in the capital, were all to influence the lives of his young grandchildren.

If nothing else, the children were much excited by Washington. The Fosters moved in the most prestigious political and diplomatic circles, and their grandchildren were fascinated observers of the capital scene. The Mexican and Chinese Ambassadors were neighbors and frequent visitors, among many others. Eleanor Dulles has written of that time and place:

> The large, four-story red-brick house, which my grandfather built, had plenty of room for living, working and entertaining. My grandmother, May Parke Foster, presided like a duchess over the tea table at five o'clock, as Senators, Justices, ambassadors, and State Department officials came in early, with plenty of time for a relaxed hour of conversation before a formal dinner. The reception rooms—the size of small ballrooms, as they seemed to us children,—were romantic with their tablets, screens, hangings and vases from the Far East and Europe.
>
> The women with their sequins and plumes and the men with their decorations and sashes were dashing and romantic. . . .

Nor were the children only observers. From a very early age, they themselves attended parties and dinners and met the glittering entourage that so often passed before them. At the age of four, for example, Foster Dulles attended the birthday party of five-year-old Benjamin Harrison McKee at the White House: a rather early first visit to the residence.[14]

Thanks to his grandfather's substantial influence, both direct and indirect, as well as the background from which his father emerged, John Foster Dulles's boyhood was simply not confined to the placid backwaters of upstate New York. There was a strong, almost rural coloration to part of his early years which indubitably left their mark on the growing child. He was always to remember small-town life with great fondness and all through his adult life would occasionally retreat to the pleasures of sailing and living off the shores and islands of Lake Ontario. There was, as well, a very fundamental religious character to his childhood which likewise held its influence over the years. Allen Macy and Edith Foster Dulles, intellectually oriented and worldly though they may have been, were deeply religious people who insisted on a rigorous training for their children. But, to these ingredients much more was added. Travels with his family and frequent stays in Washington broadened the outlook of the young John

Foster Dulles far beyond the horizons of Watertown. The capitals of Europe and the fashionable diplomatic, political and legal circles in which his grandfather moved gave him a taste of the world that very much helped determine the course of his life.

Dulles left Watertown in 1904 to attend Princeton University. The choice was predictable. His father had gone to Princeton and so had several uncles in earlier years. As his sister put it, "Princeton was just in the family blood."

At sixteen, Dulles was the youngest member of 1904's entering class, and he became its most successful. He joined the debating Whig Society and eventually won the Junior Debate Prize. He was fond of chess and became part of a circle of friends who often played. When invitations to the Prospect Avenue eating clubs were issued and some of these friends did not receive any, Dulles declined his and helped keep the group together. Aside from scholastic distinctions, his one great exploit as an undergraduate was not unlike his adventurous childhood expeditions for prized birds' eggs: After careful planning, he climbed the rainspouts of Nassau Hall one night and snatched the clapper from the bell in the tower.

Academically, Dulles accumulated solid achievements. As one of his friends put it, "Foster and I were 'polers'—quiet harmless folk who concentrated on studies." His undergraduate record was fairly routine and showed a concentration in philosophy. In particular, he seems to have undertaken extensive work with the university's renowned John Grier Hibben. As a junior, he was awarded the Dickinson Prize for the "best dissertation upon a theme in logic." In 1908, highest honors in the Department of Philosophy were bestowed. And, to cap his success, he was named valedictorian at graduation and awarded the Chancellor Green Fellowship in Mental Science.[15]

Philosophy may not have been Dulles's only significant interest at Princeton. Although his recollections might have owed something to hindsight exaggeration, he frequently pointed in his later life to early contacts with Woodrow Wilson. Wilson was president of the university during Dulles's years there, of course, but he continued to teach jurisprudence and constitutional government to juniors. Like many, Dulles was deeply impressed by his lectures and often demonstrated their impact on his own thinking in later years.[16] Dulles also found in Wilson reinforcement for the sense of social awareness and public service which he would probably have inherited in any event from his own family. As a mentor, Wilson made this an important part of his educational philosophy. "What

9

we seek in education," he once explained, "is a full liberation of the faculties, and the man who has not some surplus of thought and energy to expend outside the narrow circle of his own task and interest is a dwarfed, uneducated man."[17] Dulles went on to live the Wilsonian injunction; he even explicitly admitted at one later point in his life that "The major benefit I got from Princeton was participating in Woodrow Wilson's courses where I gained my interest in public affairs."[18]

Within the Dulles family, there seems to have been an unspoken assumption that Foster would enter the ministry and follow in his father's and ancestors' footsteps. Allen Macy Dulles's religious and intellectual concerns did appeal to his eldest son to some extent, as his undergraduate major in philosophy indicates. But, toward the end of his senior year, in the spring of 1908, he made a formal decision not to go that way. One of his sisters has recalled that while home from spring vacation, he broached the subject with the family. "I hope you will not be disappointed in me if I don't become a minister," he is pictured as saying. "But I've thought about it a great deal, and I think I could make a greater contribution as a Christian lawyer and a Christian layman than I would as a Christian minister." And that was that. His sister Eleanor has written that in talking about this decision, he emphasized to her that he simply did not feel that he could match his father's quality.

> He said he didn't think he was 'good enough'. He was not sure that he could serve in the same spirit as my father had. He questioned in his mind whether he could give his best service to a church in a small city, whether he had the deep devotion to the ideas that had been a part of his father's and mother's life and which had sent his grandfather as a missionary to India. . . .[19]

The decision to enter the law rather than the ministry could certainly not have been a mysterious one for the Dulles family. All of the children had been too close to their grandfather Foster and had seen too much of his world to have escaped his influence. His grandfather's profession hardly foreordained the patterns of Foster Dulles's life, but when those patterns displayed similarity to the older man's, it would have been obvious that his imprint had been felt.

It is even possible to speculate about a strong immediate influence by Foster on his grandson's career choice. In 1907, his many years of work for the Chinese government had resulted in his appointment as Chinese representative to the Second Hague Peace Conference. Preparing to go to Europe, he asked young Foster if he would be interested in taking time away from Princeton and attending the Conference as a secretary-clerk for the delegation. Dulles immediately accepted. Several times in later years, he recalled his experiences at the Hague with warm contentment. It became a glittering European hiatus in his college days, replete with a constant round of stellar diplomatic functions. On one occasion, he told the tale of his greatest exploit at the Conference—and told it with the relish of a man reliving a cherished experience. It seems that after all the delegates had converged on The Hague, they immediately ran afoul of a question of protocol. How were the more than two hundred men attending to be ranked? Who was to be granted the honor of receiving the first callers, and who was to be in the lesser position of doing the first calling? With some international ingenuity, a solution was discovered, and Dulles played a messenger's role in it:

> It was finally decided to cut the Gordian knot by fixing an appointed hour at which each person in attendance at the conference would arrange to have his cards left upon each other member of the conference. Accordingly, at four o'clock on a given afternoon, all of the secretaries, of which I was one, set out in automobiles loaded with about two hundred cards of each of the members of his delegation, which were then left at the hotels where the other members were residing. In this way the conference was able to get off to an orderly start and the world war was deferred for nearly seven years.[20]

How easily the young Princeton undergraduate's days at this international gathering may have served as a *coup de grâce* in his developing thoughts about a choice of career. Surrounded all his life by the worlds of the minister and the diplomat-lawyer, the young man's choice of direction for himself was almost certainly encouraged by his days at The Hague.

Of course, Dulles's career "choice" was not one which involved a total rejection of his father's model. As he himself apparently put it, he wanted to be "a Christian lawyer"—and in some respects that is what he became. To an extremely successful career as a corporation lawyer and a diplomat, Dulles did eventually add interest in church affairs and attention to certain religious ideas.[21]

Dulles's decision to become a lawyer was probably not hastily arrived at and neither was it hastily executed. Before entering law school, the twenty-year-old graduate decided to use a $600 award received at graduation to support a year of study in Europe. The entire Dulles family, as on earlier expeditions, accompanied him. They left New York in August 1908 and, after several months of traveling through the Continent, settled down in a large apartment on the Avenue de Breteuil in Paris. Dulles enrolled in courses at the Sorbonne that evidenced a continuation of somewhat divided loyalties. On the one hand, he attended the lectures of the noted Henri Bergson, whose writings on philosophy had already attracted him at Princeton. On the other, he began taking courses in international law—one of his notebooks from Paris is filled with scribbled French and English notes on international fishing rights. (Dulles allowed himself to participate in less formal aspects of the Sorbonne routine, as well. Several friends have recalled his regaling them with tales of participating in student riots! On one occasion, a massive demonstration was mounted against a scholar who had written a derogatory analysis of Joan of Arc. With a good deal of foresight, Dulles joined the mob, wearing a derby hat tightly stuffed with newspapers: it was perfect protection, he explained, against the truncheons of the Paris gendarmes.)[22]

After Paris and a few months in Madrid, where he picked up some working knowledge of Spanish, Dulles returned to the United States. In the fall of 1909, he went to live with his grandparents in Washington and enrolled at George Washington University Law School. For the next two years, he prepared to follow in his grandfather's footsteps and while doing so, came into constant contact with the Washington establishment he had observed so often before. His brief diaries and calendars indicate a constant round of socializing in the capital: debutante balls, dinners, and teas at the White House, even a number of engagements with President Taft's daughter Helen. He also came into more formal contact with Washington figures through part-time work at his grandfather's law offices. There are references in his calendars, for example, to legal work he was doing for the Mexican Embassy, to calling on President Taft in the company of Senator Gamble, and to contacts with Robert Orr at the State Department.

Neither his social activities r or extracurricular work interfered with Dulles's academic progress. In fact, within two years, rather than the normal three, he had completed his course work at George Washington University. During the spring of 1911, he studied for the New York Bar Examination while staying with his family in Auburn. Before summer had come, he had gone to Rochester and successfully weathered the test.[23]

That spring of 1911 also proved to be important for more than the passage of the bar exams. In Paris two years earlier, the Dulleses had seen a good deal of the Averys, another visiting American family from upstate New York. Back at home to study, Foster saw them regularly again and an infatuation with Janet, one of the daughters, grew quickly. On the very day of his bar examination, he returned from Rochester unexpectedly early and asked her to go canoeing. When they returned, both families were apparently amazed to find that he had proposed to her and that she had accepted. They were married a year later.[24]

1911 was the year of independence for John Foster Dulles. Twenty-three years old, he found himself with a law degree in hand and a fiancée waiting. The years of childhood and formal education had come to an end.

There had been a variety of forces at work on him in those early years. The small-town setting of his pre-college days; the religious concerns and activities of his parents and home; the intellectual stimulation of education and wide travel; the insights into law and diplomacy and politics through grandfather Foster: Each contributed something to the process of maturation and each would likewise remain at the base of diverse facets of Dulles's adult personality and thought. The combinations may seem incongruous at times, but they were certainly present. On one occasion, for example, Dulles's sister Eleanor recalled a familiar scene from childhood that captures well the flavor of those years. She was writing of summer evenings at Henderson Harbor when the children had to take turns playing backgammon with their aging grandmother. The game was played indoors, by the light, and the children apparently longed to move out into the cool night air instead. As Eleanor wrote, it was "pleasanter to be with the larger group on the porch over the lake, talking of fishing and of foreign affairs and watching the western sky dim as Orion and the Dipper came up, often mirrored in the dark blue waters."[25]

2

Wall Street and Washington, 1911–1918

WITH PRINCETON, the Sorbonne, and George Washington University behind him, John Foster Dulles went to New York in 1911 to build a career. He was a well-traveled and well-connected young man. He was intelligent, he was willing to work hard, and in relatively short order, success came.

The course of Dulles's early success says something about the nature of upward mobility in American business and government in the early twentieth century. More importantly here, it says something about Dulles's personal future. The activities of his first professional years—especially the loci of his work, on Wall Street and in Washington—established patterns that would repeat themselves continually in later years.

I

As successful as Dulles was shortly to be, there was a pause of uncertainty before potential became reality: Even while preparing for admission to the

New York Bar, he found himself awkwardly unable to find a job. With a record at George Washington that included the highest grades in the school's history, it must have seemed as if suitable employment would not be too serious a matter. For a while, it was. On his own, Dulles applied to a number of New York City law firms during the winter of 1910–1911 only to be turned down by all. "They said," one of his sisters has recalled, "they were only interested in the graduates from Harvard Law School."[1]

The shortcomings of a George Washington University degree were soon made up for by the influence of grandfather John Watson Foster. Still active in his own legal career, Foster took his grandson's career problem in hand in February 1911 and arranged for an interview with an old acquaintance in New York. Foster sent his grandson to see one of the partners in Sullivan & Cromwell in the hope of securing some "advice" and "information" concerning the New York scene. The advice became a junior clerk's position, with a salary of fifty dollars a month. This was a meager but standard beginning at this Wall Street firm—and it was, after all, a job.[2]

In reality, it was much more than just "a" job. By 1911, Sullivan & Cromwell could only be described as one of the most important law firms in the United States. The original Sullivan of the partnership had died in 1888 and the power of the firm had come to reside in William Nelson Cromwell. Born in Brooklyn in 1854, Cromwell had a shock of white hair and a prominent white mustache that gave him a striking physical resemblance to Mark Twain—and some of his exploits would have provided excellent grist for Twain's mill in *The Gilded Age.* Association with him was to permanently affect Dulles's career.

Cromwell was a legal genius. He combined a wide-ranging knowledge of the law with a shrewd business mind and placed himself close to major economic developments in the United States in the 1890s and early 1900s. Associated with giant corporations, he was particularly expert at reogranization, and his services were utilized by the Northern Pacific Railroad, the National Tube Company, and the United States Steel Company, among others. His talents won him the largest legal fees of his time.

Part of Cromwell's shrewdness, and an important source for his legal success, was to be found in his fundamental awareness of the political facets of business enterprise. Without friends and acquaintances in high places, he freely admitted, the businessman and lawyer lacked an indispensable resource. As he himself put it, "in the course of . . . more than 30 years, the firm of Sullivan & Cromwell had . . . come to know, and be in a position to influence, a considerable number of public men in political life, in financial circles, and on the press, and all these influences and relations were of great and sometimes decisive utility, and of valuable assistance . . . ."[3]

Perhaps the best example of Cromwell's political-business prowess was his work for the New Panama Canal Company between 1896 and 1903. This company had purchased the unused canal concession originally granted by the Colombian government to Ferdinand de Lesseps and hoped to reap a windfall profit by selling it in turn to the United States government. There was no question that Congress was inclined to construct a canal across Central America in the 1890s, but the Panamanian enthusiasts were worried because attention had been focused on a route through Nicaragua. To turn government interest to Panama, Cromwell was retained. He served his clients well and formulated what he himself called a "Napoleonic strategy." Of greatest importance were his extensive Washington contacts. He was able to call freely on major figures in the capital—Presidents McKinley and Roosevelt, Secretary of State John Hay, Secretary of War William Howard Taft, and Senators Mark Hanna, John Spooner, and A. S. Kittredge, among others. He also had listening posts and co-workers in both Colombia and Panama. Through his association with Senators Spooner and Hannah, and through large contributions to Republican campaign funds, Cromwell arranged for the introduction of an amendment to the Canal Bill that altered the route from Nicaragua to Panama. When Colombia proved difficult in succeeding negotiations, Cromwell's hand again became visible: Another of his clients, the Panama Railroad Company, was not uninvolved in the encouragement of a revolution in Panama. And through his friendly association with Secretary of State Hay, Cromwell received a friendly hearing for the exorbitant financial demands of the New Panama Canal Company. One journalist was distraught enough at the lawyer's role to describe him as "the man whose masterful mind, whetted on the grindstone of corporation cunning, conceived and carried out the rape of the Isthmus." While exaggerated, such a characterization hints at Cromwell's techniques. The full story is complicated and has been described extensively elsewhere, but the overall political and international setting, as well as the successful outcome, bear ample testimony to Cromwell's work.[4]

It was in William Nelson Cromwell's shadow that Dulles began his legal career in 1911. The great man may then have been barely aware of the junior clerk's existence (that would quickly change), but the impression on Dulles was enormous. In 1911, Sullivan & Cromwell was a firm close to the centers of business, finance, politics, and diplomacy in the United States and its attractions never wore thin for Dulles. For forty years, with only the briefest departures, he was to stay with the firm and build an enormously successful legal career of his own in its Wall Street offices. This was to be his real career, the one at which he spent most of his life, and it was to affect greatly almost everything else he ever did.

Work as a junior clerk in the bustling law firm brought little immediate pleasure or excitement. John Watson Foster wrote his grandson shortly after he had begun work in New York that "You must not allow yourself to tire of the drudgery of the office—that is what the new clerks have to go through I suppose." Dulles had just written him that he had "had another long day of it yesterday, working in the office till 11 p.m. on an interesting point in mortgage law," and it must have seemed that he was less than convinced of the joys of his labors. As consolation, his grandfather wrote that "You are evidently making yourself quite useful to the firm, and that is the important thing towards your success." Further, he said, he would be coming up to New York in October and would stop by at the firm and "say a good word of benefit for you."[5]

Dulles's own hard work and perhaps his grandfather's "good word" helped brighten the picture quickly. By November he was traveling to Ohio on business for the firm. In January 1912, he went further afield, to Canada and the British West Indies. He was acting as legal counsel for the New York Produce Exchange and was invesigating the likely effects on his client's business of a proposed British intercolonial preferential tariff plan.[6]

His trip to the West Indies was the beginning of several years of professional work by Dulles with clients commercially and financially interested in Central America and the Caribbean. He began to work as counsel to the Fiscal Agent of Panama, for example, undertaking part of the large legal representation of Panamanian interests that Cromwell had brought to the firm after the 1902 revolution. In addition, he became counsel to a group of French banks investing in and reorganizing Brazilian railways; the representative of a client involved in Peruvian mining; the representative of "large American financial interests" in Cuba, for whom he traveled to Havana; and legal counsel to a financial combination anxious to increase investments in Panama. His work in the Caribbean region was successful enough to bring him an offer of a new job from W. R. Grace & Co. in 1914, but he turned down the opportunity because it would have taken him out of law and put him too exclusively into a "business" position.[7]

The outbreak of war in 1914 added new geographical dimensions to Dulles's work. In April 1915, he made his first business trip to Europe. He stopped in Rotterdam where he arranged for the consignment of shipments from the American Cotton Oil Company, his client, to the Netherlands Oversea Trust. He then moved to London to prepare for similar consignments there as well as satisfactory war risk insurance. Finally he went to Paris to look into the sequestration of Mumm & Co. champagne and to consult with the French bankers involved in Brazilian railway investments. After returning home, his work for clients with European interests continued. Dulles began to handle the affairs of the American drug firm Merck & Co., for example, and was in regular contact with the State Department regarding difficulties concerning European shipments; he became associated with the Standard Paint Co. of New York and helped look after its plants and subsidiaries in Italy and Russia; and he also became associate counsel for French banks conducting war finance operations in the United States.[8] These early World War I legal activities were a foretaste of what was to become the dominant European focus of Dulles's legal career in later years.[9]

The benefits of hindsight make it clear that his early years at Sullivan & Cromwell were crucial in laying the foundation for the career that would absorb Dulles's time and interest for most of his life. This foundation had some clear identifying markings. It seemed, for example, to portend considerable professional success—given the quite rapid increase in the scope of Dulles's activities and the prominence of his clients. It also indicated that Dulles was part of a burgeoning community of Americans who had recognized the opportunities beckoning in the international economy. The United States had never been isolated from world commerce and finance, of course, having even in embryo been part of an enormous mercantilist empire. But the late nineteenth and early twentieth centuries witnessed a major expansion of global commercial and financial activism for Americans, an expansion encouraged by their own internal growth as well as the increasing integration of the international economy overseen by the British and others. A rising number of corporate and banking leaders, as well as a full complement of lawyers, decided it was neither desirable nor necessary for the United States to tend only its own garden. Buoyed by shimmering visions of cheaper raw materials, bottomless markets for exports and remunerative investment opportunities, they sallied forth. William Nelson Cromwell was one of them. Dulles's grandfather Foster was another—he who had rejected litigation over the ownership of Indiana hogs for more exciting tasks concerning money and goods in places like Mexico and China. His grandson, a relative latecomer to the ranks, followed in his path. His clients were sometimes involved in exotic fare, like French champagne and Brazilian railways, and sometimes in pedestrian, like cans of paint, but quite consistently, whatever their particular interests, they were part of global enterprise.

Such professional activities, for Dulles and many others, had important intellectual repercussions. From the ranks of such businessmen, bankers, and lawyers, for example, came many of the key "internationalists" in the United States—men whose day-to-day work encouraged a deep, abiding interest in world affairs and a concern for the role of their country in them. Dulles had already absorbed internationalism in childhood, almost by osmosis, but the early years of his career reinforced the inclination emphatically. He allowed his clients' interests to prod him, or at least accompany him, into other related activities. In late 1912, for example, he wrote a lengthy pamphlet on the Panama Canal (a logical subject for a Cromwell employee) and circulated it to every government official he could manage to reach. Perhaps benefiting from his grandfather's founding role in the American Society of International Law, he became involved in its work as well, as a speaker on Canal and general Latin American questions at annual meetings and as a writer for its *Journal of International Law.*[10]

In addition to a general internationalism, professional involvement in the world economy could also produce specific ideas and interests. Grandfather Foster had been a strong advocate of freer trade, for example, and had worked actively on the negotiation of reciprocal trade agreements in the Harrison administration.[11] Dulles inherited this concern for loosening up world trade. After returning from Europe in the summer of 1915, for example, he undertook extensive conversations with officials in Washington about the desirability of establishing an "American Trade Organization." The idea had emerged from conversations with the American ambassador at The Hague and reflected a belief that importers and exporters in the United States needed a forum for dealing with common problems. Dulles found little government support for the notion at that time and little interest on the part of businessmen who feared such an organization would involve giving up independence of action. Also at this time, he became a member of the Reform Club of New York, an organization whose work was concentrated in "tariff reform" and "other work, tending to the removal of restrictions of trade."[12] These early signs of interest in freer international trade would multiply manyfold in succeeding years.

II

The upward direction of Dulles's career within Sullivan & Cromwell was soon aided by the family ties he continued to find available after 1911. In family assistance, Dulles was twice blessed. He owed his first employment to the influence of his grandfather; he owed his first government employment to his uncle, who, when Dulles began work as a lawyer, was soon to bring a second Secretary of State into the family circle. This was Dulles's "Uncle Bert," Robert Lansing.

Lansing had been a neighbor of the Dulleses in upstate New York and had married Dulles's aunt, another daughter of John Watson Foster. The family tie eventually made Lansing something of a *deus ex machina* for his nephew. Even before becoming Secretary of State, Lansing tried to draw Dulles into government service. In 1913, while he was American head of the Arbitration Agency created to settle various claims between the United States and Great Britain, he offered Dulles a post as assistant counsel. Dulles declined the offer—because a senior partner told him it was too early in his career to get a temporary post in Washington—but he was happy to avail himself of Lansing's aid in other ways. While his uncle was counselor of the Department of State in 1914 and 1915, Dulles asked him for numerous small favors concerning the activities of Sullivan & Cromwell clients in Europe, Latin America, and China. In April 1915, he received personal letters of introduction for use during his first European business trip.[13] After Lansing became Secretary in June 1915, Dulles also arranged dinner meetings in New York at which prominent bankers and businessmen were able to meet his uncle.[14]

Lansing's appointment as Secretary of State was followed by closer contacts with his nephew. Within a year and a half, Dulles would actually be in Washington working for the Department of State—by then, it was apparently no longer too early for the young Sullivan & Cromwell attorney to gain some government experience.

Dulles's move to Washington was the end result of a gradual process that began with matter of course conversations at the State Department regarding Sullivan & Cromwell clients. Slowly, Dulles began to move beyond this routine and involve himself, if only slightly at first, in larger diplomatic questions. In June 1916, for example, Dulles heard from Emiliano Chamorro, a Nicaraguan he had come to know while representing British and American bankers in that country. Chamorro was then the Conservative Party candidate in a presidential election campaign and deeply worried about his inability to carry the field against the incumbent Diaz "dictatorship." To offset his handicap, Chamorro began painting himself as a sterling defender of American interests in Nicaragua and a worthy recipient of United States support in the election. As he put it to Dulles, "I needs must look to the State Department for a square deal in the election, and a word from it spoken in time in a clear and definitive way, I think would do. If you help to have that word said, I will be ever grateful to you."

Chamorro struck a responsive chord by contacting Dulles. "During the past few weeks I have frequently thought of your candidacy, and needless to say I welcome any opportunity to be of possible service to you and the cause which you represent," the young lawyer wrote. Noteworthy as "service" was Dulles's promise to see "Uncle Bert" within the week. Early in September, Chamorro happily notified Dulles that the American Minister had presented Diaz with a list of instructions concerning the approaching election—and in October, Dulles sent a congratulatory telegram following Chamorro's electoral victory.[15]

Of course, Dulles's influence on American policy toward the 1916 Nicaraguan election was probably minimal. Chamarro almost certainly owed his support from Washington more to wide-ranging contacts and the general State Department concern for American interests in Nicaragua than to the specific influence of the Secretary's nephew. What makes Dulles's plea for Chamorro important in the face of this, nevertheless, is the way it represented a broadening of perspective and activity on the part of the young lawyer: It was really more important to him than to Chamorro.

Dulles's further involvement in State Department activities came a few months after Chamorro's election. Spurred into action by business pressures, Dulles came close to playing a semi-official role at the behest of his uncle. It was February 1917. An election in Cuba several months earlier had resulted in a bitter dispute between an entrenched Conservative regime and a Liberal faction which felt it had been robbed of victory. When demands for investigations of returns were repeatedly ignored, various Liberal politicians led their followers in revolt. Acting on behalf of several clients who had investments in the island of more than $170 million, Sullivan & Cromwell became very concerned with these problems.[16]

Dulles was sent to Washington on February 13 "to secure such information in regard to conditions and the policy of this government as might be available." In addition he was to offer his services to the State Department. A senior partner in the firm had been contacted by Orestes Ferrara, speaker of the Cuban House of Representatives and a leader of the Liberal faction. Dulles was to consult with the Secretary of State and offer to use Sullivan & Cromwell's "good offices" to bring "to bear on Dr. Ferrara such influences as the Department of State might desire." This offer was accepted by Lansing, and Dulles proceeded to make several commutations back and forth between Washington and New York for the purpose of transmitting communications. The Liberals protested their good faith, indicating that they had no desire to take over the Cuban government by force and asking that the United States investigate the recent elections. The State Department, acting on instructions from President Wilson, refused to cooperate and decried the Liberal revolt as "lawless and unconstitutional."

In addition to his messenger's role in this imbroglio, Dulles did not forget his original purpose for going to Washington: to provide for the protection of American property endangered by the revolution. At one meeting with his uncle and the Latin American Bureau Chief, he "very strongly emphasized" the necessity of protection. The Bureau Chief promised to look into the possibility of sending a light cruiser to the northern Cuban coast. While breakfasting with Lansing the next morning, Dulles "suggested that the Navy Department send two fast destroyers—one for the Northern coast and one for the Southern coast of the portion of Cuba controlled by the revolutionaries." Lansing immediately conferred with Secretary of the Navy Josephus Daniels and that same afternoon, orders were sent for two destroyers to leave for Cuba.[17]

Barely a month after these Cuban developments, Lansing drew Dulles into formal State Department service. On March 28, 1917, as the United States and Germany were drawing closer to war, he asked his nephew to visit Central America. There was in Washington increasing concern for the protection of the Panama Canal and "It seemed . . . expedient," Lansing wrote later, "to send a special emissary on a secret mission to Panama to urge the principal officials of that government to declare war on Germany as soon as the American Congress acted." This mission soon broadened to include other stopovers throughout the area, for all of which Dulles's Sullivan & Cromwell experiences and contacts would be useful. As the secretary's nephew described the perceived purpose of his trip, he was being sent "on a confidential mission to Central America with a view to seeking to bring the Central American states into alignment with us against Germany . . . so that we could effectively protect the Panama Canal without infringing any neutral rights."[18]

Dulles's first stop was Nicaragua, where he re-encountered his friend, and now President, Emiliano Chamorro. In a report to Washington, he commented on the President's "strong sympathy" for the United States, especially noteworthy in the midst of rampant anti-American sentiment among the population as a whole. Chamorro gladly issued a proclamation suspending diplomatic relations between Nicaragua and Germany.

Going next to Costa Rica, Dulles found a delicate situation. A political leader named Tinoco had seized control of the government by force and was considered "unscrupulous" in Washington. Dulles argued that difficulties with Germany made it necessary to tone down American hostility toward Tinoco and urged that he be formally recognized. Recognition would cement the dictator's loyalty and provide "in Costa Rica a Government and people with more sincere friendliness to us than any other Central American state."

Dulles's last stop was Panama, where he found conditions generally troublesome. An election campaign was in progress, and the American emissary felt that victory for either candidate would result in "continued misgovernment by corrupt cliques with resulting financial crisis, possible civil disorder and certain unsatisfactory relations with the United States." Seeking a safer path through this far from encouraging situation, he began meeting with many of the "better class of business and professional men in Panama." If American diplomatic and canal officials would indicate their interest, Dulles found, this "better element in Panama" would be willing to put forth a third and more attractive political candidate. He personally urged such support as a way of avoiding difficulties with Panama at an uncomfortable time.[19]

Although Dulles was officially working for the Department of State on this Central American jaunt, it is interesting to note that he found it convenient for certain business purposes as well. In Costa Rica, for example, he studied the foreign indebtedness of the government on behalf of British and French bondholders. In Nicaragua, he acted as an intermediary between the Chamorro government, the Department of State, and British and American creditors, who included the Seligman Bank, in order to work out a plan for refunding Nicaragua's foreign debt in a way that would allow United States government supervision. His conversations with Chamorro centered around the creation of an American-supervised National Bank and the intense opposition of a Liberal party anxious to "restrict American control in the country."[20]

III

By the time Dulles returned to Washington in late May 1917, the United States had entered the Great War. This did much to shape his subsequent course of action. What had begun as a temporary official association with the Wilson Administration soon evolved into an ongoing relationship, one that would last for two and a half years. Not until September 1919 did Dulles return to New York and Sullivan & Cromwell.

The reasons behind Dulles's decision to remain in Washington are not at all clear. His correspondence and personal records for 1917 are sparse and reveal little about his reactions to the international crises of those days. It is possible that the entrance of the United States into the war suggested major opportunities in government for the young lawyer. It is also possible that a sense of special duty was casting its spell. There are some tattered sheets of paper in his files, such as a handwritten draft of a statement written in August 1917, that suggests he had fallen under the sway of Woodrow Wilson's dramatic leadership. Giving no indication of the reason behind his effort, Dulles wrote that "I believe it to be of the utmost importance that the nations at war with Germany should unite in a new statement of their purposes, which should be asserted to be the creation of a world of new international relationships." He referred specifically but only briefly to the Fourteen Points and other statements on war aims and said that they had "been magnificently formulated" by the President—they offered precisely what was needed to make the allied war effort take on "the character of an idealistic crusade."[21] Dulles himself certainly seemed anxious to join in a crusade under the leadership of his former Princeton mentor.

His first Washington post was as "Special Counsel in Regard to Central American Affairs" at the Department of State. It is hard to tell what his duties actually were. The only evidence of his activity available in State Department records is a memorandum he wrote of a conversation with a National City Bank representative concerning the purchase of Haitian bonds.[22] Late in the summer of 1917 he applied for admission to Officers Training School, but was rejected because of poor eyesight. He enlisted in the Army in September anyway and was commissioned a Captain in the Signal Officers Reserve Corps. He was immediately drawn into Military Intelligence and, undoubtedly because of his experience, became head of the Economic Section of the Positive Military Intelligence General Staff. This work lasted for no more than a few months. By January 1919, he was ordered to begin discussions with civilian authorities at the War Trade Board: On March 12, the Secretary of War appointed him official liaison between the War Department and that agency. In July, he became assistant to Vance McCormick, the Chairman of the War Trade Board.[23] This upward mobility in the military and at the War Trade Board seems to have been the result of several mutually reinforcing factors: awareness of Dulles's previous experience with financial and commercial matters at a prestigious law firm, day-to-day recognition of his basic abilities, and a dollop of appreciation for the fact that he was the nephew of the Secretary of State.

Created on October 12, 1917, the War Trade Board was composed of representatives of the Secretaries of State, Treasury, Agriculture, and Commerce and was instructed to administer controls over commerce provided for in the "trading with the enemy" acts. Supervising the conduct of American trade so as to prevent any benefits to Germany was a responsibility that could not be divorced from military activities, and this was where Dulles came into the picture. His role as liaison between the Board and the War Department was to provide compatability of aims and methods. As he put it, "My duty was to ensure coordination between the Blockade and Economic Plans of the War Trade Board and the Military Plans of the General Staff."[24] This "duty" eventually involved him in a wide range of commercial problems.

Primary among Dulles's responsibilities at the War Trade Board was the handling of negotiations with neutral European states, designed to insure the effectiveness of the Allied blockade of the Central Powers. As Vance McCormick summarized these negotiations:

> The important object which the United States and the Allied Governments had in mind in placing the embargo on exports to the border neutrals and in negotiating agreements with them was the restriction or prohibition of exports from these countries to Germany of essential war materials, including foodstuffs and military supplies.

Dulles became involved in lengthy negotiations with Denmark, Switzerland, the Netherlands, and Spain. With Spain, for example, the Board used Washington's ability to control cotton and petroleum exports to pressure Madrid into trade agreements concerning the exclusive provision of mules, horses, and minerals to the Allies.

Coping with the shipping of vital commodities was another concern of the War Trade Board that involved Dulles. He participated in lengthy and hostile negotiations with representatives of the Netherlands, hoping to secure the use of Dutch shipping facilities for Belgian relief supplies and food shipments to Switzerland. Under pressure from the Germans, the Dutch were afraid to agree. In a statement drafted by Dulles, President Wilson announced on March 21, 1918, that the United States was simply requisitioning all Dutch ships then in American waters. Simpler negotiations were also held with Denmark at this time: an offer of raw materials persuaded the Danes to provide shipping facilities solely for the Allies.[25]

Dulles's months on the War Trade Board also involved him in some work very different from that concerning relations with neutrals, work that would have some interesting long-range implications for him. From early 1918 on, the Board was drawn into the extensive Washington deliberations over what to do about the revolution and civil war in Russia.

Initial reaction to the March 1917 revolution had been very positive in the Wilson Administration. Perceiving liberal democratic characteristics in the Kerensky government, the President was enthusiastic about the prospects for friendship and pleased at the way in which the political changes in Russia had improved the image of the anti-totalitarian forces struggling with Germany. But the Bolsheviks who rose in October and November were another matter. After a brief period of confusion and evaluation, it became clear that Washington was vehemently opposed to what the President called "the poison of Bolshevism."[26]

The War Trade Board became involved in policy debates on the Bolsheviks in the spring of 1918. To some extent, its connection with the blockade of the Central Powers was responsible for this: part of the Allies' great concern for Russia's continued role in the war against Germany was a disquietude concerning a possible breach in the blockade that might be opened through Eastern Europe. Other factors were involved as well. Cyrus McCormick, the giant of the agricultural machinery industry in the United States, was a relative of the War Trade Board's chairman. In the years before the 1917 revolution, Cyrus and his business associates had become deeply involved in industry and investment in Russia; they had grand visions of the potential for future economic involvement there. Following the emergence of the Bolsheviks, McCormick and representatives of New York banking interests made regular efforts to influence evolving American policy. Vance McCormick became a contact and an advocate in their behalf. On May 21, 1918, he appointed a three-man committee to study Russian-American economic relations. His order demonstrated that both business and wartime exigencies were involved. On one hand, the committee was instructed to devise means "to create in Russia conditions so that the blockade of the Central Powers which the War Trade Board is enforcing by commercial agreements with western European neutrals will in Russia also be maintained." On the other hand, it was also charged with studying "methods by means of which exports from this country may safely be made to Russia and imports from Russia of articles needed by us may be provided for."[27]

Vance McCormick's appointment of this committee is relevant here because John Foster Dulles became one of its three members. In view of Dulles's intense feelings toward communism and the Soviet Union, it is interesting to note how early in his life he came into contact with the Russian problem. More immediately, his membership on this committee became an important component of his labors at the War Trade Board.

At first, the thrust of the work being done by the committee on which Dulles served was unclear. By May 1918, there was still no indication of the precise form Washington's opposition to Bolshevism was likely to take and War Trade Board members mirrored this ambiguity. On June 5, for example, the three-man committee merely issued a report calling for the appointment of a "Russian Commissioner" who would "take charge" of all economic matters involving Russia.[28] Within weeks, however, as the Wilson Administration's policy became sharper, so did the War Trade Board's. It was in late May that Czechoslovak forces traveling east across Russia to Siberia (in order to board ships at Vladivostok that would carry them to the western front in Europe) clashed with Bolshevik authorities. As the Czechs began cooperating with anti-Bolshevik Russians in Siberia, they received official encouragement and support from the Allied governments. To the British, French, and Japanese—and very shortly to the Americans—the Czechs and their Russian associates provided a perfect medium for action against the dreaded Bolsheviks. By July, elaborate plans had been drawn up which brought Allied and American forces to Siberia to support the anti-Bolshevik campaign; concomitantly, the anti-German coalition also began military operations at Murmansk and Archangel on the Baltic.[29]

In the midst of these June and July 1918 maneuvers, Dulles's committee began recommending steps that reflected the inclinations of the Administration. One proposal called for sending a War Trade Board representative from Vladivostok into the Siberian interior in order to discover the economic needs of the Czechs and their Russian supporters. It was assumed that items like clothing and small tools were vitally needed, but that a random shipment might bring goods into the wrong hands. Once needs were known, licenses for export from the United States would be issued and delivery allowed "in Siberia only to those designated by War Trade representatives."[30] By the fall, these proposals were deemed inadequate by Dulles's committee. Unsettled conditions made private traders reluctant to get involved in the area, and fewer rather than more goods would likely be sent if Washington did not step in. On October 5, it was suggested that the President "appropriate out of the funds at your disposal $5,000,000 to be utilized by the War Trade Board or such other agency as you may select, in supplementing such shipments as the War Trade Board may license private traders to make. . . ." Wilson gave his approval. A public announcement was made concerning the creation of the "Russian Bureau, Incorporated," a company whose capital stock of $5,000,000 was totally owned by the United States government. The company would export agricultural implements, railroad supplies, and clothing to Russia, in return for raw materials. The announcement was signed by Vance McCormick as the Bureau's President and John Foster Dulles as its Secretary and Treasurer.[31] At about the same time, discussions were also begun about what was becoming a confusing currency situation in Siberia: the

President was urged, and agreed, to allow the War Trade Board to try to deal with the problem through consultations with Great Britain, France, and Japan.

By the time Dulles became an officer of the Russian Bureau, he had less than a month of service remaining on the War Trade Board. But the work of the Russian Bureau went on, serving as one arm of the Wilson Administration's policy to bring about the demise of the Bolshevik movement and encouraging American economic penetration of Siberia. Within days of its organization, for example, the Bureau appointed the International Harvester agent in Vladivostok as one of its representatives and he in turn invited the National City Bank to open an office in that city.[32] While John Foster Dulles did not intensively interest himself in such later undertakings, he was to remain involved to some extent well after his departure from the War Trade Board.[33] The fact that he was so involved in any initial deliberations on policy toward Bolshevism and Siberia is important in itself: It serves as a fascinating early chapter in a long history.

When Dulles left his post as Vance McCormick's Assistant at the War Trade Board in December 1918, he did not return to Wall Street. As he had found himself involved in waging the war from Washington, so he was shortly to find himself active in shaping the war's settlement at the Paris Peace Conference.

Even before setting sail for Europe at the end of the Great War, Dulles had fashioned a career for himself that tells much about his later life. His early professional experiences in New York and Washington actually reveal in microcosm the pattern of his future. His grandfather Foster before him had enjoyed a successful diplomatic career in the nineteenth century and had then built upon it a lucrative international law practice. Dulles reversed his grandfather's timing, but was faithful to the components of the pattern. At Sullivan & Cromwell, before World War I, he began moving toward a successful corporate law practice with decidedly international overtones. In Washington, during World War I, thanks most clearly to the help of Robert Lansing, Dulles began his first real involvement in international affairs and the shaping of foreign policy. His scope and his success, both as a lawyer and a policy maker, were decidedly limited by the end of 1918—but substantial strides were not far away.

3

Dulles and the Paris Peace Conference, 1919

IT TAKES CAREFUL LOOKING to find John Foster Dulles in the official photographs of the American delegation to the Paris Peace Conference. His young face, with its wire-rimmed glasses, is tucked away in a rear corner, barely noticeable to eyes caught by the larger figures of President Wilson and the senior advisers in the foreground. But Dulles was not as unobtrusive in 1919 as the group portraits might suggest. He played a quite important role in the U.S. delegation's efforts to deal with one of the most important issues which emerged at the peace conference. He performed a number of crucial, rarely noted chores and became a respected colleague. In the process, he learned lessons and absorbed ideas which were long to play a role in his own life and thought.

I

Dulles's route to Paris was one made possible by confusions in the preparation of intelligence and research facilities for the United States delegation.

During the war, a number of agencies had grown up in Washington which were eventually to vie with each other for the honor of transferring their services to Paris. Working with Vance McCormick, for example, Dulles had had regular access to the War Trade Board's Bureau of Research. By late 1918, this bureau had been coupled with similar service facilities at the Shipping Board, the War Industries Board, and the Department of Labor to create a new Central Bureau of Planning and Statistics. Accepting the advice of its head, Edwin F. Gay, President Wilson designated the Central Bureau "as the official source through which shall be obtained economic data required by the American delegates at the Peace Conference."[1] Rivaling the Central Bureau in its desire to undertake work in Paris, however, was the famous "Inquiry." This body of experts, brought together by Colonel House, had worked all through the war to compile shelves of studies on economic, territorial, and political problems that were expected to arise during the peace negotiations. By late 1918, with the cooperation of State and War Department officials, Inquiry members had already crossed the Atlantic and were busily establishing headquarters in France.[2]

To avoid hopeless confusion and redundancy of function, Gay sent John Foster Dulles to consult with members of the Inquiry. The young lawyer was instructed to arrange for a single centralized intelligence apparatus by the time the American delegation arrived in Europe. Gay had been shrewd in sending the Secretary of State's nephew to do his negotiating, and Dulles, in turn, proved an adept negotiator in this minor broil. Given a chilly reception, he soon prevailed on his opposite numbers to accept a simple combination of personnel that allowed all parties to protect their particular niches in the bureaucracy.[3] Of most importance here, Dulles quite consciously sought to create a position of potential for himself while negotiating a settlement of the interagency rivalries. Final details provided that he would remain outside actual technical research work, and he was dubbed instead "the recognized channel of communication" with Washington's Central Bureau. He was specifically delegated to work with the economic advisers on the American delegation and to coordinate their needs with the work of the intelligence sector. This was to prove most advantageous, as Dulles himself admitted: "The practical working out of the foregoing plan is, as I anticipated, that through my personal contact with [Vance] McCormick, [Bernard] Baruch, [Norman] Davis, and [Gordon] Auchincloss and Secretary Lansing, I am posted as to the actual status of economic questions and in practical effect arrange for the work of the Economic Section with whom I meet every few days . . . ."[4]

Dulles's early contact with the American delegation's economic advisers became the foundation of an important role at the Peace Conference, for the issues they came to deal with proved of central importance. Barely had Colonel House arrived in Paris than he was predicting that "the finance and economic questions" inherent in making peace "would meet us at every turn."[5] His prophecy was quite accurate. Among the "questions" House referred to, reparations proved of greatest significance—and from his first days in Paris in January 1919 until the day of his departure eight months later, Dulles was involved with little but reparations.

Dulles first participated in the internal deliberations of the delegation. Writing position papers and taking part in meetings, he participated in the early hammering out of the American position. Then, on January 25, the Council of Ten approved the establishment of a Commission on the Reparation of Damage to allow consultation on what was expected to be a troublesome matter. At its first meeting on February 3, the American representatives listed were Baruch, Davis, Lamont, and McCormick, with Dulles identified as "legal adviser" of this team. Through mid-April, at both plenary meetings of this body and meetings of its three subcommittees, he was frequently involved.[6]

In addition, Dulles also came to be centrally active in the meetings of allied "experts" that began on February 21. These informal and secret meetings among American, British, French, and Italian economic experts were authorized by President Wilson and Prime Ministers Clemenceau, Lloyd George, and Orlando after a few weeks of unproductive open committee meetings. The experts met almost daily until May 10, and their labors were eventually responsible for the actual reparation clauses in the peace treaty.[7]

Although a draft Peace Treaty was presented to the Germans on May 7, Dulles's work was far from finished at that time. A major portion of the German Counterproposals of late May were concerned with the reparations clauses, and several weeks of new wrangling among the Allied and Associated Powers ensued concerning possible changes in the treaty: Dulles continued to participate in the work of the economic advisers.[8] After this, he went on to two other chores as well. First, he became active in the early discussion of reparations and peace terms concerning the lesser enemies. Although the treaties with Austria, Hungary, Bulgaria, and Turkey had not been signed by the time Dulles returned to the United States, he participated in some of the most substantive negotiations concerning them.[9] Second, he became a member of several important post–Peace Conference organizations. He began working on the

Interim Reparation Commission, sat alongside Herbert Hoover on the Supreme Economic Council, and was the American representative on both the Committee on the Execution of the Treaty with Germany and a special committee on the Rhineland convention.[10]

Dulles's basic role as "legal adviser" to the American team working on reparations negotiations proved to be significant. Whether true as a general definition or not, the term as applied to him became a wide-ranging one, including the functions of frequent *spokesman*, occasional *negotiator*, and primary *draftsman*. As will be seen, each of these was to involve him in important aspects of the Peace Conference work. His negotiating and drafting, for example, led him to the heart of an issue as significant as the decision to include the "war guilt" clause in the final treaty draft. Dulles's numerous memoranda and drafts of treaty clauses even formed the basis for many discussions among reparations experts and in certain respects actually foretold the specific form of the reparations settlement.

Involvement with reparations put Dulles close to some of the most important and time-consuming work being done in Paris in 1919. As he himself put it, reparations "proved, perhaps, the most troublesome single problem of the Peace Conference." This judgment was echoed by virtually all participants, usually with unconditional emphasis: to Thomas Lamont, for example, reparations "caused more trouble, contention, hard feeling, and delay at the Peace Conference than any other point of the Treaty of Versailles."[11]

As Lamont's appraisal suggests, the reparations issue became so significant because of the sharpness of disagreement concerning it among the victors. As harsh as the lines may have been drawn between the United States and its European associates on many issues, nowhere were they drawn more harshly than here. Put baldly, the Allies—Great Britain and France primarily, but Italy, Serbia, and other states as well—demanded a full measure of reparation from Germany. The Great War's destruction had been immense, and it was reasoned very simply that it was only just for the defeated enemy to make proper recompense. As Premier of France, for example, George Clemenceau clearly lived up to his "Tiger" reputation on this matter. Ready at the drop of a hat to recall his youthful emotions during an earlier German assault on France, he shared fully the desires for *revanche* that touched many of his countrymen. And Lloyd George, while his personal vengefulness may have been less, was a shrewd politician who had just been through a troubling general election. British constituents had been whipped into a frenzy of expectation by pledges to squeeze Germany "until you can hear the pips squeek"—and George was not likely to forget those sentiments. As he said of the British voters after he arrived in Paris, "Heaven only knows what I would have had to promise them if the campaign had lasted a week longer."[12]

The United States, as the "Associate" of these Allies, assumed from the beginning a distinctly different stance. For reasons that will require examination, the American delegates in Paris rejected the demand for revenge by means of harsh economic punishment. It was vitally necessary, they argued at all times, that Germany and other defeated enemies be treated *moderately*, if not leniently. On the issue of reparations, particularly, the Americans maintained that a modest rather than a heavy financial obligation should be imposed—and that this would serve the best interests of the victors themselves.

As one specific issue after another was negotiated in the process of shaping the reparations clauses of the Peace Treaty, the distance separating the United States from its Allies became all too apparent. Because the Americans and the Europeans had different end objectives in mind, predictable clashes ensued on particular issues such as the inclusion of "war costs" in the total German obligation, the estimation of a "fixed sum" to be indicated in the peace treaty, the powers of the Reparation Commission, and so forth. It was during the working out of these clashes that Dulles played his role. President Wilson himself, of course, and Colonel House to some extent, were usually the ultimate arbiters of the American positions. But the substantive work on reparations, including virtually all of the intensive negotiations and drafting, was handled by Vance McCormick, Norman Davis, Bernard Baruch, and Thomas Lamont—and into this team of experts Dulles was quickly drawn.

The first major issue over which the victor's struggle concerning reparations was joined was the question of "war costs." Even before formal meetings of the Peace Conference were underway, American delegates knew that the British, French, and others would be demanding what were called "integral" reparations. By this term, the Allies meant that Germany would assume the financial burden of *all* the costs of the war: the expense of replacing all lost or damaged property, public or civilian, *and* the money expended by governments for arms, planes, ships, and supplies used in fighting the war.[13] The Americans were horrified at the thought of including all war costs in the German obligation because of their potential effect on the dimensions of the final settlement. Studies that Lloyd George had ordered, for example, brought the British delegation to Paris with a rough financial objective of about $90 billion; Clemenceau and the French were demanding $200 billion. The

Americans, on the other hand, were convinced that Germany could pay no more than $25 to $30 billion. The wide crevasse between such an estimate and the British-French figures was almost laughable. After first hearing of the Allied goals, Colonel House confided to his diary that "I thought the British were as crazy as the French but they seem only half as crazy which still leaves them a good heavy margin of lunacy."[14]

It was quickly realized that the Allies were very much in earnest, however, and instead of contemplating such follies, the Americans started working to defeat the campaign for "integral" reparations. The arena first chosen was the Commission on the Reparation of Damage, where the meetings began on February 3. There, the war costs issue became the first order of business.

The tack adopted by the United States was a legalistic one, and the delegation's "legal adviser" was given primary responsibility. At numerous early meetings, Dulles spoke at length and elaborated two reasons for opposition to war costs. First, he argued, there was no legal basis for making the demand: Neither the principles of international law nor traditional practice supported the demand for repayment of all of a government's wartime expenses. Second, and more important, Dulles maintained, the victors were simply not free to make such a demand in any event—for, in entering into the Pre-Armistice Agreement with Germany on November 5, 1918, the United States and the Allies had made a specific commitment on reparations. Part of the Pre-Armistice Agreement stated that the Allies "understand that compensation will be made by Germany for all damage done to the civilian population of the Allies and their property by the aggression of Germany by land, by sea and from the air." In his statement to the Commission, Dulles underlined the emphasis in these words on *civilian* population. The Pre-Armistice Agreement amounted to a "contract" with Germany, he argued.[15]

Dulles's reasoning certainly did not carry all before it. None of the Allies would accept the thrust of his argument, knowing full well the limits it would place on their demands, and debate in the Commission on the Reparation of Damage became bitter.[16] Despite the rancor, however, the United States substantially succeeded in getting its own way on the issue of war costs within a month. Dulles was very much involved. The earliest crack in the Allied wall of intransigence, for example, appeared when he made an insightful suggestion to the French reparations experts on February 14. Be wary of *le jeu des pourcentages*, the play of the percentages, he told them. On a number of occasions, the young lawyer used approximate figures of reparations demands to convince both France and Belgium that their *percentage share* of total reparations would be adversely affected by the inclusion of war costs. Great Britain and the United

States, he reasoned, had expended far greater sums on the actual fighting of the war than their continental allies and would, therefore, receive a larger portion of German reparations under such a scheme. France and Belgium, on the other hand, had had far greater damages in the "civilian" category and would receive the lion's share of money if the German obligation were restricted to that type of reparation. Specifically, Dulles suggested that, with a narrow definition, France would receive 43 percent of the total due from Germany and Belgium would receive 24 percent; with war costs included, France's share would be only 24 percent and Belgium's 1.7 percent. Further, if Germany's ability to pay in the future proved to be less than the Allies expected, such a percentage disadvantage could become an absolute one. Both French and Belgian delegates shortly began to succumb to the charms of this reasoning.[17]

The opening wedge thus cut into the Allies front was widened by a second force with which Dulles had no outstanding connection. During the third week in February, the American advisers as a group radioed a full report on the war costs debate to the President, then returning to the United States on the S.S. *George Washington*. Wilson's response was received in Paris on February 24: "I feel that we are bound in honor to decline to agree to the inclusion of war costs in the reparation demanded," the President declared. "We should dissent and dissent publicly if necessary."[18] When the force of these words was informally communicated to Lloyd George and Clemenceau, Wilson's firmness weakened further their attachment to war costs.

Even after the arrival of Wilson's cable, however, the Allies were not completely prepared to abandon their demand for war costs. If men like George and Clemenceau felt some inclination to follow the American lead at this point, and there is some indication that they did, both insisted that they could not forget their vociferous constituents. Clemenceau is reported to have grumbled that no matter how large a sum he was able to secure from Germany, the French people would demand twice as much and dub him a traitor in the bargain.[19]

One more American maneuver was required to provide the British and French with a remedy for such quandaries. Significantly, this maneuver was again the brainchild of the economic experts' young legal counsel. He moved this time behind the scenes of the Commission on the Reparation of Damage, working at the secret meetings of experts that had been approved by the Big Four leadership. During these private consultations, his role was played because of the success of an initial American gambit to seize the "drafting initiative." The Americans wanted to be the moving spirit in the meetings of experts and decided that one way to accomplish this was to put forth the first specific treaty clause proposals:

These would form the framework for debate and hopefully get discussions off on a determining right foot. This American strategy set the stage for an influential role by Dulles, because it was he who was charged by his colleagues with the job of writing draft reparation clauses. From February 21 through May 10, he was to be almost constantly involved in drafting and revising—and for the first month of meetings among the experts, his drafts did form the basis of discussion.[20]

On the subject of war costs, Dulles's major contribution came immediately in his first draft, circulated on February 21. His proposed treaty clauses were lengthy, involving technical provisions concerning the collection of reparations and a series of guarantees designed to insure collection. Included, as well, was a list of the categories of reparations upon which the Allies and the United States were in agreement, i.e., various types of "civilian" damage. The key section of this draft pertaining to the war costs debate came in its last paragraph, where Dulles attempted to devise a formula for dealing with reparation categories opposed by the United States. As a suggested text, he wrote:

> Certain of the governments at war with Germany, believing that it is just and within the contemplation of the principles agreed to as governing the peace settlement, that the German Government shall, in addition to the reparation above specified for, make reparation for the entire cost of the war to the governments with which Germany has been at war and the indirect damage flowing therefrom, in order that these nations should be put back in as nearly the same position as may be to the condition which they would have been in had war not occurred by the aggression of Germany, *the Government of Germany recognizes its liability in the premises. It is agreed, however, that the ability of the German Government and nation to make reparation is limited to such an extent as will render the making of such complete reparation impracticable, and accordingly, the governments at war with Germany renounce the right to insist upon reparation other than is expressly specified for herein.* [Emphasis added.][21]

What Dulles was attempting to devise, in short, was a formula that would meet the Allies halfway; a statement that *theoretically* Germany was liable for reparation of civilian damages and war costs, coupled with a proviso emphasizing the former enemy's limited resources and the resultant necessity of a lower *actual* liability. He was not enthusiastic about the proposal in the abstract, to say the least, but it seemed a necessary evil. As he quickly explained to other members of the American delegation, he was "not in favor of this scheme as an original proposition, but presented it as a possible way out of the present difficulty."[22] It might be mentioned that in the throes of devising a "scheme," Dulles and the Americans he worked with had no appreciation of some facets of the process they were beginning. For, to telescope briefly, the trend of thinking which Dulles initiated on February 21 was shortly to lead to the enunciation of the notorious "war guilt" clause.

Dulles's proposal was of interest to George, Clemenceau, and Orlando. With wary eyes focused on bitter voters and politicians at home, they began to weigh the psychological satisfaction that might be gained from a righteous pronouncement of Germany's full liability for the war's damages: it just might equal the pecuniary rewards of receiving reparations for war costs. But their interest did not immediately translate into acquiescence in the American scheme. For five weeks, in fact, the Americans and the Allies debated about the precise wording of the formula to be incorporated in the treaty. Dulles's many proposed drafts were always seen by the British and French as too mild, it being said that they concentrated too much on Germany's inability to pay and too little on a decisive statement of the victors' just rights to receive. Exasperated, George introduced a draft of his own to the Council of Four on May 29. Mentioning the enormous losses resulting from a war caused "by the aggression of the enemy states," he went on to enunciate "the indisputable claim of the Allies and Associated Governments to full compensation."[23]

While George's draft also included a disclaimer to full compensation on practical grounds, the starkness of his claim struck the Americans as disturbing, as too brazen a contradiction of the Pre-Armistice Agreement. As Dulles himself put it to the experts, "We do not desire to proclaim a right to recover war costs irrespective of agreed limitations . . . ."[24] To work toward a solution of the problem, the American experts offered yet another draft for discussion—one which proved ingenious enough to be successful. To keep away from the direct claim of Allied "right" to war costs, the Americans veered back to a more indirect statement of German "responsibility." And, to carry the obliqueness of the treaty clause yet a degree further, the concept of *causal* as well as *financial* resonsibility was introduced. The results were two sentences of enormous subsequent importance:

> 1. The Allied and Associated Governments affirm the responsibility of the enemy states for causing all the loss and damage to which the Allied and Associated Governments and their nationals have been subjected as consequence of the war imposed upon them by the aggression of the enemy states.
> 2. The Allies and Associated Governments recognize that the financial resources of the enemy states are not unlimited and . . . they judge that it will be impracticable for the enemy states to make complete reparation for all such loss and damage.[25]

For the Americans, this formula was still not ideally satisfactory. What it offered, however, was a psychological sop to the Allies which was oblique enough to avoid an unacceptable concentration on rights to specifically financial demands.

This new formula at last proved acceptable to the Allies. Although Dulles was to be involved in six more weeks of consultations concerning revisions, few alterations of any substance were made in these crucial opening sentences of the Treaty of Versailles' reparation clauses. When the German delegation was presented with a copy of the peace treaty in May, they saw almost exactly these words in Articles 231 and 232. The "war guilt" clause had been written, and the Americans, very much including John Foster Dulles, were its initial proponents.[26]

It is clear that after long and arduous negotiations, the United States emerged victorious from the debate over "war costs." It is also clear that Dulles played a significant role in forcing the exclusion of these from the total German obligation. Although the most junior of experts, the young legal counsel found himself playing the trump cards. The relevance of *le jeu des pourcentages* was first suggested by him and helped bring an initial softening in Allied firmness. And, more importantly, the concept of proclaiming Germany's responsibility for the war as a theoretical principle not only emerged in Dulles's first draft treaty clauses of February 21, but emerged specifically from his own thinking. The absence of either of Dulles's maneuvers might have led to a very different outcome in the debate.

Whatever comfort the American delegation may have taken in the victory over war costs was destined to be of short duration, however. Within a few days, a series of concessions to the Allies began which made it clear that the outcome of the war costs debate was to be the only real victory which the United States would win in the reparation negotiations. Not surprisingly, in view of his role to that point, Dulles was very much involved in the gradual debilitation of the American position.

Even while the controversy over integral reparations was raging, for example, a closely related issue was being dealt with that was to have a substantially different outcome. As part of their overall campaign to set moderate parameters to Germany's reparations, American negotiators had been urging the desirability of including in the peace treaty a specific and modest statement of the complete German debt. As an abstract possibility, the Allies were not opposed to the inclusion of a "fixed sum" in the final treaty—but, predictably, they seriously disagreed with specific figures proposed by the Americans.

Extensive efforts were made to resolve the fixed sum dilemma between late February and late March. Subcommittees of the Commission on the

Reparation of Damage struggled, but to no avail; the Council of Four and a specially created secret subcommittee of its own did likewise.[27] In the end, it fell to the secretly meeting experts to find a route through the impasse once more—and John Foster Dulles proved to be its discoverer.

In his first draft treaty clauses of February 21, Dulles proceeded from the assumption that continued stalemate on the fixed sum issue suggested that the simplest course would be to postpone consideration. The treaty, he proposed, should create a Claims Commission to accumulate claims for damage against Germany and a Finance Commission that would determine Germany's total obligation in accord with the Claims Commission findings. Both parties were specifically envisioned as post-Peace Conference agencies. These suggestions were really basic blueprints for the Reparation Commission established by the Treaty of Versailles.[28]

As with other Dulles proposals, this one did not take hold quickly. For more than a month following its presentation, U.S. and Allied negotiators worked to find a more positive solution. By the end of March, haggling over a fixed sum had finally brought exhaustion, and there was renewed attention to the concept of a post-Conference commission. Even though the Allies were then close to accepting the U.S. position on war costs, they were still not prepared to accept the fixed sum the Americans were concomitantly demanding. To Lloyd George or Clemenceau, concerned about angry and expectant constituents, it must have seemed that the inclusion in the treaty of a modest fixed sum would have robbed them of the psychological boons which the exchange of "war costs" for "war guilt" promised: the impact of that exchange in terms of pounds or francs would have been too noticeable. And so, on March 26, with the leadership taken by Clemenceau, the decision was made to rely on the work of a post-Conference commission for fixing the amount of Germany's obligation. As the French Premier put it, "I am impressed by the ingenuity of the plan for [a] permanent commission, as proposed by our financial delegates. It lets us act as circumstances require. . . . Impossible, in my view, to discover anything more flexible"[29]

The resort to a palliative concerning the amount of Germany's obligation was as much a compromise for the Americans as for the Allies. As such, it was the first of a long series of steps down from the early victory over war costs. From early April on, in fact, one defeat after another awaited the U.S. delegation as each additional facet of the reparation settlement came up for discussion.

At the end of March, for example, the British put forth a proposal that deeply disturbed American negotiators. On March 27, Lord Sumner recommended that Germany's obligation include the costs of Allied expenses for *pensions and separation allowances*. Fully supported by Lloyd George, the proposal was based on the argument that without such an inclusion, Great Britain's share of reparations would be smaller than was just.[30]

To a man, the Americans reacted strongly against the British proposal. President Wilson dismissed Sumner's reasoning as "very legalistic," and was inclined to ignore it altogether. Dulles, in turn, wrote a lengthy memorandum for the delegation on the proposal: treating it more seriously than the President, he reached the same negative conclusion. Dulles was particularly concerned about the "great pecuniary importance" of pensions and separation allowances in terms of the total of Germany's obligation, arguing that the figure eventually arrived at might be doubled. This sounded basically as bad as the inclusion of war costs, and it is not surprising that Dulles developed the same counterargument he had used on earlier occasions. The United States and the Allies had entered a contract with Germany on November 5, 1918, he maintained, and in no way was he able to see how pensions and separation allowances could be included in the terms of that contract. "If the Allies expected Germany to understand that she was to repay the costs of these items," he wrote, "I, personally, do not see how the Allies could have chosen words less apt to convey that meaning."[31]

Faced with this hostile reaction, George did not give up the effort to include pensions in the German obligation. Aware of a great respect President Wilson had for South Africa's General Jan Smuts, George convinced Smuts to write a memorandum defending this new British proposition.[32] The maneuver was a shrewd one. On April 1, the day after reading the paper, Wilson called a meeting of the reparations experts in the library of his residence on the Place des Etats-Unis. He declared that he had been "very much impressed" by Smuts' approach and was now inclined to go along with the British. He immediately heard a chorus of protests. Thomas Lamont, for example, told him that "we couldn't find a single lawyer in the American delegation that would give an opinion in favor of including pensions." Dulles was quiet until the end of the meeting, apparently hopeful that his superiors would be able to dissuade the President. Their failure, perhaps, led him to speak just before leaving. The young lawyer attempted to argue the logic of the decision with Wilson, questioning whether the United States would be able to oppose any broad reading of the Pre-Armistice Agreement if a concession were made on pensions. What was to stop the Allies from demanding more, even war costs, once this crack was made? "Logic! Logic!" Wilson lashed out, "I don't give a damn for logic. I am going to include pensions." At which point, Dulles and the other advisors saw fit to leave. The British had carried the day.[33]

Wilson's insistent reining in of his advisers on the question of pensions took place in early April. The final draft peace treaty was presented to the German delegation in early May. During the intervening month, any number of additional clashes concerning reparations took place between the United States and its Allies—with continually dismal results for the former. During the first half of April, for example, the American delegates suffered a double-barreled defeat on the related questions of a time limit for Germany's reparations payments and the powers of the future Reparation Commission. From the beginning, the Americans had argued that Germany could be expected to pay the victors for no more than twenty-five to thirty years. It was reasoned that to require payments any longer would involve major practical difficulties and would also dangerously inflate the total debt. Once the notion of a Reparation Commission had been agreed upon, the Americans began applying their time-limit rubric to it. As the Commission worked, they argued, it should assess Germany's obligation not on the basis of what it believed the enemy *should* pay as a just and abstract matter, but on the basis of what it *could* pay in the span of thirty years.[34]

It came as a shock to the Americans to find that the Allies would not accept the concept of a time limit *cum* absolute limit on the assessments of the Reparations Commission. As one observer put it, the Allies saw the Commission as no more than a "legal adding-machine," in that it would take the categories of damage agreed to at the Peace Conference, accumulate all claims pertaining to them and simply announce a total reparations figure at a later date. What power it might have was to be confined to the technical aspects of German payments, with primary regard to *modes* of payment, i.e., should they be in gold or marks or goods and services.[35]

Clemenceau and Lloyd George held out staunchly against the American reasoning concerning a time limit—and Wilson eventually bowed. Article 233 of the Treaty of Versailles did instruct a Reparations Commission to determine the total German obligation by 1921 and draw up a schedule of payments for thirty years; but, the Commission was also given the power to extend the period of payments beyond thirty years if the sums due were not discharged in that time. As Vance McCormick disgustedly put it, "In other words, everything will be paid, whatever the period necessary."[36]

Other disagreeable sessions among the experts and the Council of Four ensued as well. For example, how to pay for the army of occupation and the provision of food for Germany during the aftermath of the war became causes for wrangling.[37] A proposed special priority for Belgium concerning receipt of payments from the enemy and the powers of the Reparation Commission to issue bonds on the collateral of anticipated payments were others.[38] None of these matters were settled easily, but none caused quite the bitterness that emerged earlier within the victors' camp. Dulles's involvement with them was also limited, in comparison to his central role in deliberations concerning war costs, a fixed sum, and the pensions and separation allowances matters.

After May 7, however, stormy frontal clashes came once more. On that day, Germany's representatives received a draft peace treaty at the Trianon Palace Hotel in Versailles. First in a series of brief memoranda and then in a forty-thousand- word set of Counterproposals delivered on May 29, the Germans attempted to force changes in the treaty terms. More than one-fifth of the Counter Proposals dealt with reparations, and the German words immediately hit responsive chords among the victors—among the British to some extent, but primarily among Americans.[39]

One German complaint, for example, concerned the fear that various sections of the Peace Treaty would so strip Germany of productive resources and capital that payment of extensive reparations in the future could not possibly be expected. Norman Davis sympathized with the German concern and on June 1 wrote a memorandum for the American delegation urging steps to guarantee "a requisite working capital" for Germany in the postwar period. On the same day, Dulles wrote along similar lines, specifying the desirability of giving Germany a definite sum for the purchase of necessary food and raw materials and suggesting that a certain number of ships be left to the defeated enemy.[40] While Davis and Dulles had unanimous backing in American quarters, little was accomplished in talks with the Allies. When Dulles offered numerous draft replies concerning provision of ships, food, coal, and raw materials, all suggestions were met with imperious resistance. The reply sent to the Germans on June 16 contained only a general rubric that "the resumption of German industry is an interest" of the victors and that, therefore, "commercial facilities without which this resumption cannot take place" would not be withheld.[41]

The Americans fared better with efforts to soothe German fears in another respect. In their May 29 communication, the Germans had pointed to the alarming power of the Reparation Commission as too serious an intrusion on postwar sovereignty: it would have *greater rights in Germany than a German emperor has ever had,*" they argued. The Americans suggested that Germans were unrealistically frantic and needed a more careful explanation of Reparation Commission functions. Dulles was instructed to write such an explanation, and the Allies were persuaded to include it almost verbatim in their June 16 reply. Dulles tried to argue two points for the Germans: first, that the Commission was a necessity in view of the great complexity involved in reparations payments over many years, and second, that it was a necessity that would be of *benefit* to Germany. As he wrote, the Commission "is instructed to exercise its powers *constructively* to insure in the interest of all as early and as complete a discharge by Germany of her reparation obligations as is consistent with the due maintenance of the social, economic and financial structure of a Germany earnestly striving to exert her full power to repair the loss and damage she has caused."[42]

Finally, the Germans had also expressed great desire for the inclusion of a fixed sum in the peace treaty. In view of earlier American desires in this direction, it is not surprising that this was met with immediate enthusiastic support. Within two days of receiving the Counter Proposals, Thomas Lamont, Norman Davis, and Dulles had all written memoranda urging the importance of including a precise set figure in the treaty. At a June 3 delegation meeting, after the President had described reparation as "the biggest point" in the German complaints, unanimous agreement was heard along the same lines. Armed with draft texts, Wilson confronted his Council of Four colleagues—but as in the past, to no avail. Lloyd George pleaded primarily the pressures of time as an excuse—to set a fixed sum at this date, he argued, was "like asking a man in the maelstrom of Niagara to fix the price of a horse"—but it has usually been argued that ongoing domestic political pressures were still tying his hands on this issue. The French were similarly opposed. One friend of Dulles's on the French delegation explained that "Mr. Clemenceau wants to get over the crisis of public opinion until the Peace Treaty has been actually signed and the summer has gone. Then he will let his people into any figures that may be necessary in the early autumn." The most that could be gotten into the June 16 reply to the Germans was a vague offer to consider any plan for dealing with the specifics of reparations that Germany herself might put forward within a period of two months following the signature of the peace treaty.[43]

By the middle of June 1919, it was clear that the Americans had been far from successful in implementing their ideal plans for a reparation settlement with Germany. A major initial victory over "war costs" had been more than overpowered by a string of defeats concerning a fixed sum, the inclusion of pensions, a time limit, and the powers of the Reparation Commission. For good or for ill, John Foster Dulles had been intimately involved with the shaping of this settlement. As has been shown, he was usually close to the center of debate and discussion concerning reparations. He had come to Paris as a young intelligence officer and within weeks had been drawn into the small circle of economic and financial advisers that was to handle the most volatile issue of the Peace Conference. The records of the Paris meetings are replete with his many memoranda, his almost innumerable drafts of proposed and actual treaty clauses, his extensive statements in meetings both large and small, and his provocative and influential suggestions for dealing with particularly thorny problems. While it could never be said that Dulles was the great moving force in reparations negotiations, to be sure, especially in view of the end product that was the Treaty of Versailles, it would likewise be impossible to deny him recognition as an important figure on the scene.

II

Dulles's intensive involvement in reparations negotiations must have been personally satisfying. A young, moderately successful lawyer before going to Paris, a junior cog in the wartime Washington bureaucracy, he had become a respected "expert" and a counselor to a President and major diplomats. Dulles had not been a stranger to the world of diplomacy as a young man, to be sure; his family's lifestyle, thanks particularly to his grandfather's career, had given him many opportunities for observing world affairs at close quarters. But in 1919, Dulles was no longer simply observing—he had become himself a participant.

If Paris was satisfying, it also proved significant. Dulles's role at the Peace Conference was the culmination of two and a half years of government service that were to leave deep impressions. Perhaps most important in this respect is the way in which the work of 1919 provided a key intellectual experience for him. While not alone responsible, his role as legal adviser to the American reparation experts helped to develop certain patterns of thought that were long to remain part of him. By the time he returned to the United States, a Dulles world view—not really discernible before—had begun to take shape.

Like many at the Paris Peace Conference, Dulles got caught up in the heady experience of thinking about the future during what looked like a crucial moment in international affairs. With the bloodletting over, he and other policy makers envisioned a malleable world in need of reshaping. What kind of world would it be desirable to create? How should it be done? Dulles may have thought extensively about such questions before, but there is no real evidence of it until 1919.

His views on such matters, like those of some of his senior colleagues, evolved primarily in connection with his work on reparations. He and the Americans in general advocated a moderate reparations burden, with a fixed sum dischargeable in about twenty-five years, and they saw this as a fundamentally desirable goal. Their extensive arguments and negotiating efforts found them stating again and again the reasons behind their proposals and, as such, served as a revealing medium for the expression of core values and concerns.

In a most basic sense, the Americans opposed placing a heavy reparations burden on Germany because they feared this would threaten the economic and political stability of the world. Their anxiety in this respect was great and emerged from three overlapping concerns: a degree of altruistic interest in the fate of war-shattered Europeans; the conviction that an unstable, troubled postwar environment would find the Germans and other peoples rushing into the arms of "bolshevism"; and attentiveness to the quite traditional politico-economic relationship of the United States and Europe.[44]

Aside from the element of humanitarianism, which has often been commented on and which almost surely did play something of a reinforcing role in shaping U.S. inclinations, most scholarly attention in recent years has been paid to a powerful ideological thrust in American policy. Even before the end of the war, of course, Washington officials had demonstrated a clear distaste for the turmoil that had erupted in Russia. An initial enthusiasm by some for the March 1917 revolution had been transformed into deep suspicion and hostility toward the Bolshevik leaders who entered the scene later in the year. Within months, Wilson and Secretary of State Lansing were aiding and abetting a variety of international efforts to suppress the hated radicals of Petersburg and Moscow. From Siberia in the East to the Ukraine, Eastern Europe, and Archangel in the West, the United States and its Allies in the struggle against Germany found themselves devoting considerable attention, money, and manpower to a new "enemy."[45]

At the Paris Peace Conference, concern over the extent of Bolshevik power was great—some have written, indeed, that the spirit of Bolshevism haunted the meeting rooms in which the Allies were working. The minutes of the Council of Four, for example, are replete with accounts of wide-ranging discussions among the major political leaders concerning the Russian situation and its impact on European problems. There were detailed examinations of current military conditions; elaborate prognostications of the dangers of Bolshevik expansion in Hungary, Austria, and Germany; extended deliberations concerning the use of blockades and food supplies for the purpose of influencing various political and military situations. Each of the victors, in fact, went so far as to establish elaborate intelligence networks to keep themselves posted on the rapidly changing situation in Eastern and Central Europe. American military representatives, as well as subordinates of Director General of Relief Herbert Hoover, fed a steady stream of reports into United States headquarters in Paris; special fact-finding missions to particularly crucial areas were regularly organized as well.[46]

This preoccupation with the dangers of Bolshevism certainly affected the American approach to German negotiations. The President and his advisers came to argue that Germany must not be treated too harshly lest the Allies rob themselves of the fruits of victory by allowing the new Bolshevik enemy to make great inroads in Central Europe. Still in Washington, for example, on the brink of negotiating an armistice, Wilson gave voice to a gnawing concern: grappling with a natural desire for punishing the enemy, he tried to keep this feeling in check because "if we humiliate the German people and drive them too far, we shall destroy all form of government, and Bolshevism will take its place." Dulles's uncle, Robert Lansing, shared this view. In a prophetic letter to Elihu Root at just this time, he too struggled with German policy:

> . . . how far should we go in breaking down the present political organization of the Central Empires or by military operations render them utterly impotent? . . . *We have seen the hideous consequences of Bolshevik rule in Russia, and we know that the doctrine is spreading westward. The possibility of a proletariat despotism over Central Europe is terrible to contemplate* . . . The situation must be met. What is the best way? How does it affect our policy toward Germany? [Emphasis added.]

In answering his own questions, Lansing invariably emphasized the need to treat Germany moderately. "We must look to the future," he said, "even though we forget the immediate demands of justice. *Reprisals and reparations are all very well, but will they preserve society from anarchy and give to the world an enduring peace?*" (emphasis added).[47]

Once the Peace Conference was underway, American policy makers were not likely to forget the linkage between fears of Bolshevism and the determination of reparations. During one discussion in the Council of Four, for example, President Wilson attempted to explain a softening attitude toward Germany and revealed basic concerns most clearly: "We cannot expect as much from a disorganized and demoralized Germany as from the pre-War Germany, which might have taken pride in meeting our demands. *We owe it to the cause of world peace to save Germany from the temptation to abandon herself to Bolshevism*; we know too well the connection between the Bolshevik leaders and Germany"[48] (emphasis added).

In Paris, as in Washington, Wilson was hardly alone in citing the potential danger of strengthening Bolshevism by weakening Germany. Secretary of State Lansing, for example, gave eloquent testimony to the President's logic during an address in the French capital:

> East of the Rhine there are famine and idleness, want and misery. Political chaos and outlawry have supplanted the highly organized government of imperial Germany. Social order is breaking down under the bitterness of defeat and the hopelessness of the future. *Like the anarchy which for a year had made an inferno of Russia, the fires of terrorism are ablaze in the states of Germany. . . . It is no time to allow sentiments of vengeance and of hatred to stand in the way of checking the advance of this conflagration*, which will soon be at the German borders threatening other lands. We must change the conditions on which social unrest feeds and *strive to restore Germany to a normal though it be a weakened social order.* [Emphasis added.][49]

Up and down the ranks of the delegation, support could be found for this position of building a viable democratic government within a revived Germany. This was particularly true among the economic experts who handled the substantive negotiations of the reparations settlement. At all times, these experts were cognizant of the effect their work could have on the political and economic stability of Germany. In one of the first memoranda drawn up in Paris, for example, Paul Cravath explained his recommended policy of moderation by stating that "the Allies would not desire so to burden Germany with obligations as to force her people into revolution."[50]

As evident as is the United States' concern about spreading Bolshevism, however, it was only one part of a general American preoccupation with the stability of the international order. American policy, in fact, was almost bifurcated in this respect. It is arguable that a moderate treatment of the defeated enemy in 1919 would have been sought even if there had been no nightmares of Bolshevism. Even discounting the possibility of revolution in Central Europe, Germany's failure to restore itself to some semblance of its former stature could still have awful repurcussions on the commercial health of Europe and the rest of the world.

There is no question that key Americans at the Peace Conference viewed the restoration of normal economic and financial conditions on the world scene as a major goal. Colonel House, after a meeting with Tasker Bliss and Marshall Foch, confided to his diary that all three men had found themselves in agreement on the necessity of a speedy peace "so that the wheels of industry should be started in motion throughout the world." Even more emphatically, Secretary of State Lansing declared that *"To restore the peaceful intercourse between the belligerents, to open the long-*

closed channels of commerce, and to give to the war-stricken peoples of Europe
the opportunity to resume their normal industrial life seemed to me the first and
greatest task to be accomplished" (emphasis added).[51]

Further, United States policy makers had a clear appreciation of the importance of Germany to the restoration of economic health and stability. Europe, it was argued, was at the center of the world economy—and Germany was at the center of Europe. If a vengeful reparations burden were imposed on Germany, the Americans believed, it would prevent the satisfactory recovery of her economy and would, in turn, prevent the recovery of Europe. In explaining the American commitment to the policy of including a fixed sum in the peace treaty, for example, Thomas Lamont wrote:

> The American delegation consistently urged this course of procedure . . . because, chiefly, *a definite settlement of the question would soonest bring about settled financial conditions in Europe and soonest yield improved credit and financial stability* to France, Belgium, and such other Allied states as were, in part, dependent upon German reparations for the balancing of the budget. [Emphasis added.][52]

And in a lengthy memorandum that reveals much concerning American objectives in Paris, Norman Davis was even more precise in his explanation of the desirability of a fixed sum:

> *The German situation and its treatment is the key to the whole financial situation of Europe. . . . if Germany is not at work and consequently is in a chaotic condition and unprosperous, it is impossible for the rest of Europe to get to work and be prosperous.* It is most essential for the future stability of Europe that confidence and credit be restored at the earliest possible moment, and these can never be restored as long as any large nation in Europe is struggling under a financial burden which the investors of the world think she cannot carry. There is nothing, in our opinion, which could be done which would go further toward re-establishing confidence, credit, and the normal economic and industrial life, than to make an agreement with Germany which the business people of the world think is just and can be carried out. . . . [Emphasis added.][53]

Davis was joined by most of the delegation in his concern for building a suitable credit base upon which international economic stability could rest. In fact, this can be seen as a major preoccupation of all significant American policy makers in Paris. Even the President, in an address cabled to Congress in May 1919, wrote that "America has a great and honorable service to perform in bringing the commercial and industrial undertakings of the world back to their old scope and swing again, and putting a solid structure of credit under them." And Wilson worked most energetically in the furtherance of this "service." During the Council of Four discussions of the Reparation Commission's powers to issue bonds, he vehemently refused to give up an American veto power over issuance. The world's credit base was at stake, he argued, and the United States had to have the power to oversee it. In a discussion with Norman Davis, the President explained:

> *The aspect of the subject which interests me is the world aspect of it.* Unless these securities that Germany is going to give are known to be worth something they cannot be used as a basis for credit, and somebody else will have to supply the credit. Now they cannot be made worth anything unless Germany has the means of going to work and producing. . . . And therefore *the thing has two sides to it; not only the aspect of Germany and France and Italy—but the World aspect* . . . . [Emphasis added.][54]

It is clear that the concerns of American policy makers for the potential impact of the German peace settlement on the stability and health of the international order stemmed from more than a one-dimensional fear of encroaching Bolshevism. The nightmares of revolution were there, to be sure, but they were joined by other very disturbing visions of chaotic industry, trade, and finance. Undoubtedly, the circumstances of the international scene in 1918 and 1919 frequently tied fears of Bolshevism and distraught economies together in the minds of policy makers. Discussions of each were sometimes in such close proximity as to make them virtually indistinguishable. What else can one make, for example, of Colonel House's diary record of a meeting with Lord Robert Cecil in April: "We both see the world crumbling about our feet, and see the need not only for peace, but the lifting of all trade restrictions and the bringing the world back to normal. Even after peace is made our trouble will not end, for it will be many weary months before it will be possible to start industries and get the currents of commerce properly flowing."[55] Nevertheless, this frequently conjunctive relationship should not blur the existence of *distinct* factors. Bolshevism and the dangers of revolution compounded enormously the strains on the international capitalist system, interfering with the drive for rehabilitation of credit and commerce and industry—*but* they were hardly the only causes of strain on the system and the Americans in Paris knew this. It is entirely logical to maintain that these policy makers would have been anxious over the treatment of Germany, anxious particularly over the reparations settlement, even if "Bolshevism" had never reared its head. They were all too well aware that dangers other than radical revolution existed in potential form in Germany.

To go a step further in this discussion of American objectives in formulating policy on reparations in 1919, it is of fundamental importance to emphasize that U.S. policy makers did not envision themselves as merely contemplating abstract conundrums: they believed unswervingly that vital *American* interests were at stake as the politico-economic contours of Germany and Europe were being shaped. Basically, American policy makers argued that instability or chaos in Europe, whether it resulted from spreading revolution or the inertia of economic dislocation and stagnation, would cause terrible reverberations within the United States economy. It was in pursuit of American self-interest, not just idealistic notions, that they sought to forge a safe reparations settlement.

The explicit awareness of how deeply American interests were intertwined with the peace settlement in Europe is evident on every hand. One of the clearest expressions of the position was made shortly after the Peace Conference by Thomas Lamont. Bemoaning the failure of the Senate to appoint an American representative to the Reparations Commission, lest this be seen as some form of approval for the Treaty of Versailles as a whole, Lamont argued:

> The powers of this permanent reparations commission, as set up in the treaty, were so great, and the *effect of its decisions upon the financial and commercial workings of the Allied and Associated countries, including America,* was likely to be so far-reaching, that obviously it was necessary that the delegates should be men of the highest capacity, courage and wisdom. . . . Our failure to name a delegate for this commission has been not merely a great disappointment to our former associates in the war, but has, I believe, been largely responsible for *the continued economic unsettlement in Europe, with its unfortunate reflex upon our own industrial and commercial business.* [Emphasis added.]

Lest anyone not understand the connection between European and American industry and commerce, Lamont spelled it out. The United States had to involve itself in the rehabilitation of Europe, he wrote, because "America is already in the situation. She cannot disentangle herself. *Europe is her greatest customer, her greatest purchaser of grains, cotton, copper and all other raw materials. If our own industry and commerce are to be restored, if we are to get back to our former prosperity, then, indeed, must we lend our own efforts to European restoration*" (emphasis added).[56]

Those above Lamont in the ranks of the delegation felt no differently on this subject. During one speech in Paris, for example, Secretary of State Lansing pointedly emphasized that his concern for restoring Germany and preventing revolution there had no particularly altruistic roots. "It is not out of pity for the German people that this must be done without delay, but because we, the victors in this war, will be the chief sufferers if it is not done."[57] And on many occasions, Woodrow Wilson gave evidence of an extensive appreciation of the ties that bound the United States to

Europe. In early August, the President addressed Congress and talked extensively about the vital necessity of approving the peace settlement. He began by admitting that the normal routines of American life had been far less disturbed by the Great War than those of the Europeans. But, he insisted, it was as important to the United States to assist in the restoration of normal life across the Atlantic as it would have been to encourage restoration internally:

> . . . *our industries, our credits, our productive capacity, our economic processes are inextricably interwoven with those of other nations and peoples,*—most intimately of all with the nations and peoples upon whom the chief burden and confusion of the war fell. . . . *We must face the fact that unless we help Europe to get back to her normal life and production a chaos will ensue there which will inevitably be communicated to this country.* . . . We, and we almost alone, now hold the world steady. . . . It is in this supreme crisis—this crisis for all mankind,—that America must prove her mettle. . . . She saved Europe by her action in arms; she must now save it by her action in peace. *In saving Europe, she will save herself,* as she did upon the battlefield of the war. . . .
>
> And, if only in our own interest, we must help the people overseas. *Europe is our best customer.* We must keep her going or thousands of our shops and scores of our mines must close. *There is no such thing as letting her go to ruin without ourselves sharing in the disaster.* [Emphasis added.][58]

A month later, during two addresses in St. Louis, Wilson referred particularly to the reparations settlement and the Reparation Commission in this context. He was outraged at the refusal of the Senate to appoint an American representative to the Commission and could not understand how his opponents could so blithely disregard American self-interest:

> Is there any merchant present here or any manufacturer or any banker who can say that our interests are separate from the rest of the world, commercially, industrially, financially? There is not a man in any one of those professions who does not admit that *our industrial fortunes are tied up with the industrial fortunes of the rest of the world.* . . . *I am looking after the industrial interest of the United States.* I would like to see the other men who are. They are forgetting the industrial interests of the United States, and they are doing things that will cut us off, and our trade off, from the normal channels, because *the reparation commission can determine where Germany buys, what Germany buys, how much Germany buys.* . . . *It is going to stand at the center of the financial operations of the world.* [Emphasis added.][59]

As John Foster Dulles took part in reparations negotiations, he came to reason precisely like his senior colleagues. By the end of the Peace Conference, he was explaining his attitude toward reparations and describing the motivations beneath his policy recommendations in a way indistinguishable from what they would have said.

51

The similarity of assessment was actually apparent very early. In a January 29, 1919, letter to his former Washington superior, he offered some suggestions for resolving deadlocks already evident in Paris: his ideas might "not be practicable," he wrote, "but we here are very much impressed by the urgency of settling the indemnity question, which is operating in considerable measure to arrest *the renewal of trade and industry.*" Describing the quietude in European industry, he concluded that "the idleness of the world is, in my opinion, a most critical fact" (emphasis added).[60]

During most of the succeeding months of the Peace conference, Dulles did not carry through on the thrust of this letter. Like many of his colleagues, perhaps, numerous day-to-day problems did not encourage time-consuming elaborations of motivations. But, during the final days of negotiations concerning Germany, he did once more begin to place specific policy proposals in a more general explanatory setting. On June 3, for example, he wrote the third in a series of memoranda analyzing the German Counter Proposals. Where two initial pieces had been specific catalogues of German desires and possible responses, his third was an effort to *explain* the importance of incorporating a fixed sum in the final treaty. To Dulles, Germany's request for a fixed sum came at a particularly crucial moment. It added great impetus to a long-term American desire because of "a comprehension, daily becoming clearer, of the *critical financial situation of Europe.*" Brushing aside British and French arguments about clamoring voters, Dulles argued that "the financial and economic situation of Europe is so serious that no government would adopt merely as a matter of domestic politics, a policy which is not defensible on its merits. The only political consequences to be taken into account are those relating to *the stability of government in general.*" Further, he went on, "what the world requires immediately, is a new basis of credit."

> Europe's need is immediate. Any substantial delay in securing from Germany an obligation having a substantial present value may involve *consequences which will approach a disaster....*
>
> We therefore strongly recommend that the opportunity offered by Germany's counter-proposal be taken advantage of to fix a definite obligation which Germany will assume in a manner at least semi-voluntary. ... Under such conditions there is every reason to believe that *the German people will again become a stabilizing productive and consuming factor in the world's economy.* [Emphasis added.][61]

Dulles's words in this memorandum are those of a man in easy accord with the opinions of his superiors. On the one hand there can be no question that he was thoroughly persuaded that reparations could have a great impact on the European and world financial situation. On the other hand, his statement of concern for the "stability of government in general" suggests that he was also not untouched by the fears of Bolshevism which were common in Paris in those days. His personal records and diary for the Peace Conference, in fact, show that he participated in occasional meetings and discussions concerning revolutionary difficulties in Russia, Hungary, and Central Europe in general: in July, for example, he worked with the Finance Commission to devise a means of preventing Bela Kun from utilizing the Hungarian bonds and securities which his regime had confiscated. He maintained some contact with the War Trade Board, as well, being drawn by Vance McCormick into occasional planning for a blockade of Russia, pressure on neutral states regarding trade with the Bolsheviks, and arrangements for using Russian assets in the United States to finance the operation of Siberian railroads.[62] Spread out over the eight months of his work in Paris, such activity did not leave Dulles unaffected.

Shortly after the end of the Conference, Dulles also revealed that he was as cognizant as anyone of the way in which American self-interest was involved in the reparations settlement. It was September 1919, and the Senate had refused to approve the appointment of a temporary American representative to the Reparation Commission. Fearing that this boded ill for the future, Dulles forwarded a lengthy memorandum to the Foreign Relations Committee expounding on the folly of not supporting American involvement in such a crucial agency. "Senators who profess interest in the economic and financial welfare of the United States" could not seriously be acting in this way, he wrote:

> The Reparation Commission is in essence a committee on the reorganization of Allied Europe. Even were the United States not directly affected as it is by the carrying out of that reorganization, the United States is deeply interested in the successful accomplishment of the organization itself.
>
> Allied Europe is financially indebted to the United States in a sum approximating thirteen billion dollars. It should be our customer annually for several billion dollars worth of our products. Upon the successful financial and economic rehabilitation of Europe depends Europe's ability to repay what she owes and her ability to buy from us what we wish to sell.

It was "sound common sense," Dulles concluded, to assist in the revitalization of a "valued customer . . . temporarily embarrassed."[63]

When John Foster Dulles began to explain his position on reparations in a way fundamentally like that of high-ranking representatives in the

American delegation, he was unknowingly testifying to the essential significance of the Peace Conference in his own personal history. Paris in 1919, for him, proved to be the scene of penetrating *intellectual* experiences. Under the pressure of events and perceived opportunities and in the shadow of his senior colleagues, Dulles developed a strong interest in certain issues and problems and a particular approach to dealing with them. This effect on the patterns of his thought would be discernible for many years.

Basically, like others in policy making positions with him in 1919, Dulles came to be preoccupied with the value of order and stability in the international arena. He was aware of a host of problems at the Peace Conference which had the potential for creating chaotic world conditions: the reparations settlement most importantly, general postwar debts and credit arrangements, territorial and boundary changes, the Bolsheviks and other revolutionaries in Eastern and Central Europe, among others. Over and again, he and his colleagues worked to nip in the bud the awful potential for disorder. They sought to heal the raw wounds of the Great War by creating a global political economy of peace and prosperity, peace and prosperity as they defined them at least.

Dulles's personal approach to grand-scale conceptions of ideal political economies, to be sure, was frequently quite particularistic in its focus on issues predominantly economic in nature. He may have had a vision which considered all sorts of possibilities, in other words, but it would be easy to take away from the formal record of his thoughts in Paris the idea that economic problems would be the most important stumbling blocks to peace and order. It was not that he ignored political or social or even ideological issues, by any means, but simply that he spent far more time discussing industrial, commercial, and financial matters—and that his route to other issues frequently lay directly through these.

Such an approach was very natural for the Dulles of 1919, of course. As a young lawyer in New York, his corporate and banking clients had begun to engender in him a tendency to pay close attention to world economic developments. Then at the War Trade Board and at the Peace Conference, he had worked almost exclusively, for many months, on a variety of technical commercial and financial problems. The similar concentration on economic problems by several of Dulles's senior colleagues in Washington and Paris, further reinforced his interest in economic issues. Men like Norman Davis and Thomas Lamont had world views with a strong economic cast. So did Woodrow Wilson. Despite the endless emphasis of scholars on the President's moralism and idealism, some studies have indicated that he was not so cloud-bound as to be ignorant of commerce and finance.

On a number of occasions, for example, Wilson displayed no doubts about the causes of the Great War in which he had played a significant role. As he put it to one audience:

> Why, my fellow citizens, is there any man or any woman, let me say is there any child here, who does not know that *the seed of war in the modern world is industrial and commercial rivalry?* The real reason that the war we have just finished took place was that Germany was afraid her commercial rivals were going to get the better of her, and the reason why some nations went into the war against Germany was that they thought Germany would get the commercial advantage of them. The seed of jealousy, the seed of the deep-seated hatred was hot, successful commercial and industrial rivalry. [Emphasis added.]

Nor did Wilson lose sight of what he saw as the obvious roots of war once the fighting had ended. In a seldom-quoted address in Turin, Italy, made during his triumphal tour before the opening of the Peace Conference, he clearly demonstrated how consistent he could be. "This is a great industrial center," he told his audience on January 6, 1919:

> Perhaps you gentlemen think of the members of your Government and the members of other Governments who are going to confer now at Paris as the real makers of war and of peace. We are not. You are the makers of war and of peace. *The pulse of the modern world beats on the farm and in the mine and in the factory. The plans of the modern world are made in the counting-house.* The men who do the business of the world now shape the hands of those who conduct the commerce of the world. . . .
>
> I have only this to suggest, therefore. We go to Paris to conclude a peace. You stay here to continue it. We start the peace. It is your duty to continue it. *We can only make the large conclusions. You constantly transact the details which constitute the processes of the life of nations.* . . . [Emphasis added.]

Seven months later, in a message to Congress, the President reiterated the thrust of this speech and also indicated explicitly his belief that political and social problems were dependent upon economics.

> Politically, economically, socially the World is on the operating table, and it has not been possible to administer any anesthetic. It is conscious. *It even watches the capital operation upon which it knows that its hope for healthful life depends.* It cannot think its business out or make plans or give intelligent and provident direction to its affairs while in such a case. . . . There can be

no confidence in industry, no calculable basis for credits, no confident buying or systematic selling, no certain prospect of employment, no restoration of business . . . until peace has been established. . . . [Emphasis added.][64]

Not that a preoccupation with the importance of economic affairs should be taken to signify exclusive attentiveness to U.S. interests, either for Dulles or his senior colleagues. American policy makers knew very well that the kind of international order which they were seeking would yield important commercial and financial benefits for the United States. But, rightly or wrongly, they also persuaded themselves that what they wanted would be politically and economically beneficial to governments and peoples in Europe and virtually every corner of the globe. The Americans of 1919, like many before and after them, were able to enjoy all the sense of certainty and accomplishment that came with this equating of what was good for the United States and what was good for the rest of the world. It was never necessary to weigh "ideals" against "interests" when the scales seemed always balanced between them. Dulles came to share this sense of equivalency by the time of the Paris Peace Conference and he rarely doubted its applicability in later years.

There is some irony in the Dulles world view that emerged from the Paris Peace Conference. In 1917, falling into line in the "idealistic crusade" which he said his President was leading "magnificently," Dulles had called for "the creation of *a world of new international relationships*"[65] (Emphasis added). By 1919, he and other Americans were talking quite differently and can be seen, perhaps at most, as trying to march backward into their brave new world. Lansing now talked of the need "to *restore* the peaceful intercourse between the belligerents"; Wilson wanted to bring "the commercial and industrial undertakings of the world *back* to their *old* scope and swing again"; and Dulles used words like "*renewal*" and "*rehabilitation*" (emphasis added). What had seemed at the beginning to be a world system in need of basic transformation had become at the end a system appealing enough to deserve reconstitution. Their pronounced anti-Bolshevism, as well as their yearning after a reestablishment of viable economic relationships, both testify to the fact that the Americans in Paris had come to feel a fundamental loyalty to the prewar international order.

Of course, in the case of Wilson and a number of his senior advisers, it has long been clear that there never had been any question of a total rejection of the prewar order. The President, for instance, obviously thought of himself as a reformer not a revolutionary. Neither his domestic nor his world role entailed any real challenge to the most basic values and institutions of the status quo. Internationally, in particular, his proposals would have altered somewhat but not eliminated the nation-state system, capitalism, and the traditional pursuit of national interests. His rhetoric could be very dramatic, even religious and millennial in tone, to be sure, but it was rhetoric which teased a listener into expectations beyond what might actually be delivered. The inherent moderation lurking behind the radiant rhetorical banner became clearer as one looked at actions instead of words. It became especially clear when the end of the Great War produced an atmosphere of turmoil and crisis. Wilson and other Americans decided then that calm, orderly change likely must be even slower than they might earlier have estimated.[66]

Although the record of Dulles's thoughts during the Great War is quite limited, he seems to fit in with the Wilsonian dichotomy of teasing rhetoric and modest substance. His 1917 praise for the President's efforts on behalf of a new world order appears with hindsight to have been a rhetorical flourish made in the exciting early stages of American involvement in the war. By 1919, however, the core of the world order Dulles had known was in danger of collapse, as far as he was concerned, because of a double-barreled threat of outside pressure and internal weakness. This was enough to throw into clear relief his inherent conservatism. He followed his American colleagues and, for not the last time in his life, dug his heels in substantially behind the position one might have expected on the basis of earlier statements.

4

Dulles as Lawyer, 1919–1929

GERTRUDE STEIN ONCE CALLED the young Americans and Europeans who had come to maturity in the era of the Great War the "lost generation." Battered and bemused by the bloodshed and disillusionments of an awful conflict, these young men and women had been permanently scarred—they had wandered through the rest of their lives.

Stein was perceptive about the young members of her own circle, but her label should not be applied too freely. There were young Americans and Europeans who survived the Great War both physically and emotionally unscathed. Some, like John Foster Dulles, even prospered. When Dulles returned to New York in September 1919 to renew a lifestyle he had left two years earlier, his prospects were glowing. He had left Sullivan & Cromwell in 1917 as a most junior member of the firm; he returned in 1919 as a full partner, with his fortunes as a lawyer and businessman about to skyrocket.

Dulles's interlude of work in Washington and Paris had much to do with the stunning success that came to him during the 1920s. On the one hand, government service had made him a seasoned expert on subjects that were likely to be of interest to Sullivan & Cromwell and its clients. Through work at the War Trade Board and the Peace Conference, he had acquired a wide-ranging knowledge of European economic and financial conditions. In addition, his knowledge was not confined to abstracts or paper. Working with the Interim Reparation Commission and other post-Conference agencies in Paris during the summer of 1919 gave him practical day-to-day experience in an area that was soon to be of major importance to American corporations and investors.

Dulles emerged from World War I with more than expertise and experience. Perhaps unconsciously following the example of William Nelson Cromwell, Dulles returned to Wall Street with a full, far-ranging network of friends and contacts in high places. For decades after 1919, he would be able to draw on the ears and friendship of high-ranking government and cabinet officials in Washington, London, Paris, The Hague, Brussels, Berlin, Prague, Vienna, and Warsaw. And in business circles on both sides of the Atlantic, his contacts were equally numerous.[1] Washington during the Great War and Paris during the Peace Conference proved to be incubators of sorts for the careers of politicians, diplomats, and businessmen. Having been in both places himself, Dulles was really part of a brood that was on the threshhold of power: his "siblings" gave him a conduit to information and occasional influence that could not but be a help to his legal career.

I

Dulles may not have intended to return to New York as early as he did. His official resignation from various government posts in Paris came in August 1919 and received mildly sensational coverage in American newspapers as an unexpected development. Press reports tied the young lawyer's departure to the recent refusal of the United States Senate to appoint a temporary American representative to the Reparation Commission.[2] Dulles was, in fact, concerned about the Senate action and was troubled particularly by the prospect of a lack of American impact on vital negotiations concerning German labor, coal, dyestuffs, and shipping. At one point in early August, he even sent a troubled cable to Secretary of State Lansing asking for his uncle's guidance as to what he should say to his European colleagues in view of the Senate decision.[3]

If Dulles's August resignation was a protest, however, it was only partially one. It is quite clear that he was planning to leave Paris before he heard of the Senate action. As early as March 1919, he had talked to William Nelson Cromwell about returning and participating in a reorganization of the firm which would make him a full partner. After the President asked him to remain in Paris, Dulles wrote to Cromwell that "I am hoping that these matters can be cleaned up so that I shall get away in early August...." Even when accepting appointments to various Paris committees during the summer, he always cautioned the State Department about his intentions. On one occasion, he wrote that he would be happy to serve on the Committee on the Execution of the Treaty with Germany "if I can properly do so consistently with my intention of returning to the United States at a fairly early date."[4] Concerned though he may have been about the Senate's coolness toward the peace settlement, in other words, Dulles's personal plans never hinged solely on actions in Washington.

And if there was any prematurity at all about Dulles's return to New York, it was never apparent in his work. Within a scant few weeks, he had thrown himself into a fast-paced stride at Sullivan & Cromwell. He began work on a series of projects that substantially set the course of his work for the next several decades.

Immediately on returning to his firm, Dulles undertook legal work for the European Textile Corporation, a newly organized syndicate of American cotton brokers and textile manufacturers. In January 1920, he traveled to Eastern Europe for the company. As one of his letters of introduction explained, "This syndicate is composed of Messrs. G. H. McFadden & Brothers, cotton brokers, the American International Corporation, Lockwood Green & Company and Lawrence & Company. Representatives of each of the above firms will accompany Mr. Dulles, hoping to make satisfactory arrangements with mills by offering cotton and taking a part of their finished product in payment...." The trip was obviously successful because European Textile had become a multi-million dollar operation by the end of the year.[5]

Dulles's trip to Europe for cotton and textile clients involved other business as well. As he wrote to a friend, he was going "to make some investigations and carry on some negotiations on behalf of American bankers who desire to invest in Germany, Poland and Czechoslovakia." From Central and Eastern Europe, he did in fact report to Assistant Secretary of the Treasury Norman Davis on numerous investment opportunities. At least some of these were attractive to his banker clients, and an investment enterprise, the Overseas Securities Corporation, was organized as a result. Dulles went on to serve as its legal counsel.[6]

Also within the early months of his return to Sullivan & Cromwell,

Dulles began advising a government agency concerned with American exports. Congress had authorized the creation of the War Finance Corporation in 1918, giving it the right "to make short-term loans, of five years' duration or less, to American exporters unable to obtain funds on reasonable terms through regular banking channels." Unstable economic conditions following the Armistice led to an extension of the corporation's life and continued use of its $500,000,000 capitalization. From late 1919 until its liquidation in 1924, Dulles served as its legal counsel. In the course of his relationship, almost $400,000,000 in short-term loans were made to corporations and agricultural interests to assist in encouraging exports. Major aid was rendered to cotton, grain, and livestock brokers, but large loans were also forthcoming for corporations like International General Electric and International Harvester.[7]

Ties with the European Textile Corporation, the Overseas Securities Corporation, and the War Finance Corporation were all developed within six months of Dulles's return to Sullivan & Cromwell. They typified, though on a small scale, the nature of his legal enterprise for the next three decades. All involved activity in the general areas of international trade and international investment; all involved connections with corporations and banking houses that were interested in the international economy.

Dulles's legal work for corporations during the 1920s alone, for example, was very extensive. Although complete information about his activities at Sullivan & Cromwell is not available, evidence can be taken from, among other things, his correspondence and appointment calendars and several business publications of the day. A relatively full outline emerges, with Dulles's 1920s clients including all of the following:

The American Agricultural Chemical Company, manufacturer of chemical fertilizers, glues, and numerous related products.[8]

The American Bank Note Company, engravers and printers of bank notes, bonds, and stock certificates. Beginning as a strictly American operation, this company gradually absorbed similar operations around the world. In 1920, for example, Dulles assisted in the takeover of the British firm, Bradbury, Wilkinson & Company, Ltd.[9]

The American Cotton Oil Company specialized in extracting vegetable oils and byproducts and had extensive international interests. Dulles originally undertook legal work for this company before World War I.[10]

The American Radiator Company, which maintained plants and sales offices around the world.[11]

Babcock & Wilcox, Inc. Dulles served as a director of this internationally active firm engaged in the manufacture of equipment used in the chemical, alcohol, and refining industries.[12]

The Carib Syndicate, Ltd., an oil investment company for which Dulles worked to secure various exploration and drilling concessions from the government of Colombia.[13]

The Coronet Phosphate Corporation.[14]

The Cuban Cane Sugar Corporation. Brought to the firm by William Nelson Cromwell years before, this company became one of Dulles's personal clients during the 1920s.[15]

The European Textile Corporation, for which Dulles continued to work until at least 1926.[16]

The Gold Dust Corporation. The "gold" in Gold Dust referred to two of the American consumers' more coyly named commodities: "Fairy" and "Sunny Monday" soaps. An offspring of the American Cotton Oil Company, Gold Dust began production on its own in 1923, keeping Dulles as general counsel until late in the 1930s.[17]

The International Nickel Company was probably the most important corporate client with which Dulles was associated during the 1920s. With net income in 1920 of $5 million, it ranked as a giant in world business. William Nelson Cromwell had worked with the firm for years and brought Dulles onto its board of directors in 1925. In this way, Dulles also came to be associated with INCO's many other interests around the globe: the International Nickel Company of Canada, Ltd.; the Huronian Company, Ltd.; the Société Minière Caledonienne (New Caledonia); and the Nickel Corporation, Ltd. of Great Britain.[18]

Jones Brothers Tea–Grand Union Stores, which produced teas, coffees, and other products and maintained a large chain of retail outlets in the United States.[19]

The National Railroad Company of Haiti.[20]

The Overseas Securities Corporation. Dulles's continuing role as director and counsel of this company involved periodical haggling with the State Department during the 1920s. When first organized, Overseas Securities had purchased a large interest in the Possehl works, near Vilna, Poland. In 1923, the Polish government moved to seize control of Possehl on the grounds that it had and continued to be controlled by German interests. Dulles appealed to Washington for support of the supposedly American interests involved in Overseas Securities, but the State Department seemed in doubt about the individuals behind this company and asked for a complete list of owners and directors. Over the space of several years, Dulles proved reluctant to provide the State Department with this information and no support for the difficulties in Poland was forthcoming. From the nature of its communications with Dulles, Washington's information had apparently suggested that the real money behind Overseas Securities was German and that the United States had no responsibility for defending its interests. Dulles's unwillingness to provide detailed information, coupled with his extensive concomitant activity in Germany at the time, suggest that this was in fact the case.[21]

The Port of Para Corporation, an American company undertaking the construction of large harbor facilities in Brazil.[22]

Slater Manufacturing Company, producers of woolen and cotton goods.[23]

The United Cigars Store Company, producers and retailers of tobacco products.[24]

The United Railways of Central America, another client originally obtained by William Nelson Cromwell. Dulles became associated with the firm in 1924.[25]

In addition to the relatively routine legal work undertaken for the above corporations, Dulles's partnership in Sullivan & Cromwell brought a number of special corporate responsibilities during the 1920s.

Early in the decade, for example, he was retained by a large number of firms to process claims against the government of Germany. Corporations such as the drug giant Merck & Company, and the Duluth Superior Milling Company, among others, were anxious to recover war-risk insurance premiums that had been paid to German firms during the early years of the Great War. Dulles's expertise in the intricacies of the economic settlement that was part of the Treaty of Versailles and his postwar connections within Germany brought him much work in this area.[26]

Another unusual series of cases brought Dulles into extensive legal work for the New York Life Insurance Company, the Mutual Life Insurance Company, the Equitable Life Insurance Company, and the Guardian Life Insurance Company. During the years preceding World War I, all of these firms had done extensive business through Russian branches. Russian laws required that the full reserves backing life insurance policies be invested within the country, principally in government and railroad bonds. As a result, a firm like New York Life had more than $60 million invested in Russia by 1917. Following the Bolshevik revolution, all of these insurance company investments had been seized by the Soviet government. Compounding the companies' problems, a substantial number of the individuals insured in Russia had fled the country after 1917—and the families of many had proceeded to file claims for insurance benefits upon their deaths! The companies all began protesting payment, considering the loss of the reserves earmarked for these policies, and a long process of court litigation ensued. Dulles became one of a team of prominent lawyers engaged by the firm (a team which also included Charles Evans Hughes), and the battles continued into the next decade. [27]

One other group of corporate connections during the 1920s deserves separate mention because of the special activities in which Dulles became involved on their behalf. Beginning very shortly after his return to Sullivan & Cromwell, he developed a fairly sizable clientele among American public utility companies and, in particular, public utility holding companies. Some of these clients, (such as the North American Edison Power and Light Company, and the Detroit Edison Company) had interests confined to the United States. Others, like the Electric Bond and Share Company and the American and Foreign Power Company, combined domestic and international business. Dulles attended to both categories: in addition to domestic business for Electric Bond and Share, for example, he was involved in that company's acquisitions in Central America; for the American & Foreign Power Company, he handled negotiations and dealings in Mexico, Guatemala, and Panama. [28]

During the late 1920s, in the great heyday of insanity engaged in by the New York Stock Exhange, Dulles's public utility clients also involved him deeply and embarrassingly in the madness of Wall Street. Electric Bond & Share, for example, became intensively involved in stock manipulations and speculations during 1928 and 1929. It actually became one of the major non-banking sources of money flowing into the Wall Street call market: on an average in 1929, it was investing and lending about $100 million a day. On July 26, 1929, Harrison Williams, a friend of Dulles's and an executive in numerous public utility holding companies, organized the Shenandoah Corporation. It was a basically speculative undertaking that put out an initial stock issue of more than $100 million. Dulles became a member of its small board of directors. Incredibly, Shenandoah proceeded to spawn its own offspring in only three weeks. On August 20, it created the Blue Ridge Corporation, with an initial stock issue of $142 million. Dulles was also a member of its board of directors. One of the students of the stock market aberrations of the late 1920s has described the launching of Shenandoah and Blue Ridge as "the pinnacle of new era finance" and a "gargantuan insanity." With little to support them but speculative mania, both corporations quickly tumbled into the abyss of the market crash. Shenandoah's stock, which had started selling at twenty-six dollars had fallen to fifty cents by 1932! [29] (Dulles's involvement with the debacle reminds one of e. e. cummings' comment that the 1920s were years of "many dollars and no sense.")

II

Dulles's decision to return to Sullivan & Cromwell and become reassociated with American corporations interested in the international economy is reminiscent of the career choice made by his grandfather twenty-five years earlier. Unsure of his future in diplomacy and not quite content with its range in any event, John Watson Foster had decided in the mid-1890s to build a private practice in international law. As he explained it, he was going to take advantage of experience and contacts to work on "great questions" for "large interests."[30]

The timing of both grandfather and grandson was excellent. Foster's practice in the late nineteenth and early twentieth centuries flourished. He had begun his legal work at a time when American activity in the international economy was experiencing major new growth. Dulles's timing was even more fortunate. During the 1920s, the interest of American corporations and banking houses in global enterprise burgeoned—more international activity ensued than had characterized any previous peacetime period.

Major international expansion for American business and banking during the 1920s owed much to the impact of the Great War. Where that conflict had devestated the economies of other great states, it had heaped enormous benefits on the United States. No physical damage at all was inflicted on American farms and factories. Mammoth exports of manufactured and agricultural products resulted from the wartime exigencies of the European allies; and the same wartime pressures had forced those same Europeans to turn to their former debtor for major financial assistance. The results were stunning. American sales to the European allies increased by almost 200 percent between 1914 and 1917; by 1919, total exports were nearing $8 billion, twice the value of imports in that year. On the financial side, the United States was transformed from a major debtor to a major creditor nation. In 1914, American indebtedness to foreigners had been $4 billion greater than foreign debts to Americans; by the end of 1919, such debts to Americans exceeded American obligations by $12.5 billion![31]

Aware of the meaning of such statistics, American businessmen and bankers eagerly anticipated further development of economic power in the postwar period. As an island of stellar prosperity in the midst of an economically troubled sea, what else could be expected? American corporations could go on to maintain and perhaps further increase sales abroad; they might also significantly expand branch operations outside the United States. And American banks might assume international financial leadership, turning New York into the money capital of the world. In their exhilaration, American businessmen and bankers were like the F. Scott Fitzgerald hero who remembered the mood of the postwar days by saying, "We felt like children in a great bright unexplored barn." In economic terms, the barn was as big as the world. [32]

John Foster Dulles's great success as a lawyer during the 1920s stemmed very much from the fact that he involved himself with both the corporations *and* investment banking houses that were increasingly active on the international scene. His work in the financial world, in fact, must have taken up the major share of his professional schedule.

To draw up a list of Dulles's banking clients during the 1920s is almost the same as drawing up a list of the major houses of the time: J. P. Morgan & Company; the National City Company; Kuhn, Loeb & Company; Dillon, Read & Company; the Guaranty Company of New York; Lee, Higginson & Company; Harris, Forbes & Company; Brown Brothers and Brown Brothers, Harriman; Goldman, Sachs; the First National Corporation of Boston. These among others turned to Dulles for legal assistance. His work with these key American banks also involved him in regular contact with important European houses. Even before World War I, he had been overseeing investments in Latin America for French and British investors. In the 1920s, he broadened his contacts with Europeans, becoming involved with such institutions as the Crédit Lyonnais in France and the Dresdner Bank in Germany.

One initial facet of Dulles's postwar work with the American banking community was in the area of foreign trade financing. Although anxious to continue substantial purchases of American agricultural and manufactured products after the end of the Great War, European countries found themselves economically too weak to afford such trade. Huge American government loans had made it possible to make necessary purchases during the war, but the end of fighting brought an end to government largesse. Already in 1919, American banking houses began looking into the possibility of filling the void left by their government. In October of that year, for example, Dulles was writing to a friend in the French cabinet about a meeting of businessmen and bankers he was to attend in Atlantic City. The goal of the meeting was the creation of "a large American corporation whose securities could be sold here against the collateral in the form of notes, mortgages, shares, etc. deposited with it by foreign firms and corporations dealing with credit." Obtaining credit in this way, such foreign corporations could proceed to purchase the capital goods and raw materials they would need to place their operations on a revived and stable footing. As Dulles told his friend, "There are three or four banking houses, with whom I am very closely in touch who, I think, would be prepared to back such a proposal. . . . "

Later, in 1920, Dulles was also invited to a meeting of the American Bankers Association, where the problem was once again discussed. Preparing to attend this meeting, Dulles wrote to the President of the organization that the expertise in European finances he had gained at the Paris Peace Conference had been supplemented "by a recent private trip to Europe, including Central Europe," where he had studied "particularly the problem involved in the nations' financing imports from the United States." [33]

The plans for a grand-scale foreign trade financing corporation never really took form. Maintaining contact with banking houses, however, Dulles simply became associated with other undertakings. Most importantly, he provided legal counsel for a substantial number of the banks that threw themselves with such gusto into foreign loans during the 1920s. In the space of less than ten years the new giants of international finance that were located in New York, Boston and Chicago found themselves lending more than $10 billion to governments and corporations outside the United States. They did this by purchasing great quantities of bonds and securities issued by these governments and corporations—and then reselling them to eager American investors. [34] Dulles was particularly active in handling the legal facets of such bond and security transactions, keeping watch over the details of the bankers' contracts with the foreign issues and relevant government regulations as well.

The loans and securities issues on which Dulles worked during the 1920s evidenced truly worldwide interests, touching virtually every area of the globe.

Latin America, for example, which had been an area of special interest to him in pre-Great War years, continued to receive attention from Dulles during the 1920s. Among the bond and security issues with which he was associated were the following:

A 1923 sale of Republic of Panama bonds, arranged by the Guaranty Company of New York. [35]

A 1924 sale of bonds by Argentina, arranged by Brown Brothers.[36]

A loan of $30 million to the Government of Chile, transacted in 1926 by Hallgarten & Co.[37]

A 1926 loan of $3 million to Banco Agricola Hipotecario, of Colombia, by Hallgarten & Co. and associates.[38]

A $10 million loan to the government of Colombia, arranged by Hallgarten & Co. in 1926.[39]

A loan of $5 million to the Dominican Republic, transacted by Lehman Bros. in 1926.[40]

$1 million to the City of Santiago, Chile: Hallgarten & Co.[41]

A 1926 loan to the government of Bolivia, arranged by Lehman Bros.[42]

$11 million to the Province of Buenos Aires, arranged in 1927 by Hallgarten & Co.[43]

$6 million to the City of São Paolo, Brazil: arranged by Lazard Frères.[44]

A 1927 loan of at least $20 million to the Republic of Colombia, arranged by Hallgarten & Co.[45]

A Goldman, Sachs loan of $15 million to the State of Minas Geracs, Brazil: 1927.[46]

A 1928 loan of at least $22 million to the Republic of Colombia, arranged again by Hallgarten & Co.[47]

$1.2 million loan to the Province of Cordoba, Argentina: arranged in 1928 by the First National Corporation of Boston.[48]

A 1928 loan of $5 million to the Banco Agricolo Hipotecario: arranged by Hallgarten & Co.[49]

A 1928 loan of $20 million to the State of Rio Grande do Sul, arranged by the First National Corporation of Boston.[50]

$40 million to the Province of Buenos Aires, arranged in 1928 by Hallgarten & Co. and the First National Corporation of Boston.[51]

Latin America was only one area of interest to Dulles's banking clients during the 1920s. Early in the decade, they showed strong inclinations to move forcefully into many regions. In the Far East, for example, Dulles became associated with a number of loans to the government in China:

In 1919, a loan of $5.5 million by the Pacific Development Company, an enterprise begun by the Chase National Bank and Hayden Stone and Company.

A 1920 loan arranged by J. P. Morgan & Company.

A 1922 loan arranged by J. P. Morgan & Company.

A 1924 loan by the Pacific Development Company.[52]

And in the Middle East, Dulles undertook some limited legal work for William Nelson Cromwell and his investing associates: in 1923, for example, they were considering the placement of some capital with the Ottoman–American Development Company. [53]

But Latin America, the Far East, and the Middle East never figured as the real centers of Dulles's banking activities during the 1920s. Europe, instead, became the focus of his work in this period just as it had been the focus of his government work during the war. He provided legal services to banks engaged in financial transactions with European governments and corporations on a regular and extensive basis. Among the transactions with which he was associated were the following:

A $15 million sale of Czechoslovakian bonds in the United States during 1920. [54]

A loan of $2 million to Burmeister & Wain, Ltd. of Copenhagen, by Brown Brothers in 1921. [55]

A $3 million loan to the Copenhagen Telephone Company, by Brown Brothers, in 1925. [56]

A $3 million loan by Brown Brothers to the City of Helsingfors, Finland, in 1925. [57]

A 1925 loan of $7 million to a syndicate of Danish municipalities, arranged by Brown Brothers. [58]

A $7.5 million loan to the Cunard Steam-Ship Co., Ltd., negotiated in 1925 by Brown Brothers. [59]

A loan of $5 million to the Farmers Credit Union of South Jutland, Denmark, by Brown Brothers, in 1927. [60]

A 1927 purchase of General Electric Company of Sicily bonds, by W. A. Harriman. [61]

A loan of $36 million to the City of Rome, arranged in 1927 by Hallgarten & Company. [62]

A W. A. Harriman loan of at least $10 million to the Terni Societa per l'Industria e l'Electtricita of Italy, arranged in 1927. [63]

A 1927 loan of $15 million to the City of Copenhagen, by Brown Brothers. [64]

A $5 million loan by Brown Brothers to the Mortgage Bank of the Kingdom of Denmark, in 1927. [65]

The purchase of 400,000 shares of Credit Anstalt of Vienna by Goldman, Sachs. [66]

A 1927 loan of $70 million to the government of Poland, arranged by the Bankers Trust Company and associates. [67]

A $30 million loan to the Kingdom of Norway, negotiated by Brown Brothers in 1928. [68]

A loan of $55 million to Denmark, supervised by Brown Brothers in 1928. [69]

An $8 million loan to the County of Akershus, Norway, by Brown
   Brothers, in 1928.[70]
A loan of $1.5 million to Glommens and Laagens of Norway, by
   Brown Brothers, in 1928.[71]
A 1928 Brown Brothers loan of $10 million to the City of Antwerp.[72]
A loan of $3.5 million to the Province of Upper Austria, arranged by
   Blyth, Witter & Company in 1928.[73]
A 1929 loan to the Polish Mortgage Bank.[74]

In addition to thése European financial activities, Dulles developed a
specialized expertise during the 1920s. The intensive knowledge of the
German economy accumulated during his work at the Paris Peace Conference was turned to professional advantage when American bankers became particularly interested in that country several years later. Although
Germany was but one country in the world anxious for American dollars,
the proportion of the total investments alloted to German governments
and German corporations places it high on the list of the United States'
new debtors by 1929. Of the $9.4 billion in foreign securities held by
American citizens at the time of the stock market crash, $1.2 billion were
of German origin—more than 10 percent of the total. Considering that
the first major public offering of German securities in the United States
was not made until 1924, the financial dimensions of the subsequent five
years' activities becomes even more impressive.[75] It was in this hectic
realm of American—German financial transactions that Dulles became
especially active. Among the many loans and security sales on which he
worked were the following:

The German External Loan of 1924, recommended by the Dawes
   Committee: the first major loan to Germany after the Great War. In
   the amount of $100 million, the loan was managed by J. P. Morgan
   & Company, with the National City Company; Guaranty Com-
   pany of New York; Lee, Higginson & Company; and Kuhn, Loeb &
   Company.[76]
A 1925 loan of $8.7 million to the City of Munich, arranged by Harris,
   Forbes & Co.[77]
A loan of $5.5 million to Electrowerke, A.G., arranged by Harris,
   Forbes & Company.[78]
A $10 million loan to Deutsche Raiffeisenbank, A.G., arranged by
   Harris, Forbes & Company in 1925.[79]
A 1925 loan of $3 million, by Lehman Brothers, to Leonhard Tietz
   Aktiengesellschaft.[80]
A $10 million sale of bonds for the First Mortgage Bank of Saxony,
   managed by Brown Brothers.[81]

A 1926 loan of $5 million to the City of Nuremberg, arranged by the Equitable Trust Company, the Guaranty Company of New York, and Lee, Higginson. [82]

A $10 million loan to the Union of German Mortgage Banks, arranged in 1926 by Brown Brothers. [83]

A 1926 Brown Brothers loan of $3 million to Manfeld Aktiengesellschaft für Bergbau und Hüttenbetrieb. [84]

A 1926 loan of $7.5 million to Westphalia United Electric Power Corporation. [85]

A $20 million loan to the Berlin City Electric Company, arranged by Lee, Higginson and W. A. Harriman. [86]

A sale of State of Bavaria Bonds arranged by Brown Brothers in 1926. [87]

A 1927 loan of $4 million to the Hamburg Street Railways. [88]

A $5 million loan to the City of Breslau, arranged in 1927 by the First National Corporation of Boston. [89]

A $2 million loan to Nassauische Landesbank of Germany, by Halsey, Stuart & Company. [90]

A 1927 loan by the First National Corporation of Boston, in the amount of $14.5 million to the City of Frankfurt. [91]

A loan of $30 million to the State of Prussia, arranged in 1927 by Harris, Forbes. [92]

A $3–8 million loan to the Communal Bank of Saxony, negotiated in 1927 by W. A. Harriman. [93]

A $20 million loan to the North German Lloyd Company, arranged in 1927 by Kuhn, Loeb & Company; Guaranty Trust Company; and Lee, Higginson. [94]

A 1928 Brown Brothers loan of $8 million to the Hamburg Elevated, Underground and Street Railways Company. [95]

A $15 million loan to the City of Berlin, arranged by Brown Brothers in 1928. [96]

A $7.5 million loan arranged in 1928 by Goldman, Sachs to the Gewerkschaft der Constantin der Grosse. [97]

A $4 million loan to the Thueringer Gas Gesellschaft of Leipzig, negotiated in 1928 by Blyth, Witter & Company. [98]

A $3.5 million Brown Brothers loan to the City of Hanover in 1929. [99]

A $5 million sale of Hansa Steamship Line securities, supervised by the Guaranty Company of New York in 1929. [100]

The German Government International Loan of 1930, recommended by the Young Committee. In the amount of $98 million, the loan was managed by J. P. Morgan & Company, with the National City Company; Guaranty Company of New York; Lee, Higginson

& Company; Chase Securities Corporation; and Kuhn, Loeb & Company acting as other originating houses. [101] This 1930 loan and the similar transaction recommended by the Dawes Committee in 1924 were the two largest loans made to Germany at any time in the 1920s.

As the dates of the financial transactions on which Dulles was involved reveal, the enthusiasm of American bankers for foreign loans moved toward fever pitch as the 1920s progressed. Each year brought increasing activity: where, in 1923, $458 million in long-term capital left the United States, 1928 saw a flow of $1.6 billion. It is now generally recognized that the enthusiasm of American banking houses was greater than their good judgment in encouraging such enormous transactions. Carried away by the heady experience of new-found financial power, they seemed more concerned with simply using that power than using it sensibly. The situation became absurd at times. As one study of the period reveals, "Some 36 houses, most of them American, competed for a city of Budapest loan and 14 for a loan to the city of Belgrade. A Bavarian hamlet, discovered by American agents to be in need of about $125,000, was urged and finally persuaded to borrow $3 million in the American market." American bankers were also quite clearly enamored of the great profits that could be made from the sale of foreign securities in the United States. As numerous critics put it during the next decade, the bankers had arranged transactions with little real attention to their viability, confident that they would reap their commissions and be free of the unstable bonds or securities before serious difficulties became apparent. [102]

Compounding any instability that may have been inherent to the enormous American loans of the 1920s was the general economic posture which the United States assumed at the time. Despite regular opposition from more internationally oriented businessmen, Washington emerged from the Great War with little interest in altering the protective tariff system that shielded American industry from potentially harmful foreign competition. In fact, the Republican powers of the first postwar decade managed to substantially increase the difficulty of marketing imports in the United States, moving through several steps to the notorious and essentially prohibitive rates of the Smoot–Hawley tariff of 1930. By doing so, the government made it difficult for even the most reputable foreign debtors to make long-term payments on loans, bonds, and securities. Where, in the end, were these debtors to obtain the dollars necessary for these payments? [103]

Between implicit economic weakness, inflated indebtedness, and a long-range scarcity of dollar resources for non-Americans, it would have taken a miracle to prevent the great 1920s transactions of American banking houses from coming to grief. As events would prove, there was to be no miracle.

It should be clear by this point that John Foster Dulles lived and breathed in the international economy during the 1920s. He was, fundamentally, an international business lawyer. His many clients ranged from corporations interested in world markets and foreign subsidiary operations to major banking houses undertaking investments around the globe.

The range, stature, and activities of his clients during the 1920s had several important effects on Dulles's life. Some would become fully evident only over time: the continuing evolution of a network of highly placed friends and contacts, for example, or the accumulation of further experience in international financial and commercial transactions, and the sharpening of his sensitivity to the general importance of those transactions. Other effects were more immediately apparent, including his dramatically successful career. A junior clerk in 1911, he had already made significant progress when he became a partner in Sullivan & Cromwell at the end of 1919. And his star went no where but up from there. In 1926, the senior man at the firm, Royall Victor, died in a boating accident, and a vacancy at the top was unexpectedly opened. William Nelson Cromwell, semi-retired, chose Dulles to fill it. At a very early age, Dulles thus became senior and managing partner of one of the most important law firms in the United States. In 1931, *Fortune* magazine did an article on the young lions of American corporate law: Dulles was among the handful profiled.[104]

Great success brought a closeness between Dulles and the American businessmen and bankers with whom he worked so regularly. A community of interest emerged from his day-to-day involvement with their economic enterprise. Private and public statements reveal, for example, that Dulles felt considerable pride in the accomplishments of his corporate and financial associates. He was capable of the most sweeping compliments. In commenting on extensive foreign landing by American bankers, for example, he could write that this work was "an amazing achievement and one to which our present prosperity is largely ascribable." On another occasion, he argued that "our bankers have given an extraordinary demonstration of the beneficent use of financial power."[105] (The reasoning behind these statements will be examined more thoroughly in chapter 5.) Dulles seemed particularly impressed by the fact that

73

American businessmen and bankers were undertaking new roles and responsibilities in the 1920s, that they were helping to put the United States into what he thought was a proper leadership position within the international economy. He wrote and spoke several times about his role in the "Polish Stabilization Loan" of 1927, in this respect. This loan was the end result of several years of work by Dulles with the Bankers Trust Company, Blair & Company, and the Chase Securities Corporation. The Polish Government had been persuaded to begin an elaborate survey of national resources and economic potential and had concluded that a major influx of foreign capital was desirable for extensive development. Working with the Federal Reserve Bank of New York and central banks in Great Britain, France, and Germany, private American houses had then arranged a large initial credit. Dulles was fond of describing the way this would allow Poland to make important economic progress and emphasized that this was "the first such operation to be realized under distinctively American leadership in all of its phases."[106]

Pride in the work of his business associates during the 1920s helps to explain Dulles's concomitant willingness to take on their critics. He proved to be an eloquent defender of corporations and banking houses on a number of occasions. His glowing descriptions of the new international activism of investment bankers, for example, already quoted, were designed at least in part to refute numerous criticisms that were becoming prevalent by 1928 and 1929. As he was to indicate, he could not understand those misguided individuals who argued that bankers should concentrate all their resources on domestic investments.[107] He seemed especially sensitive to criticism or interference from Washington. Initial relations between American banking houses and the government had been very friendly following the Great War. A great deal of practical, routine assistance was provided by officials as bankers felt their way toward intensive international enterprise. During 1921 and 1922, the State Department did negotiate an agreement with key houses providing for advance notice to Washington of new foreign loans and securities issues, but it seemed as if the government was really just interested in being kept informed. Over the space of several years, however, the State and Commerce Departments began to press for more than information. On a regular basis, officials began applying government guidelines to private banking transactions—and in a number of cases they actually withheld approval and prevented consummation. If a loan was contemplated to a government that had not completed a war-debt funding agreement with the United States, or to a monopolized or cartelized industry, or to a government flagrantly violating American "open-door" principles, it became clear that Washington was likely to frown on the undertaking.[108]

Gradually the bankers began to chafe under the government supervision, and Dulles became an adept spokesman concerning their discomfort. In late 1925, for example, he helped to arrange a special meeting at the Council on Foreign Relations, where the only subject of discussion was "the broad and general question of whether the State Department should exercise any supervision whatsoever over foreign financing." Assistant Secretary of State Robert Olds was confronted by angry bankers who where anxious to make sure that Washington knew of their concerns. Several months later, Dulles went further and drafted a critical article on "Our Foreign Loan Policy" that was published in *Foreign Affairs* in late 1926. In his article, he described the nature of the Department of State's approach to international financial activities in a way that set the stage for basic disagreement. The power to approve or disapprove foreign loans, Dulles argued, was a real hazard facing American economic interests on the global scene. Those bankers who worked within the international economy were far more competent to evaluate financial transactions than government officials:

> Control over foreign loans implies . . . control of the foreign commerce of the United States. . . . Thus control of foreign loans involves a vast power over our national economy. . . . It is, therefore, of the utmost importance, particularly during these formative years when our nation first occupies a creditor position, that power to control foreign loans should be exercised only with the utmost conservatism and in such a manner as to establish a strong precedent against the use of this power to carry out disputable and individual economic or political theories.[109]

His praise and defense of American businessmen and bankers are useful barometers for understanding the John Foster Dulles of the 1920s. They suggest, among other things, that Dulles was not one to leave business at the office. He was absorbed by his professional concerns to the point where they served something of an intellectual function. The way he thought about the world, the problems he saw, the solutions he proposed: all, as the following chapter will more fully indicate, were affected by his day-to-day work with corporations and banking houses.

5

A World View Takes Shape, 1919–1929

ONCE A WEEK, Sinclair Lewis's George F. Babbitt would direct his portly frame to a luncheon meeting of the Zenith chapter of the International Organization of Boosters Club. Adorned with a "Boosters–Pep" button, Babbitt would attend "orgies of commercial righteousness" that were typical activities for many real-life American businessmen during the 1920s. As Lewis had Babbitt describe the ideal American male's social tendencies, he was a "God-fearing, hustling, successful, two-fisted Regular Guy, who belongs to . . . the Rotarians or the Kiwanis, to the Elks or Moose or Red Men or Knights of Columbus or any one of a score of organizations of good, jolly, kidding, laughing, sweating, upstanding, lend-a-handing Royal Good Fellows, who . . . get out and root for Uncle Samuel, U.S.A."

Once every two weeks, John Foster Dulles would attend a meeting of the Council on Foreign Relations or the Foreign Policy Association. With no button marring the neatness of his Brooks Brothers suit, he would drink and talk with fellow lawyers and executives, with prominent academics and influential political leaders. There is no indication that Dulles ever came within earshot of a gathering of Elks or Moose, but he had many other organizational ties. At various times, he was either a member or closely followed the work of the American Society of International Law,[1] the Carnegie Endowment for International Peace,[2] the National Economic League,[3] the American Peace Society,[4] the Federal Council of Churches' Commission on International Justice and Goodwill,[5] the Bar Association of the City of New York's Special Committee on Private International Law,[6] the American Arbitration Association,[7] the National Committee on the Cause and Cure of War,[8] the National Council for the Prevention of War,[9] and the American Foundation, awarder of the annual Bok Peace Plan prize.[10]

I

George Babbitt and his Booster buddies have become folkloric representations of the American businessman of the 1920s. Though fictional, their group portrait is readily accepted as a realistic portrayal of paunchy, red-faced men with narrow, provincial minds, of money-chasers with no more cultural or intellectual drive than the chomped cigar stubs ever-present in their mouths. But it is too easy to generalize from Sinclair Lewis's characters. Though Babbitts may have lived and breathed in some quarters, the lifestyle of John Foster Dulles, corporation lawyer, indicates another possible pattern for the businessman of the post–World War I era. Dulles's New York, or the Philadelphia, Boston, and Chicago of some of his associates, was in many ways a world away from Zenith. The environment of the metropolis encouraged a modicum of involvement in the realms of art and ideas for many members of the business community. In Dulles's case, daily life beyond the office involved theater and opera and numerous opportunities for intellectual exchange with writers and academics at the meetings of the organizations to which he belonged.[11] Coupled with travel, such a lifestyle entailed at least a patina of sophistication.

Another distinguishing characteristic of Dulles and those like him was a deep-seated interest in the world beyond the United States. It is easy to picture Lewis's bumbling Babbitts as staunch "isolationists"; Dulles, on the contrary, like many others involved in business and banking, had gilt-edged credentials for membership in a community of "internationalists" in the United States. His travels abroad were extensive, his organizational ties at home revealed obvious sympathies, and there was no major internationalist "cause" during the 1920s which he refused to support. He showed his Wilsonian loyalties by remaining a firm enthusiast of the League of Nations and American participation in it.[12] He went on in the early 1920s to become a sympathetic supporter of disarmament negotiations after the Washington Conference.[13] In mid-decade, he was active in encouraging American membership in the World Court.[14] And by the late 1920s, he was speaking glowingly on behalf of the Kellogg-Briand Pact.[15]

Dulles's internationalism is also reflected in his political loyalties during the 1920s, where his primary concern for what major candidates thought about world affairs led to an interesting seesaw pattern of party activism. His initial postwar attachment to the Democrats he had so recently worked with was not strong enough to survive the nomination of James M. Cox, and he remained ambivalent about his 1920 vote for some time. As he wrote to Eduard Beneš, "I am awaiting future developments to decide whether I shall this year be Republican or Democrat." By election day he had decided to support the party of his grandfather, having been persuaded by prominent Republicans like Elihu Root and Herbert Hoover that Harding would work for membership in the League.[16] In 1924, Dulles turned back to the Democrats when his former co-worker John W. Davis was nominated. Davis was an ardent Wilsonian and a lawyer like himself, and Dulles worked closely with him on the internationalist policy statements that were forthcoming during the campaign.[17] Davis's loss in 1924 and Herbert Hoover's nomination in 1928 brought a final transfer of party loyalty for Dulles. A senior colleague at the Paris Peace Conference, Hoover maintained contact with Dulles all through the 1920s and seemed to the New York lawyer to be an almost perfect candidate as far as his foreign policy commitments were concerned.[18]

Still, for all the apparent differences, there is some kinship between Lewis's George Babbitt and the John Foster Dulles of the 1920s. In one very basic sense, the resident of Zenith can serve as a model against which to measure this particular corporation lawyer from New York. Beneath their obviously divergent lifestyles, both Babbitt and Dulles were thoroughly caught up in the business ethos of the 1920s: each in his fashion lived and breathed in the world of commerce and finance and was fundamentally attentive to economic affairs.

Consider Dulles's particular brand of "internationalism." In view of his family background, his early career in New York, Washington, and Paris, and his postwar clients, the *fact* of Dulles's interest in world affairs can really be simply assumed. But what were the *specific* components of that interest? As Dulles looked at global horizons and American foreign policy, just what caught his eye and prodded his mind?

Neither Dulles's views on the foreign policy *causes célèbres* of the 1920s nor even his political activities are as helpful as they might be for elucidating the specific nature of his internationalism. They simply were not that important to him. His attentions to the disarmament issue and the Kellogg-Briand Pact, for example, were fleeting and almost peripheral in nature. Like other businessmen at the time, he seems to have been swept along by waves of popular enthusiasm and never developed any real staying power on such issues.[19] In the case of the attempt to "outlaw" war, in fact, his original attraction soon became disenchantment.[20] Even Dulles's support for the League of Nations and the World Court would have to be described as occasional. His enthusiasm was great and more independently arrived at in these cases, but he was vocal in their support only during relatively confined periods of time.

Though there was a peripatetic quality to some facets of Dulles's internationalism during the 1920s, other ingredients demonstrated striking consistency. Most importantly, there was nothing fleeting about his concern for the relationship between the United States and the international economy. Picking up on the interests he had begun to develop before and during the Great War, he made them the predominant focus of his thought. What emerged, though of greater scope than Babbitt's, was a mindset Sinclair Lewis would have recognized.

A decade of intellectual preoccupation with international economic affairs began for Dulles through his interest in reparations. Back at Sullivan & Cromwell after late 1919, his attention to the working out of the German settlement was great enough to indicate he had not shaken free from his Paris milieu. Concern over reparations was a compound of natural curiosity and outside forces. Washington, for example, contacted him often for interpretations of specific reparation clauses.[21] More importantly, Dulles's own clients were not likely to let him lose interest in the German settlement. As he began his work for corporations, banks, and even a government agency very much interested in business across the Atlantic, he had little choice but to keep a constant eye on one of the key problems facing the European economy.[22]

Dulles worked hard at keeping abreast of reparations developments. Beginning in early 1920, he made at least one business trip to Europe each year, seldom missing an opportunity to observe the convolutions of the German settlement along the way. "I have now been in Germany intermittently since about the first of March," he wrote to Assistant Secretary of the Treasury Norman Davis in April 1920, "and during this time I have had occasion to talk with many Germans on the question of reparations. I have also given considerable attention to general economic and political conditions for the particular purpose of being able to judge the practical operation of the reparation obligations."[23] During such travels, Dulles always took advantage of the numerous contacts he had developed during his Paris days. In July 1921, for example, a trip to Europe brought consultation with the American Commissioner in Germany, members of the British and French embassy staffs in Berlin, the German Minister for Foreign Affairs, one of the French representatives on the Reparation Commission, and other government officials in France, Belgium, the Netherlands, and Czechoslovakia. As he summarized this itinerary in a letter to his brother Allan, "I have had an interesting trip, partially on business . . . particularly studying my old friend Reparations."[24] Activity with regard to reparations was encouraged by others as well. He was a welcome visitor for European government officials, for example. On one occasion he responded to the appeal of the German Chancellor for help in ending the French and Belgian occupation of the Ruhr: during two weeks of traveling, he talked to and unofficially negotiated on behalf of the German government with high-level officials in Brussels, Paris, and Prague.[25]

Like many members of the American delegation to the Paris Peace Conference, Dulles took a rather surprising approach to the reparations problem immediately after returning to the United States. Although their proposals had been defeated time and again during negotiations with the allies, and although the final settlement was a far cry from what had been seen as a necessary ideal, the Americans who had been involved maintained initially a naive faith in the future. Rather than predicting catastrophe resulting from the reparations burden imposed on Germany, they tended to look at the Peace Conference in a bittersweet mood. When Colonel House summed up his feelings on the day the Treaty of Versailles was signed, for example, he wrote in his diary, "How splendid it would have been had we blazed a new and better trail! However, it is to be doubted whether this could have been done . . . at this time."[26]

There was a wistfulness in House's comment that Dulles shared. He even managed to turn it into real optimism in late 1919 and early 1920. After all, he came to reason, the reparation settlement might not be as horrendous as it seemed. For all its imperfections, the treaty clauses had established what he called a "remedial agency" in the Reparation Commission. If the Commission could be made to work effectively, it might yet salvage the future. Dulles's positive attitude toward the potential of the Reparation Commission led him to consider seriously returning to Europe as temporary American representative in late 1919, an offer made by the Wilson Administration when Norman Davis proved unwilling to take the post at that time. And when the Senate was hesitant to sanction involvement in the Commission before ratification of the full Peace Treaty, Dulles fired off a strong lengthy memorandum to the Foreign Relations Committee in which he detailed the potential benefits of membership.[27]

So prepared for optimism was Dulles that he even became a strong critic of one of the few Paris workers who offered an immediate indictment of the reparation settlement. When John Maynard Keynes published his *Economic Consequences of the Peace,* Dulles pounced on his conclusions. He had worked with and liked Keynes in Paris, and they were to remain friends for many years, but the young American was not ready in early 1920 to endorse the Briton's critique. In a letter to *The Times* of London, written during a business trip in Europe, Dulles took Keynes to task for being too pessimistic. He wrote that Germany could rehabilitate its economy even under the weight of reparations—and that if its peacetime prosperity were restored, it would be "but fair and just" that the former enemy should contribute toward reconstruction in other devestated countries. The source of optimism was Dulles's view of the Reparation Commission and the powers given to it in what he called the "discretionary" or "elastic" clauses of the peace settlement. As he put it to Keynes, "Time after time the Treaty instructs the Reparation Commission not to make demands upon Germany which interfere unduly with, or are destructive of, Germany's economic life." Flexibility did not extend to any possible reduction of debt, of course, but Dulles seems to have thought there was still enough ground for hope.[28]

Keynes was interested in Dulles's views and called them "the first serious and responsible criticism with which I had had to deal." He was also perceptive about the feelings of his former colleague when he went on to write him that "I fancy that we agree pretty much at heart about what happened in Paris and only differ as to the tactics and procedure of the immediate future."[29] More quickly than Keynes might have guessed, Dulles was to recognize how much alike their views actually were, for the optimism of the American was soon to suffer severe shocks. Even before returning from his early 1920 business trip to Europe, he realized the greater accuracy of Keynes's prophecies.

It was a disturbing journey for Dulles, but one during which he did not flinch from learning his lesson. He had arrived in Germany on March 1 and spent several weeks studying the country in, as he put it, "various stages of disorder." He had watched closely the "Kapp-Luttwitz Putsch" in Berlin and had followed the fleeing Ebert Government first to Dresden and then to Stuttgart. In Stuttgart he had witnessed the calling of a general strike and had then traveled through the Ruhr to observe conditions under the "red guards." While he was impressed during his travels by the "moderateness and orderliness of the great mass of the German people," his overall mood was despondent. "Germany today gives one the impression of being almost at a standstill economically," he wrote to Norman Davis. "The plant and equipment are still here, but very little is operating. . . . There is none of that atmosphere of energy which is customary in industrial areas; on the contrary there is abnormal quiet." Significantly, Dulles saw one root cause for the depressing economic situation: the deadening influence of "the reparation clauses of the Treaty as they are now being applied. Uncertainty as to the nature and extent of obligations and the vexatious misapplication of the economic clauses of the Treaty make it difficult to get either capital or labor into operation."[30]

Dulles's travels through Germany in March 1920 undercut the premise of his optimistic scoldings of Keynes. He had learned to his disappointment that the Reparation Commission was not using its powers to encourage rehabilitation of the German economy. He was realistic enough to recognize the foolhardiness of expecting substantial payments under the "standstill" conditions that had resulted.

Although they were late in coming, wariness and distress concerning the reparations settlement did surface in Dulles following his 1920 travels. For several years, in fact, he became a depressed observer of the European scene and a pessimistic forecaster of the future of the American economy. Dulles did not muster the intense anger of a Keynes at this time, but the American's critical reactions would have made sense to the British economist and still today suggest insightful analysis of the reparations problems.

Most importantly, Dulles came to view reparations as an unhealthy and troublesome extension of the Great War's insanity. As he put it at one point, "A hurricane has swept the world. We survey the wreckage which lies in its train." To clear away the wreckage and rebuild would require major alterations in the reparations settlement, as well as in the closely related allied debts to the United States. Steps would have to be taken to eliminate the unhealthy influence of reparations and war debts on the international economy. At best, Dulles argued, "paper debts and credits which can never be collected . . . constantly disturb the political and financial situation." At worst, the resulting disturbance could wreak fundamental havoc: as he put it on one occasion, reparations were like a "gaping wound that is draining the vitality of modern civilization." Explaining this to the Belgian Prime Minister during the Ruhr occupation of 1923, he said "that I thought there was no question but what Germany was fast approaching disintegration and that unless some solution were found within the very near future, the problem of reparation would disappear forever and there would be substituted political problems which would disturb Europe for years."[31]

The problems caused by reparations seemed no less dangerous to Dulles in the early 1920s than they had in 1919. Already at the Paris Peace Conference, of course, he and his senior associates had been convinced that the reparations settlement imposed on Germany could have great impact on the future of many countries. The payment of heavy reparations by the defeated enemy, they argued, was likely to prevent the restabilization and reconstruction of Germany. Because Germany was so crucial a component of the European structure, real economic recovery on the part of the Allies would be prevented in turn. And, to follow the 1919 declination through, continued devastation across the Atlantic would have an awful impact on a United States economy which had become so dependent on its relationship with Europe.[32]

Dulles continued to believe throughout the 1920s that reparations were of great practical importance to the United States, and he offered regular restatements of his initial conclusions. Barely back from Paris, for example, he sent a lengthy memorandum to the Senate Foreign Relations Committee clearly explaining his vigorous support for American membership on the Reparation Commission:

> The Reparation Commission is in essence a committee on the reorganization of Allied Europe. Even were the United States not directly affected as it is by the carrying out of that reorganization, the United States is deeply interested in the successful accomplishment of the reorganization itself.
>
> *Allied Europe is financially indebted to the United States in a sum approximating thirteen billion dollars. It should be our customer annually for several billion dollars worth of our products. Upon the successful financial and economic rehabilitation of Europe depends Europe's ability to repay what she owes and her ability to buy from us what we wish to sell.* [Emphasis added.]

In 1921, in a memorandum on the Treaty of Versailles prepared at the request of Secretary of Commerce Herbert Hoover, Dulles wrote that the reparation clauses had "established, in effect, a receivership of Germany, Austria, Hungary and Bulgaria. The manner of exercise of the power vested in the Reparation Commission *can be of the utmost consequence to the United States in determining the nature and character of the trade relations of a vast portion of the human race*" (emphasis added). And in 1924, in a partisan blast on behalf of John Davis, Dulles took Harding-Coolidge policies toward reparations to task for neglecting key American interests:

Here was a problem upon the successful completion of which depended not merely the welfare of our late comrades in arms and the re-entrance into the family of nations of our former enemies, but *upon which depended in a marked degree our own happiness and prosperity. Until this problem was settled on a sound and permanent basis, not only would Europe remain in financial distress and political unrest, but our own goods would not move in normal lines of trade and repayment of the Allied war debts would necessarily be halted.* [Emphasis added.][33]

Nor was Dulles any more impressed by the Republican handling of the allied debts issue. These European obligations "have hung as a cloud over the debtor nations," he wrote, "depreciating their exchanges and internal credit and diminishing the possibility of our getting the maximum benefit out of our relations with them. The present condition of uncertainty should not be perpetuated. Our treasury is getting nothing out of it and our trade is losing by reason of it."[34]

Deeply concerned about the impact of reparations and Allied debts on Europe and the United States, Dulles did not fail to approach these problems in a basically pragmatic fashion. Throughout the early 1920s, he suggested many actions that he believed would lessen future difficulties. Some of his proposals were minor, indicating the distance that still separated him from Keynes, while some were more far-reaching. In a fundamental sense, his ideal program was predictable. Throughout the 1920s, he simply took the American schema of the Paris Peace Conference and reemphasized its basic goal. Any program that would yield German economic recovery should be supported, he argued consistently. As his superiors had argued in 1919, Germany was the key to the general situation: restore health and prosperity there, and the benefits would flow outward to Europe and the world in a logical pattern.

Hoping for a revival of Germany, Dulles put early and heavy emphasis on the necessity of involving the United States. Before he had even left the Peace Conference, he had assumed the importance of an American role on the Reparation Commission, and he was never to change his mind. He urged the Senate Foreign Relations Committee to approve the appointment of an American delegate to the Commission throughout 1919 and 1920. In 1921, after his friend Louis Loucheur moved again into the French government, he urged him to work for this goal: "The first objective," he wrote, "should be to secure immediate official American participation in the coming financial conferences between the Allies and Germany." And in 1924, when lambasting the Republicans for John W. Davis, he reiterated his point:

It had been apparent from the day when the Commission was first conceived at the Peace Conference that an American upon that Commission would hold the balance of power, that his impartial and detached judgment upon the problems of the Commission would permit of their solution. It was equally apparent that if America held apart, the hereditary jealousies and honest differences of the nations of Europe would prevent any solution.[35]

If an "impartial and detached" United States had become more actively involved with reparations during the 1920s, Dulles knew just what policies he would have wanted it to foster. To accomplish the rehabilitation of Germany and the restoration of a stable and prosperous Europe, he would have had the United States take the lead in putting reparations, and Allied war debts, into proper perspective. Washington could have helped encourage a recognition that these legacies of the Great War were aberrant and dangerous phenomena in the international economic and political arenas. American policy makers could have led the way to tamer governmental attitudes, in particular, in a way that would have replaced political frenzy on these questions with a cooperative, businesslike approach.

Proper perspective on reparations and war debts was of real significance to Dulles, for example. Where routine indebtedness arose from a transaction in which the debtor was intially enriched by a transfer of wealth, and his ability to repay was at least partially based on this enrichment, the Great War had been anything but enriching for Europeans. "On the contrary," Dulles maintained, reparations and Allied debts "merely measure wealth which has been destroyed." The Allied debts to the United States, as a case in point, simply recorded "the fact that the industrial efforts of the United States were intensely concentrated in pouring into Europe a vast flood of munitions and equipment, food and transport, which were there consumed in the fiery furnace of war." In view of this, "We must, thus, recognize that the debts are different, not merely in degree, but in kind, from those with which we are accustomed to deal."[36]

The unusual nature of reparations and Allied debts led Dulles to believe that the worst possible policy for governments to adopt was to assume that payments would be made and to press on after them with a vengeance. There were two villains for him in this respect: France, in its behavior toward Germany, and the United States, in its behavior toward the Allies. Dulles believed the French were particularly dangerous in their unreasoning actions. Dreaming of "mythical milliards," they had "fallen prey to illusion" and had desperately built budgets around the 52 percent of reparations they assumed would eventually come to them. "They dealt only in terms of billions and placed their hopes in paper schemes and paper budgets"; they never realized that "except for war, it would have been impossible to have had the vast transfers and quick consumption of economic values which are recorded by paper entries. In time of peace, the process cannot be reversed or undone." Worse still, French governments built an aggressive policy on this illusory foundation, going so far as the madness of the 1923 Ruhr occupation. As for the United States, Dulles disapproved of the blustering greediness of both Congress and the White House for repayment by the Allies and strongly criticized efforts to punish tardy European debtors.[37]

Such French and American policies, multiplied to a lesser degree by other governments, had to be moderated as far as Dulles was concerned. All involved parties would have to realize that the pursuit of their own best interests should keep them from trying to force full payment of reparations and Allied debts. Instead, concerted efforts would have to be made to adopt saner and safer policies. Most importantly, Dulles urged a general agreement to *depoliticize* reparations and Allied debts. Reparations, for example, he described as "the football of European politics" in the early 1920s. Efforts to deal calmly with the problem were subject to failure every time the political winds shifted direction in Paris, Brussels, or London. In the midst of the Ruhr occupation, Dulles met with his friend Louis Loucheur in France and argued that the most aggravating facet of the crisis was the tendency of Prime Minister Poincaré to punish Germany for political ends. Avoiding the collapse of Germany and horrible problems for Europe, he said, would require "the creation abroad of conviction that debt would be dealt with *on financial and not political lines.*" To get much-needed money into Germany, "it would take some time to convince the investing public that reparation was really on *a business basis* and not a political weapon which might be used to destroy Germany" [emphasis added]. Only a calmly deliberated and "businesslike" approach to reparations promised an end to disturbances of the European and international economies.[38]

As he considered what sound economic factors should influence reparations and Allied debt policies, Dulles reached one regular conclusion: the total sum of each should be considerably reduced. With respect to Allied debts, for example, he arrived in 1923 at the point where he could state quite simply: "From an economic standpoint, I believe that it would enhance the general good if these debts were cancelled." As for reparations, a decrease in the Germany obligation seemed a clear necessity. To an audience at the Foreign Policy Association in late 1922, he said, "I think it is safe to predict that reparation will never be settled nor economic stability be restored in the world until Germany's liability is brought back to an amount approximating the material damage which she has done. . . ."[39]

Dulles's ideal scheme for reducing reparations and Allied debts was a package plan which would have eliminated the dangerous aspects of each in one amalgamated blow. In mid-1922, in this regard, he thought he sensed an increase in common sense on the part of the Allies. "The most striking feature of the European situation today," he wrote for the Council on Foreign Relations, "is the willingness to clear away paper debts and credits which can never be collected, but which, by their existence, constantly disturb the political and financial situation. The Allies have avowed themselves ready to wipe out the war debts which exist between them and France is prepared to reduce the German indemnity to modest proportions. . . ." To bring such a desirable end to fruition only required meaningful American cooperation. For, the Europeans were reasoning, they could clear the boards amongst themselves only if the United States concomitantly agreed to cut back its expected due. "They only ask," Dulles wrote sympathetically, "that we cancel that which in no event will be paid" and the United States could follow no wiser course than "to avail of the present temper of Europe to effect a general settlement which will enormously enhance our own prosperity."[40]

It bears repeating that as Dulles developed these lines of analysis concerning reparations and Allied debts during the 1920s, he did not at the same time evidence the bitterness of his friend Keynes. Disturbed and wary though he may have been, Dulles did not swing totally away from the optimism that had been with him in 1919. After a period of serious uncertainty in the early 1920s, in fact, his troubled sense of confidence was actually substantially restored for the balance of the decade, at least with respect to reparations. The major reason for this can be found in the Dawes Plan of 1924. The Ruhr occupation fiasco of 1923 had brought home to government leaders on both sides of the Atlantic the connection between reparations difficulties and what the American Ambassador to Berlin had called the "quiet bleeding to death" which much of Europe was suffering in the aftermath of the Great War. To deal with the German debt and pave the way for economic recovery, the concerned governments decided, in the words of Secretary of State Charles Evans Hughes, to "invite men of the highest authority in finance in their respective countries" to fashion "an agreement on the amount to be paid by Germany, and upon a financial plan for working out the payments." The bankers met under the chairmanship of the American Rufus C. Dawes and developed a program which included provisions for more moderate German payments in the future, the creation of a committee to deal with the difficult currency transfer problem, and a major international loan to encourage rehabilitation and currency stabilization in the former enemy.[41]

Dulles, of course, had seen the need for something like the Dawes committee long before 1924, and he followed its work closely. He received much confidential information through one of its members, and his frequent business associate Thomas Lamont of the Morgan bank. Dulles was initially disturbed that the political conditions hedging in the committee had prevented it from cutting the German debt or arranging a temporary suspension of reparation payments. "If the plan fails to prove workable," he wrote, "it will be because of the defects which flow inevitably from the limitations which were initially imposed upon the committee's power." Nevertheless, he believed the Committee had done well. Reducing payments, trying to deal with currency transfer, and encouraging recovery by means of a major loan were most desirable steps as far as he was concerned. They represented precisely the measures sensible businessmen would have recommended, and it was their businesslike nature that brought Dulles's enthusiastic praise. In an article written for *The Boston Independent*, then edited by his friend Christian Herter, Dulles said that the Dawes Plan "should at least serve to *lift the problem of reparation out of the domain of politics and put it permanently upon a business domain. If so, there will have been made the most important advance since the Armistice*" (emphasis added). Indeed, without that advance being made, Dulles argued that "the financial disintegration of Europe cannot be arrested." The move toward the depoliticization of the German debt remained the most important aspect of the Dawes Plan to Dulles and always helped to explain to him the easier air surrounding reparations through the rest of the 1920s.[42]

II

Dulles's thoughts concerning reparations and Allied debts were in the vanguard of internationalist thought in the United States during the 1920s. Among business and legal colleagues concerned about American foreign policy and world affairs, for example, his attitudes were as advanced as any prevalent at the time.[43] Occasionally, as in his call for cancellation of the Allied debts, he was even well ahead of most "liberal" Americans. He regularly demonstrated a desire to work with Europeans, victors and losers alike, and to forge accommodating American policies to help solve their problems.

It is true, of course, that Dulles's criticisms and suggestions, liberal or not, were of little significance to American and European policy makers. He was a distinctly sidelines figure after his departure from the Wilson Administration, and his wide-ranging contacts never translated into real influence. Nevertheless, his views on reparations and debts command examination. Despite their lack of external impact, they became crucial elements in Dulles's own intellectual development. To a substantial degree, his thoughts served as stepping stones to a more wide-ranging world view than had been apparent prior to or during World War I. As he considered reparations and debts problems, he moved gradually toward more extensive commentary on a whole cluster of problems plaguing the international economy of the day, most of which he saw affecting the interests of the United States.

Dulles's more generalized thoughts on the international economy developed in a fashion very similar to his views on reparations. His initial mood, in 1919 and 1920, was optimistic. The United States has prospered handsomely during the war years, and the armistice brought no immediate bursting of the economic balloon: perhaps the future held yet more glittering growth. Such exhilaration was soon followed by despondency, however, as cracks in the postwar economy appeared and widened. From late 1920 until well into 1923, Dulles became increasingly distraught about his country's economic prospects. Terms like "panic," "severe business depression," and "desperate" began to figure in his vocabulary as he described economic conditions of the time. As his travels through Germany had opened his eyes concerning the realities of the reparations settlement, so too did the standard economic indicators of the early 1920s reveal the severe commercial and financial problems specifically faced by the United States. Businessmen and government officials were all too aware, for example, that their country's gross national product suffered a $3 billion drop in 1921 and that the wholesale price index had fallen from 227.9 in 1920 to 150.6 in 1921. Exports particularly suffered: from a high of $8.3 billion in 1920, they fell by more than half to $4.5 billion in 1921 and $3.8 billion in 1922.[44]

On one occasion Dulles summed up his understanding of such statistics in graphic terms. It was early in 1922 and he was recalling for his audience the brighter economic atmosphere of the previous three years:

> With the signing of the Armistice, we found ourselves in a position of extraordinary economic strength. We had repaid all we had owed abroad before the war. In our Treasury we held Allied notes for $10,000,000,000. Privately we held foreign obligations for some $3,000,000,000 more. We were producing great crops of wheat, cotton and sugar, which were commanding the highest prices ever known. Our manufacturing facilities had been vastly expanded. We had great shipyards which had already given birth to a formidable merchant marine. Our foreign trade had doubled or tripled and our banks were daily establishing new branches throughout the world. Europe was disorganized, ravaged by war. We were in tact (sic).

"It was an exhilarating picture for an American," he said and yet it had vanished like a mirage in three short years. The merchant marine was idle; the shipyards were being scrapped; American banks were closing offices in European capitals; cotton, wheat, sugar, and copper production were being sharply curtailed because of 1921s vast unsold stocks; newly installed manufacturing equipment was standing dust-covered in the factories; unemployment was climbing and foreign trade was falling. "Why has all this occurred? We seemed to have everything; we have surrendered nothing, yet all seems to have vanished. For a time all that we touched seemed to turn to gold. Yet like King Midas, we are now faced with starvation."[45]

But Dulles never really puzzled over the causes of America's economic problems in the early 1920s. He offered his own elaborate explanations on a number of occasions. Most fundamentally, Dulles cited the unavoidable aftereffects of the Great War. "The world, economically, has been torn assunder," he said at one point, and commercial and financial dislocations were dismally logical consequences.[46] On the body of Europe especially, the war had left both scars and still-gaping wounds. Considering Europe's centuries-long importance in the international economy, the damage could not but reverberate across the oceans.

There were two ways in which the damage inflicted on Europe by the Great War specifically affected the United States, in Dulles's estimation. In the first place, devastation on the Continent sharply limited the ability of Europeans to buy as much as American manufacturers and farmers were anxious to sell to them. The awful destruction of the Great War forced continental governments to turn to the printing presses for temporary remedies during the early 1920s, and a mad inflationary spiral began which is still looked back on in bewilderment. To Dulles, European inflation was directly responsible for difficulties in the American economy:

> The great mass of people, wage earners, clerks and persons dependent upon fixed salaries, can only slowly and tardily readjust their position so as to get a fraction of what should be their proportionate share of the new money. . . . The great mass of the people have become impoverished and, being impoverished, are forced to economize. The increased buying of the few newly rich by no means offsets the economies of the millions. . . . This reacts directly on the United States. It means that less cotton, less copper, less sugar, less wheat is consumed because the average standard of living has greatly fallen.

On another occasion, in an article written for the *New York Evening Post* after one of his business trips to Europe, he again described rampant inflation across the Atlantic as "fraught with serious consequences for the United States":

> It is the United States which produces and finances many of the world's great crops and raw materials, such as wheat, cotton, sugar, copper, etc. As foreign currencies depreciate, the financial ability of the rest of the world to purchase these commodities declines. Until this decline is checked, a continually increasing burden is thrown on American producers and American bankers, and ultimately we may have to curtail our production to the strict needs of our domestic market, with consequent unemployment and loss of invested capital.[47]

To compound its impact on European absorption of American exports, inflation across the Atlantic seemed likely to affect the United States in a second important way. As Dulles expressed it, "We can put the situation in one sentence. Europe, by inflating, is destroying its ability to buy from us, and is increasing its ability to compete with us." If the wages paid to European workers were not keeping pace with the rate of inflation, he argued, then in effect the costs incurred in the production of goods on the Continent were actually declining: cutting costs would make it possible to undersell competitors in various world markets.[48]

As he looked at the double-barreled threat of European devestation and inflation in the early 1920s, Dulles could only argue that the prognosis for the American economy was very serious. The potential for increasing exports to Europe, in fact, was actually worsening. After a trip in mid-1921, for example, he returned to New York deeply worried that Europeans would soon cut back even further on purchases of American food and raw materials, *"the export of which has for generations been the keystone of our economic structure."* (emphasis added). He had talked to a number of British and German financiers who were considering extensive economic collaboration with the Soviet Union for the purpose of acquiring cheaper natural products. In describing to one audience his reaction to such planning, Dulles said:

> If you will recall that even in prewar periods, the United States exported approximately 60% of its cotton, 50% of its copper, 50% of its oil and 25% of its grains, you will appreciate the gravity of the situation that confronts us.
>
> Our economic health is dependent upon having customers for our natural products. Temporarily we became a manufacturer, shipper and broker for the world. These are gains which we have already lost since the Armistice. We have shriveled back to our prewar stature and *are now threatened with the loss of even that prewar trade which is to us not a luxury but a vital necessity.* [Emphasis added].[49]

With regard to the competitive advantages of European producers with lower costs, Dulles was equally despondent. Alongside the vision of American manufacturers being undersold around the globe, in fact, he could not but place the fear that even the internal markets of the United States would soon be invaded—unless protected by undesirably high tariffs. As he phrased it in 1922, "we are gradually, indeed, rapidly being isolated. We cannot sell abroad. Our ships have nothing to carry. Our banks have no foreign transactions to handle. We must produce only for our own consumption and we can only retain our home markets by virtue of prohibitive tariffs which, in a sense, are protecting, but in another sense imprisoning."[50]

In their pessimism, Dulles's early 1920s thoughts on the relationship between the United States and the international economy were at one with his thoughts on reparations. World horizons in general looked ominous to him as he considered the future state of the American economy. But Dulles's more general concerns coincided with his opinions on reparations, in that neither moved to total negativism. He had approached reparations in a generally pragmatic fashion, regularly suggesting policies which he believed would help allay the problem, and he took basically the same line concerning wider economic difficulties. He believed, quite simply, that he knew what would be required to solve American economic problems in the early 1920s and offered numerous suggestions for meeting the requirements.

Dulles's proposed remedy for the United States' economic ills was consistently simple in conception, and his own words describe it best:

> The development and discussion of the postwar period have fully demonstrated that *the prosperity of this nation is dependent upon the economic and financial revival of Europe.* . .
>
> We are a nation of great national wealth, producing wheat, cotton, copper and like products far in excess of our own needs. We have billions of dollars owing us from European nations. Our financial relief requires a Europe which shall be able to buy from us and even, perhaps, pay her debts to us. Therefore, our national policy, dictated by our national self-interest, calls for the economic rehabilitation of Europe. [Emphasis added.][51]

How to attain such a goal was the rub, of course, but Dulles never lacked for suggestions during the early 1920s. He began with the basic postulate that none of the economic problems of the time would be solved unless the United States actively worked to find a solution. As he put it on one occasion, "The United States, in its own interest, must grapple with this problem. It is not enough that we occupy the languid role of 'observer' while Europe discusses. . . . We must have a definite objective of our own and a well-conceived plan for attaining the objective."[52] Given American activism in the international political and economic areas, a wide range of policy commitments seemed desirable to Dulles at various times from 1920 to 1923. At one point, for example, he argued vigorously for the necessity of an international economic conference at which the problems left in the wake of the Great War could be tackled: he insisted that the United States should take the lead in arrangements, because "there is probably no nation in the world which has a more direct practical interest in such a conference." One item that Dulles would have wanted on the agenda of any international gathering was the future of the gold standard. Wild currency fluctuations after the war had interfered seriously with trade, Dulles believed, and he regularly urged a return to a gold base as a way of resetting traditional ties. "We must restore a situation where we all talk the same trade language," he said. "There must be a financial common denominator. . . . If the mark be stabilized at 1 cent gold, if the franc be stabilized at 5 or 10 cents gold, that alone will shortly permit of a tremendous trade revival."[53] Other suggestions offered by Dulles ranged broadly across political and economic horizons. More businesslike arrangements for reparations and Allied debts; progress in disarmament in order to permit a balancing of budgets; more equitable American tariffs that would allow easier European access to American markets and hence easier recovery: these among others seemed to him desirable techniques for dealing with the economic travails of Europe and the United States.[54]

Hindsight makes it clear that one of Dulles's proposals for dealing with European devastation and its impact on the United States economy became of particular importance to him. Only one item in a long list during the early 1920s, its gradual realization eventually made it the key factor for him in turning dismal economic conditions into burgeoning prosperity. Specifically, Dulles became especially attentive to the financial underpinnings of American trade during the 1920s. Quite soon after the end of the war he was arguing that the real problem facing the American economy was not a shortage of demand, but a shortage of buyers with the cash needed to buy. "There was, to be sure," he wrote, "great need abroad for our goods, but they could not be bought and paid for unless the foreign purchasers could procure dollar exchange. . . ." Given the devastated and debt-ridden condition of the European economies, supplies of dollars (or even gold) were simply not sufficient—plummeting United States exports were the result. Quite simply, Dulles contended, the United States should find a way to provide Europeans and others with enough financial assistance to allow them to buy in traditional quantities from the United States while at the same time repairing the damages of the war. If the United States could help temporarily encumbered trading partners through difficult straits, the partners would recover and the United States would continue to prosper.[55]

As indicated in Chapter 4, Dulles quickly became professionally involved with various efforts to provide such financial assistance to Europe. He worked as counsel to the government's War Finance Corporation, for example, and also sought to develop privately operated foreign trade financing corporations in the United States. When neither of these became sufficiently encompassing to forestall a serious breakdown of established trade patterns, Dulles found himself turning to traditional financial circles, the great private banking houses of New York and other cities. Already during a business trip to Europe in 1920, he was writing to the Assistant Secretary of the Treasury of his hope "that private capital operating through individual enterprise would suffice to finance Europe's essential requirements from America and gradually bring about normal exchange conditions."[56]

After a slow start, to be sure, things worked out as Dulles had hoped. Beginning in late 1923, the investment banks that were so frequently to be his clients began lending enormous sums of money to governments and corporations outside the United States. From 1924 to 1929, more than $7.5 billion in long-term capital alone flowed out of the country as great quantities of high-interest foreign bonds and securities were offered to the public by the major houses. It was the most extensive financial foray into the international arena that Americans had ever undertaken in peacetime.[57]

The international lending activities of his banker clients helped work the same change of mood in Dulles's overall thoughts on the state of the American economy as the Dawes Plan had done to his view of reparations. During the mid and late 1920s, his enthusiasm for the banks became almost unbounded. Of all the solutions he had proposed for the economic travails of the early postwar world, it was the financial assistance of the bankers to devastated Europe that seemed to him to have turned the trick: he saw the prosperity of the roaring 20s as the result. The pessimism that had permeated his expressions gave way to a scintillating optimism.

On several occasions late in the 1920s, during the last golden months before the collapse of the prosperity marvel, Dulles elaborately explained the reasons for his pleasure in the work of the American bankers. His pride-filled scrutiny is useful as a guage of his high mood at the end of the

1920s and also suggests much concerning the dominant strains in his thought.

The title of one important address is itself a measure of the man: it was called "The Power of International Finance" and was delivered to a meeting of the Foreign Policy Association in March 1928. Dulles conceived of his address as a response to an increasing number of criticisms of American bankers, criticisms leveled against them for having loaned some $11 billion to foreign governments and corporations since the end of the Great War. To those who argued that such foreign loans were unsafe or undesirable in contrast to many worthwhile investment opportunities within the United States, he was hoping to paint a picture of unappreciated benefits. As he put it, "we can very usefully make a somewhat more searching inquiry into the question of why we loan money as we do, why we loan the amounts that we do, and what becomes of the proceeds."

For Dulles, the place to begin his inquiry was with a careful look at American trade figures—in particular, the relationship between exports and imports. Department of Commerce statistics revealed that in the nine years preceding 1928, the United States had exported $47 billion in goods. "That means," he argued, "that in some way the foreigners who took our goods had to lay their hands on $47,000,000,000 in order to pay our exporters for the goods which they sent abroad." The most logical source of dollars for foreigners was the sale of goods to Americans and imports to the United States had earned $36 billion toward payment for exports. Foreigners had earned in addition $3 billion for rendering services, such as shipping, to the United States, but they had also had to pay $3 billion in interest on war debts and other loans from this country. A simple arithmetic operation showed that foreigners had earned a total of $39 billion from the United States and had incurred a debt of $50 billion for goods received and interest due.

How, Dulles asked, were America's trading partners to cope with a balance of trade that greatly favored the United States, to make up the difference between what they were earning and what they were spending in their commerce with this country? During the 1920s, he argued, there had been only one way in which they could. As he put it, the difference between exports and imports was $11 billion . . . *"and $11,000,000,000 is precisely the amount of foreign securities which our bankers have sold during the nine-year period."* The large amount of additional dollar exchange required by foreigners to carry on trade with the United States had simply been advanced to them by American bankers.

Lest anyone fail to appreciate the significance of this process of balancing the United States—world trade books, Dulles carefully underlined its impact on the domestic economy:

It is essential in considering this matter of foreign lending to remember that dollars, as such, are of no interest to any foreign borrower. Dollars are spent here. It is here that they have value in the form of purchasing power and can be used to liberate one from debt. A foreigner would never borrow merely for the purpose of importing dollar bills into his own country. They borrow dollars as they require dollar purchasing power or to pay debts in this country. We may rest assured, when we see the reports of these vast loan figures, that *the proceeds of these loans are invariably utilized in this country to pay debts here, to buy goods here, and indeed a great part of the proceeds of these loans goes into the hands of the farmer for the wheat and the cotton which he exports*. [Emphasis added.]

It was especially important to remember, Dulles argued, that under the circumstances prevailing in the immediate postwar years—devastated European economies and wild international inflation—there would have been *no other way* in which the United States could have sold the same quantities of goods. Without American financial assistance, formerly valued European customers would have continued throughout the 1920s the pattern of sharply decreased trade that had characterized the first postwar years.

Instead of criticizing American bankers for undertaking a major extension of credit to customers outside the United States, then, Dulles insisted that those bankers had performed a vital and useful service. "It is the highest function of finance," he said, "to move goods from the place where they constitute a surplus to the place where they will fill a deficit, and in performing this service during the past nine years our bankers have given an extraordinary demonstration of the beneficent use of financial power." Or, as he put it in concluding his address, "That is the story of the past nine years. It is a simple story. Its details can readily become monotonous. But *it is the story of how Europe has been saved from starving and we from choking*" (emphasis added).[58]

III

During World War I and the Paris Peace Conference, Dulles had also been engrossed by economic questions. His day-to-day work and virtually all of his written expressions of opinion, in fact, seemed to revolve around specific and narrow topics. Occasionally, however, the dominant subject of his thought carried him in a variety of directions: all of the talk of trade, debts, and industrial recovery sometimes involved concerns that went beyond the precisely economic. This characteristic of the Dulles mindset, which was little more than implicit by 1919, became quite obvious in the

1920s. A continuing preoccupation with commercial and financial matters came to serve in these years as an axis around which revolved a more
wide-ranging world view, incorporating political interests as well as
philosophical and ideological values.

Dulles was capable of placing subjects like reparations, Allied debts,
and American trade into a broader context. He was inclined, in particular, to elaborate on the assumptions of 1919 by moving quickly to
analyze questions involving the general peace and stability of the international order. In considering the reparations problem, for example, he
could move from a description of economic difficulties, serious enough in
themselves, to potential political and military crises. To Belgian Prime
Minister Georges Theunis, he described the conceivable repercussions of
the Ruhr occupation by saying:

> . . . that I thought there was no question but what Germany was fast ap-
> proaching disintegration and that unless some solution were found within
> the very near future, the problem of reparation would disappear forever
> and there would be substituted political problems which would disturb
> Europe for years.

The linkage implied here figured in many of Dulles's other assessments of
international issues during the 1920s as well. Although the Locarno pacts
between Germany, Great Britain, France, and other continental states
would be interpreted primarily as political agreements concerning security questions, for example, he insisted that "in the international field,
politics and economics cannot be divorced":

> It was economic and financial need which exerted the pressure which
> led Great Britain, France and Germany to find an agreement in
> Locarno. . . . Even a few weeks ago competent political advisers predicted
> that there would be failure to arrive at a security pact. This prediction
> would undoubtedly have been verified had not economic needs
> demonstrated the absolute necessity of an assurance of political peace
> which would permit of economic good will. Germany was faced with the
> rapidly increasing burden of payments under the Dawes Plan; Frances was
> faced by a financial crisis of the first magnitude, while Great Britain was
> continuing to suffer business and trade stagnation and increasing
> unemployment on a scale which seriously threatened her future.
>
> Under the circumstances, it was essential to create mutual political
> confidence and the assurance of permanent peace in order that there
> might be an opportunity for business revival.[60]

At one point in the 1920s, Dulles even developed a grand-scale
analysis of global conflict which took the strength of economic forces as a
core premise. Although his ideas would receive extensive elaboration a

decade later, their initial statement offers an important gauge of his thought at this earlier time. He was speaking to a "Conference on the Cause and Cure of War" organized by major American women's groups in 1924 and chose as his subject "economic imperialism." It was a fascinating address. For many, he said, it was easy to imagine conflict being caused by "some greedy group of men, who seek in a ruthless way to aggrandize themselves at the expense of other peoples and who are indifferent as to whether their actions may provoke war." His reading of history and contemporary affairs convinced him, however, that the real danger stemmed from any "group of individuals who have attained great wealth and power, who influence, or are in a position to influence, governmental action, and who have become conservative and seek to resist any change which threatens the position which they have acquired." It was those who had "the desire to retain" rather than "the desire to acquire" who really contributed to international tension. They attached themselves to governments which were usually "rigid, reactionary and truculent"—and such governments frequently brought war. As cases in point, Dulles discussed the ruling classes of Austria-Hungary and Russia before World War I and even went on to suggest that Great Britain's international behavior in the 1920s was revealing similar patterns. "Theoretical analysis" Dulles concluded, "would therefore tend to indicate that under modern conditions, and particularly in our Western civilization, the greatest danger to peace is the setting up of strong government as allies of some wealthy and governing class which sees its position threatened by some basic change of social and economical order."[61]

There were obvious sources for the kind of world view which Dulles was developing during the 1920s. The legacy of the Paris Peace Conference was important, for example. His interest in certain specific issues as well as his intense overall concern for the state of the international economy had sprouted, if not germinated, there in an obvious way. There was, as well, the clearly relevant atmosphere within which he did his day-to-day work in the decade following the Great War. As head of one of the United States' most prominent law firms, specializing in international business, Dulles dealt constantly with the intricacies and problems of world commerce and finance: Sullivan & Cromwell served as a virtual hothouse environment for the growth of particular kinds of thought patterns.

Interesting testimony to the importance of Dulles's day-to-day legal activities as an influence on his thought can be seen in the special concern he showed for the role of the businessman on the world scene during the 1920s. Many of his statements make it clear that in comparison to businessmen, Dulles found many government leaders of this time sorely wanting in policy making abilities. Be the problem reparations, Allied debts, inflation, or dwindling trade, he saw few sensible programs forth-coming from American and European governments. When the economic traumas caused by the Great War were apparently overcome in mid-decade, in contrast, Dulles concluded that this was primarily the handi-work of private economic leaders on both sides of the Atlantic. Working against great odds, he argued, businessmen and bankers had created an international environment of peace, stability, and prosperity.

The Dawes Plan for reparations brought forth a typical example of Dulles's high praise for the role of businessmen and bankers. In one speech describing the origins of the plan, he recalled that Allied govern-ments had attempted to encourage substantial loans by American bank-ers to the German government in order to speed up payments by the lat-ter. The bankers had insisted that loans would be "impractical" unless meaningful alterations were made in the onerous reparations burden, however. Unwilling to consider changes at that time, Dulles maintained, the Allies had attempted to push on without the bankers and had even-tually become mired in the dismally conceived and executed occupation of the Ruhr. Following this, Dulles argued, "The politicians came back to the bankers and said, 'After all, perhaps we need your help. Won't you tell us now on what conditions you will loan money to Germany?'" The result was the Dawes Plan.

> *The terms were drastic, but they were addressed to politicians who were humbler than they had been and who had more respect for the usefulness of bankers,* and the terms were met. Under the Dawes Plan there has oc-curred a revival of Germany which in the character of its achievement is unprecedented, I think, in the whole history of the world. [Emphasis added.][62]

For Dulles, the Dawes Plan was typical of the fortuitous role that businessmen and bankers could play in international affairs. His praise for them became effusive by the end of the 1920s. Had the United States come to enjoy stunning prosperity in the aftermath of the Great War, he would ask? Thank the bankers and the Federal Reserve Board for main-taining the proper money conditions for international financial transac-tions, he would answer. Had Europe been able to rise from suffocating ashes? Thank "American ambassadors of finance" who had brought their skills and assistance to Germany, Austria, Hungary, Poland, Belgium, and Italy. These diplomatic representatives of American banking houses had helped pave the way for reconstruction:

> A people impoverished, requiring foreign credit for necessary imports of raw materials, a request for credit, the stipulation that the credit would

be contingent upon terms, the acceptance of those terms, the reestablishment of a sound financial and budgetary position, the creation of the external credit, the purchase of our goods and their movement to where they
fill a great need.

That is the story of the past nine years.[63]

Of course, not all was righted by the late 1920s. Dulles still saw governments causing problems for businessmen on too many occasions. The
Departments of Commerce and State in his own country, for example, for
all their usefulness in business enterprise showed an unfortunate propensity to meddle in the affairs of private bankers. And the Reparation Commission occasionally seemed bent on interfering with German payments
on business loans. Nevertheless, Dulles seemed hopeful by 1929 that
government intrusion into business affairs would remain largely in properly deferential limits and that business involvement in international relations would be increasingly beneficial.[64]

It should be emphasized that Dulles's preoccupation with international economic affairs, including his special admiration for the contributions of businessmen and bankers, was much more than just one component of his day-to-day work as a lawyer. Dulles's attendance to the
interests of his clients, which was energetic and successful, never determined the perimeters of his intellect. His concerns ranged considerably
further afield, though their bent was frequently encouraged or reinforced
by his sense of what was good for the corporations or banking houses retaining him.

Dulles was especially prone to assess world affairs in the 1920s with an
eye to the national interests of the United States, as many of his
statements make abundantly clear. He was also quite prepared to discuss
the interests of non-Americans. Indeed, he was convinced that the
ultimate focus of his concern was the well-being of all people in a peaceful
and prosperous world order. Exorbitant reparations, for example, were
bad for the United States, but damaging to Europe as well: in fact, they
were like a "gaping wound that is draining the vitality of *modern civilization*"[65] (emphasis added). From the very beginning, his interest in encouraging general reconstruction in Germany and Europe stemmed at
least in part from a desire to help masses of suffering people. He felt, to put
it closer to the terms in which he discussed it, that the United States had a
responsibility to help bring the world back to health and order. When he
wrote to Norman Davis about the possibility of financial assistance in the
spring of 1920, for example, he said that it would be unfortunate to allow
temporary money problems "to prevent the very real wealth of America
being available to meet *the great opportunities and responsibilities* which now

present themselves" (emphasis added). Or, as he put it in an interview in
The New York World later that year:

America is the crux of the economic and financial situation. An attitude of aloofness makes it excessively difficult for the nations of Europe
to settle their own affairs. It threatens seriously to retard the movement of
the entire world towards political reorganization and economic reconstruction. We cannot commit ourselves to such a policy. *We must realize
our tremendous responsibility to ourselves and to the world.* [Emphasis
added.][66]

Such a sense of responsibility for helping others had surfaced, of
course, in Dulles and other Americans, during the Great War. It went
then hand in hand with consistent attentiveness to the more conventional interests of the United States itself. Both were part and parcel of the
Wilsonian crusade to reform the international order, just as Wilson's
ideals were themselves part of deeply rooted assumptions held by many
Americans about their relationship with the rest of the world.[67]

Dulles's thought during the 1920s represents in one sense a flowering
of the 1919 hybrid—of the combination of quite traditional politico-
economic interests with a moral-ethical thrust. Of course, it was a rather
curious flowering, taking place on a stem which had been bent decidedly
in one direction. Like any number of his wartime colleagues, Dulles found
himself in the 1920s talking more and more about specifically American
needs and less and less about what would be good for others. He clearly
continued to believe that the proposals he put forward would yield
equivalent benefits for all, but now usually treated this belief as an *assumption* and let it stand as an implicit ingredient in his writings.

In a fascinating way, he understood precisely what he was doing. In
Paris, for example, he had never been led to question whether the
idealistic goals of the American delegation could be genuinely served
while pursuing the practical interests of the United States, whether the
two might actually be contradictory at points. Such thoughts did cross his
maturing mind during the 1920s. Looking at the constant emphasis of his
own writings, the idealist in him even seems to have chafed somewhat
under the bridle of national interest. In early 1922, he gave a speech to a
national student organization in which he argued the desirability of
American participation in an international economic conference. After
recounting at great length the financial and commercial benefits which
might accrue to the United States as a result of such a meeting, he hit a
note which might reveal the awkward self-consciousness of a Wilsonian.
"I have talked a good deal about the selfish interests of the United States
and of our material needs," he said. "I realize that such an audience as this
would more gladly respond to an appeal conceived in the loftier vein of

moral duty and aid to others less fortunate than ourselves." But by the time of this speech, Dulles had already consciously and explicitly devised a means of soothing qualms of conscience and shared it with his audience. "Those of us who are idealists," he said, roping himself into the category, "must realize that it is the driving force of self-interest that most frequently achieves practical results. . . . And *fortunately we can very properly appeal to our selfish interests without being false to our highest ideals*" (emphasis added).[68]

This could not fail to be a satisfying dichotomy for Dulles. On the one hand, he was prepared to recognize the significance of self-interest and national interest in determining views on international affairs and the foreign policy priorities of the United States, while on the other hand he convinced himself that what he thought was good for clients and the United States would yield benefits for the rest of the world as well. How fortuitous that the tide of pragmatic self-interest should have an altruistic undertow. Like many other American businessmen of the 1920s who convinced themselves, as one put it, that their enterprise had something of "glorious service to all humanity" about it, Dulles demonstrated that Adam Smith's invisible hand was still casting its spell.[69]

The end intellectual result for the Dulles of the 1920s was a species of perhaps typically American *Realpolitik*. His statements and writings took on a hard-headed, pragmatic thrust in which Wilsonian "idealism" was buried too deeply for most to see. Perhaps the conclusion of one of Dulles's own speeches indicates this more clearly than any description. He was speaking in 1924 about the problems which France had regularly caused for "a program of world reconstruction" in the aftermath of the Great War. Discussing the broad problems of the European and American economies, as usual, he cautioned against errors in judgment which might lead to criticisms of France that would be too severe. Primary among such errors, he argued, was:

> . . . the assumption that any difference between ourselves and a foreign nation is due to the inherent righteousness of our own cause and the inherent perverseness of our neighbor. Moral distinctions, though pleasing to those who draw them, are hard to sustain in fact, and I know of no historic reasons to justify our approaching these problems of international relations with the complacent assumption that we are a party to a clashing of the forces of good and evil, and that solution is to be found in the moral regeneration of those who hold views contrary to our own.

No, Dulles insisted, world affairs were more practically oriented than this. Nations acted in accord with their own concepts of what was good for them and it made no sense to wear blinders concerning the motives of one's own nation or any other. Far better to recognize the realities of national behavior—to recognize that:

> *The foreign policies of today are determined with primary regard to their bearing on finances.*
>
> Let us look at our own position. We are a nation of great national wealth, producing wheat, cotton, copper and like products far in excess of our own needs. We have billions of dollars owing to us from European nations. Our financial relief requires a Europe which shall be able to buy from us and even, perhaps, pay her debts to us. Therefore, *our national policy, dictated by our national self-interest, calls for the economic rehabilitation of Europe. . . . Generally speaking, we want the rest of the world to grow rich—so that we may get some of its wealth.*
>
> *I doubt if there is anything particularly moral about our position. It is true that our program does involve an improvement in conditions in other nations, but our interest in this improvement is not so much altruistic as due to the fact that they are at once our customers and our debtors. . . .* [Emphasis added.][70]

In basic intellectual terms, Dulles had taken some interesting steps during the 1920s. Thirty-one years old at the end of the Paris Peace Conference, he had avoided what might have been a common route for a man returning to corporate law at that stage of life—to devote all mental energies to clients and profession. Instead, Dulles had kept faith with Woodrow Wilson's Princeton philosophy and continually turned a portion of his time toward analysis of larger interests. He even went beyond just thinking about international affairs to the more demanding task of writing and speaking about them. The body of his work during the decade, though not great, is large enough to indicate a mind that never confined itself to the strict routines of Sullivan & Cromwell. His own inclinations, it should be added, were reinforced by organizations and editors ready to take him seriously. He was recognized as an expert on reparations and general world economic problems in many quarters. Throughout the decade he spoke before such groups as the Foreign Policy Association, the Council on Foreign Relations and the International Chamber of Commerce, and he prepared articles or reviews for publications such as *Foreign Affairs*, *The New Republic*, and *The Nation*.[71]

The result of Dulles's efforts during this decade was a world view of greater scope and complexity than that apparent in 1919. He had been an active man with a no doubt active mind before and during the Great War, but his particular tasks had never required more than quite specific expressions of opinion. Even at the Paris Peace Conference, he had only barely and occasionally moved beyond tightly conceived statements. In the 1920s, there was real growth beyond this. Dulles's experience and his professional status created opportunities which he was ready to grasp. He developed a clear ability to express his thoughts on a wider range of issues than had seemed to attract his attention in the past.

Not that this made Dulles some high-powered intellectual. Development in and of itself would hardly have guaranteed this. In fact, the substance of his thought remained relatively shallow and its thrust relatively immature during the 1920s.

The structure of Dulles's world view was rather simplistic. Its constant emphasis on international economic problems produced some spin-offs in other directions, but not enough to belie the fact that it had a relatively narrow base and focus. Dulles may have been a world watcher, but his thoughts always demonstrated the angular vision that came with a perch in a Wall Street tower.

Dulles's tendency to operate in specifically defined channels was compounded by a slack, almost nonchalant, critical faculty. It had been apparent already at the Paris Peace Conference that the Great War was not going to have the kind of burning impact on Dulles that it had had on some. Perhaps because of his own personal security and success, his was not a mind scarred deeply by confusion or doubt, his were not the thoughts of one of the "lost generation." Still, within the particular perimeters of his vision in 1919 and the early 1920s, Dulles's statements and writings had a certain bite to them. He had serious, perceptive things to say about some of the problems of the early postwar period and an incisive way of expressing himself. But not for long. His thrusting analysis was soon parried by developments which would not have so easily fooled a more rigorous mind.

In particular, Dulles seems to have allowed the apparent prosperity of the American economy to carry him through and beyond the anxieties felt immediately after the end of the war. He basked in the rosy glow of seemingly secure good times and even waxed rhapsodic about the brilliance of those leaders, especially businessmen, who had helped make it all possible. In the process, he let down his analytical guard in any number of ways. He lost sight of the legacy of the Great War's destruction, forgetting that it was merely being papered over, as it were, by a series of massive credit arrangements. He allowed his diligent, but Wilsonian, attentiveness to American economic interests to lead him to the conclusion that if things were going well for the United States, then they had to be going well elsewhere in the world. And he allowed his rather specialized view of his own country's economy—his great familiarity with its place in international commercial and financial transactions—to blind him to developments or problems evolving beyond his usual field of vision. Any and all of these were common enough among reputedly astute Americans during the 1920s, not to mention Europeans, but it is no mark of intellectual distinction for Dulles to have shared the shortsightedness of others.

Dulles's rosy perceptions, it should be added, strongly reinforced the essentially conservative bent of the world view he had just begun to articulate in 1919. The tendency of Wilsonians to talk less and less about significant reform and change, discernible throughout the Paris Peace Conference, was eventually carried by Dulles through all of the succeeding decade. He had made some pointed references to alterations in economic behavior shortly after the war, but even these limited proposals were quieted before long. In their place came the glowing portraits of the status quo which Dulles penned in the late 1920s, portraits based on glib assumptions about the permeability of prosperity. Why talk about reform when everything was working so splendidly? Why change an international order within which so many were peaceful and prosperous?

How ironic such an attitude would seem a few short years later.

6

Dulles as Lawyer, 1930–1939

THE GOLDEN PROSPERITY of the late 1920s was, of course, already tarnished while John Foster Dulles was marveling over it. In only a short time, its intrinsic weaknesses brought collapse. Heady economic glory gave way to the disasters of the 1930s, and every economic indicator soon shouted the dimensions of the debacle: 13 million Americans unemployed by 1932, national income down from $81 billion to $49 billion between 1929 and 1932, one hundred thousand businesses failing in the same three years.[1]

The areas of Dulles's day-to-day activity offered their own dismal statistics. At the New York Stock Exchange, the Dow Jones index for thirty industrials in January 1933 was 83 percent below the same index for September 1929: there was a room at the Union League Club in New York, which Dulles occasionally frequented, that was dedicated to the irony of Wall Street and literally papered with once-valuable securities. In the banking community, with which he was so involved, the terrain was very bleak. By 1931, two hundred U.S. banks were failing every month and almost $2 billion in deposits were lost in that year alone. One of Dulles's associates has recalled that in the 1930s "the goose didn't hang very high in the investment banking business." His quaintness veils a serious understatement: foreign securities issues, which had been a Dulles specialty and had totaled more than $1 billion in 1928, plummeted to a comparatively meager $51 million by 1932.[2] Dulles's other clients had problems too, as corporate profits in the United States fell from $8.4 billion in 1929 to $3.4 billion in 1932. And in the area of foreign trade, which was important to many of those with whom Dulles was associated, total American exports dropped a staggering 62 percent over the same period.[3]

In this decade of bust, as in the boom that preceded it, the essence of John Foster Dulles's life is to be found in his role as a lawyer. More of his time was spent on the commercial and financial problems of his banking and corporate clients than on anything else. The tone of his life in the 1930s and the place of this period in his overall development cannot really be appreciated without examining these business and legal activities.

I

Someone has written that the onset of the Depression must have seemed like a slowly bursting bubble to those who lived through it. The end result was a virtual collapse of entire economic systems, but the frightening proportions of failure were only gradually apparent. Dulles's continuing work for major American banking houses during the 1930s offers an interesting example of this. In a cycle that was typical of the time, he experienced an initial shock following the crash of the New York Stock Exchange, or other spectacular crises, then the reemergence of hope and a scurrying after plans and programs that would strengthen economies, and finally a realization that the bottom had practically dropped out and a search for whatever palliatives might be available.

Dulles's special area of interest in international finance during the 1920s had been Central and Eastern Europe, and it was precisely in this area that the most serious problems for American bankers first emerged in the 1930s. The economies of Hungary, Austria, and Germany were among the earliest to be hit by crisis after 1929. Their general malaise soon infected the rest of the developed world. By May 1931, the imminent collapse of Austria's largest bank, the Kreditanstalt, seemed to threaten the prostration of an important link in the world financial network.[4]

Initial reactions to the financial crisis in Central Europe were panicky.

In Great Britain, the Governor of the Bank of England feverishly insisted that something must be done to "save the ship before she sinks." In the United States, President Hoover quickly began soliciting suggestions from important economic figures—and at one point had John Foster Dulles tell him that he "regarded the situation as critical" because "there is danger of the whole system breaking down." Immediate alarm then gave way to cooler analysis, at least temporarily, and a scramble for remedial programs began. During June, central banks in the United States, Great Britain, and France arranged several credits of more than $100 million for the Austrian National Bank and the Reichsbank in Germany. President Hoover then secured general consent for a one-year moratorium on intergovernmental debt payments, hoping to alleviate pressure on many economies. In July, representatives of the major powers began meeting in London to devise a common program for the Central European crisis.[5]

To Dulles, the troubled air of mid-1931 was reminiscent of the problems of earlier days. As plans were made for dealing with the financial crisis, he seems to have been on the lookout for another Dawes or Young Plan—and was hoping that his firm would be involved with such transactions once again. Carefully keeping in touch with developments in New York and Washington himself, he relied on Robert E. Olds, head of the Sullivan & Cromwell office in Paris, to keep up with events in Europe. In July, Olds reported to Dulles in a way that indicated the nature of their interests:

> As you may surmise, all of us here are deeply interested in following as closely as possible the developments in the financial crisis precipitated by the collapse of German credit. . . . Various rumors fly about and the situation seems to change almost from hour to hour. . . . If the political factors can be overcome, it would seem reasonable to assume that further advances to Germany in some form or other will take place, perhaps through an international banking consortium organized at the instance or with the tacit approval of Governments. Under these conditions it would, of course, be highly desirable for us to get into the picture. . . . We shall lose no opportunity to edge in if we can.

Olds's ability to "edge" Sullivan & Cromwell into any new arrangements seemed considerable. Among the contacts he reported to Dulles were important officials in the French Cabinet and the Bank of France, and the American Ambassador to Paris. Having served as Assistant Secretary of State several years earlier, Olds also found it easy to arrange meetings with Secretary of the Treasury Mellon and Secretary of State Stimson during their July visits to Europe. In New York, Dulles felt the same concerns as Olds and was certainly not without contacts of his own. "We here are very much interested in this and in its possible developments," he wrote, "and I am trying to keep in fairly close touch with the situation." Thomas Lamont of Morgan's was keeping him supplied with all fast-breaking news, "with the result that we [Sullivan & Cromwell] have established much the best service on these matters of any one in New York." Dulles was thinking of a hurried trip to Europe to get first-hand impressions and, in the meantime, was "trying to keep in touch with the Washington attitude here in New York through Eugene Meyer, Governor of the Federal Reserve Board."[6]

Although poised and ready to act, Dulles and Sullivan & Cromwell were not to repeat their involvement in the Dawes and Young Plans. No such plan emerged in 1931. The American, British, and French officials meeting in Paris all feared that the amount of money required to stabilize finances in Germany and Austria would be too great, and the French compounded the problem by showing a reluctance to help Germany in any event. Their conference was adjourned with the classic decision to form a group of experts to "study" the situation.[7]

Unable to involve his firm in a major government-supported program, Dulles did become active in one strictly private scheme to stave off complete financial crisis in Central Europe. Between late July 1931 and May 1932, the New York house of Lee, Higginson headed a syndicate which advanced close to $500 million in short-term credits to the German Government. Dulles became legal counselor for the syndicate. Heinrich Brüning was German Chancellor during the months of these credit operations and, in later years, some of Dulles's associates looked back on the financial arrangements as ones designed to prevent the control of the German government by the National Socialists and Adolf Hitler. Dulles did come to know Brüning well during negotiations for the credit operation and maintained contact with him after his emigration to the United States.[8]

The credits provided to the Brüning government were very large, but they were far from sufficient to deal with the economic crisis confronting Central Europe by 1932. Month by month, economic leaders on both sides of the Atlantic could see stalemated governments and private bankers with limited resources attempting to cope with ever-worsening conditions. The Depression spread all too obviously around the globe, and any hopes for a quick recovery of momentum were drowned in the realization that the commercial and financial structure which had been built during the 1920s had actually collapsed. Many of the same foreign governments and corporations that had sold $11 billion in bonds and securities in the United States during the first ten years following World

War I were now unable to meet either interest or principal payments on their obligations.

The process of defaulting on bonds and securities began neatly on January 1, 1931, when the government of Bolivia announced that it was unable to continue service on its debts. Bolivia's lead was followed by many Latin American countries during the next year, and by early 1932, Hungary became the first European country to default. Crucial backstepping from obligations by Germany came in phases between 1932 and 1934, while Czechoslovakia and Poland defaulted on their extensive debts between 1934 and 1936. Overall figures by the end of the decade underline the financial devastation involved. In 1938, 75 percent of $1.7 billion in outstanding bonds and securities were in default in Latin America and 60 percent of almost $4 billion in Europe.[9]

It was not surprising that Dulles, who had been so involved with the great promotion of foreign securities in the United States during the 1920s, should soon become involved with the grand-scale defaults of the 1930s. His role as a lawyer for major American banking houses, in fact, was as great in the negative phase of the interwar period as it had been in the positive. Fees from banker clients continued to contribute substantially to the income of Sullivan & Cromwell—although the pleasure of profit for the lawyers was tempered by a long view that took into account the day-to-day decline of the international economy.

In December 1931, the State Department informally contacted a number of prominent bankers concerning the alarming increase in Latin American defaults. Responding to a suggestion from Washington that "consideration be given to the establishment of some central organization to study the situation and promote its ultimate improvement," a meeting was arranged under the auspices of the Council on Foreign Relations. The Assistant Secretary of State, the Economic Adviser of the State Department, and numerous bankers and lawyers attended. John Foster Dulles was asked to preside, testimony to the extent of his banking activities.

Meeting with the bankers, State Department representatives tried to encourage the creation of a unified American agency similar to Great Britain's Corporation of Foreign Bondholders. This British agency had been organized in 1868 to provide a common front for banker negotiations with defaulting governments and corporations, one which would be sufficiently organized to attract maximum home government support. A few of the bankers meeting in late 1931, Dulles among them, were persuaded that the time had come for Americans to take such an organizational step. In a report prepared for the Secretary of State, Dulles wondered whether Washington could possibly support a myriad of fully independent bankers: "The Department of State would doubtless feel much freer to aid the situation if it could deal with or through some central organization of high repute. . . ." But most of the investment bankers valued their independence too greatly to allow submergence in a unified agency. "With substantial unanimity" they argued that their own primary responsibility to those who had purchased foreign bonds through them could not be delegated to others. Their own knowledge of the particular circumstances of each defaulted issue, besides, led most to argue that they could best deal independently with individual problems.[10]

While Secretary of State Stimson confirmed his Economic Adviser's inclination to "follow the subject along," it was to take several more years of crisis in foreign investment to coax reluctant bankers into a common fold.[11] Instead of a unified council representing all foreign bondholders, most bankers continued to operate totally independently. At best, they organized ad hoc protective committees to deal with particular default problems. One of the first of these committees was organized shortly after the meeting at the Council on Foreign Relations when the government of Hungary suspended service on virtually all of its international obligations because of a scarcity of foreign exchange. If any exchange did become available, Budapest announced, it would be applied to service on a specified list of bond issues. American bankers were very disturbed by the Hungarian problem. At the most elementary level, they had sold $67 million in Hungarian securities in the United States during the 1920s; to compound the problem, Budapest's list of preferred issues included none that had been sold by them. To cope with a serious financial problem and what they saw as a deliberately discriminatory program, a group of houses that included the Bankers Trust Company, Brown Brothers, Harriman, and Lee, Higginson, decided to coordinate activities and appeal for State Department Assistance. The bankers chose John Foster Dulles to advise them on legal matters.

Legal counsel's opening gambit was a letter to Secretary of State Stimson on February 16, 1932, asking for government support to achieve a "rejection of the program contained in the Government's announcement with respect to the proposed application of available foreign currency to certain other long term loans (none of which are issues brought out by American bankers), on the ground that the program is unfairly discriminatory. . . ." Stimson was willing to help and sent a cable to Budapest on February 25, 1932, instructing the American representative there to "point out to Hungarian authorities the desirability of not crystallizing priorities until actual need for decision regarding foreign exchange arises and in any event until full opportunity for presenting case is afforded." But the combined pressures of bankers and State Department were not enough. As late as 1935, all American-held Hungarian bonds were in default. Even later arrangements made with the Hungarian government provided for service of only 1.5 percent interest on formerly 7 percent bonds. The road to resurrecting some value from Hungarian securities was a long one, and its end was far from satisfying for Dulles and his clients.[12]

Considering the intensive connection with German financing that Dulles had forged during the 1920s, it would have been strange if he had found himself uninvolved with Germany's economic difficulties in the succeeding decade. One particular medium for Dulles's continuing involvement with Germany was his role as American delegate to a series of "debt conferences" arranged by the Berlin government in 1933 and 1934. Attending with Albert H. Wiggin and Shepherd Morgan of the Chase National Bank, Dulles worked for banker clients who had arranged the sale of more than $1.2 billion in German bonds and securities in the United States.[13]

Germany's difficulties with foreign debts began well before the first debts conference was convened in mid-1933. Faced with serious foreign exchange shortages as early as July 1931, Berlin had created a payments scheme in which only 50 percent of interest and principal payments on debts were to be made automatically. Of the other 50 percent, as much would be paid as possible after necessary imports of food and raw materials were arranged; the balance would be paid in scrip or "blocked currency" that might he redeemed in marks or held pending the availability of the particular exchange medium involved.

For two years, the German mode of debt service worked well. It proved possible to redeem a substantial amount of the blocked currency, so that creditors received the major part of interest and principal due them on a regular basis. By June 1933, however, newly appointed Reichsbank President Hjalmar Schacht was convinced that the system would shortly break down. When he greeted the bankers attending the first debts conference in Berlin, there was an icy undercurrent in his statement that the overall problem of his country's debt should be considered "on the hypothesis that Germany would declare a virtually complete transfer moratorium."[14]

The delegates to the conference, of course, unanimously protested to Schacht the foolhardiness of a complete German suspension. As Dulles summed up his own opinions and the general reaction, "a sweeping transfer moratorium would have political and economic repercussions which would so diminish Germany's capacity to get foreign exchange that there would be danger that the . . . position of Reichsbank would be rendered worse rather than better. . . ." Germany might damage her international credit beyond repair. Perhaps reacting to the onslaught of criticism, Schacht went on to suggest an alternative German policy. It might be possible to continue debt servicing for certain countries, he told the assembled bankers, and specifically cited "the possibility of treating various national groups of creditors differently, on the basis of the particular balance of trade between Germany and each respective country." Nations with whom Germany had a favorable balance of trade might thus expect continued payments, since the Reichsbank would find itself with a surplus of that country's exchange medium.

Schacht's suggestion was followed by a six-month recess in the debts conference, a timing device that allowed representatives to consider Germany's problems and await word of what governments might do at the forthcoming London Economic Conference. Dulles and the American bankers needed no time to mull over the German proposal, however. Their reaction was immediate and very hostile. As Dulles wrote to Secretary of State Cordell Hull, Germany seemed to be moving toward a policy that would specifically discriminate against the United States, since the data submitted by Schacht had indicated "that of the principal creditor countries the United States was the only country with which Germany had an adverse trade position." This was a senseless policy for Germany to adopt, he argued, involving as it did a punishment of the United States for providing the goods and raw materials that Germany desired. He returned to New York discouraged and chagrined. "Perhaps," he wrote his sister Eleanor, "the best thing is to let the whole situation bust up and let each fellow handle the matter independently."[15]

Dulles's inclination to allow the German situation to "bust up" was temporary and he returned to Berlin for another session of the debts conference in December 1933. The London Economic Conference had failed by that time to alleviate Germany's or any other country's economic problems, wilting as it did in the face of Franklin Roosevelt's refusal to cooperate in stabilizing gold prices and currency exchanges.[16] With the situation unchanged, Schacht announced that the Reichsbank had no choice but to alter debt servicing arrangements. The delegates refused to sanction any alteration in the 50 percent cash, 50 percent scrip program, but Schacht simply announced a German government decision to pay only 30 percent in cash. In addition, and of greater importance, Schacht let it be known that the Germans had taken the bull by the horns and negotiated two short-term special trade agreements with Switzerland and the Netherlands, which provided privileged treatment for holders of German scrip in those two countries.

Dulles and his American colleagues reacted with expected vigor to these special trade and debt agreements. If such preferential treatment of certain states became accepted policy, Dulles told Schacht, American creditors would develop great hostility toward Germany. Among other repercussions, "it would be doubtful whether the American issue houses would be disposed to continue representation at the Reichsbank Debt Conferences." Dulles made some headway. Over the bitter opposition of some European delegates, Schacht arranged a special meeting between his old New York friend and the German Minister of Economics. The Minister, in turn, called a special meeting of the Cabinet at which Dulles was allowed to explain the American position. The upshot was a minor German concession, embodied in a letter from the Reichsbank President to Dulles: in the future, the Americans would be notified of any trade agreement negotiations and would be given an opportunity to voice concerns or protests.[17]

Pleased with this sign of German good will, Dulles immediately began working for a more solid success. In a report circulated to American bankers and bondholders, he urged that "prompt efforts should be made to secure some cooperation from the United States Government in laying before not merely the German Government but other interested foreign Governments, notably Switzerland and the Netherlands, the American position to the effect that the conclusion of preferential agreements based on trade concessions is unfair and in the long run contrary to the best interests of all the creditors." Perhaps Congress or the President could provide "some effective means of exerting pressure" on Germany that would yield more positive results. American securities holders, Dulles concluded, should realize "that it is not only Berlin, but to a considerable extent Washington, that holds the power of decision as to their treatment."

Dulles and the American bankers did reasonably well in securing Washington's cooperation during a brief recess in the debts conference. By the time they returned to Berlin in January 1934, a State Department communique had been delivered to the German government and had made "a considerable impression." Meetings with Schacht and members of the German government continued, with "vigorous and well-conceived support" from the State Department behind the scenes. When the British government and creditors began protesting German policies too, fearful of their own potential handicaps in a system where debt service depended on proper trade relations, Berlin was dissuaded for the time being. The Swiss and Dutch agreements were allowed to lapse, and no new ones immediately took their place.[18]

Returning from Berlin in early 1934, Dulles thought the worst of the German problem was over. An optimistic report to bondholders indicated that "a major danger" had been prevented. Consolidation of this success was necessary, but the future looked bright. Within months, however, Dulles's optimism was mocked. Already during the conferences, the American Ambassador to Berlin, William Dodd, had found it hard to understand the bankers' pleasure in German actions. Schacht's December 1933 letter had provided no effective veto for Germany's creditors over future trade agreements, he argued, involving as it did only the inconsequential obligation of listening. Commenting on Dulles's report particularly, Dodd wrote Washington that "judging from past performance" by Germany "It is somewhat difficult to discover the basis for this optimism."[19] Dodd's cynicism proved accurate. Even before the end of 1934, the German government established such restrictions on payments from the Reichsbank that all cash payments on all dollar loans, including the formerly privileged Dawes and Young Loans, were terminated. In the long run, 32 percent of all the American money lost as a result of international defaults during the 1930s was lost on specifically German bonds and securities.[20]

The Depression's awful impact on Dulles's banking clients was displayed in another case of enormous notoriety. It was one that involved Dulles in a legal enterprise of great dimensions—geographically, financially, and chronologically.

In March 1932, surveying a crumbling economic empire from his elegant Paris apartment, the legendary Swedish "Match King" Ivar Kreuger committed suicide. At the time of his death, Kreuger controlled business interests capitalized at almost $1.5 billion. His holdings ranged from match production monopolies in many countries to iron ore and chemical companies to great quantities of diverse government bonds. Impressive on paper, however, Kreuger's empire was actually dangerously weak. The economic problems of the early 1930s had been compounded by what the accounting firm of Price, Waterhouse termed "gross misrepresentation," i.e., faulty and faulted bookkeeping dating as far back as 1924.[21]

Financial leaders around the world reared in panic at the news of Kreuger's death and what it portended. Government committees were created in Sweden and other countries to investigate the economic disaster while private bankers and investors quickly scurried to organize "protective committees" that might offer some aid in the anticipated deluge. In New York, one such committee was formed by a group of bankers holding $50 million in 5 percent debentures of Kreuger & Toll, an investment holding company Kreuger had organized for his government bond speculations. Under the leadership of George M. P. Murphy and with the cooperation of Lee, Higginson, Kreuger's primary American bankers, this committee began operations by appointing John Foster Dulles legal counsel.[22]

The obvious objective of any protective committee would be the safeguarding of the value of particular securities held by certain individuals and institutions. In the case of the Kreuger & Toll 5 percent debentures, this was an incredibly difficult job that was to involve Dulles in close to a decade of business machinations.

Dulles's initial advice to the Murphy Committee was to be attentive to the situation in Sweden, Kreuger's home base. Fearful that the Swedish government would attempt to manipulate Kreuger's holdings in a way that would benefit primarily the Swedish and International Match Companies, Dulles sent a Sullivan & Cromwell junior partner on an investigating expedition. With the cooperation of important European holders of Kreuger & Toll debentures, Dulles's committee successfully pressed for the appointment of a representative on the Swedish government agency that had been established to deal with Kreuger's tangled affairs. Jean Monnet, who had worked with Dulles on the Polish Stabilization plans of the 1920s, was eventually accepted by Stockholm as a spokesman for Kreuger & Toll interests.[23]

With the rear somewhat protected, Dulles next entered New York Federal Court and successfully persuaded the presiding judge to declare Kreuger & Toll bankrupt in the United States. This move was a necessary preliminary to carefully assessing the company's assets in this country. Gordon Auchincloss, another former associate of Dulles's, was appointed receiver by the court and began gathering data on the company's holdings in August 1932.

Auchincloss's findings were as bad as the Murphy Committee may have feared. The paper value of Kreuger & Toll assets was impressive, he reported in early 1933, but the real value on world markets of the day was virtually nil. The more than $100 million in German, Hungarian, Kingdom of Serbs, Croats and Slovenes, Republic of Latvia, and Kingdom of Rumania bonds that represented the company's major holdings would not fetch a small fraction of their original worth in an auction at that time.[24]

Contemplating the grim realities, Dulles and his clients decided that an auction of Kreuger & Toll assets was out of the question in 1933. As an alternative to doing nothing, they began pressing the Swedish government and the Swedish and International Match Companies about the possibility of a fundamental reorganization of all of Kreuger's enterprises. While reorganization would involve no immediate return for Kreuger & Toll debenture holders, it might promise the reestablishment of viable and profit-making corporations in the long run. A formal series of meetings to consider possibilities took place in Stockholm in September 1933, and found all but the Kreuger & Toll forces uninterested in going further. Kreuger's other enterprises, encumbered with debt though they may have been, were hoping to recoup losses from continual production and profit-making. They saw no reason to allow their resources to be siphoned off by the totally unproductive and particularly instable investment holding company.

Unwilling to accept initial defeat, the Americans represented by Dulles agreed to pay expenses for further meetings. As chief negotiator the Murphy Committee chose Norman Davis, who was enticed away from government service and disarmament talks by a retainer of $75,000 and the promise of a like amount if a successful reorganization scheme were forthcoming. Davis began negotiations in Stockholm in late 1933, brought them to New York in October 1934, and completed them in New York in April 1935—and never earned his second $75,000. Neither his own work, Dulles's active assistance, nor the friendly interest of Washington (in the person of Ambassador to Sweden Laurence Steinhardt, who became a good friend of Dulles's during the Kreuger & Toll operations) could melt down the resistance of the various Swedish and International Match forces. By July 1935, the negotiations were ended by a terminal agreement under which Kreuger & Toll transferred any interests and securities in the match industry to the Swedish Match Company for the sum of $2.5 million. Nothing more was ever gained from other components of Kreuger's empire.[25]

After the financial settlement with Swedish Match, the Kreuger & Toll debenture holders moved reluctantly toward an auction of assets. In late 1935 and early 1936, financial agents traveled through Europe scouting potential bidders in government offices and corporation headquarters. Virtually none seemed to exist. Then, in April 1936, in a last desperate effort to avoid a disastrous conclusion, Dulles's clients came up with a new maneuver. A formal petition was filed with the Securities Exchange Commission to allow the creation of a new holding company, the Kreutoll Realization Company. The new venture was created to purchase all Kreuger & Toll assets at an auction and then hold them for disposal at some future and assumedly more propitious date. In October 1936, the auction was held, and Dulles cast virtually every successful bid: his clients, now organized as Kreutoll Realization, put up all but $34,000 of the $9 million raised *in toto*.

With the auction of its assets, Kreuger & Toll ceased to exist as an enterprise in the United States, and Dulles's initial service for its debenture holders was ended. By that time, however, he had already begun work as legal counsel for Kreutoll Realization and continued to serve it in the years ahead. In 1937, for example, he oversaw the purchase of $22 million in Yugoslavian bonds by a Yugoslavian bank willing to pay $4.4 million. In 1940, he successfully appealed to the State Department for pressure on the government of Greece concerning a delayed interest payment on some 1930 bonds.[26] The major portion of his work on affairs involving Ivar Kreuger's enterprises had come to an end with the Kreuger & Toll auction, but something more than just the memory lingered on. (As late as 1964, a Sullivan & Cromwell partner was still attentive to Kreutoll Realization's situation: in discussing the history of the company, he mentioned that $23 million in Hungarian Land Reform bonds had still not been sold and represented a continuing "asset" of the company![27])

Dulles's work on behalf of banking clients with financial difficulties was enormously profitable for himself and Sullivan & Cromwell. His legal fees for work on the Murphy Committee and Kreuger & Toll debenture holders alone, for example, came to more than $540,000 by the end of the 1930s.[28] But the difficulties being faced by valued clients sometimes became too great even for the lawyers on the scene, and Dulles's role as head of Sullivan & Cromwell brought him into contact with several such situations. In an October 1934 letter to William Nelson Cromwell, for example, Dulles reminded his titular superior "that in the course of our discussion on Firm policy which took place last spring, we both felt that in view of the crippled condition of many of our clients, particularly those that have been active in the financial field, it might be necessary and desirable in the interest of the Firm to help some of them get a fresh start, if this could be done under circumstances which gave promise of successful activities along lines which could lead to desirable business for the Firm." During the initial discussion Dulles alluded to, Sullivan & Cromwell partners had tried to decide how to deal with what seemed to be the imminent collapse of the prominent First National Corporation of Boston. They had considered the possibility of putting $50,000 into a similarly named new venture. By October, Dulles had given careful thought to a new project along the same line and was seeking Cromwell's financial cooperation.

He had in mind the support of a partnership between two old friends and business associates, Jean Monnet and George Murnane. Monnet, who was of course to become most prominent in international affairs at a later date, had already known Dulles for fifteen years by 1934. The two men had initially met in Paris in 1919, where Monnet had been an assistant to the French Minister of Commerce. After some work for the

League of Nations, he had become closely associated with Dulles in 1926 and 1927 while working with the Bankers Trust Company, Chase National Bank, and the Federal Reserve Board on the Polish stabilization plan. Subsequently, Dulles succeeded in having him selected as the foreign liquidator in the Kreuger & Toll dissolution. Monnet, Dulles advised Cromwell, "is one of the most brilliant men that I know" and "an intimate friend."

George Murnane, too, was an old friend by 1934. He had been a New York associate for years, first through his work with the New York Trust Company and then as a partner in the Lee, Higginson investment banking house. He was to remain one of Dulles's closest friends for the rest of his life.

"I have long felt that they would make an ideal combination," Dulles wrote in description of his plan, "and the fact that they are apparently coming together is largely due to my efforts in the belief that if they did so they would be exceedingly successful in becoming engaged in enterprises which in turn would produce a large amount of legal business." The two men had in mind the organization of a New York firm that would act as "financial agents" for various enterprises. Dulles was proposing that Sullivan & Cromwell put up $50,000 in support of the plan, half of which he was willing to supply himself. Cromwell cabled back agreement and Monnet–Murnane came into existence shortly thereafter.[29]

Aside from the interest of the early association of Dulles and Jean Monnet, Sullivan & Cromwell's financial support of Monnet–Murnane serves as another clear indication of the blighted contours of the financial community. "The crippled condition of many of our clients"—it was all too obvious to John Foster Dulles.

II

As extensive as his ties to them were, major banking houses comprised only one portion of Dulles's regular clientele during the 1930s. Substantial work for American and foreign corporations which had begun during his early days at Sullivan & Cromwell even before World War I continued into the Depression years. His corporate activities around the world gave him an even fuller appreciation of the condition of the international economy than banking work alone would have provided.

A number of Dulles's corporate clients during the 1920s continued into the 1930s. He remained a member of the Board of Directors and Executive Committee of the American Agricultural Chemical Company; a

Director and Executive Committee member of the Babcock & Wilcox Corporation; a Voting Trustee and Director of the Gold Dust Corporation; a Voting Trustee and Director of the Grand Union Company; a Director and Executive Committee member of International Nickel Company of Canada, Ltd. and International Nickel Company; a Director of S. Slater & Sons, Inc.; a Director of Tobacco Products Company; and a Voting Trustee and Director of the United Stores Corporation.[30]

Dulles also maintained ties with a number of clients among public utilities and public utility holding companies during the 1930s. He remained legal counsel and member of the Board of Directors for the Detroit Edison Company and the North American Edison Power Company, for example, and became a Director and Executive Committee member of the Electric Shareholdings Corporation (a $20 million investment trust); a Director of the Milwaukee Electric Railway and Light Company; and a Director of the Western Power Company.[31] He became particularly active on behalf of these clients after the passage of the Public Utility Holding Company Act in 1935—a bill which grew at least in part out of the mad stock market machinations of people such as Dulles and corporations such as his utility holding company clients during the late 1920s. During bitter congressional debates concerning the regulatory act, the companies involved mounted an enormous lobbying campaign to persuade sympathetic Congressmen that it was a dangerous departure from free enterprise. William O. Douglas, then a young member of the Securities Exchange Commission, which was to be given supervisory powers over the companies, remembers John Foster Dulles as one of the primary organizers of this campaign. There is no hard information to indicate that Dulles actually played this role, but his sympathies were clearly opposed to congressional action. When sufficient majorities in Congress ignored business pressure in this case, Dulles went on to put in months of work accumulating and transmitting the information about his clients that was required by the S.E.C. For the first time in his career, he was forced to cancel a business trip to Europe—in order to deal with the flood of utility company work.[32]

Aside from continuing corporate clients and work with public utility holding companies, a considerable amount of new work with corporations developed for Dulles during the 1930s. Information about these clients is relatively sketchy, as it is for earlier years, but it does underline further the wide range of Dulles's legal career and its truly international scope.

In 1930, for example, Sullivan & Cromwell was consulted by W. A. Harriman and Company concerning a concession for an electric light and power distribution system obtained from the Polish government several years earlier. Having invested substantial sums of money in lengthy engineering surveys, the company had discovered that the Poles were in the process of negotiating with a French firm for a similar project. Dulles, among other actions, cabled the details of the problem to the State Department and requested that the American Embassy at Warsaw "be authorized to take a friendly interest in the situation." According to Averill Harriman, this was only one of a number of occasions on which Harriman and Company, as well as Brown Brothers, Harriman, called on Dulles for legal services.[33]

Also during the 1930s, Dulles became involved with the platinum interests of Adolf Lewisohn & Sons. Although almost no details are available, this was a relationship which Dulles himself described at one point as "exceedingly complicated." In particular, it involved Sullivan & Cromwell in negotiations with the Soviet Union before the official recognition of that country by the United States in 1933.[34]

In another case involving the Soviet Union, Dulles continued legal work for several major American insurance companies involved in court battles concerning pre-1917 policies covering Russian citizens. Deprived of their sizeable investments in that country by the Soviet government, New York Life, Equitable Life, and other companies had attempted to forego payment on a substantial number of claims by Russians who had left their country following the Bolshevik revolution. Litigation continued throughout the 1920s and came to a temporary end only in 1931. A settlement was arranged by New York Life in that year with the largest group of Russian policy holders. For an undisclosed amount the beneficiaries agreed to assign any and all claims against the Soviet government to the New York Life Insurance Company. The firm seems to have anticipated an eventual negotiation with the Soviets concerning its $67 million in confiscated investments.[35]

In addition to involvement with American firms concerning various international business problems, Sullivan & Cromwell had a full complement of foreign clients during the 1930s. Among those with which Dulles was personally concerned were some that had first drawn on his services during the 1920s. With the North German Lloyd and the Hansa Steamship Lines, for example, Dulles maintained contact concerning bond transactions that had been arranged in the plusher days of the 1920s.[36] New clients outside the United States included one close to a domestic interest: court work was undertaken for the Société Intercommunale Belge d'Electricité, a large public utilities company in Belgium.[37] Considerably further east on the Continent, Dulles was also legal counselor for Hans Petschek. A wealthy Czechoslovakian who spent much time in the United States, Petschek had financial interests all over Europe. For one of his concerns, the United Continental Corporation, Dulles served as a Director and Chairman of the Board during the 1930s[38] (A decade later, during the early Cold War crises there, Dulles was to be greatly concerned with the internal affairs of Czechoslovakia because of his continued representation of Petschek's business interests.)[39]

Yet another European client, one which involved Dulles in a notorious legal hassle, was the Bank of Spain. Late in 1938, this bank retained Dulles and Sullivan & Cromwell as legal counsel in the United States for the purpose of bringing suit against the Federal Reserve Bank of New York. Seeking $15 million, the Bank of Spain was hoping to compensate itself for a financial loss that had grown out of that country's bloody civil war. In early 1938, representatives of the embattled Barcelona government had approached the United States Secretary of the Treasury concerning possible purchases of Spanish silver. The silver contemplated for sale was not the property of the government itself, however. It belonged rather to the privately owned and operated Bank of Spain, which, since 1874, was the institution empowered to issue currency in that country. The bankers claimed that the United States Treasury agreed to the purchase without formal corroboration of their willingness to sell. In subsequent days, approximately $15 million in silver was stolen from the Bank of Spain and shipped to the United States, where cash and check payments were made to the representatives of the Barcelona government.

What the bankers were seeking in United States courts was damages for the inappropriate conduct of government agencies like the Treasury Department and the Federal Reserve Bank of New York, to which the shipped silver had been delivered. They claimed that United States officials were aware of the private control of the Bank of Spain, that they should not have been willing to engage in such a sales transaction with any but Bank of Spain officials, and that most importantly, no payments should have been made to any but individuals empowered to accept by the Bank.

Dulles seems to have hesitated before undertaking the legal work for the Spanish bankers. Perhaps the emotional climate of the day concerning events in Spain made him wary of doing work for an institution that might have seemed to be an arm of the Franco government. Perhaps not, however. After seeing the Secretary of State and receiving assurances from the Treasury Department that no substantive foreign policy issues were involved, he accepted the retainer. His legal counterpart, working for the Federal Reserve Bank, was former Secretary of State Henry L. Stimson.

Within a year, the case for the Bank of Spain had been lost and Dulles's public image had been tarnished. As will be described below, he was to be haunted for many years by the charge that he and his firm had been willing to undertake legal work for the fascist Franco regime. His constant disclaimers concerning the strictly "private" nature of the Bank of Spain made little dent in the charges.[40]

III

Dulles's career as an international lawyer was seldom deemed worthy of comment in the later, more public years of his life. While he was Secretary of State, biographical summaries of his earlier life would jump quickly from his work at the Paris Peace Conference to his church-related work in the early 1940s and his tentative relationship with the State Department during the Truman years. Only one aspect of his professional work ever received anything like real public attention—and it was such that Dulles would gladly have done without it. This involved his supposed ties to German industry and finance during the 1930s, with the concomitant issue of his relationship to the Hitler regime and fascism in general. The raising of these matters was invariably handled in exposé-style journalism and was accompanied by bitter denunciations of his pre–World War II business conduct.

Perhaps the first example of the muckraking of Dulles's legal activities came during the 1944 presidential campaign. Dulles was publically recognized then as Thomas Dewey's major foreign affairs advisor, and the possibility of his becoming Secretary of State while Germany had yet to be defeated seemed too disturbing to some journalists. Drew Pearson fired an opening salvo against him which was immediately supported by Walter Winchell as having the potential to "rock America." In what one subsequent defense of Dulles called "most scurrilous and venomous attacks," Pearson and Winchell charged that the senior partner of Sullivan & Cromwell had rendered consistent legal services to "the banking circles that rescued Adolf Hitler from the financial depths and set up his Nazi party as a going concern." They specifically suggested that Dulles had had professional ties with Baron Kurt von Schroeder. Further, Pearson maintained, Dulles had shown a strange affinity for other fascist types. He had "argued personally for Dictator Franco of Spain" and had had "legal relations with Count René de Chambrun, son-in-law of Laval, now arrested." Outside journalistic circles, Senator Guffey read the same charges to his colleagues on the floor of Congress.[41]

Later examples of such charges abound. In early 1947, while receiving press attention for his role at the Moscow meeting of the Council of Foreign Ministers, Dulles's legal association via cartel relationships with the German industrial giant I. G. Farben was discussed on national radio by commentator Raymond Walsh. A Soviet-controlled broadcast in Germany at the same time referred to his ties with the Schroeder bank and, in fact, broadened the charge against him to include general profascist sentiments in the years before World War II. Citing sections of 1939 statements, it was suggested that Dulles had seen no threat from the fascist powers and had been a consistent apologist for their aggression. In 1949, too, while Dulles was running for a Senate seat against Herbert Lehman in New York, much was made of his 1930s activities: Lehman and others leveled a bombshell charge of anti-Semitism against him, and Harold Ickes, for one, raised questions about his earlier German associations.[42]

These charges concerning Dulles' professional activities before World War II are important and deserve examination. If accurate, they suggest an important conclusion concerning Dulles's nature as a lawyer and an individual. Even if such work comprised only a small part of his long and wide-ranging legal career, it would be so morally reprehensible as to deserve singular attention. If untrue, the charges could be laid to rest as the ravings of cranks and political enemies—which is certainly the fate Dulles wished them during his lifetime.

Dulles never hesitated to issue firm denials of the charges. While he refused to get involved in public altercations—for fear, he said, of giving too much importance to his accusers—he regularly issued private rejoinders. As Chairman of the Federal Council of Churches' Commission on a Just and Durable Peace in 1944, for example, he assured its executive committee that the charges were untrue and agreed to resign the post if they thought any damage might be done to the Commission work. In 1947, answering an accusatory letter in *The New York Post*, he wrote that "Frank Kingdon's article is totally misleading and merely paraphrases the smear line which has been adopted by the Soviet communist newspapers. See, for example, the Moscow *New Times*, issue of February 28, 1947." A few months later he started specifying denials, writing "I have never had anything to do with, or even met, Baron Kurt von Schroeder. I was never attorney for the Franco regime. I was never attorney for Count de Chambrun . . . neither I nor my firm has ever represented in any way I. G. Farben. . . ."[43]

Dulles's denials were buttressed from other sources as well. When the first charges were made against him in 1944, the editorial staff of the *Christian Century*, then actively supporting the work of his Commission on a Just and Durable Peace, hurriedly issued a biting editorial against the attackers.

The Christian Century, moved by a sense of outrage at this sort of attack upon an outstanding Christian statesman, has taken pains to inquire into the allegations and innuendoes which form the substance of this assault upon his character. From authentic and trustworthy sources we are able to deny outright many statements of alleged fact and the innuendoes which certain statements of fact were made to carry.

They denied any ties to German banking circles by Sullivan & Cromwell and added that "during the past ten years neither Mr. Dulles nor his firm has represented any Axis national. This was not a coincidence; it was a matter of deliberate policy." In contrast to the charges, the editors emphasized Dulles's wartime associations with the Allies, his legal work for the British, French, Dutch, and Belgians. Years later, other members of Sullivan & Cromwell also denied the charges. Allen Dulles, for example, who had found himself smeared by the same brushes, recounted the closing of Sullivan & Cromwell's Berlin "office" in the early 1930s: the rooms maintained for the firm in the Hotel Esplanade had been closed "because of Hitler. You couldn't really do an honest piece of law in Germany after the Hitlerian laws began to be passed and the Hitlerian discipline clamped down on the country. And I remember very well the reason for the closing. There was no particular incident, except that we didn't feel you could practice law there."[44]

In the face of such denials, what should be made of the charges against John Foster Dulles? In some ways, it is tempting to deny them outright. It is clear, for example, that the heavy direct involvement of Dulles and Sullivan & Cromwell in German business and banking during the 1920s and early 1930s was *not* continued into the Hitler era. There is no reason to doubt the closing of the Sullivan & Cromwell office in Berlin. There is no clear evidence indicating legal work for I. G. Farben, no definitive proof linking the London or New York Schroeders to their German namesakes, no proof at all linking Dulles directly to Spain's Franco.

It is true that with the advantage of access to his personal papers, pointed questions might once have been put to Dulles. He might have been asked, for example, why the closing of Sullivan & Cromwell offices in Berlin and the supposed cessation of legal work there had been followed by continued business trips to Germany. His own correspondence and passports indicate visits to Berlin in 1934, 1935, 1936, 1937 and 1939. In early 1936, his itinerary in Berlin included consultations with Hjalmar Schacht, an old friend and Hitler's choice to head the Reichsbank; H. F. Albert, partner in a German law firm with which Sullivan & Cromwell had had frequent dealings; and officials of the Hansa Steamship Company concerning financial matters.[45] Questions might also be raised concerning the purported independence of the London-based J. Henry

Schroeder and Company. Because the British members of this family were cousins of the German, some journalists and authors have suggested that that bank served as a financial link between German industrialists and the banking centers of Great Britain and the United States.[46] On another front, the actual independence from the Franco regime of a key institution like the Bank of Spain might be questioned. Having raised these matters, however, one would be forced to conclude that the evidence for definitive statements is either so ambiguous or so limited that it is far from sufficient. The type of bitter denunciation of Dulles's business conduct that was made after the 1930s could simply not hang on such alone.

In another respect, however, there is good reason not to leave the question of Dulles's associations with Nazi Germany too hastily. A thorough study of his legal work suggests that there are some major activities which may be of key importance in this regard. To telescope somewhat, something of the spirit if not the letter of the critiques of Dulles and his business associates proves to be correct after all.

Pertinent here are Dulles's close associations with some of the most significant of the international cartels that emerged in the world economic arena during the 1920s and 1930s. Anxious to subject world markets to what they considered safe and profitable controls, producers from many countries negotiated a wide range of formal operating agreements during the interwar years. Common among them were marketing arrangements that divided world sales on the basis of territorial prerogatives or quotas, price-fixing programs, patent, and process-sharing procedures designed to eliminate technological advantages for any single participant, and actual joint operation of subsidiaries in which stock and management were shared in agreed proportions. Most of these agreements were designed to rationalize and stabilize industries thought to be strongly competitive or even chaotic. Cartel organizers argued that the existence of many independent corporations in many countries, competing intensely with each other for limited markets, raw materials, and technological advantages, created an international economic milieu in which uncertainty and wasteful competition were grievous burdens. They set off to negotiate gentlemanly agreements with counterparts in other states so that an orderly, predictable, and profitable economic system could emerge.[47]

Cartel agreements became particularly pervasive during the crisis-filled days of the 1930s. With devastating weaknesses and irregularities in world economic enterprise, industrial stability became especially appealing. Further, as many governments developed autarchic commerical and financial policies that created serious barriers to normal economic activity, corporations that relied heavily on international activity used cartel associations as devices for piercing such barriers. The result was that few products used by industries or average consumers escaped the influence of cartels during the 1930s. Estimates as to the number of cartels in operation by World War II range from a minimum of 250 upwards to more than 1200. A League of Nations study concluded that 42 percent of world trade between 1929 and 1937 was under the control or strong influence of cartels. Another later study surmised that 87 percent of all mineral products, 60 percent of all agricultural products, and 42 percent of all manufactured products sold in the United States in 1939 were cartelized.[48]

John Foster Dulles was very much involved with the increasing importance of cartels during the interwar years. Already in the 1920s, he was expressing annoyance at what he took to be a naive American suspicion of such economic entities. By the 1930s, his role at Sullivan & Cromwell made him an active participant in both the creation and ongoing functioning of at least two of the major international cartels of the time.

The first and most clear-cut case of Dulles's involvement with international cartels stems from a business association already mentioned. From 1922 to 1949, Dulles served as a Director and member of the Executive Committee of both the International Nickel Company of Canada, Ltd. and its American counterpart, the International Nickel Company. INCO was the largest producer of nickel in the world, with combined assets in excess of $290 million by the end of World War I. In the early 1930s, during the period of Dulles's association with the company, a series of agreements were negotiated with the other major nickel producers of the world. First was an arrangement with two major French producers. In 1931, the Société Anonyme Le Nickel and the Société Anonyme Caledonia Charbonnages Minerais et Metaux de la Nouvelle Caledonie organized the jointly owned "Caledonickel" in France. In the same year, International Nickel entered a formal agreement with this new entity designed to eliminate competition in the distribution and sale of commercial nickel. A "Main Agreement" going into effect on January 1, 1932, with an expiration date of December 1943, granted International Nickel exclusive market rights in the United States and Canada while dividing the balance of world markets by negotiated quotas. Prices for commercial nickel were also fixed by the agreement. A second step in early 1933 brought an agreement between an International Nickel subsidiary and Norddeutsche Affinerie, a German nickel refiner, making International Nickel the distributor of the German firm's nickel production. And third, in 1934, International Nickel and its French associates reached a formal agreement with Germany's I. G. Farben. In a "Main Agreement" and a "Patent Agreement" a series of understandings was reached: International Nickel maintained its exclusive market privileges in Canada and the United States, while markets in the rest of the world were divided between International Nickel, the French concerns and I. G. Farben on the basis of newly negotiated quotas; license rights to a newly patented I. G. Farben nickel refinery process were granted to International Nickel, and the latter agreed in return to supply I. G. Farben with supplies of nickel-bearing materials; sales of I. G. Farben's production of the mineral were to be handled by International Nickel and Caledonickel distributors; and price schedules were also arranged. The original term of the agreement was to have been from January 1934 to December 1943, but a revised "Supplemental Agreement" was negotiated in 1937, increasing I. G. Farben's market quotas.[49]

John Foster Dulles was quite clearly associated with International Nickel throughout these worldwide negotiations. As member of the Board of Directors and Executive Committee determining such policies, and as senior partner of the law firm retained by International Nickel as "legal counsel," he can be described as intimately associated with the establishment of the world nickel cartel. When the United States Department of Justice brought suit against International Nickel for violations of the Sherman Act in May 1946, in fact, Sullivan & Cromwell continued its traditional role and handled the legal defense against the antitrust action. Of particular interest in this regard is the fact that the defense tactic chosen admitted freely the existence of the enumerated 1930 agreements. The brief against the Department of Justice action rested only on a challenge to the charge that the Sherman Act had actually been violated. In 1948, after two years of consultations between counsel and government officials, "a complete accord" was reached which resulted in a "consent judgment" against International Nickel without formal trial proceedings.[50]

International Nickel's network of agreements offers only one example of Dulles's role in building cartel associations during the 1930s. On another front, he was connected with negotiations among the world's major producers of chemicals and helped to organize what is often referred to as the "Grand Alliance" of the interwar years.

An enormous range of products and a constant flow of technological innovation made instability part of the very essence of chemical enterprise. Chemical producers believed that they faced enough uncertainty without having to cope with the routine difficulties of intra and international competition and had negotiated numerous cartel agreements as early as the 1870s. Substantial stabilization of the industry on a global scale, however, was interrupted by the outbreak of the Great War. In the aftermath, the damaged condition of traditional powers in the field and the emergence of new young giants in the United States and Japan made it necessary to build anew during the 1920s. Complex new interrelationships were gradually constructed and the rationalizing process was nearing completion by the late 1930s. Hundreds of separate agreements had been arranged among virtually every major chemical producer in the world by then. Germany's I. G. Farben, Great Britain's Imperial Chemical Industries, Ltd., Belgium's Solvay & Cie., France's Establissements Kuhlmann, Italy's Montecatini, Czechoslovakia's Aussiger Verein, Japan's Mitsui, and the United States' Dupont and Allied Chemical & Dye were all tied to each other in varying degrees.[51]

Dulles's involvement with this process of cartelization of world chemical producers stems from his 1930s association with one of the oldest of the field's giants, Solvay & Cie. of Belgium. Solvay's power developed on the basis of crucial technological innovations in the production of alkalies during the 1870s. A new ammonia soda process allowed the company to enjoy great advantages in supplying the chemical needs of glass, soap, paper, synthetic fiber, textile, petroleum, food, and drug companies. A worldwide network of operations was gradually created. In 1872, Brunner Mond (one of the eventual components of Imperial Chemical Industries) was organized by Ernest Solvay and granted the exclusive license to the alkali process for the entire British Empire. Similar steps were taken around the world. In addition, Solvay began undertaking cooperative projects with other major chemical producers. With I. G. Farben, for example, Solvay owned stock in the Czech firm Aussiger Verein and jointly operated the German Solvay Company. After the organization of Imperial Chemical Industries, too, Solvay's involvement in Brunner Mond brought it 25 percent of the stock and directorships in the new British giant. And in an area that would eventually involve John Foster Dulles, Solvay controlled a similar 25 percent of stock and directorships in Allied Chemical & Dye in the United States.

Through subsidiaries and direct stock control, Solvay & Cie. thus reached into every area of world chemical production by the 1930s. Its scope and influence were yet further enhanced by participation in significant cartel arrangements. In the United States, for example, the Solvay–American Investment Corporation was a holding company whose principle financial resource was 500,000 shares, or 25 percent, of the outstanding common stock of the Allied Chemical & Dye Company. Dulles and Sullivan & Cromwell were legal counsel to Solvay–American and participated in the creation of both informal and formal cartel arrangements between the Belgian and American companies. This was not always easy. Allied Chemical occasionally showed signs of resisting the impulse toward industry-wide cooperation shared by its "competitors."

During the 1930s, in fact, the company developed a reputation for old-fashioned, dog-eat-dog competitiveness. In one instance in 1933, which specifically involved Dulles, President O. F. Weber and associates on the Board of Directors maneuvered a stockholders meeting into refusing to reelect the Solvay–American representatives to the board for the subsequent year. Within weeks, a special committee representing holders of 25 percent of the common stock was organized calling for a special stockholders meeting and the ouster of several members of the newly elected board. Weber quickly publicized the fact that the committee really represented the Solvay–American Investment Corporation, and, in fact, its legal counselor was John Foster Dulles. A campaign was mounted against the special committee on the theme of the dangers of "foreign interests" having a share in the management of the company. Pledging a fight against "foreign domination," Allied's officers secured endorsements from a number of prominent business leaders "warning the American people against the possibility of foreign domination of the American chemical industry." The special committee denied the relevancy of this campaign, calling it a "red herring," but it did put off its frontal assault on the Allied Board indefinitely.[54] Twenty-five percent of the common stock was a strong handle, but not strong enough to turn the trick.

Dulles maintained constant contact with Solvay & Cie. officials in 1933 and succeeding years and remained legal counsel for Solvay-American itself. An opportunity to reverse the hostile move of 1933 came two years later when O. F. Weber retired and H. F. Atherton took over as President and Chairman of the Board of Allied Chemical. While there is no precise indication of what took place, Dulles and Solvay-American representatives began a series of meetings with Atherton which, as subsequent events demonstrated, concerned Solvay's role in the U.S. giant and Allied's relationship, in turn, to the international cartel system. George Murnane, lifelong friend of Dulles and partner in a banking firm which Dulles had helped found, was elected a Director of Allied at the April 1936 stockholders meeting. With Murnane as a conduit, Dulles and other Solvay officials began a regular relationship with H. F. Atherton: meetings took place periodically over succeeding years. In addition, and it would seem as a result, it was precisely in 1936 that Allied Chemical reestablished and reinforced its ties to various chemical cartels. It was in 1936, for example, that Alkasso, whose principal member was an Allied subsidiary, renegotiated agreements with Imperial Chemical, I. G. Farben, and Solvay & Cie. The interrelatedness of cartels in chemicals is demonstrated by the fact that in that same year, Allied entered separate agreements involving dyestuffs production with I. G. Farben.[55] The maverick days were over, and Allied Chemical had adopted the gentlemanly behavior of its counterparts in the industry.

Dulles may have been involved with yet a third major interwar cartel as well. In the mid-1930s, he was a Director of the Consolidated Silesian Steel Company, whose only asset was stock in the Upper Silesian Coal and Steel Company. While nominally Poland's largest industrial concern, two-thirds of Upper Silesian's stock was owned by the German industrialist Friedrich Flick and one-third was owned by Americans: Consolidated Silesian was the entity that represented both the German and American interests.[56]

While Dulles's ties to Consolidated Silesian are unquestionable, the relevance and significance of those ties is unclear. As to association with cartels, it is suggestive. World steel producers had developed after 1926 one of the most highly structured of all international cartels. Major American companies like United States and Bethlehem Steel conducted negotiations with European counterparts like Germany's Vereinigte Stahlverke and the British Iron and Steel Corporation, Ltd. In addition to the giants of the field, producers of any relatively significant quantity of steel in smaller states were also drawn into the myriad cartel arrangements and those of Poland were no exception.[57] It is, to repeat, significant that Dulles was a Director of the holding company which controlled all of the stock of Poland's largest steel producer.

And in addition to the cartel issue, it is clear that Dulles was formally associated through the Consolidated Silesian Coal and Steel Company with one of Germany's major industrial figures. Friedrich Flick, it should be recalled, was a significant supporter of the Hitler regime after 1933 and was eventually tried as a war criminal at Nuremberg.[58]

John Foster Dulles's ties to the International Nickel Company and the international nickel cartel, to Belgium's Solvay et Cie. and its elaborate cartel relationships in the world chemical industry, and to the Consolidated Silesian Coal and Steel Company and its possible relationship with the international steel cartel were important components of his legal and business career during the 1930s. They have considerable relevance for evaluating the nature of his career in the decade before World War II. In a technical sense, Dulles was always correct in his vehement denials of the charges that he had been willing to associate himself professionally with German business and financial concerns that had clearly lent support to the morally repugnant Hitler regime. He personally was never associated with the J. Henry Schroeder banking interests, for example, and even his brother's position in that sphere is not legitimately suspect because no definitive proof exists to tie those banks to Germany in the 1930s. Dulles's cartel activities, on the other hand, make the righteousness of his later denials of German associations grate somewhat harshly. His two definite attachments with the International Nickel Company and Solvay et Cie. spanned the years when these clients were developing and maintaining cartel relationships with, among others, Germany's I. G. Farben. As legal counsel, director, and executive committee member for both companies throughout the 1930s, it is clear that Dulles was actively and specifically engaged in arranging those cartel relationships. Dulles's denials of ties to a prime German economic entity like I. G. Farben were technically correct in the sense that he was not directly employed by the German company—but those denials in no way suggest the possibility of the real and significant relationships among cartel associates. If, as Dulles and his supporters always later maintained, he felt considerable repugnance toward the Hitler regime and guided his firm to a decision that it was impossible to do legal business in Nazi Germany, his qualms were hardly categorical in execution. As one historian has suggested, a far more accurate gauge of the sentiment of American businessmen toward Germany during the 1930s is a measurement of their actions rather than their words: this is certainly applicable to John Foster Dulles.[59]

Cartel associations underline clearly some of the key characteristics of Dulles's career during the interwar years. In one respect, they are examples of truly worldly professional activities, of a kind which make it possible to say that Dulles was, in a most fundamental sense, an international lawyer. They also exemplify the specific thrust of this particular lawyer's career: years of orientation toward the interests of major corporations and banking houses.

7

Depression, 1929–1934

"IT WAS NICE WHILE IT LASTED," Charlie Wales reminisced. "We were a sort of royalty, almost infallible, with a kind of magic around us." But 1931 was not 1929, and Charlie, the protagonist of F. Scott Fitzgerald's "Babylon Revisted," was all too painfully aware of the changes. From the moment he returned to Paris and walked across the long green carpet of the empty Ritz bar, silence and depression engulfed him. Gone were the throngs of fellow American businessmen feasting on the bull markets at home; gone was the bartender who had come to work in his custom-built car. If Charlie and his compatriots had been kin to royalty once, they had become emperors without clothing.

The plight of Charlie Wales offers insights into the experiences of John Foster Dulles. Fitzgerald's story succeeds in pulling one away from the clichés of the Great Depression toward the realization that the impact of economic crises on individuals might take subtle as well as drastic forms. Breadlines and Hoovervilles were not the stuff of everyday life for a relatively successful businessman like Wales—nor for a very successful lawyer like Dulles. Still, the depression of the Depression had a way of piercing the armor of continuing affluence.

There is no ignoring the fact that Dulles continued to enjoy wealth and success throughout the 1930s. He remained senior and managing partner of Sullivan & Cromwell, busier than ever. Yet Dulles, like Charlie Wales, was anxious. Looking at what he said and did during this decade, it is impossible to escape the conclusion that he was more often than not a shaken and worried man. Why?

One clear reason for the lack of alignment between Dulles's mood and his personal fortune is that he was never content to look only at his bank balance. During the 1920s, his day-to-day legal activities had combined with a wide-ranging interest in world affairs to yield constant attention to developments in the international arena. His desire for a broad understanding of the world scene evidenced always a keen interest in the forest as well as the trees. In the 1930s, the forest was no longer pleasant to behold.

The larger whole into which Dulles had most often placed his specific professional preoccupations had been the international economy. As a lawyer for banks and corporations, his responsibilities had a way of expanding into a general attentiveness to developments in world commerce and finance. He had been particularly concerned about the way in which the United States was affected by those developments. He was convinced that his country's tremendous productive capacity absolutely required substantial external outlets. When problems arose that threatened American export ability during the 1920s, he worried greatly. European devastation, currency instability, American tariff policies, among other things, attracted his regular attention. Still, solutions for problems had been found, and Dulles had rejoiced. By the end of the decade, he was speaking glowingly of the "amazing achievement" by which the United States had developed a fruitful economic relationship with the rest of the world.[1]

Almost identical themes are present in Dulles's thoughts during the early 1930s, but the variations on them were profoundly different. Where the saga of the twenties had been one of victory over threatening odds, that of the thirties recounted omenous failure. Increasingly during this decade, Dulles saw the United States threatened with economic isolation and hence stagnation, unable to make the world economy run smoothly again in the service of American interests. The sense of magic and infallibility that seemed once to have existed had gone.

I

Like many Americans in the early 1930s, John Foster Dulles was slow to realize the depth of the economic crisis engulfing much of the world. For what hindsight suggests was a remarkably long time, he held fast to a "prosperity is just around the corner" faith. This is especially curious in Dulles's case because he was aware so early of problems on the horizon. Already in April 1929, for example, in a speech to the International Chamber of Commerce, he voiced some trepidation about the incredible feats of the New York stock market. High interest rates were drawing foreign funds into the United States at an unprecedented rate, he said, "creating an abnormal demand upon the foreign central banks for dollar exchange which their citizens would use not to pay for American goods, but to loan to brokers at 10%." Temporarily, the gold reserves of European banks would offset the extra and non-trading demands for dollar exchange—but only temporarily. "This situation cannot long continue," Dulles warned, "without a collapse which will mean the realization of the dangers which were forecasted ten years ago." The wherewithal to purchase American goods would simply not be available to foreigners, and this could only create major problems for the American economy. A few days after this speech, obviously contemplating the same troublesome scene, Dulles expressed related sentiments to a business associate: "I feel that unless there is a good deal more soberness about stock market activity . . . we are headed for serious difficulty."

Furtive glances at the market did not a Cassandra make, however. Like many an analyst in 1929, Dulles had a way of quickly tucking his worried thoughts away. His International Chamber of Commerce address concentrated almost entirely on the "amazing" achievements of the American economy and American bankers in the postwar decade. The problem he had mentioned was almost in the nature of an afterthought, the citing of a bit of tarnish on an otherwise golden image. If a problem existed, indeed, solutions were also at hand: the Federal Reserve Board, Dulles argued, in yet another example of its wisdom, was already grappling with the gold and dollar exchange matter. By May, things were actually improving. As he put it, "I think the situation is . . . a good deal better now than it was a few months ago."[2]

Even the disasters of October 1929 did not shatter Dulles's optimism. With his office on Wall Street, and his clientele such as it was, he certainly knew what was happening. From "Black Tuesday" on, he would have followed developments carefully. Aside from being aware of the overall catastrophe—that within two weeks the total value of all stocks traded on the exchange had fallen 40 percent—he would have had all too many specific crises to contemplate. The Blue Ridge Corporation, for example, in part his own investment trust brainchild, had dropped from 24 to 3 by October 29! Yet through the rubble, Dulles moved rather blithely. On November 1, in a letter to a banking colleague in London, he wrote wryly, but positively: "I assume that you have been following with interest, which I hope is entirely academic, the recent convulsions of our stock market. On the whole I think it is a healthy development and if anything should lead to an improvement in conditions abroad and probably also it may bring nearer the time when foreign financing can be done here."[3]

This reaction was not just that of a stunned moment either. It lingered for more than a year. In February 1930, for example, Dulles took time out from a business trip to speak to The American Club in Paris. Even at this date, he began his address by outlining the "tremendous" accomplishments of the postwar years. So successful had businessmen been that "now business faces a better future than ever before!" Almost reluctantly, Dulles went on to admit that "the sky is not entirely cloudless." There were various "uncertainties" facing American business. Deliberations in Washington seemed to be opening the way for a new round of tariff building that might interfere with international trade. There were problems developing too concerning adequate supplies of gold for trade purposes, with the United States accumulating too large a portion of the existing stock. Gold was, in turn, only part of a larger problem that Dulles had long been discussing by this date: what he referred to here as "the inequality of prosperity which exists between the United States and Europe." As in earlier years, he was concerned about the inability of Europeans to pay for all they were buying from the United States. Billions of dollars in American loans had helped lubricate the trade mechanisms of the 1920s, as he well knew, but how long this could continue was a provocative question under the circumstances of early 1930.

Ten years earlier, the citing of similar "clouds" had led to the issue of real storm warnings. In 1930, the clouds were whisked away. Tariffs? Yes, they could be a nuisance, but the rising tariffs of the 1920s had not prevented a real increase in American trade. As long as the new plateau became known and stable, "whatever it is, there is no reason to believe that American business cannot adapt itself to it once conditions can be definitely foreseen." Gold? The Federal Reserve Board, in cooperation with European central banks, had adopted a healthy "international point of view" and was trying to create credit and money conditions conducive to a redistribution. As for inequality of prosperity, Dulles offered no optimistic resolutions. He did briefly suggest that the United States should buy more from Europe—but he seems not to have been bothered by the fatuous nature of this thought.[4]

Later in 1930 Dulles had still not lost his optimistic mood. Following through on the interests of earlier days, he studied carefully the workings of the Young Plan for reparations. What he saw might have troubled him. The Brüning government in Germany, to which Dulles's banking clients were still lending dollars, was becoming increasingly nationalistic and talking about the need to curtail reparations payments. Nazi "demagogues," with electoral victories going their way, were saying the same in even more extreme fashion. And yet, to Dulles, such developments were not very disturbing. Confronted with the question of whether Germany might unilaterally renege on her debts, he declared flatly that "the danger is not there." His words on the subject to a meeting of the Foreign Policy Association are revealing:

> We have a reparation "settlement" which apparently has failed to "settle." Within Germany we find her internal finances in serious embarrassment and an economic situation which finds expression in anti-foreign agitation. In France we find disillusionment regarding Briand's policy of conciliation and a disposition to revert to the Poincare policy of the strong hand.
>
> One could easily become pessimistic in the face of such a situation did not analysis show that the existing difficulties are largely psychological. . . . All that renders the situation potentially serious is the psychology of pessimism and defeatism which prevails in Europe, and particularly in Germany. In such an atmosphere all of our economic troubles become doubly serious and hard to bear, whereas *the history of the past decade has taught us how rapidly our economic ills evaporate in the face of confidence* . . . . [Emphasis added.]⁵

Dulles's "confidence" during 1930 put him squarely in the ranks of the businessmen and government officials with whom he worked so regularly. Such positive expectations were common among most of them. Were commodity prices falling dramatically? What of it? Secretary of the Treasury Andrew Mellon was declaring that "I see nothing in the present situation that is either menacing or warrants pessimism." Had unemployment tripled? Charles Schwab of Bethlehem Steel still insisted that "never before has American business been as firmly entrenched for prosperity as it is today." Were American exports falling from $5.2 billion in 1929 to $3.8 billion in 1930? In mid-year, the President could pronounce that "we have now passed the worst and with continued unity of effort we shall rapidly recover."⁶ That there were problems, Dulles and others were willing to admit—without allowing such recognition to induce pessimism. Lingering euphoria prevented thoughts about such problems from reaching their logical conclusions.

The economic realities of 1931 dislodged that euphoria. Crisis succeeded crisis and Dulles's mood, like others, succumbed. He was particularly affected by grave problems in the financial world. General business reverses during 1930 brought a dramatic decline in international credit transactions: American bankers who had offered $1 billion in 1928, for example, provided only $190 million in 1931. Worse yet, bankers in Europe and the United States found it more and more difficult to secure payments on outstanding loans. As early as November 1930, the Banque Adam in Paris was forced to close its doors. The new year brought further developments as a similarly overextended Credit Anstalt in Vienna began tottering. When major banks began meager efforts to assist the Austrian institution, panic ensued. By May and June 1931, reverberations were spreading, and runs began on banks in Hungary, Czechoslovakia, Rumania, Poland, and Germany.[7]

Dulles was as aware as anyone of the unfolding crisis and made no secret of his newfound fears. His record of a meeting with Herbert Hoover in mid-1931 makes this quite clear. Dulles had been called to the White House for consultation on a plan for remedial action to deal with the tumbling financial dominoes in Central Europe. The brainchild of the Administration was a "moratorium" on inter-governmental debt payments, designed to relieve strained European treasuries. When meeting the President on June 13, Dulles's first words were "I regarded the situation as critical." In a memorandum left with Hoover, he elaborated:

> The present depression is unique in that it came at a time when all of the nations were burdened with enormous public debts, created at a time of inflated values, and so recent in origin as not yet to have been digested in the world's economic system. There is growing apprehension that declining values will so increase the effective burden of this debt that it will in large part prove insupportable and bring about *a wide-spread collapse of public credit, carrying away billions in American investments and banking advances, as well as the possibility of an adequate export trade.* [Emphasis added.]

To Dulles, Allied debts and reparations were two items of major importance in the overall structure of international finance. Unless more palatable arrangements could be worked out for these, there was *"danger of the whole system breaking down"* (emphasis added).[8]

This was new talk for Dulles, reminiscent of the dark moods of the early 1920s. In months ahead, he would find reason for allowing the darkness to deepen yet further. Hoover's moratorium, for example, proved to be a fairly empty gesture. The United States, Great Britain, and France bickered over its specific terms in a way that reflected the latter's abiding suspicions of Germany. While they were bickering, their central bankers also dallied: talk of major aid to German and other Central European banks during the summer of 1931 never really got off the ground. Meanwhile the crisis spread. Britain's plight was evidenced by its departure from the gold standard in September, an event which triggered a 50 percent decline in value of the pound in the following three months. Sensing a route to a special trade advantage, twenty-five other countries abandoned gold shortly after. This put the dollar under a good deal of pressure during the fall of 1931 and contributed to the drastic decline in American exports for the year as a whole: from an already low $3.8 billion in 1930 to $2.4 billion in 1931.[9]

Such developments did not encourage optimism. Dulles watched anxiously, as government officials and central bankers debated action during the summer, only to be disappointed. No major programs to aid Germany, no major new undertakings for Sullivan & Cromwell emerged. The message seemed clear. By fall, Dulles was expanding on his first panicky comments to President Hoover, in a way which indicated that he now understood the scope of international economic problems. He had gone to Europe on a business trip in October and while there had undertaken a fact-finding study for the Federal Reserve Board. Anxious to take advantage of Dulles's contacts and experience, the Board asked him to study "European financial conditions as affecting American exports." There was particular interest in the possibility of expanding the sale of cotton and other agricultural products in countries like Germany, Poland, and Czechoslovakia.

Dulles sent the Board both specific information on Central Europe and a broadly conceived analysis of what he saw as a problem-filled future. His major theme was the unfortunate but inevitable interrelationship of financial crisis and plummeting trade. As he put it in his opening paragraph:

> The prevalent depression, with its enforced or optional economy by the consuming public, constitutes, of course, a basic deterrent to the turn-over of goods. This is true whether the goods be domestic or foreign. But superimposed upon this general situation, and aggravating it as regards the international movement of goods, are the extreme precautions now felt to be necessary to protect the various currencies from depreciation.

"Under ordinary conditions," Dulles wrote, "nations do not feel required to operate on a self-contained basis." Normally, there was always enough "fluid capital" available to deal with temporary adverse trade balances. Borrowing and repaying on short-term or long-term bases, the businessmen of many nations were enabled to fit easily into the smoothly running international economic machine. International creditors were wildly demanding repayments, which seriously threatened the financial condition of the borrowing nation. The result was catastrophic in its impact on international trade.

> Short term credit is not, at the moment, looked upon as sufficiently stable to play its previous role as buffer between international debit balances and gold shipments. *Each nation accordingly feels it must, as nearly as*

may be, operate on a self-contained basis and be free from dependence on foreign credit with the menace to currency which this now implies. The English slogan "Buy British and support the £" typifies the prevalent viewpoint. [Emphasis added.]

Dulles's broad analysis was firmly buttressed by the specific information he offered. Studies of economic conditions in Germany, Poland, and Czechoslovakia had convinced him that no real trade opportunities existed for the United States. Determination to maintain the value of the mark "in the face of great difficulties," for example, "moulds Germany's commercial policy. It requires that imports be held at a minimum, even though this involves unemployment, reduction in the standard of living, and exhaustion of domestic stocks." In Poland, Dulles did find a desire to import more American cotton in order to increase production in the depressed textile industry. Unfortunately, this desire was countered by "a reluctance to do this at the expense of creating a short-term debt position which might impair the carefully husbanded reserves of the Bank of Poland."

Economic conditions in Central Europe, Dulles was basically arguing, were thoroughly uninviting for the United States. Former, and potentially valuable, markets were being closed to American producers as various governments determined to maintain as nearly self-contained economies as possible. Only by allowing the absolute minimum of imports into their countries did such governments hope to avoid yet more dire financial problems than the beginning of the Depression had thrust upon them. Short-term and long-term financing were considered simply too dangerous for financial stability. And as Dulles was aware, if they were unwilling to borrow they would be unable to buy. The statistics he gathered for his report showed this all too clearly. American cotton sales in Czechoslovakia had been $42 million in 1930, for example, and had fallen to $24 million in 1931.[10]

His report to the Federal Reserve Board, coming on the heels of discussions with Hoover and his advisers, obviously indicates that Dulles had finally recognized the evolving phenomenon of the Depression. Optimistic blinders had been belatedly but thoroughly discarded, and no illusions remained about the seriousness of the problems facing the international economy. He saw at last that the economic marvels of the 1920s were not just trembling, but collapsing.

In the months and years after 1931, Dulles made up for his delayed reaction by frequent discussions of the Depression crisis. He spoke and wrote regularly about the devastating problems being experienced within the international economy and about the inevitable repercussions for the United States. In a 1932 memorandum fowarded to the State Department, for example, he penned a sweeping indictment of the protectionist devices being devised by many governments:

> The existing system of currency controls, quotas, clearings, etc. is more and more throttling international trade and commerce. Each new restriction by one State has been met by a counter-restriction by another State. The result is a virtual elimination of triangular operations and the reduction of trade to isolated barter transactions. The resultant damming up of products in their countries of origin has a steadily depressing influence on the domestic price level. This in turn, reacts upon price levels in adjoining States. . . .

These techniques for protecting currency stability and credit strength had become "an intolerable interference with and stifling of individual initiative and enterprise."[11] The end result, Dulles felt, was likely to be a rigidly and dangerously compartmentalized global economy: as more states pursued autarchic policies, i.e., sought self-sufficiency in a seemingly threatening international environment, mutually beneficial commercial and financial transactions would become increasingly difficult.

Nor was it individuals alone who were being stifled. As in the past, Dulles never lost sight of the impact of international economic problems on the United States. In a particularly revealing article for *Foreign Affairs*, for example, he bemoaned the collapse of New York as a major international credit center:

> The decade 1920–1930 saw New York become the financial center of the world. At the time we took considerable satisfaction in supplanting London in its time-honored role. Today the use which we made of that opportunity is looked back upon as one of the less creditable incidents of a now discredited period.

There was more than embarrassment here, of course. The drastic decline of foreign financing in New York was an enormous problem. After all, Dulles wrote:

> . . . foreign financing is . . . desirable from a broad national viewpoint that the American market should be available to foreign borrowers. That our exports are largely promoted thereby must be conceded. Indeed, at this juncture, when foreign bonds cannot be sold to the public, our Government has apparently contemplated stepping into the breach by loaning abroad many millions of public money so that foreigners will have dollars wherewith to buy and consume our agricultural products [a

141

reference to the evolving Export–Import Bank] . . . dollars are used by foreigners to acquire goods for which domestic consumers would otherwise have to be found.

Also, Dulles concluded, there were other ways in which the broad national interest was being served by foreign financing. "We must bear in mind," he wrote, "that there are many and important, even though intangible, advantages in being an owner and potential buyer of foreign securities." As an example, he cited the recent maneuver which saw Canada returning to the London market for the sale of its bonds after twenty years of working with American bankers:

> The event is hailed by the English press as inaugurating closer political and economic relations between England and Canada and a probable tie of the Canadian dollar to sterling rather than to the American dollar. *When one nation develops close financial relations with another and realizes that it may have occasion to go to it for financing, it shapes its commercial and fiscal policy with a view to maintaining the lender's good will.* England has long derived advantages from such relationship. It is equally possible for us to do so. [Emphasis added.]

Such a technique of influence, such a method of power, should simply not be denied the United States. After all, Dulles concluded, "It is so clearly our destiny to play an international role. . . ."[12]

Nor did Dulles limit himself to discussions of trade figures and slipping global influence: the ramifications of these developments seemed too obvious to miss. Shortly after the appearance of his *Foreign Affairs* article, for example, he wrote another piece describing the apparent ineffectiveness of New Deal programs to deal with the domestic crisis caused by the Depression. Something had to be done, he argued, to terminate one of those regular "periods of privation which, even though generally of brief duration, are so intensive as *to threaten social revolution*" (emphasis added[13]). At just the same time, he began thinking along related lines about the political and psychological traumas evolving in the international arena.[14]

II

During the 1920s, Dulles's diagnoses of ills facing the American and international economies had always been followed by prescriptions. This remained true of his approach in the 1930s, but with some variation in timing. His slow response to the onset of Depression was mirrored in the fact that his recommendations for dealing with it only gradually matured.

As already suggested, for example, Dulles seemed to think that very little in the way of action was necessary in 1929 and 1930. Clouds overhead did not darken his optimism. "Convulsions" in the stock market were actually seen as a useful purgative. As for wider-ranging problems, suggestions were made, but of such a broad and imprecise nature as to raise questions about how concerned their formulator actually was. To argue, for example, that Europeans were facing once again the problem of how to pay for all they were anxious to buy from the United States was quite routine for Dulles by this date. But where earlier years had brought sometimes elaborate descriptions of desirable actions by businessmen, bankers, and government, Dulles was content in 1929 and 1930 to refer to the desirability of an "international point of view." Even the serious matter of rising tariff barriers was brushed aside by his conviction that American businessmen could cope with almost any rates once they were known. At worst, Dulles seemed to think the U. S. economy was facing a problem of negative "psychology"—if better vibrations would be set in motion, problems would "evaporate."[15]

Positivism and bland homilies disappeared in 1931, to be replaced by floundering and then pessimistic resignation. Confronted with the financial crisis in Europe in June, for example, Dulles seemed confused. He could tell President Hoover that the situation was "critical," but then proceed to argue that the real problems were still a negative "state of mind" and "unreasoning apprehension." Having concluded this, he proposed an extremely complicated plan involving a temporary moratorium on only 75 percent of reparation and Allied debt payments and the discount of future annuities. As Under Secretary of the Treasury Ogden Mills told him, his plan was too convoluted for even most politicians to understand and would not serve any useful psychological purpose. One significant aspect of Dulles's rejected proposal was that it was offered as a substitute for what he considered the too extreme suggestion of a straightforward one-year moratorium.[16] While he was becoming more convinced that major problems did exist in the international economy, in other words, he was not yet prepared to advocate major actions to deal with them.

Through the summer, Dulles tended to float with events rather than give much thought to how they might be shaped. He approved of the Hoover moratorium once it had been announced and was critical of the French government for being difficult about details. As talks within government and banking circles were held concerning further steps, he and his partners were clearly hoping that a major new loan and "plan" involving Germany would emerge: this suggests he believed such action desirable. Then, when the much more modest "standstill" agreement was worked out to alleviate short-term credit pressure on Germany, Dulles also seems to have approved.[17]

None of the palliatives of mid-1931 turned the trick, of course. As the depths of the economic crisis became more obvious, Dulles's drifting stopped for awhile—at a nadir which found him feeling powerless and very pessimistic. The clearest evidence of this can be found in his October 1931 report for the Federal Reserve Board. Detailed study of trade patterns in Central Europe had convinced him that governments were attempting to create "self-contained" economies. How could policies so damaging to the United States be altered? Given the option of proposing any plan in a hypothetical fashion, Dulles's recommendations turned out to be minimal and revealed a real lack of confidence about the possibility of taking any effective action whatsoever. He began, for example, by suggesting the possibility of Federal Reserve Board credits to foreign central banks. That would make possible currency stabilization and, in turn, freer trade. While this had been done quite successfully in the 1920s, however, Dulles was not convinced it would work again:

> The difficulty in resorting further to this procedure, is that this type of support of foreign currencies, on a scale which, under to-day's conditions, would be adequate to accomplish the desired result, would involve a very large commitment and one out of proportion to the benefit which our country would derive therefrom. For to the extent that a foreign currency is supported *in general,* the benefit is general, not only to American exporters but to hosts of others, exporters, creditors, etc., throughout the world.

An alternative recommendation envisioned the establishment of a government banking organization which would in effect finance American exports by allowing foreigners to buy goods with their own currency. This organization would hold the foreign currency, and pay dollars to the American exporters. In time, when economic conditions were back to normal, the foreign currency would be gradually disposed of for dollars. But problems sprouted here too. Foreign governments would have to be persuaded that this American agency would not suddenly dump the non-dollar exchange and create financial havoc: no mean feat. In addition, Dulles seemed concerned about the possible costs of such a program if depressed economic conditions continued. Should the mark or zloty or crown tumble in value, potentially large American holdings could be worthless. In sum, he was not too sanguine about success:

> In view of difficulties and objections above alluded to, the plan obviously is not one which can be unqualifiedly recommended, and I do not submit it as such. I submit it as exemplifying the only principle on which we can, today, expect to stimulate largely the foreign consumption of American goods. *The remedy may be worse than the disease,* but in any event it may be useful to have diagnosed the situation. [Emphasis added.][18]

The diagnosis that Dulles was offering in late 1931, in fact, reveals just how greatly his mood had changed. On the one hand, not surprisingly, the international landscape looked bleak. On the other hand, such a perception of the immediate seemed to be projected indefinitely into the future. So thorough was the obliteration of earlier optimism that Dulles was unable even to imagine solutions to existing problems.

Depressed resignation did not last indefinitely. Coming at the end of 1931, it represented a perhaps natural swing to the opposite extreme of Dulles's earlier conviction that little action was necessary to deal with economic difficulties—a swing made so extreme by delayed realization of how critical those difficulties actually were. This reversal of attitude was then followed by another Dulles twist, with a coming to rest somewhere between the two poles. Gradually, he decided that remedial actions were possible and that both American and international economic conditions could be improved. The actions he envisionsed were a great deal more demanding than the rather flighty dicta of 1929 and 1930, but he believed at least that they could work if given a chance.

From 1932 on, Dulles developed a range of proposals for dealing with critical economic problems. Even more than in the 1920s, when he was similarly forthcoming, they varied a good deal in their precision, their logic, and probably in their importance to him.

Troubled as he was, for example, with a glint of panic flashing now and then, Dulles could fall prey to knee-jerk conservative reactions which he might ordinarily have recognized as wide of the mark. This comes through in a number of critiques of the domestic policies of the Roosevelt Administration. In a March 1933 letter to *The New York Times,* he could reach the absurdly simplistic conclusion that "the present phase of our crisis is primarily one of Government finance." What other explanation could there be, he asked, when it was obvious that the federal government had "drained the lifeblood out of sound institutions in order to operate an extravagant public budget. . . ." How such lifeblood had been drained Dulles did not make clear, but he insisted that the government's budget should be cut "radically" in order to protect the inherent resources of the American economy and the initiative of American citizens.[19]

A year later, Dulles was still taking the government to task for both inadequate and actually harmful programs:

> There is a general awareness of the fact that something is wrong with our economic system as it has heretofore been functioning. The "New Deal" is popular because it implies an intention to do something about changing a system which, with all its advantages, has serious defects. We have not, however, progressed beyond the "something" stage. . . . There

145

is no clear appreciation of what is wrong and why, or as to what changes are possible consistently with preserving features which we all wish to see preserved. The result is a hodge-podge of measures principally aimed at superficial symptoms, frequently inconsistent with themselves or inconsistent with the functioning, in beneficial ways, of our present system.

Though this was an interesting and perceptive base, Dulles built little more than frothy recommendations upon it. He cited the need for what he called "a control of token values sufficient to prevent the enhancement of paper values at a rate which does not correspond to economic realities." He was critical of the inflationary policies being pursued by the Roosevelt Administration through currency manipulation and other devices. Drawing a comparison with Germany in the 1920s, he argued that Americans were afraid to engage in routine economic transactions for fear that anything earned in sales would quickly become valueless. To circumvent the problem before it became unmanageable, he urged giving greater powers to control money to the Federal Reserve Board.[20]

Critical comments on Hoover and Roosevelt budget policies suggest a mind preoccupied with surface problems and blind to the more profound causes of the Great Depression. Though Dulles had his lapses, his experience and perceptivity usually led him to deeper analysis and more dramatic proposals. In November 1932, for example, during a business trip to the Continent, he spent some time with his brother in Paris. Allen Dulles was then involved in preparations for the Geneva Disarmament Conference and also closely in touch with those State Department officials making arrangements for the Economic Conference to be held in London the following year. The two brothers talked at length about the economic difficulties plaguing the United States, apparently spending most of their time discussing the barrenness of the once fertile fields of Germany and Eastern Europe. Foster Dulles then drew up a "Memorandum Concerning the Central European Situation" which Allen presented to Norman Davis, the American representative on the League of Nations Financial Committee and head of the delegation to the Disarmament Conference. Copies also went to Herbert Feis, Economic Adviser of the State Department, and to Harvey Williams, the American participant in the Financial Sub-Committee working on preparations for the Economic Conference.

The point of the memorandum was to suggest a way of overcoming the "throttling" of interstate credit and trade activities in the crucial Central European area. As he had concluded in his report for the Federal Reserve Board, Dulles believed European governments and business leaders were afraid of engaging in what had been normal borrowing and lending transactions in the 1920s. Because of this, the wheels of commerce had come to lack necessary lubrication and had ground to a halt. What could be done about it? Wary of the charms of bankers that had led them to accept credit and thereby created their financial problems after 1930, Dulles argued, private and state debtors would have to be convinced of the safety of credit transactions again. One way of calming their fears would be a significant downward adjustment of their outstanding financial obligations. Creditors would have to realize that "the attempt to perpetuate a creditor position which has become excessive generally results merely in exaggerating the ultimate loss." As a specific recommendation, therefore, Dulles urged readjustment of outstanding debts *in return for* "the abandonment of the existing system of abnormal trade and currency control." Such a bargain would provide immediate foreign exchange relief and, more importantly, make possible a resumption of "normal" trade relations. This would reduce still further the difficulties of debtor states because they could sell more to others; likewise it would reduce problems of creditor nations such as the United States, whose productive capacity was being hamstrung by lack of markets.

In the Dulles recommendations, to go one step further, international creditors were to be assisted by an organization that possessed a perspective broad enough to make possible such arrangements. The Finance Committee of the League of Nations was to supervise negotiations between creditors and debtors and oversee the operation of a four-part program:

> 1. An examination, under the auspices of the League of Nations, of the foreign currency debt of the countries in question with a view to an adjustment thereof, in agreement with representatives of the creditors, to meet the necessities of each case;
> 2. The acceptance of the debt adjustment by sufficient creditors to warrant making the plan effective;
> 3. Coincidentally with the debt adjustment becoming effective, the simultaneous abolition by the debtor countries concerned of their abnormal trade and currency controls;
> 4. The League, in the interest of the foreign creditors, would exercise such supervision of finances of the relieved debtor as may be useful to insure attainment of the desired economic results.[21]

Nothing came of Dulles's suggestions. When Allen passed on his brother's thoughts to Norman Davis and Herbert Feis, little positive reaction was forthcoming. Feis was "in agreement concerning the necessity of organizing the American creditor groups with a veiw to prompt and united action," but was not optimistic about going further. "He seemed to be somewhat skeptical as to whether a program as comprehensive as that suggested in the memorandum could be carried through at this time," Allen reported.[22]

Still, the memorandum was important in the long-range evolution of Dulles's own views. It testifies certainly to his perceptions of the scope of economic problems: involving the League in major international financial transactions, perhaps even in supervising the economies of certain debtor states, was a grand-scale proposal whose genesis was found in a sense of very great problems. In addition, Dulles took the thoughts that were ignored in 1932 and tucked them away in his own mind. Over succeeding years, he would grow increasingly convinced that the United States, acting unilaterally, would never be able to cope with policies of self-containment and economic nationalism being practiced by so many governments. He would come back again and again to the idea of utilizing the remedial possibilities of an international organization, an organization which by its intrinsic nature might help counteract the fragmentation of the international economy.[23]

Though he could shoot wildly from the hip or propose dramatic and unlikely schemes in the early 1930s, Dulles was usually the relatively calm and moderate analyst he had been in the 1920s. In fact, he continued to advocate more than anything else actions which would have fit very clearly into the conventional wisdom of his circle of internationalist American businessmen and bankers during the first postwar decade. Government officials and individual business leaders, he argued, should develop "an international point of view" and work for the betterment of their specific national interests by working for the betterment of all. It was foolish to pursue nationalistic or protectionist policies of an extreme variety and to play fast and loose with currency manipulation and restrictions, tariffs, quotas, and debt payments. Narrow, autarchic policies might provide short-term rewards, but would eventually cause a shattering of the great global economy and stultified opportunities in the future.

The drift of Dulles's thoughts is evident in his reactions to many specific events and problems. In mid-1933, for example, he began serving as a representative of several American banks at a series of debts conferences arranged by the Reichsbank in Berlin in order to work out satisfactory arrangements with creditors. To the dismay of the Americans attending, Reichsbank President Hjalmar Schacht immediately began hinting that Germany might start treating its various creditors on the basis of current favorable trade balances. Such a bilateral policy would have left Dulles's clients high and dry because Germany exported far less to the United States than she imported from her. Dulles vigorously protested to Schacht, whom he had known well for more than a decade, insisting that Germany's imports were so large precisely because "we produced the raw materials which Germany required for her manufacturing industries." In a report sent to Secretary of State Hull, he described how he went further in talking to Schacht and detailed the inevitable implications of such a possible German policy for American and general international trade. "I . . . pointed out," he wrote, "that practical experience showed that where any system of direct clearings was introduced, *the result was to break down and diminish international trade"* (emphasis added). In the long-term interests of all, Germany should maintain a flexible and even-handed trade and debts policy.

Dulles continued to keep a wary eye on Berlin during the succeeding stages of the debts conferences he attended in December 1933 and January 1934. At one point, after some secret discussions with the German Cabinet about possible special arrangements with Switzerland and the Netherlands, he felt he had succeeded in keeping bilateralism at bay. His report to his clients described the warding off of "radical curtailment both of German debt payments and also of German imports of our goods." His overview of the situation also evidenced his perception of the current threats to ideal international economic relationships:

> The German attitude evidenced realization that mistakes, particularly of method, had been made in the past and that a resulting situation of great gravity had arisen. Its solution compelled Germany to choose between two political groups and two economic systems. The Continental Group—France, Belgium, Switzerland, The Netherlands and Czechoslovakia—all were pressing for the system of relating trade facilities to debt payment by a series of bilateral arrangements. Great Britain and the United States pressed for the system of equality of debt treatment and the nonparticularization of trade relations. Within Germany, important officials in the Ministry of Economic Affairs, which has primary responsibility in the matter, believed in the "Continental" system. Nevertheless, faced by this difficult choice, Germany definitely (though not irrevocably) elected to meet the British and American viewpoint. . . .[24]

Success with Germany, as Dulles had feared, was short-lived. Only months into 1934, Berlin, like many other capitals, shifted decisively toward autarchic debt and trade policies—the "Continental" system. Even the British continued to back away from freer, multilateral practices. As one observer at the time described it:

> . . . the various mercantilist expedients were once again adopted. Tariffs, exchange restrictions, quotas, import prohibitions, barter trade agreements, central trade clearing arrangements—all the fusty relics of medieval trade regulation, discredited through five hundred years of theory and

hard experience, were dragged out of the lumberrooms and hailed as the products of the latest enlightenment.[25]

Actually, Dulles was convinced that the sources of autarchic economic policies were not all to be found in Europe. He had deep reservations about the wisdom of his own government. Hull he respected as a far-sighted advocate of freer international trade, but the Secretary of State seemed to be surrounded by men of more dubious credentials. He was outraged, for example, at the debacle of the London Economic Conference. Herbert Hoover had wisely made plans for the meeting in the hope that it could tug into the 1930s some of the spirit of international cooperation that had helped produce the economic success of the 1920s. But Hoover's hopes had been "sabotaged by the Roosevelt Administration which did not want to assume any international commitment which might interfere with its monetary experimentation upon the United States." The American refusal to participate in an international currency stabilization effort, Dulles believed, had helped persuade others to scurry into thickening economic shells. In later years, he even argued that Roosevelt's aloofness had made it easier for Hitler to gain decisive power in Germany.[26]

"It was nice while it lasted," Charlie Wales had said, and John Foster Dulles would not have disagreed. Out of the ashes of the Great War, he had, with some doubts, discerned the emergence of a golden age in the international economy; golden, at least, as far as the United States was concerned. Dulles believed that major breakthroughs in American trade and investment abroad had contributed substantially, indeed crucially, to galloping prosperity at home during the 1920s. He was convinced as well, of course, that the benefits which had accrued to the United States had helped produce an international atmosphere in which peace and prosperity were enjoyed by many.

And then the deluge. Production and employment crises in many nations, compounded by major financial difficulties, began straining the sinews of the international economy to the snapping point in the early 1930s. A United States which had battened on global financial and commercial transactions when times were good suffered accordingly.

As he had celebrated the gold of the 1920s, so Dulles bemoaned the tarnish of the Depression. What else could be expected? The international economy, and the position of the United States within it, was nothing less than the world in which Dulles lived. For twenty years before the onset of the Depression he had worked in it day after day, as a corporation lawyer,

150

as a government official, and then as a lawyer again. There was no way in which such a man would have moved ostrich-like through a time of economic troubles. His corporate and banking clients were obviously affected by commercial and financial problems and would alone have given him pause to worry. Reinforced by his habit of analyzing broader national and international issues, the anxieties were bound to multiply.

Given a range of possible channels for his fears, Dulles moved in but one direction. He stuck firmly to the internationalist catechism he had recited in earlier years. To the talk of others about turning inward, about currency manipulation, protectionism and economic self-sufficiency, he reacted with consistent disdain. What the United States needed was more financial and commercial interaction with the rest of the world, not less. And, also as in earlier years, he continued to assume that free and flexible economic interrelationships would benefit others as much as Americans.

The success of the mid and late 1920s remained a model in Dulles's mind. Economic relationships had not been perfect then, by any means. He himself had regularly criticized the behavior of his own and other governments on matters like reparations, Allied debts, and trade policies. Yet by and large, things had worked out well. Central bankers in key capitals had shown a praiseworthy willingness to cooperate, governments had bent toward each other to negotiate agreements like the Dawes Plan, and private bankers had boldly provided ample fluid capital for rehabilitation and trade development. Such actions had served as a kind of therapy and had relaxed an international economy suffering the spasms of war, had allowed fruitful commercial and financial interrelationships to grow.

But the spasm of Depression in the early 1930s was followed by no such relaxation. Dulles saw instead central banks becoming too politically hedged to deal effectively with financial crises, acceding to governments now bent on self-protection at the expense of others. The muscles of the world economy grew ever tighter, as obstacle upon obstacle to freer movement was erected. By the time Dulles had come to grips with the crisis in his own mind and had reached conclusions about what had happened and what needed to be done, it was too late. Where he called for "an international point of view," economic autarchy became the order of the day. Where he suggested a cooperative League of Nations program to deal with debts and ease trade, he found governments unattentive. Where he hoped for a revival of multilateral spirit at the London Economic Conference, he saw confusion and selfish disunity. All in all, he was witness to the emergence of world economic patterns diametrically opposed to those he saw as vitally necessary for American as well as general prosperity.

It was not a pleasant time for a man of Dulles's convictions. The magic aura of earlier years was replaced by what he himself called a "situation of great gravity." Zest and pleasure gave way to constant pricks of anger and anxiety, made all the sharper by the belief that he knew what needed to be done—made all the sharper, as well, by real fears of yet worse things to come.

8

"To Occasionally Philosophize": 1934–1939

In 1934, CLIFFORD ODETS WROTE A PLAY about the contemporary scene and called it *Paradise Lost*. He was scathing in his denunciation of what he saw around him. In his own country, he lashed out at "This system!—the one which breeds poverty. . . . Gets you all down to the margin. Dispossessed like me, like another sixteen million in a walking death. . . ." Abroad, he saw nothing to lighten the despair. "The world has a profound dislocation," he had one of his characters say. "Idiots out prowling the dynamite dumps by night! One struck match and we all blow to hell!"

John Foster Dulles had his eyes focused on the same phenomena. He was more bemused than condemnatory in his expression, but there was a certain kinship of theme in the words of the playwright and the lawyer. As early as March 1935, Dulles had seen enough of the unfolding Depression to write that "our institutions and our individuals have been severely tested. Many have been found wanting."[1] By the following year, his anxiety had had a chance to reverberate. "It is bewildering that the world should again be moving toward war," he wrote. "We know that we ourselves want peace and we feel that . . . peoples everywhere at heart desire it. . . . Yet . . . we sense that we are inevitably moving on toward war."[2]

There was no mistaking the signs as far as Dulles was concerned. In 1919 and periodically during the 1920s, he had made clear his belief that economic crises could have awful political and military repurcussions. Now, in 1933 and 1934, his careful following of the news, his transatlantic travels, his talks with Washington friends and business contacts around the world persuaded him that this was exactly what was happening. The economic tremors of the Great Depression were shaking the foundations of the international order, he felt, and political and military sparks were bound to fly. To his own deep dismay, nothing that happened for the rest of the decade surprised him or forced him to change his mind.

To some extent, Dulles went on as before in dealing with his redounding anxieties. He wrote speeches, articles, and reports offering a variety of recommendations for dealing with the grave commercial and financial problems of 1933 and 1934. But he started going beyond his usual approaches as well, prodded by problems that were clearly beyond the usual ones of the 1920s. As he put his thoughts on paper, he worked with them more intensely than in the past. Not just refining or honing, he stretched his ideas by grappling with them over and again. In the process, he lifted himself to a higher level of abstraction than was his norm, becoming virtually philosophical in inclination. In 1934, for example, he wrote an article called "The Road to Peace." It was followed by lengthier works with titles like "Peaceful Change Within the Society of Nations" and *War, Peace and Change*. Dulles carried a striking number of his earlier concerns up to these loftier heights, as it turned out, but they took on quite a different appearance as they rose.

I

The first sign of a novel loftiness in Dulles came in an article he wrote for the *Atlantic Monthly* in late 1934, which appeared as "The Road to Peace" in the October 1935 issue. "I have had in mind for some time thoughts as to the problem of preserving peace," Dulles had written to one of the editors, and his manuscript quickly revealed a sweepingly conceived line of analysis. A few early paragraphs contained its essence:

> The true explanation of the imminence of war lies in the inevitability of change and the fact that peace efforts have been misdirected toward the prevention of change. Thereby forces which are in the long run irresistible

are temporarily dammed up. When they finally break through, they do so with violence.

None would dispute the abstract proposition that, as the world has changed in the past, so it will continue to change in the future. We have not attained a state of fixation such that the world is immutably frozen in its present national lines.

. . . There is [however] a general disposition to ignore the occasion for change in each particular year. We forget that the changes which we recognize to be inevitable over a hundred years must occur sometime. They may occur gradually, year by year, or else, if they are allowed to occur infrequently, when they come they will be so momentous as to cause a great shock.

To Dulles's mind, the world required methods or routines of "peaceful change" if recurring wars were to be avoided.[3]

Stark though Dulles's initial foray may have been, he obviously felt deeply the need to understand the problems of war and peace. He was to spend years elaborating on these earliest impressions. Between 1934 and 1938, for example, he produced several speeches and memoranda on the same basic themes, a lengthy draft of an article that went unpublished and finally a book-length manuscript. The latter was published by Harper and Brothers as *War, Peace and Change* in early 1939. It was a thoughtful book, though sometimes painfully turgid, and received a particularly favorable reception in European intellectual circles—at least until its theories were drowned out by the sound of gunfire.[4]

Throughout the years he spent developing his analysis, the obvious core of Dulles's thoughts was his dread of a new international war. In 1938, for example, he wrote of the steady encroachment of "the war system," of his fear that "we were in the grip of some evil force which it is beyond the power of man to master." A nightmare to many by then, such visions had been disturbing Dulles for five years. To make matters worse, he was also sensitive to the particular horrors of twentieth century war. The blessings of modern science and technology had produced "totalitarian warfare," in his phrasing, a phenomenon capable of contaminating whole societies in the filth of its denouement. As the Great War had demonstrated, people could no longer look on war as exotic entertainment. All had become "participants in the bloody arena."[5]

Spurred by such visions, Dulles proceeded on the basis of a logical assumption: the nature of this "bloody arena" would have to be understood if ways of destroying it were to be found. Just why did nations go to war? Only an awareness of belligerent motivations would serve as a foundation for remedies, would allow human ingenuity to develop substitutes for the techniques of the warmakers.

Dulles went to the basics of his world view in trying to understand what war was all about. He tapped his own perceptions of human nature. Human beings were the building blocks of nations, he argued, and human beings were "all selfish." In one of many citations from *The Federalist Papers* he knew so well, he accepted Alexander Hamilton's description of man as "ambitious, vindictive and rapacious." Throughout history, men had struggled to acquire what he summarized as "wealth, power and position." They had so taken these goals to heart that more often than not they became the rationale of human existence. Even worse, many men had come to define themselves according to their "material and social status"—according to how much wealth, power, and position they had *relative* to other men. The result was frequently a world of Hobbesian nightmare. Greed and ambition drove men to compete with one another, to take from one another, to dominate one another.[6]

In Dulles's mind, the international order was like the smallest unit of human society. One encountered groups or nations rather than individuals, but the behavior patterns were the same. Only now those behavior patterns produced war. Governments, like the isolated strivers of which they were extensions, sought to improve the wealth, power, and positions of their citizens. In doing so, they resorted to the use of force. Taking from others became the standard method of nations on the make and fighting back the standard response of those anxious to keep what they already had. As Dulles saw it, "force, actual or potential, has historically proved to be the only mechanism which can be relied upon to effect international changes."[7]

This characteristic of the international order was further compounded for Dulles by the fact that it seemed to be permanent. The wellsprings of human nature were not easily diverted. His reading of history convinced him that there would always be some nations, different ones at different times, that would want to grow richer or stronger than they were. Their drives would provide a constant impetus toward change on the international scene. Just as surely, these "dynamic" states, as Dulles labeled them, would be resisted by others of a "static" inclination, "those who are sufficiently satisfied with what they have—in the way of possessions or opportunities—not to want any important change. . . ."[8]

Certainly Dulles saw this pattern of static versus dynamic behavior around him during the 1930s, so much so that it spurred his fear of a new wave of international conflict. In everything he wrote on the theme of war and peace at this time, he specifically pointed to the actions of Germany,

Italy, and Japan as typical of "dynamic" inclinations through all time. The Japanese were "a people of great energy"; Italy, after "a phase of decline," was experiencing a "qualitative revolution" in which "industry, discipline, and willingness to sacrifice seemed to replace slothfulness and laxity"; Germany, though suffering an inevitable period of "moral and physical decadence" after the Great War, had gone on to see its "energy . . . quickly restored." Energized as they were, these three nations were flexing their muscles and seeking changes in the contours of the international scene. Japan was demanding respect for the principle of racial equality and was physically expanding in East Asia. Italy too demanded respect, to make up for "past indignities and slights," and was staking a claim to influence in the Mediterranean. ("Ethiopia became a victim," Dulles wrote, "not because of its intrinsic worth—which is problematic—but because its conquest would be symbolic of Italy's new structure. . . .") And Germany, "publicly branded" at Versailles, chafing under the constraints of the treaty signed there, lashed out in a variety of ways: by creating a monstrous military establishment, by annexing Austria, by swallowing Czechoslovakia.

As the counterweight of the 1930s, Dulles saw "static" nations like Great Britain, France, and the United States. Satisfied as they were, these nations vigorously resisted changes in the international order that might alter their relative status. In fact, their tendency would be to resist *all* change for as long as possible. In doing so, Dulles argued, they actually made war more likely. Resistance created yet greater determination to bring about change on the part of the "dynamic," a determination that might easily take irrational and dangerous forms. "Excessive external restraints," Dulles wrote, create "unsound internal conditions. . . . Energy is developed to an abnormal pitch by recourse to emotion and semi-hypnotic influence. . . ." The problem was not unlike that of an average human being experiencing prolonged repression: "He becomes abnormal or at least develops antisocial complexes."[9]

The road to peace, Dulles argued, lay in finding a way of avoiding the explosive confrontations between fire-breathing dynamic states and others that were rigidly static. Confrontation itself was unavoidable. Some nations, like some individuals, would always seek growth and change; others would always prefer that things remain the same. But surely it was possible to devise methods for dealing with clashes more peacefully? Could not human ingenuity come to grips with "the task of reorganizing society, within the limits permitted by human nature, so as to substitute for force some other procedures."

Dulles believed it was possible to begin such a reorganization toward

"Peaceful Change Within the Society of Nations." His first prerequisite was that governments contented with the status quo should recognize "the inevitability of change." They and their citizens could not expect to control permanently the wealth or advantages that were theirs at any given moment. "Wealth, power and position constantly change," Dulles wrote. "Fortunes made by economy, foresight and industry are lost by profligacy, stupidity, and idleness. Prestige and influence are lost by incompetence and unworthy discharge of responsibility." In essence, Dulles urged the presently well-endowed to realize that "the changes which we recognize to be inevitable over a hundred years must occur sometime." Accepting such a fact of life would help to create an atmosphere in which changes could occur slowly, even selectively. As Dulles put it in an analogy he used over and again, "The river which periodically bursts its banks we do not hold in check by a frontal dam. We go back toward the sources and canalize them so as to effect a peaceful diffusion." There was the alternative of railing against all change by waging battles in bloodly arenas, but history had shown that this would simply not prove successful in the long run.[10]

One of the things which persuaded Dulles that nation-states could adapt to methods of peaceful change was his conviction that virtually all had arranged their *domestic* routines in precisely this way. Most societies, he argued, had managed to create a peaceful internal order by the twentieth century. People had gradually learned the insanity of a regime in which force was the standard tool for bringing about changes in wealth, power, and position. "Even the bravest and strongest could get small satisfaction out of a system wherein his personal safety, his enjoyment of his possessions and even his spiritual liberty, depended upon constant vigilance and the willingness and ability to resort to physical force and when there was the constant apprehension that a braver and stronger would appear." Gradually, very gradually, men had found other ways, less destructive and uncomfortable, to settle disputes over conflicting desires.

Dulles predicated two broad "principles of solution" to which human beings within societies had turned, "through conscious decision or unconscious evolution." He cited first "those efforts which are primarily directed to *states of mind*. It is sought to mould the human spirit so that desires will either be so diluted in intensity or so metamorphosed (sic) in character that conflicts of desire will be minimized." Men had encouraged "spiritual desires" in each other, such as a sense of duty to one's fellow man, which were not limited by the physical resources of a society's environment; all who shared such a desire could be satisfied without having to resort to force to take something away from someone else. To Dulles, the social peace which existed in many nations depended in part on "duty" and "unselfishness" as spiritual elements in the roster of human wants.

Human wants were not all spiritual, of course, and men had also turned to various forms of *law* and *authority* to lessen yet further the violent tendencies plaguing them. "A scheme of society" was sought which would assume "the presence of conflicting desires," but provide "substitutes for force" as a way of working them out. Governments, Dulles argued, had emerged at least in part as a response to this problem. As he described it, the government created within a state:

> . . . had the duty to familiarize itself with the various desires and needs of its group, to appraise the possibility of their being satisfied and reconciled, and to prescribe rules of conduct, consonant with the *mores* of the community, which would be calculated to permit the maximum of satisfaction, or the minimum of dissatisfaction. Once such rules are promulgated, the alternative procedure of violence can be, and is banned. The authority is given by the group the right and the means to enforce its rules and to compel, in lieu of individual resort to violence, the utilization of the peaceful procedures laid down by the authority.

Courts, for example, provided a peaceful routine procedure through which a person might seek the punishment or diminution of a rival. Legal codes might be used to foster "the creation and maintenance of opportunity" for dynamic individuals within a society (Dulles was quite vague here, but he may have had something like antitrust legislation in mind); taxation might become a tool for "a peaceful taking away, or a restraint of exploitation, for the benefit of the so-called underprivileged." Governments might also seek to create an environment fuller in resources (by acquiring territory or industrialization and foreign trade?), hoping to lessen the number of occasions on which men would be forced to dispute because of limited means of satisfaction.

Perhaps the key function of authority and law within societies, in Dulles's estimation, was the balancing of demands for change against demands for preservation of the status quo. Effective authorities, he argued, tamed dynamic and static forces by conceding something to each. Those individuals satisfied with their position and possessions were protected and allowed "some period and degree of effortless enjoyment." At the same time, those dissatisfied because of a lesser stake in the existing order were offered, through established routines and laws, "a possibility of peacefully diminishing the advantages of those who have. . . ."

As Dulles summarized it, absolute stability or security for any one group was recognized as impossible. There was, nevertheless, compensation in a "particular form of security": "freedom from violent attack upon person and property." The cost for this, to go full circle, was acceptance of "insecurity with respect to indefinitely retaining, exploiting and passing on without impairment or subtraction all that one had or can acquire by measures short of force." Great numbers of human beings had come to accept the logic of such arrangements within their respective societies. While some would certainly have preferred absolute and permanent control of power and possessions, most had accepted change as a fact of life. They had thus avoided a buildup of demands to the point where they could be affected through none but violent and ruthless means. Only occasionally in modern times, Dulles argued, had powerful groups within societies failed to face reality and held out absolutely against change. He specifically cited the French and Russian revolutions as evidence of the results. Far more often, explosions had been avoided. The result: "There are millions of people who live for years in close association and interdependence, without thought of force as the solvent of their conflicting individual desires. . . ."[12]

Unfortunately, Dulles believed, what was true of human relations at certain levels was not necessarily true at all. "We must recognize," he wrote at one point, "that relations between States have not been brought under the rule of law in the same way as relations between citizens or social groups within the borders of States."[13] The elimination of force as a tool of diplomacy, as a means of bringing changes in relative wealth and power, had simply not taken place in the international arena.

Nor was the elimination likely to be affected, given the nature of existing programs to hasten it. As he looked back over the peace efforts of the twentieth century, Dulles could see little but naive and dangerous failure to understand the fundamentals. Virtually every effort to "preserve the peace" had been founded on the hope that everyone could be persuaded or forced to leave everything as it was. Boundaries, treaties, armies, etc.: freeze them and harmony would reign, the argument had run. In the League of Nations, for example, Dulles had come to see "an implied guaranty of the status quo of all members." Plans to extend indefinitely the Washington agreements of 1922 had amounted to an effort by some to use "naval ratios as a permanent strait jacket." By renouncing the use of force, the only existing means of effecting change, the Kellogg-Briand Pact had become a campaign to "perpetuate the world as it is."

Given Dulles's assumption that change was inevitable, that certain dynamic individuals and states would always seek growth and develop-ment, it is not surprising that he saw such peace efforts as doomed to failure. Or worse. An organization like the League of Nations, rallying efforts to resist assaults on the status quo, was actually more likely to pro-voke war than to prevent it. As he summed up his impressions of recent peace efforts at one point, "the steps we had taken were inadequate and tended excessively to perpetuate the status quo, and it became obvious that any given status, however admirable it might be at the beginning, could not be indefinitely prolonged without bringing about a clash with human needs, which are constantly changing."[14]

Dulles considered himself enough of a realist not to be provoked into ranting against this past. After all, he argued, it was quite logical that many had fallen into the trap of "confounding peace with stability."

> Those whose lives fall in pleasant places contemplate with equanimity an indefinite continuation of their present state. "Peace" means to them that they should be left undisturbed. It is those who seek change that are the disturbers of the peace. "Aggression" becomes the capital interna-tional crime and "security" the watchword. The popular demand for peace is thus capitalized by those who selfishly seek to have the world con-tinue as it is.

Under such circumstances, it was perfectly logical that "the presently endowed nations"—France, Great Britain, and the United States—were the most avid formulators of "peace" projects:

> If other countries like Germany, Japan and Italy adhere only reluc-tantly if at all to such projects, it is not because these nations are inherently warlike or bloodthirsty. They too want peace, but they undoubtedly feel within themselves potentialities which are repressed and they desire to keep open the avenues of change. They appraise the 'peace' plans presented to them as shemes to eliminate the only effective mechanism of change.[15]

II

Past failures to chart "The Road to Peace" did not translate into perma-nent hopelessness as far as Dulles was concerned. If men would draw the logical conclusions from repeated errors, then efforts could be directed toward finding new approaches. In particular, the time had come to turn away from the schemes to freeze the status quo, to turn *to* the methods that had worked so well within smaller units of human society. "It is now in order," Dulles wrote, to consider how earlier solutions "can be pushed forward into the international field so as to bring the influence thereof to bear on the particular factors which our analysis showed to be conducive to totalitarian warfare."[16] What should prevent governments from seeking to eliminate force as a tool for effecting change in the same way that individuals had through centuries of evolution?

During the several years he spent "philosophizing" on the theme of war and peace, Dulles developed a variety of specific recommendations to substantiate his call for a new and wider use of old solutions. Some were in the nature of random jottings, usually made once and then forgotten. On one occasion in 1935, for example, he called for improved international leadership. "It must be recognized by statesmen that a policy which is truly conducive to peace is seldom a popular policy," he wrote; the best public leaders would have to be more far-sighted in their approach to the possibility of change in the international arena. On another occasion, Dulles proposed changes in the technical routines of international relations, such as a turn to bilateral as opposed to multilateral treaties. As he put it, "One of the great vices of the post-war structure is that so many states are parties to each item of settlement that it is almost impossible to see how, as a practical matter, changes can be evolved through peaceful processes."[17]

Other recommendations appeared more regularly in Dulles's writings and were presumably more important in the evolving pattern of his thoughts. Several times he suggested greater attentiveness to what he had earlier dubbed the "ethical" approach. He was convinced there were ways in which the state of mind or the thought patterns of man, the *international* animal, could beneficially be altered. As one case in point, he cited the desirability of giving men causes that went beyond the interests of their particular nations. Where a sense of duty had helped diminish clashes between individuals, for example, psychological or emotional counterparts might help do the same on a larger scale. "Devotion to an ideal and willingness to sacrifice therefore are among the finest of human traits," Dulles wrote. "Also, they are among the most dangerous." There was no reason why they should be put only at the service of nation-states.

> Social philosophies, such as communism, capitalism, fascism or democracy, already are becoming idealized to many and are recipients of their devotion and sacrifice. If such idealizations were divorced from nation personifications, and if force were renounced as a means of propagation, they might provide a new ideological phase which, with all its dangers, would be an acceptable alternative to the clash of nations which confronts us.

162

In addition, religions maintained some vitality in the modern world and these might be utilized in this fashion. It mattered little precisely which specific causes were adopted. "It is sufficient to know," he wrote, "that many such potential causes exist, and to point out that their great opportunity is now here."[18]

Another proposal that cropped up several times in Dulles's writings during this period was the vitalization of Article 19 of the League of Nations Covenant. This provision authorized the Assembly of the League to regularly "advise the reconsideration . . . of treaties which may have become inapplicable and the consideration of international conditions whose continuance might endanger the peace of the world." No power was given the Assembly to actually alter treaty terms or international conditions; it had only the right to study and recommend. But, argued Dulles, the Assembly was thereby "accorded a moral position in those respects which constitutes at least a sound first step. . . ." The component of Article 19 that especially recommended it to Dulles was that it looked toward "a periodic but measured alteration of the *status quo,* designed to strike an acceptable balance between the dynamic and static desires of the national group."[19]

The recommendation that Dulles put forward most often called for the creation of "economic fluidity" on the international scene. Many of the detailed suggestions concerning commercial and financial matters that fed into this were certainly familiar to a lawyer of Dulles's bent, and this may help to explain why he returned to them so often. Whatever the reason, "economic fluidity" came to rest at the core of his every discussion of the grand-scale problems of war and peace during the 1930s.

Already in his *Atlantic* article, Dulles provided an outline of economic proposals. What he was trying to encourage, he wrote, were:

> . . . national policies which permit a *diffusion of economic advantages. Exports and imports, emigration and immigration, and the international flow of capital,* even though these must necessarily be regulated, can bring about a large measure of *international flux* without shock to national boundaries. Economic isolation, on the other hand, greatly exaggerates the importance of national boundaries and means that evolutionary forces can find satisfaction only through changes of boundaries, the form most difficult of peaceful accomplishment. [Emphasis added.][20]

As this brief description indicates, Dulles saw international economic reform as a valuable tool for piercing the rigid barriers of the international scene. In particular, if offered a way of peacefully dealing with the dangerous obstacles that national borders had come to represent. "The boundaries of nations are in theory immutable and each nation has the right, which in practice is largely exercised, to convert its boundaries into barriers against intrusion from without, whether it be of goods or people or even ideas." The global landscape was pocked by such barriers: among the examples Dulles cited were restrictions on immigration and visitation; "restrictions of imports through tariffs, quotas and embargoes; restrictions on exports; restrictions on alien ownership of real estate and upon alien investment in many types of enterprise." All too often, such restrictive boundaries brought down the wrath of dynamic individuals and states anxious to expand their opportunities. One way to make war less likely in the future was to build "safety valves" into the barriers that boundaries represented. Or, as Dulles put it on another occasion, to allow "apertures" to be "cut in the boundaries of sovereignty." "Our requirement is that there be sufficient outlets for human energy so that it will diffuse itself peacefully and not be suppressed and compressed within a rigid envelope until a bursting pressure is attained."[21]

Dulles elaborated in a variety of ways on his suggestion that "economic fluidity" be used as a "safety valve" in international relations. On several occasions, for example, he used his own nation's history as "a striking example of what can be attained."

> This union was formed by states originally exercising the same sovereign rights as any other nations, states jealous of and even hostile towards each other and desirous of building up what they hoped to be their own prosperity by a convenient usage of their boundaries to restrain intercourse with one another.

As such, the United States of the late eighteenth century was something of a microcosm of the international scene of the 1930s. The Constitution, however, had provided an ideal *modus vivendi* for potentially warring political units. Boundaries of individual states had continued to encase varying governments acting independently on social, educational, and religious issues, independently collecting taxes and independently maintaining court systems. But, at the same time, enough "safety valves" were cut through these boundaries to avoid the pitfalls of, for example, a European environment in which many states were totally sovereign. The authors of the Constitution "found an essential basis for peace in the renunciation by each of the right to interfere with *the interstate movement of people, goods and ideas*" (emphasis added). As long as such free movement was possible, actual boundaries became "a matter of quite secondary importance."

It is sufficient that the resident of one state can invest his money in another or call on capital from another to finance his own investment; that he can sell goods to or buy from another and, if he chooses, travel freely back and forth and enjoy an unrestricted exchange of ideas. . . . Where, in a given State, there is found a density of population and a high degree of energy, there also exist sufficient opportunities to project that energy beyond the state line, so that alteration of the boundary itself is no objective.

Dulles placed great stress on the applicability of the American example to international relations. He would often discuss the international potential of "federalism" in future years. It was certainly his belief that if Germany, Italy, or Japan had been faced during the 1920s and 1930s with an international order in which boundaries contained "safety valves" to allow for the diffusion of energies, assaults on peace by those nations might not have occurred. In sum, "if boundaries permit what is known in the American States as *'interstate commerce'*, then we have cut apertures through the boundary barriers which are probably sufficient to assure that the dynamic forces within one state will currently diffuse themselves without threatening a violent change of boundaries" (emphasis added).[22]

If the early history of the United States supported Dulles's emphasis on the utility of "economic fluidity," so too did its more recent past. By the mid-1930s, Dulles was referring often to the support that Woodrow Wilson, his greatly admired former chief, would have given to the programs he was suggesting. Dulles argued that Wilson had been fully aware of the unavoidability of change in the international arena—and of the resistance which invariably greeted it. Concerned particularly with the rigid façade of territoriality that defined nation-states, Wilson had sought "to mitigate the obstructive character of national boundaries and to provide areas within which the dynamic forces could peacefully diffuse themselves." Freedom of the seas; a mandate system that would provide an "open door" to commercial and financial opportunities in underdeveloped quarters of the world; extensive removal of tariff and currency barriers: such were the programs sought by Wilson in order to create "an elastic world." In such an environment, boundaries would cease to act as absolute restraining walls against dynamic nations and peoples. Force, therefore, would no longer be automatically turned to as a tool for bringing about change.

To Dulles, it was significant that when Wilson came to outline his goals in the Fourteen Points address, he placed freedom of the seas, the mandate system, and the reduction of trade barriers *before* the League of

Nations. The President had been realistic enough to know that "the elimination of war was appropriate only as channels were otherwise provided for the peaceful diffusion of dynamic forces." Wilson, and Dulles after him, could hope for the successful maintenance of peace by the League only if there were first created "a world which is elastic and fluid in its organization."

Almost twenty years after his first government service, Dulles was suggesting that the Wilsonian program be vitalized. "That program has not failed," he declared, "it has never been tried."[23]

In another frequent variation on his basic theme of "economic fluidity," Dulles outlined a dichotomized program that would well serve his purposes. It became a significant facet of his general perspective on international affairs in succeeding years:

> We cannot treat all boundaries alike. A distinction must be made between those that enclose a highly developed and industrialized society and those which enclose areas which are as yet inadequately developed. The former cannot be suddenly exposed to new competitive conditions without serious disturbance. When a social system has been created which itself provides the peaceful outlet for a large quantum of human energy, then we would not advance our program were we to effect international changes which were so radical and abrupt as to close these domestic outlets.[24]

This was not to say that nothing could be done by developed states. Quite the contrary. Economic and political leaders in these countries would have to realize that "there can be *a broader and longer range vision of what is the best interest of the domestic economy*; there can be avoidance of minor obstructions which provide irritations out of all proportion to their substantive importance" (emphasis added). As a specific example, he cited the problem of international monetary exchange: "purely national moneys, which are unstable and nonexchangeable in relation to other moneys, constitute a most severe restraint to travel, the movement of goods and people, and the participation, through investment, in natural advantages and greater opportunities which are abroad." Why could there not be international agreement among the economic powers to maintain "national monetary units in some reasonably stable relationship to each other? Or why not "some substantial removal of barriers to the exchange of goods?" "International trade can be greatly facilitated by a gradual reduction of duties and elimination of quotas on lines which reflect the principal of reciprocity": this was an avenue which the great powers were especially capable of following. Or, why not easier facilities for the emigration of interested individuals? All such very specific reforms, in Dulles's estimation, would greatly reduce the obstacles that too frequently blocked international pathways—and all were reforms that developed societies could and should accomplish.[25]

He argued that among certain nations there already existed "a sense of comradeship and of friendliness" that provided a valuable precondition for freer "interstate commerce."

> Such a spirit exists between the Scandinavian countries. It exists between England and the self-governing Dominions. It exists between Canada and the United States. In each of these cases there is, *in embryo, a "polity," which transcends national lines and which is no less real because it is informal.* Such *oases* constitute very precious contributions to the cause of international peace. If through bodies of study and enquiry, set up on geographical bases, a community spirit could be developed, this might well serve to enlarge and multiply still further those groups of nations which felt a sense of comradeship and common polity. . . .

Or, as he put it to Henry Stimson at another time, "evolution along the ways I have in mind could first best occur as *between the United States and the British Empire or parts thereof,* and if and as progress were soundly made, additional nations or peoples might be brought in. . . ." Several years later, Dulles and his brother even drew up an elaborate proposal calling for a customs union between the United States and Canada.[26]

As extensive as such "apertures" in the international boundaries of the 1930s might appear, they seemed only a beginning to Dulles. "When we move on to those nations which are less highly developed, and particularly when we consider colonial areas, a much more ambitious program is practical." In such areas, he argued, boundaries did not protect highly developed societies which would be threatened by a sudden removal of traditional frameworks. "There would seem to be no insuperable obstacle to *opening up vast areas of the world* through the application of the principles of the 'mandate' system as proposed by President Wilson." The administration of all such areas should be designed to serve the interests of their inhabitants as well as insure that the resources found therein could play a role in the preservation of international harmony. Of special significance was the creation of an "open door" atmosphere, in which the markets, investment opportunities, and raw materials of these "vast areas" would be available on a basis of free and equal competition. Dulles was suggesting, of course, as had Wilson before him, sweeping away the imperialist system, at least with respect to its crucial economic ingredients. Following through on his earlier analogy from the American federal system, he felt that such an "opening up" of the underdeveloped areas of the world could make more viable the easy and peaceful "interstate commerce" so important to him.[27]

III

The substance and tone of his writings in the mid-1930s make it clear that the intellectual identity of John Foster Dulles was going through an important stage in its evolution. By the end of this decade, the distinguishing markings of his thought would be more complex than they had been in 1919, the 1920s, or even the early years of the Great Depression. There was growth and development beyond early stages and toward those characteristics often associated with him in the later years of his life.

The subject matter of Dulles's analytical efforts was broadened and defined in a more encompassing, mature fashion. From 1911 on, he had gradually established himself as a skilled corporate lawyer and a respected observer of certain facets of world affairs. He had, in particular, used the expertise gained in government service and day-to-day work at Sullivan & Cromwell to fashion commentary on varying conditions in the international economy. After 1934, Dulles took this special interest and used it as a springboard to more wide-ranging concerns. He developed, in particular, an explicit, extensively articulated preoccupation with what he saw as the fundamental problem of his times: a cycle of economic and political crises that had plagued the international order since the late nineteenth century. He had had a glimpse into the maw of that cycle during the Great War, but had been fooled like many into believing that it had been ended in the 1920s. Now it had regained its fury and he, older and hopefully wiser, sought to understand it and deal with it.

The denser substance of his writings helped produce an analytical thrust that went beyond his earlier style as well. Where he had primarily written as a corporate lawyer-critic, he now took on the garb of a philosopher. He wrote sweepingly and extensively about the nature of man, the patterns of human society, and the roots of conflict in human and international relations. "I think it is useful to occasionally philosophize on these matters," he wrote a friend, but the adverb was really an understatement. In the space of four years, he wrote hundreds of pages on his philosophical and political theories. He then capped them off with the first book of his career, a piece of work that received respectful and sometimes admiring attention from American and European intellectuals.[28] The body of his work as a whole had a scale of concerns and language of analysis that was far grander than anything he had produced before.

In addition, Dulles made his philosopher's role stand cheek to jowl with that of "reformer." The bottom line of his analysis was always the discovery of *solutions* for grave contemporary problems. If there was a vicious cycle of crises affecting the international order, how could it be tamed? Dulles thought he knew. Stepping back from the turmoil, he urged his contemporaries to follow him down "The Road to Peace," to "create a new world system in which war would be eliminated . . . some world mechanism, which would permit of changes corresponding to the changing needs of social justice."[29]

Of course, Dulles's new intellectual identity as a philosopher-reformer of international relations did not require shaking off his earlier roles. His career at Sullivan & Cromwell went on busily, and concern for the problems of other days continued. Dulles built onto his earlier work and thought instead, adding layers that molded themselves to the solid substratum of his past.

The overlapping of Dulles's intellectual roles is displayed in many ways. One is the regularity with which familiar subjects and ideas cropped up in the new-style writings of the mid and late 1930s. Although he gave them a grander setting, for example, Dulles remained preoccupied with the core significance of economic developments in international affairs. As in earlier years, the commercial and financial ties between nations were often the specific foci of his attention. Much of his broad theoretical analysis of the drift toward the war in the 1930s actually took off from a consideration of problems that had long been of concern to him: the great problems that currency irregularities, tariffs, and quotas posed for peaceful world commerce and investment. Such problems, for Dulles, were all too frequently precisely the ones that escalated into major political and military confrontations. His discussions of the difficulties caused by Germany and Japan were solidly based on this assumption. In a 1937 address to the International Chamber of Commerce, he said:

> Take the case of Germany. Inability to get foreign exchange blockades her almost as effectively as she was blockaded during the war. There is a shortage of food and a lack of raw materials. There is the same sense of being encircled by hostile faces.
>
> I sometimes think such international restraints create a condition akin to claustrophobia. The desire for outlets to the outside world becomes a form of mental disease. . . .

And in a letter to Lord Lothian several years later, he suggested a similar predicament for Japan:

> . . . I agree that the basic difficulty in Japan was the universal economic nationalism to which you refer. Except for that the Japanese probably would not have been greatly interested in China. They would doubtless have much preferred to get raw materials and find markets elsewhere. As, however, these possibilities gradually shrank, they then looked to China feeling that if the western white races put trade barriers up against them at least they should have a free hand with the adjoining yellow race.[30]

Dulles's sense of a political economy of international tension was a significant facet of his world view. As in the 1920s, his elucidation of details translated into general conclusions. In a very significant introduction to his remarks on Germany before the International Chamber of Commerce, for example, he said:

> The conclusion is inescapable that it is a well-ordered domestic economy which provides the greatest assurance of peace. The problem of international peace is but an extension of the problem of internal peace.[31]

The legacy of many years of work in international finance and commerce is especially evident in Dulles's recommendations for dealing with the major world problems of the 1930s. Once he had established a theoretical framework, his most specific and concrete proposals were always economic in nature. Even in the rudimentary *Atlantic Monthly* article of 1935, he cited the value of economic elasticity, i.e., easily interchangeable currencies and freer trade, in creating the kind of world system he had so grandiloquently described. In an address at Princeton several months later, he emphasized purely economic projects: freedom of the seas, reduction of tariffs, a mandate system that would provide an open door to underdeveloped areas. In later writings, including *War, Peace and Change,* he elaborated yet further on the desirability of "interstate commerce"; the need for currency and tariff reforms by economically sophisticated societies; the potential of "opening up" the raw materials and investment opportunities of less advanced regions.[32] While Dulles certainly made other proposals, none appeared as regularly and as prominently as these from 1934 to 1939.

It is interesting that Dulles seems to have been aware of this tendency in his writings. On one occasion in 1936, someone wrote suggesting that his analysis concentrated too heavily on economic issues and did not deal with problems of international politics and prestige. Dulles didn't flinch. "I think this is fairly subject to the criticism that it puts too much emphasis on the material and economic aspects," he wrote back. "The factors which you mention are certainly real but somewhat elusive to deal with. I want to think about them further."[33] Of course, it may not be surprising that a man who had spent his adult life as a lawyer for international banks and corporations should find noneconomic problems "somewhat elusive"—or even that he had not found much time to "think" about them. His writings on international affairs throughout the 1920s and early 1930s had already witnessed this characteristic.

Another 1930s link to earlier preoccupations with things economic was Dulles's continuing suspicion of governments. During the 1920s, he had regularly decried the meddling of politicians in the day-to-day routines of the world economy. Bankers and businessmen were more rational, he had argued. If they had been able to deal unilaterally with problems like reparations, Allied debts, and foreign investments, fewer tremors in international relations would have resulted. By the mid-1930s, Dulles had come to believe that sensible businessmen were also more *peaceful* in inclination. Many of his theoretical discussions argued for the creation of a world order in which the wilder impulses of politicians could be tamed. He often emphasized the desirability of giving wider rights and opportunities to individuals, as opposed to nations. "It is, after all," he wrote in 1937, "not the State as such but the human being within the State which has *natural rights,* and if we can give human beings, wherever they are, *reasonable access to opportunity wherever it is located,* then we shall have . . . created a principal organ of world evolution" (emphasis added). It was on such a foundation that Dulles often built his case for a diminution in the rigidity of boundaries. Fewer trade restrictions and easier currency convertibility, for example, would help make individuals "less boundary conscious." People could be "made to feel that opportunity beyond their boundaries is reasonably available to them, and that they need not pay the price of blind allegiance to their sovereign in order to obtain opportunity outside their present boundaries." If a world order more open to individual pursuit of opportunity could be created, "we would have put a stop to the development of mass abnormalities which, akin to claustrophobia, are primarily consequent upon a sense of restraint and repression. Such feeling of being restrained, even if it be imaginary, urgently requires a cure."[34]

Chagrin at government interference with the "natural rights" of individuals in the international arena was an important component of Dulles's world view during the 1930s. As an intellectual conclusion, it translated directly into day-to-day behavior. One cannot help but notice the overlapping of such thoughts and Dulles's concomitant work with international cartels. Chemical, nickel, and steel producers had clearly found national boundaries and government regulations obstacles to their pursuit of opportunity. As a lawyer for companies in these fields, Dulles helped devise means for piercing the rigidity of global horizons. He himself certainly saw it this way. As he wrote to Lord McGowan, a cartel associate by way of Imperial Chemical Industries, Ltd.:

> The word "cartel" has assumed here the stigma of a bogeyman which the politicians are constantly attacking. *The fact of the matter is that most of these politicians are highly insular and nationalistic and because the political organization of the world has under such influence been so backward, people who have had to cope realistically with international problems have had to find ways for getting through and around stupid political barriers.* [Emphasis added.][35]

Nor is the presence of "old" thoughts in "new" writings merely an example of coincidental intellectual momentum in Dulles. There is an important integral relationship involved, in which the experiences of the past very much provided the *source* for the thoughts and actions of the "present" that was the mid and late 1930s. As Dulles moved in new directions, as he turned to philosophical speculation and grand-scale schemes for reform in international relations, he drew on the warp and woof of his own life for inspiration. Both consciously and unconsciously he found a great deal there.

Clearly, for example, Dulles's writings in the 1930s had some linkage with the intellectual interests of his youth. Following somewhat in his father's steps, he had majored in philosophy at Princeton. A commencement prize even carried him to Paris for some postgraduate work under Henri Bergson. There is no tangible evidence of Dulles's philosophical bent for more than twenty-five years after his departure from the Sorbonne, but its later materialization suggests that a proclivity was buried, not abandoned.

Another source of crucial and particular significance was Dulles's early-life experiences with Woodrow Wilson. As a young man, Dulles had seen in Wilson a dynamic and crusading leader trying to move the troubled world of his time toward a more peaceful and prosperous order. In 1917, he had written of his own "passionate belief" in his President's work: the seeking after "a new system of international relationships; the creation of a world safe for democracy where free peoples can peacefully work out their own destinies and where occasion and opportunity for war will be eliminated." Partially cool for more than a decade after, the ashes of this passion were stoked in the 1930s and the warmth revived. Wilson was gone, but his "splendid vision" was alive, and Dulles gave it a central place in his writings. Lines of analysis and specific recommendations put forth during the Great War were explicitly commended to readers of a later day.

As he began assuming a reformer's stance, Dulles would not have doubted the importance of Wilson as a role model.[36]

Another fundamentally important source for the thoughts of the 1930s was Dulles's long experience in the world of world capitalism. At various times in the interwar years, Dulles showed himself to be one of a breed of reform-minded businessmen anxious to alter the patterns of international relations in a way that would allow a more efficient functioning of admirable economic mechanisms. As already discussed, he was occasionally disturbed at the way in which political and military affairs were allowed to interfere with commercial and financial routines. The earliest evidence of this is in his criticism of foolishly politicized reparations policies. Indictments of government interference with trade and investments followed quickly and reached a peak in the autarchic atmosphere of the early Depression. In a more positive direction, at least from his own perspective, Dulles also revealed his values in his extensive involvement with international cartels: working with like-minded businessmen, he helped to create economic entities that could rise above shortsighted government policies. His writings of the mid-1930s reinforced and systematized such impulses: calls for freer trade, currency reform, and the "opening up" of colonial regions of the world, among other things, were logical extensions of earlier ideas.

Taken as a whole, Dulles's interwar comments on difficulties plaguing the international economy are important sources of his reform ideas. Concern over commercial and financial problems translated into a desire for fewer political and military clashes and a more "businesslike" tone to international relations. (Wilson's proposals, appealing to Dulles in general, became especially attractive because they would do much in this particular direction if accomplished—i.e., given the former President's emphasis on freedom of the seas, lower trade barriers, and the mandate system.)

Feeling this way, Dulles was an interesting embodiment of the enlightened businessman envisioned by Karl Kautsky during World War I. Writing from the perspective of a German socialist, Kautsky had predicted the emergence of something like an anti-Babbitt mentality among men involved in world trade and finance: deeply impressed with the merits of capitalism, they would seek to reform some of the troublesome and dangerous tendencies often but not inextricably associated with it. Dulles's desires to move away from war, autarchy, and traditional imperialism were precisely the sort of things Kautsky anticipated. So were his specific recommendations. Kautsky expected moves for reforms that would allow the rational processes that characterized capitalism at its best to be continuously extended—which is what Dulles was essentially calling for in citing the merits of a "businesslike" perspective, free "interstate commerce" and international cartels.[37]

An awareness of sources encourages sensitivity to some of the basic assumptions and values inherent in Dulles's evolving world view during the 1930s.

It becomes clearer, for example, that Dulles's later, more grandly clothed proposals involved as much as ever a belief in the overlapping of lofty idealism and national self-interest. During 1919 and the 1920s, his analysis of international problems had led him to suggest a variety of solutions which he presumed were of enviable duality: on one hand, they offered remedies for specific economic problems being faced by the United States and on the other, as luck would have it, they offered advantages for war-ravaged countries. This duality remained a part of Dulles's world view throughout the 1930s. He himself could hardly have escaped the conclusion that many of his suggestions for dealing with the grand-scale problems of war and peace would have been very helpful in dealing with the severe economic difficulties being faced by his own country. In the early years of the Depression, he had spent much time describing those difficulties, with particular emphasis on their international dimensions. Proposals for freer trade, investment, and currency convertibility—which he made so frequently—could be directly turned to easing such national problems. Indeed, not surprisingly, many U.S. government officials, from Franklin Roosevelt and Cordell Hull down, reached a similar conclusion and took to couching their proposals in lofty language. Dulles certainly understood the linkage, drawing as he did on the same rhetoric. On one occasion, for example, he expressed to the Assistant Secretary of State his strong support for the Reciprocal Trade Act. He hoped the government could do more to stimulate popular interest in the program—to get people to "realize that the advantages are to be appraised not merely in terms of immediate economic benefit but in terms of war and peace."[38]

The body of Dulles's writings in the mid and late 1930s also makes abundantly clear the fundamental moderation, indeed conservatism, that undergirded his thoughts in earlier years. As with Wilson before him, for example, Dulles's approach to the phenomenon of "change" can serve as a key medium for fixing his essential political identity. In much of what he wrote in the five years after "The Road to Peace," he made change and the inevitability of change his core concepts. His analysis of the world crisis of the 1930s began with the contention that certain dynamic nations, as certain individuals, always sought to improve their wealth, status, and power. Others, content with their place and perquisites in the world, opted for an indefinite perpetuation of the existing order. When the static held out resolutely against the dynamic, economic and even military battles could be sparked. On the basis of this assessment, Dulles proposed that nations accept the logic of "peaceful change" as an alternative to the traditional dance of death.

What is striking in Dulles's schema is his clear appreciation for the *conservative functions of reform*. While he was trying to convince the statically inclined to accept the inevitability of change, and to roll more peacefully with the times, there was a warning built into his advice that revealed his own essential attachment to the status quo. If "orderly change" were not accepted, Dulles counseled, then violent change would always eventually ensue. Given this historical certainty, would it not make more sense to accept the less threatening of the only two alternatives available in human society and international relations and to fashion methods of *moderate* change that would defuse pressures for *revolutionary* transformations? Dulles's "peaceful change" proposals, in other words, were fundamentally *preventive* devices designed to avoid radical alterations which he explicitly dreaded.

Dulles frequently revealed his opposition to sweeping change. Already in "The Road to Peace," he had laid out his priorities very clearly:

> . . . nations which are dissatisfied with their international status must recognize that there must be a large measure of stability. We cannot, of course, invite chaos or encourage the idea that any dissatisfied nation may take for the asking from those who have. It must be recognized that changes, if they are to come peacefully, will come slowly and only after justification therefore is abundantly apparent. Indeed, changes may often be delayed beyond the time when their desirability and inevitability may seem self-evident. Patience is indispensable to peace.[39]

He was also explicit about his specific perception of "peaceful change" as the rational *alternative* to "chaos." As he put it in one early piece: "We forget that the changes which we recognize to be inevitable over a hundred years must occur sometime. They may occur gradually, year by year, *or else*, if they are allowed to occur infrequently, then when they come they will be so momentous as to cause a great shock." He saw it as clearly desirable to avoid this. What he wanted, he said in *War, Peace and Change*, was a global order characterized by an *"organic elasticity which will cushion the world against shock"* (emphasis added).[40]

The fact that Dulles essentially backed himself into a reformist position offers further testimony to the importance of his Wilsonian and business roots. If Dulles had been impressed by Wilson as a crusading leader, he must also have been conscious of his chief's strong commitment to moderate change and his active hostility to overly dynamic elements like the Bolsheviks. He certainly became quite involved in the implementation of the Russian phase of antiradicalism that was an inherent twin of the President's reformism. And in Kautsky's prognostications concerning the emergence of enlightened capitalists, there was always the assumption that further rationalization of the existing world system would help prevent the radical alterations being urged by Lenin and others. For Wilson as a political leader and for sophisticated businessmen taking off from a preponderantly economic base, in other words, the shared objective was to right several aberrant features of the international system while leaving most of its essential components intact.

This is Dulles's kind of logic. In his own mind, he was developing an alternative to the dangers of the rigid sovereignty system, but an alternative that did not require a radical transformation. Where some might take his diagnosis and prescribe "the abolition of the entire concept of national sovereignty and the unification of the world into a single nation," Dulles believed less would suffice. If nothing else, a "grandiose" scheme was "so remote that it can scarcely be expected to secure the adherence of those who seek peace as a practical objective." More to the point, the total razing of boundaries was unnecessary. "If boundaries permit what is known in the American States as 'interstate commerce,' then we have cut apertures through the boundary barriers which are probably sufficient to assure that the dynamic forces within one state will currently diffuse themselves without threatening a violent change of boundaries."[41]

It is interesting to note, especially in view of its long-range significance, the most extreme example of Dulles's commitment to minimal change: his attitude toward the underdeveloped world. It was during the 1930s that he first revealed a belief in the utility of the underdeveloped world that was directly in line with that of Wilsonians and Kautsky's anticipated leaders. Until this time, Dulles's writings had been overwhelmingly European-American in geographical forcus. In the midst of economic and political crises, he became conscious of the potential of other regions. Asia, Africa, and Latin America, which may simply have been taken for granted before, came to be seen as "vast areas" in which the clashing desires of great powers could be tamed. Let these areas be "open" for commercial and financial penetration by all, and nation-state rivalries would remain peaceful. The dynamic forces of the day would find ample opportunities for their satisfaction as long as no one group had exclusive "imperial" privileges.[42] (This was, of course, the thought behind Wilson's hopes for mandates within the League of Nations.)

The point here is that what Dulles's proposals would not have changed was as significant or more significant that what they would. While great powers would presumably relate more peacefully to each other in such a system, the essential nature of their combined relationships with the underdeveloped areas would remain the same. Nothing at all was proposed that would have prevented the latter from continuing as useful appendages of the great power hierarchy, locked into what would still be a fundamentally exploitative relationship. There could be lip service to considering the needs of inhabitants, but such concern was inherently incidental to the main purpose of the program. What benefits might emerge for these great numbers of people would always be a function of a second-class status that was structurally induced. It could not be otherwise in a system that would alter the format of exploitation, but not the substance.

All in all, then, Dulles's analyses revealed a man who circled the phenomenon of change as if it were suspicious quarry, one whose recommendations were quite clearly designed to tame the beast's more extreme potential. By way of definition, of course, such a pattern of reasoning and programing is what separates conservatives and liberals from radicals, reformers from revolutionaries.

Not that there should be anything surprising about finding such a perspective in John Foster Dulles. In the 1930s, after all, he was an extremely successful and wealthy international lawyer as well as a citizen of the most powerful single nation in the world. While troubled by certain irrational features in the world order which surrounded him, he was too much a beneficiary of that order's essential institutions and values to question them in any truly fundamental fashion. To the nation-state system and capitalism, he proved basically loyal. For radicals who did question the fundamentals, he responded with a conviction built on a series of elemental assumptions: that the existing world order required reform, but not radical transformation; that it contained within itself the capability for reform; and that it was well worth reforming.

9

The War Years, 1939–1945: Church . . .

THE DIRECTION OF HIS THOUGHTS during the mid and late 1930s suggests that John Foster Dulles was running both forward and backward at the same time.

He was moving forward in the sense that he was developing the subject matter and thrust of his intellectual efforts. With a few sudden, long strides, he laid out the boundaries of a more broadly conceived, more complex world view than had been obvious in earlier years. He was moving backward in that he absorbed into his new-style writings elements of his youth that had lain dormant for years. His father's scholarly bent and his own inclination toward the study of philosophy at Princeton and the Sorbonne can easily be seen as deep-rooted forces that had a slowly evolving but significant impact.

At the very end of the 1930s and during the early 1940s, Dulles carried this pattern yet further—he went on advancing the theories and analysis which had emerged after 1934 while finding inspiration in ever-deeper recesses of his early life. The strong religious atmosphere of his home in

Watertown and the church foundation of his father's and mother's careers had had little visible effect on him after his decision not to enter the ministry. But by 1940, their power to move him became obvious once more. He found himself willing to consider time-consuming work with organizations like the Federal Council of Churches. More importantly, moral themes began to figure prominently in his writings, and religious enthusiasm was soon making more vibrant the speculations of the philosopher he had already in part become.

I

Actually, a tendency toward the passionate and dramatic surfaced in Dulles before any extensive church-related ties had been formed. It became evident in his reactions to the outbreak of war in 1939.

The basic thrust of Dulles's comments on the exploding European scene was consistent with his previous discussions: that the war was the logical endpoint of the path international relations had taken after 1919, that until "static" and "dynamic" forces in the international arena were balanced, men and nations would go on fighting for "wealth, power and position." The tone of his analysis changed considerably, however, almost as if he were absorbing something from the charged atmosphere around him. He had usually offered views in a temperate fashion. His style had been that of a rather aloof philosopher, his language laden with ponderous abstractions that must often have muffled the ring of his ideas. When war erupted in Europe, this began to change in a way that would become increasingly obvious and important as the war years went on. His syntax became more emphatic and precise when describing the defects of the existing international order. The unfolding crises of the 1930s, he told the Foreign Policy Association, were "a repetition of the senseless cyclical struggle between the static and the dynamic. Such struggles are but the inevitable, ever recurrent, incidents of any rigid system." Or, as he put it to the Economic Club of New York a few days later, "I am satisfied that the present world system—which alternates between periods of rigidity and of violent explosion is self-destructive."[1] There was also a more powerful thrust to his proposals for remedial action. Recommendations that had been proffered with protestations of moderation were still forthcoming, but were now couched in more dramatic language. "The vitally important issue," Dulles told one audience in October, "is *the realization of a new world order* which will put our political knowledge to work and end a system which makes these violent revolts both inevitable and recurrent." Why?

The fundamental fact is that the nationalist system of wholly independent, fully sovereign states is completing its cycle of usefulness. . . . The world has become an interconnected economic unit, managed by a series of unconnected powers. Millions upon millions of human beings today find their well-being and livelihood depend upon power elsewhere which is exercised without any responsibility toward them. Thus today, more than ever before, are the defects of the sovereignty system magnified, until now it is no longer consonant with either peace or justice. It is imperative that there be transition to a new order.[2]

In addition to altering the tone of his presentation to some degree, Dulles made one significant addition to his analysis during 1939. Prodded perhaps by the escalating debate among his countrymen, he started discussing the way in which the United States should respond to conflicts in Asia and Europe. He had publicly avoided the specifics of this issue during the years he was developing his grand-scale theories. Now he was ready to leap into the fray.

There was nothing vague about Dulles's position on American foreign policy in 1939. "I see, neither in the underlying causes of the war, nor in its long-range objectives, any reason for the United States to become a participant," he told one audience in October. If Americans allowed themselves to be drawn in, it would be "as is the moth into the flame." This, of course, was a position based solidly on his earlier analyses. Given his sense of what all the great powers of the 1930s were trying to do, given his perception of the world system they epitomized, endorsement for American involvement in European or Asian wars would have been simply illogical. Here were conflicts that were "the self-destructive byproducts of the present world order." What could be gained by participation? Had any of the combatants shown any desire to reform that world order so as to avoid future explosions? No, Dulles believed. Interwar peace efforts had demonstrated that "the official mind still has no conception of a world order other than that one which identifies peace with the status quo." No one had sought, even experimentally, to work out "a practical, workable system under which the barriers and restraints of sovereignty may be made yielding to the inevitable requirements of change." Because of this, Dulles believed it would be "senseless" for the United States to "exhaust" itself in such an effort. "Were we now to act affirmatively," he told one audience, "would it not be to re-establish . . . an order which by its nature is self-destructive and a breeder of violent revolt?" Could there be any merit in an effort that "would be designed merely to recreate with England and France a military domination which would be used to enforce peace under conditions such as prevailed during the first post-war decade and out of which our present troubles arise?"

Considering costs in terms of blood and treasure, "I say that the time has not come to throw all that we hold most dear into a struggle which can have no constructive result."[3]

Dulles's general inclinations concerning the proper course for American foreign policy in 1939 were strongly reinforced by his particular dissatisfaction with what he considered the unwise leadership being exercised in Washington. Franklin Roosevelt and his advisers were too much creatures of the existing world system, Dulles believed. Their "entire effort" in dealing with global conflicts "has been to identify peace with a maintenance of a *status quo.*" "Except for that orphan child of the administration, the Hull trade policy," he told the Economic Club of New York, "I cannot find any word or act which evidences adequate perception of the true nature of peace." Dulles found this particularly "incomprehensible" in a program from "so-called 'liberals.' "

> They are the first to recognize and insist, in internal affairs, that property and contract rights cannot be immutable. They demand some political mechanism which will invalidate contracts obtained by coercion, which will prevent wealth from being integrally inherited, which will appropriate private property required for the public good, and which by taxation will take away from those who have for the benefit of society as a whole. They realize that unless such devices exist revolution will be inevitable. And despite the fact that revolt always has hideous aspects, they consider it morally justified. Yet in the field of international affairs these same liberals preach the doctrine of the sanctity of vested interests and identify peace and morality with the indefinite perpetuation of a *status quo* system.

The end result was that the Roosevelt Administration had opted for a policy in which Americans, "through power of money and armament, are to create a new world bloc committed to the doctrine of *the divine right of things as they are*"[4] (emphasis added).

Dulles's perspective on world affairs was unusual in the United States of 1939. He defied easy categorization and found himself misunderstood on many occasions. Some reacted with outrage to Dulles's version of the underlying trends of international relations. They took his critical comments on the nature of British, French, and American foreign policy as an indication of support for Axis behavior. As early as 1935, but especially in 1939, he was denounced in some quarters as a pro-fascist and as an apologist for Nazi and Japanese aggression.[5]

It is easy to see why some of Dulles's statements spurred anger in the raging atmosphere of the day. At one point in October 1939 he told an audience:

> For fifteen years following the World War, Great Britain and France dominated Europe. They, with the United States, achieved a power so overwhelming that their political and economic policies vitally affected all other peoples of the world. . . . Yet that power was exercised purely selfishly to the end of perpetuating in their own people a monopoly of advantage. We see in Japan, Italy and Germany the fruits of such a system.

A few months earlier, he had made a similar charge about the motives of status quo powers. The only thing heard from London, Paris, and Washington was talk about "sanctity of treaties," "law and order," and "resisting aggression." He said, "Such phrases have always been the stock in trade of those who have vested interests which they wish to preserve against those in revolt against a rigid system."[6]

Certain listeners took such statements to mean that the Allies rather than the Axis powers were responsible for the international crises of the day. Dulles seemed to be implying that Axis campaigns were legitimate responses to overbearing behavior by the beneficiaries of the status quo. But most critical reactions to Dulles's analysis were based on a misreading of his position. What he was attempting to do in the mid and late 1930s was to understand why Germany, Italy, and Japan were behaving as they were. His efforts at explanation, right or wrong, involved neither admiration nor endorsement. This was obvious from the beginning. Already in 1935, he and the editors at *Atlantic* hesitated over the publication of "The Road to Peace," given the outbreak of the Italian-Ethiopian crisis. For his part, he "was somewhat reluctant to see it come out . . . when *it might seem to be a defense of Italy.*" Nevertheless, the article appeared. "If my generalizations were true a year ago," he explained to a friend, "they would still be true. As a matter of fact, there is a good deal to be said on behalf of Italy, although there is a great deal to criticize in the way in which Mussolini has gone about it." From this point on, Dulles tried to guard his rear beforehand by including specific disclaimers in almost everything he wrote. In *War, Peace and Change,* he followed his catalog of German, Japanese, and Italian responses to the rigidity of the status quo by writing: "The foregoing recitals are not by way of defense. What has happened to China and Ethiopia and to many Austrians and Czechs is repugnant to civilized mankind." And in March 1939, speaking to the Foreign Policy Association, he described leaders in the Axis capitals as "evil creatures."[7]

Such criticism of Axis behavior is perfectly consistent with the thrust of Dulles's analysis throughout the 1930s. At all points, he tried to make it clear that it was the existing *system* of international relations that was at fault, not one or another particular nation. If he did not exalt the purity of the Allies by 1939, it was not because he felt their opponents deserved his praise instead. As he put it at one point:

> . . . I do not blame personally the rulers of England and France for what they did or what they failed to do. They were the creatures of the system of which they formed part. Neither do I condone the violence, cruelty and intolerance which characterizes the present leadership of Germany, Italy and Japan. Indeed, this merits our most thorough condemnation But, as we have seen, a system of irresponsible power always creates the mass discontents out of which evil leadership arises.[8]

It seems clear, in other words, that Dulles was not a pro-fascist in the late 1930s. He was, instead, an observer determined to remain above the fray, ready to hurl philosophical bolts at both camps while denouncing what their combat represented. Of course, this did not (and perhaps does not) clear him of questionable behavior in all eyes. Some of those who did understand Dulles's writings still concluded that he was operating with blurred moral vision. Though they may have recognized the shortcomings of Great Britain, France, or the United States, reasonable men could still insist that the particular horrors perpetrated by the fascist powers required moral distinctions and clear loyalties. For those who did, Dulles's even-handedness was unacceptable. Henry Stimson, for example, who had praised the work of 1935–36, thought Dulles was off base by 1938–39. "I am not sure that you have not oversimplified your analysis," he wrote, "and that your attitude is not too much detached from certain ethical and psychological factors. . . ."[9] And one wonders what Stimson and others would have added if they had been aware of the ongoing business contacts that formed a steady complement to Dulles's intellectual conclusions. His association with major German and Japanese industrialists by way of the chemicals cartel, for example, gives pause even today.[10]

There were other ways in which Dulles's 1939 statements were subject to misinterpretation as well. His recommendations for American foreign policy prompted both praising and damning reactions from those who occasionally mislabeled him an "isolationist." Robert Taft and William Borah were among some who were happy to think that Dulles was of like mind after war broke out in Europe; Wendell Willkie and James P. Warburg were typical of others who had the same reading of Dulles's position but reacted critically to it. In the postwar years, some went on to lambaste him for urging a cowardly and irresponsible path on his fellow citizens, with a number of critics arguing that he was a prominent member of the American First Committee.[11]

"Isolationist" is a label that simply fails to stick. Dulles did provide legal services during the incorporation of America First, but was never a supporter of its efforts. Later misunderstandings probably arose because his wife provided regular financial aid to the group. But Mrs. Dulles was independently wealthy, and her contributions in no way implied her husband's endorsement. More importantly, Dulles was intellectually unsuited to isolationism. For almost three decades, he had been a vigorous proponent of American activism in the international arena. Now, in 1939, although he opposed U.S. involvement in European and Asian conflicts, he never advocated a withdrawal into some Fortress America. Rather, it was the particular circumstances of these conflicts that led him to spurn involvement. He simply did not accept the idea that he was an isolationist because he opposed involvement in the pointless debacle that the war represented to him. What most separated him from the isolationists was the fact that his opposition to intervention was strictly conditional. He made every effort to make it clear to his listeners that he could envision circumstancs under which he would certainly change his mind. "I am not an 'isolationist,' " he said at one point, "indeed I have generally been called an 'internationalist.' . . . I would not oppose affirmative action if our policy were based upon a genuine understanding of the causes of the present crisis and was intelligently designed to achieve a world order whereby recurrent crises might hereafter be avoided." Or, as he put it to William Borah when refusing an invitation to testify before his Senate committee:

> My general feeling is that if the world is bound into a cycle of recurrent violence, then I should like to see the United States avoid involvement. I fear this is the situation in Europe today. However, I am 'isolationist' only in this sense and believe that if any program could be evolved which would break the cycle and give some promise of re-establishing a real era of peace rather than mere armistice, then we should play our part. [12]

Further testimony to the conditional nature of Dulles's anti-interventionism is found in a number of 1939 comments on the very different reactions he had experienced a quarter century earlier. "I was willing and eager to see the United States go into the World War under the leadership of Wilson," he said on one occasion. "I felt that he had perceived and might correct the inherent defects in our present world system." But 1939 was not 1917, and FDR was not Wilson. In a number of specific and pejorative comparisons, Dulles maintained that "today . . . I do not find in our public opinion, official or private, any comprehension of the true nature of the problem. Our reactions seem to me to be impulsive and emotional, wholly lacking either that intellectual content or that intelligent idealism which alone would justify the risks which would be involved."[13]

II

Given the thrust of his ideas, it would not be impossible to imagine Dulles remaining out on some personal intellectual limb after 1939. His biting criticisms could have evolved into ongoing cynicism concerning British and French war aims and the actions of the Roosevelt Administration. With a thriving law firm able to absorb as much time as he was prepared to give it, Dulles might have gone on to act like an Old Testament prophet taken off to a desert: brooding over the fact that the mainstream was out of touch with his thinking, he could have issued occasional dicta on the logic of descending doom.

Though conceivable in the context of 1939, such a scenario would have been out of character for Dulles, and it did not materialize. He had never really been content with total devotion to legal work, nor had he ever accepted a strictly sideline role as a naysayer. In the past, his speeches and his writings, as well as his travels and organizational ties, had evidenced inclinations more positive and social. Particularly during the mid-1930s, he had inched more and more beyond the offices of Sullivan & Cromwell. He had tried to communicate with others about the international problems then raging and had been especially anxious to share his ideas for their solution. As it turned out, such tendencies from the past had more momentum than the aloof cynicism of 1939. They reasserted themselves and soon carried Dulles far beyond the forays of earlier years.

It was the tenor of Dulles's approach rather than its substance which changed first. In several of his comments on the sorry gap between Roosevelt's leadership and Woodrow Wilson's stunning ideals, he had hinted at a desire to be inspired again. He had spoken not as if he were unalterably determined to sit out the cyclical struggle underway around him, but almost as if he were hoping that the Wilsonian spirit would somehow touch the policy makers of London, Paris, and Washington. The implied yearning, fleeting and wistful though it was, soon grew much stronger. During 1940 and 1941 Dulles made his adjustment to the fact of war and did it by turning his attention from the past and present to the future. If fighting was going to take place, and if even the United States were going to become involved, was there any way in which the sacrifices could be made productive? Was there some way in which the postwar world could be made better? What reforms could be sought that might make the future more peaceful and economically secure? Such questions were decidedly related to those Dulles had grappled with at previous times. As he turned back to them during the early years of World War II, he was clearly responding to a personal intellectual drive that was too basic to be lost in the despair of 1939.

That Dulles felt this kind of intellectual drive is evident as one looks at his continuing efforts to communicate with others. Shortly after the outbreak of war in Europe, he reaffirmed his connections with the internationalist community in the United States, with groups and individuals that had been active throughout the 1920s and 1930s and were now trying to adjust their efforts to the circumstances of war. In January 1940, for example, he became a member of the Commission to Study the Organization of Peace, a new offshoot of the League of Nations Association. Through radio broadcasts and published reports, the Commission hoped to motivate the American public to a mature concern for the shaping of the postwar world. At about the same time, Dulles also agreed to participate in a secret Council on Foreign Relations project involving studies of postwar issues for the Department of State. Earlier ties with the National Council for the Prevention of War were maintained too.

In his work with these groups, Dulles hoped to find an opportunity for what he saw as serious consideration of postwar problems and meaningful planning for the future. At one of the first meetings of the Commission to Study the Organization of Peace, he offered a compendium of the ideas elaborated in *War, Peace and Change*, focusing particularly on the relevance of Wilsonian programs to the 1940s. Wilson was "the greatest stateman of modern times," Dulles wrote:

> He . . . conceived a peace founded upon a dilution of national sovereignty. No nation could claim a legal or moral right to perpetuate its own status, but treaties and international conditions would be subject to change, on the initiative of an international body. . . . The colonial areas would be wholly withdrawn from the operation of the sovereignty system. There would be "freedom of the seas" and provision for the levelling of the trade barriers.[14]

Similar interests led Dulles to association with the Federal Unionists, a new group founded by Clarence Streit. Streit and his adherents sought a federal union of the United States, Western European nations, and Great Britain and its self-governing dominions. They believed that a common defense establishment, a custom-free economy, and a common monetary, postal, and communications system would help prevent future wars. Dulles was intrigued by all this. Like Streit, he believed the federalism that was part of the early history of the United States could serve as a model for international developments in the twentieth century, and he seems to have enjoyed toying with the intricacies of adaptation. At one point, he spent many hours with Streit drafting a proposed congressional resolution inviting the United Kingdom, Australia, New Zealand, and South Africa to join the United States in a "Provisional Federal Union."[15]

None of these groups proved very satisfying for Dulles. Over time, they absorbed less and less of his interest. In sharp contrast was his association with the Federal Council of Churches. Here, an intermittent 1930s connection blossomed into an intense working relationship in the early 1940s. This transformation and its aftermath proved to be a significant development in Dulles's life. The religious elements of his childhood family life were emphatically revitalized and stood again from this point on as an influence of real relevance for his thought and behavior.

When, as a student at Princeton, he had decided to study law instead of entering the ministry, Dulles paved the way for a long period of what he himself called "nominal" religious ties. For three decades after 1908, he kept his church connections limited and dispassionate in comparison to the milieu of his youth. He became a member and elder of the Park Avenue Presbyterian Church in New York, but he was attentive there primarily in administrative and financial matters. This was the case with other church activities as well. Periodic involvement with the New York Synod of the Presbyterian Church, for example, came with legal representation of its interests during several General Assemblies. In 1922, he also provided counsel during the incorporation of the Federal Council of Churches.

One agency of the Federal Council did spur more intellectual concern by Dulles, though its formal religious ingredients were not noticeably responsible. From the early 1920s, he was sympathetic toward the work of the Department of International Justice and Goodwill. As the usual voice for the Council on global issues, the Department enunciated a Wilsonian and internationalist position that Dulles found attractive. By 1936, in fact, he had developed friendships with several churchmen in the agency and even allowed himself to be persuaded to attend a special World Conference on Church, Community and State at Oxford in July 1937. For a passing moment, he seems to have felt that church leaders and intellectuals active in the international ecumenical movement might be valuable allies in pushing for the world reforms he was then advocating. The meetings at Oxford proved very exciting, as men like Reinhold Niebuhr, R. H. Tawney, Paul Tillich and T. S. Eliot listened attentively to his ideas. He was placed in charge of a drafting committee for a statement on "The

Universal Church and the World of Nations," and the end product read like a polished version of his 1935 *Atlantic* article. [16]

As positive as this experience may have been, Dulles went through several more years of quite limited involvement in church activities. He did continue to find the positions of the Department of International Justice and Goodwill admirable, including its public statement on the outbreak of war in Europe. [17] In addition, Dulles found the Federal Council useful because it provided him with an occasional public platform for the elaboration of ideas. In July 1939, he attended a small conference in Geneva where he exchanged opinions with European Protestant leaders. And in early 1940, at a time when his rather unusual point of view may well have cut down other invitations, he was asked to address a National Study Conference on "The Churches and the International Situation." [18]

Nevertheless, there was a hesitancy in Dulles's relationship with Protestant leaders. Until late 1940, other things kept him at arm's distance. For one, he was too busy elsewhere with older organizational ties and, especially, his work at Sullivan & Cromwell. Turning down several requests in 1939, one of them an invitation to be chairman of International Justice and Goodwill, he explained that business and other interests were absorbing all his time. [19] More importantly, he long remained unsure about the alignment between his own ideas and those common in church circles. Particularly after the outbreak of war in Europe, he found evidence of attitudes with which he could not feel comfortable. Henry Sloane Coffin, president of Union Theological Seminary, began articulating a pro-Allied position and became a vocal member of the Committee to Defend America by Aiding the Allies. Coffin argued that the war in Europe revolved around a "moral issue . . . between the triumph of unscrupulous and brutal tyranny and forces which promise an orderly world in which free man can breathe." He and Henry Van Dusen went so far as to circulate a statement on the war at the Philadelphia National Study Conference in February 1940. Although admitting that all nations bore some responsibility for the "ultimate causes" of conflict in Europe, this statement went on to elaborate the particular horrors of fascism and totalitarianism. Allied victory in the war would more likely lead to a new and more peaceful world order, it concluded, which "the best elements in all belligerent nations are hoping and praying for. . . ." [20] Dulles was initially impressed by the reference to a reformed international order, but soon came to the conclusion that he could not live with unbridled enthusiasm for the Allies. As he wrote Van Dusen in March, he would not accept the idea that the war "involved a great moral issue, with right wholly on one side of the Allies and wrong wholly on the side of Germany."[21] When Coffin circulated a second statement in May, urging "moral and material" aid to Great Britain and France, Dulles quickly voiced further disagreement. "The premise of the proposed Statement," he argued, "appears to be that we should adopt as a permanent feature of our foreign policy an effective guaranty of the British and French empires." Finding a way to move the world away from imperialism seemed a more logical goal. Furthermore, he told Coffin, he was distressed by the tendency to bestow a church sanction on the Allied war effort.

> During the years when it was possible to think calmly of these matters, I resolved that I would constantly strive not to identify national self-interest with righteousness. It seems to me that the proposed statement cannot be reconciled with that resolution. It says, in effect: we do not want the Nazis to threaten our hegemony in Latin America; we do not want later on to risk having to face Germany, or perhaps Japan, without strong military allies. Therefore, it is suggested, it is God's will that we should now invoke hatred and cruel violence to help decide the war in accordance with our self-interest. This may sound practical politics, although I doubt it. But I am even more doubtful that it is Christian. . . .[22]

Coffin's prestige in Protestant circles and the willingness of many to sign his public statements surely kept Dulles suspicious about the wisdom of closer association. As it turned out, however, there were other church leaders who shared his misgivings about reacting to the war in Europe in the spirit of a religious crusade. Leaders of the Department of International Justice and Goodwill, in particular, turned their energies to keeping the Federal Council from moving in this direction. As they maneuvered, they turned to Dulles for advice and kept him fully informed. He, in turn, responded with ideas and interest.[23]

Faced with a serious division of opinion, the leadership of the Federal Council of Churches worked hard to find ground on which all could stand. By turning their attention to the future, they succeeded. During Executive Committee and special study group meetings in the spring and summer of 1940, it became clear that however deep their disagreements might be on the causes of the war and the nature of the belligerents, they shared common long-range goals. A conscious decision was reached to allow each individual to decide for himself what position to take on the nature of the war and the desirable response of the United States to it. Protestant leaders would turn their *joint* efforts to what could be done once the war was over.[24]

It was at this point that Dulles finally began to draw closer to the Council. Having gone through his own time of disequilibrium and emerged with a preoccupation with the future, he must have felt more comfortable with the Protestant leaders he had come to know. He was invited to an informal dinner in October 1940 at which discussion focused on devising a way to channel Protestant thinking on the postwar world. A consensus emerged on the desirability of organizing a major study commission. Dulles must have been enthusiastic about the idea, because he agreed to draft a statement urging creation of such a group and to present it to the biennial meeting of the Federal Council, scheduled for December in Atlantic City. The delegates there responded with their support and approved the creation of a "Commission to Study the Bases of a Just and Durable Peace," designed to "clarify the mind of our churches regarding the moral, political and economic foundations of an enduring peace." They also endorsed a motion naming Dulles its chairman. [25]

III

Work with the Commission on a Just and Durable Peace figures as an important chapter in Dulles's life. He served as its chairman from 1940 to 1946 and gave it a great deal of his time and energy. More importantly, the group's identity from the very beginning was an extension of his own. Though designed differently, the Commission proved to be a highly personalized undertaking in which style and substance were both largely determined by his inclinations. There was a Committee of Direction composed of two dozen Protestant leaders with which he worked. There were also several hundred members eventually within the full Commission to whom he brought ideas and "statements" for approval at periodic conferences. But Dulles was an enthusiastic chairman, and hours of effort brought him to meetings so well prepared that his colleagues invariably let him lead the way. As one of them put it, "It was recognized that this was really a one-man show. It was really his Commission. It produced a series of documents. . . . Every one of them originated on one of his yellow lawyer's pads, on which he wrote his memoranda. . . . The Commission really was a rubber stamp for John Foster Dulles's ideas." Frequent media reference to the "Dulles Commission" underlines this description. [26]

Dulles and his co-workers set a twofold task for themselves. They wanted first simply to get Americans thinking about international relations and the desirable ingredients of a future peace: as they put it in an early published statement, they would try to "educate and crystallize public opinion" about the difficulties inherent in the struggle for "a just and durable peace." Secondly, they were anxious to suggest ways in which those difficulties could be tackled. They wanted to "provide the spiritual background without which none of our major problems can be solved," to inculcate "certain broad moral principles" with which the future plans of governments and peace conferences could be made to conform.[27]

With the benefit of hindsight, it is clear that Dulles drew the "broad moral principles" he wanted to emphasize from the body of his own work during two preceding decades. All of the major injunctions which became central to the work of the Commission on a Just and Durable Peace emerged directly from his earlier analyses and recommendations. Immediately after the group began functioning, it took up his emphasis on the need for "some new world order," some "better world order." This became a fundamental "guiding principle" for all subsequent work and was emphasized over and again in Commission statements. "The society of nations" had been a "society of anarchy," it was argued, plagued by surges of "power politics" and "the scourge of recurrent war." It would be "indefensible" for governments to recreate an environment conducive only to a "constant repetition of self-torture" in which men inflicted "misery," "violent death" and "starvation of body and soul" on each other.[28]

Dulles's Commission also accepted his earlier conclusion that the logical way to produce a new and better world order was to alter the established system of totally independent nation-states. Dulles wrote in 1941, as he had in the 1930s, that "the sovereignty system is no longer consonant either with peace or with justice." Many Commission publications developed this theme. Real peace, one maintained, would require "a willingness to accept, in certain areas, a surrender or pooling of the exclusive perquisites of national sovereignty and a sharing of economic advantages." One of Dulles's speeches in 1942, which was widely circulated, took off from the same premise: it called for a "dilution of sovereignty" and argued that this would make possible "that resumption of political evolution which is necessary if the world is to get life and happiness, rather than death and destruction."[29]

Working with his co-members, Dulles did go beyond his previous recommendations when it came to suggesting methods for accomplishing key goals. Most importantly, in this respect, he became an early and vigorous advocate of a new international organization. The League of Nations had proved a failure, but certain alterations of design and rededication to tasks originally undertaken in 1919 could spur enthusiastic support from many doubters. "The fact is that the world has become an increasingly interdependent affair," Dulles argued in 1941. "It is an anachronism that there should not be in it some organism that owes a duty to the whole." He actually defined the encouragement of American support for such an organism as "the most important matter" before his church commission. The vast majority of subsequent communications took off from this base. In the words of one of them, it was necessary to have:

> . . . some form of organization that will exist by the consent of all of the nations, that will accept a duty to seek first of all the general welfare, that will be composed of men who put the general welfare above loyalty to their particular nation, and which organism can express judgments that will command the moral support of all.

Between 1941 and 1945, the Dulles Commission elaborated a number of basic chores for this desired organization. Reflecting similar preoccupations by other internationalist groups in the United States, many of the publications prepared by Dulles and his associates actually concentrated on delineating the shape of what might come. Some parts of their blueprint tended toward the grand and sweeping. A new organization, for example, should seek to protect "the right of individuals everywhere to religious and intellectual liberty." Others were more specific and reflected assumptions common to many observers. It was regularly urged that a world organization encourage disarmament efforts, for instance, or provide "procedures for controlling military establishments everywhere." Still other proposals stemmed very specifically from Dulles's own established views, though they were not necessarily unique because of this. The Commission issued regular calls for procedures that would make it possible "to adapt the treaty structure of the world to changing underlying conditions"—something directly in line with its chairman's earlier emphasis on the potential value of Article 19 of the League of Nations Covenant. There was also frequent emphasis on the need to encourage "the goal of autonomy for subject peoples" and to allow a new international organization "to assure and to supervise the realization of that end." For years, Dulles had emphasized the significance of Wilson's mandate system, and his church commission provided a chorus for his efforts along these lines. Finally, regular reference was made to the role a world organization could play in "bringing within the scope of international agreement those economic and financial acts of national governments which have widespread international repercussions." This had been a constant theme for Dulles throughout the 1930s and it proved to be central to his wartime work with the Federal Council of Churches as well. [30]

Though the thoughts and goals that Dulles shared with his co-workers were not new, what was done with them certainly was. Where its chairman had usually directed earlier efforts at limited audiences, the Commission on a Just and Durable Peace aimed for stimulation of a vast segment of American public opinion. Indeed, publicity efforts and public relations campaigns became the dominant ingredient in Dulles's church-related work during World War II. The lion's share of his energy in this sphere, and no doubt that of other Commission members, was channeled more often than not in one direction: toward taking a few basic ideas that were agreed upon very early and elaborating and publicizing them in such a way that would have maximum popular appeal.

The pattern established at the beginning was followed consistently thereafter. Immediately after the December 1940 Atlantic City Conference, Dulles began meetings with about two dozen leaders who styled themselves a Committee of Direction. This Committee decided that their first task was to establish "definite lines of communication running from the Committee . . . through the full Commission and then on to churches and Christian groups throughout this country." Acting on Dulles's suggestion, they also made some quick decisions about what should be communicated. During April and May, a memorandum of "Preliminary Views" was published, along with a handbook entitled "A Just and Durable Peace." The latter was designed to encourage discussion at the grassroots church level and gathered numerous statements by world religious and political leaders; it also included lists of questions to consider and a bibliography for further reading. Forty-five thousand copies of the handbook were made available to churches in this first effort at large-scale publicity.[31]

Following this perhaps modest beginning, Dulles and his colleagues built up steam. They gradually learned the ropes of public relations work and expanded their repertoire of techniques. They continued to rely heavily on Federal Council publication of pamphlets and on distribution of these through the intricate network of the Protestant denominations. Some printings ran to 700,000 copies. They worked, as well, to encourage media attention to their efforts. Given the size of the Protestant population in the U.S. and the status of the Federal Council, this may not have been difficult. At all events, countless newspaper stories and editorials appeared during the war years, and attention in mass-circulation periodicals such as *Newsweek*, *Time*, and *Life* was not infrequent. Self-propelled news coverage and commentary was increasingly supplemented by the Dulles Commission as well. Space in newspapers was purchased and solicited for articles and advertisements; radio time was arranged for the announcement and presentation of new statements. All in all, millions were reached, and Dulles and his colleagues felt well-satisfied with their efforts at communication with the public.[32]

The subject matter of these intensive publicity efforts involved a series of variations on basic themes. The United States should accept its long-range responsibility as an important protagonist in the international arena. It should try to turn the horrors of war into a brighter future by working for reforms in the political and economic behavior of nation-states. It should work particularly to diminish the exclusive perquisites of sovereignty, looking toward the encouragement of organic interdependency among the peoples of the world. These Dulles precepts, shared or adopted by his Commission colleagues, were repeated over and again.

The details of specific Commission pronouncements varied a good deal, depending on circumstances and the tack chosen for a particular situation. Sometimes, items were triggered by diplomatic developments. An early publication followed the August 1941 meeting of Franklin Roosevelt and Winston Churchill off Newfoundland, for example. The Dulles memorandum circulated by the Commission expressed serious reservations about what had quickly become famous as the "Atlantic Charter." Dulles applauded the value of two government leaders offering "their conception of a new world order," but was more than skeptical about the long-range value of this specific effort. He wondered if the Charter was anything more than a string of airy words. No real actions had been proposed to vivify recommendations concerning equal trade privileges, equal access to raw materials or disarmament. "Unless we propose concrete measures," he insisted, "statements of good intentions . . . will be looked upon with grave and warranted skepticism." Doubting commitment, Dulles also worried about the lack of imagination in Roosevelt and Churchill. He believed that there ran through the Charter "a single, unifying conception, namely, that the postwar world should reproduce and stabilize the political organization of the prewar world." Was there no room for growth? No provision for *change* as opposed to the mere *stabilization* of prewar practices and institutions? He often argued that there was. In this piece, he pointed to the possibilities of "regional," "continental," or "hemispheric" integration, citing especially the desirability of "a federated commonwealth of some type" in Europe.[33]

A number of other Dulles Commission statements also emerged as responses to specific international developments. The Moscow Conference of October 1943 was followed by a public letter praising the intergovernmental decision to build a new world organization. In the fall of 1944, a critical appraisal of the Dumbarton Oaks Proposals was drafted by Dulles, worked on by his colleagues, and approved at the biennial meeting of the Federal Council of Churches. And Dulles's personal appraisal of the Yalta Conference was adapted in toto by his Commission and given wide circulation in March 1945.[34]

The Dulles Commission did not simply react to global political developments. It often determined its own itinerary. On several occasions, for example, National Study Conferences were arranged in order to disseminate ideas to large numbers of Protestant leaders. The first of these was held at Ohio Wesleyan University in March 1942. The 350 in attendance included fifteen bishops, seven seminary heads, eight college presidents, and numerous prominent laymen: one Methodist bishop said it was "intellectually . . . the most distinguished American church gathering I have seen in 50 years of conference-going." Discussion sessions were organized around four themes, the political, economic, and social bases of a just and durable peace and the role churches might play in bringing about such a peace. Delegates also heard formal addresses from a leader of the World Council of Churches, the Chinese Ambassador to Washington, the President of the League of Nations Assembly, a State Department representative, and Dulles. On the last day of the meeting, a memorandum entitled "Thirteen Guiding Principles" was endorsed. It embodied the activist and reformist views Dulles and his Committee of Direction had earlier settled on, calling in particular for the creation of "a true community of nations."[35]

Among other things, a conference like that of March 1942 helped attract media and general public attention to the Commission on a Just and Durable Peace. This was true of other specially designed campaigns as well. In early 1943, Dulles began prodding his associates to undertake what became their biggest public relations effort. He was "deeply impressed by the critical nature of this hour," he wrote, and was becoming apprehensive about the long-range commitment of Americans to international collaboration:

> I see a strong possibility of continued isolation which will be based upon the huge military power that we will have developed by the end of the war. We will have a two-ocean navy; we will have strategic bases both in the Atlantic and the Pacific; we will have a huge capacity for airplane and tank production, and we will be facing a world where cooperation will be difficult. Under the circumstances, I foresee a drift toward dependence upon our strength alone.

He proposed a major campaign to "force" a positive decision to the question "Will the American people now commit themselves to a future of organized international collaboration within the areas of demonstrated world interdependence?"[36]

As usual, Dulles swayed his associates. The resulting effort was impressive. A set of propositions christened "Six Pillars of Peace" was drafted, outlining the need for international organization and suggesting initial functions like those previously agreed upon. Maximum fanfare was provided for presentation to the public. John D. Rockefeller, Jr., with whom Dulles had been working at the Rockefeller Foundation, agreed to host a luncheon of "leading civic leaders" for the launching. Radio time was purchased for descriptive addresses by Dulles; articles were prepared for church and other periodicals; 60,000 copies of the "Six Pillars" statement were circulated to Protestant ministers. Dulles also arranged for columns on each of the pillars to appear in hundreds of newspapers: he persuaded prominent figures like Sumner Welles, Arthur Sulzberger, and Senator Joseph Ball to draft these and lend their support to his Commission's drive.[37]

Another chapter in the Six Pillars of Peace campaign came in a National Mission on World Order that was mounted in October and November. Dulles and Senator Ball addressed a kickoff gathering of five thousand at New York's Cathedral of St. John the Divine. Commission teams then spent three weeks traveling to more than a hundred cities urging support for their program. Meetings were held in many churches with service organizations and students' and women's clubs. Dulles estimated that more than 20,000 people eventually participated in the discussions of local Pillars of Peace Committees, which were created as a medium for continuing grassroots study and discussions.[38]

Media attention to the Six Pillars was great, and Dulles was very pleased. "It has made a very profound impression," he wrote to a friend: hundreds of editorials had appeared in American newspapers; wide press coverage in Europe had been "more favorable and sympathetic than I could have expected." But the newsworthiness of his Commission's efforts did not have quite as much impact as Dulles had hoped. In one quarter especially, Washington, D.C., he had anticipated more receptivity than had become apparent by 1943.

Dulles's concern for public relations work on behalf of his proposals for international reform had always involved a conviction that government leaders needed persuasion as much as anyone else. In August 1942, perhaps encouraged by a request for ten copies of a Commission publication, he wrote to Sumner Welles about "the possibility of some closer collaboration of our Commission with the Department of State." It would be useful for policy makers to know the "broad moral principles" Protestant leaders were concerned about, he said; some formal communication "would assure the Department of State of an opportunity of knowing the trend of thinking of Christian leaders in relation to its plans and . . . on the other hand, would give increased assurance that Christian groups could strongly support the international planning of our Government." Welles's reaction was positive, and it began a friendly relationship with Dulles that lasted several years. It did not turn into the relationship with the Department that the latter had wanted, however. Welles asked for the names of Commission members with whom discussions could be held on various matters, but Leo Pasvolsky, Secretary Hull's special assistant for work on an international organization, killed the plan before it ever got off the ground.[39]

Shortly before the start of the Six Pillars campaign, Dulles tried again. Once more he received Welles's personal endorsement, but was told nothing more could be arranged. He even tried appealing directly to the President. In a meeting at the White House on March 26, 1943, Roosevelt said he was unfamiliar with the new statement and took time to read it! He then praised it as "splendid," yet told Dulles not to say anything to reporters about their conversation. He did add that "he would like, at some near future date, to make some public reference to what we were doing . . . ."[40]

Dulles's involvement in Republican Party affairs had long before evidenced critical attitudes toward the Roosevelt Administration. Lack of meaningful receptivity at the State Department and the President's non-commital response in early 1943 added coal to the fire, and Dulles was more prone than ever to be critical in the future. In mid-1943, he was writing to a relative that the change of U.S. involvement in a new world organization was being threatened by "the absence of any political leadership." To Henry Van Dusen, he was very pointed:

> It is perfectly clear to me that the present Administration . . . does not possess the competence to deal with the problem of bringing this war to an acceptable end and making quick and orderly transition to some better post-war order. Roosevelt is at home when it comes to uttering fine generalities, but when it comes down to the concrete, there is complete chaos and confusion, conflict of authority and lack of decision.[41]

If Dulles was unable to supplement public attention to his Commission's efforts with Washington's enthusiasm, he was more successful in adding an international dimension to them. Like many of the Federal Council leaders with whom he was working, Dulles had been impressed by an ecumenical spirit which had begun to flower in the 1930s. He hoped that war would not prevent some further integration of a terribly divided Christendom and actually seems to have thought that progress would be more likely if church leaders in other Allied nations would lend support to the well-developed programs of his U.S. Commission.

In July 1942, he traveled to England at the invitation of British church leaders in the hope of beginning some transatlantic cooperation. Nothing materialized. It proved to be a fascinating visit for Dulles, but, as he put it, "more on the secular than the religious side." He had lengthy meetings with almost every member of the War Cabinet, including Anthony Eden and Ernest Bevin, but found little direction and enthusiasm in church circles. Something more substantial emerged the following year. Fourteen British church leaders, including the Archbishop of Canterbury, issued a statement entitled "A Christian Basis for Reconstruction" in July 1943. It was modeled closely on the Six Pillars of Peace, and the Dulles Commission quickly endorsed it and circulated copies.[42]

Dulles had plans to move beyond cooperation with the British as well. Some materialized, some did not. In mid-1943, he thought of attending a Stockholm meeting being sponsored by the emerging World Council of Churches. He wrote enthusiastically to Sumner Welles about being able to exercise "more authoritative and effective influence" if he had "closer personal contact" with the European situation in wartime. Perhaps he could even go on from Sweden to Moscow! It is unclear whether Dulles backed out of this plan for his own reasons or because of problems with government travel priorities.[43] At all events, he spent part of July 1943 in Princeton instead of Stockholm—at an "International Round Table" which made it possible for Protestant representatives from a number of countries to consult as a group rather than singly with a traveling Dulles. Considering the fact that they were meeting in wartime, the diversity of the group was impressive. Churchmen included the General Secretary of the British Council of Churches; Protestant leaders from Canada, Australia, and New Zealand; the former president of Doshisha University in Kyoto; the president of Ginling College, China, as well as American representatives. Dulles also brought political figures to his alma mater as sources of information and ideas. Representatives of the Swiss and Netherlands governments participated, as did the Director of the Chinese News Service in New York.

For three days, discussion revolved around earlier Commission on a Just and Durable Peace pronouncements. A published statement drafted by Dulles and endorsed by those in attendance elaborated the essential substance of the Six Pillars. In addition, several secret memoranda dealing with the Soviet Union, Germany, and Japan emerged from more detailed discussions: they provide now a fascinating glimpse into the way in which

Dulles and his colleagues tried to bridge the gap between their "guiding principles" and concrete issues.[44]

IV

The essential substance of Commission on a Just and Durable Peace proposals remained quite consistent throughout World War II. The mood or tone in which public relations efforts were carried out did not. Dulles and at least some of his colleagues went through a clearly discernible cycle of emotions: their expectations shifted ground, and the thrust of their communications with the public was altered considerably.

In Dulles's case, early work with the Commission found him in an intensely religious, almost beatific frame of mind. For a while at least, he seems to have found a comfort in church quarters that he did not feel in the crisis-ridden world outside, and it induced a new tone in his public statements. The angry Old Testament prophet of 1939 became in late 1940 and 1941 a rather soft-spoken messenger for gentler New Testament words.

Appropriate scriptural allusions began to punctuate his writings. His December 1940 address in Atlantic City urged Federal Council of Churches leaders to avoid being sucked into the international conflicts of the day. "Let them rather draw the world unto them," he said, "knowing that as they in truth form part of Christ's church, then they are that Tree of Life whereof the leaves serve the healing of the nations." In another statement, he wrote that "When Christ portrayed the ultimate passing of judgment upon the nations, and their separation as a shepherd dividing his sheep from the goats, it was those nations which had shared that were called to inherit the Kingdom."[45]

The sudden emergence of Biblical imagery was just one obvious sign of Dulles's increasingly religious proclivities. The general terminology in which he now discussed international relations was equally revealing. One of the first questions he put to his Committee of Direction was "What is the distinctive contribution which Christians can make toward a better world order?" In answer, he suggested that the healing potential of Christlike qualities could help counteract the hatred that ran rampant in war: he listed those qualities as "minds that will think calmly, visions that will see clear, and hearts that comprehend the essential unity and brotherhood of man." In addition, he reminded his colleagues of the crucial importance of Christ's most basic injunction: instead of heeding the dictates of "short-range self-interest," man should "seek . . . first the Kingdom of God and His righteousness." As early as 1937, in one moment at Oxford, Dulles had marveled at the ability of some to have a "genuine belief in Christ's life and teachings as a guide to human conduct"; by early 1941, he was clearly ready to declare himself one of the believers.[46]

Dulles's references to specific Christian values frequently led into discussion of general "moral" considerations and their relevance in appraising alternative directions for international relations. "Moral law, no less than physical law, undergirds our world," was the first point made in the Commission's early publication *Thirteen Guiding Principles*: it would be necessary for Americans to endorse "a moral way of international living" if a just and durable peace were to be achieved. On another occasion, Dulles told Sumner Welles that he did not think it was the function of his church group to offer "technical proposals" to the State Department, but that he and his colleagues did feel they could develop "certain broad moral principles with which concrete plans should conform."[47]

It was not long before the dulcet tone of Dulles's earliest religiously inclined words grew more vibrant. Only months after American entrance into the war, the chairman of the Commission on a Just and Durable Peace succumbed to the emotionalism of many of his countrymen. In the electric atmosphere of 1942 and 1943, when many were led to worry or dream about the future in dramatic terms, Dulles did likewise. He took his message of Christian and moral concern and fired it with a striking missionary zeal.

In the introduction to a mid-1942 pamphlet, for example, Dulles described his study group's "purpose" as being "that the American people be filled with *a righteous faith and sense of mission in the world*" (emphasis added). He looked back on the eighteenth and nineteenth centuries, when the United States, Great Britain, and France had been "imbued with and radiated great faiths"—"Manifest Destiny", the "White Man's Burden," and "Liberty, Equality, Fraternity". While such "faiths" were not totally pure or beneficent in results, he admitted, "they served to make these nations the three Great Powers of the World." There was no reason why this could not remain the case. It was true that the destruction of the First World War and a preoccupation with material things had come close to exhausting "our spiritual springs" and turning the Allies into "burnt-out peoples." But a new faith, one in a program of international reform, could revive the fire of the past. We "need a faith," Dulles said, "a faith that will make us strong, a faith so profound that we, too, will feel that we have a mission to spread it through the world."[48]

Dulles's "righteous faith" lent itself to something like millennialism in 1942 and 1943. It was not unusual for him to whirl verbal banners, to try to rouse marchers for the great crusade that would bring a bright, peaceful future. During his Commission's late 1943 National Mission in World Order, for example, his speaking tour found him at his most zealous. "We seek to revive in our people a sense of destiny in the performance of a great work of creation," he said on numerous occasions. "Vision" and a "sense of great purpose" were needed. Without them, the United States would lose "its soul," "our children and grandchildren will not breathe an air suffused with the elixir of creative effort." With them, tomorrow beckoned: imbued with a sense of "the power of creation, we shall see a world in which most of humanity has been torn away from all established institutions. Almost everywhere a new society must be built. This is not only a calamity, *it is an opportunity, the like of which men never saw before"* (emphasis added).[49]

Dulles's vibrant late 1943 exhortations represent a high point in the cycle of moods through which he moved during his work with the Commission on a Just and Durable Peace. As it was, the striking rhetoric was already somewhat out of synchronization with inner feelings that had begun to change.

All through 1943, in fact, Dulles gave private but clear voice to thoughts which increasingly belied his public talk of exhiliration and dramatic missionary undertakings. By year's end, he had grown much less optimistic, shifting emphasis from his notion of "opportunity" to his fear of "calamity."

As early as the unveiling of the Six Pillars of Peace in March 1943, Dulles had spoken of his sense of "the critical nature of this hour." As the Allies began to discern the likelihood of victory, he thought he could see a return to the old game of power politics among them: the Soviet Union's grasping behavior concerning Finland and the Baltic states and its interest in Poland; Great Britain's jockeying for position with Free French leader Charles de Gaulle; the unresolved conflict between "the so-called 'Red Army' faction and the Kuomintang" in China. These among others suggested that governments and leaders had learned nothing from their present traumas and that the world would be "doomed" to a "continuance of the war system." Dulles's perception of evolving Allied behavior grew no more positive in succeeding months. In October, for example, when many were impressed by the Moscow Declaration's promise of a new international organization, he demurred. This step went "only part of the way," he insisted, and could turn out to be little more than an empty gesture: none of the great powers had shown any firm commitment to new-style international behavior. "To move from words into functioning institutions infused with the spirit of Christian fellowship remains a political and spiritual task of immense proportions."[50]

Given his sense of ambiguous, even antagonistic, behavior by the Allies, Dulles began to voice more regularly his fears concerning the fate of an anticipated new world order. In particular, he became preoccupied with what he saw as one potential disaster that would almost certainly trigger the collapse of all his Commission's wartime dreams: the possibility of deepening disillusionment on the part of the American people. What if, at the end of the Second World War, Americans reacted as they had after the First? Shocked that catastrophe had barely changed the nature of the world, that power politics and national greed had emerged unscathed, many had tried to isolate themselves from the rest of the world in the 1920s, Dulles believed. Surely this could happen again. The settlement of immediate postwar issues might easily create situations that "will shock the Christian conscience."

> All humanity is in an abnormal mental state. Inevitably hatred, vengefulness, fear and greed are in the ascendency. Essential facts are unknown and what appear to be facts reflect the distortions or selections of war propaganda and censorship. Many of the major decisions are within the power of others than ourselves and the necessities of continuing war collaboration compel compromises as to post-war arrangements . . . .

In addition, any world organization created by the victorious Allies might "adopt and sanction such postwar settlements and seek to perpetuate them."[51]

Dulles worried greatly about the potential for disillusionment under these circumstances. American interest in international reform was a fragile thing, he wrote in December 1943; its persistence "depends upon whether, in the light of concrete developments, the world body will be judged by Christians to be an organ through which they can in fact satisfy their sense of mission and of destiny. The present Christian unanimity about international collaboration can readily disintegrate on that point." In a meeting with Franklin Roosevelt in February 1944, he made the same point:

> I said that we were concerned about the aggregate of objections which would arise against particular settlements. We feared this would create decisive opposition to the "general world organization" if it was essentially military and repressive, to "hold the lid on" a lot of objectionable detailed

settlements. I knew, from my experiences in Paris in 1919, that it would be impossible to get settlements of boundaries, treatment of enemies, reparations, etc. which could seem perfect and not involve compromise.

If such "decisive opposition" emerged, Dulles was convinced there was no hope for a viable organization or any kind of new world order: the enormous economic and military power of the United States would have to be harnessed to the Commission's expectations, he believed, if they were to have any chance for success.[52]

Dulles felt that his Commission on a Just and Durable Peace should try to shape American public opinion so as to prevent a "relapse toward political aloofness." He and his colleagues could help lead the way toward a constructive perspective on the great problems of the day. They could, on the one hand, encourage realistic expectations about the likelihood of major, immediate reforms at war's end. On the other, they could continue to engender hope, with the conviction that long hard work would allow for modest beginnings. There was a fine line between realism and hope, but Dulles would have argued that it existed and that maturity came with finding it.

Dulles urged such a course on his colleagues in December 1943, and a month later public relations efforts were started. A "New Year's Statement" was widely circulated incorporating the cooler message that had been adopted. "We do not demand the impossible or the impracticable," it emphasized. Dulles himself gave several well-publicized addresses, urging Americans to "judge critically the practical possibilities of converting . . . words into deeds." On one occasion at Princeton Theological Seminary, he emphasized the importance of remembering that "the society of nations is in a most primitive stage of development. . . . Each member goes his own way and individual power, whether or not actually used, primarily determines whether one or another gets what he wants or keeps what he wants. . . ." Because "no society moves at a single bound from the primitive stage of anarchy to a highly developed order," Americans would have to be patient in anticipating progress at the end of the war. "Like Pilgrim, we must stumble forward," he said in May.[53]

Dulles saw little reason to alter his revised opinions during the balance of 1944 and early 1945. At the time of the Dumbarton Oaks Conference, he reacted with alarm to press and public expectations of the creation of some "super-state." To encourage heady dreams was to court inevitable disillusionment, he warned. "I am rather skeptical as to whether much can be done on the global level beyond consultation," he wrote Lionel Curtis at Oxford. "I fear that the beginning we make will be extremely imperfect," he told another acquaintance.[54] He occasionally detailed his opinions as well. To a National Study Conference in Cleveland in January 1945, he offered a catalogue of emerging problems: it touched on Greece and Poland and expressed serious disenchantment with Roosevelt, Churchill, and Stalin.[55]

Continuing skepticism produced continuing themes in the Dulles Commission's public relations efforts. An early 1945 "Message to the Churches" began with emphasis on the limits of anticipated postwar reforms. It urged American Christians "to be tolerant of results which, in themselves, will often be unsatisfactory." Such tolerance might encourage Washington to work harder for modest successes, might lead government "to work in such mire as much of the world is today" and worry less about the criticism which would be "heaped upon it when it comes back with some of the mire adhering to its hands and feet."[56]

Still, he made sure not to go over the line into what he would have seen as counterproductive cynicism or fatalism. "The main thing is to get started," he said on one occasion, after listing his numerous objections to the grandiose and seemingly unrealistic Dumbarton Oaks Proposals. To a mass meeting in Washington, held days before the opening of the San Francisco Conference, he was particularly clear in urging a balance of enthusiasm for doing something with practicality about particulars. "We are . . . at a stage where we must begin at the beginning. That means something very elemental," he said. The nations of the world were like so many "savage chieftains or frontiersmen" who had just begun to "gather around the campfire" for discussion. Because of this, "there are no shortcuts" to meaningful international order. Alluding to earlier experiences, he also stated that "this time it is of the utmost importance that we be realistic."[57]

V

Leadership of the Commission on a Just and Durable Peace was one of the activities that produced important changes in Dulles's life during World War II. In earlier years, Dulles had shown few inclinations to become a widely known public figure. Though no recluse, his had been a familiar name in fairly circumscribed circles of globally oriented businessmen and lawyers, government officials on both sides of the Atlantic, and organized internationalists. He had generally limited his speaking engagements to groups like the Council on Foreign Relations or the International

Chamber of Commerce; he had written for prestigious but limited circulation periodicals like *Foreign Affairs* and *The New Republic*.

The Commission on a Just and Durable Peace helped change all this for Dulles. As leader of a major Protestant study group, he found himself with a vast potential audience; before very long, he was busy cultivating it. When he spoke after late 1940, it was often to audiences of several hundreds—and the increasing use of the radio held out the possibility of thousands and even millions. When he wrote, the Federal Council of Churches would print up to 700,000 copies of his pieces. Newspapers carried stories about his work and used excerpts from his writings; mass circulation periodicals such as *Life* and *Reader's Digest* began carrying his material as well. When, during the 1944 election, Dulles served as foreign policy adviser to Thomas Dewey, his visibility received yet a further boost.[58] His prominence increased much more in the future, of course, but from the early 1940s on, he was a public figure recognizable to many.

What of the identity of this more public figure? Had it changed significantly as Dulles moved from being a corporate lawyer-internationalist to a lawyer who was a prominent lay religious leader?

There are some signs that do suggest significant change. The great amount of time spent on church-based activities was a totally new factor in Dulles's adult life, and its impact is easily discernible. His language was permeated with scriptural allusions, and his analysis frequently placed into a context of religious themes and concepts. Earlier, one would not have found Dulles speaking of "Christ-like qualities" or the need for Christians to find a "sense of mission" in tackling international problems.

In general, this new ingredient in Dulles's work involved an intense and explicit emphasis on moral and ethical considerations. As the first of the Commission's "thirteen Guiding Principles" put it, in fact, "moral law, no less than physical law, undergirds our world." And Dulles was quite prepared to define the major implications of that moral law. The most basic ingredient for him, and the one which he emphasized over and again during the war years, was the need to share and cooperate instead of pursuing only self-interest. One discussion of the need for a new world organization argued that it should "exist by the consent of all of the nations . . . accept a duty to seek first of all the general welfare . . . [and] be composed of men who put that general welfare above loyalty to their particular nation. . . ." This concept was often specifically related to Christian values. The first memorandum drawn up by Dulles and his Committee of Direction emphasized the need to "seek ye first the Kingdom of God and His righteousness" and indicted earlier American behavior which, "alike in economics, politics and international relations, was organized around motives of short-range self-interest." What was required instead was "the uplifting of human motivation through the regenerating spirit of Chirst."[59]

And yet, do the new vocabulary and missionary zeal that figured so noticeably in Dulles's wartime work represent anything more than a *stylistic* change—flashy new veneer on an old base? There is much to suggest that, as with the novel elements that had emerged in his life during the mid-1930s, Dulles was capable of moving *on* without leaving *behind* his own past.[60]

The substance rather than the tone of Dulles's thoughts reveals this most clearly. Granted that he was working from a new platform, Dulles remained preoccupied with the core problem that predated his heady church ties: how was the United States, how was the world, going to cope with the cycle of economic and political crises that had been unfolding in the twentieth century? As he put it to Arthur Sulzberger of *The New York Times* in 1941, he was trying to encourage Americans to find "the will and capacity to break the recurrent cycle of war and the economic maladjustments which have characterized recent times."[61] His speculative work in the 1930s represented one spirited attempt to tackle that problem, his leadership of the Commission on a Just and Durable Peace another. He reworked his ideas over and again during the war years and frequently whipped them into new shapes, but he never really removed them from this encompassing intellectual context.

Dulles's tendency to approach international problems by way of economic difficulties was still present in the 1940s, as was his related propensity for recommendations that dealt predominantly with commercial and financial matters. In an early 1942 article for *Fortune*, he illustrated his by then clear conviction that economic problems could lead to political and military clashes. "The outbreak of the second world war was preceded by trade strangulation without precedent in time of peace," he wrote. "No one can doubt that this was a contributing cause of the war. As Secretary of State Hull has so frequently pointed out, if national boundaries become unnatural barriers to the movement of men, trade and investments, the boundaries inevitably become subject to attack." Nor was it only the great and obvious problem of war that was involved as Dulles considered the importance of economic affairs and relationships. In an interesting section of an early Commission memorandum, he advised Americans not to be smug about their own championing of individual freedom as against the fascist emphasis on national power and the search for economic opportunity. "This, of course, is morally right," he wrote, "but it costs us nothing and, indeed, coincides with self-interest. . . ."

> We must further realize that to seek to extend the individual right to freedom of thought, of conscience, of worship and of expression is empty unless there is also . . . "an opportunity for livelihood, without which intellectual and spiritual freedoms have little practical content."[62]

As for remedies, the very first publication of the Commission on a Just and Durable Peace proposed a single step on which to concentrate for the time being, one which urged a limitation on national actions that had "wide economic repercussions." International measures should be taken to prevent any government from taking a step which:

> 1) excludes others from markets in which to sell; 2) prevents others from acquiring raw materials, food stuffs or manufactured goods they need; 3) restricts immigration and emigration; and 4) alters the value of metals (gold and silver) commonly used as monetary bases and the relationship and interchangeability of different moneys.

As a step in this direction, the Committee proposed unilateral action by the United States Congress. That body was urged:

> 1) To recognize, by resolution, the principle that legislative action within the four fields . . . enumerated may involve international repercussions and a consequent duty to exercise our power with a decent regard for all who may be seriously affected; and accordingly that no such legislative action (other than of a war emergency nature) should be taken until the Congress first obtains a report as to the effect of the comtemplated action upon people elsewhere.
>
> 2) To establish a new administrative unit, under the Executive and correlated to the State and other interested Departments, having the duty to study economic interrelations and to make, as occasion arises, the reports contemplated by the preceding paragraph. . . .
>
> 3) To request the President, in so far as he deems it compatible with the public interest, to invite other nations now to take parallel action, pending the time when it may be practical to take joint action.[63]

Such a strong emphasis on the need for economic reforms in the global arena remained a constant ingredient in Commission proposals. The published evaluation of the Atlantic Charter, for example, included tough criticism of Roosevelt's and Churchill's failure to offer meaningful pledges concerning international collaboration on trade, money, and freedom of the seas. In one 1942 address, Dulles may have underlined the point with the greatest clarity. He was sketching his own vision of what a new international organization should do and listed only three initial chores:

> 1) I would have the Executive Organ create a Monetary or Banking Corporation . . . empowered to provide monetary media through which needed exchange of goods between nations could be facilitated. . . .
>
> 2) I would have the Executive Organ authorized to charter commercial companies, as seemed to it desirable, to engage in the business of effecting international movements of goods from one country to another. . . .
>
> 3) I would have the Executive Organ authorized to negotiate compacts with the several nations whereby their tariffs and trade quotas would be fixed. . . .

Through the enactment of these three proposals, Dulles saw the possibility of an international order similar to the structure of the British Empire of the nineteenth century. Great Britain "then chartered great companies to develop world trade. She became the world's banker and, through control and handling of gold, established what in effect was an international money." Of course, he admitted, England's operations had been "imperialistic" in nature and had had "consequences" it would be undesirable to reproduce. Still, a similar structure, international in scope and beneficent in nature, "dedicated to seek the general welfare," would be most welcome:

> Those who would come under the regulations of the central Executive would be those of commercial knowledge and experience. . . who appreciate the need of a common ordering of such activities as those they would be engaged in. It may be noted in this connection that Chambers of Commerce and similar organizations have for many years been the outstanding advocates of some form of international planning and regulation of trade, and that the heads of the various central banks of issue came into an intimacy of cooperative effort which made of them a kind of supranational guild. [64]

(This speech is also interesting because it reveals, at least implicitly, the continuation of Dulles's earlier tendency to take swipes at political leaders who lacked the finesse and percipience of businessmen in the international arena. [65])

Primary concern with economic problems and programs links up with another element of continuity in Dulles's work with the Commission on a Just and Durable Peace. As in earlier years, that concern formed the core of an essentially moderate approach to dealing with international affairs.

In spite of some appearances to the contrary during the war years, Dulles's concrete proposals for global reform continued to be hedged about with quite specific and narrow perimeters. He spoke frequently of the need to "begin at the beginning" in working for changes in international behavior, using words like "elemental" and "rudimentary" in his descriptions of desirable first steps. After his 1942 discussion of the "functional" economic tasks a new international organization might undertake, he explained the need for a realistic approach: "By these three initial steps we will have begun that dilution of sovereignty which all enlightened thinkers agree to be indispensable. . . . We will have avoided the mistake of assuming, at the beginning, tasks so vast, so difficult and so unexplored that failure is likely. . . ." He was perhaps even clearer when explaining to a friend his reactions to Clarence Streit's "Union Now" plans. Though intrigued by them, he found himself ultimately unimpressed: "I think the educational value of what he is doing is very great, but I doubt very much that it is practical or perhaps desirable to attempt a political union as close as he suggests. *Personally, I would favor economic and financial union, letting the political union work out of them if and when this becomes a natural development . . ."* (emphasis added).[66]

Dulles's limited sense of what needed to be done to the routines of international relations had been and remained a function of his limited disenchantment with the status quo. From the beginning, his enthusiasm for peaceful change had stemmed from the way it would allow a maximum conservation of the existing order's desirable features where war and revolution would entail wholesale destruction.[67] Aside from his overriding preoccupation with the elimination of obstacles to "interstate commerce," in particular, he revealed no real resistance to the capitalist system, the concept of the nation-state, or the traditional pursuit of national interest.

There was certainly no lack of concern for the interests of his own country during World War II. Even when Dulles was at his loftiest, in his discussions of the importance of moral leadership and missionary drive, he was really developing a theme that had much to do with his thoughts about what was good for the United States. Though it was not necessarily material interests he had in mind, he would have seen the psychological or emotional advantages he was dealing with as tangible and desirable in and of themselves. This was obvious in his 1942 discussion of the way the United States, Great Britain, and France had once been "imbued with and radiated great faiths." Though this caused some problems, "at least they served to make these nations the three Great Powers of the World." Likewise, during the National Mission on World Order in late 1943, when he talked about the need to revive "a sense of destiny" in Americans: "Half of the population of the world—one billion people—will face tomorrow the task of rebuilding their economic, social and political order," he said then. "Where will they turn for guidance, example and inspiration? One hundred years ago, fifty years ago, they surely would have turned to us. But they will not do so as we are today. . . ." How greatly he hoped that Americans would stir themselves in order to stir others—so that they might feel again "the power of creation and a *satisfaction* which far surpasses that of possession" (emphasis added). [68]

As an extension of these kinds of statements, Dulles implicitly and occasionally explicitly argued that if Americans did not stir themselves to lead the way to a new and better world order, no one else would. This offered, of course, something of an ultimate psychological payoff for his countrymen: they could feel the burden of responsibility, but enjoy all the feelings of authority and indispensability that could go with it. Dulles certainly had no doubts about the potential ability of the United States to determine the direction of the postwar world. As early as the Paris Peace Conference of 1919, he had urged Americans to take hold of the future and work to mold it as they thought best; his writings in the 1920s had included similar injunctions. [69] Now, in 1942, he reemphasized his belief that "for at least a generation we have held the preponderant economic power in the world, and with it the capacity to influence decisively the shaping of world events." He went on to argue that that *American* capacity *had* to be used if peace and prosperity were to be achieved in the future. As he put it in his Six Pillars of Peace address, the key concern of his Commission was to persuade the American people to make the decision in favor of "organized international collaboration." "It is that decision which our proposals are designed to force, and it must be made *now* or the opportunity for such collaboration will inevitably disappear. . ." (Dulles's emphasis). [70]

Although Dulles's church-related writings tended to emphasize the psychological rewards available to Americans, he was certainly never blind to more substantive political and economic goals. In October 1941, he reacted critically to the somewhat self-righteous cast of the Atlantic Charter pledge not to seek special advantages for the United States and Great Britain:

> . . . I . . . believe that our national policy will in fact very greatly "aggrandize" our nation to some extent "territorially", and to a great extent "otherwise". The statement may be correct if emphasis is put on the word "seek". It may be that our aggrandizement will not be of our "seeking", but nevertheless it will be a fact. We have acquired for ninety-nine years far-flung naval bases in the Atlantic. We have taken over Greenland and Iceland, and through the guise of developing commercial aviation we have driven the German and Italian airlines pretty much out of South America

and are developing there what in reality are United States military air bases. We are greatly developing naval and air bases in the far distant Pacific islands and in the northwestern extremes of Alaska. These, coupled with our two ocean navy, will put us in a position to dominate the Far East. I do not think there can be any question but what the United States will come out of this period with a combination of naval power, air power and stategic bases controlling both the Atlantic and Pacific Oceans and South America to an extent that we will have acquired a dominant position in the world comparable to that of England during the last century. It seems to me that this is in fact "aggrandizement, territorial or otherwise."

Not that Dulles was objecting to the likelihood of these developments—he simply saw no reason to pretend to reluctance or pure altruism. "There is little alternative in this world between going forward and going backward," he wrote, and "going forward is certainly preferable. . . ."[71]

A similar down-to-earth perspective on what was essentially traditional great power behavior was evidenced in Dulles's 1942 visit to England. Worried about "turmoil and confusion" in Europe after the war, Dulles told Anthony Eden and Stafford Cripps that London and Washington, not some world organization, should come to "rather definite views as to what should be done in Europe" and then do it "firmly, backing the element in each country who shared those views"; he told Clement Attlee they "should make up their mind as to what should be done and then go in and do it." In discussions of underdeveloped areas, as in the 1930s, he developed a somewhat nontraditional American approach in a way that revealed how limited its challenge to the existing order actually was. To Eden and Colonial Secretary Lord Cranborne he said, "What you have got to do is have some of your important people say that from now on we are going to have a new deal and open up the door to these colonies and start off on a new basis." As to why this needed to be done, however, Dulles said only that the British would have "to pocket their pride" in order to secure "American postwar collaboration in the development of the great colonial areas of the world." This suggested nothing beyond the old Wilsonian conception of leaving the fundamental, exploitative relationship of great powers and underdeveloped regions untouched and concentrating on eliminating the conflicts among the former.[72]

Toward the end of the war, Dulles grew clearer and clearer in his supportive references to the customary pursuit of national interest by the United States. They emerged as what seemed to him natural complements to his very modest expectations concerning a new international organization. In a Cleveland address discussing developments in Poland

and Greece, he expressed chagrin that "*the United States* has not shared responsibiity for the practical decisions which must be taken in the liberated areas" and that "that responsibility has been apportioned in great part to the Soviet Union and in small part to Great Britain." This aloofness must not continue, he insisted; "*Our government* ought to participate actively in the decisions now being taken in Europe, decisions which, *more than any Security Organization,* will determine whether there is to be a Third World War" (emphasis added). To a Detroit audience a few weeks later, he was even more emphatic. "*We* shall have to get down into the arena of international politics as never before, and in that arena *we shall have to battle hard for our safety and our opportunity.*" Those who looked to a United Nations Organization for solutions to all postwar problems should remember that "that world organization at its beginning will serve primarily to promote consultation among nations . . . . World organization will not assure *us* either *opportunity abroad or safety at home.* It will not of itself reverse trends which, wherever we look, imply danger to us. *We shall have to do that ourselves*" (emphasis added).[73] As expressions of Dulles's views on the eve of the San Francisco Conference, these can serve as clear harbingers of his behavior there.[74]

It is true that during the early stages of his Commission on a Just and Durable Peace activities, one would have had to look closely to appreciate the bedrock of moderation and traditionalism on which Dulles's analyses were resting. He was inclined then to grandiloquent phrasing about "a new world order," about Christian ethics and concern for others. His exuberance and missionary zeal gave a ring to his words which would easily have distracted a listener or reader from the more down-to-earth characteristics of his particulars. As has been shown, Dulles's optimism faded as the war continued, and a more temperate and realistic tone replaced his millennialism. After this, from late 1943 on, the more essential substance of his proposals became clearer.

It is worth mentioning that the combination of consistent basic values and shifting tones in the Dulles of World War II provides an interesting parallel to his own and other Americans' experiences during World War I. Though he did not testify to it as fully as he would in the 1940s, Dulles had gotten caught up in the great Wilsonian crusade of 1917. Like many then, he had spoken as if he wanted and anticipated some basic transformation of the existing world order. By the time the Great War ended, however, he and others who had been stirred by this missionary urge had fallen back on a far more modest position and were hoping desperately for a recreation of the world they had known before the shooting had begun. Dulles may have continued to hope for the reforms then, but his hopes were modest and rarely discussed. [75]

It is interesting that Dulles was himself aware of the way his experiences in two world wars were linked. In an early 1944 letter to a colleague, he wrote:

> The other night I glanced through a thick volume which the Carnegie Endowment got out in 1919, reprinting all of the statements which had been made during the last war about the peace to come. Anyone who thus refreshes his recollection cannot but be highly skeptical of the present repetition of all the hopes and promises . . . which so quickly evaporated with the armistice. I am confident that afterevents will prove we were right in making our central theme a warning against that. [76]

Given the obvious presence of so much intellectual baggage from the past, it is tempting to say that his work with the Commission on a Just and Durable Peace brought little more than a stylistic change in John Foster Dulles. In a 1944 meeting at the White House, Franklin Roosevelt told Dulles that he could see the logic of his proposals, but that he should "put some steeples on them" in order to rally public support. [77] It could be argued that in general terms that is what Dulles had been doing while working with his church commission: adding lofty moralistic spires to a structure he had built long before.

And yet, these steeples *were* important. Though they do not signal the emergence of some totally "new" Dulles in the 1930s, they serve as landmarks to a stage in the process of his long-range development. Dulles did change during World War II, but, in a very human way, he did not change completely. Just as in the mid-1930s, his past met his present and an intertwining relationship resulted: his past remained at the core of his identity, but the new surrounding layers clearly changed it in some significant way.

Essentially, the steeples represent revised explanations which Dulles developed for older concerns. The revisions were made to satisfy both himself and others.

Dulles's early writings on world affairs, from World War I through the 1930s, consisted of two basic ingredients: the identification of particular political and economic problems facing the United States and Europe on one hand and the suggestion of particular remedies on the other. As he presented his recommendations, he relied almost completely on logical and legitimate self-interest for explanatory purposes. He argued, that is, that it was politically and economically advantageous for certain steps to be taken—for reparations to be reduced, for central bankers to cooperate, etc. Reference was occasionally made to altruistic or moral reasons for proposals, but these were either down-played or dealt with as if they were really just secondary assumptions. In fact, Dulles could quite curtly reject the idea that ethical considerations played any meaningful role in international relations. [78]

In the mid-1930s, Dulles began to alter somewhat his approach to the international problems which had long concerned him. His usual concentration on specific political or economic problems affecting the United States was replaced by grand-scale theorizing about war and the need for global reform. In turn, Dulles raised to a higher plane the arguments he offered for various proposals. He shifted his emphasis to the broad ethical concerns he had downplayed in the 1920s. He never doubted that grave political and economic problems facing the United States were involved, but Dulles as philosopher chose to concentrate on the way in which his proposals would bring *world* peace and prosperity: if there was coincidence involved now, it was that the former could be seen growing out of the latter. [79]

Then, during World War II, Dulles moved yet further. He made global reform a religious, as well as an ethical, imperative. His writings took on a lofty tone as they were worked through the routines of his Commission on a Just and Durable Peace. Peace and prosperity became crucial temporal goals in a divinely ordained scheme for mankind. Christ's words and the Christian tradition, which put emphasis on caring and unselfishness, were used to buttress arguments that had been made in other ways in other years.

Not that Dulles lifted himself in toto to some cloudy realm of idealism. In good Calvinist fashion, the outgrowth perhaps of his Presbyterian roots, he made it quite clear that if his goals and methods were morally right, they were also practical. He never ceased discussing his reading of specifically American needs and evidenced no sense of contradiction in combining this with his loftier arguments. As he put it to one audience, "We can carry on with confidence, knowing that . . . the Christian approach is the realistic approach." Moreover, his very definition of "morality" in international behavior testifies to his sense of being able to join the altruistic and the pragmatic. "We believe," he told a 1942 study conference, "that the principle of cooperation and mutual concern, implicit in the moral order and essential to a just and durable peace, calls for a true community of nations." Americans and others he said on another occasion, would have to learn "a moral way of international living." Just what did Dulles have in mind when enunciating such broad generalizations? Extrapolating from his own examples, there is no doubt that as far as the *specifics* of the lifestyle he envisioned were concerned, he wanted men and nations to behave as he had been urging them to for more than two decades! All of Dulles's past recommendations were incorporated neatly into the "new" message: nations would have to avoid commercial and financial practices that were harmful to others, including self-serving manipulation of currencies and tarriffs; underdeveloped countries and colonies would have to be opened up for the use of all; serious efforts would have to be made at disarmament. [80]

If the hardiness of Dulles's early politico-economic agenda is noteworthy, however, so is the fact that it was thriving in a very different environment from the one in which it had first emerged. Dulles *had* added steeples to it, had decided to go beyond the "undertow" of the 1920s and label his program "moral" and "Christian." What emerged during World War II was related to earlier views, therefore, but was like a reflection of them in a distorting mirror, with elements reversed and altered in prominence. That Dulles could rearrange his thoughts in this way suggests something more than a change of style in the man. During his years of work with the Commission on a Just and Durable Peace, he was actually taking what had seemed an almost vestigial component in his early world view and working with it to a point where it functioned on a day-to-day basis: the result was the development of a substantive facet of his intellectual identity.

Of course, development may be limited or extensive, may lead to a modicum of strength or dominance. Which was the case in Dulles's work with the Commission on a Just and Durable Peace? Granting the restoration of the almost atrophic moralism of an early world view, did this give it *priority* over *other* more consistently functioning components? This is a question impossible to answer with an eye only on the church-based work of the war years. True, the traditional images of the man might prompt an easy affirmative answer: the heady, religious rhetoric of the early 1940s does suggest that Dulles was reaching the borders of his later reputation, that he had begun to analyze international affairs from a strikingly moralistic perspective. But that rhetoric, even granting thorough conviction behind it, can be misleading if viewed apart from the full complex of Dulles's day-to-day lifestyle. The role of prominent Protestant lay leader was only one of several which he played during World War II, after all, and it is really necessary to see how he spoke and acted in other guises before reaching conclusions about either the depth or the staying power of his evolving moralism. As will be shown, the Dulles world view of the war years—and after—could appear quite different as it took shape in varying contexts. Its core components were generally visible at all times, but the relative significance and interrelations of each to the other, as well as the resulting appearance of the whole, could change markedly.[81]

In broad outline at least, whatever their depth or staying power would turn out to be, the thoughts that Dulles's church-related work inspired were typical of one of the most time-honored of American modes of viewing international affairs. The Dulles combination of altruism, duty, and pragmatism was in the great tradition of the nineteenth century sense of "manifest destiny"; his words and themes, allowing for individual quirks and the circumstances of the 1940s, would have been understandable to earlier spokesmen like Thomas Jefferson, John Quincy Adams, and Josiah Strong.

Dulles himself was probably most conscious of his indebtedness to one particular historical model, Woodrow Wilson. Though he had demonstrated an affinity for his former leader many times before, Dulles was never so much like Wilson as during association with the Commission on a Just and Durable Peace. The twenty-five years that separated their experiences meant little in comparison to the way both men tried to cope with the horrors of war by blending religion and political economy. The United States would have to exercise "spiritual leadership," Wilson had said during the Great War, and "lead the way along the paths of light." Such leadership might be possible without resort to war itself. As Wilson told one gathering of businessmen in 1916:

> Life your eyes to the horizons of business; do not look too close at the little processes with which you are concerned, but let your thoughts and your imaginations run abroad throughout the whole world, and with the inspiration of the thought that you are Americans and are meant to carry liberty and justice and the principles of humanity wherever you go, go out and sell goods that will make the world more comfortable and more happy, and convert them .o the principles of America.

But this might not suffice, and real involvement in European conflicts might be necessary. If so, Wilson argued, the country should wait "for the great opportunity when the sword will flash as if it carried the light of heaven upon its blade."[82]

Dulles never spoke quite like this during the 1920s and 1930s. Moving only so far in these years, he went from sharing his former leader's attentiveness to the economic interests of the United States to being highly enthusiastic about grand-sounding schemes for international reform. Only during the 1930s did he add to his own work the moral and religious tone that had been so resonant in Wilson's. In doing so, like Wilson before him, he allowed his cynicism about a war to be transformed first into tolerance for participation and then into crusading zeal. Nothing suggests that Dulles did this in order to become more like Wilson, indeed that would seem most unlikely, but unconsciously at least he came closer than ever before to the mixture of styles and substances represented by that significant role model.

Also like Wilson before him, Dulles found the mixture of economics, political theory, and religion an easy one to brew and a palatable one to serve. Neither a "moral" perspective nor religious terminology were alien to his experience; even more than the philosophical inclinations of the mid-1930s, they meshed with important facets of his childhood and young adult life. Dulles of course, like Wilson, was the son of a Presbyterian minister. He had grown up in a home permeated by church concerns and activities; until his last year at Princeton, he had even planned to enter the ministry himself. In terms of basic intellectual drives, this background could only have eased the transition of analysis that one sees from the 1920s through the mid-1940s. In a more shallow but interesting way, it also gave him a facility for quick and comfortable adaptation of language. Drawing from deep wells, he clearly found it easy to utilize rhetoric that would be readily familiar to Protestant ears in the United States. When he attended the Oxford Conference on Church, Community and State in 1937, he had not had experience with religious audiences or issues in years. Yet, his statements during and after the meetings sound like those of an old hand. In one piece he described the "dynamic" movements underway in Germany, Italy and Japan as new religions. In each, "it is the State which is now deified. To it all else must be subordinated. . . ." This was a tragic development, he argued, because worship of such a "false god" involved sacrifices which were "degrading to the human soul." He suggested that Christians should revitalize their convictions, as he himself would have to do, and win again the faith of men. If it could be shown that Christianity "genuinely contributes to the solution of the vital problems which press upon us," then the loyalty of the masses could be weaned away from temporal deities. Unless this happened, he predicted the triumph of "paganism".[83] What is particularly striking about this kind of writing at the time of the Oxford Conference is that it disappeared as suddenly as it had emerged. For at least three years, Dulles totally avoided similar themes and terminology, until he decided to turn to them with more lasting enthusiasm in late 1940. The ease with which he could drop into and out of such a rhetoric demonstrates quite clearly that this was familiar territory for him, one not often visited in recent years, but hardly forgotten.

10

The War Years, 1939–1945: ... and State

DULLES'S LIFE DURING WORLD WAR II was neither exactly like nor totally unlike what it had been in earlier years. It was as if the tremors of war had disturbed the crust of his world and produced an altered landscape: some of its landmarks were old, but changed in placement and appearance; others were new or older yet, but had only just been tossed up to the surface from deep within.

What produced the tremors? Why had Dulles decided to address the question of reform in the international order so seriously? Why did he fashion a philosopher-reformer's role for himself? What made him inch more determinedly toward a public arena represented by the Commission on a Just and Durable Peace and its Protestant audience?

Certainly the atmosphere of the times had much to do with it. Here was a perceptive man in a day when even the dull would have been aware of major world problems. Already in the more tranquil 1920s, Dulles had noted various difficulties in commercial and financial affairs and had suggested ways of dealing with them. Now, as economic crises threw off glar-

218

ing political sparks and the sparks set off the blast of war, he simply let his mind follow what for him was a logical course: he allowed more analyses and proposals for reform to grow out of a long-established concern for the condition of the international order. The scale of his work became grander, to be sure, as did its infrastructure in terms of associates and organizational ties, but both were presumably in proportion to what he took to be the scale of the problems.

Yet more than the air of crisis changed Dulles's life before and during World War II. Tremors came from within as well as without. In particular, Dulles seems to have reached a point where he no longer found his work at Sullivan & Cromwell as nearly self-sufficient as it had been in earlier days. In a variety of ways from the mid-1930s on, he began to reveal a yearning after something more, something different.

Not that he was in any way ready to leave the firm and his business activities. Though he trimmed to some extent the number of corporations with which he was connected during World War II, he remained a director or trustee of the American Agricultural Chemical Company, the American Bank Note Company, Babcock & Wilcox Corporation, the Bank of New York, Inc., the Grand Union Company, and the International Nickel Company of Canada, Ltd.[1] His involvement in international financial transactions too, which had been so extensive throughout the 1920s and 1930s, altered in complexion in the early and mid 1940s, but clearly continued. Instead of counseling large U.S. investment houses in security offerings or default recovery efforts, he now took on foreign governments as clients and handled a variety of tasks for them in the United States. He was one of the lawyers called on by the Anglo-French Purchasing Commission, for example, when it was trying to navigate some of the fine points of American laws and banking practices. He was periodically retained by the governments of China and the Netherlands as well (though for purposes that remain unclear).

In two cases that absorbed considerable amounts of his time over more than four years, he agreed to represent the National Bank of Belgium and the National Bank of Poland. In both cases, suits were filed to attach the considerable New York reserves of the Bank of France in order to force a return of gold which the Belgian and Polish governments-in-exile felt was legitimately theirs. In 1941, the Bank of France had turned over to the Reichsbank some $65 million in gold that it had been holding for Warsaw and some $225 million in gold that it had been holding for Brussels. The suits were initially successful, and the results upheld by the New York Court of Appeals and even the U.S. Supreme Court: as a result, more than $500 million in Bank of France funds were attached. After the liberation of France, negotiations were hastily undertaken and arrangements made for the formal return of the Belgian and Polish gold. [2]

This kind of continuing legal activity was important for Dulles and testifies to the ongoing significance of Sullivan & Cromwell in his life. Still, it is impossible not to recognize that as busy a lawyer as he remained, Dulles was not as totally involved as he had been in earlier years. When he began writing his philosophical articles and a book, when he allowed himself to be coaxed into leadership of a major church study commission, he took an increasing amount of time away from his firm and his clients. In one way or another, perhaps only subconsciously, he began reevaluating and then redirecting the routines and dynamics of his daily life.

Why he did this remains unclear, if nothing else because he himself never spoke of it. Perhaps the frustrations of the Depression and the calamity of war encouraged reassessment of the past and future. His sister Margaret recalled the "tremendous impression" that the Oxford Conference on Church and State made on him in 1937: he had gone with "the kind of hopelessness of the difficulties of the economic world," she said, and had been exhilirated by church leaders who were "full of idealism as well as practicality."[3] Perhaps the yearning for different directions would have come anyway, even in a time of peace and prosperity, simply because he had reached a stage in his life when something new would have seemed attractive just because it was new. Dulles was fifty years old in 1938, after all, and had long since reached the pinnacle of his profession: how easy it is to imagine him, at this time, directing a more and more curious eye to other fields.

Whatever the spur, Dulles responded—and kept on doing so. His writing and his drift toward lay leadership among American Protestants were reinforced in the early 1940s by yet further moves in new directions. Where earlier years had seen occasional dabbling in politics, there now ensued time-consuming and intense activity; long-past forays into the world of diplomacy were remembered and sought again. Both would alter Dulles's life greatly by the end of World War II.

I

Dulles's interest in being personally active in politics had been strong in early life and had then waned in the years of his greatest legal and business success. He had gone from running political errands for his grandfather Foster's Republicans to relatively intimate friendships with leaders such as Herbert Hoover and John W. Davis in the 1920s. Indeed, the peak of his political involvement was his role as foreign policy adviser to Davis in 1924. Then, for more than a decade, Dulles kept his distance. Interest in politics was there, but it took the form of financial donations—more and more regularly to Republicans—and very occasional letters expressing opinions about particular campaign issues. [4]

Dulles's interest shifted back into high gear in the late 1930s and remained there for the rest of his life. Thomas E. Dewey was the catalyst for this change. The two men met in 1937. Dewey had been a Special Prosecutor for a sensational investigation on organized crime in New York and was asked to come to Sullivan & Cromwell as head of its litigation department. At the same time, impressed by his youth and the media's attention to him, local Republicans talked to him about campaigning to become District Attorney. He decided to try out the political waters before moving to Wall Street. In 1938, having triumphed in his first foray, Dewey was persuaded to become candidate for the New York governorship. He lost by 60,000 votes, but the hard times through which the G.O.P. was going made that seem a hair's breadth from victory, and he was quickly touted as a viable vote-getter for the 1940 presidential election.

Dewey and his close friends claim that he was stunned by the speed with which national opportunity had come. A bit confused, but ambitious, he began in 1939 to draw a few advisers together to think out possibilities. Dulles was one of the first, and his early talks with Dewey began a close relationship that remained important for both men until at least 1951. [5]

For Dewey, Dulles came to serve as a sort of "elder statesman," one of the three of four "guiding figures . . . at the core" of his political clique. Dulles was "up to his ears" in work on foreign policy issues, in particular: Dewey virtually never spoke on international affairs without his advice and generally used a Dulles draft as well. There is no question that Dulles would have become Secretary of State if any of Dewey's 1940s campaigns had been successful. [6]

For Dulles, Dewey was gradually to become the man who could carry him into the realm of political power and diplomacy. Indeed, he may well have been the man who actually revived Dulles's interest in these things, the man whose surprising success prodded him into thinking about arenas in which he had not been active for some time. Dewey looked like a bright, attractive man with great potential. He was fully supportive of the kind of international activism that Dulles assumed was a necessary policy for the United States and a necessary platform for the G.O.P. Actually, given Dewey's initial experience in local politics and his own description of Dulles's association with him, it could easily be argued that the young candidate absorbed his views on foreign affairs directly from Dulles: this would have made him an appealing public spokesman for the older lawyer.

Not that Dewey served as Dulles's only iron in the political fire. Once his interest had been revived, he showed an openness to a variety of possible associates. He liked Dewey and very much wanted him to be President in the 1940s, but his own political and diplomatic ambitions were never circumscribed by Dewey's fortunes alone. Dewey's efforts to win the 1940 nomination were unsuccessful in spite of some good signs. A lead in the polls over Senators Arthur Vandenberg and Robert Taft did not keep the District Attorney from being dramatically outflanked by a late entry, that "simple barefoot Wall Street Lawyer" Wendell Willkie. Dewey was immediately bitter, but Dulles was not. He simply tried to merge two teams. He sought to build a bridge to Willkie, offering help on "certain measures which will, I think, put behind your movement some of the worth while things which we had in the Dewey pre-Convention Campaign." With his brother Allen, he even drafted a "Statement of an American Foreign Policy" for the successful candidate. But Willkie had no desire to use Dulles as a close adviser. He told him he would "call on you much" and called him not at all. The neglect hurt somewhat. About midway in the campaign, Dulles sent William Nelson Cromwell a list of suggestions for contributions to the G.O.P., totaling $10,000: "I believe it aggregated $20,000 in the last Presidential campaign," he added cryptically.[7]

Following the election, Dewey continued to plug away at political affairs. In spite of the fact that he was no more than a District Attorney in 1941 and that a year later he became a private citizen, he publicized his opinions on international affairs. February 1941 saw him endorsing the Roosevelt Administration's Lend-Lease proposals, for example. Using Dulles drafts, he gave regular addresses in succeeding months, one to the prestigious Economic Club of New York. In spite of some sideline machinations by Willkie, Dewey won the Republican nomination for Governor of New York in 1942 and went on to trounce his opponent.[8] This gave him a strong position from which to deliberate future moves, one which he knew had served other men as a way station to the White House.

Meanwhile, Dulles had been doing more than writing Dewey's speeches. He started meeting and corresponding with G.O.P. insiders around the country and developing potentially useful ties with key people at the *New York Times* and the *New York Herald Tribune*. He began assembling his own group of close advisers, drawing in particular on men from the Foreign Service whom he had known since Princeton days or had met in connection with work on behalf of clients.[9]

Dulles worked primarily for and around Dewey, but it is impossible to say whether he felt inextricably bound up with the younger man's efforts at this stage, or whether he would have been prepared again to move more independently. The depth of his ties was never really tested, because Dewey enjoyed greater success from this point on. Dewey's first major success after his election as Governor, of course, came with the winning of the presidential nomination in 1944. His impressive showing in the Wisconsin primary in April sent most other candidates scurrying, and he racked up a strong first-ballot victory at the Chicago convention in June.

Given the state of the G.O.P., the nomination could easily have been lost by poor maneuvering in 1943 and early 1944. The party was in utter disarray. Roosevelt's highly successful leadership of the Democrats had produced an aura of gloom and doom in Republican quarters, and party leaders grew increasingly quarrelsome. Most bickering took place between the loyalists of individual leaders—Taft, Vandenberg, Willkie, and others—and stemmed primarily from personality clashes and struggles for control. Some of the struggling did involve substantive policy matters, though not as much as often imagined. There were disagreements about the degree of American involvement in international affairs that would be necessary once the war was over and others about the scale and functions of a new international organization. Arthur Vandenberg once described the protagonists on these questions as "what we might loosely call the 'Eastern internationalist' school of thought" as opposed to "the 'Middle Western nationalist' school." The merits of different stances, shallow though the distinctions may often have been, were thrashed out continuously for many months prior to the 1944 convention: in editorial columns of newpapers close to the G.O.P., in meetings of the national committee, in organized study committees, and in a specially arranged conference at Mackinac Island in September 1943.[10]

Dulles shrewdly refused to be drawn into the Republican melee and protected himself and Dewey from a good deal of unnecessary enmity as a result. He carefully kept in touch with such varied party leaders as Willkie, Stassen, and Taft (a friend since Dulles's law school days in Washington). He let it be known, but with almost philosophical detachment, that he saw the policy quarrels as both pointless and dangerous for the G.O.P. Just prior to the Mackinac Island Conference, he responded to Senator H. Alexander Smith's query about his views:

> I have thought for some time that as a matter of political strategy the Republican Party ought not to allow the issue to appear to be one between isolation and collaboration. So long as in the public mind that is the issue the Republican Party, irrespective of anything that can be said, will be

looked upon as tending more toward isolation than the Democratic Party. *I think that that issue is a false issue. It is perpetuated by the Democrats for their own purposes.* [Emphasis added.]

The real conflict was not between isolationists and internationalists, but between those who called for recognition of the "mutually helpful interdependence of independent nations" and those who called for "some form of world government with its own military force." Somewhere in the statement forthcoming from Mackinac, Dulles suggested, "this thought might be introduced":

> We are convinced that the result which we all want would not be gained by the United States merging its identity into some supernational agency created from paper plans. No world government could function except on the foundation of a world-wide community of spirit. This does not exist to a degree which would justify any nation in commiting its destiny to a body asserting world-wide authority. World government is not, however, the only alternative to world anarchy. Much can be done, by building between nations a cooperative relationship. . . .

By arguing along these lines, "the Republican Party might get away from the tentacles of a false issue that had been imposed upon it by its political enemies."[11] It might also allow the party to stop its internal bloodletting. His talks with party leaders had convinced him that the so-called "isolationists" were unnecessarily frightened. Republican "internationalists," like Dulles himself, were simply not world-staters. As far as views on the American role in the international community were concerned, he wrote Dewey's 1940 campaign manager, "most of the differences are imaginary rather than real." Dulles believed the G.O.P. factions would recognize their basic affinity if they talked calmly about fundamentals. "I wish very much that a few influential Republicans could be gotten together for a real discussion of international policy," he said. "The great trouble is that most of those who talk do not really know what they are talking about." The right people would quite easily "find a formula which would be constructive and sane, and on which the great bulk of the Party could unite."[12]

Dulles's perception of a degree of basic unity within his party was shared by a few others. After one stormy National Committee meeting in April 1942, Arthur Vandenberg realized how much sound and fury had been unnecessarily expended. A party resolution had been adopted which described the international "responsibility" of the United States and pledged Republican support for efforts to create "understanding, comity and cooperation among the nations of the world." Vandenberg couldn't understand why Taft and others had fussed so much in the process of accepting this resolution. It "was mere shadowboxing with platitudes," he wrote. "*I* agree with this general statement. *I* do not see how *anybody* could disagree with it. I think that Senator Taft made a great mistake in going to this Chicago meeting and opposing this declaration and in thus *giving* Willkie the pretense of a 'victory.'" It was also Vandenberg who later admitted that "so-called 'isolationists' and so-called 'internationalists' are not *necessarily* very far apart and *really* may be 'brothers under the skin!'"[13]

In fact, it was Vandenberg who gave Dulles the chance to test out his theory of what "a few influential Republicans" could accomplish for party unity. At Mackinac, Vandenberg and Senator Austin of Vermont had been asked to work out a draft foreign policy plank for the 1944 platform. When Dewey emerged as the obvious front runner, the Senators approached him for ideas; Dewey, in typical fashion, directed them to Dulles.

Dulles and Vandenberg, in particular, in a correspondence that began in May 1944, resolved issues quite satisfactorily. There was some sparring over specifics, but of a very calm variety. The first Vandenberg–Austin draft, for example, contained what Dulles referred to as a suspicious "joker." The two Senators had written, "We believe that the peace treaty must be just to be enduring," and Dulles thought this sounded too much like "the Republican line in 1920. . . . Apparently the reason for the inclusion . . . is designed to provide an alibi for not joining in organized international cooperation. . . . " Dulles was also suspicious of the Vandenberg–Austin statement that "we wish to see sovereign rights and self-government restored to those who have been forcibly deprived of them." This was too unrealistic to Dulles. It adopted what he termed "the most questionable language of the Atlantic Charter," and failed to take into account Allied interests in the postwar governments of the enemies and political realities in areas such as Eastern Europe.

In addition, Dulles drew attention to what he thought were important omissions in the Senators' draft. First, "there is no reference to economic policies." Citing a recent Dewey address, he suggested pointing to a Republican desire" to establish and maintain in our relations with other nations conditions calculated to promote worldwide economic stability not only for the sake of the world, but also to the end that our own people may enjoy a high level of employment in an increasingly prosperous world." He went on to express the desire to include statements on the necessity of American involvement in postwar international affairs and a specific reference to postwar collaboration among the principal powers with regard to enforcement of peace treaty terms against the former enemies.

But Dulles never really worried about the platform turning out well. The Vandenberg–Austin draft had contained the Mackinac statement supporting "postwar cooperative organization" to prevent aggression and "attain peace with organized justice in a free world," and he found it easy to live with that. Further, his critique of the draft platform brought almost complete acquiescence from the Senators. As Vandenberg put it to Dulles, "I am delighted to discover, first of all, that there is no fundamental disagreement between us. Reduced to the most elementary vernacular, I should say that my Republican Mid-West is perfectly willing to sanction 'international cooperation' just as long as it knows that we aren't going to 'haul down the flag' and that we aren't going to be international 'saps' in 'giving America away.'" Apparently, Dulles's ideas did not threaten these heartland sensibilities. Vandenberg proceeded to accept virtually all of the Dulles alterations and additions. Only concerning one issue did he hold out, and this reflected his political savvy about his own particular Michigan constituency: with respect to the return of sovereign rights, he wrote that the G.O.P. could at least "express the general '*wish*'"! "I do not consider it a commitment to 'restore the prewar status of Poland and the Baltic States.' It is, however, a gesture in this *general* direction so far as practicable: and I think we are entitled to take advantage of this tremendous political potential."[14]

Following an extensive correspondence, Vandenberg and Dulles met together to put finishing touches on the foreign policy plank. Both expressed concern to each other about "leaving so delicate a matter to the mercies of a 'mass meeting,'" and managed to eliminate all of their problems by the opening of the Chicago convention. There, while some chagrin was evident among lingering Willkie supporters, the Vandenberg–Austin–Dulles handiwork encountered no real problems.[15] Dulles had solid evidence for his belief that a few calm and well-informed leaders could find the basic "formula" around which the party could unite. In 1948 and 1952, he would not forget.

It was inevitable that Dulles would play an important role in the 1944 campaign. Dewey would have preferred concentrating his fire on accumulated domestic problems, but the strategy of the Democrats and the apparent interest of the public both forced regular attention to foreign affairs. Under these circumstances, the G.O.P. candidate turned, as ever, to his senior adviser.

Dulles was obviously anxious to get involved, and he gave unstintingly of his time and words. Although he never spoke or wrote to anyone about personal ambitions, it would not be hard to imagine him thinking about the probable reward for his efforts. Dewey was recognized as Roosevelt's most serious electoral opponent and was seen in a variety of quarters as having a fair chance of winning in November. Given the Dulles family's striking history and the added inducement of being able to work with a President who had practically absorbed his views on foreign affairs from him, Dulles surely must have considered the possibility of becoming Secretary of State.

Dulles also seems to have been sincerely convinced that it was important to replace Franklin Roosevelt. All through the early years of his work with the Commission on a Just and Durable Peace, he had complained about "the absence of any political leadership" in the direction of international reform. He was highly skeptical of Roosevelt and pictured him as a dilettante and procrastinator: "Indeed, it is difficult to perceive if he has any foreign policy other than drifting into war and out of war," he wrote on one occasion. In December 1943, he sharply lambasted the President's lack of concrete planning in a letter to Henry Van Dusen:

> It is perfectly clear to me that the present administration has not drawn upon and does not possess the competence needed to deal with the problem of bringing this war to an acceptable end and making quick and orderly transition to some better post-war world. Roosevelt is at home when it comes to uttering fine generalities, but when it comes down to the concrete, there is complete chaos and confusion, conflict of authority and lack of decision.
>
> Lack of statesmanship is going to force us to win this war in the hardest way, and also, I fear, is going to undermine any really constructive planning for the future.[16]

Dulles's concern by 1944, and possibly his ambition, yielded an intense partisanship that seemed strikingly and dramatically new in a man who had maintained a low political profile in earlier years. For the first time, he revealed personal characteristics that became hallmarks of his political style in years to come—a mixture of honesty, dishonesty, caution, and opportunism. These were hardly unique pieces of armor in the political arena, of course, but the wearing of them certainly seemed new to the public persona of John Foster Dulles.

Though Dulles developed a thrusting political style, his partisan zeal was probably surpassed by Dewey, who began swinging away at Roosevelt during the usually quiet summer doldrums. In mid-August, newspapers began carrying rumors about proposals that would be discussed at the upcoming Dumbarton Oaks meetings on international organization. Dewey told the press on August 16 that he was "deeply disturbed" by the drift of reports. "These indicate that it is planned to subject the nations of the world, great and small, permanently to the coercive power of the four nations holding this conference." Condemning this "rankest form of imperialism," he insisted that "the equality and rights of small nations and minorities" would have to be guaranteed.

Dewey had evidenced no interest in the rights of weak nations before 1944, and Dulles's later behavior at the San Francisco Conference indicated no genuine concern on his part, so the August maneuver was almost surely designed to take the Administration off-guard and garner some news coverage at a quiet moment. If so, it worked and paid some handsome, though temporary, dividends. The very evening of the statement, Secretary of State Hull called together an emergency meeting of advisers. "I expressed to them my concern that Governor Dewey's statement might throw the postwar organization into the political campaign, with disastrous consequences," Hull has written. Spending a sleepless night thinking over the problem, Hull tried to cope with it at his own news conference the following day. He publicly assured Dewey that his fears were "utterly and completely unfounded," and declared that he was willing to meet with the Governor in order to work out a "nonpartisan approach" to the whole problem of international organization. Dewey probably threw Hull a curve when he took up his offer the following morning and designated Dulles as his representative for discussions. The Secretary was at a cabinet meeting when he heard this and had a hard time persuading a skeptical President that it made sense to go along with talks if they would protect an international organization from partisan attacks during the campaign.

Dulles worked hard in preparing for his meeting, in spite of the fact that he was suffering at the time from a painful attack of thrombophlebitis. He traveled to Albany for consultation with Dewey, back to New York for a tête-à-tête with Willkie (who agreed to see him but not the Governor) and to Washington for preliminary talks with Senators Vandenberg, Taft, and Austin. Then, on August 23, he began three days of arduous discussions at the State Department. The Secretary of State later wrote that he had "seldom worked harder on any project than on the preparation for and conduct of the conversations with John Foster Dulles." As Dulles put it, "I had hoped that we would agree within a few hours. Actually, we had three days of almost continuous conference. The Secretary seemed to me very stubborn. Perhaps I seemed that way to him."

Their three days together yielded both agreements and disagreements. Hull clearly came to the meetings hoping to get Republican agreement to lift international organization and other "postwar problems" out of the political arena. (As Under Secretary of State Breckinridge Long put it, he was hoping to "bind the political opposition.") He immediately gave Dulles a copy of the State Department's latest draft plan for the new world organization and reviewed virtually every contemporary issue in the nation's foreign affairs. Dulles was not prepared to be bound just for the sake of information. In return for continuing access to the State Department and the opportunity to offer suggestions, he expressed his willingness to cooperate in a "nonpartisan" fashion on the specific matter of international organization. Even here, and most certainly in other areas, Dulles and Dewey insisted on maintaining a residual "right to debate generally all aspects of foreign policy." Stern partisanship would be limited, in other words, but discussion would not be totally stifled.

A rather tenuous agreement had been arranged between the Dewey camp and the Roosevelt Administration. Its limits were clearly reflected in the final communique issued by Hull and Dulles on August 25:

> Secretary Hull and Mr. Dulles expect to continue to confer about developments as they arise.
>
> The Secretary maintained the position that the American people consider the subject of future peace as a nonpartisan subject which must be kept entirely out of politics.
>
> Mr. Dulles, on behalf of Governor Dewey, states that the Governor shared this view on the understanding, however, that it did not preclude full public nonpartisan discussion of the means of attaining a lasting peace.
>
> The question of whether there will be complete agreement on these two respective views and their carrying out will depend on future developments.[17]

With this particular imbroglio out of the way, the campaign began in earnest in September. Dewey and Dulles had one overall image that they wanted the electorate to grasp at the beginning: that of a youthful standard bearer in the vanguard of a "young and vigorous" party anxious to lead the United States to an active role in world affairs. Both men were obviously aware of the lingering images of Harding–Coolidge "isolationism" and were anxious to dispel them immediately. The Republican platform had endorsed an international organization, and the candidate's acceptance speech was as forthright as anything the President had said on the subject. Indeed, the Dewey–Dulles strategy envisioned going the Democrats one better, by arguing that the Republicans could provide more dynamic leadership than a worn-out Roosevelt. "A vital and necessary part of the American dream is that America shall, by her conduct and example, give leadership and inspiration to all the world," Dewey said in one speech. "We're still young. We're still in the fullness of our strength." But Roosevelt and his advisers were "stubborn men, grown old and tired and quarrelsome in office," men whose "tired, shaky fingers" could not do the job which was waiting.[18]

The Democrats were hardly likely to let the Republican line go unchallenged. Vice-presidential candidate Harry Truman quickly developed the theme of Roosevelt's "tried and experienced leadership" and his intimate working relationship with other world statesmen. Henry Wallace went on the attack and charged that for all Dewey's protestations, isolationists were still loyal to the Republican cause. The President himself entered the fray on September 21, in a speech to the Teamsters annual convention in Washington. After sarcastic swipes at Dewey, he referred to the variety of "peace-building tasks" that were only a short way down the road: similar chores "were faced once before, nearly a generation ago," he said, and "were botched by a Republican Administration. That must not happen again."[19]

Democratic discussion of the G.O.P. position was unfair, for a number of reasons. Roosevelt and others were for all practical purposes dragging the international organization issue into the campaign by reference to the Wilsonian struggle of an earlier day, in spite of the fact that they had pressed to fence it off in August. Given the likelihood that Dewey and Dulles had been acting opportunistically when the problem first arose, this may have been a fitting comeuppance, but it was still precisely the kind of partisan maneuvering the President self-righteously attributed to his opposition. More importantly, the innuendoes of isolationism just didn't make sense. Dewey had been as direct as Roosevelt in discussions of an international organization—or as inclined to hedging. Both men, after all, were denizens of a political arena in which the innocuous usually triumphed over the meaningful. Dewey had also evidenced his supportive intentions quite clearly to the Administration. Dulles and Hull consulted regularly by phone about meetings at Dumbarton Oaks; a former Ambassador to Germany served as a day-to-day Republican liaison with the State Department; and a strong positive statement had been released the day of the publication of the Dumbarton Oaks Proposals.[20]

Dewey and Dulles compounded the effect of Roosevelt's innuendoes by their own unwise follow-up. In early October, they dealt clumsily with a flap about a peace-keeping force that would be available to a new world organization. The big question for many reporters and Congressmen was whether the American representative on a Security Council would have blanket authorization to commit U.S. troops or have to wait for congressional approval in each individual case. Dulles at first wanted no part of the debate, fearing that any position would alienate someone. He wrote Vandenberg of his hope that "this issue can be postponed until after the election, when we will know where we are and when partisan emotionalism will have died out." Even when *Life* magazine and Senator Joseph Ball, among others, pressed for a clear position, Dulles and Dewey ducked. This left the President with an opportunity he felt he could not pass up, and he publicly declared himself in favor of blanket approval. Only after strong media and opinion-poll reaction did Dewey try to rush in and take the same position.[21] By then the damage had been done. Although a view on this question was hardly a meaningful gauge of general foreign policy commitments, it was easy for the public to see Dewey's hedging as evidence of timidity and even isolationism.

Outmaneuvered by Roosevelt on the peace-keeping force issue, and angered by the general image-foisting of the Democrats, Dewey, Dulles, and other Republican strategists thought about trying some unsavory politicking of their own. They considered the possibility of raising pointed questions about the President's supposed failure to act on early warnings of the Japanese attack on Pearl Harbor. The extent of intelligence sophistication in Washington had been an issue ever since December 7, 1941, and investigations had long been promised. Many Republicans had been charging suspicious White House behavior, and Dulles wondered as early as August 1944 whether something could be made of Roosevelt's actions. General George Marshall, however, appealed to Dewey not to raise the issue lest the Japanese learn of the American ability to break their diplomatic codes, and Dewey agreed to avoid it.[22]

There was also some thought given to playing on the anxiety of Polish-Americans about the future of their homeland. Vandenberg had made clear his interest in exploiting the issue as early as March, being particularly conscious of the large ethnic bloc in his home state of Michigan. During platform deliberations, Dulles expressed doubts about the long-range possibilities of doing anything to stop the Soviets from getting their way in Poland and about what would therefore be the emptiness of any G.O.P. promises. By October, nonetheless, he and Dewey were ready to try something. Several initial meetings with Polish Ambassador Ciechanowski yielded somewhat ambiguous assurances of Republican concern for his London-based government. Shortly after, Dewey decided to go further. He made a number of public statements criticizing the suspicious secrecy of Roosevelt's diplomacy and calling for the creation of an "independent and sovereign" Poland led by "the true Government" in exile in England. The President was an older hand at appealing to ethnic minorities, however, and easily outmaneuvered the Republicans. He fed leaders of Polish-American organizations and even Prime Minister Mikolajczyk a string of vague, quite blandly misleading assurances about boundaries and U.S. support: it proved to be enough to keep the overwhelming support of a bloc of voters usually loyal to the Democrats in the past.[23]

In their efforts to develop some telling position against Roosevelt, Dewey and Dulles saved their heaviest fire for one particular issue: the supposed susceptibility of the Democrats to communist control. Other G. O.P. spokesmen had started developing this theme well before the 1944 campaign, but the standard bearer and his key foreign affairs adviser delivered a series of their own wild, red-baiting punches. On September 26, Dewey changed his image of Roosevelt from that of a frail and passing leader to that of a wild-eyed, dangerous radical. All the talk about the President's indispensability was absurd, Dewey argued; Roosevelt was indispensable only to political machines, suspicious labor leaders like Sidney Hillman, "Mme. Perkins . . . and Earl Browder, the ex-convict and pardoned Communist leader." On October 8, he described a Roosevelt victory as one "essential to the aims of the Communists." Later in the month, Dulles drafted a particulary unsavory piece that would be used by Dewey in Boston on November 1. "Mr. Roosevelt has so weakened and corrupted the so-called Democratic Party that it is readily subject to capture and . . . the forces of Communism are, in fact, attempting that capture," he wrote. The quarreling among tired men who had held power for too long had "opened up rifts through which alien forces can readily enter," he went on, and it was certain that "the Political Action Committee of Sidney Hillman and the Communists of Earl Browder" would rush in. In contrast, the Republican Party was described as "young and vigorous." There was no danger, Dulles concluded, "that, if the Republican Party is elected, its power will slip, through tired, shaky fingers, into hands which destroy that free America for which our sons are fighting and dying." Dewey's finishing touches to this draft described the kidnapping of the Democratic Party and argued that "the Communists are seizing control of the New Deal, through which they aim to control the Government of the United States."[24]

Dulles, and no doubt Dewey, knew that such accusations were absurd. Not a word about what would have been a cause of great concern is found in any of his statements or correspondence prior to the campaign, and the charges were promptly dropped on election day. Nevertheless, with what he once described as "the smell of powder" in the air during the campaign, Dulles was quite prepared to bend the truth. He had already shown himself ready to exploit the Pearl Harbor and Polish issues; red-baiting simply involved going a step beyond this kind of opportunism, into the realm of presumably time-honored political dishonesty.

Not that either Dulles or Dewey were incapable of putting a sincere and clear position before the public. There were some occasions on which this seemed necessary—or at least safe. For example, there was the question of American planning concerning postwar Europe, an old preoccupation for Dulles and a newly discovered cause for Dewey. Charges were periodically made about the "indecision" and confusion of the Democrats concerning Europe, Dewey building a particularly strong point around the idea that the foolish Morgenthau Plan had probably resulted in a greater German determination to continue fighting. Dewey made it clear, using Dulles's words, that he saw one of his key future tasks as the devising of a method "to prevent Germany and Japan from taking vengeance on the world twenty-five years from now." In a strictly procedural sense, he urged that a formal association among the principal Allies be empowered to enforce the terms of the peace for at least twenty-five and perhaps fifty years. In a more fundamental sense, Dewey also outlined what those terms of peace should be. With respect to Germany, he said that the "core" of the solution was "to sterilize the possibility of another aggressive war. . . ." He suggested, in particular, the internationalization and neutralization of the Ruhr. "The heart of Germany, the whole essentials of war, lie in the Ruhr," Dewey said, and it "must forever be forbidden to make military weapons for use by a reviving, aggressive Germany." Dewey also went on to state his view that "the whole economic rehabilitation of Europe is essential." This was closely related to the issue of defeated enemies, he argued, because "the Ruhr is Europe's great mass production area, and if Europe is to attain a sufficient degree of economic stability the benefits of Ruhr production have to be available to all the countries of Europe." The Ruhr might actually become the core around which a reformed and more integrated Europe could take shape, something which Dewey endorsed as a sound alternative to rebuilding the same old "firetrap."[25]

Election day brought Roosevelt his fourth presidential victory, with 25,600,000 votes to Dewey's 22,000,000. Dewey had done better than any defeated candidate since 1916, but that still left him the defeated candidate.

With respect to foreign policy questions, at least, Dewey's campaign efforts had just not worked. It can be argued that his hedging on the international organization issue was a little too obvious for many voters, that his opportunism was easily surpassed by a more nimble Roosevelt, and that his red-baiting was too crude. Even his moments of real candor did not help: forthright discussions about the postwar importance of Europe to the United States just did not seem to spark any public interest.

And yet, it is probably true that greater skill in Dewey, or better advice from Dulles, would still have yielded disappointing dividends. Would anyone really have been able to successfully challenge a popular President at the crucial stage of a war that was being won? As Dulles put it a week after election day, "I felt from the beginning that we could hardly win against the 'Commander-in-Chief' unless we got some breaks, such, for example, as the ending of the German war by early October." Arthur Vandenberg was in accord: "I think we were defeated by war psychology. It is next to impossible to beat the Commander-in-Chief in the midst of . . . a highly successful offensive; and it is doubly impossible when the Commander-in-Chief happens to be Santa Claus."[26]

II

In spite of defeat, the 1944 election campaign was an important episode in John Foster Dulles's public career. Though later developments might have transpired as they did anyway, in some other fashion, it was clearly this particular campaign which served as a crucial launching pad—both for his continuing political activities and for a reentry into the realm of diplomacy.

Politically, 1944 saw Dulles adding to and carefully piecing together the nuts and bolts he had been accumulating in the preceding few years. The result was a fairly impressive power base. He had begun reinvolvement in Republican Party affairs in 1940 as a marginal figure tied to a marginal candidate. Intervening years saw him becoming particularly adept at developing extensive contacts with many G.O.P. leaders around the country. Unlike Wendell Willkie, he kept himself open to discussions with people of divergent views and went out of his way, even after Dewey's nomination in 1944, to at least see and listen to many: as a result, men such as Taft, Warren Austin, and Clement Eaton would be sympathetic to Dulles in the future. Arthur Vandenberg would be especially helpful as time went on. Thrown together by the inevitable details of a major campaign, Dulles and the Michigan Senator quickly came to like and respect each other. After their first consultation on the platform, Vandenberg had written, "I think the really *important* thing is that you and I find ourselves in such substantial wholehearted agreement. I have the feeling that this will prove to be greatly useful in the days to come." By the week

234

following the election, he was saying that a compensation for the Dewey defeat "from my point of view—has been the privilege of coming to know you. I feel that we are already 'old friends.'. . . I beg of you always to feel free to send me your advice and suggestions." Dulles's response was that "one very great satisfaction has come to me from the campaign . . . and that is the opportunity I have had to become acquainted with you." His actions in succeeding months evidenced a clear determination to build on this initial opportunity.[27]

It deserves mention as well that by 1944 Dulles had a wide range of friends and associates in quarters that were nominally nonpolitical, but that were not necessarily irrelevant to his personal political future. In the late 1930s, he had followed in his grandfather's and William Nelson Cromwell's footsteps and become active in the work of the Carnegie Endowment for International Peace and the Rockefeller Foundation. Both organizations broadened his circle of acquaintances among the potentially influential and provided useful touchstones for occasional access to media and financial support.[28] Through these and other avenues, Dulles developed interesting lines of communication to such important newspapers as the *New York Times* and *New York Herald Tribune*. He was also successful in attracting the enthusiasm of Henry Luce. Time–Life publications became an important media outlet for Dulles in 1942 and gave him favorable coverage many times in the future. In August 1944, for example, *Life* ran a long feature story about Dulles which must have done much to increase his public visibility when coupled with his advisory work for Dewey and his concomitant leadership of the Commission on a Just and Durable Peace. The story both indicated and reinforced the fact that Dulles had become a moderately well-known and influential figure in his own right.[29]

Of course, by itself the political and quasi-political power that Dulles had in hand could not have built a bridge across the chasm of 1944's defeat. Held and tended, such power might have become something over time, but it would have been useless in the short run for an adviser who had no personal political office to fall back on. Circumstances came to Dulles's rescue, however. Well before he would have been able to command it, he was able to have his defeat and yet eat too at the political and diplomatic tables which had obviously become appetizing to him. Five months after election day, he found the opportunity to take up his first formal diplomatic chores in twenty-five years: he was invited to serve as adviser to the American delegation at the upcoming San Francisco Conference, called to draw up plans for a new international organization.

How did the Republican adviser of a defeated presidential candidate secure a diplomatic appointment from an ostensibly hostile Democratic Administration? Part of the explanation is to be found in the search for a "bipartisan" foreign policy by that Administration. Haunted perhaps by memories of Woodrow Wilson, Roosevelt, Hull, and many key advisers had regularly shown themselves anxious to develop a practical rapport with the opposition party in Congress concerning foreign affairs. Peace treaties, postwar programs, and even an international organization would be safer than in 1919 if a cooperative working relationship between the two parties could be built on a mutual recognition of transcendent international imperatives. Key House and Senate leaders were regularly invited to the State Department during 1943 and 1944 for briefings and consultation about postwar planning and, as has been seen, an effort was even made to prevent noisy partisan debate during the 1944 campaign. The latter effort was less than fully successful and revealed the tentativeness of Roosevelt's commitment when election sparks were in the air, but it did serve to focus considerable public and media attention on the basic notion of "bipartisanship" and to make John Foster Dulles one of the Republicans most noticed by the men in power.[30]

Even with bipartisan inclinations in Washington, it took vigorous pressure from Arthur Vandenberg to bring Dulles an appointment from the victorious Roosevelt. Vandenberg had been the prize Republican catch for the Democrats. As an articulate spokesman for Midwestern "isolationists," he had been seen as of great potential importance, especially when he revealed that his own readings of international affairs had persuaded him that the United States would have to play an important leadership role at the end of the Second World War. Vandenberg was shrewd enough to know his value to the Administration and had played the prima donna, always slow to come around and always exacting a price for doing so. Sometimes he simply required deferential ego-stroking, sometimes minor modifications in the wording of policy statements. In early 1945, he upped the ante. Invited to join the delegation to San Francisco, he hemmed and hawed about not wanting to be tied to the Dumbarton Oaks Proposals. "I cannot go to this conference as a stooge," he insisted, and waited until the White House agreed that he could be a "free agent" before accepting his invitation. He also pressed for an invitation to Dulles, whom he had come to like and respect. "I wish you were going to be with me," he wrote. "If you want a job as 'Advisory Council' [sic] I prayerfully petition your occupancy of the room next to mine in Frisco . . . ." Dulles was somewhat coy, but made it clear enough that he would be interested in going to San Francisco. He wisely let Vandenberg do his stalking for him, however, and in late February the Senator told Secretary Stettinius that Dulles might replace an ailing Clement Eaton. Hearing nothing, he waited until the first official meeting of the delegation on March 13 and announced that he wanted "to take John Foster Dulles as my lawyer." Stettinius was then frank and doubtful: "He said he had great respect for Dulles but that the President greatly dislikes 'Tom' [Dewey] and Dulles and that it might be obnoxious." Vandenberg continued to press, however, with Dulles looking on anxiously. Probably because Stettinius was willing, an invitation was finally secured in early April.[31]

Dulles was anxious to go to the San Francisco Conference, but he prepared for it with real misgivings. He began voicing his doubts long before he knew he would be going, in fact as soon as he had had his first glimpse of the Dumbarton Oaks Proposals. The planners had come up with blueprints for a "super-state," he said in October 1944; they looked "over-elaborate and too inflexible," and were especially forbidding for their "almost exclusive emphasis upon military force." Such a scheme could not possibly succeed, he felt, and to put it forth would only invite dangerous disillusionment when the failure became obvious. Far better to move slowly toward a more potent international organization, to rely on "a gradual process . . . from within a loose framework."[32]

This emphasis on the need for elementary beginnings had emerged as a Dulles theme in 1943 and had gained in strength in late 1944 and early 1945.[33] As in the past too, Dulles tried to have his Commission on a Just and Durable Peace continue to walk the fine line between cynicism and constructive criticism. As he explained to Bishop Oxnam, they had a "task of considerable delicacy." "The Dumbarton Oaks proposals ought to be greatly improved and we must take a position which will promote that without at the same time creating so much opposition that they will be defeated if not improved." The result was a series of statements that must have seemed to some to be running warm and cold at the same time. To a large Brooklyn church meeting, for example, Dulles said:

> . . . The Dumbarton Oaks Proposals fall short of . . . what is necessary to assure peace with justice. Too much reliance is placed upon force, the use of which is not related to any definition of what is or is not proper national conduct. The arrangement partakes too much of a military alliance. The proposed organization is inadequately endowed with curative and creative functions such as were sought for it by our Six Pillars of Peace. . . . I can say now that the conscience of many Christians cannot with silence accept the errors of commission and omission.

After this catalog of problems, however, he immediately added a balancing counter. "On the other hand," he said, "we must not, in the search for perfection, withdraw our support of the best which may now be practical."[34]

Privately, Dulles began to talk to Arthur Vandenberg about specific steps which might be taken to improve the existing blueprint. "I fear . . . there is not the possibility of making much change," he wrote shortly after the Senator's appointment to the American delegation. "There will doubtless be some additions, e.g., a preamble, a provision for a Commission to deal with colonial trusteeships, etc. . . . But changes of scope, purpose and structure will, I fear, be few. The present over-elaborate and over-ambitious scheme will, in the main, be kept." The two men did agree that if they "concentrated on one or two carefully chosen points," they might be able to make some improvements, and in the weeks before they both went to San Francisco they worked with this thought in mind. Vandenberg decided that the new organization should make a more explicit commitment to seek "justice" in various situations, and he sought to wedge the word into several strategic locations in the proposed charter. Dulles toyed with several other ideas: incorporating Article 19 of the old League Covenant, for example, which encouraged peaceful revision of treaties; and a proposal for making future amendment and revision of the Charter easier.[35]

It is not clear whether Vandenberg and Dulles expected the San Francisco conference to revolve around negotiations concerning such low-key issues as these. If they did, they quickly encountered many surprises. They, like most delegates and observers alike, would not have been prepared for the noisome and frustratingly time-consuming conflicts that began to crop up everywhere. Even before the meetings were formally under way in late April, the great powers began to argue among themselves, and the lesser powers began to argue with the greater powers. Then for eight weeks in California, far longer than anyone had expected, meetings dragged on and tempers mounted. President Truman impatiently delayed his departure from Washington to address the closing session of the Conference several times as he waited for troublesome issues to be settled. And, most importantly, while some of the controversies were on minor technical points, others proved to be of basic significance.

Troubled waters should have been expected, perhaps. During preparations for the meetings, one dispute arose over France's role in the Conference as compared to that of the original convening powers—Great Britain, the United States, the Soviet Union, and China. On another front, there was consternation within the American ranks over the possibility that Foreign Minister Molotov might not attend the conference, thus implying a Soviet denigration of its importance. There was consternation in the Soviet ranks too, over American hedging concerning a Yalta commitment to allow the Ukraine and White Russia to be separate members of the new organization and to invite them to San Francisco. Then, the moment proceedings began in California, there was chagrin on all sides over who was to act as "Chairman" of the gathering. The United States and most other nations believed Edward Stettinius should fill the role, following the tradition of allowing the host country to have this honor; the Soviet Union believed the unity of the major Allies should extend to the chairmanship of the conference and that each should take turns in the position.

As it turned out, none of these problems held a candle to the deluge that followed. For nine weeks, from late April to late June, the real battles took place.

The first substantive issue that emerged in San Francisco concerned the relationship between regional organizations and the new international body. It was quickly recognized as a crucial question, with the potential for affecting the entire future of the new organization. Early in the proceedings, an amendment to the Dumbarton Oaks Proposals was approved by the great powers which provided that "no enforcement action should be taken under regional arrangements or by regional agencies without the authorization of the Security Council with the exception of measures against enemy states in this war. . . ." The specific exception envisioned in this amendment was a series of security treaties applicable to Germany which had been negotiated by the Soviet Union with Great Britain, France, Yugoslavia, Czechoslovakia, and the Lublin Polish government. In the face of this Allied agreement, forces within the American delegation began to feel that special dispensation for independent action should also be granted to the Western Hemisphere security system that had been forecasted at the Chapultepec Conference in March 1945. With initial prodding from Nelson Rockefeller, whose role at San Francisco was to serve as liaison with Latin American delegations, Arthur Vandenberg forcefully entered the debate and demanded that something be done to protect the Monroe Doctrine and the historic Pan American system: if alterations were not suitable, he argued, he would not be able to guarantee approval of the Charter by the United States Senate. To complicate negotiations in this area, the American delegation members most distraught over the problem also felt that while the Western Hemisphere would have to be accorded special status within the United Nations, the door would have to be closed to any subsequent exceptions. A basic solution was devised after two weeks of very bitter confrontations between a United States–Latin American camp and most other delegations, but the United Nations as an *international* organization was permanently weakened by the trap door to regionalism that was thereby built into the Charter.[36]

An issue which developed shortly after the regional problem was that concerning the interpretation of the Yalta agreement on voting arrangements in the Security Council. Although it did not greatly affect the nature of the United Nations, the conflict here caused the most sparks during the San Francisco Conference. It was a multi-level problem really, in which various blocs at the Conference clashed over the voting procedures respecting three functions: how would the members vote when deciding to initiate *discussion* of a problem, to undertake an *investigation* of a problem, and to adopt *recommendations* for the settlement of a problem. Concerning the latter two, the great powers were in agreement on the Yalta formula, which maintained that these were substantive matters which would require the unanimous agreement of the permanent members of the Security Council; hence, the great powers would have "veto" power over decisions. The smaller powers, however, were disgruntled by the Yalta formula and waged an arduous campaign to eliminate the veto when recommendations of *peaceful* means of settlement were involved. If a decision were being made to use force to settle a problem, they agreed that the veto would have to apply, but it seemed intolerable to them to blanket all powers of recommendation in this way. Only during the last days of the Conference did the great powers secure general acceptance of their position, after what Senator Tom Connally described as "the most laborious, sweaty and almost bloody fight."[37]

One of the reasons for the acceptance of the Yalta formula on Security Council voting was an emerging awareness among the smaller powers of a battle that was going on within the ranks of the great powers themselves over a related question. It was on June 1 that the Soviets announced they were interpreting the Yalta agreements to mean that any decision of the Security Council to *discuss* an issue was a *substantive* matter, because it might be the first in a progression of steps toward more serious action, and that, therefore, such a vote would require the unanimous consent of the permanent members. U.S., British, and Chinese representatives expressed strong disagreement with this position, vehemently arguing that the Soviet interpretation was erroneous and that the veto could not apply to mere discussion. The most hostile days of the Conference followed. Only an urgent direct appeal to Marshall Stalin brought a June 6 Soviet acquiescence in the looser interpretation of the Yalta accord.[38]

Other dramatic confrontations dotted the San Francisco landscape as well. Much discussion went on concerning the establishment of a Trustee-ship Council within the United Nations. In the face of concerted efforts by small states and dependencies, American representatives at the conference were very anxious lest anything interfere with American control over former Japanese mandates in the Pacific; Great Britain and France were incensed over efforts to rush what they saw as unprepared peoples toward independence; and the Soviet Union was anxious to secure some influence for itself in this organ. There were also considerable fireworks over evolving plans for the Economic and Social Council of the new organization. American leadership was provided to a bloc of states that viewed with alarm the discussions going on in San Francisco: "fantastic" and "radical" programs were severely criticized, and much effort went into making sure that the Council would not be able to interfere in questions that were substantially within the "domestic jurisdiction" of sovereign states. Very late in the Conference, there was also a short-lived explosion over a Soviet attempt to limit the discussion privileges of the General Assembly.[39]

Even if Dulles had not anticipated all of these stormy scenes, he quickly demonstrated his willingness to jump into them. The official records of the Conference as well as his own personal materials indicate that he spent an incredibly busy two months, and that there were few issues with which he did not come into contact at some point. In terms of its superstructure, his role was very much like the one he had played at the Paris Peace Conference of 1919. It involved first, last, and always extensive participation in American delegation discussions of issues and strategy. Though Dulles was far from the most vocal member of the team, his views on major controversies were always heard and his legal skills often came into play in putting negotiating tactics into shape: this was true regarding general discussions and drafting exercises connected with the regional organization issue, the Security Council veto and "domestic jurisdiction" safeguards, among others. Dulles was particularly prone to writing memoranda for delegation use which summarized troublesome issues and sometimes laid out alternative courses of action.[40] Outside the American delegation, Dulles moved on many levels. He was charged with representing the United States on a number of the major standing committees of the Conference: Committee I/1/A, for example, in whose meeting the "domestic jurisdiction" issue was discussed and Committee II/3/A, where debate about the Economic and Social Council took place.[41] He also participated in many of the meetings of the Four and Five Power "Informal Consultative" committees, where many controversies were ultimately thrashed out: on May 26 and June 2, for example, he helped argue the U.S. case concerning the Security Council veto.[42] Dulles was also very helpful to the Americans because of his enormous network of friendships and contacts, gained through many years of international legal and business experience. Vandenberg once told him that he seemed to know more people at the Conference than anyone else in the American delegation. Dulles seems to have enjoyed the chance to draw on and renew his acquaintances. He even arranged to have a small dining room available at the St. Francis Hotel so that he could hold private luncheons—with Lord Halifax one day, Georges Bidault another.[43] On any number of occasions, the delegation asked him to use his network or to try to develop contacts to allow for unofficial discussions and pressure, and he was perfectly willing to be accommodating. During the weeks when the regional organization issue was at the center of the storm, he carried on informal meetings with Latin American, French, British, and Soviet delegates.[44]

Dulles's work as strategist, drafter, spokesman, and negotiator offers significant insights into his thoughts at this moment of return to the diplomatic arena. Beneath all of the hectic activity, there are many indications of the way his mind was digesting new experiences and relating them to the conclusions or assumptions of earlier days.

Dulles's personal approach to the various San Francisco controversies was usually adapted to the particular idiosyncracies of each. With rather striking consistency, however, his analyses and recommendations were linked by a few core concerns. As in the latter months of his work with the Commission on a Just and Durable Peace, Dulles regularly reiterated his modest expectations concerning a new international organization. A beginning would be made, he felt, but it would be "elemental"; indeed, to avoid disillusionment as a result of fledgling failures, care would have to be taken to realistically limit the tasks thrown on the shoulders of the new body. Another theme revealed in his church-related work also figured in his San Francisco thoughts, though it emerged with new clarity and force: his concern for the interests of his own country. Dulles had never made any secret of his attentiveness to the politico-economic needs of the United States, even during the early war years when he was inclined to speak primarily in terms of moral and Christian duty to others. For reasons that will deserve discussion, he never spoke of his religious considerations in San Francisco and returned to a style of analysis that put virtually exclusive emphasis on pragmatic national interest. One quite new concern also emerged at the United Nations Conference, albeit to some degree a subspecies of his concentration on what would be good for the

United States. It was in San Francisco that Dulles began to piece together an increasingly cynical and suspicious portrait of the Soviet Union. The intellectual underpinnings of what became his strident Cold Warrior views were still very immature in mid-1945, but hindsight highlights the signs of what was coming.

The first major controversy with which Dulles became involved was that surrounding regional security pacts, and his approach to it clearly reveals each of these overarching concerns. Dulles was one of the small number of Americans who would have preferred ignoring this entire question in San Francisco. As a result, he spent as many hours in torturous wrangling with his own colleagues as with the British, Chinese, Soviets, and Latin Americans. He argued in essence that this was an issue which offered an unenviable combination of the unnecessary and the dangerous: great effort would have to be expended to accomplish what might simply have been taken for granted and, once begun, careful programing would be required if serious consequences were to be avoided.

Dulles's discussions of the dangers inherent in the regional organization issue offer clear evidence of his perception of American interests at this point and his evolving suspicions of the Soviet Union. He was dubious of seeking some special status for a Pan-American security arrangement, he said, because it might easily lead to the United States being frozen out of other quarters of the globe. In particular, it might give unnecessarily tempting opportunities to the Soviet Union, a country whose power Dulles had come to respect by 1945, but whose traditional preference for regionalism as opposed to internationalism he fully recognized.

Just the appearance of a push on this issue could have unfortunate results, Dulles argued; it would create a disturbing "psychology" among peoples of great significance to the United States. As he put it in one memorandum, it "might suggest to Western Europe and to China that the U.S. intends to retreat into hemispheric isolation and might leave those European and Asiatic states to fall into Soviet-dominated regional arrangements." If the push were successful, but not properly channeled, the consequences would grow worse. He was particularly worried about the possibility of some general Charter rubric on regional organizations which would have exempted them from supervision by the Security Council. If the Americans had to accept this in order to get universal respect for the Pan-American system, he felt, the price would be far too high. This "would open the door to, and invite, a whole series of regional agencies whose potential use of force would deprive the Security Council of any real authority in the world." He could easily see the emergence of "a European regional arrangement which will include Western Europe as well as Eastern Europe and which *the Soviet Union will dominate* and where *we* will *through the Security Council* have no voice" (emphasis added). All in all, he could see no reason to go out of the way to "advocate a procedure which would . . . jeapordize both the World Organization and *our own strategic relations as regards Western Europe and China*" (emphasis added).[45]

His sense of potential dangers led Dulles to opt for doing as little as possible about this issue. Why push, he asked his colleagues? It was, after all, "a highly remote contingency" that the Latin Americans would ever actually move to implement the vagaries of the Act of Chapultepec: "it is extremely doubtful that in fact the issue will ever become real." The U.S. could promise that when and if it did, efforts would be made to have the arrangements "fitted into the new organization." In the meantime, the less said the better. It could simply be taken for granted that United States' interests in the Western Hemisphere would be secure in the postwar period. If a problem arose, the veto in the Security Council would prevent any type of interference by the new world organization of which the U.S. disapproved. If use of the veto by others prevented the Council from taking action that the U.S. did desire, then the "inherent right of self-defense" would allow unilateral or regional action to deal with a threat. As he put it in one delegation meeting:

> . . . at no point would the member states give up their right to use force in all circumstances . . . they pledged to refrain from the use of force in a manner inconsistent with the purposes of the organization. Since the prevention of aggression was a purpose of the organization, action to prevent aggression in the absence of action by the Security Council would be consistent with the purposes of the organization. . . . If a European country vetoed action to prevent aggression in the Western Hemisphere, we would be entirely free to use force.

Or, as he phrased it in a memorandum, "Any member remains free to use force to maintain its security. The right of self-defense is unimpaired."[46]

Dulles was not prodded to demand more by the early acceptance of an exemption from Security Council authority which favored countries other than his own. Like most Americans in San Francisco, he accepted the logic of treating as special entities a series of bilateral security pacts involving French and Soviet efforts to protect themselves from future German aggression. Unlike most Americans, he did not think this required a similar exemption for the Western Hemisphere. He would probably have preferred the avoidance of special pleading by any state, but he was not overly worried by the efforts to deal with the former enemy. Better to leave arrangements no more complicated than this. After all, he argued, "while the Soviet Union would have a free hand in Eastern Europe" under the accepted clause, "we would still have a voice in Western Europe" via the Security Council. To push for broader exemptions would threaten this far more important Western European position by inviting a regional arrangement in which the United States could not logically expect to be a member. "From his point of view," therefore, "the question was whether it was worth it to us to save our position in Western Europe or whether we should trade this off to assure American solidarity . . . whether or not to build on hemisphere solidarity alone and throw away all of Europe or whether to save our voice in Western Europe."[47]

But Dulles did not get his way. He had allies in Harold Stassen and Leo Pasvolsky, but their combined influence was not nearly as great as that of Arthur Vandenberg, especially when coupled with the urgings of military spokesmen like Henry Stimson (back in Washington) and John McCloy. The delegation as a whole was persuaded to push for some tangible recognition of the Monroe Doctrine and the anticipated offspring of the marriage contract represented by the Act of Chapultepec. Accepting the unavoidable, Dulles became deeply involved with the inter-delegation bickering that was designed to produce an appropriate Charter clause. He spent hours in subcommittee meetings, using his highly respected legal ingenuity to devise acceptable language. What he and his associates came up with was an addendum to a clause on the inherent right of self-defense, one which would specify that the right referred to unilateral action *and* "arrangements, like those embodied in the Act of Chapultepec, under which all members of a group of states agree to consider an attack against any one of them as an attack against all of them." The advantage of this approach, he told his colleagues, was that the specific mention of Chapultepec "prevents throwing the door open to less sound and historical arrangements"; in fact, he recommended that there be "a veto power on that, i.e., that no new groups can be created . . . without the approval of the Security Council."[48]

It is curious, but the Americans do not seem to have envisioned serious opposition to their scheme. Though Dulles would have had to admit that it was a clear case of special pleading, he seems to have persuaded himself that others would go along. Even the Soviets, about whom he was obviously suspicious, were seen as likely to be accommodating. They, Dulles argued:

> . . . accepted the fact that they would be able to deal in their own sphere
> and he believed they felt that, working through a world security system,
> they might be able to influence areas outside their direct control. He

thought this might mean that we could get an exemption for the Western Hemisphere without actually being driven out of Europe. The Russians, wanting to get as much as they could in the way of influence outside their own sphere, might be willing to accept the best they could get.[49]

No one cooperated. All of the other organizing powers expressed their disapproval of the American draft clause, with the British being the most vocal. New drafts were shunted back and forth for several days, with general agreement on the concept of regional action to deal with armed attacks or emergency situations, but a total impasse on a specific reference to Western Hemisphere plans. Finally, in a May 12 meeting with the British delegation, Vandenberg made the testy remark that a Senate reservation to the Charter would be necessary if the Act of Chapultepec were not explicitly mentioned. To what must have been his surprise, Eden said he "would have no objection to such a reservation." Within hours, the Senator persuaded his American colleagues that this would probably be the simplest way to break the logjam, and an agreed-upon text for what became Article 51 was soon prepared.[50]

Aside from its relevance to his sense of American needs and his perception of the Soviet Union in mid-1945, it should be obvious that Dulles's approach to the regional organization issue says much about his belief in the inevitably rudimentary nature of a new international organization. His emphasis on the "inherent right of self-defense" and the ability of the United States to *assume* its freedom of movement for protection of its interests coincided completely with his earlier statements. Though hypothetically desirable, he had argued in 1944 and early 1945, there was no way nations were going to be rushed into surrendering the perquisites of sovereignty. This was particularly true of the great powers, he argued in San Francisco. As he explained it in one memorandum, "the Permanent Members are under *no restraint whatever* in the use of force for their own security. They are under a moral obligation not to use 'security' as a pretext for aggression. If they disregard that moral obligation, *nothing can be done about it*" (emphasis added). Arthur Vandenberg said he was shocked by this reasoning, that he found it "totally disillusioning" to think that "we have the right to do anything we please in self-defense," that every state was "a law unto itself." Though he did not respond directly, Dulles would probably have seen his friend's assessment as both romantic and unrealistic.[51]

In the standard narratives, regional organizations and voting arrangements in the Security Council are always described as the two great issues of the San Francisco Conference. Dulles was involved with both of these basic concerns.

During the early stages of debate over the veto, Dulles returned again and again to his advice about realistic expectations for the new organization. In the best of all possible worlds, he implied, he would have endorsed the unlimited right of the Security Council to investigate a problem and to make recommendations for its solution. Given "the present state of the world," however, "the only practical procedure" was to settle for less; "it was impossible . . . to advance beyond the position that had been achieved. . . ." As he put it in a memorandum, "It is natural that the nations which would have to bear by far the greater part of the burden of maintaining or restoring peace and security should want at all stages to preserve as between themselves a unanimity without which effective action is difficult if not impossible."[52]

To be sure, there were limits to Dulles's willingness to bend with the winds of pragmatism. He did want to publicly express hope for future improvements in this area. He talked about the possibility of a "liberalized" approach to the veto developing over time and urged the United States delegation to go "on record" as being supportive of the principle of a more open approach than that embodied in the Yalta formula. Dulles was also adamant about not backtracking from the American understanding of that Yalta formula. He was as shocked and angered as anyone when at the late date of June 1, Andrei Gromyko dropped his bombshell about a Soviet interpretation of Yalta which granted veto power over whether a subject would even be *discussed* by the Security Council. While he had accepted the need for unanimity in decisions to investigate problems or recommend solutions for them, Dulles drew the line here. Discussion was the most elementary of steps, and if it were not automatically allowed, his hopes for even an "elemental" beginning would not be realized. As a result, he joined his colleagues in a unanimous decision to firmly oppose the "ridiculous" Soviet interpretation.

The dispute dragged on for almost a week, and Dulles's concern increased as a wait began for word of accommodation from Moscow. Prodded to a degree by Arthur Vandenberg, with whom he consulted virtually every day, he was soon in a hypercritical mood and ready to make one of his biting criticisms of Soviet behavior. It came in a memorandum written in the heat generated by a long conversation with Vandenberg and Stassen on June 4. The issue of a veto over discussion was too important to allow for compromise, Dulles insisted. First, it involved "a basic ideological conflict" whose resolution would do much to determine "what kind of a body the Security Council is to be. . . ." "The Soviet political system does not encourage or even admit of free discussion of the kind we rely upon to clarify different viewpoints and bring out ways of solution," he argued; such an approach could not be allowed to set the overall tone of the new organization. Second, "this matter of veto has come to assume . . . a *symbolic* importance beyond the issue itself—important as that is" (emphasis added). Because of this, acceptance of the Soviet interpretation would "seriously impair the future influence of the U.S. in world affairs." Here Dulles imagined a variety of forbidding scenarios. For example, the Soviet Union might jump to misleading conclusions because of an American concession: it "would be deemed by it to be a sign of weakness. It might make it extremely difficult for the U.S. again to prevail in any international negotiations with the U.S.S.R. and it would tempt the U.S.S.R. to keep on crowding the U.S. until dangerous friction developed." To this picture of Moscow prepared to "crowd" the United States, Dulles added other unflattering lines. Nations other than the Soviet Union might misread an American acceptance of a veto over discussion as well:

> Many if not most of the nations of the world are under strong pressure by the U.S.S.R., both directly and through internal penetration. They are wondering whether or not there is any nation which feels strong enough to stand up for what it believes as against the U.S.S.R. If the U.S.—the greatest and most powerful nation of the world, with the possible exception of the U.S.S.R.—is not willing on this issue and at this juncture and with all of the support that is available, to stand firm, then these other nations will themselves in other matters readily fall in with the U.S.S.R. policies. The result will be to leave the U.S. in a position of greatly increased and dangerous isolation. [53]

Though the Soviets eventually agreed to withdraw their demand for veto rights over "discussion," other problems soon arose to disturb the Americans in San Francisco. Dulles and his colleagues found themselves engaged in something like a steady guerrilla struggle over the question of "domestic jurisdiction," for example.

Dulles's position was intriguing here and demonstrates the way he could alter his position under the pressure of circumstances. Throughout the late 1930s and his work with the Commission on a Just and Durable Peace, he had been critical of the way so many governments failed to appreciate the broad international implications of actions that seemed essentially domestic in nature. Currency regulations, trade policies, or immigration restrictions, he had often argued, could have as great an impact on people across the globe as on those within the nation establishing them. In the economic field especially, this had been a major preoccupation for him. He had often urged the need to begin diluting formal sovereignty in this respect, to allow some kind of internationalization of once exclusively domestic jurisdiction. The first concrete proposal put forward by his church commission, in fact, called on Congress to establish an "administrative unit" to watch over the "international repercussions" of contemplated U.S. legislation. [54]

When Dulles became a member of the American delegation to the San Francisco Conference, he found himself forced to cope with the "domestic jurisdiction" question from an official rather than an outsider's position. He tried at first to make the two identical. During an early delegation review of the Dumbarton Oaks proposals regarding limits on the authority of the Security Council over such issues, Dulles waded into the discussion with all the assurance of his long experience. He said he had "objected to this paragraph at the time of his discussions with Secretary Hull in the fall of 1944. It was . . . a contradiction in terms to say that a matter which threatened the peace of the world was solely a matter of 'domestic jurisdiction.' How could that be? . . . The Security Council should have authority to consider any matter which threatened the peace of the world." But Dulles was stepping on sensitive toes by saying these things in this setting. Washington had shown no inclination to allow outside interference with what it would have defined as the internal affairs of the United States, and the Senate in particular had traditionally and jealously guarded the country's sovereignty. Arthur Vandenberg and Tom Connally quickly demonstrated the latter to Dulles. Without a protecting reservation, Vandenberg said, "there would be no possibility of getting the Charter approved by the United States Senate." Dulles pressed the issue further: "the trouble with international law was that it had reserved the right of any state to do as it pleased," he argued. "He wondered whether something might not be gotten through the Senate." But the two Senators were adamant. As Vandenberg put it, "this was one of the 'fantasies obsessing the Senate.'" [55]

Dulles bowed to the inevitable. When the Dumbarton Oaks clause was raised again, two days after the initial discussion, he made no objections. The delegation as a whole approved a slight alteration in wording, but allowed the overall rubric limiting the international organization's jurisdiction to stand. Dulles then turned his considerable legal expertise toward safeguarding the American position against inroads on many fronts. During his months in San Francisco, he was often called upon to help deal with potentially troublesome proposals or undesirable phrasing in proposed amendments and clauses. On May 23, he was caught up in a discussion of a move to have the new organization "promote full employment"; he helped devise strategy to guarantee that this would "not constitute a threat to the internal security of any state. . . ." And nowhere was vigilance required more than in negotiations concerning an evolving Economic and Social Council. Many delegation members grew steadily more piqued at an "avalanche" of "radical" proposals for the new agency's responsibilities; Arthur Vandenberg moved from dismissing some of them as "dream stuff" to alarmist warnings about an effort to "communize" the world. Dulles joined hands with his colleagues in their efforts to prevent the Council from "encroaching upon domestic matters" and becoming "a super state."[56]

Did Dulles find it difficult to work as an American watchdog as far as "domestic jurisdiction" was concerned? If he did, there is no evidence of it. Neither the official minutes of the conference nor his private records reveal any signs of strain after the first delegation discussion of the question. In one way or another, he seems to have found it possible to accept the thrust of official American policy here. Perhaps this is not surprising. That policy, after all, meshed quite easily with some of the basic concerns Dulles himself had demonstrated in other situations during the San Francisco Conference. He surely would have sensed the link between some of the early statements made in his delegation and his own arguments about the need for a realistic, elemental beginning for the new organization. There must have been a familiar ring to Tom Connally's words at one point, for example—that "we were covering virgin territory, and it would be best to proceed conservatively in order to accomplish anything at all." Here was one of those situations in which what might have been desirable in an abstract sense would have to give way to what was practical. Likewise, Dulles might easily have seen that Washington's concern for the inviolability of its policies on trade, currency, labor, and immigration was but another facet of attentiveness to the national interests of the United States. He himself had shown no special desire to avoid meddling with American independence and freedom of movement in the past, concentrating instead on the way in which cooperation with others could bring economic and political benefits. What might have begun to emerge in the work on "domestic jurisdiction" questions was an awareness that the fundamental goal of national interest was more important than the methods which he had usually advocated for serving it.[57]

There were yet any number of other issues with which Dulles became involved during the San Francisco Conference, and each would suggest something of the drift of his thoughts during those months. Two deserve mention because they both reinforce the images already evident and connect with important later developments in Dulles's life and thought.

Marginal participation in discussions of trusteeship, for example, demonstrates Dulles's attentiveness to American interests in 1945 and is relevant to his extensive subsequent involvement with the underdeveloped world. Initially, he took a somewhat more liberal approach to this question than his hypersensitive colleagues. In one of the early Washington meetings of the delegation, Secretary of War Stimson was troubled by an anticipated requirement for information about strategic territories the United States was planning to control in the Pacific. Dulles argued that there was "not a real difficulty" here; he saw no reason why the new organization's efforts "to look into the condition of colonial peoples" should interfere with American military requirements. At a later date, however, Dulles showed the same inclination to fall into line that he had in deliberations on regional organizations and domestic jurisdiction. On June 23, Vandenberg and some of the military advisers became upset about an interpretation of a Charter clause that would have required regular reports to the Secretary General about "conditions" in territories like Hawaii and Alaska. Though Dulles does not seem to have been personally disturbed by this prospect, he went along with the general delegation effort to make sure it did not transpire. He also showed himself fully supportive of the U.S. policy to avoid citing "independence" as the ultimate goal for subject peoples. As he put it in one meeting:

> . . . the concept of independence might not assist in the establishment of future peace. Just as in the last war when there was criticism of those who set up many independent states in Europe, we would be subject to the same type of criticism. It would be progress if we could speak of self-government integrated within an overall framework. Mr. Dulles added that the church groups with which he was associated were satisfied in all their statements with self-government or autonomy as objectives of the trusteeship system and had never insisted on independence. [58]

Further evidence of one of Dulles's other core concerns, his evolving suspicions of the Soviet Union, can be found in his work on the question of a right of withdrawal from the new organization. This was a topic that came up in the earliest meetings of the U.S. delegation but was not resolved until the closing days of the Conference. All, Americans and others alike, seemed to assume that of course a nation should have the right to withdraw membership under a variety of circumstances. This did not prevent lengthy haggling as to whether that right should be expressly stated or simply assumed, with those favoring the latter course arguing that this would lend a more positive tone to the Charter. As individuals and a delegation, the Americans seesawed in their position, eventually opting for an assumed right supported by an interpretive statement in an official Commission report.

Dulles personally began and ended the Conference in favor of this approach. For the space of a few weeks midway through the proceedings, however, he argued the case for an explicit withdrawal clause—and did so on the basis of his chagrin at Soviet behavior. He made his clearest statements in a May 17 memorandum, written at a moment of great annoyance with Moscow's seemingly perverse delay in endorsing a clause on regional organizations which everyone else had finally approved. Dulles wanted the U.S. to have an unquestionable right to leave the United Nations, he said, because he worried about "the use which the Soviet Union may make of its position as a Permanent Member of the Security Council." There were two major problems as far as he was concerned. First, "Available evidence indicates that the U.S.S.R. does not now practice genuine cooperation with Great Britain or the U.S. *within the orbit of its physical might.*" He had been told by State and War Department officials that agreements regarding Poland, Rumania, Yugoslavia, Austria, and Germany "have not been lived up to...." He assumed that something similar might soon develop "in relation to Manchuria, Korea and parts, and possibly all, of China." If so, it would have a staggering impact on the United Nations: it "would remove from the effective concern of the World Organization a vast area embracing about half of the population of the world and extending from the Pacific to the Atlantic." Second, what if the Soviets sought to use the organization "to stir up unrest in the rest of the world?" Their privileged position in the Security Council would give them both "a high forum for spreading their views" and a chance to intimidate "small nations" which might think they "cannot share in active participation in the functioning of the World Organization or get protection from it without having the goodwill of the Soviet Union." Dulles made it clear that he was "by no means convinced" that the Soviets would behave as he feared. There were, however, "so many present warning signals" that for a while he urged making sure there would be a foolproof escape hatch from the new structure. [59]

III

Dulles left San Francisco in late June, after eight weeks of hectic activity. He had been involved with virtually every major issue that came before the Conference and had usually been a party to the inner debate and negotiation that was spurred by each. To his colleagues in the U.S. delegation, he had seemed an important figure. Vandenberg, surely one of the kingpins of the team, had called him "my lawyer." Sol Bloom dubbed him "our brains," and Clement Eaton wrote, "It is the general opinion, in which I concur with all my heart, that you have made the most noteworthy contribution of any single individual to the successful writing of the Charter."[60]

But Dulles was more modest in assessing his influence than some of his colleagues. The closest he came to a boast was a letter to one friend in which he claimed that he had "played a more important role than some of the Delegates." His modesty was justified. For all his ubiquitousness in delegation, committee, and subcommittee meetings, it cannot be said that he enjoyed real authority in San Francisco. On several key issues, clearly, his early advice was simply rejected. He would have preferred to ignore the regional organization issue—the delegation decided it could not. He would have favored a narrow reading or even rejection of the "domestic jurisdiction" loophole—the delegation decided to move in the opposite direction. It was really men like Vandenberg, Connally, and Stettinius who determined the basic features of American policy in San Francisco, with occasional *obiter dicta* from Truman or Stimson back in Washington. Dulles's role, like many other delegates, to be sure, came *after* the basics had been laid down: at that point, his legal skills could be brought into play for deciding tactics, devising appropriate wording for clauses, and acting as spokesman-negotiator for the delegation. This was interesting but of more marginal significance to the proceedings.

The real importance of Dulles's work at the San Francisco Conference, as at the Paris Peace Conference a quarter-century earlier, is to be found in what it says about Dulles himself rather than American foreign policy or great power relations in 1945 *per se*. In this respect, it is quite valuable, particularly when coupled with his evolving political activities of the war years. Both help fill in the picture of Dulles in these years, of the way he spent his time and the things which concerned him. Both are especially important because of what they say about the way he made the transition from thought to action and because of the way they offer different vantage points from which to assess the philosophical-religious inclinations that had culminated in the Commission on a Just and Durable Peace.

One thing that his political and diplomatic activities help illuminate is the thrust of Dulles's ambition in the early 1940s. Dulles has often been pictured as a man virtually born with the intention of becoming Secretary of State. Given his grandfather's and uncle's experiences, his own role in the Wilson Administration, and his great success in the international economy between the wars, the proposition has a certain verisimilitude. If he did always have his eyes set on some position of high political-diplomatic power, however, there is little real evidence of it through the first fifty years of his life. There is no indication at all, in fact, that Dulles ever spoke of ambitions along these lines, and his actions certainly did not demonstrate any drive in this direction. If he was bent on making it in Washington, his role as foreign policy adviser in the unlikely John W. Davis campaign of 1924 was certainly ill-chosen. Only during the early days of World War II did Dulles's behavior begin to signal an interest in traditional political and foreign-policy making power. Only then did he take the public persona he had begun to develop as an advocate of international reform and a Protestant lay leader and give it more precise direction by channeling it into national politics. Initial forays on behalf of Dewey in 1940 grew into major campaigns. Dulles was no dabbler in G.O.P. and national politics by 1944, but a man expending great time and energy in pursuit of electoral victory and its fruits. Nor did defeat deflect the now risen ambitions. A month after election day, he was happily writing his brother that "as soon as Secretary Stettinius was appointed he asked me to come down to Washington, and I spent the greater part of the day with him" discussing prospects for the new international organization: "I think we may find a basis for continuing to work in contact with each other in relation to that particular matter." Then, all through early 1945, he slyly but clearly worked at getting himself appointed to the San Francisco Conference.[61] All in all, though it is impossible to pinpoint a precise moment of origin, it is quite clear that Dulles had a whetted appetite for political and foreign policy-making power by 1944–1945.

Evidence of his G.O.P. and San Francisco activities also helps to highlight the multiple facets of Dulles's thoughts and his talk of his thoughts in these years. Here was a man with a considerable range of interests. International commerce and finance, global reform programs, Republican political efforts, international organization, and campaigns to direct American Protestant sentiment: though many links existed between these various components as Dulles dealt with them, there was also a diversity which made him an individual active in several relatively distinct arenas.

It is particularly interesting to see how Dulles in one arena compares with Dulles in another. In a way that could never be appreciated by looking only at his work with the Commission on a Just and Durable Peace, it can be seen that Dulles had the tendency and the ability to deal with different audiences and situations in different ways. He was able to adapt his actions and even his language according to his estimation of circumstances. His political role, especially his behavior in the 1944 election, had a virtually Machiavellian stripe to it that one sees little evidence of in the church settings he moved through at the same time. As a Protestant leader, he could urge again and again the importance of Christ-like hearts and minds and the primacy of the "moral law" that undergirded the universe. As a striving Republican, he was quite capable of devising strategy that was beneath the ethical standards taken for granted by his church associates.

In San Francisco, Dulles revealed a more important schism between his various roles. As a member of the United States delegation, both the tone of his words and the thrust of his advice would almost surely have caused some surprise among his colleagues at the Commission on a Just and Durable Peace. Some of the most noticeable ingredients in his war-time statements were not to be seen or heard. Gone was the steady counterpoint of scriptural references; gone too was the more substantive emphasis on the need for a reformed world order, involving especially the shift from pursuit of selfish national interest to Christian cooperation and sharing. In their place in San Francisco, Dulles offered statements and advice that were far more in tune with the traditional resonances of the global political arena. His discussions of issue after issue, from regional organization to "domestic jurisdiction" to withdrawal, were all couched in the time-honored vocabulary of *Realpolitik,* with emphasis on the political, economic, and strategic facts of international life as they affected the great powers. The resulting shift in the overall tone of his statements— i.e., traditionalist as opposed to ethical-religious—carries with it a more basic variation in goals as well. In particular, of course, Dulles demonstrated a far more blatant concern for the specific interests of the United States than he had in the bulk of his preceding church-related work.

In the immediate aftermath of the San Francisco Conference, there came yet other interesting indicators of Dulles's multifaceted behavior in varying contexts. He devised markedly different appraisals of the new organization and its Charter for the several types of audiences that sought his opinions. The Executive Committee of the Federal Council of Churches heard Dulles wax rhapsodic. "The Charter . . . fulfills our hopes even beyond our expectations," he said; its "new and lofty conceptions" could turn it into "a Magna Carta for the world." For the Senate Foreign Relations Committee, he developed a more subdued approach. He left no doubt of his support for the United Nations, but discussed it in far more traditionalist terms. The Senate need not worry about going too far too fast, he said in particular: "We remain the master of our own destiny. The Charter does not subordinate us to any super-government. There is no right on the part of the United Nations Organization to intervene in our domestic affairs. There can be no use of force without our consent. If the joint adventure fails, we can withdraw." And in communicating with some old friends in the internationalist organizations he had worked with occasionally for twenty-five years, he took yet another tack—something like a mixture of pleasure and world-weary skepticism. He gave this judgment to Phillip Brown of the American Peace Society: "Of course, of itself it assures nothing, but at least it is an inspiring document which starts off with a good spirit behind it, and it will afford mankind on opportunity if it really wants one." These and other statements in the weeks immediately after San Francisco, reveal an ongoing repertoire of styles which Dulles had developed by mid-1945 and which he was quite prepared to use almost simultaneously. [62]

Given the full range of Dulles's wartime activities, it seems clear that the "steeples" which were so evident on the thoughts of the Protestant lay leader were landmarks to only one portion of his identity. Though he could be moved by his sense of "moral law" and Christian duty to talk of sharing and cooperation, he could be moved by other things to talk in other ways as well: by the economic interests of his clients, by the politico-economic interests of his country, by his own political and diplomatic ambitions.

What of the relative power of these various drives? Did Dulles accord one or another some clear priority during the war years? Not in any decisive fashion. In a perhaps very human way, he seems to have allowed the different drummers to whom he was attentive to produce varying rhythms in varying circumstances. Sometimes his multiple motives simply existed side by side and independently, each functioning in some, but not all situations: e.g., his concern for discerning the nature of moral law was important to his role as a Protestant lay leader, but irrelevant to his Republican activities. Sometimes his perceptions of various goals reenforced each other in his own mind: e.g., his clear continuing conviction that international economic reforms would yield both peace and prosperity for all and the solution to major economic problems faced by his own country. And sometimes, finally, they could pull in opposite directions. The "domestic jurisdiction" controversy was the most interesting example of this possibility. When faced with his colleagues' clear determination to safeguard their sensibilities about meddling in the internal affairs of the United States, he abandoned his own and his church commission's long-held belief in the importance of whittling away at this kind of narrow, virtually autarchic outlook. As has been shown, he stated his own position at first and then backed off and actually worked as a guard dog for the contrary-minded. Dulles may have behaved in this way because of his sense of the broadly political importance of cooperating with administration leaders or men like Arthur Vandenberg. He may, alternatively, have been persuaded of the greater importance of protecting American interests, particularly given the general feeling of skepticism about the evolving shape of the Economic and Social Council: the goal of American national interest may have transcended attachment to the specific mode of Christ-like cooperation for achieving it. In either case, it seems clear that this was a situation in which Dulles demonstrated his ability to drift away from the ethical standards he could so eloquently discuss.

Dulles himself seems neither to have been disturbed by variations in his motives nor even cognizant of some of the contradictions implicit within them. Frederick Libby of the National Council for Prevention of War, in fact, once admitted to some confusion as to the identity of the real Dulles and was quickly reassured by his old colleague: ". . . I find myself in general agreement . . . when you are speaking as the chairman of the Commission on a Just and Durable Peace," Libby wrote. "It is when your client is our State Department that I find divergence between our positions." To which, Dulles replied:

> . . . I am not aware of having departed, in an official capacity, from what I have advocated as Chairman of the Commission on a Just and Durable Peace. On the contrary, at San Francisco and at London I stood strongly for the principles which the Commission had advocated and to a considerable extent those principles became the official American position. Of course, one who has official responsibility must conduct himself somewhat differently from one who, as a private citizen, stands on the side-lines giving advice. I am sure you realize that.[63]

In 1945 Dulles clearly saw himself moving into the future with consistent principles. He continued to operate with a series of basic assumptions that had figured in his thoughts since 1919: that the political and economic affairs of the international arena required stabilization and reform; that this would be fundamentally desirable for all, Americans and non-Americans alike. He did give vent to headier sermons on the general permeability of advantage as the years went on and added political ambition to his critic's role, but neither would have struck him as inherently contradictory. He never stopped discussing the needs of his own country after all, and went on joining idealism with self-interest as long before. And as far as politicking was concerned, it could easily have been seen as a matter of altering personal day-to-day activities, not fundamental ethical or politico-economic concerns. At various times prior to the mid-1940s, it might have been seen as such. If in 1924 some would have wondered about the tenuous linkage of a pragmatic, "realistic" perspective with a religious and moralistic emphasis, Dulles would have wondered too. "Our national policy, dictated by our national self-interest, calls for the economic rehabilitation of Europe," he said then. "I doubt if there is anything particularly moral about our position. It is true that our program does involve an improvement in conditions in other nations, but our interest in this improvement is not so much altruistic as due to the fact that they are at once our customers and our debtors. . . ." As late as 1940, he would still have been pointed and dubious. "I do not know of any nation which accepts for its sovereignty limitations based upon moral standards," he explained in a letter about his lack of enthusiasm for the Allied war effort. "Each nation professes that its action is in accordance with moral standards, but actually this constitutes an attempt to cloak self-interest in ways which will appeal to those of its members who have moral standards. . . ."[64]

Dulles lost this sense of the subtle, yet significant tension between various kinds of human and national motives in the 1940s. Had he not, in his own day-to-day experiences, succeeded in blending what had seemed divergent tendencies—becoming an outspoken Protestant leader while remaining a highly successful corporation lawyer and analyst of the politico-economic interests of the United States? Had he not thereby added an intense ethical and religious thrust to a still solid base of traditional concerns? His certitude about the logic and legitimacy of doing this was thus built into the brick and mortar of his own existence by the 1940s and was to remain with him for the rest of his life.

11

Putting on the Cold War Armor, 1945–1946

GERMANY SURRENDERED ON May 8, 1945, Japan on August 15. Unbridled celebrations were inevitable. In Times Square, Piccadilly, Red Square—and almost anywhere else that people could gather—thousands thronged and danced and sang: photographs of them are like time capsules filled with exploding joy.

If John Foster Dulles joined in the revelries that came with the end of war, the effects wore off quickly. Like some other government leaders or informed observers in the Allied countries, he was essentially too realistic to get caught up in the frenzy of celebration for very long. He had had his moments of excitement in 1942 and 1943, when he came close to turning his Commission on a Just and Durable Peace into the vanguard of a millennial crusade, but he had checked himself and reverted to the calmer, sometimes cynical mood in which he had first contemplated the Second World War. All through 1944 and early 1945, he tried to defuse what seemed a great potential for disillusionment: Americans and others should be temperate in their expectations, he urged, and should prepare themselves for a long, hard struggle on behalf of future peace and prosperity. "All humanity is in an abnormal mental state," he wrote at one point. "Inevitably hatred, vengefulness, fear and greed are in the ascendency." On another occasion, in February 1945, he said: "Half of the population of the world—one billion people—face today the task of rebuilding an economic, social and political order. All of their established institutions have been swept away."[1] There was potential for vast, almost cataclysmic trouble here, and Dulles had no hope of finding some facile way of avoiding it.

With a mind set like this, Dulles was never shocked as the problems he had anticipated began to unfold at the war's end. "We have entered upon a critical and difficult period," he told American Protestants in yet one more widely circulated statement, this one in November 1945. "Common threats to the general welfare" were to be found on every hand, "all too plentifully":

> There are the economic dislocations and maladjustments that produce human want and fear. There are political maladjustments that repress natural human aspirations. There is the menace of militarism and the necessity for controlling such forces as atomic energy. There is exploitation and repression of dependent peoples. There are denials of human rights and fundamental freedoms.

The essence of this litany was repeated many times in the months just after the end of the war. "We are at the beginning of a long and difficult negotiation which will involve the structure of the post-war world," he wrote in October 1945. Those who had just celebrated the end of bloodshed, he said in November, "are experiencing one phase of the cycle whereby, in the past, war has always perpetuated itself."

> This time we must break the cycle. We have what may be mankind's last chance. With the development of atomic power, traditional conceptions of security are obsolete. The most powerful nation might now be conquered in a day. Another great war will release forces which might even leave the earth lifeless like other planets.

Men confronted "an unsettled world" with "unruly elements" threatening to get out of hand, he said in December. In fact, as he put it dramatically in April 1946, it was "a world which seems largely a vacuum, so far as faith and order are concerned."

> Asia, Africa and South America are lacking in healthy societies. Most of Continental Europe is in postwar demoralization, accentuated by indecisive and incoherent attitudes toward Germany. The capitalistic centers, notably the British Empire and the United States, have developed

some major defects. One of these is imperialism, with its by-product of racial intolerance. Another is the failure to maintain steady production and employment.[2]

At the end of the First World War, Dulles had expressed similar concerns about the grave problems that might follow a long period of bloodletting. Then, he had gone back to Sullivan & Cromwell and issued occasional storm warnings from an observer's vantage point on the sidelines of the global diplomatic arena. At the end of the Second World War, he was neither anxious nor forced to move to this kind of position again. His ambition, his skills, and the internal dynamics of Washington politics in the 1940s, on the contrary, conspired to move him closer and closer to the center of the stage of American foreign policy making and international relations.

In particular, President Truman and each of his successive Secretaries of State came to Dulles again and again in the aftermath of the San Francisco Conference. In order to strengthen bipartisan support for their foreign policies, they offered him a variety of positions which cumulatively demonstrate the direction he was taking. On the United Nations front, he went on to serve as a member of the U.S. delegations to the early 1946 session of the General Assembly in London and at succeeding sessions in New York in 1947, Paris in 1948, and back in New York in 1950. He was also quickly drawn into the work of the Council of Foreign Ministers, attending its meetings in London in 1945, in Moscow and London in 1947, and in Paris in 1949. His most extensive official responsibilities came with his appointment as "consultant" to the Department of State for negotiation of the Japanese Peace Treaty, an undertaking that preoccupied his time and energy from April 1950 until early 1952. In addition, Dulles was consulted more informally on a number of occasions. Participation in State Department discussions of Germany, the organization of NATO, the Berlin crisis, and Korea brought him periodically into a kind of inner circle of American policy makers: indeed, his influence within that circle was greater than any number of the more prominent members of the Truman Administration.

All in all, Dulles moved rapidly to the high plain he had set his sights on only in the early 1940s. Decisive power remained very much out of his hands between 1945 and 1952, to be sure: he was often "in" but not "of" the central directorate of foreign policy makers. Still, he was close enough to the core for satisfaction. As an indication of this, and of longer range ambitions, he began to reapportion his time among what had become the various major interests of his life. The Federal Council of Churches was the first to feel the effect. Though the Commission on a Just and Durable Peace lingered on into 1946, its raison d'être became more ambiguous in the postwar era: Dulles found little reason to turn to it with the intensity he had shown earlier, and no other church-related undertaking came even remotely close to attracting a similar commitment. Sullivan & Cromwell began to decline in importance for him as well, albeit more slowly. He remained managing partner of the firm until 1949 and active with a certain number of important problems and clients, yet it was clear that he was no longer according this work the primacy that it had held in earlier years. His own timetable would have had him severing ties completely in 1948, to become Tom Dewey's Secretary of State. As it turned out, this did not happen until his appointment as consultant for negotiation of the Japanese Peace Treaty in 1950. Afterwards, thanks to Dwight Eisenhower, he never had to return.[3]

Besides diplomacy, only political activities absorbed as much time as Dulles had given them prior to the end of World War II. Ongoing association with Dewey, continuing efforts to keep in touch with all wings of the G.O.P., gradual acceptance as a Republican figure equal in status and authority to Arthur Vandenberg: these were all part of Dulles's political life after 1945, and none would have been possible without serious commitment. It may have been an increasingly heightened partisanship that led Dulles to give unstintingly of his time to politicking while he was backing away from church-related work and corporate law. He would no doubt also have been fully aware of the way in which his role within the Republican Party was inextricably bound up with his foreign policy making ambitions.

As Dulles edged toward power after 1945, what did he want to do with it? This is a central question for any understanding of his evolving thoughts on international affairs, of course, particularly important because it concerns the period immediately preceding his tenure as Secretary of State. No simple answer would be truly satisfactory and in many respects the entire balance of this volume is designed to cover the subject in its complexity and subtlety. To telescope somewhat, it could be suggested that Dulles wanted to do two things as he participated in the shaping of American foreign policy.

First, he was anxious to deal with the range of problems he had been studying for more than a quarter of a century. Most basically, he wanted to break the vicious cycle of economic crisis and war that had plagued mankind and to see the dawn of an era of peace and prosperity. To do this, he wanted a strong, mature United States to accept its responsibilities. Americans, he felt, could lead others away from economic autarchy and its inevitable political and military repercussions, could lead others toward a more integrated and rational community of nations. Such thoughts were very much on Dulles's mind when the fighting ceased in 1945, and they remained there for the rest of his life.

Second, Dulles proved anxious to deal with major problems that were new to the international arena, those which arose for the first time after the war's end or whose seriousness only became apparent to him at that time. In the 1945–1952 period, this translated most significantly into great concern for the menace of the Soviet Union and what Dulles came to see as the international communist conspiracy. There were other emerging interests as well, though some became fully obvious only after he became Secretary of State: these would include attentiveness to left-wing leaders and movements in general and to the sometimes related question of rising nationalism in the underdeveloped world.

Dulles's reputation would suggest that his "new" concerns after World War II quickly eclipsed his "old." His image seems strikingly clear: that of a Cold Warrior par excellence who demonstrated again and again an overwhelming preoccupation with the dangers posed by the warlords of the Kremlin. This is an "image," however, and it can be argued that it is far too simplistic. It has emerged in a way that takes too little account of who Dulles was and what his life experiences had been prior to the onset of the Cold War. It has emerged, as well, because of too much attention to the man's public statements and inadequate efforts to dig deeply into what was said and done behind the façade.

Dulles *was* an anticommunist in his sentiments—and sincerely so—but there are important qualifications that must be made to the conventional image. He was, first, a man who came late in life to strong convictions on this matter. When he did, second, he proved quite capable of adding a melodramatic quality to his public statements about it which did not always mesh with his private feelings. Both of these factors will be specifically considered in this chapter. And, third, he was much more than *just* an anticommunist and probably not even *primarily* an anticommunist: one can easily imagine many of his basic thoughts on international affairs and many of his proposals for American foreign policy emerging after World War II even without the provocative presence of the Soviet Union. This will become clearer in succeeding chapters dealing with Dulles's approach to the specific problems that developed in Europe and the Far East after 1945.

I

Dulles's first systematic effort at analysis of the "international communist conspiracy" came in a lengthy memorandum drafted in the spring of 1946. Pressed by Arthur Vandenberg and induced by Henry Luce, he polished his writing and agreed to publish his appraisal in *Life* magazine: it appeared in two lengthy instalments in June 1946, under the title "Thoughts on Soviet Foreign Policy and What to Do About It."

Dulles clearly hoped his articles would provide an educational shock to its readers. As he put it to one editor, "I am very hopeful that through this presentation the American people can be aroused to the danger they face in time to ward it off without another war." The "danger," as he saw it, was the effort of Soviet leaders to achieve world domination. Some of his opening sentences laid out his perspective quite clearly:

> The makers of Soviet foreign policy take seriously the fact that the world *is* "one world" and that peace *is* "indivisible." These phrases, which are catch-words and slogans for us, are the basic premises of Soviet foreign policy. The primary purpose of that policy is to achieve peace, security and opportunity for the Soviet Union. Those are the usual goals of every foreign policy. But, since, to the Soviet leaders, the world is one world and since peace is indivisible, peace and security are considered by them to depend upon *eradicating the non-Soviet type of society which now dangerously divides the one world into incompatible halves.* That also, they think, will be good for the world, for the Soviet type of proletariat dictatorship, originated to promote the welfare of the masses and to end the exploitation of man by man is considered the ideal kind of government. [Emphasis added.]

This Soviet push for global power was built upon what Dulles saw as ruthless intolerance for those things that Americans prized in their way of life. If successful in creating their *"Pax Sovietica,"* Kremlin leaders would "eliminate what, to us, are the essentials of a free society"; their efforts were "repugnant to our ideas of humanity and fair play."

For Dulles, Soviet behavior was a three-pronged menace. Looking toward maximum authority, policy makers in the Kremlin had divided the world into an "Inner Zone," a "Middle Zone," and an "Outer Zone." Each prompted the development of different techniques, though all were linked as far as long-range goals were concerned. By the Inner Zone, Dulles meant those territories that had already been formally incorporated into the U.S.S.R. "on the basis of historic, strategic or ideological considerations." From an uncertain base in 1917, this geographic core had grown enormously. It stretched "in a great arc" from parts of Finland to Sakhalin and the Kuriles. And looking at Moscow's behavior in the Middle East, Dulles concluded "There is no reason to believe that expansion has come to an end."

Control of the Inner Zone was direct and total. Though this was the preferred arrangement for Soviet leaders, it was not yet possible away from their home base. The Middle Zone was "territory which surrounds the Inner Zone, which is not yet ripe for incorporation into the U.S.S.R." In the west, it included Soviet-occupied Germany and virtually all Eastern Europe; in Asia, it was Outer Mongolia, Manchuria, the northern half of Korea, and China's Sin Kiang province. Dulles thought concentrated efforts were being made to add to these territories Greece, Iran, Turkey, Kurdistan, and the southern half of Korea. The shared characteristic of such diverse components, in Dulles's mind, was that all were amenable to the influence of the Soviet army. In some cases, military occupation was actually the case. Elsewhere:

> Where there is no present occupation, there is fear of it and the governments there, while nominally independent and in some respects actually independent, are under strong inducement to *put their foreign policy, their armies and, most important of all, their secret police and censorship into the hands of persons who take much guidance from Moscow.* Thus the Soviet leaders assure that the character of these governments will be friendly. [Emphasis added.]

Troubled though he was at the dynamics of Moscow's intrusion into the affairs of its near neighbors, Dulles's greatest concern seems to have been for the still longer Soviet reach toward the Outer Zone. Comprising all the rest of the world, it was "sufficiently distant, physically, from Soviet land power so that 'friendly' governments cannot be achieved by direct power methods." Undaunted by this predicament, however, Soviet leaders had devised a variety of methods to bring different areas more and more under their sway. In some parts of the Outer Zone, for example, Soviet leaders sought to undermine existing systems through nominally national communist parties. Maneuvering in normal political channels or disrupting the political and economic life of their societies when it suited them, these local communist parties attempted to serve the larger aims of Soviet foreign policy. Dulles was especially troubled by the obstructive efforts of the French and Italian communists with respect to "a political or economic union of the Western European powers." Moscow "wishes to keep these nations divided lest, united, they develop an influence which might counter that of the Soviet Union in the European Middle Zone." Acting on orders, Dulles maintained, local communist parties became strident and influential voices of Soviet opposition within France and Italy.

Elsewhere in the Outer Zone, when formal communist parties were illegal or ineffective, Soviet leaders opted for "influence . . . through small, well-disciplined minorities. These work their way into positions of influence in large factional blocs and can even be a balance of power where major political parties clearly divide the voting strength." In Latin America, for example, "extreme left wing agitators" were taking advantage of postwar economic difficulties to encourage unrest among susceptible workers. And on a larger scale, the Soviet Union was making a successful drive to turn the recently created World Federation of Trade Unions into a conduit for its political influence. Dulles saw the W.F.T.U. as comprised of "the left wing of labor" and argued that "the communists and communist sympathizers among them exert concerted influence along lines favored by the Soviet Union."

Finally, Moscow was paying special attention to those large portions of the Outer Zone that were less than fully self-governing. Seeing 750,000,000 people in colonial dependency as a great opportunity, "Soviet leaders stimulate the independence movements and give them moral leadership. They encourage revolution, rather than evolution, as being apt to result in governments which will break completely with those who now govern." Dulles seemed particularly concerned about Soviet efforts to "woo" the Arab world in the mid-1940s. At the Security Council, they "went to extremes" in pushing for the withdrawal of French and British troops from Syria and Lebanon. Dulles commented ruefully on the way this encouraged further "unrest in French Morocco, Algiers and Tunisia."

Given his contention that Moscow's goal was ruthless repression of all, it is no wonder that Dulles spoke of the great "danger" facing the United States of 1946. His description of the Soviet Union portrayed it as an awesome foe. To its global pretensions, bad enough in themselves, he saw added an ability to devise perversely shrewd policies. How could Americans not be deeply worried by a great power bent on ends so averse to their own perceived desires—and so ready to develop such a variety of tools to meet diverse geographical and political situations? For Dulles, the "spectacular successes" of Soviet leaders underlined the frightening dimensions of this combination. Cementing their control at home, they had gone on to realize "most of the extreme aspirations of the Tzars." They had surrounded themselves with subservient states and become a powerful force "everywhere" in the world. As Dulles put it: "Few men in political life anywhere act without first thinking about whether they will please or displease the leaders of the Soviet Union. Never in history have a few men in a single country achieved such world-wide influence."[4]

Reading Dulles's *Life* articles recalls George Kennan's hindsight reaction to his own famous analysis of Soviet foreign policy (written just a few weeks earlier): "Much of it reads exactly like one of those primers put out by alarmed congressional committees or by the Daughters of the American Revolution, designed to arouse the citizenry to the dangers of the Communist conspiracy."[5] The Dulles pieces do tend to the melodramatic. Alarmist in tone, they have a powerful thrust that links up easily with their author's later reputation.

But Dulles's "primer" emerged from a gestation that was quite different from Kennan's. The foreign service officer's analysis was a distillation of suspicious reactions that had surfaced during early days in the field and were verbalized again and again until, in finely polished form, they finally caught influential eyes in Washington in 1946. Dulles's *Life* articles had no such neat and highly cultivated roots. He had come much more slowly to his conclusions, and only after June 1946 did he go on to hone them to their notorious sharpness. In earlier years, he had simply not had any steady perspective on the Soviet Union's international role. During most of the interwar period, there had not even been much interest. His concern arose through subtle but significant stages. It came to rest only in April 1946, when he sat down to appraise systematically what had begun to seem an interrelated series of postwar problems. Only then, he confessed to colleagues on the Commission on a Just and Durable Peace, did he feel "clear enough in my own mind about Russian foreign policy to feel like giving leadership in any particular direction."[6] The intellectual convolutions which led up to this moment make Dulles a fascinating, though surely not unique, figure in the United States of the 1940s. His experience contrasts with that of men like Kennan and suggests another pattern for the emergence of the American Cold Warrior.

Of course, Dulles's experiences more than a quarter-century before the drafting of his *Life* articles provided the real roots of his Cold War attitudes. As a lower-echelon member of Woodrow Wilson's Administration between 1917 and 1919, he had witnessed and shared the first reactions to the Bolshevik Revolution.

He had been surrounded then by men who felt revulsion at the violence and chaos associated with the communists. The Bolsheviks in Russia and their counterparts in Eastern Europe were perceived as threats to Western civilization, giving rise to anguished deliberations in many capitals. Secretary of State Lansing, Dulles's uncle, was typically vitriolic, offering numerous descriptions of "anarchy" and "the fires of terrorism," while warning that "the flames are sweeping westward." Although he did not speak like Lansing at that time, Dulles almost certainly shared the perspective he represented. As a government functionary in Washington and then Paris, he joined in a variety of policy debates and programs specifically aimed at crushing the revolutionary menace. His work at the War Trade Board in 1918, for example, included participation in a scheme designed to stymie the Bolsheviks in Siberia: the Russian Bureau which he served as treasurer became a conduit for shipping goods to favored Czech and Kolchak forces.[7]

There was a momentum in Dulles's attentiveness to Bolshevism that carried him somewhat beyond his government service. During a 1920 business trip, he went to great lengths to witness first-hand the activities of the "Red Guards" in Germany. The result was several alarmed letters about the collapse of business and order. But the sense of crisis, for Dulles and others, waned after 1920. While the mood of disapproval surely lingered, it did so in a decidedly lower key. Time had shown that the Bolsheviks would need their greatest energy to control affairs within Russia itself and that even Eastern Europe could be saved from the deluge. The Soviet Union actually became a backwater of international affairs as far as Dulles was concerned, and he seldom commented on its place in the world order of the 1920s and 1930s. He went so far as to criticize the "absurdity" of nonrecognition of the Soviet government by the United States as early as 1924, although he made it clear that "recognition does not imply amity or friendship." Other than this, observations on Russian affairs were limited to an occasional word on business matters. He found distasteful the Bolsheviks' "obvious disregard of contractual obligations," a conclusion brought home by his work for the New York Life Insurance Company.[8]

The significant role of the Soviet Union in World War II forced another twist in Dulles's perspective. He slowly grew more attentive to Moscow's role in international affairs and even started to become vocal about issues that would soon be seen as intrinsic to the Cold War. What he had to say during the war often contrasts sharply with the position that emerged in 1946, however. His views were quite complex and especially intriguing because of his later reputation. Particularly important was his tendency to see a problem with two relatively distinct faces: one, the Soviet Union as a great power and a force in world affairs and, two, the Soviet Union as the almost coincidental seat of communist ideology.

Dulles became explicit about *communism* as he developed his own grand reform schemes. He began to perceive it as a rival "faith." All of his work with the Commission on a Just and Durable Peace, for example, was designed to chart a route away from the cycle of economic crisis and war which he believed inherent in the existing world order. Like Woodrow Wilson before him, he approached the problem from a reformer's perspective and favored moderate, peaceful changes to accomplish a long-range goal. Communism, on the other hand, like "fascism," Dulles considered "an alien faith," committed to "worldwide realization through world revolution." Its approach and methods went against the very grain of his own identity.

Dulles did not comment often on the revolutionary faith of communism during World War II, but when he did he clearly indicated his sense of it as an explicit alternative or a dangerous challenge to his own proposals. In May 1941, he wrote about the early work of his church commission to Arthur Sulzberger: "I am convinced that if we are to be successful in overcoming revolutionary movements, such as those which spring from Russia and Germany, we must have some affirmative and dynamic program of our own." And as he put it to one business associate, "I hope to avoid . . . in this country" the kind of "loose thinking and . . . strong tendency toward Marxism" which he perceived among church leaders in England; he confessed to feeling "somewhat discouraged, as I have so far been unable to find any economists who have thought through a solution of such problems as unemployment without coming to a rather extreme form of state socialism." On another occasion, he laid out the dichotomy in way that testifies to the precision of his perception. In looking toward a new world order, he wrote:

> There are two ways of transition. One is through catastrophe. This is the Russian program. Lenin foresaw that another general war would complete that which the World War had so well begun. He saw that it would so disrupt and sicken society as to lead to mass revolt. . . .
> The other way of transition is a peaceful and gradual one, which will build upon, rather than destroy, the experience, culture, personal liberty and material comforts which the old order has given us. . . .[9]

While Dulles's comments on communism were sharp, they were few and far between. Compared to his extensive analysis of other problems, they suggest a reservoir of hostile attitudes existing somewhat below the surface—present, but generally out of sight. In contrast, his comments on the Soviet Union were extensive and remarkably temperate. He was not blind, of course, to the presumably symbiotic relationship of communist ideology and Soviet statehood. Occasionally, very occasionally, he even linked the two in some explicit way, as in his comment on the Russian–Leninist program for a new world order. In the context of the war years, however, it was overwhelmingly more common to find Dulles separating the two factors and opting for a less simplistic, ultimately more ambiguous reading. What he perceived was a powerful nation whose existence and actions in the world arena were much more (or much less) than a straightforward function of an encompassing ideology.

Where Dulles had ignored or made testy comments about the Soviet Union earlier, the war years brought different reactions. There was dawning respect, for example. Great military campaigns spurred tribute to "Russia's magnificent performance," leading at one point to his statement that "if we win this war it will be largely with the help of the Russian and Chinese man-power." As he put it in early 1944, "We have, in this war, come to a new understanding of Russia. The devoted and sacrificial and immensely successful effort of the Russian people shows values to which we had been blind." There was also awareness of the long-range impact of this. The vast armies that would help bring victory would make of the Soviet Union "a formidable force" when peace arrived, Dulles concluded as early as January 1942. He paid more and more attention to such a new variable in his estimations of the post-war world.[10]

What he saw when looking forward did not please him. Quite early, he became convinced that Americans were allowing wartime enthusiasm to blind them to certain characteristics of the Soviet Union that were bound to cause problems. "We tend to be much too idealistic, particulary in terms of the other fellow," he wrote in March 1943, "and we are in for some rude shocks, particularly from Russia." Camaraderie under fire would give way to serious disagreements in the victors' camp.

What else could be expected, Dulles felt, given significant differences in the respective nature of Allied societies? Where the United States and Great Britain prided themselves on political freedom, the Soviet Union had developed a thoroughly undemocratic order. Where "religious and intellectual liberty" existed in the West, none was to be found in the Soviet Union. While Americans thought often in terms of "the moral law," the Soviets attended solely to "material force." And where free enterprise and capitalism were the accepted economic traditions in the United States and Great Britain, state socialism or communism dominated the Soviet Union.[11]

What else but serious disagreement could be expected, as well, given the very different desires of the Soviet Union and the United States for the postwar world? Already in the summer of 1942, while on a church-related visit to England, Dulles found himself regularly discussing Soviet plans for Eastern Europe. American Ambassador Winant informed him of British inclinations to give in to territorial demands that would have let the Russians "have a large slice of Poland and Bessarabia and the Baltic States." His friend Eduard Beneš also talked with him about his intention of keeping Czechoslovakia on friendly terms with the Soviet Union and about his belief that "Poland has got to agree to shrink up so that they will not offend Russia." In Dulles's estimation, Americans were not likely to accept Soviet desires in this area very happily: they clashed too obviously with the democratic principles around which the great war effort was being rallied. As he put it in February 1943:

> . . . we have an interest which is sentimental, and derived also from large immigration, in the small Baltic countries, such as Finland, Latvia, Estonia and Lithuania. There is also a very strong Polish population and a strong sympathy for Poland. These Baltic and Polish peoples will look to the United States to champion their cause as against what may be strategic conceptions of Russia.

This early awareness of Soviet desires for Eastern Europe did not fade as the war went on. It remained in the forefront of Dulles's perception of Soviet foreign policy, a regular source of concern.[12]

Nor was Eastern Europe the only region in which Dulles envisioned American dissatisfaction with long-range Soviet goals. "It seems to me," he wrote in early 1943, "that provocation is inherent in our two nations' different attitude toward the areas of Russia's contact with the rest of the world in both the east and the west." He noted the China situation in particular, arguing that with peace "the old struggle between the so-called 'Red Army' group and the Kuomintang group will probably break out and then have to be resolved. As before, Russian sympathy will undoubtedly be with the Red Army group, and, as before, our sympathies will preponderantly be with the Kuomintang group and the Soong dynasty."[13]

Yet other contrasts between Soviet and American thinking on the postwar world stemmed from their differing approaches to a new international organization. Dulles became quite involved with planning for the United Nations and was very conscious of limited Russian enthusiasm. "The different Russian philosophy makes it extremely difficult to produce anything which Anglo-Saxons would regard as fundamentally sound and inspiring," he explained on one occasion. The key problem seemed to be that the Soviet Union had "made it clear beyond possibility of doubt that she is not going to renounce any of her sovereignty."[14]

Sightings of such unattractive ingredients in Soviet society and foreign policy would provide the ammunition for many of Dulles's blasts in the Cold War. It is significant, however, that they were approached very differently during World War II. Though one can never doubt Dulles's essential distaste, he dealt with his perceptions of Soviet characteristics in a consciously temperate fashion that is in sharp contrast to subsequent patterns.

Both a sign and a source of Dulles's calm approach was his usual wartime habit of drawing a distinction between communism as an ideology and the Soviet Union as a state. Almost invariably in these years, his hostility to the former simply did not link up with his evaluation of the latter. Soviet leaders were not yet seen as ideologues seeking global communism via world revolution. When Dulles discussed their goals, he did so as if he were appraising a rather traditional great power. As he put it decisively in early 1944, "The Russian revolution swept away the Czars and all of their institutions. But *the foreign policy of the U.S.S.R. today is that of Peter the Great.*" The result was a pursuit of *national* interest which had varying components in Dulles's analyses. Among the earliest he identified was the devotion of Soviet leaders to the future protection of their country. "A vital objective of Russia, as for the rest of the world, is that of achieving security," he wrote in mid-1943. He argued along these lines that "nations that have the power to do so will usually seek strategic boundaries unless satisfied that their security can equally or better be served in some other way." This translated into special concern for Eastern Europe, where Dulles recognized the importance of "the strategic conceptions" of Soviet leaders. Beyond this goal, Dulles did believe that Moscow was aiming for a general expansion of its power and influence, but that it had a perspective with definite geographical limits. Quite regularly in 1944 and 1945, he would sight the desire of Soviet leaders to create a "sphere of influence" along their borders, particularly in the west. "Their political thinking at the moment," he said in November 1944, "runs primarily in terms of regional arrangements." In contrast to his own desire for true international collaboration, he wrote on another occasion, the Russians favored "separate, regional responsibility."[15]

These goals of Soviet foreign policy were troublesome as far as Dulles was concerned, but they were not uniquely so. They contributed to an international situation in which the United States would have disagreements with the Soviet Union that would not be very different from those with other great powers. Dulles was disturbed by Great Britain's tendencies to pursue a "sphere of influence" policy, for example, and commented regularly on it. He was bothered by talk of a British–Russian deal over Eastern Europe, by London's jockeying for position with Charles de

John Foster Dulles at age 7 (left) and his younger brother Allen.

The Princeton University graduate, 1908.

With his wife, Janet Avery Dulles, at
Schönbrunn, April 1928.

In Berlin, 1933.

The delegates to the Princeton Roundtable organized by the Commission on a Just and Durable Peace, July 1943. Dulles is in the front row, 7th from the left.

Secretary of State George Marshall (left) and Dulles during the United Nations General Assembly meetings, Paris, 1948.

Secretary of State Dean Acheson (front row, third from left) and Dulles during the Paris Council of Foreign Ministers session, June 1949.

The Dulleses listening to election returns, November 1949.

In the General Assembly,
1947.

With General Douglas
MacArthur, June 1950.

Inspecting the 38th parallel, Korea, June 1950.

With Syngman Rhee, June 1950.

With Japanese Prime Minister
Yoshida, January 1951.

With a model of the Kobe
shipyard, Japan, December
1951.

A photograph utilized on thousands of postcards during the 1949 Senate campaign.

Gaulle, and by British reserve concerning the new United Nations Organization. In one critical commentary in 1945, he singled out Churchill and Stalin as figures equally responsible for the emerging regional tendencies he opposed. Looking at the Prime Minister, it could be said that "the present arrangement is primarily due to the fact that Mr. Churchill's great ambition lies, not in establishing world order, but in preserving an Empire which, he has asserted, will not be voluntarily liquidated so long as he is the King's first minister."

Nor, for that matter, was the Soviet Union totally unlike the United States. During World War II, Dulles revealed an occasional and intriguing awareness of analogies to Russian behavior in the American past. In February 1944, he responded to one too self-satisfied citizen by writing:

> "Aggression" is a subtle thing. Does it include economic aggression? Some nations are in a position by economic pressures to coerce others. We have not infrequently done this over the past. And does it include political interference in another country which brings about revolutionary change of government from which a foreign nation is a beneficiary, as, for example, *Texas, Panama and, perhaps now, Poland?* [Emphasis added.]

Somewhat earlier, Dulles had written a doubtlessly unappealing letter to Henry Luce about some articles on American foreign policy and international law.

> I confess to being one of those lawyers who do not regard "international law as law at all" because, among other things, *no nation is, or feels bound to conform to any course of action other than its own interest* and, as Mr. Jessup says, international law "can be twisted to suit any national interest." He suggests that we [the U.S.] are an exception. But that is not accurate. [Emphasis added.]

In a later speech, he gave an example of the reasoning behind this contention:

> Most of the expansion of the American nation has been through war or the threat of war. Was that illegal and should the United States have been forever confined to its original strip of territory along the Atlantic seaboard? How about the way we got Texas? To turn to current politics, how about the rebirth of Russia and the dynamism of the U.S.S.R.? There are no legal principles which enable us to redetermine the boundaries of Poland.[16]

In addition to these comparisons, Dulles made clear in other ways that he did not yet perceive the Soviet Union as a singularly dangerous force in international affairs. Much of his wartime work with the Commission on a Just and Durable Peace offers testimony to the unstrained approach he had developed. The attempt by Dulles and his colleagues to walk a line between inspirational leadership and intelligent idealism is especially pertinent. Throughout the last two years of the war, they were anxious to push for postwar reforms that would yield a more peaceful and prosperous world order, yet were so conscious of the dangers of mass disillusionment that they repeatedly emphasized how slow progress was likely to be. The key goal they set was ongoing collaboration and consultation among the Allies, designed to lead toward a better future. Nothing should be allowed to interfere with this, they argued, not even imperfect peace settlements or sometimes distasteful behavior by one or more great powers.

This line of reasoning had obvious implications for appraisals of Soviet foreign policy. In February 1943, Dulles sent Lord Astor a draft of the Six Pillars of Peace proposals. An accompanying letter catalogued the European and Asian problems that might develop because of Soviet goals, only to insist that British–American compromises with those goals would be eminently desirable if they led to continuing collaboration. Unless that goal were kept in mind, Dulles pointed out, "*we will almost surely become concentrated upon difficult problems of detail and of manoevre and will exaggerate their importance* and I feel very apprehensive as to the outcome" (emphasis added). He expressed similar thoughts to Franklin Roosevelt a month later when presenting the "Six Pillars of Peace" pronouncement. The President discussed problems with Eastern Europe and religious freedom, indicating that "he did not like the word 'compromise' but that there were some things that had to be compromised if collaboration was to be maintained." Dulles assured him that this was his Commission's precise concern:

> . . . that was a reason why we had expressed our propositions in terms of collaboration as an end in itself and that we were seeking to make people realize that collaboration, rather than any particular results of collaboration, was the thing that was of prime importance and that inevitably collaboration involved give and take and no one of the collaborators getting everything precisely in his own preferred way.[17]

This self-conscious "realism" concerning collaboration's immediate rewards marked Dulles attitudes toward the Soviet Union in sharp contrast with those of later years. None of Moscow's goals were yet perceived so negatively as to dampen his enthusiasm for cooperation, nor his conviction that cooperation was possible. Nor were these attitudes of short duration. Dulles's initial reactions to the Yalta agreements make it clear that what was said in 1943 was still being thought in early 1945. Where in later years he would use those agreements as a whip with which to lash

Democratic policy makers, his first assessment was one of relative praise. True, the specifics of the accords were unpalatable in part, particularly the territorial acquisitions of the Soviets and the lack of attention paid to the wishes of the Poles. Nevertheless, the crucial ingredient in Dulles's mind was that those specifics had been agreed upon by the three major Allies, consulting with each other in a way that boded well for the future.

> The Crimea Conference showed a revival, within the great alliance, of a will to collaborate for peace, as for war. . . . A new era was opened . . . in that the United States abandoned a form of aloofness which it had been practicing for many years and the Soviet Union permitted joint action on matters that it had the power to settle for itself. These are two momentous precedents.[18]

It should be indicated that the general context of his church commission's specific comments on Soviet foreign policy is also revealing of the nature of Dulles's wartime perceptions. Those comments were always part of surveys of world problems likely to emerge at war's end, part of, that is, the surveys Dulles offered to convince his colleagues and listeners that international peace and order were not going to be easily achieved in the immediate future. When his calculations included critical comments on Moscow's behavior, Dulles was clearly suggesting that he saw postwar difficulties coming from that direction. Nevertheless, the surveys *as a whole* reveal that he considered the behavior of the Soviets no more serious than a substantial number of other problems. Some of Dulles's statements, in fact, suggest that the Soviets were almost certainly *less* problematic in his mind. In February 1945, for example, he took one analytical tour of the globe which concluded that "in whatever direction we look, we face hard problems." In Europe, he saw no real signs that the conflict-causing attitudes and institutions of centuries would be spurned at war's end; in Latin America, he thought he could discern sure signs of social and economic "distress" that could affect the United States and perhaps the rest of the world; in Asia, he suggested the serious repercussions of a possible wave of "anti-foreign" sentiments; and in the United States, he feared lack of commitment to creative world leadership on the part of his fellow citizens. Included in this overview, following remarks on Asia and before those on the United States, was a paragraph that argued that the development of "more friendly relations with the Soviet Union" was a problem demanding serious attention. This speech as a whole, which is quite typical of his efforts during the war years, reveals the way in which the Soviet Union was only one item in the *range* of problems Dulles perceived. Unlike the statements of later years, there is no suggestion at all that Soviet leaders were in any way responsible for the other difficulties touched on. And, in addition, the placement of the problem of Russian–American relations after all but one other suggests that it was simply not in the forefront of Dulles's concerns.[19]

In the midst of Dulles's calm wartime appraisals of the Soviet Union, there were occasional flashes suggesting his special hostility or concern. Some of his contributions to the 1944 Republican presidential campaign are especially noteworthy. In the heat of battle, he demonstrated a capacity for hyperbole that would frequently be in evidence in later years. A draft for Dewey's last campaign speech is striking for its contention that Roosevelt had softened the Democratic party up for domination by communists. "He has felt he must say that he does not welcome the support of any person or group committed to Communism. That is as may be," Dulles wrote. "The important facts are, first, that Mr. Roosevelt has so weakened and corrupted the so-called Democratic Party that it is readily subject to capture, and, secondly, that the forces of communism are in fact, attempting that capture."

This was nonsense and Dulles must have known it since he never made such charges outside the campaign arena. A similar contrast between partisan and nonpartisan perceptions can be seen in a brief flurry concerning Dewey's charge that Roosevelt was not doing enough to aid freedom in Eastern Europe. When Walter Lippmann questioned the wisdom of such an assault, Dulles came to his candidate's defense. In spite of the lack of American power in countries like Poland, he wrote Lippmann, "all Poles who want their country free will be heartened by knowing that some of us still believe in what Mr. Roosevelt professed, in 1941 were our 'principles.' " "Moral force" could be used to aid Poland in its struggle with Soviet desires. This contention clashes with the more "realistic" position Dulles was fashioning for his church commission at precisely the same time. In conjunction with his other campaign contributions, it suggests that the smell of political powder could bring out the melodramatic in Dulles. Of course, Dulles's campaign performance may also demonstrate a respect for the utility of waving the red flag, a sense that anticommunism was an emotional issue that could pay handsome political dividends.[20]

II

Dulles's perspective on the Soviet Union altered yet again when he returned to government service in April 1945. As an American delegation adviser at the San Francisco Conference, which saw the founding of

the United Nations, he came into direct contact with Soviet representatives for the first time. This was quickly followed by his attendance at
the London meeting of the Council of Foreign Ministers (September
1945) and the first session of the United Nations General Assembly
(January–February 1946). The experiences of these eleven months
nudged Dulles into an analytical limbo. The relatively uniform temper-
ance of the preceding four years was replaced by a fairly fast-moving
counterpoint of hot and cool. Some developments suggested a Soviet
Union far more dangerous than he had imagined, a nation led by communists bent on revolutionary meddling in every quarter of the globe.
Other events, some as late as March 1946, seemed more typical of the rational policy makers he had earlier discussed: troublesome, but with ambitions limited to the creation of a rather traditional sphere of influence
along their borders. Such variant observations produced a basic am-
bivalence in Dulles between April 1945 and May 1946.

As Dulles's initial jump back into the fray, the San Francisco Conference was the most disturbing of his new diplomatic experiences.
Several developments led him to wonder if his preconceived notions
about Soviet indifference to international organization had been too
shallow. On the one hand, he believed he had underestimated Moscow's
determination to thoroughly cut off its desired sphere of influence from
the rest of the world. It was prepared to "deny any effective cooperation
with reference to its potential orbit," he concluded on one occasion; such
a policy "would remove from the effective concern of the World Organization a vast area embracing about half of the population of the world and
extending from the Pacific to the Atlantic." To compound this problem,
some developments led him to theorize about a yet more dangerous thrust
in Soviet policy toward the U.N. Could it be that the Soviets were hoping
to use the new body as "a high forum for spreading their views"? "Since he
had come to San Francisco," he told the U.S. delegation on May 8, "he
had concluded that they [Soviet leaders] would want an organization in
order to get the maximum possible voice *outside* their own sphere of influence. . . he believed they felt that, working through a world security
system, they might be able to influence areas outside their direct control."
Or, as he put it in a memorandum, there was much to suggest that the
Soviet Union wanted to "use the World Organization to stir up unrest in
the rest of the world." A related concern was his feeling that the Soviets
were trying to push the United States into accepting undesirable initiatives. Weeks of disagreement about the Security Council veto left
Dulles convinced that the U.S. had to stand firm on its position. Failure
to do so would be seen in Moscow "as a sign of weakness. It might make it
extremely difficult for the U.S. again to prevail in any international

277

negotiations with the U.S.S.R. and it would tempt the U.S.S.R. to keep on crowding the U.S. until dangerous friction developed."

Dulles's reactions to Soviet behavior at San Francisco provide the first signs that the two-faced problem he had considered during the war was being simplified in his mind. Though he does not seem to have been conscious of it, his very generalized condemnations of *communism's* striving for world revolution were being linked more symbiotically with analyses of *Soviet* foreign policy. The result was a far more troubling estimation of Moscow's ambitions, a great step beyond earlier assumptions about the desire to build a tightly defined sphere of influence.

In the months following San Francisco, Dulles made other biting comments on the motives behind Soviet foreign policy. Following his February 1946 return from the first meeting of the General Assembly, he was prepared to catalog any number of examples of Soviet expansion beyond some hypothetical sphere. For a group at the Council on Foreign Relations, he offered a staccato-like blast:

> ... The Russians, chiefly through "moral" leadership, are making political capital of explosive situations, stirring up trouble in Italy, the Balkans, Greece, and Egypt. In Italy the Communist party is strong. The present Bulgarian government is supported by the Soviets. In Greece, Britain is finding it exceedingly difficult to maintain a preponderant influence. The Russians are making inroads on the Arab League. They are holding out for Tripolitania and will certainly demand a change in the status of the Dardanelles. They have recently championed the cause of Syria and Lebanon more strongly than Syria and Lebanon themselves. In the Security Council they played the role of protector of oppressed peoples.

At the same time, he was becoming more scathingly critical of Soviet *methods*. In December 1945, he wrote to a business associate who was concerned about the state of Russian–American relations. "The leaders of the Soviet Union are dynamic and they are atheistic," he said. "That means that they do not have the restraints which inhibit those of static qualities, or moral restraints of the kind which tend to inhibit us." As a case in point he cited a recent Molotov speech which ascribed tough U.S. policies "to the fact that we felt we had the atomic bomb as a weapon to fall back on." This charge suggested a frightening ingredient in the Soviet mindset to Dulles. "Actually, of course, any use of the atomic bomb against Russia never entered our minds," he wrote. "The fact, however, that it entered Molotov's mind indicates what might have been the case had their position been reversed." Such concern was heightened during one January meeting of the General Assembly which Dulles often referred to in later months. In debate on a Refugee Resolution, the Soviets sought to justify the "purging" of free political expression from camps in which Poles, Yugoslavs, and other East Europeans were living:

> Other states espoused the practice of tolerance and freedom of political belief and expression. This led to one of the most dramatic episodes of the Conference, a debate where Mrs. Roosevelt, with moving simplicity, pleaded for tolerance, and where Mr. Vishinski, with the explosive power of a great prosecutor, denounced tolerance as a dangerous weakness.

(In his *Life* articles, Dulles recalled Vishinsky railing: "We do not want to accept tolerance. We paid too much for it.") The debate was "rather frightening," Dulles reported. He later maintained that it spurred some of his most serious doubts about the Soviet Union. In March, a radio interviewer asked him if "communism" and "democracy" could peacefully coexist. "That is a $64 question and I'm not sure I know the answer," he said. A recounting of the Vishinsky statement was then followed by the observation that "there is no doubt that we can get along in a world that is partly communistic. We have gotten along for a great many years in a world which contained many who believed in things that seemed to us strange and alien. The real problem is, do the leaders of the Soviet Union think that their society can exist in a world which also contains the freedoms in which we believe." In addition to the Vishinsky speech on tolerance, Dulles cited a statement by a Russian who was soon to be one of the secretaries of the United Nations: he "has said to me that he has real doubt as to whether the two societies can exist peacefully side by side."[21]

In spite of suspicions and criticisms such as these, Dulles shied away from thorough denunciation of Soviet foreign policy during the hectic months of 1945 and early 1946. In fact, the dominant tone of his commentary remained positive and temperate.

At San Francisco, his sharp salvos were usually followed by cool afterthought. One written discussion of Moscow's irritating and threatening behavior was summed up as follows:

> I want to make clear that I am by no means convinced that the Soviet Union intends to adopt such a policy as is above outlined. The actions . . . which cause present concern may largely be explained by distrust which carries over from twenty five years of isolation and hostility in the rest of the world, and also by the fact that probably there are military elements within the Soviet which are somewhat beyond the control of civilian policy. I think we must, as a working hypothesis, proceed on the assumption that Russia will come to practice genuine cooperation. We must be tolerant and give that assumption every chance to come true.

And in a post-Conference address to the Philadelphia Foreign Policy Association, he ran through a list of problems that had not been caused or exacerbated by Soviet leaders. He even waxed rhapsodic about an increasing spirit of cooperation which he had sensed in the closing days of the meeting:

> . . . overriding all of our differences there was a resolve to reach a common goal. . . . The dominant spirit was one of working together, not working against. Gradually, the differences came to seem less and less important. In the end, there came a profound sense of unity and of fellowship. I saw men who had engaged in tough debate embrace, while tears of joy dimmed their vision.[22]

This calmer, optimistic ingredient affected Dulles's policy recommendations at San Francisco and those recommendations, in turn, reflect the positiveness that still lay at the core of his thinking. On two controversial issues, regional security arrangements and the Security Council veto, he urged the American delegation to adopt a firm stand in opposition to Soviet efforts. If the United States made its position clear enough, strongly enough, he concluded, it would get what it wanted. With respect to regional security, he wrote, "we could get an exception for the Western Hemisphere without actually being driven out of Europe. The Russians, wanting to get as much as they could in the way of influence outside their own sphere, might be willing to *accept the best they could get*" (emphasis added). He was even more assured about the wisdom of firmness on the veto issue.

> It seems extremely unlikely that the U.S.S.R. would refuse to join the organization solely on the ground that the Conference had clarified the Charter in the sense of the interpretation of Yalta agreed to by the U.S., U.K., France and China. Whether the intentions of the U.S.S.R. are good or evil—and I assume that they are good—it will need to be a member of the Organization. It seems incredible that it would stay out because the United Nations here at San Francisco denied the Soviet Union a right hereafter to veto discussion by the Security Council. . . .[23]

All in all, Dulles's proposals emerged from a conviction that Soviet leaders were rational men, basically pragmatic in orientation, and likely to be accommodating when necessary. They were vexatious, but not yet part of some implacable Soviet-communist menace.

It is significant that similar perceptions ran through all of Dulles's thoughts during the September 1945 meeting of the Council of Foreign Ministers. While a member of the American delegation, Dulles was only rarely its spokesman, and he spent many hours simply listening to discussions and jotting down notes on the speeches and negotiating positions of various governments. By the end of the gathering, he had pieced together an outline of the principal issues and an overview of what he saw as very disagreeable Soviet behavior. A peace treaty with Italy was the first important item on the Council agenda. It produced almost unrelieved contention: the Soviets pushed for Yugoslav control of Trieste, the Americans for a boundary following ethnic lines; the Soviets demanded substantial reparations, the Americans opposed them; the Soviets claimed rights to supervise a trusteeship over Tripolitania, the Americans called for international supervision through the United Nations. When discussion of treaties with Balkan countries began, tension grew even worse. Moscow was angered by U.S. disapproval of existing governments in Bulgaria and Rumania and pushed vigorously for recognition of them. As Secretary of State Byrnes held out for democratization, in Rumania particularly, the Soviets opted for obstructionism: they triggered a breakup of the meeting over technical questions concerning French and Chinese participation in discussions. By the end, the foreign ministers could not even agree upon a common closing statement.

Though the weeks in London produced more tension and far less accomplishment than those in San Francisco, Dulles's attitudes and actions concerning the Soviet Union were more temperate than they had been in the spring. Throughout lengthy meetings of the American delegation, he made no denunciations of Russian foreign policy. And on those few occasions when he was specifically asked for advice, that which he gave reflected a positiveness that would become rare before long.

When Soviet anger about nonrecognition of the Rumanian government first became obvious, Dulles and Charles Bohlen urged Byrnes to be tactful. The Secretary was balking at negotiating a peace treaty for Rumania until a democratic government was created there that would fulfill the American understanding of Yalta's Declaration on Liberated Europe. Dulles urged a "non-provocative" approach instead, entailing a statement that the United States government would reserve final judgment on peace terms until fuller information on conditions in Rumania was available. The emphasis on Yalta terminology, he told the Secretary, "implied an attack on the Groza government that it was not necessary to put in a formal conference document and . . . to do this would force a Soviet defense of Groza." Byrnes held firm, however. Though it did not alter policy, Dulles also went on to express his "doubt as to the long-range efficacy of non-recognition in such a situation as Roumania. I said that it seemed like starting over again our policy of non-recognition of the U.S.S.R.—and on much the same grounds—which had proven a barren policy."[24]

On another issue, Dulles and Byrnes again disagreed on strategy, though it was Dulles who took the tougher line in this case. When the Soviets pressed for the exclusion of France and China from discussions of Balkan peace treaties, on the basis of a procedural agreement arranged at Potsdam, the Secretary of State was reluctantly prepared to accede in order to keep negotiations afloat. On at least two occasions, Byrnes tried to get Dulles's agreement to this. As the latter described it, "He expressed the hope that I would agree with him and would go along together on this program." Dulles would not cooperate: "I stated that I could not agree; that in my opinion there was no value . . . in a procedure which would publicly humiliate and alienate France and China. . . ." Adding clout to this, Dulles decided that he "had to tell him that I could have no assurance that the Republicans would not make an issue if he agreed to the narrow treaty-making procedure desired by the Russians."

But Dulles's threat of partisan attack was not based on a desire for a stern and uncompromising American policy toward the Soviet Union, as some studies of the London Council meeting suggest. His attitude toward the France–China issue was fundamentally *conditional*, and he made this very clear to Byrnes. What bothered him about the Soviet demand was that it might lead to a permanently narrowed treaty-making procedure. If Moscow would formally agree to an "ultimate enlargement" of the treaty process "to include all the nations which had been at war," Dulles told Byrnes, *then* he would be prepared to *accept* the exclusion of France and China in London. In particular, he wanted Soviet acceptance of a full-scale "general peace conference" as the eventual end step in procedure.

Dulles's position here, in other words, was more open than is at first apparent. Still basically diplomatic, he was prepared to agree to an unappealing Russian demand in return for acceptance of an American demand. In addition, he felt confident that adroit U.S. handling of the matter would bring a successful compromise. "I said that I felt confident that the Soviet would in due course accept the conference idea," he told Byrnes. As at San Francisco, he was approaching Soviet policy makers as if they were reasonable men with whom real negotiation was possible.[25]

Dulles's ex-post-facto musings on this Council of Foreign Ministers meeting were a logical extension of these attitudes. When the London meetings broke up without having made any progress on the peace treaties with the defeated enemies, he did admit to Edward Stettinius that he was "discouraged and unhappy." More usually, his perspective was quite positive. In a national radio broadcast on October 6, he emphasized the silver lining in the London clouds. Disagreements among the Allies might have come "as a shock to the American people," he argued, but it was good that the public had come to realize that those disageements existed. Before September 1945, people had been fed "a war diet of soothing syrup" and were lulled into "the impression that complete harmony had been achieved."

> The reality was that there was unity in so far as related to joint effort against common enemies. But behind that there have always been the differences which are now coming to light.
>
> It is not healthy, and I am glad that it is no longer necessary, to try to cover up the fact that we have differences.

Dulles himself had long anticipated the emergence of such differences, of course, having described them as inevitable during the later stages of his work with the Commission on a Just and Durable Peace. As such, he was not inclined to be too critical of any one of the Allies, not even the Soviet Union. Moscow's behavior had been frustrating and angering, to be sure, but it was also very natural. In describing the Soviet intransigence on Rumania and the resulting deadlock in the meetings, Dulles told his radio audience:

> Let me hasten to say that I have no feeling that the Soviet delegation . . . did anything that was not within their rights. In every important negotiation, public or private, there comes a moment when the negotiators test each other out. It was inevitable that a time should come when the Soviet Union would want to test us out.

And what had happened with respect to Rumania could be expected on other issues too, with no greater cause for alarm.

> The American people should see what has happened in its true proportions. We are at the beginning of a long and difficult negotiation which will involve the structure of the post-war world. The Soviet Union wants to know what our political attitude will be toward the states which border them, particularly in the Balkans. They want to know what our attitude will be toward sharing with them the control of defeated Japan. They want to know what our attitude will be toward giving them economic aid.

As this statement suggests, to go an important step further, Dulles returned from London with a relatively clear sense of the scope of these natural Soviet testing instincts. Where San Francisco had prompted comments on an unlimited communist striving for global influence, London reenforced the more limited appraisal of earlier days. In particular, Dulles squarely returned to his sense of the Soviet Union as a proponent of a spheres of influence system for the postwar world. Commenting in his radio report on the failure to settle so many issues, he said:

> It is possible . . . that we shall not agree on the postwar settlement. If that happens, it would lead to *different nations carrying out their will in particular areas*. That is not necessarily a permanent disaster, but it would be most unfortunate. It would tend to divide the world into *blocs and spheres of influence*. [Emphasis added.]

Obviously unappealing to Dulles, this was still a problem very different from those caused by an open-ended communist menace. Indeed, in the fall of 1945, Dulles continued to assume it was a problem that could be handled. As he put it in October, "nothing that has happened so far makes me feel that we may not all come to agree." The Balkan treaties might prove to be an exceptional stumbling block, concerning as they did an area where Moscow's "interest was perhaps more directly engaged than that of the United States." Certainly further efforts at negotiation were eminently logical.[26]

Such expectations remained a strong counterpoint to Dulles's more pessimistic thoughts for some months. As late as March 1946, after his return from the first meeting of the General Assembly, he steered clear of complete adherence to the ideas that would become dominant in his *Life* articles. His chagrin at Soviet intransigence in the new world organization was matched by a conviction that *"no one of the great powers* trusted the others sufficiently to hand over to them control of its destiny." Nor did he see Soviet leaders as responsible for all of the serious problems discernible beyond the United Nations. His wartime tendency to grasp the complex origins of international dilemmas continued in two statements of the Commission on a Just and Durable Peace which Dulles drafted at this time. While both contained brief mentions of the need for improvement in U.S.—Soviet cooperation, their overriding emphasis was placed on other matters: the search for methods to control atomic energy; the need to avoid a spirit of revenge in working on peace settlements; the desirability of attending to human rather than strategic needs in settling new boundaries; the fostering of progressive programs for colonial peoples; the preparation of an International Bill of Rights to deal with racial and sexual discrimination; the search for new methods of international economic cooperation; and the encouragement of the new United Nations Organization, among others. Although Dulles would very shortly begin speaking and writing as if all of these problems were either created or exacerbated by the Soviet Union, there was no hint of that stance in these statements. The all-encompassing international communist conspiracy had not yet been delineated.[27]

Dulles set out to resolve the indecisiveness inherent in his more recent statements on the Soviet Union during April 1946. On one of his regular retreats to Duck Island in Lake Ontario, he consciously sat down to think out a more precise and consistent position. As usual, he produced a long, roughly-written essay wholly focused on Soviet foreign policy. Over the next month, he asked his brother and Arthur Vandenberg to look this over. He polished it quite quickly and by mid-May had accepted Henry Luce's offer of publication in *Life*. (Although Vandenberg advised him that Luce had paid $25,000 for each of two Churchill articles, Dulles accepted $5000 for both parts of his. He donated the money to the Federal Council of Churches.)

Writing his *Life* articles gave Dulles a much clearer sense of direction as far as evaluating Moscow's actions was concerned. Before, he confessed to his colleagues in the Commission on a Just and Durable Peace, he had "not felt clear enough in my own mind about Russian foreign policy to feel like giving leadership in any particular direction." Now he thought he had "a clear understanding of the fundamentals" and was ready to move.[28]

Dulles's sense of having grasped "fundamentals" in a coherent fashion involved opting for the harsher of his divergent portrayals of Soviet diplomacy, of course. The *Life* articles completely rejected the notion that Soviet leaders were essentially Russian in nature. They rejected the thought that these leaders could be described as troublesome men whose troublesomeness had limits, whose primary concern was to create a quite traditional sphere of influence along their borders. Peter the Great had been laid to rest, Dulles concluded in these pages, and had been replaced by the spirits of Marx and Lenin: the result was that communism was on the move, marching to the drummers of the Kremlin and bent on world conquest.

In the months following the appearance of his *Life* articles, Dulles made it clear that the thoughts behind them were not just those of an anxious moment. The more strident themes of his revised analysis were repeated over and again, to different audiences and on different occasions. In early June, A. J. Muste wrote of his qualms concerning the direction of recent discussions in the Commission on a Just and Durable Peace. Though critical of conditions within Soviet society, Muste thought Dulles did not appreciate the way in which American atomic power engendered arrogant attitudes and behavior in Moscow. Dulles thought this was nonsense. With only thinly veiled disdain, he wrote:

> I think you are drawing a good deal on imagination when you try to explain Soviet methods as being due to fear of us and of our atomic bombs. Resort by Soviet leaders to measures of forceful coercion has been

characteristic for nearly 30 years within the Soviet Union and long preceding the atomic bomb. The objectionable feature of their foreign policy is that they are attempting in foreign affairs to do precisely what they have been doing at home for nearly 30 years.

Similar dialogue took place a few months later when Dulles was invited to speak to the Detroit Committee on Foreign Relations. The leader of the group had explained that it had had extended discussions of Soviet–American relations and had tentatively concluded that the "United States and Russia can 'get along' . . . that Russia wants only to secure her borders, is internally unprepared for another war and consequently doesn't want one and, has no intention of grabbing off new territory or trying to evangelize the world." They now wanted someone with recent experience of working with the Soviets to share ideas with them. Because he had addressed the group during his more temperate days, its members were probably unprepared for Dulles's response. "The point of view which your Committee holds reflects, I fear, a good deal of wishful thinking," he wrote. "Even Henry Wallace recognizes that the Russians are 'teaching that their form of communism must, by force if necessary, ultimately triumph over democratic capitalism.' "[29]

Actually, Dulles's correspondence following the *Life* articles pales alongside some of his public statements. Using the colors and tones that would so much be associated with him in future years, it was in speeches or newspaper and magazine pieces that he most often chose to develop his newly clarified theories. One September appearance before a national convention of Presbyterian leaders is especially noteworthy. His language and theme were both striking and destined to be repeated frequently. He began by commenting on the "strain and tension" in the international atmosphere. Unlike so many earlier statements, however, he maintained here that this was not the result of a wartime coalition falling apart in traditional fashion. No, he said, "This time . . . what is happening is more than that. *We seem to be witnessing a challenge to established civilization—the kind of thing which occurs only once in centuries.*" Drawing on his wartime interest in Arnold Toynbee's work, he elaborated:

> In the tenth century after Christ the so-called Christian world was challenged by an alien faith. The tide of Islam flowed from Arabia and swept over much of Christendom. . . .
>
> Now another ten centuries have rolled by and the accumulated civilization of these centuries is faced with another challenge. This time the challenger is Soviet communism.

Lest any of his listeners doubt what he now saw as the fundamental differences between "civilization" and "communism," Dulles carefully laid them out:

The faith and institutions of Soviet communism differ vastly from those of the Western democracies. The official creed of the Party is an abstruse materialism. The form of government is dictatorship. The economic life is an extreme form of state socialism. The official methods are ruthless and intolerant. *The spirit is revolutionary. The scope of its effort is universal.*

Dulles underlined the "universal" dimension of the Soviet challenge, in particular. Soviet leaders:

. . . proclaim to 750,000,000 dependent people their right to be independent, and publicly and secretly they encourage revolutionary efforts to throw off the yoke of what they call Western imperialism. By intensive Spanish and Portuguese language propaganda in Latin America they prod the peoples there, upwards of 100,000,000, to arise from political apathy and to take power—as communists. Through Chinese communists they hold out to 400,000,000 Chinese the promise of change from corruption and incompetence which have become traditional in some circles of Chinese officialdom. To the 350,000,000 of continental Europeans, economically wrecked by two world wars, they offer a plan which, they promise, will sustain productivity more surely than an individualistic economy.

Thus the Soviet communist party challenges the supremacy of the so-called Christian world.[30]

III

The changes that had taken place in John Foster Dulles's discussions of the Soviet Union between 1941 and 1946 were substantial and obvious. Virtually all of his attitudes evident during the Second World War survived the fighting by less than a year. Where the Soviet Union had been of marginal concern to the Dulles of earlier years, it had become one of his major concerns by mid-1946. During the war, he had envisioned a substantial range of international problems, of which the Soviet Union was one. Now he described many but interrelated problems, all essentially linked to and subsumed by the overriding difficulty of the Soviet Union. During the war, he had perceived the Soviet Union as a quite traditional great power: while he thought its goals were unlike those of the United State in the mid-twentieth century, he admitted that they were not unlike those of the United States in the past, nor of other great powers at the moment. By mid-1946, in contrast, Dulles was describing the Soviet Union as the embodiment of a great communist menace, the center of a revolutionary assault on all of Western civilization. No longer were Soviet leaders seen as men with regional ambitions, anxious to create a sphere of influence along their borders in Europe and Asia. Now they were painted as despots seeking world domination, the fomentors of crises that girdled the globe. And, to go one step further, these alterations in Dulles's appraisals produced other changes as well—in the mood and tone of his presentation. Where he had reacted critically but calmly in earlier years, his reactions had become stridently negative and alarmist by 1946.

Though these shifts in the thrust of Dulles's writings may be obvious, the reasons behind them are much less so. It is difficult to explain precisely why such a substantial swing in mood and attitude occurred. Dulles himself was not helpful. During these years, he seems very seldom to have been aware of the changes through which his ideas and pronouncements were going. The only effort he made at self-analysis was a letter to a Yale professor who was an occasional correspondent, written at the time of the Henry Wallace uproar in the fall of 1946. Dulles had been generally positive in comments on Wallace up to this time and even began this letter by saying that he had admired his "fine aspirations and many good ideas." Wallace's recent statements, however, particularly the Madison Square Garden speech in which he urged a friendlier policy toward the Soviet Union, were described as "unrealistic." They "reflected the attitude which we all had when we began negotiations with reference to the peace at San Francisco." The problem was that Wallace had unwisely stuck with his attitude, while others had changed:

> Having actually participated in negotiations with the Russians at that and several succeeding conferences, the Wallace approach proved impractical.
>
> It is a good initial approach to say that if you pat the dog he will not bite you. If, however, after several times patting the dog he still nips you, then it is necessary to think of another approach. Wallace has been sitting behind the scenes and has not had to go through the experience of having his hand nipped.[31]

While Dulles had apparently convinced himself that his own changing point of view on the Soviet Union's international behavior had come about because of too much "nipping" at a friendly hand, his explanation should be taken with a grain of salt. If nothing else, it describes a cathartic process that Dulles himself did not actually go through. For all his "experience" of working with the Soviets, he was quite slow to change his own message. San Francisco and the London Council of Foreign Ministers meeting simply did not produce fundamental changes of perception and even after his contact with the Russians at the London United Nations Organization meeting in January 1946, he spoke for three months as if no crisis had arisen because of Moscow's behavior. If his overall point in September is at all relevant to his own experience then, it implies a clearly delayed reaction to the bites of the threatening Soviet dog. In fact, like other statements in later years, Dulles's letter has a substantial component of hindsight to it. Written in September, it came months after the real process of his rethinking had been completed. By then, he had written his *Life* articles and had gone some way toward polishing his stertorous denunciations. It is difficult to determine how much Dulles was reading back *into* the previous intellectual experience and whether he was imposing some pattern in retrospect.

Dulles's minimal and questionable effort at explaining changing attitudes is compounded by the fact that it is not always possible to tell whether he fully believed all of the more extreme things he began writing in 1946. The frequency with which he would reiterate his points over time, as well as the force and color of his tone, suggest conviction and sincerity, to be sure, but they do not prove it. Some ingredients in his ongoing thoughts and public statements trigger suspicion when compared with others. Was there a degree of manipulation and posturing behind the revised Dulles appraisals?

If Dulles's statements on the Soviet Union after mid-1946 represent the real state of his thoughts, what would explain the evolution through which he had gone? The most obvious answer is that Dulles became convinced that Moscow was resisting, and blatantly resisting, the kinds of international reforms which he wanted to see accomplished in the postwar era.

Dulles, of course, had a highly developed personal sense of what needed to be done in the aftermath of World War II. He had put years of effort into describing his conception of the international order's major problems, years of thought into identifying the steps that might be taken to solve them. The result was the kind of agenda he elaborated so extensively in the writings of the late 1930s and the public relations efforts of the early 1940s: a revised and altered international organization; the freer movement of money, goods, and people; procedures for peaceful alteration of treaties, etc. He always made clear his conviction that progress toward a "new world order" would be slow, but he did expect something to happen; particularly during the war years, he allowed his "realistic" sails to be billowed out by the exhilirating winds of anticipation.[32]

As for many, the events of 1945 and 1946 made it clear to Dulles that neither the dawn nor the day of a new world order had arrived. In the aftermath of his work in San Francisco, he was capable of saying some highly positive things about the birth of a new international organization, but the more usual tenor of his words during and after the conference belied occasional heartiness. And if the new U.N. could not prompt any steady sense of progress, no other postwar developments were likely to do so. The increasingly obvious physical devastation wrought by the war, bickering over peace settlements in Europe, and uncertainty about the future in Eastern Asia, among other things, prompted new anxiety rather than satisfaction. As he put it in a November 1945 statement for his church commission, "In great areas civilization is now imminently threatened by privation, starvation and consequent chaos." There existed "all too plentifully" evidence of "economic dislocations and maladjustments . . . political maladjustments . . . the menace of militarism and . . . exploitation and repression of dependent peoples. . . ." Nor were the leaders of the victorious Allies doing much to increase international cooperation in dealing with these grievous problems. "The distrust, the differences of political method, the differences of moral judgment are just as great today as they were six months ago," Dulles told one audience. "Indeed, if anything, the differences have increased since the unifying force of common enemies has disappeared." All in all, one of his church statements concluded, "A world of fear, hatred, cruelty, misery, and violent death is closing in on the prospect of a world of fellowship and love."[33]

What Dulles saw by early 1946 convinced him that major responsibility for the worsening of the international situation rested on the shoulders of Soviet policy makers. They seemed bent on spurning even the most elementary regard for diplomatic conduct and what passed as the general conventions of international law; they certainly seemed more determined than anyone else to resist the kinds of reforms which he felt were so essential for peace and prosperity. Unappealing actions in Eastern Europe turned out to be like a pebble thrown in a pond, Dulles came to argue, yielding ever wider ripples of threatening behavior. Soviet policy on Germany was uncooperative and suspicious; Soviet coolness toward the United Nations was disappointing; Soviet desires for former Italian colonies was disturbing; Soviet espionage activities, in Canada for example, were sensational; Soviet maneuvers regarding Greece, Turkey, and Iran were frightening. Where others yearned for "a world of fellowship and love," he concluded, Moscow's leaders hoped that chaos and human anguish would pave the way for the triumph of their power and ideology.[34]

This raises another question. If Dulles moved to sharply critical views because he saw the Soviet Union as the great threat to world peace and propserity by 1946, what is the explanation for this kind of perception? His views on the Soviets from April 1946 on, after all, were highly simplistic, even melodramatic. During the late stages of World War II and the early months of the postwar period, on the contrary, his writings had shown a real sensitivity to the complex roots of old and new problems plaguing the international order. He had sensed potential difficulties with Moscow, but had placed his discomfort into a much broader context—one that included references to the likely ramifications of the war's physical and emotional impact, of the self-serving behavior of other great or near-great powers, of his own country's occasional irresponsibility and of the gestating yearning for self-determination in the underdeveloped world, among other things. Why did he move away from this more subtle and realistic perspective in 1946? Why did he opt for using the Soviet Union as an all-purpose lightning rod for his anxieties about the state of the global arena?

Several factors may have been involved. Each suggests a certain predisposition toward the kind of overreaction that emerged in Dulles.

First, Dulles shared with many a clear philosophical bias against communism and an understandable, though not necessarily accurate, presumption that it stood at the core of the Soviet Union's "ideology." Like fascism, communism was an "alien faith" to him. It looked to revolution and a total rejection of the past as a solution for problems, he felt, whereas he wanted to preserve many features of the status quo and change others slowly and peacefully. Essential conservatism was a fundamental component of the Dulles world view, and it spawned periodic blasts at more radical philosophies over the years. In the post–World War II period, general anxieties would have been more easily channeled into a preoccupation with the villainy of the Kremlin because of it. Thus, Dulles may have gone through a process similar to that of Woodrow Wilson during the First World War, a process he had personally witnessed. Wilson too had seen himself as a "reformer" of the international order and had lashed out at the Bolsheviks when anticipated changes did not take place. He too had opted for putting "blame" for failure on the shoulders of the radicals he distrusted, conveniently avoiding any impugning of his own nation and its associates, his like-minded colleagues, and his own recommendations.

The role of philosophical or ideological bias in producing his strident Cold Warrior attitudes would have been reinforced by what had become Dulles's occasional preoccupation with American exceptionalism. His work with the Commission on a Just and Durable Peace, in particular, showed a steadily increasing emphasis on the weighty responsibility which the United States had toward the rest of the world. If Americans could regain the "great faith" and "sense of mission" which they had in the past, he had argued many times, they would be able to provide "guidance, example and inspiration" to an anguished humanity; by leading the way to a reformed world order, they would create an era of peace and prosperity and feel the exhilirating "power of creation." In the months that followed the end of World War II, Dulles continued to embroider this theme and put more emphasis than ever on the indispensability of United States leadership. If the new international organization was going to become a potent force for peace, he argued in early 1946, for example, "the spiritual and intellectual power must, above all, be supplied by the American people. The success or failure of the United Nations depends on that more than on any other single factor." If the peace settlements with the former enemies and new working relationships among the victors were going to be just and harmonious, he said in October 1945, this too would depend on the United States: "We are the only great nation whose people have not been drained, physically and spiritually. It devolves upon us to give leadership in restoring principle as a guide to conduct. If *we* do not do that, *the world will not be worth living in. Indeed, it probably will be a world in which human beings cannot live"* (emphasis added). A month later, he dubbed Americans, especially American Christians, "a minority" which "must save the world."[35]

Already during the war, this kind of preoccupation with the global "mission" of the United States had had its impact on the quality of Dulles's analyses. It signaled the beginning of the end of the generally aloof and worldly, *Realpolitik* attitudes of the 1920s and 1930s, the decline in particular of a sophisticated skepticism about the moral pretensions of governments and patriotic citizens. As he himself became more personally concerned with religious and ethical questions, Dulles found it less difficult to imagine that the United States as a society within the international arena could be so concerned as well. As he began to couple attentiveness to traditional political and economic issues with emphasis on moral considerations, he began to assume that the United States could do both as well. To some degree, Dulles's indictments of the Soviet Union from 1946 on may represent the other side of the coin of this shift. If some nations could be moral in their behavior, in other words, others could be immoral! And in Dulles's mind, an immoral nation could be identified, quite simply, as one that opposed what the United States was seeking: Americans, after all, were trying to teach the world "a moral way of international living," and how else but as immoral would one define resistance to that desirable objective?

292

Dulles's occasional resort to moralistic assessments of American behavior helped to create a predisposition toward sweeping denunciation of the Soviet Union. Such a readiness to drift into simplistic analysis, which existed at least several years before 1946, became a standard ingredient of what appeared after that date. It also contributed to the melodramatic tone for which Dulles became so well known. His stark, strident pronouncements on the international communist menace were, in fact, something like mirror images of the heady descriptions of the United States which began to appear in 1942 and 1943.

The atmosphere around him also contributed to the particular direction Dulles's thoughts took in early 1946. Many of the political leaders with whom he was regularly in contact by then had already begun to speak to each other, and sometimes to the public, about a rising and pervasive Soviet menace. There had been quarrels over Eastern Europe and Germany, mounting tension in Iran, and discoveries of spies in Canada in the first months of 1946—and Washington was buzzing with embryonic denunciations of a global conspiracy. One of the interesting facets of Dulles's thoughts on the Soviet Union, indeed, is the fact that he came somewhat more slowly to his conclusions published in *Life* than had so many. Kennan, Acheson, Harriman, Truman, and others beat Dulles to the punch, in spite of *his* later reputation, and they probably helped speed up his movement. Aside from seeing the direction in which their thoughts were running, Dulles's position as colleague within the policy-making establishment of the day made him essentially dependent on them for information and assessments of international developments.

Some of the people closest to him must have helped more than others. His brother Allen had already decided the Russians were implacable foes and told Foster that a draft of his *Life* articles was too tepid and optimistic! So too did Arthur Vandenberg. The Michigan Senator was a prolific correspondent, and Dulles had already been barraged with anti-Soviet statements by the time he sat down to rethink his position. When Vandenberg read his friend's draft, he praised it but said that it demonstrated a calmer demeanor than his own: "You are a philosopher in your ivory tower. I am a sadist who thirsts for a practical show-down. Perhaps you had best stay in your tower—and not let me tempt you to toss bricks. Bless you!" He did try to tempt, however, and urged revisions. Dulles should say more about "Pal Joey" and his "cells" in the United States, "at work upon our very vitals;" he should add something about atomic weapons and the Soviets "who would use our atomic secrets against us without conscience or compunction." I am more than ever convinced that Communism is on the march on a world-wide scale which only America can stop," he concluded. He urged Dulles to help stop that march, and his pleas added more force to the movement underway in his friend's mind.[36]

Dulles's essential conservatism, his sense of American exceptionalism, and the mood of people near him may have helped to push him away from the temperate and subtle understanding of the Soviet Union that had generally been his. In the circumstances of early 1946 and after, any or all might help explain why he, like many, went beyond reacting to events with concern to overreacting in a simplistic and melodramatic fashion. Of course, none of these factors can be weighted in any precise way as far as relative significance is concerned. Dulles himself never admitted to the relevance of any of them and may not even have considered the possibility that they could be relevant. In addition, their ultimate significance is limited by a certain degree of uncertainty concerning the real depth of some of the more melodramatic statements he was prone to make about the Soviet Union. Were they always a precise reflection of his inner thoughts?

This question is worth raising because of a number of characteristics of Dulles's behavior that began to emerge in the 1940s, coincidental with his more publicly oriented work among Protestant churches and Republicans. On one hand, Dulles had demonstrated well before 1946 a capacity for *overstatement*. This was revealed particularly clearly in his work with the Commission on a Just and Durable Peace. He freely admitted that he felt exhilirated by "air suffused with the elixir of creative effort" and poured great energy into drawing up blueprints for the postwar world. His excitement, his missionary zeal, produced statements with a highly dramatic tone. However, it was a tone that often outran the basically moderate nature of his own core reform concepts.[37]

Dulles's tendency to overstatement is not attributable to a mood of incautious excitement alone. Some of his hyperbole must be seen as part of a more consciously manipulative style, an effort to adapt both the tone and substance of statements to certain audiences or circumstances. During the 1944 campaign, for example, Dulles found it useful to fashion purple indictments about radical and communist subversion of the Democratic Party. Hoping to strengthen Dewey's chances by rousing the public's ire, he had written speeches quite unrelated to his own more temperate perspective. His work at the San Francisco Conference the following year revealed a related characteristic. Struggling to promote programs and charter changes that would serve the specific interests of the United States, Dulles demonstrated in the private deliberations of the American delegation a set of concerns sometimes significantly different from those the general public might have expected from the chairman of the Commission on a Just and Durable Peace. It became apparent that the highflown moralism of many of his church-sponsored statements was at least in part a façade—that Dulles the diplomat did not speak the way Dulles the church leader did.[38]

Neither of these tendencies may be surprising in a man who had had a long career as a successful lawyer and a shorter but more intense experience as a political strategist. Both, so to speak, came with the territory in which Dulles worked. Surprising or not, both tendencies remained in evidence after World War II and clearly affected Dulles's discussions of the Soviet Union. The increasingly charged atmosphere of 1945 and 1946 would certainly have made Dulles more susceptible to melodramatic overstatement, for example. As other voices grew more shrill, his own could do so without quite seeming to. The importance of a crisis atmosphere is also suggested by the fact that in private correspondence Dulles remained capable, though less and less frequently, of calmer deliberations than he would offer in public. But Dulles was not just a chameleon, reacting only in some instinctive way to a changing environment. He also continued to play to different audiences, tailoring his statements as he saw fit. On May 22, 1946, he wrote the editor of *Readers' Digest* of his hope that "the American people can be *aroused* to the danger they face . . . " (emphasis added). Not two weeks later, he took a calmer tack with Walter Lippmann, who criticized the *Life* manuscript as too alarmist in tone. "I agree with you that the great question is whether the American people can see the truth and not react foolishly. . . . I pondered this for weeks and finally came to the decision . . . to trust the American people to exercise *reasonable self-restraint*" (emphasis added). Dulles adopted a similar approach in relating to a figure like James P. Warburg, trying to put himself in the same category as this more temperate analyst of world affairs. In a September 1946 letter in which he tried to answer some Warburg criticisms, Dulles wrote that it would be "far-fetched" to argue that Russia was "seeking to conquer the world": "I myself have no such suspicion. What I have said was, that the leaders of the U.S.S.R. seek communism throughout the world." This was fancy footwork, even for a lawyer, especially given the contents of an address which he gave in Philadelphia only a week earlier. In one of his most melodramatic blasts, he had compared "Soviet communism" to the "tide of Islam" in the tenth century and had described its challenge as "ruthless," "revolutionary" and "universal." (Some time later, Dulles sent Walter Lippmann a copy of another talk on the similarity of the Soviet menace and the assault of

Islam. He went out of his way to explain that he "was speaking then with the Archbishop of Canterbury at a religious service and *consequently emphasized primarily the moral and social aspects of the struggle* . . . ." [emphasis added].)[39]

Several reasons for the manipulation or exaggeration of views suggest themselves as one looks at Dulles's concerns and activities during the mid-1940s. Though he would have shied away from admitting it, he could hardly have been unaware of the impact of partisanship. As a Republican in 1944, he had hoped to turn anticommunism into a tool for his party. The thought lingered on. In September 1945, he wrote Arthur Vandenberg about a speech the Senator was planning on "opening up the U.S.S.R. to newspaper correspondents." "The more I think of it," Dulles said, "the more I think that can make a pretty good issue."[40]

Partisanship on behalf of self may have played a role too, in a way that Dulles might not have consciously recognized. He had moved more determinedly into the public and political arenas during the late 1930s and early 1940s and had shown clear interest in taking on some significant government responsibility. That interest had made him conscious of the importance of his own image as well as his party's. Within the Protestant community, he had shaped his statements in such a way as to insure maximum appeal—not doing complete violence to his personal views by any means, but demonstrating a willingness to bend with the winds of sentiment he perceived in his audience. Dulles the political animal, Dulles the man of ambition, did not forget the importance of building a power base after World War II. Many specifically political activities as well as indirect measures like comments on the issues of the day, including the Soviet Union, suggest that he was not totally unlike a leader *manqué* who was willing to adapt his leadership to the direction in which he thought his potential followers would want to go.

Finally, it would not be irrelevant to see Dulles consciously playing to his audiences because of concern for what he would have seen as broad national and international interests. Already in 1944, he had begun to worry that Americans would be inclined to draw back into their shells at the end of World War II. As chairman of the Commission on a Just and Durable Peace, he had repeatedly emphasized the dangers of isolationism bred of disillusionment, as in the 1920s. Drawing on a logic that he had been moved by all his life, he urged average citizens *and* government officials to sanction active U.S. involvement in the international arena—for the sake of American peace and prosperity, for the sake of global reform. Like the lawyer that he was, he wanted to present the strongest case possible for this involvement. Emphasis on the dangers inherent in the postwar atmosphere, with "communism" as a particularly potent word, may well have seemed shrewd to Dulles in 1946. It certainly did for other policy makers at that time.[41]

None of this means that John Foster Dulles was a man who thoroughly and deviously altered his beliefs for political, personal, or even idealistic reasons. He was no Machiavelli, twisting his public words into a form that would serve a purpose, willing to ignore what he knew were his own private thoughts. No. It is quite clear that Dulles did indeed change his mind about the Soviet Union during early 1946. After a period of reflection and inner debate longer than many American policy makers allowed themselves, he concluded that Soviet policy makers were more ambitious than he had earlier believed. In addition to their desire for a sphere of influence along their borders, they seemed bent on expansion into many areas of the globe. One might easily disagree with the altered perspective and question the emotional and intellectual reactions which led to it, but neither disagreement nor questioning would deny the reality of Dulles's experience.

Still, to say this much is not to say also that Dulles was only a simple man baring his soul to other policy makers and the public. Having changed his mind about the Soviets, he was fully capable of doing one or both of two things as he presented his revised views to others: first, unconsciously overstating his description of an international communist conspiracy and exaggerating its dangers; second, consciously tailoring his statements to what he perceived as the needs of the moment or the idiosyncracies of his audience.

12

Focus on Europe, 1945–1948: I

"I HAVE HAD some interesting times lately, particularly at San Francisco and at London," Dulles wrote an old classmate in November 1945. "However, working in this rarified atmosphere makes me wish that we could occasionally relax in the spirit of our Princeton days. Certainly the world is in a mess and it is not very easy to see the way out." There is a note of nostalgia in these words that is unusual for Dulles, one prompted perhaps by the special mood of a moment of recollection. Under all other circumstances in the immediate postwar period, as through virtually all of his earlier life, Dulles would more normally have given voice to clear convictions about what needed to be done to clear up the "mess." If the end of fighting had produced "a critical and difficult period," as he thought it had, he was rarely retiring about sighting what seemed to him the logical path through it. If Soviet leaders, perversely compounding the host of problems that would have emerged in any event, were mounting "a challenge to established civilization—the kind of thing which occurs only once in centuries," then Dulles was almost invariably ready to suggest ways of meeting the challenge. [1]

In a fashion that owed much to patterns set in the late 1930s and war years, Dulles offered his postwar proposals for ameliorative actions in two relatively distinct ways. On one hand, his reading of certain kinds of occasions and audiences led him to continue developing the grand, sweeping style that had surfaced so noticeably in his philosophical writings and in his work as a Protestant lay leader. Using a tone and language that were often dramatic, he would issue broadly conceived obiter dicta on the travails facing humanity in general. On the other hand, there were always situations in which Dulles chose to be more specific, in which particular problems were analyzed and more precise remedies put forward. This had been true, though less noticeable, even in his early work with the Commission on a Just and Durable Peace, and it continued as a crucial facet of his mental processes after 1945. In any ultimate sense, of course, broad pronouncements and specific prescriptions were linked: they were both the product of Dulles's mind, and he himself would not have seen them as anything but symbolic. Still, simultaneous stylistic variations are interesting and may have something significant to say about how his words and proposals should be interpreted.

I

Many of Dulles's generalized recommendations continued to be built upon the core concept of United States leadership in the international community. He had argued many times during World War II that if Americans did not show others how to break the recurrent cycle of war and economic crisis, the cycle would continue. This remained his message after the fighting had ended. "Our nation was designed to help others," he said in December 1945:

> The founders of our nation dedicated us to show how men might organize a good society. They conceived of that, not as a selfish enterprise, but as a way whereby our conduct and example might aid humanity. That purpose ws expressed in almost those words in the opening paragraph of the Federalist Papers and the theme constantly appears in the utterances of the founding Fathers.

What he was talking about, he said in February 1946, was "the great American experiment" of the eighteenth and nineteenth centuries, when "we acted under a sense of moral compulsion, as a people who had a mission to perform in the world."[2]

As Americans sought to refire their "sense of purpose and . . . capacity to inspire and uplift," Dulles saw a few key goals toward which he wanted them to lead. They should continue to encourage "greater trust and fellowship" among nations, particularly the great powers. As early as 1943, he had insisted on the fundamental necessity of "organized world collaboration" if "another war" and a "world of anarchy and power politics" were to be avoided. He was not likely to back away from this conception at the moment when it was most necessary for it to come into play. "The hour of victory inevitably starts the disintegration of a war coalition," he wrote in November 1945: "The common enemy, which compelled united action, is gone. To take its place, new occasions for unity must quickly be seized upon." (Sensitive like many to the new relevance of the atomic bomb, Dulles added to this statement the sentence, "We must unite or perish.") In an address at Union Theological Seminary, he said, "Fellowship, and not fear, is the cement with which world order must be built." At Princeton University in February 1946, he said that wartime "fellowship" was "worth preserving": "There must be spun a web so precious that no one wants to tear it. It must be made more advantageous to agree than to disagree."

As a specific mechanism for encouraging fellowship, Dulles believed Americans should continue to emphasize the value of cooperation in the performance of "curative and creative tasks." His testimony before the Senate Foreign Relations Committee in July 1945 argued that the new United Nations Organization would encourage the undertaking of "great tasks of human betterment which will hold the members together in fellowship and friendship."

> That is the great hope of the future. Unity, such as that we want to preserve, is the reaction to a common peril and a common effort to overcome that peril. Germany and Japan were the peril which drew us together. With the complete defeat of Germany and Japan that peril will seem to have disappeared. Then our unity, too, will disappear unless we find new, compelling tasks to pursue in common. It is such tasks that the San Francisco Charter proposes to the United Nations. It brands intolerance, repression, injustice and economic want as common perils of the future just as Nazi Germany and Imperialist Japan are the common perils of today. It proposes that we stay united to wage war against those evils.

He made similar points in February 1946. "Self-interest is a dominant human motive," he explained then. "It can serve as a cement which binds men together in fellowship. It can be a repellent, which sets men one against the other. The art of peaceful statesmanship is to find ways whereby the welfare of the members can be served better by working together than by working apart." This is what the United Nations promised:

> It can serve to advance human welfare in all of its phases—spiritual, cultural and material. It can promote basic human rights and fundamental freedoms. It can fight disease. It can help to solve the vast colonial problems. It can develop world trade. It is given almost unlimited opportunity to advance the welfare of the member peoples. Thereby it could create a fellowship of common effort which would make the parties want to settle such differences as emerged in the Security Council.

As usual, Dulles did insist that it was going to be up to the United States to push the new world organization in this direction. It required "the spiritual power which could be supplied by the American people. The success or failure of the United Nations depends upon that more than any other single factor."[3]

When Dulles began to produce vivid dissertations on the dangers represented by the Soviet Union, in 1946 and 1947, he altered the thrust of his general recommendations. He continued to emphasize the crucial responsibilities of the United States, but the nature of its leadership he now perceived somewhat differently. This was logical, of course. Further talk of encouraging "fellowship" would have been inappropriate in conjunction with warnings about a communist offensive akin to the tenth century "tide of Islam"; additional urgings of "collaboration" on "curative and creative tasks" would not have meshed with the portrayal of leaders "bent on eradicating the non-Soviet type of society." Cooperation for the sake of peace and prosperity remained a fundamental ingredient of an ideal world order in Dulles's mind, but it became a long-range goal more than a serious proposal for immediate action: at best, it became a step that could come only further down the road, after other more pressing actions had been taken.

The dominant theme of Dulles's broadly conceived proposals during 1946 and 1947 became the means by which Americans could deal with the "challenge" to "civilization" stemming from Moscow. As he outlined his ideas, he allowed the highly colored nature of his analysis of Soviet behavior to make more dramatic than ever his emphasis on the duties and role of the United States. "By the providence of God and the circumstances of history, the American people are now given a world opportunity and responsibility of unparalleled scope," was one typical comment. "If we as a nation measure up to the task set before us, a better world order than mankind has known can come into being. If we fail, the whole family of nations will suffer untold tragedies. . . ."

If Americans were going to fulfill their destiny, Dulles believed they had to open their eyes to the perilous condition of the international arena. Too many were relaxing in the quietude of the homefront after years of shooting and bloodshed; too many were coasting along in some postwar euphoria, believing that peace and prosperity were inevitable now that the Axis had been defeated. This was strikingly wrong, Dulles argued increasingly, and it was imperative for his countrymen to recognize the "alarming" nature of the global scene. As he put it to Arthur Vandenberg in September 1946, "I feel that the American people will have to revise their ideas about the peace and realize that we are in for, perhaps, a good many years of struggle which will be worldwide in scope. . . ." Once they grasped this, he was sure they would act accordingly. He wanted full public disclosure of the problems encountered in the early meetings of the Council of Foreign Ministers and the United Nations, for example, because "it is good for us to see the realities that used to be concealed. It *will* shock us, but it *may* shock us into doing what needs to be done. The American people have always stood up to hard tasks once they knew what was required of them."[4]

What were the "hard tasks" Dulles would have identified? First, there was the costly and unappealing need to "maintain a strong military establishment." As early as December 1945, he had told *Look* magazine that "we are demobilizing too fast, in terms of numbers and in terms of quality." This was dangerous, he had said then, because the United States was surrounded by "an unsettled world, where many respect only physical force"; if that force were not available, "unruly elements" could "emerge and take control. . . ." As time went on, he occasionally reiterated this somewhat vaguely defined explanation. "I favor the immediate enactment of legislation which, through draft if necessary, will enable the United States to maintain a strong army," he told the *New York Times* in June 1946. He did so because "in much of the world, provisional order is only maintained because the U.S. Army is there. Were it to be withdrawn or were it to be there only in token strength, forces of unrest would take control. . . ." More regularly, Dulles came to associate the general need for military strength with the specific threat posed by the Soviet Union. He put it typically and clearly in his *Life* articles:

> . . . if we neglect our military establishment that may lead to a dangerous misjudgment of us by the Soviet leaders. They believe in force. They take it for granted that those who have precious things will, if they are able, main-

tain a force-in-being to protect them. They assume that a man who does not put a lock on the door of his house has nothing in it that he greatly values. There can be little doubt but what Soviet leaders became much more confident and ambitious when, immediately after the fighting stopped, we let our military establishments deteriorate.[5]

But armed strength was only part of what would be required in order to deal with the communist menace, Dulles felt, and perhaps the easiest part at that. After all, he said at one point, "the Soviet challenge is double-barreled." The immediate problem of physical expansion could be dealt with by physical safeguards, but what about "its other phase—the ideological phase. . . ." Here the depths of the crisis confronting the United States and the difficulties of dealing with it became even more apparent. In the aftermath of an incredibly destructive war, the world had become "largely a vacuum, so far as faith and order are concerned," and the communist notion of "social revolution" had become vastly appealing: Soviet strategists were quick to move to salve the spirits of millions of "weary people" who were "sick, nigh unto death" of the efforts needed "to keep body and soul together."

If Americans were going to deal with this challenge, they were going to have to fight ideology with ideology. They would have to demonstrate the essential worth of their traditions and lifestyle, Dulles argued, and lay claim as in the past to "moral leadership in the world." They certainly possessed the best of credentials for this task as far as he was concerned. The slightest reflection should give them confidence in the basic moral principles on which their society was built. Two hundred years of progress at home had produced a "society of freedom" in which individuals had reaped enormous benefits, he wrote in his June 1946 *Life* articles. Over and over, he said a few months later, it had been demonstrated that "our dedication . . . is to the progressive realization of the dignity and worth of man in every area of life—political, economic, social and religious. . . ." To their credit Americans had often carried this dream beyond their own borders as well. They had aimed, he said in October 1946, at "the world-wide achievement of man's individual freedom, under God, to think, to believe, and to act responsibly according to the dictates of his own conscience." Or, as he put it in a statement published by the Federal Council of Churches in July 1947, their goal had been:

> . . . a world of free societies wherein all men, as the children of God, are recognized to have certain basic rights, including liberty to hold and change beliefs and practices according to reason and conscience, freedom to differ even from their own government and immunity from persecution or coercion on account of spiritual and intellectual beliefs.

The task immediately facing Americans was to reassert their dedication to these enormously appealing principles and to underline their relevance to an evaluation of sharply different Soviet values. "The moral issue must be clarified," he told students at Northwestern University in June 1947, and applied to the circumstances of the post–World War II era.

> That issue is not the issue of economic communism against capitalism or state socialism against free enterprise. It is not an issue of relative national power. Those are not moral issues. The moral issue is the issue of the free state as against the police state.
>
> A police state is a state where a few, who control the police power, proclaim a pattern of political, social and economic life and then use the police power to perpetuate it, detecting and crushing all who do not conform to their pattern.[6]

Of course, Americans would have to do more than simply reiterate high-sounding moral principles or engage in "sterile denunciation" of communist promises. They would have to breathe life into their beliefs, "to demonstrate anew the value of a free society." "That kind of society has been smeared throughout the world," Dulles wrote, and much would have to be done to prove that "the abuses which Soviet propaganda tilts at are much the ghosts of a dead past." In the United States itself, "we can demonstrate that our political and religious faith is a curative thing, able to heal the sores in our body politic." Why should "the blight of bigotry" be with us still, he asked on several occasions? "Racial intolerance, discrimination, and oppression are a standing negation of democracy and Christian morality," he wrote in the fall of 1946, and we must "do away with the widely prevalent double standard of personal relations and citizenship applied to Negro Americans." There had been "slow," but "real" progress along these lines, but it would be necessary to "press on."[7]

Problems outside the United States were staggering in their dimensions, but Dulles believed Americans would have to demonstrate that their system and beliefs could help deal with these too. The United States should continue pushing for the abandonment of "political imperialism." Progress had already been discernible within the United Nations, with Great Britain and the Netherlands in particular being encouraged to accept "the principle that imperialism and strategic advantage must yield to the right of independence," and more would have to be done to make sure that "words" were translated into "deeds." Even more pressing in its implications for the United States was the need to contribute "to the relief and reconstruction of a dislocated world." In "Europe . . . Asia, South America and the colonial areas," he said in January 1947, "there are vast tasks of reconstruction to be undertaken. Old societies need to be rebuilt.

Sick societies need to be made well." Americans should show that they could respond positively to these tasks. As he put it in his *Life* articles:

> If we believe in a humane society, we will help those in other lands who are destitute. If we believe in a society of human freedoms, we will keep life and vigor in those who, if they live, will support and defend that kind of society. We will show the world that it is a good thing to have free people as neighbors.[8]

Dulles's broadly drawn agenda for dealing with the Soviet Union in 1946 and 1947, then, incorporated a few key tasks for his countrymen: they should maintain impressive military strength, they should reassert the moral principles of the "great American experiment," and they should show that those principles could serve as a better foundation than "police state" communism for solving global problems. If Americans faced up to these responsibilities, he was convinced that the Soviet challenge to civilization would be deflected. In the bargain, indeed, the overall process of dealing with it might actually produce beneficial results.

Dulles believed that the maintainance of physical strength would impress Moscow and keep it from attempting any additional territorial expansion. He did not accept the notion that there is "an inevitability about Soviet foreign policy," he wrote in 1946:

> Soviet leaders today are not as fanatical as were their predecessors. . . . Under Mr. Stalin, Soviet moves abroad seem to have been marked by an effort to calculate chances. Soviet foreign representatives have sometimes taken extreme positions, but Mr. Stalin has pulled back and relieved the tension when unexpected opposition was encountered.

Dulles dealt with the importance of using military power to influence Moscow's behavior on many other occasions as well. In an address to the Inland Daily Press Association in February 1947 he warned that a slackening of strength "would cause Soviet leaders to push on recklessly":

> The greatest danger of war is from possible Soviet miscalculation. Political leaders who are dynamic and who have had great initial successes often become overconfident. They are apt to take ever greater risks until they find to their chagrin that they have made a bad calculation and have gotten into trouble which they never wanted or expected. I believe that Soviet dynamism will keep within tolerable bounds; but that will be because it comes up against something that is vigorous, not because it encounters mushiness.[9]

Clarifying and utilizing moral principles would help counteract the Soviet ideological offensive, something that physical strength alone would not make possible. On the one hand, Moscow itself would receive the clear message that both barrels of its threat were going to be dealt with by the United States. He wanted to see "a moral resistance so solid that to assault it would evidently be futile," Dulles said at one point; he wanted to demonstrate "that our way of life is so vigorous and deeply rooted that others will renounce, as both impractical and as undesirable, the task of uprooting it," he wrote in his *Life* articles. On the other hand, those to whom Moscow was appealing would also be impressed. "We must show that our free land is not spiritual lowland, easily submerged," he argued, "but highland that, most of all, provides the spiritual, intellectual and economic conditions *which all men want*" (emphasis added). A rededication to moral principles would give Americans "spiritual and intellectual vigor" again and "the leadership which that bestows"; it would develop a faith that *"would bring into being a world which is responsive to that faith,"* instead of to communist enticements (emphasis added). After all, as Napoleon had once observed, " 'In war, moral considerations make up three-fourths of the game.' "[10]

All in all, Dulles argued in 1946 and 1947, physical and moral resistance would allow the United States to deal with the grave problems confronting it. And if those problems forced Americans to behave in a more mature and responsible fashion, then perhaps it was good that they had materialized. This latter sentiment was very much the product of his enthusiasm for the historical analyses of Arnold Toynbee, it should be added. Dulles had started reading *A Study of History* in the early 1940s, after meeting Toynbee in connection with cooperative work between British and American Protestant leaders. He had been impressed and had begun incorporating some of the work's conclusions in statements drafted by the Commission on a Just and Durable Peace, particularly those on the need to revive a "dynamic faith" in the ideals of American society. Now, in the early years of the Cold War, Dulles used his sense of Toynbee's arguments more than ever. He allowed them to lend a grand historical sweep to his own writings. "Every civilization faces, and ought to face, periodic challenges," he wrote in *Life*. "That is the kind of world God put us in," he said in early 1947. "Western democracy has for many centuries held unquestioned supremacy in the world. It is natural and even healthy that we should now have to evaluate again our place in history, to clear away some of the barnacles that have gathered and to reinvigorate the basic and worthy features of our historic faith. . . . Otherwise we shall be merely one more great nation gone decadent and ripe to be plucked." He certainly had no doubt but that the time for plucking could be put off. "We have the ideals, we have the 'knowhow,' we have the power," he said. "Since the collapse of the Roman Empire, there has never been a nation which possessed so great a superiority of material power as does the United States. Also, as we have shown, we still possess deep springs of faith on which we can draw for ideals which respond to the aspirations of men everywhere."[11]

II

After reading the draft of one of Dulles's broadly conceived prescriptions for dealing with the Soviet menace, Arthur Vandenberg felt somewhat dissatisfied with the extreme loftiness of its proposals. In several letters, he urged his friend to offer readers something more than "moral tonic." "We cannot win this supreme contest for the world's soul without getting on our knees," he wrote in one, "but neither can we win it by *staying* on our knees." "I'm for sweetness and light, too," he said in another, "but also for the good old K.O."[12]

Vandenberg should have known that emphasis on religious and moral dynamism was only one facet of Dulles's identity. The Senator himself said in one of his letters that he could see that "the primary appeal of your thesis is to the moral judgments of *the particular constituency which is your preoccupation*," i.e., in this case, the Commission on a Just and Durable Peace and its Protestant audience (emphasis added).[13] As in the past, however, Dulles thought he had other "constituencies" as well. Responding to different audiences and varying drives within himself, he always went beyond highflown moralism to far more particular and far more traditional recommendations involving political and economic actions. Sometimes these proposals served as accompanying detail for the sweeping strokes of "sweetness and light"; more often they emerged in their own distinct form and were especially prevalent in the more private realm of his personal correspondence and behind-the-scenes discussions with church colleagues, political associates, and government leaders. As Dulles developed his more substantive proposals after World War II, he revealed again and again the crucial concrete foundation on which he stood while observing the global arena. As it turned out, it was the base he had been comfortable on for more than a quarter of a century, one he had come to know long before lofty, cloudy realms had caught his eye.

Dulles offered many recommendations involving more traditional political and economic measures after 1945, but none were as crucial to him as those looking toward *the alteration of the structure and environment of continental Europe*. Europe and its relationship with the United States had been a preoccupation almost as long as he had been thinking about international affairs, and it is not at all surprising that it remained so during and after World War II. His unfolding thoughts and actions became testimony as much to the momentum of his past as to the concerns of his future.

Essentially, Dulles saw postwar Europe as the most appropriate laboratory within which to demonstrate the striking virtues of the international behavior he had described in the 1930s. With American cooperation, Europeans could reform themselves and stand as a model for a more peaceful and prosperous world order. Most importantly, they could develop more flexible and cooperative relationships with each other. The danger of rigid boundaries separating tightly packed territorial compartments might be defused, for example, by a gradual dilution of total sovereign control over economic affairs. This would foster freer, and more profitable, commercial and financial relationships and put an end to irresponsible autarchy. In the bargain, it would reduce political tension and greatly lessen the likelihood of future wars in an area that had shown itself prone to explosion time and again.

In early discussions of the postwar world, Dulles used Europe as a negative example. On several occasions in 1939 and 1940, he specifically pointed to the outbreak of war there as the inevitable consequence of a fundamentally faulty structure. In a memorandum sent to Wendell Willkie during the 1940 campaign, he was equally emphatic:

> We should avoid any political commitments in the affairs of Continental Europe. The nations of Europe, in the face of repeated warnings, have sought to perpetuate precisely that political system which, as the Federalist papers demonstrate with such logic and wealth of historical precedent, is bound to lead to recurrent wars. We have there—or did have—some thirty "independent, unconnected sovereignties in the same neighborhood" and "to look for a continuation of harmony between them . . . is to disregard the uniform course of human events and set at defiance the experience of the ages." We cannot, if we would, impose upon Europe a system conducive to peace. It may be that, through agony, they will evolve toward some system of interconnection, which could have been achieved peacefully had not short-sighted selfish policies prevented. We must not commit ourselves to a restoration of the pre-war status which contains within itself the seeds of its own violent destruction.

A year earlier, he had specifically contrasted the dangers of the European environment with the advantages of the federal system that early Americans had devised, a system in which "boundaries become *structurally* porous and elastic" because "each state renounced the right to interfere with the movement, as between themselves, of people and goods."[14]

Dulles shifted emotional gears during 1941 and began approaching many issues in a more positive fashion. If the past had demonstrated the follies of America's transatlantic neighbors, he quickly came to argue with respect to Europe, what could be done to right the situation for the future? He had no doubts at all. "We should seek the political reorganization of continental Europe as a federated commonwealth," he wrote in September 1941. "There must be a large measure of local self-government along ethnic lines. This can be assured through federal principles which in this respect are very flexible. But the reestablishment of some twenty-five wholly independent sovereign states in Europe would be political folly."

Dulles expanded on this basic premise many times, and it became one of the most concrete and consistent ingredients in his wartime blueprints for the future. Without its accomplishment, in fact, he seemed to feel that the new world order he was hoping for was not likely to appear. Peace would certainly not come to the Europeans themselves. "Continental Europe at once suggests itself as *the area* within which regional political evolution should most logically be resumed," he wrote in March 1942:

> There exists in Europe a high degree of interdependence. The trade, industry and economic life of the European peoples is closely interrelated, especially in their eastern area. There is much social and intellectual intercourse. On the other hand, there persists a very high degree of political independence. Of the total number of independent sovereign nations, about thirty, or nearly half, are to be found in Europe. War, there, is a chronic condition.

Two years later, at lunch with Jean Monnet, he agreed with his old friend's conclusion that "if Europe remains as twenty five or twenty eight separate states with two great Powers (U.S. and Russia, with Britain as a possible third power) they will be merely torn apart by rival jealousies and maneuverings."

Nor would the horrors of war be confined to the Europeans alone. Decisions regarding the Continent's future would, "more than any Security Organization . . . determine whether there is to be a Third World War," Dulles believed. And the United States was particularly vulnerable to such reverberations. As he explained it when discussing his reactions to the Atlantic Charter:

> Twice within the last twenty-five years the United States has become deeply involved in the wars originating between the independent, unconnected sovereignties of Europe. It has been demonstrated that the world has so shrunk that European wars can no longer, as during the last cen-

tury, be confined to Europe. Therefore, it is not merely of self-interest to Europe, but of vital concern to us, that there be not restored in Europe the conditions which inherently give rise to such wars. From a purely selfish standpoint any American program for peace must include a federated continental Europe.

The same point was made in a draft speech for Tom Dewey during the 1944 campaign: "The old negative policy of 'avoiding European entanglements' is no longer good enough. The world has grown so small, and force has become so explosive, that we cannot avoid becoming involved in Europe's troubles. Two World Wars have shown that. We must exert in Europe a positive influence for peace." [15]

The equation of war with the exercise of excessive and irrational sovereignty was one Dulles had begun making in the interwar years and his steady application of it to the European scene of the 1940s was one sign of strong continuity. So was his ever-present emphasis on the particular need for reform in the economic area. As so often in the past, Dulles used commercial and financial practices as the major specific components of his recommendations. "The interdependent life of Europe can be brought under rules of a common authority which will so order that life that at least the economic efforts of the people will be more productive," he wrote in March 1942. Unless more cooperation were forthcoming regarding trade and currency policies, unless freer "interstate commerce" were allowed in Europe, then "there is no alternative to periodic reductions of living standards and destruction of life through wars and their incidents."

Dulles often indicated the kinds of economic developments he wanted to see in Europe's future by taking another series of swipes at politicians. Some Europeans had recognized the need for responsible cooperation, he argued on one occasion:

> Organized labor has worked in intimate and fruitful association. The individuals controlling the commerce and industry of the different European countries work readily together. Through the cartel system the great industries of Europe have achieved cooperation as complete as was possible in the face of the antagonistic and disordered economic and fiscal policies of their respective governments. Also, during interludes of peace, large seasonal movements of labor across national boundary lines were customary.

Unfortunately, "insular and nationalistic" government officials had set up clutches of "stupid political barriers" to interfere with the functioning and maximization of these tendencies. "The fact of the matter is," Dulles wrote a Wall Street colleague in 1942, "that economic unity in Europe has primarily been held back by a small group of self-seeking politicians in

every nation. . . . Because a lot of politicians want to hold on to the trappings of sovereignty, are we to allow a condition to persist which makes
recurrent war inevitable and which now, apparently, also inevitably involves our being drawn into such wars?"[16]

Dulles's wartime discussions of the need for changes in the European
environment involved, perhaps inevitably, a degree of preoccupation
with the future of Germany. With the accumulated observations of many
years behind him, he saw the fate of the defeated enemy as a key factor in
the evolution of the postwar world. Well before V-E Day he had sketched
in a rough agenda that he would have liked victorious governments to
follow.

His basic goal with respect to Germany was simple and straightforward enough. As he put it in an interview in December 1944, "Germany
should be subjected to controls sufficient to make the German people
unable to conduct a modern war." Variations on this theme reflected different facets of Dulles's experience and world view. To some degree, he
demonstrated the important personal legacy of the Great War and its
aftermath. Germany should be controlled by a Commission of U.S.,
British, and Russian members, he urged in 1944, with representatives of
France, Belgium, and the Netherlands; this Commission should operate
totally independently of any new international organization; it should
"supervise" military and industrial capacity and be prepared to do so for
at least twenty-five and perhaps even fifty years. Dulles explicity cited
these measures as alternatives to the ones embodied in the Treaty of Versailles, which were followed haphazardly after 1919, and he argued that a
different course was necessary if the postwar 1940s were to avoid a repetition of the mistakes of the past.[17]

Dulles's wartime thoughts on Germany also revealed the deep imprint
of the immediately preceding years' intellectual experiences. From the
very beginning of his efforts to chart a desirable course for treatment of
the enemy, he related it to his overall concern for global reform and to the
encouragement of freer interstate commerce in particular. He was
especially anxious to place consideration of Germany into a broad context. The question of what to do with Germany was "part and parcel of
the whole European problem," he wrote one associate as early as October
1941; a Commission on a Just and Durable Peace subcommittee on German policy might more wisely be called "a group studying the European
question," he said on another occasion.[18] Operating with this kind of encompassing perspective, Dulles always then went on to argue that any
consideration of Germany was intimately connected with the issues of
continental unity and reformed economic relationships. "Germany

ought to be integrated into a unified Europe," he believed, and the commercial and financial spheres were the logical ones in which to seek that unification. As one of his Commission statements put it during the closing months of the war, the peace settlement "should be inspired by the desire to secure the maximum of collaboration among the peoples of Europe and encourage the economic development of Europe as a whole including Germany." This kind of vision implied "some political decentralization of Germany," Dulles felt, perhaps even "dismemberment," but that might actually be beneficial as long as broader economic cooperation was achieved. While in London in 1942, he specifically told Anthony Eden of his interest in the possibility of "allowing separatist tendencies to develop in Germany." "Partitioning of Germany in her economic life and to some extent political and cultural life . . . is not something I want to reject out of hand," he told church associates in March 1944. The key thing was to guarantee that a breakup of Germany would be concomitant with the integration of the Continent as a whole. "I think it vitally important that there be a large measure of economic freedom between the separate states and the non—German areas upon which new states would abut," he wrote in 1942. "Otherwise economic pressures will force a new centralization." [19]

As Dulles thought about the future of Europe during World War II, he operated in what was essentially a speculative limbo: with the exception of the inevitable question of what to do with Germany, he dealt with the issues that he chose to analyze because they linked up in some way with his personal interests and concerns. The end of the war changed this. Rather than responding to essentially internal stimuli, Dulles's thoughts, like those of many concerned and informed people, began to drift into channels created by events taking place in the real world. Postwar Europe was actually taking shape and the decisions, problems, and crises inherent in the process became almost unavoidable foci.

Eastern Europe attracted a great deal of Dulles's attention during the closing months of the war and for quite some time afterwards. Though his interest owed something to the events of 1919 and his extensive business activities in the area during the interwar years, the intensity of his concern was greatly increased by the circumstances of 1945 and 1946. Poland, Hungary, Rumania, Bulgaria, Yugoslavia, and other countries became sometimes interlocking stages on which were acted out classic postwar dramas. What kinds of societies would rise from the ashes? How would they compare to prewar orders? Who would control them, internally and externally? The potential for a series of skirmishes and explosions was especially great because the natural tendencies of people within Eastern European societies to struggle among themselves about the directions their futures would take were exacerbated by the traditional meddling of great powers in the affairs of weaker states. The Soviet Union, of course, had made it clear throughout the Second World War that it would insist on playing a greater role in the region than had been possible in the inter-war years: it showed itself ready to move in a flexible and frequently ad hoc way in 1945 and 1946, but it left no doubt about the broad thrust of its power. In variable and no doubt confusing fashion, the British and the Americans sought to keep the eastern half of the Continent from falling under Moscow's control: there was no way in which their political and economic actions could fail to produce sparks within the Grand Alliance. Therefore as Dulles followed the news and listened to the government leaders with whom he now regularly worked, he had little choice but to see Eastern Europe as a region in which problems of at least temporary priority were to be found.

Dulles's approach to Eastern Europe during the early war years had been a logical outgrowth of his previous experience: he simply viewed it as one part of the Continent as a whole. Though he may have acquired a sense of certain regional characteristics during his interwar work concerning Poland or Hungary or Rumania, by the early 1940s he showed no signs of thinking of the area as something special and apart. While in London in 1942, for example, his frequent references to the need for European federation always encompassed both halves of the Continent. Talks with Eden, Attlee, and Cripps touched on the possibility of a series of interlocking regional arrangements, including one between Poland and Czechoslovakia and another involving Greece, Yugoslavia, and other southeastern countries. Dulles made clear his preference for an across-the-board association but was interested enough in any possibility to speak with Eduard Beneš and other Eastern European representatives in London about potential developments.[20]

Already in London, however, Dulles may have begun moving away from the conception of Eastern Europe as one integral part of a larger continental whole. It was there, if not earlier, that he became impressed with the evidence of Soviet expectations concerning its future role in the region. U.S. Ambassador Winant, for example, divulged some of the behind-the-scenes details of British–Soviet negotiations concerning Polish, Bessarabian, and Baltic State territories; without strong American opposition, he told Dulles, London would have given way to what was clearly a strong Russian appetite. Dulles sensed something of the same perception of rising Soviet power in his conversations with Beneš. The

Czech leader expressed deep dismay at the failure of the U.S. and other western countries to come to his aid in 1938 and made it clear that he could see no choice but to rely on friendship with Moscow after this war. He was also critical of the London Poles' intransigence regarding the Soviets; for their own safety, he said, they would have "to agree to shrink up so that they will not offend Russia."[21]

This kind of inside information reinforced what might have become evident through a simple alertness to day-to-day news. It was not long before Dulles realized and admitted that Eastern Europe was by and large likely to be a region with special problems in the postwar years—that it was unlikely to fit neatly into the Continent-wide reform schemes he himself had in mind, that it was probably not even going to be possible to apply the elementary principles of the Atlantic Charter to postwar settlements there. In a meeting at the White House in March 1943, for example, he and Franklin Roosevelt spoke about the virtual inevitability of unappealing developments regarding Poland, Bessarabia, and Rumania. A few weeks later, Dulles expressed a similar, but even broader, conclusion to Sumner Welles: he predicted potential shocks as efforts were made to reconcile "the views of the U.S.S.R with the national aspirations of peoples such as those of Finland, Latvia, Lithuania, Estonia, Poland, etc."[22]

Dulles tried to devise a special strategy for dealing with this special region. His overall counsel was for Americans to be "realistic" in their expectations. Because of Soviet interests, settlements in Eastern Europe were going to fall short of what the United States would want if it were able to control affairs. Americans might try to influence developments and soften the harshness of particular settlements, but they should approach matters calmly and in a clear spirit of compromise. This would aid the peoples of Eastern Europe on the one hand and the rest of the world on the other, because it would make possible the crucial continuance of great power cooperation .

Dulles made the gist of this approach clear in his early 1943 meeting with Roosevelt. As they looked at Poland and Bessarabia, the two men agreed that "some things . . . had to be compromised if collaboration was to be maintained"; they indicated a joint "fear lest too much 'idealism' in these matters should lead to a rejection of collaboration as a permanent principle." A few weeks later, Dulles expressed similar thoughts to Sumner Welles:

> While I certainly do not feel that we should abandon the ideals of the Atlantic Charter, I place organized cooperation between Britain, Russia and the United States as a prime essential to durable peace. Without this

the ultimate fate of the peoples in question will, I think, be much worse than if their future can be dealt with within a framework which Russia can feel assures continuing peace and minimizes the necessity for her action being dictated wholly by strategic considerations. It seems to me that if this is true then some reasonable compromise may have to be accepted as part of a realistic treatment of the situation.

And so on through the end of the war. In early 1945, he made clear his appreciation of Moscow's perceived needs in Eastern Europe. He recognized that " ' territorial propinquity' " could create its own "sense of vital interest," as he said in one speech, and he wanted to be sure to be "conciliatory and understanding of the ideals and vital needs of others."

There was a loophole in Dulles's "realism" concerning Eastern Europe, and it was to prove large enough for him to fall through in the early postwar period. The whole notion of "compromise," after all, entailed the assumption that the Soviet Union would be willing to allow American or British input with regard to settlements along its borders; as he described it when discussing the Yalta agreements, he wanted the Russians to permit "joint action on matters that it had the power to settle for itself." Whatever the factors shaping Soviet policy, this was not an operating procedure that Dulles would often see after the closing days of World War II. Even more threatening to ongoing equanimity were Dulles's expectations for the long-range evolution of Eastern European affairs. Though he was prepared to be conciliatory about "decisions taken in the heat of war," he made it clear that "we must keep open the possibility of revising such decisions in the light of truer insights." We should be tolerant "provisionally, of practical situations which fall short of our ideals," he told a church conference in January 1945:

> . . . The vital word in that sentence is the world "provisionally." We cannot agree to solutions which fall short of our ideal if thereby we become morally bound to sustain and perpetuate them. That would be stultifying. It is the possibility of *change* which is the bridge between idealism and the practical incidents of collaboration. . . . There must be "potentialities for correcting mistakes." . . . It must be made clear that collaboration implies not merely a spirit of compromise but equally a right on the part of every nation, to persist in efforts to realize its ideals.[23]

Moscow was not likely to look to the future of its border regions with a similar perspective.

As it turned out, Dulles's hopes for Eastern Europe did not make it as far as the "bridge" of change he was anticipating. Though he never really offered any detailed picture of the kind of short-run compromise settlements he was prepared to support, his perceptions of developments that took place shortly before and after the end of the war in Europe make it clear that he did not believe what the Soviets were offering, even at this early stage, was sufficient to justify his endorsement.

During the San Francisco Conference, for example, Dulles began receiving information from Washington policy makers about Moscow's lack of cooperation regarding Eastern European affairs. During one of his private luncheons with Arkadii Sobolev, Counselor at the Soviet Embassy in London and a delegate in San Francisco, the two men talked about the declining cordiality between their governments: the Russian pointed to a U.S. desire to wage "class warfare," typified by "the failure . . . to grant large Soviet credits," but Dulles said that he had been told it was because Moscow was "not carrying out a number of political agreements which had been made about Europe. . . ." In a memorandum prepared for the delegation at about this time, Dulles roughly indicated his sources and their conclusions:

> Available information indicates that the U.S.S.R. does not now practice genuine cooperation with Great Britain or the U.S. within the orbit of its physical might. There have been many agreements beginning with the Moscow agreement of 1943, with reference to cooperating on the problems which would be created by the liberation of Europe. There have been specific agreements for cooperation with reference to such countries as Poland, Roumania, Yugoslavia, Austria, occupied Germany, etc. It appears to be the judgment of members of the Department of State, who follow these matters, and also of the U.S Army, that these agreements have not been lived up to by the Soviet Union, and that in fact where the Soviet Union is able to do so it takes unilateral action.

The indirect information about Eastern Europe that Dulles was receiving in San Francisco was supplemented by personal observation when he attended the Council of Foreign Ministers session with Secretary of State Byrnes in September 1945. Aside from extensive discussions of Italy, the agenda in London was dominated by questions relating to peace settlements with Finland, Rumania, Bulgaria, and Hungary. Dulles's files, which he eventually put into four large bound volumes, were filled day after day with data on the extent of Russian interest in these countries and the variety of techniques they were prepared to use to get their way. In addition to specific treaty proposals circulated prior to discussion, he was also given copies of many of the cables and reports coming to Byrnes from U.S. representatives in Eastern European capitals and Moscow: for example a September 16 Burton Y. Berry report on the undemocratic origins and procedures of the Groza government in Rumania and a September 28 memo from Averill Harriman about Soviet goals in Bulgaria and other countries.

By the time he returned to New York in early October, Dulles had what he thought was a clear picture of Eastern Europe as a region being cut off from the rest of the Continent by the Soviet Union. Nothing that happened in succeeding months altered this opinion as far as he was concerned. The *Life* articles that he drafted in March 1946 offered a full dress description of this area as part of the "Middle Zone" created by Moscow. He noted that this was territory "not yet ripe for incorporation into the U.S.S.R., but . . . close enough to it to be amenable to the influence of Soviet military power." He wrote further:

> This zone is, or recently has been, occupied by elements of the Soviet army. Where there is no present occupation, there is fear of it and the governments there, while nominally independent and in some respects actually independent, are under strong inducement to put their foreign policy, their armies and, most important of all, their secret police and censorship in the hands of persons who take much guidance from Moscow. Thus the Soviet leaders assure that the character of these governments will be "friendly."

To leave no doubt about the geographical perimeters he envisioned, Dulles listed its European components: Poland, the eastern half of Germany, Czechoslovakia, Eastern Austria, Hungary, Rumania, Bulgaria, Yugoslavia, and Albania.[24]

Dulles's perception of the Eastern Europe scene by 1946, of course, had thus been absorbed into his evolving portrait of an encompassing Soviet communist menace. As such, it suffered from the same weaknesses that afflicted the grander vision. His own inherent ideological and emotional biases and his general acceptance of Washington's interpretations of Moscow's actions helped produce a simplistic overview of what was going on along the borders of the Soviet Union. Like the other American policy makers with whom he was more frequently coming into contact, he glossed over or never saw the complexities of the Eastern European region. In particular, he does not seem to have grasped the substantial differences in the internal circumstances of individual countries between 1944 and 1947 and the flexibility or confusion of Soviet policy to which this might have testified. For example, he should have known that the situation in Czechoslovakia was very different from that in Rumania, given his contacts with Beneš and other leaders in the former and his access to information about the latter, but there is no hint of this in his statements. Consciously or unconsciously, he allowed his sense of certainly about the nature of the forest to overpower his interest in looking at the trees.[25]

Simplistic though it may have been, Dulles's perception of Eastern Europe as a region essentially controlled by the Soviet Union did not lead him to urge on the United States any strenuous remedial actions. It seems a sharp contrast to his later reputation, but 1945 and 1946 found him quicky accepting the realities of the situation and demonstrating a preference for going on to deal with other problems. He made no secret of his distaste for the behavior of Russian policy makers and occasionally outlined his own hopes for ideal postwar settlements along their borders, but he seems to have known that he was really only going through the motions. At a time when he was spewing forth great numbers of proposals for American or United Nations actions, he said absolutely nothing about taking concrete steps to deal with the myriad of Eastern European situations.

Dulles first revealed his adaptability to Soviet behavior in Eastern Europe during the San Francisco Conference. Receiving reports from State Department and Army colleagues in the U.S. delegation, he had a clear sense of what was happening: at one point, in fact, he specifically used the phrase "their own sphere of influence" to refer to Soviet interests in Eastern Europe. He does not, however, seem to have given a moment's thought to altering the situation. The only thing that clearly worried him was the possibility that the Soviets might want to go *beyond* the sphere of influence they were constructing, and he developed for the first time a rather explicit dichotomy of Eastern versus Western European concerns. As he put it in one memorandum on the regional security agreements issue, he wanted to avoid suggesting "to *Western* Europe and to China that the U.S. intends to retreat into hemispheric isolation and might leave those European and Asiatic states to fall into Soviet-dominated regional arrangements." This would bring about a spread of the "situation such as prevails in eastern and middle Europe," he said on another occasion.

At the London Council of Foreign Ministers meeting, where the focus of attention was considerably narrower and closer to the Eastern European region than in San Francisco, Dulles revealed the same perspective. There was never any doubt about his personal disapprobation for Soviet plans and behavior in Finland, Hungary, Bulgaria, and Rumania, but neither was there any question of his proposing policies beyond a resistance on principle. He spoke vaguely about the possibility of a general peace conference improving on the moral tone of specific settlements, but he seems to have had little real hope of this actually happening. His recommendations regarding Rumania, in fact, suggest a more emphatic resignation than his delegation colleagues. The U.S. should try to be "non-provocative" in what it said about the Groza government, he told Secretary of State Byrnes; the interest of the Soviet Union was "perhaps more directly engaged than that of the United States," he added at another time. More importantly, he made clear his "doubt as to the long-range efficacy of non-recognition in such a situation as Roumania. I said that it seemed like starting over again our policy of non-recognition of the U.S.S.R. . . . which had proven a barren policy." Dulles's reference to the "long-range" obviously implies the view that circumstances in Rumania were going to remain unsatisfactory from an American viewpoint.

In a post-mortem on the London meetings, which he conducted for his Commission on a Just and Durable Peace, Dulles came as close as he ever did in these years to offering a capsule prescription for dealing with the Eastern European situation. He said that Americans had "stood firm" on behalf of self-determination and democratic government and that "there is a good chance that if we continue to stand firm, those principles will, in the main, prevail." He had what many might have considered a curious definition of "in the main," however. As he put it:

> There is, of course, a risk that if we do that, [stand firm on principles] all of the United Nations may not join in treaties of peace with the enemy states. It might be, for example, that the United States, Great Britain and France would make a separate treaty with Italy and that the Soviet Union would make a separate treaty with the Balkan countries. *Each might accept, but not join in, the results agreed to by the others.* [Emphasis added.]

In essence, Dulles himself followed the route he outlined here. On the one hand, he occasionally indicated the basic principles with which he thought all peace settlements should conform. In a pamphlet published by the Federal Council of Churches in November 1945, for example, he called for territorial settlements in accord with the "natural long-term aspirations" of inhabitants; the avoidance of "wholesale displacements of peoples"; limited reparations; and progress toward the provision of basic civil liberties, among other things. On the other hand, he showed himself completely ready to live with the consequences of refusing to compromise on such matters. He made it clear to Secretary of State Byrnes in the fall of 1945 that he was uncomfortable with a Truman Administration interest in some kind of "collective action" agreement to protect the Dardanelles. As Byrnes told the President, "Mr. Dulles . . . was somewhat wary about our undertaking a guarantee of passage in waters so far from our shores." His *Life* articles, drafted in early 1946, contained not a single prescription for the Eastern European problems of the day. Nor are proposals to be found anywhere in his extensive correspondence with Arthur Vandenburg during the latter's attendance of the 1946 Paris sessions of the Council of Foreign Ministers and the follow-up Peace Conference there. His assessment of the treaties with the lesser enemies that were eventually forthcoming reflects this lack of interest in an American initiative. Though it was carefully worded and lukewarm praise, to be sure, he publicly said of the American delegation's efforts that through "patient firmness" they had secured treaties "with Italy and the satellites which, while not ideal, involve no flagrant new injustices."[26]

An aura of calm resignation carried over into Dulles's legal work, as well. Sullivan & Cromwell undertook representation of the Petschek and Gellert families of Czechoslovakia in 1945: both had had extensive property interests that had been effectively wiped out by postwar nationalization and confiscation legislation, and Dulles sought to secure reasonable compensation. In a voluminous correspondence with U.S. Ambassador Laurence Steinhardt (with whom he had once worked on the Ivar Kreuger disaster), Dulles plotted a low-key and ultimately successful strategy. He accepted the fate of the properties as an accomplished fact, never railed against Prague's policies or suggested that Moscow was in any way involved, and simply applied himself to untangling currency and bureaucratic difficulties. In the end, he and Steinhardt secured an $8 million settlement for the Petschecks alone.[27]

There was an exception to the rule of Dulles's calm resignation regarding Eastern Europe after World War II, and it was noteworthy enough to serve as one prop for his later reputation. When Dulles put aside diplomacy or business or intellectual analysis and turned his attention to partisan politics, the shifting of gears produced a far more strident and melodramatic approach. On such occasions, Dulles could sound as if he were demanding more substantive action by the United States. The precedent was set during the 1944 presidential campaign. His initial inclination had been to spurn Arthur Vandenberg's advice regarding an appeal to Eastern European ethnic groups in the United States and to accept the fact that the Republicans were not likely to be able "to restore the prewar status of Poland and the Baltic States. . . ." By the time the campaign was in full swing, however, he had changed his mind. A number of meetings were held with representatives of the London Polish government at which expressions of interest in their cause were forthcoming. More importantly, Dewey began using Dulles's speech drafts that criticized Roosevelt's failure to do anything meaningful regarding various Eastern European questions, and he specifically mentioned Poland, the

Baltic States, and Rumania. When Walter Lippmann expressed some doubts about this kind of politicking, Dulles wrote a wounded letter about the need to emphasize "principles."[28]

The 1944 experience was a relative shadow of what would emerge as time went on, of course. There were occasional G.O.P. blasts about Democratic failures in Eastern Europe during the usually muted foreign policy debates of 1948 and then a great explosion of purple prose and rhetoric on the subject all through the 1950s.[29] Whatever the implications of these kinds of political assertions, however, it seems clear that in the 1940s, at least, they were essentially hollow. On the crucial question of action, Dulles simply backed off and resorted to vague generalities. This is not surprising. It was the outgrowth of the uniformly calm approach to Eastern European questions that he took when away from the political arena. It also testified to the fact that his mind and concerns were really focused elsewhere.

III

Though Eastern European controversies frequently dominated headlines in late 1945 and early 1946, they never completely diverted Dulles's attention from the problems of the Continent as a whole. The broader scene had drawn his attention for too long and had led him to articulate his concerns too strongly to ever be eclipsed by the special problems of a particular moment.

His attention in the immediate postwar period was focused, perhaps inevitably, on the devastating impact of physical destruction across the Continent. "I feel apprehensive as to what we will find in Europe for years to come," his brother had written to him from his aerie in Berne during the closing days of the war: "If Hitler succeeds in nothing else, like Samsom, he may pull down the pillars of the temple and leave a long hard road of reconstruction."[30] This proved an accurate prediction.

Though he had seen it all once before, in 1919 and the early 1920s, Dulles was no more inclined to accept it the second time around. There was something particularly appalling about the descent of "privation, starvation and consequent chaos" on Europe, he felt. His attendance of the first Council of Foreign Ministers meeting in the fall of 1945 and the first session of the General Assembly in early 1946, as well as travels away from his London base, afforded him the opportunity to see the situation first-hand. "It is impossible to find words to portray such numbing misery as I glimpsed on the Continent," he told a radio audience in March 1946:

". . . peoples have been exhausted by the physical and moral strains of war and, since fighting has stopped, the daily problems of keeping alive seem to have become even more burdensome." He soon made it clear that he was as convinced as he had been in the 1920s that the United States should step in to help alleviate the strains. He wanted the Republican Party to declare its support for "grants-in-aid to avert the immediate menace of chaos through misery," he wrote to Representative Charles Halleck in November 1945. The same month, he drafted an introduction to a Commission on a Just and Durable Peace pamphlet which said that "the people of our nation should take whatever remedial and sacrificial action they can to alleviate the appalling conditions which are the aftermath of war."

As with many, Dulles focused on aid to Great Britain as the first concrete measure of an American commitment to the rehabilitation of Europe. Negotiations for a major loan began in Washington in September 1945. The British were desperately seeking large-scale dollar credits to help them make the transition to economic recovery. The cost of fighting the war had been incredibly draining, requiring among other things the liquidation of fully one-half of their overseas investments. Until their greatly shrunken export capacity recovered, they knew they would face staggering balance-of-payments problems. The Americans were willing to offer assistance, but they exacted their price. After three months of grueling negotiations, they secured what they thought were major concessions on currency and trade policies in return for a low-interest $3.75 billion credit.

Dulles's personal approach to the British loan was a mixture of enthusiastic endorsement of the basic concept and discomfiture with some aspects of its execution. An example of his overall support came in a major address to the National Association of Manufacturers in December 1945, where he declared that a major credit to Great Britain was certainly "in the national interest." Few other countries could so capably utilize assistance. "There are some areas where the need is great but where, if we dump everything that we could spare, it would only slightly and temporarily mitigate the distress," he said. "On the other hand, there are areas such as Great Britain, France, Holland and Belgium where a relatively small amount of help might quickly get productive machinery going again and revive hope and self-confidence." Such areas should receive "a priority rating" from Americans "because aid extended . . . will contribute the most to the healthy environment we seek." This did not mean complete satisfaction with the way in which the Truman Administration was arranging things, however. Dulles was disgruntled by the failure to consult with leading Republicans during negotiations with the British, for example. He also felt that Truman's people were unreasonably demanding. "Personally, I was against putting economic clauses in the loan agreement," he wrote a British friend. "I believe that if conditions permitted of freer trade and freer currency, your government would pursue that course voluntarily. If conditions did not permit, it was a mistake to have you bound." Not surprisingly, given the thrust of his wartime proposals for Europe, he also complained about the way in which the British loan was being treated as a foreign policy entity unto itself. "What is the *total program* of which the British loan forms a part," Dulles asked in a letter to Arthur Vandenberg? He wanted Republicans to press for creation or clarification of a broad surrounding context. [31]

To his dismay, Dulles soon learned that many of his fellow Republicans did not support the idea of a loan as he did. What was worse, their opposition tended to be based on factors not even related to the few particular grievances that he would have shared. After a December 1945 letter outlining a desirable G.O.P. policy on the loan, for example, in which he simply assumed that basic endorsement would be forthcoming, Dulles received a jolting response from Arthur Vandenburg. Was it really desirable for the United States to open a "pawnshop," the Senator asked? The British certainly didn't seem the most attractive of "customers." The loan terms proposed had "too many side doors and back doors and escalators," for example. "There seems to be a convenient and expedient 'if' or 'but' attached to each prospective British obligation." There was already talk of not wanting to repay the loan as well, coupled with a certain inclination "to 'shylock' us even before the papers are signed." And what of the lineup that might begin outside the pawnshop once the British loan was consummated, he also asked? The Russians were surely likely to appear in it, and Vandenberg simply didn't think "a majority of this Congress would vote a postwar loan to Russia—at least *not* until the 'iron curtain' reels up for keeps."

> Yet it seems that if we *grant* a loan to England and then *deny* one to Russia . . . we have thereby made further cooperation among the "Big Three" practically impossible (which, incidentally, would be the *end* of UNO). In other words, if we are going to ultimately *deny* a Russian loan, *perhaps* it would be better *not* to open up the "pawnshop" at all. [32]

Events contradicted this argument as Congress and the Truman Administration had no difficulty continuing to spurn Russian requests for aid and loans even after the British loan. Dulles utilized his own position as a leading Republican to overcome the "restless and unhappy and highly critical" mood he saw in his party and feared might exist in the country at large. On the public front, he buried his own grievances and came out foursquare behind the proposed arrangement. He brought the Federal Council of Churches into line, for example, by persuading it to endorse and circulate a March 1946 statement he had written, entitled "Faith and Works." The very first action it identified as a priority was for the United States to "consummate the proposed credit to Great Britain": "We recognize that the proposal . . . represents the kind of practical assistance which is imperative for world order," it explained. Attempting some fanfare, Dulles personally delivered a copy of the statement to President Truman on March 16, taking the opportunity to underline his endorsement. Dulles was equally emphatic, but more expansive, before an audience at the Council of Foreign Relations. "The British are in dire need of the American loan," he said, reporting on his just-completed visit, and "if Congress were to refuse the loan the nationalization of British industry would be intensified and the position of the Socialist and Communist parties would be bolstered."

He also worked behind the scenes. In meetings and correspondence, he tried gentle persuasion on G.O.P. leaders like Vandenberg and Representative Charles Eaton. Here he had some success, though it could not be said that he accomplished anything single-handedly. By the end of April, he was able to write the Senator from Michigan: "I was delighted that you came out for the British loan. I think I know how much mental anguish you went through . . . but I feel it was a courageous and statesmanlike thing." In July, he wrote Eaton something similar, adding however that he was "sorry that more of our Republican brethren did not follow you. . . ."[33]

The loan agreement passed the Senate on May 10 and the House on July 13, 1946. For many, the way was now cleared for greater attention to other problems. In Dulles's case, there was an almost immediate shift of concentration to two of the profound concerns that had emerged during the war years: the rehabilitation and integration of continental Europe and the devising of a system for effective long-range protection against Germany.

Hints of Dulles's concern, as well as his approach, began to crop up in the summer and fall of 1946. He carried on a running correspondence about integration with his old confidante Ferdinand Mayer, for example. On July 15, he told Mayer that "the important thing is to keep developing in people's minds the idea that the unification of Europe is a goal toward which to move." A few months later, he was laying out his own reading of some of the specific questions that would have to be tackled in working toward that goal, e.g., would a united Europe include both the eastern and western halves of the Continent? Would it include Great Britain? Would there be free trade, free immigration, and a common money? Would Germany be included as a single state or enter as several newly created ones? The latter question demonstrated his old tendency to link consideration of the defeated enemy with broader concerns about Europe as a whole. In September 1946, he reacted to some suggestions sent to him by James Warburg with words that could have been spoken at any time during the previous three or four years:

> As regards your concrete proposals, my impression is that they too much isolate the German problem from the problem of a peaceful and prosperous Europe. I have felt for some time that to get such a Europe requires getting increased economic and political unity. The important question is whether, as a practical matter, such unity can come, even in Western Europe, if a central German government has exclusive control of the resources which constitute the economic heart of Europe [particularly the Ruhr and Rhine areas.]

Dulles said something similar to Arthur Vandenberg a few days earlier, in appraising James Byrnes' dramatic statement of American policy in Stuttgart. He was glad that the Secretary of State "went to Germany and took a strong position there," he wrote, but he thought it would have been *"better to envisage the German problem in the setting of an increasing political and economic unity for western Europe"* (emphasis added.)[34]

This joining of German and European problems became more and more important to Dulles, and by the end of 1946 he had made it the centerpiece of his pronouncements on international developments. He became determined to coax public and political attention in this direction and undertook a series of speaking engagements and follow-up interviews and press conferences.

In terms of visibility, the peak of his efforts was reached in a highly publicized address to the National Publishers Association on January 17, 1947. In a neat progression of thoughts and proposals, Dulles testified both to past concerns and future objectives. He began by reiterating his previous assessment of Europe as "the world's worst fire hazard." "Twice within the last 30 years the edifice has virtually burned to the ground," he said. "The human and material losses have been colossal and irreparable." How could this senseless destruction be avoided in days to come, he went on to ask? Basically, by preventing yet another reconstruction of the same old continental environment. It was time to follow the advice of the American founding fathers, Dulles argued, to search for "harmony" in a more integrated, federalized structure. It was especially important to alter traditional commercial and financial patterns in order to bring about "economic unification." "A Europe divided into small economic compartments cannot be a healthy Europe. All of Europe's economic potentialities need to be used at maximum efficiency and European markets should be big enough to justify modern methods of cheap production for mass consumption."

Dulles admitted that thorough economic integration would have to evolve slowly, but he insisted that it was time to make a beginning. In particular, he argued that Americans and Europeans should approach the unavoidable task of shaping a peace settlement for Germany with an eye on this larger ultimate goal. "Whoever deals with Germany deals with the central problem of Europe," after all, he said; it should be appreciated that "the German settlement may decisively determine whether the movement will be toward economic unification or toward rebuilding the old structure of independent, unconnected sovereignties." As a specific example of what he had in mind, Dulles offered his earlier suggestion for the "Europeanization" or "internationalization" of the Ruhr–Rhine area. "The Basin of the Rhine, with its coal and industrious manpower, constitutes the natural economic heart of western Europe. From that area ought to flow vitality not merely for Germans but for Germany's western neighbors. If that happens Western Europe, at least, with its 200 million people, could develop into a more prosperous and stable land."[35]

His address to the National Publishers Association was widely reported in the media and prompted numerous commendations. Walter Lippmann devoted a full column to praising its suggestions, the *New York Herald Tribune* editorialized on its value, and warm letters arrived from old associates like Bernard Baruch. If Dulles needed any encouragement to continue broadcasting his ideas, he thus received plenty: as he put it to Arthur Vandenberg, "The favorable extent of . . . reaction has been beyond my expectation." In succeeding weeks, he utilized his German–European proposals in several other speaking engagements, one of which was carried nationally by the C.B.S. radio network; he also carried on his usual extended correspondence and held a number of press conferences in which the subject figured prominently.[36]

To his surprise perhaps, Dulles's German and European recommendations found a receptive audience in Washington. In broad outline, they really blended quite easily with official U.S. policy as it had been enunciated during 1945 and 1946. With the dramatic and quickly abandoned exception of the Morgenthau Plan, there was never any doubt about a basic American desire to treat Germany in a moderate if not lenient fashion. The handling of complex endless negotiations about reparations and allowable levels of industry certainly made it clear to the other Allies that the crucial question of the defeated enemy's economic future was not going to be resolved on the side of destructiveness or vindictivenes if the United States could prevent it. Truman Administration figures had also demonstrated a steady appreciation for the way in which the treatment of Germany could contribute to the broader goal of rehabilitation in Europe as a whole. Phrasing it negatively, Robert Murphy said as early as September 1945 that "extreme, ill-considered deindustrialization of Germany may well have the effect of creating and extending chaos in Europe." A specific, more positive outgrowth of this pattern of reasoning was the persistent push for wide-ranging utilization of Ruhr and Saar coal: as Dean Acheson put it in May 1946, "United States economic policy for Europe . . . requires that increasing amounts of German coal be made available to help recovery in France and other Western European countries." Nor was there any Washington resistance to the possibility that a German contribution to continental reconstruction would produce greater integration among formerly disparate and antagonistic societies. The Americans clearly favored the reintegration of the defeated enemy into a reformed, stable, and prosperous system. Will Clayton outlined this scenario in the fall of 1945, and a few months later George Kennan called for a "rescue" of the western zones and the "integrating" of them "into an international pattern of western Europe rather than into a united Germany."

By the summer of 1946, Washington was moving toward this goal on several fronts: it was urging creation of an Economic Commission for Europe within the United Nations to coordinate individual economic programs into an overall continental recovery plan; it was negotiating with the British and French about a merger of occupation zones and more intense application of German resources to Western European problems; and it continued to lay down broad statements of goals, such as the July State Department pronouncement that "it is general U.S. policy to favor the reestablishment of economic intercourse between all European countries, and to oppose economic as well as political autarchy either of countries or blocs. . . . As an ultimate objective, the U.S. desires economic integration of Germany and integration of Germany into the whole European Economy."[37]

His obvious alignment with official U.S. policy on Germany and Europe may be more apparent in retrospect than it would have been in early 1947, however. Like many at that time, he might have questionned the ability of the Truman Administration to achieve the goals he supported; he might even have wondered if the President actually had a clear perception of any long-range goals. There was considerable confusion in the conception and execution of American policy in 1945 and 1946. Some of it came from internal weaknesses: confusing lines of authority, for example, and an essentially immature capacity for delineating *specific* programs that would make it possible to reach *broadly* defined goals. In the case of German policy, these were especially evident. There was a notorious lack of coordination between the War and State Departments and an obvious lack of clear, detailed plans for the administration of the defeated enemy. Though it is now clear that the Americans avoided doing anything that would seriously interfere with eventual reconstruction and reintegration, they did relatively little of a more positive nature in the first eighteen months immediately after the war and could easily have been seen as floundering and uncertain. Their own shortcomings were compounded by outside problems, of course. The French were particularly uncooperative as far as German policy was concerned, making it clear again and again that they favored much more punitive treatment; the Soviets shifted ground dramatically on the level-of-industry question, in order to accommodate their emerging interest in securing reparations through current production; and the Germans themselves were far from quiescent, displaying a sometimes disturbing variety of political and economic inclinations in their party and labor union activities.

On the broader continental front, matters were easily as complicated. How would the American interest in integration be affected by developments in Eastern Europe? Would that half of the Continent be allowed to drift off on its own? Would the same be said for the Soviet-occupied zone in Germany? And what would be the impact of the pronounced drift toward nationalization of basic industries in many European countries? Or the increasing tendency to resort to bilateral as opposed to multilateral commercial agreements? These and other questions were of fundamental importance to the evolution of the postwar European environment, and therefore of fundamental importance to American policy makers. The answers to them were simply not going to be determined by those policy makers alone, however: even if they had had a more mature program and apparatus, they would have confronted Europeans who were not prepared to give up their role in shaping their own future. [38]

Walter Lippmann caught the combination of alignment and contrast between Dulles's early 1947 recommendations and official United States policy. Commenting on the January 17 address to the National Publishers Association, he wrote that Dulles's "German European program is entirely consistent with the best hopes and intentions of the State Department and General Clay's conduct of military government." He went on to praise Dulles for laying out those hopes and intentions more "coherently and systematically" than the Truman Administration had done.

He has made explicit what had been implicit. He has stated positively and constructively what has thus far been obscured or confused by an excessive preoccupation with details, with temporary difficulties of the occupation, with small expedients, and with the quest for tactical advantages in the general diplomatic conflict with the Soviet Union. [39]

Dulles soon learned firsthand of State Department interest in the kind of general European policies he had outlined. He and Arthur Vandenberg consulted in early February 1947 about the lack of a Republican member in the U.S. delegation to the forthcoming Moscow Council of Foreign Ministers meeting. In view of their extensive combined involvement in earlier sessions, the two men were surprised that neither had been invited to participate in seemingly crucial negotiations concerning Germany. Dulles feared that "this foreshadows a decline in bipartisan cooperation" and wondered if it would be possible "to keep in step" with the Administration in the future. Vandenberg was not anxious to go, apparently preferring the expanded role that Republican control of the newly elected Congress would give him; he did, however, drop a heavy hint to Secretary of State George Marshall that if he wanted to take a Republican to Moscow, it should be Dulles. A week later, Dulles himself sent a letter to Marshall, directing attention to his recent statements on Germany and asking for an opportunity to talk about evolving U.S. policy. He went to the State Department on February 24. After a half-hour discussion, "the Secretary got up and said he had to leave to see the President. . . . He then added: 'Would you go with me to Moscow?' " Dulles said he was "completely surprised," but quickly recovered enough to clarify the situation. "You know my views," he told Marshall. "If we are going to quarrel I had better not go along"—to which Marshall replied "that my views had much merit and that he did not think that they would create any serious difference between us."

Dulles tried to confirm the likelihood of this kind of agreement before formally accepting the invitation. Talking with Ben Cohen, Counselor for the State Department, he was told that "while there was some difference in emphasis and wording, he thought there was no basic objection to the viewpoint I had indicated in my January 17th speech." Pressing further at yet another meeting with Cohen, Dulles "expressed some concern that anti-French views of Murphy and Clay might make difficult a solution in terms of strengthening Western Europe." Cohen reassured him that "their views were not basic and were offset by views of others, such as Matthews." The next morning Dulles called Marshall and agreed to join the U.S. delegation. Less than two weeks later, he was on his way to Moscow.[40]

13

Focus on Europe,
1945–1948: II

I

CONCERN FOR THE FATE of Germany and Europe was very much at the center of Dulles's thoughts during 1946 and 1947. Why?

Noting some of his more sweepingly conceived statements, especially those written with large public audiences and the media in mind, it seems obvious that Dulles was driven in part by his evolving fears of the Soviet Union. He had come to feel, like many, that the rapid propulsion of Soviet power into countries along its borders had transformed Central and Western Europe into the next terrain on which Cold War maneuvers would be carried out; if the "iron curtain" were to be kept from falling over yet more of the Continent, remedial and protective action had to be taken.

Dulles did not anticipate any sudden new Soviet *military* moves in 1946 and 1947 and was not one of those who had nightmares about Red Army columns sweeping toward the English Channel. What he feared was a slower, more subtle process in which the *spirit* of the Germans, French, British, and others would be broken. Plagued by physical destruction and postwar social and emotional malaise, Europeans might be attracted to the alternative *ideology* of communism: they might then collapse into a Soviet sphere of influence without ever being blatantly forced to do so.

Fear of a Soviet ideological challenge in Central and Western Europe was a specific example of broad concerns Dulles had voiced before. As suggested at various points above, in fact, he had demonstrated through most of his life a predisposition against the kind of revolutionary philosophy ostensibly represented by the Soviet Union. In sketchy form while working in Woodrow Wilson's Administration and more verbosely in the reform-oriented writings of the 1930s, he clearly revealed his preference for slow and modest as opposed to explosive and drastic alterations of the status quo. His World War II work as Chairman of the Commission on a Just and Durable Peace had seen a particularly obvious flowering of this kind of inclination. Many of his statements took off from the premise that Americans needed to revitalize the dynamic faith that had once been theirs in order to fend off threats from extremists of many stripes. If they wanted safety at home and opportunity abroad once the fighting ceased, he had insisted, other peoples would have to be persuaded of the ongoing relevance of "the great American experiment." This theme had been developed in the postwar period as well and meshed easily with evolving suspicions of the Soviet Union. "We must show that our free land is not spiritual lowland, easily submerged," he had written in his *Life* articles, "but highland that, most of all, provides the spiritual, intellectual and economic conditions which all men want." This would offer an alternative to communism for those so desperately seeking models for the future.[1]

Witnessing to the liberal faith remained an important ingredient in Dulles's proposals for Germany. Citing yet again the need for "spiritual and intellectual vigor," he told the National Publishers Association that "the forthcoming Moscow Conference will show whether we have the wisdom to prescribe healing of such vast dislocations as everywhere surround us." Millions of people would be watching the United States grapple with the particular problem of Germany, waiting to see if Americans could move from the realm of airy promises to actual performance. It would be a concrete test with enormous potential repercussions:

> We Americans believe that our individualistic society best qualifies men for leadership. Such a society, we believe, provides the richness of diversity and of experimentation and the stimulus of competition. That, I

say, is *our* belief. But it is no longer the belief of others. They are skeptical. They are frightened by the unruly aspect we present and they suspect us of a certain moral and intellectual bankruptcy. They are attracted by the apparent smoothness and efficiency of a society where conformity is the rule and where all men walk in step. That is why Soviet communism can seriously challenge us for world leadership. . . .

I am confident that out of the physical vigor of our people and the intellectual stimulus of our free society can come the constructive ideas for which the whole world stands in wait.[2]

Despite his protestations of confidence, Dulles frequently used rather vivid images to describe what would happen to the United States if it did not meet the Soviet ideological challenge in Europe. "We are in a position of danger," he told the Women's National Republican Club in February 1947. "We are a small island of prosperity in the midst of a sea of misery. We risk being engulfed by waves of bitterness and resentment which are being agitated and organized against us." If the United States did not prove its mettle in Europe, he argued on another occasion, the broadening appeal of communism would "threaten us with an isolation which, sooner or later, would gravely endanger us." He was also quite prepared to elaborate on the dangers to all of western civilization. When Secretary of State Marshall asked for a summary of his views at their February 24 meeting, Dulles offered a sweeping overview:

. . . the European settlement must seek to strengthen economically western Europe; that that was the area of vital importance to us, that we had fought two wars to keep political freedom alive in that area, and that in essence we would have lost those wars if it fell under a Soviet type dictatorship which suppressed human liberty. I pointed out that the economy of Central Europe, including Scandinavia, was being integrated into, and drained into, that of the Soviet Union, and that if this tendency extended on into Western Europe, western civilization and personal freedom, as we had known it, would be impossible.[3]

If Dulles's postwar recommendations for Germany and continental integration emerged in part from rising Cold War fears of the Soviet Union, they had other important sources as well. In particular, they were a logical outgrowth of several decades of deep concern about Europe's problems and their impact on the United States.

Dulles's interest in the economic health and stability of Europe went back, at the least, to 1919 and the early 1920s. As a young adviser at the Paris Peace Conference and a legal counselor for New York investment houses, he had shown again and again his fervent hope for repair of the Great War's horrendous damage. He had made abundantly clear his conviction that his own country's prosperity was ultimately dependent on equivalent prosperity across the Atlantic. His concern for integration or federalization had deep personal roots as well. During the 1920s, he had urged political leaders to behave in a more "businesslike" fashion and to develop an "international point of view"; he had singled out for special praise the cooperative policies of central bankers in Washington, London, Paris, and Berlin. In the 1930s, he had developed these thoughts into more precise constructs. Troubled by portents of war, he had pressed for "economic fluidity" and freer "interstate commerce," for the "dilution of sovereignty" over the movement of money, goods, and people. Such reforms in European as well as global international behavior would yield a multitude of rewards: almost certain elimination of the likelihood of war, full and secure prosperity for participating nations, and, coincidentally, solutions for the grave economic problems facing the United States during the Great Depression.

The specific European proposals that Dulles elaborated after World War II link up very clearly with such long-established concerns. As early as December 1945, he told the National Association of Manufacturers that the United States should be prepared to offer material assistance to countries such as "Great Britain, France, Holland and Belgium where a relatively small amount of help might quickly get productive machinery going again and revive hope and self-confidence." He wanted the U. S. to help create "a healthy Europe," he said in January 1947; if nothing else, "Western Europe . . . with its 200 million people," should be assisted so that it "could develop into a more prosperous and stable land." He wanted to use the rich resources of the Ruhr, he told another audience to "generate economic vitality for all of Western Europe."[4]

There was particular emphasis in the early 1947 recommendations on structural reforms that would create a more *peaceful* Europe. Economic revival was crucial, Dulles felt, but if it occurred within a continental environment that was essentially identical with what had existed before 1939, it would inevitably disintegrate into the explosions of yet another war. "Whoever deals with Europe deals with the world's worst fire hazard," he said. "Repeatedly it bursts out in flames." Yet after each destructive conflagration, "the structure has been rebuilt substantially as before." It was time for Europeans to learn to live at peace with each other. A federal system, particularly concerning economic affairs, would provide the right kind of infrastructure: the first steps of an ongoing process could be taken by dealing with the Ruhr and its widely needed coal and iron.[5]

If European interrelationships in general required reform, Dulles believed it was especially vital to rethink the role of Germany within the whole. His perception of Germany's role, indeed, was one of the most important sources for Dulles's post–World War II European proposals. How could Germany be tamed, he came to ask? How could its demonstrated propensity for using its power to wage war be brought under control? Plans for a federalized Continent and for economic integration were designed to accomplish these ends.

This is abundantly clear in all of Dulles's discussions of the internationalization of the Ruhr. The fate of this one area seemed to him to embody in microcosm Germany's alternative potential directions for the future. "The Basin of the Rhine, with its coal and industrious manpower, constitutes the natural economic heart of western Europe," he argued. If control of the Ruhr were placed in the hands of some sort of federal agency, the heart could beat within a healthy body and "generate vitality for all of Western Europe." If the faulty patterns of the past were utilized once more, however, "experience unhappily shows" that it could "stoke the terrible fires of war."

Internationalization of the Ruhr really seemed the only safe and sensible alternative as far as Dulles was concerned. It certainly was preferable, for example, to any thoughts of "industrial disarmament" or "pastoralization" (favored by the American public and even some segments of the Roosevelt Administration, despite opposition from most of the Presidential advisors). Could anyone seriously consider "trying to cover with manure the natural industrial basin of Europe," he asked? "It would be futile and stupid." What a waste it would be for all Europeans to have to settle for an uncertain and dimmer economic future. In addition, even granting the wild assumption that the Allies would "indefinitely" provide "immense charity to prevent mass starvation," the Germans would almost surely rebel: it would take "huge armies . . . to repress restless people deprived of the work for which they are fitted," and the record of the past did not suggest that the victors were likely to accept that burden.

Dulles was no more impressed by the alternative procedure of resurrecting a unified Germany and restoring essential control of its resources to the Germans themselves. The experiences of the 1930s had demonstrated that "relying upon treaty provisions, like those of Versailles, to prevent use for military purposes" was a very faulty safeguard beyond a short initial breathing-space. Enforced, the Treaty of Versailles "would have kept Germany impotent for a thousand years"—but who would guarantee that any new treaty would actually be enforced any more than that of 1919? Nor was a potential German ability to turn resources directly into military assets the only problem Dulles saw in a straightforward restoration of the defeated enemy's traditional sovereignty. Given the inherent power of their economy, he wondered if it might be only a matter of time before the Germans would be tempted to seek "by economic pressures, a mastery of western Europe which they could not achieve by arms." The French, Dutch, and Belgians, among others, might succumb to such pressure. Alternatively, neighboring countries might try to shape a peace settlement that would allow them to "annex bits of Germany" and live with "economic separation" more securely. Either way, Western Europe would be condemned "to an unhealthy and precarious future."

No, Dulles believed, measures like the internationalization of the Ruhr offered a better route for Europe's and Germany's future. Such measures would begin a process of structural change that would help avoid the recurring disasters of the past. They would help produce "economic forces operating upon Germans" which were "centrifugal and not centripetal," by which Dulles meant that there would be "natural forces which will turn the inhabitants of Germany's states toward their outer neighbors" in a positive and cooperative rather than aggressive fashion. The solution to an old, old problem would then begin to emerge: "a form of joint control which will make it possible *to develop the industrial potential of western Germany in the interest of the economic life of western Europe*, including Germany, and do so *without making Germans the masters of Europe*" (emphasis added).[6]

Not surprisingly, Dulles's analyses of the 1946–47 political and economic problems of Europe involved as much appreciation for their relevance to the interests of the United States as his thoughts on ideological questions. While he was convinced that it was to their advantage for Europeans to reform their interrelationships, he never doubted that this would greatly benefit his own country as well. Did anyone really believe that Americans would be able to avoid bloody and costly participation if yet another war rocked Europe's future? "Formerly, Europe could have its wars without involving us," he said in February 1947, but the experiences of the twentieth century had demonstrated the effective disappearance of the Atlantic moat.

> The United States has both the moral right and the political power to seek a German settlement which will promote the peace and prosperity of Europe. We have bought both with the blood of our youth which, twice within our generation, has been plentifully shed in Europe. It would be an inexcusable failure of statesmanship if we used the present opportunity merely to rebuild the old European deathtrap.[7]

Nor did 1947 find Dulles losing sight of the fundamentally important economic relationship that existed between the United States and Europe. For almost thirty years, he had emphasized the way in which commercial and financial ties with peoples across the Atlantic accounted for much of whatever stability and prosperity Americans had enjoyed. In the 1920s, he had worried about the way in which a "starving" Europe would yield a "choking" United States, with the latter unable to market its enormous agricultural and industrial production; in the 1930s, he had bemoaned the autarchic compartmentalization of the Continent and the impact of a steady decline of normal international transactions on a depressed American economy; in the early 1940s, he had drawn blueprints for a "new world order" which had always assumed the value of more cooperative financial practices and "freer interstate commerce" for the United States. Now, in the aftermath of World War II, he was as sensitive as ever to the global economic needs of his own country and was particulary conscious of the role Europe might play in meeting those needs. The United States was in a "new position," Dulles told the National Association of Manufacturers within months of the end of the war. "It is one of great opportunity, but also of great peril." He could be excited as he looked at the inherent economic strength of the country, he said, particularly because "we have achieved a new high in productive power." He could be frightened as he considered the obstacles which might block utilization of that strength, however. Here again was the same problem that had plagued post–World War I Americans. More ready than ever to market their abundance abroad, they found themselves "surrounded by peoples who are largely destitute." Who would be able to pay for all that was there to be sold? Dulles propsed dealing with this grave, reemerging problem by providing emergency U. S. government aid for troubled European economies. Citing Great Britain, France, Holland, and Belgium as particularly important, he advised negotiations with the governments of these countries in which American policy makers would *"tell them what it is we have decided to do in our interest"* (emphasis added).[8]

His thoughts on the European scene of 1946 and 1947 provide another and particularly important example of the shallowness of traditional images of John Foster Dulles. In approaching problems and proposing solutions, Dulles went far beyond any simplistic Cold Warrior's style. Though it is clear that hypersensitivity to Soviet ambitions and a communist ideological challenge colored his perspective, it is equally obvious that he saw much else involved as well. Desire for reform of the political economy of Europe, grave doubts about the trustworthiness of Germany, and attentiveness to the traditional needs of the United States, among others, served as key stimuli for the thoughts and proposals that were so regularly forthcoming.

Nor did any of these factors have an inevitable or intrinsically subservient relationship to the frequently more colorful anticommunist side of the postwar Dulles. He was understandably prone to blending a variety of arguments on behalf of certain proposals in order to achieve results and would no doubt have argued, if pressed, that the problems he discussed were mutually reinforcing and susceptible to the same kinds of remedies. He was also, however, sensitive enough to his own past to know that some strains in his thought had a more independent and fully developed life of their own. Speaking to a church audience on behalf of what was to become the Marshall Plan, he cited a history of personal and church support for European integration that clearly predated the "Cold War":

> When, in 1941, the British Christians at Malvern and our own church groups advocated that Europe become a federated commonwealth, we were not inspired by any hostility toward the Soviet Union. We saw European unification as a peace imperative. Today we advocate the same thing, namely European unity, in the same spirit, namely the spirit of peace.[9]

Such a statement, meshed with the content of other extensive discussions on the same subject, is an important signpost to the complex foundations from which Dulles's analyses could spring. It is also suggestive of the powerful momentum of traditional, pragmatic interests. All on its own, it could be argued, attentiveness to the politico-economic implications of European integration and German policy could have produced the very same proposals for action which Dulles called his own in 1946 and 1947. In reality, this kind of concern never did operate in a vacuum after World War II and was always coupled with ideological involvements. But recognition of the role of the latter should not obscure sensitivity to the potency of what had long preceded it.

II

Even before he left for Moscow, Dulles may have had a sense of what was likely to happen at the next session of the Council of Foreign Ministers. On the day he was invited to join the American delegation, State Department Counselor Ben Cohen had told him that "it was the Department's view that the present conference would last about five or six weeks and would not make any great accomplishment other than to clarify and reduce the issues." Cohen was close to target. The U. S. team was in the

Soviet capital from March 10 to April 25, and it came home with no dramatic successes to its credit. Indeed, on the latter count, even modest accomplishments were nonexistant in a series of meetings that were characterized by deep suspicions and frequently hollow diplomatic posturing.

Given the strikingly different goals of the various Allied delegations, positive results could hardly have been expected. The primary focus of peacemaking efforts was now on Germany, and no other subject seemed capable of producing divisions of such fundamental importance to each of the victors.

The Americans went to Moscow determined to deal with a number of problems that were becoming more alarming to them almost daily. They were especially worried about ongoing postwar economic weakness in Germany and in Germany's western neighbors. A whole cluster of difficulties might result from this, the Americans felt: they were conscious of its striking effects on trade patterns of great concern to the United States; they felt that it was relevant to the debate going on within many European countries about the future of capitalist institutions and alternative socialist mechanisms; and they believed it portended problems with the "communists," those in Moscow and/or the various national communist parties, who might seek to use economic problems to their political advantage. To some degree, there was also fretting about the way slow European recovery was costing American taxpayers so dearly—in relief and occupation costs in Germany, for example. To deal with problems like these, George Marshall and his advisers set their sights on a more unified and economically stronger Germany. They had begun moving in this direction months before, but continued their efforts in Moscow through alternate use of four-power and bilateral negotiations. During discussions of the administrative structure of the occupied defeated enemy, for example, they pushed for more efficient coordination, in particular for treating Germany as "an economic unit" rather than four distinct entities: they had begun a merger of the American and British zones months earlier and made no secret of their desire to go further. On other occasions, they pushed vigorously for an escalation of the levels of industry that had previously been agreed to for Germany. Especially with reference to coal and steel, American delegates began to argue that more production was required in order to bring speedier recovery for Germany itself and for Germany's near neighbors as well. And as something of the reverse side of this coin, they continued to shape their policy on reparations so as to do the least damage to the German economy and the United States Treasury: they sought to minimize Germany's overall obligation and insisted that before any reparations could be forwarded, imports of food and other goods should be paid for out of revenues from German production and exports.[10]

In a way that could hardly have surprised them, the Americans found that their Allied partners often felt very differently about Germany's future. The most highly publicized disagreements involved the varying goals of the Soviet Union. While they favored the closer integration of the occupation zones and more potent central administrative agencies the U.S. was advocating, the Russians saw these steps leading in a very different direction. They were, on one hand, deeply suspicious of the obvious American desire to integrate a reviving Germany into a reviving western Europe. It is still impossible to say definitively just what their own alternative vision of Germany's future international relationships was: they may have thought in terms of a more aloof, essentially neutral state whose demonstrated tendency toward aggression would be monitored by all of its former antagonists; they may have envisioned a relatively independent state in whose affairs they themselves might eventually become more influential. Whatever their goals may have been, they clearly had no intention of allowing all of Germany to gravitate toward an evolving Western alliance dominated by the United States. In discussions of central administrative agencies, they were not likely to accept George Marshall's proposal for decisions by majority rather than unanimous vote—this would have deprived them of an essential mechanism for preventing their own gradual exclusion from influence on Germany. The Soviets had very different expectations for the long-range economic impact of proposed changes in the occupation of Germany as well. Their concern for the burdens of the American taxpayer was doubtless nil, and they were much more attentive to their own recovery than that of France or Belgium. Hence, their interest in fostering a more potent and efficient Germany was joined to a desire to secure greater reparations for themselves and a number of Eastern European states: they wanted no part of American policies that would have rehabilitated the German economy while at the same time curtailing sharply reparations from current production.[11]

Though often ignored in the aftermath by policy makers preoccupied with perceptions of communist "obstructionism," France's reactions to American proposals in Moscow were usually as cool or even cooler than the Soviets'. The French had a few precise desires with respect to Germany, and U.S. schemes seemed to them uniformly inappropriate. Rather than greater unity in the defeated enemy, Paris representatives preferred to think in terms of continued weakness through division. They maintained enthusiasm for compartmentalization into zones of occupation and, in fact, were anxious to go further, with essentially permanent amputations of German territory: they were determined to secure effective control of the Saar for themselves, for example, and wanted to move toward creating a special international regime for the Ruhr. Nor were they keen on the form of economic revitalization of Germany that the Americans favored. They desperately wanted to secure greater quantities of coal for their own use, but were leery of any moves toward recovery in so suspect a neighbor. Overall, the French took the narrowest and hardest line of any delegation in Moscow. Feeling as they did, they could offer little agreement in the quadripartite negotiations, thus very much contributing to total failure there; they also felt forced to resist virtually all meaningful concessions in strenuous bilateral discussions with George Marshall and other Americans.[12]

Only the British offered anything like cooperation to the United States. This was not surprising. Suspicious of the Soviets, concerned about economic developments in Western Europe generally, and especially troubled by the onerous costs of running their own occupation zone, London's representatives had a vantage point very much like that of their Washington counterparts. Joint efforts to deal with German problems had begun almost a year earlier, and even in the midst of the Moscow meetings, Geroge Marshall and Ernest Bevin seemed to have put as much effort into preparing new plans for bizonal unity and economic recovery as into seeking broader four-power programs. Given Soviet and French policies, they surely knew that for the time being their two-party efforts were all they were likely to achieve.[13]

Secretary of State Marshall logically held center stage for the Americans when it came to public statements and formal exchanges during the Moscow session of the Council of Foreign Ministers. Dulles and other members of the U.S. team played more low-profile roles, giving advice and helping to piece together positions and strategies during behind-the-scenes delegation meetings. In this setting, Dulles moved in predictable fashion. On his own, he demonstrated again and again the importance of the various concerns which had figured so noticeably in his early 1947 analyses of the European scene. Some of his personal recommendations, in fact, were simply carried from home and placed full-blown into the more formal diplomatic setting; others emerged for the first time or were clarified in Moscow, but meshed completely with earlier ideas. There were no surprises in the interplay between Dulles and his colleagues in the U.S. delegation either. The basic similarity of his own and official thinking on German and European affairs very much continued during early 1947, and Dulles even seems to have come to appreciate it more than in the past. There were occasional signs of impatience with the Truman Administration regarding specific programs, but he generally found it easy to support the policies that evolved in Moscow.

Dulles had no difficulty in accepting the overall thrust of U.S. policy regarding Germany, which was to be expected since he himself had been urging some of its elements for at least three or four years. As early as 1943, he had indicated a suspicion concerning the potential problems caused by demands for reparations, a suspicion that had lingered on after the experiences of the 1920s and early 1930s. In 1944, he made clear his own interest in using Germany in order to restore economic health and stability to Europe as a whole: one of the immediate virtues of continental integration, he had argued, would be the availability of German resources to adjoining economies. And in his major early 1947 pronouncements, he had brought the latter issue to a head by urging the "internationalization" of the Ruhr: "The Basin of the Rhine," he had said in one speech, "with its coal and industrious manpower, constitutes the natural economic heart of western Europe. *From that area ought to flow vitality not merely for Germans, but for Germany's western neighbors*" (emphasis added).[14]

In Moscow, similar arguments were forthcoming from Dulles. He felt that the existing administrative structure in Germany was "exceedingly inefficient" and that "what is left of Germany ought to be politically and economically united." "Germany remains economically and politically divided by zones of occupation," he said on one occasion. "That is bad—not just for Germans, but for Germany's neighbors, the French, the Dutch, the Belgians, the British, and others. All of them, in one way or another, are injured by the present state of the German economy." The time had come to take whatever actions were necessary "to prevent Germany from continuing to be a 'slum' in the heart of Europe," and he showed himself ready to support most U.S. proposals to this end. Not surprisingly, he was personally most interested in developing and then widely using the resources of the Ruhr for this purpose. Without the Ruhr's resources, he argued, "it is impossible to rebuild either France, Belgium or Holland." The single question of "what happens to the coal of the Ruhr," he said on another occasion, "can be and is now the most important decision in Western Europe."

Dulles lined up behind the more negative component of American policy too and joined in opposition to what he considered counterproductive reparations demands. A March 30 memorandum on reparations from current production laid out his personal position quite clearly for his colleagues:

There appears to be little possibility, in fact, of giving the Soviet Union anything approaching *what* it wants *when* it wants it, out of the Western zone unless in effect the United States is prepared to pay for it. There is a large current and accumulated deficit in the balance of payments. The coal situation is very tight and Germany's current production could not be stepped up without cutting off coal from France, Belgium, The Netherlands, etc. The Western zones have not yet achieved, and will not for some time achieve, the level of industry presently allowed and needed for their own minimum livelihood.

He offered similar arguments in a letter to Arthur Vandenberg at about the same time, concluding with a point he knew would make an impression on many of his friend's congressional colleagues: "The Soviets would now like to squeeze our zone by having it produce consumer goods for Russia. That of course would mean an indefinite postponement of the ability of the United States Zone to pay for its food imports. *In effect we would be paying reparation to Russia*" (emphasis added).[15]

It deserves emphasis that Dulles's support for American policies toward Germany was not always total. He had a number of qualms that periodically disturbed him in Moscow and went on concerning him long after he returned home. Most importantly, he was frightened by what might happen if adequate safeguards were not built into the programs that were designed to yield a revived and healthy Germany. Was it safe to allow the remergence of an economically healthy, unified, and totally *independent* Germany? Dulles thought not. This would set in motion a reversion to a prewar European environment which was too faulty to tolerate, as far as he was concerned. He had said for years that the old structure as a whole was a Pandora's box of inevitable economic weaknesses and political-military clashes. As well, the re-creation of something very much like a prewar Germany, supposedly reformed but structurally unaltered, seemed to him now to promise the most frightening particular scenes within an overall nightmare about Europe's future. Looking only a short way down the road from early 1947, for example, his thoughts during the Moscow Conference conjured up at least three conceivable disasters for world peace and American interests if this route were taken. In one, he predicted that fright at a U.S. push for an economically potent and independent Germany "would certainly drive France into the arms of Russia. . . ." The "dominant French sentiment is fear of Germany," he argued in one early meeting of the American delegation. If it looked as if the defeated enemy were going to remerge with its traditional trappings of power and sovereignty, then Paris would look wherever it had to for allies who would be equally disturbed. And though the shift of France "into the

Soviet bloc" would be bad enough in its own right, it would engender yet greater problems:

> . . . Spain and Italy would almost certainly become communist-dominated, the Mediterranean would be lost, northwest Europe would be effectively flanked, and the U.S. position in South America would be greatly weakened because of the great influence there of the Latin cultures of Europe (France, Spain, Italy.)

Though it bespoke confusion about ultimate Soviet motives, Dulles offered another frightening scenario in which the Russians would endorse rehabilitation and independence for Germany as a preface to their own takeover of the country. Moscow was confident of the "possibilities of political penetration in an adjacent and partly occupied area," he told the American delegation; the Russians felt they had "a good chance to get control of all of Germany," he wrote Arthur Vandenberg, "which would for all practical purposes mean control of the continent." And finally, even if it were possible to discount fears of potential French or Soviet behavior, he felt there were more than enough grounds to worry about what Germany herself might do if given another opportunity to play a lone hand. Over and over, he spoke of the dangers of creating a situation which could be exploited by the "militant and vengeful persons who will surely again be found in Germany"; of the way in which Germans could so easily be tempted to "play both ends against the middle" in their relations with the Soviet Union and the Untied States; of the way in which Germany might use great and independent economic power to "become the master of Western Europe."[16]

No, Dulles argued, Europe, the United States, and the world should be protected against all of these eventualities. In his address to the National Publishers Association, he had made clear his desire to find a way of developing "the industrial potential of Western Germany in the interest of the economic life of Western Europe . . . without making Germans the masters of Europe." Now, in Moscow, he wanted to follow through. He would like to "solidify and strengthen Western Europe" without creating "an economically and politically united Germany," he told his delegation colleagues; he "did not want all the German eggs in one basket," he said on another occasion, vulnerable to exploitation by either the Russians or the Germans themselves.[17]

As it turned out, Dulles found that some of his colleagues shared his sense of the dangers inherent in recreating a powerful Germany—at least in a general way. Among the extensive delegation briefing papers prepared in advance by the Department of State, there was one that analyzed a French proposal for international supervision of the Ruhr: it identified

U.S. policy with this general concept and cited, among its justifications, the need to prevent an "unfettered German control of the vital coal and iron and steel resources" which "would leave many European countries . . . at the mercy of Germany." George Marshall made essentially this point in the April 10 meeting of the Council, saying that the U.S. wanted "to ensure against the militant use of these resources by a revived Germany," while at the same time allowing them to "be equally employed in the interests of European states, including Germany." The Secretary of State expressed related fears during his April 15 meeting with Marshall Stalin as well. "The United States deeply desired economic unity," he said then, but was "seriously concerned at the idea of a centralized, and by that he meant dominant German Government which would control industry, education, finance, and other matters. The United States felt that such a German Government would constitute a real danger for the peace of the world."[18]

The problem, from Dulles's point of view, was that his colleagues were not prepared to follow through on such concerns. Too often, they were willing to voice their fears and then let them hang fire. Dulles's own favored solution for the dilemmas likely to stem from a united and independent Germany came straight from the heart of his earlier analyses: the internationalization of the Ruhr. He brought it up as a vitally needed project at the very first delegation meeting he attended. Given potential dangers from French fears, Soviet appetites, and latent German ambitions, he argued, "the European settlement should seek primarily to solidify and strengthen western Europe (Britain, France, Belgium, and Holland) and keep France from falling into the communist bloc. *This can best be done by integrating the Ruhr area economically into western Europe and not now risking it in an economically and politically united Germany*" (emphasis added). This kind of alteration of the Continent's economic landscape, he continued to believe, especially if treated as the first in a series of steps, would set up natural and ongoing barriers to the forces of discord that had been dominant for many years. In particular, it would so alter the political, economic, and psychological *structure* of Germany that that country's potential for aggressive behavior would be effectively tamed. The Allies might hope to create "a Germany which . . . would never again want to make war," Dulles argued; internationalization of the Ruhr would create "*a Germany which could not again make war even if it wanted to*" (emphasis added).[19]

But Dulles's American colleagues were not especially impressed by his proposals for the Ruhr. After urging such a step on March 7, he waited more than four annoying weeks before it received any serious consideration. And then, when it came in a special delegation meeting on April 7, it did not produce the result he had wanted. He had offered a detailed proposal for the creation of a Ruhr Commission with members from France, the Netherlands, Belgium, Switzerland, Czechoslovakia, Poland, Denmark, and Italy; the Commission would be given authority over "allocation" of "coal and other heavy products (to be defined)" and instructed to guarantee "equitable distribution as between domestic use and export to one or another place." Several hours of discussion among the Americans, however, produced only an agreement to "make a general, but not concrete, suggestion of some form of international control." As a result, Marshall brought the matter before the other foreign ministers on April 10, but left it so broadly defined that no further action or even discussion was likely to be forthcoming."[20]

Still, Dulles may have been realistic enough to conclude that some official interest in his Ruhr project was better than none. Though he confessed to a bit of pique and disappointment to Arthur Vandenberg and George Marshall, he never offered sharp criticism and never allowed incomplete success on this one matter to cancel out his overall support for American policy on Germany. He had and retained some qualms about what Truman Administration policy makers were doing, but he shared enough of their beliefs to give them loyal support, especially in public. He had endorsed a drive for more efficient administration and economic rehabilitation of Germany before the early April "decision" on the Ruhr, and he went on doing so; he had opposed heavy reparations before, and he went on doing so; he had believed in the need to use Germany to help rebuild her neighbors, and he went on doing so.

III

Instead of being depressed by the dismal failure of their six-week effort, American policy makers returned from Moscow in an energized mood. Secretary of State Marshall delivered a radio report in which he tried to prepare the nation for some kind of dramatic new action. "The recovery of Europe has been far slower than had been expected," he said. "Disintegrating forces are becoming evident." He described "the impoverished and suffering people of Europe" as "crying for help, for coal, for food, and for most of the necessities of life. . . ." The United States had gone to the Moscow Conference hoping to forge remedial programs with its Allies, Marshall argued, but over and over the obstructionist behavior of the Russians had prevented meaningful action. Now the time of waiting was over. If the Soviets were not willing to cooperate, then the United States would move ahead with whatever support from other countries it could muster. "The patient is sinking while the doctors deliberate," he said. "So I believe that action cannot await compromise through exhaustion. . . . Whatever action is possible to meet these pressing problems must be taken without delay." As an indication of what he meant, he had already instructed George Kennan and the State Department's Policy Planning Staff to speedily prepare a study of European reconstruction problems. The runways were being cleared for some major new initiatives."[21]

Dulles returned home just as ready for action and just as prepared to go on without further thought of joint action with Moscow. In his own radio report, delivered the day after Marshall's, he too detailed examples of Soviet perfidy regarding German and European needs. The Conference's failure had been "a grave disappointment" to the United States and "a tragedy to millions in Europe," he said. This should not, however, be allowed to stand in the way of taking effective steps from this point on. "We cannot let ourselves be stymied merely because we cannot get agreement," he insisted. "It is up to us to show, in every available way, that free institutions are the means whereby men can save themselves from the sea of misery in which they find themselves."[22]

Of course, it should be realized that many of the words coming from U.S. policy makers in the aftermath of the Moscow Conference were part of a somewhat self-righteous and rather dishonest public relations effort. If the Americans went to Moscow with no real expectation of accomplishing anything regarding Germany, which is what Counselor Ben Cohen told Dulles in February, then their talk of "grave disappointment" was patently exaggerated. One newsman who had heard the advance scuttlebutt in Washington said the policy makers he was listening to in April seemed to want it both ways: they reminded him, he said, "of a Vermont farmer who annually would say something like this—we killed a pig today, didn't weigh as much as we thought, but then we never thought it would." Furthermore, U.S. policy makers had begun to talk of paying less attention to securing Soviet cooperation and of devising new, more independent measures concerning Europe and Germany a good many months earlier than April 1947. Already at the Paris Council of Foreign Ministers meeting in May 1946, the Americans specifically warned the Soviets that continued refusal to cooperate concerning Germany would lead to the "inevitable alternative of treating Western Germany as economic unit and integrating this unit closely with Western European economy." Initiatives shortly thereafter demonstrated the seriousness of the warning, with arrangements being made that summer to begin a merger of the U.S. and British occupation zones. In the very midst of the

Moscow Conference itself, the Americans continued their push toward a more independent, more "Western" approach to Germany. Marshall and Bevin carried on numerous talks about Bizonia, especially about coal production and overall levels of industry, and Marshall made a further effort to coax Bidault and the French into the merger fold.[23]

Dulles, it should be added, was personally no more forthright than others when he implied that the failures of the Moscow Conference had given him the idea of shaping European policies without concern for securing Soviet cooperation. The thrust of all his early 1947 public statements certainly showed a clear inclination along these lines before he even knew he would be going to Moscow. He repeated many times the major point he made before the National Publishers Association in January: U.S. policy should seek "to develop the industrial potential of *western* Germany in the interest of the economic life of *western* Europe . . ." (emphasis added). Dulles also played a two-faced role in Moscow itself, going along with the supposed American policy of seeking all-German economic and political unity, but moving quite differently behind the scenes. On one occasion, taking advantage of an old acquaintanceship with Georges Bidault, Dulles tried to persuade the French Foreign Minister that a merger of the western occupation zones would be wise. He developed similar arguments in a March 29 letter to Arthur Vandenberg. He was coming to feel that the reparations controversy should be handled by the time-honored "study" routine, he wrote: "Such a study will be very complicated and the outcome uncertain. Meanwhile, the present zonal basis will continue, which, I think, is good. It is useful to have more time *to consolidate the Western Zones* and not expose them yet to Communist penetration" (emphasis added).[24]

Dulles's proposed agenda for dramatic action after the Moscow Conference offers further testimony to the relatively meaningless nature of negotiations there as far as he was concerned. As early as his radio report of April 29, he simply picked up the major recommendations he had already formulated in January. First, he argued, something would have to be done about the continuing irrationality and wastefulness of leaving Germany in shattered condition. Second, in order to make a degree of German unity and rehabilitation safe and widely beneficial, it would have to be brought about with an eye to the defeated enemy's past propensities. In particular, there should be a broad-flanking movement toward reform of as much of the Continent's economic life as possible, with a substantial breakdown of traditional barriers to the movement of men, goods, and ideas: this would allow an integration of Germany into a larger whole and hence a structural safeguard against future aggression; it would also provide general stimulation to many individual economies. As Dulles put it, studies of "the problem of Germany" had convinced him that "there is no economic solution along purely national lines. Increased economic unity is absolutely essential to the well-being of Europe." As an example of what he had in mind, he also referred again to the way in which internationalization of the Ruhr could serve as an extemely desirable first step in a longer-range process.

Dulles did return from Moscow with a somewhat greater sense of urgency about his proposals, although this may have stemmed from the way months had gone by without effective action as much as alarm at Soviet behavior. He referred regularly, in fact, to growing qualms about foot-dragging in Washington during May and early June. In one letter to Senator Ferguson, he said that "the failure of the Moscow Conference raises very sharply the question of what American policy should be in relation to Western Europe." Unfortunately, "neither the President nor the Secretary of State have given any indication." He could not imagine this being tolerated for very long, either by Republican leaders or average citizens: "We are pouring into that part of the world a great deal of money, but the money does not seem to be geared into anywhere near a constructive program." In a talk to the Council on Foreign Relations, he referred to the "present paralyzing uncertainty" of the European situation and went on to urge again his own solutions regarding Germany, economic reform, and the Ruhr.[25]

As might be inferred from some of these comments, Dulles did not find the loudly touted "Truman Doctrine" a very meaningful effort toward dealing with European problems in the spring of 1947. Though he gave the President's proposals his initial support and at one point congratulated Arthur Vandenberg on his "brilliant" handling of congressional maneuvers, he left little doubt about his sense of the program's limits and dangers. "I have never been keen about it," he told Vandenberg in July, explaining that "the Soviet Union with very little expense and effort can bleed us badly in Greece." Aside from the practicality of Greek–Turkish aid, which he went on questioning when the issue arose at the United Nations, Dulles seems to have been even more concerned about the way such a high-profile effort would defuse the drive for European recovery and unity: swipes at the periphery were not an adequate substitute for concerted efforts to deal with core problems.[26]

By June 5, Dulles learned that his impatience had been somewhat inappropriate. In his famous commencement address at Harvard on that day, George Marshall began to reveal the extent of planning regarding Europe, which had in fact been underway in Washington for some time. Building on reports that had come from a foreign-aid study group in the

State Department, George Kennan's Policy Planning Staff, and a State–War–Navy Coordinating Committee, among other sources, the Secretary of State testified to deep concern for a revitalization of Europe and invited leaders across the Atlantic to cooperate in formulating plans that the United States would try to support. Within days, British Foreign Secretary Bevin and French Foreign Minister Bidault were consulting about timing and procedures. The foundation of the Marshall Plan had been constructed.

Though Dulles might have been chagrined at being left in the dark about the months of Administration planning which lay behind Marshall's initiative, he gave voice at first only to strong support. He personally commended the move in meetings with both the President and the Secretary of State within a week of the Harvard address. By late June, he wrote to Counselor Ben Cohen that he was "delighted" at the way "the Department's program . . . seems to be developing momentum. What we need is to take and keep the initiative, and that I think we are beginning to do." Before July 1, he had also drafted and had published a memorandum expressing the strong support of the Federal Council of Churches for a meaningful program of American aid to Europe, one which would, in particular, help eliminate "such evils as excessive nationalism and the use of boundaries as barriers to the healthy movement of goods, people and ideas." So strong was Dulles's first enthusiasm for what became the Marshall Plan, in fact, that it involved a number of stabs at taking credit for the nurturing of the concept in Washington offices. Writing to an Indiana relative, he praised the taking of the "initiative" by the U.S. and said, "I think I have perhaps been somewhat helpful in this respect"; in a letter to the new editor of *The Christian Century*, he wrote, "May I remark in passing that you are, I hope and believe, right in your 'suspicion' that I have had something to do with the shift in emphasis from the so-called 'Truman Doctrine' . . . to the program of economic aid based on increasing economic unity in Europe, which I discussed at great length with Secretary Marshall at Moscow. . . ."[27]

It was not long before Dulles's initial enthusiasm began to buckle, however. Neither the Secretary of State nor any other Administration leader made efforts to communicate with him about the evolving details of the Marshall Plan during the summer and fall of 1947, and something of a forced isolation in New York may have encouraged his increasingly independent and skeptical perspective. At all events, he was not impressed by the proposals that European leaders produced for American consideration during July and August, and he felt that some of the bright promise of Marshall's initiative was being dimmed. When Washington failed to push for improvements in these plans, he grew even more concerned. As early as July 21, he complained to Arthur Vandenberg about "our policies—or lack of policies" regarding Europe and argued that "considerable revisions" would be required to "whip" sketchy proposals "into shape. . . ." He remained firmly committed to the idea of U.S. aid for European reconstruction and spoke forcefully for passage of the European Recovery Plan legislation, which was unveiled in December, but he had serious reservations: he made it clear to many correspondents and audiences that he felt that neither the Europeans nor the Truman Administration were going as far as they should to deal with the problems they confronted.

The most important shortcoming in evolving plans as far as Dulles was concerned was the gap between theory and action regarding continental unity. Marshall's original proposal had "caught men's imagination and stirred them to quick action" precisely because of its call for cooperative effort, he said at one point; it had promised "to cure what is fundamentally wrong . . . the division of western Europe into many small economic compartments." Unfortunately, the intitiative of June had been poorly worked out in succeeding months. Governments on both sides of the Atlantic had been responsible. "In Europe the leaders, public and private, see and say that Europe cannot be a vigorous and healthy economy without increased unity," he told the Foreign Policy Association in early 1948. "But also, they say, their day-to-day problems are so urgent that it is very difficult for their governments to devise and carry through long-range projects. So, little has been done. . . ." In Washington meantime, the Truman Administration had not done enough to coax and press the Europeans. Dulles told the Senate Foreign Relations Committee that continental leaders were in effect saying "You must push us," but the Americans were simply standing in place and waiting. The result was that the European Recovery Plan legislation sent to Congress in December contained "only vague suggestions" of the vital unity goal.[28]

One glaring example of the overall failure to satisfy transcendent reform needs in Europe, in Dulles's view, was the lack of meaningful action regarding Germany. As he had said so often before late 1947 and early 1948, he saw Germany's future as intimately entwined with that of Western Europe as a whole: if Germany's economic strengths, particularly in areas like the Ruhr, were structurally integrated into a Western federation, then recovery and peace would both be feasible; without integration, recovery or peace (or both) would be in jeopardy. Though Dulles sensed a general commitment to this kind of logic in Washington, he did not see the driving commitment that would be needed for its transition into effective policies. His disappointment in the details of evolving Marshall Plan legislation had been compounded by his experiences at the short, unproductive session of the Council of Foreign Ministers held in Paris in December 1947. Dulles had made his usual arguments about the significance of Germany to his American delegation colleagues, with particular emphasis this time on the reverberations of Sovietization in the eastern portion of the country, but had not succeeded in sparking the kinds of dramatic initiatives he felt were necessary. Speaking to the Senate Foreign Relations Committee a month later, he extrapolated from his Paris experiences and argued that the United States was doing a dismal job of using the influence that its victor status gave it in Germany:

> . . . productivity in western Germany is at a level far below that which prevails elsewhere in Europe. The currency there is the most inconvertible of all currencies. There is little incentive and stagnation replaces a healthy movement of goods, people and ideas. The area is infiltrated by communism. Our government there had not cooperated with neighboring countries to the degree suggested by the State Deparment's program for "mutual cooperation" on the part of European governments. Today, western Germany is the bottleneck of European recovery, and that means us.[29]

Not surprisingly, Dulles took his discussions of shortcomings and bent them into recommendations for alterations in U.S. policies toward Europe. In virtually every statement dealing with the European Recovery Plan, he insisted that something more concrete should be done regarding economic cooperation. He told the Senate Foreign Relations Committee that "the basic purpose of the program ought to be set forth more clearly." In "unambiguous language," Europeans should be told "what it is we are aiming at" with respect to unity; it would not be amiss to include "targets," in fact, "both production targets and also such targets as increased political, economic and monetary unity." And lest transatlantic confreres imagine they could disregard any terms eventually incorporated in enabling legislation, Dulles urged a system of measuring out aid in proportion to progress toward indicated goals: "It should be set forth explicitly that continuing aid is contingent upon continuing cooperation by the peoples and governments of participating countries, and that the degree of aid should broadly speaking be measured by the degree of cooperation." (Touching on the same point before the Council on Foreign Relations, he said the E.R.P.'s administrator could "be instructed to open up or close down the spigot depending on how much progress was made" toward specified objectives.)

Dulles laid out related plans for Germany as he discussed the Marshall Plan. His proposals to the Senate included the following injunction:

As regards Germany, the Administration should supply similar production targets and assurances that, in so far as lies within our governmental power, we shall seek to integrate its economy into that of western Europe to the mutual advantage of both, and establish such international controls as will assure that German economy will neither be diverted to war purposes or be usable as an economic weapon against other peoples.

He made the same point many times in these months. To the Foreign Policy Association, he argued that:

In Germany, we have a unique opportunity for leadership. There we ourselves are a western European government. We can exercise a decisive influence in the Ruhr area which is the natural economic heart of Europe. If there is to be economic unity in Europe, that is the place to begin and it is a place where it lies within our power to begin.[30]

His broad proposals for more concrete steps toward continental unity and the integration of Germany, Dulles felt, would significantly improve the Truman Administration's programs. The E.R.P. "needs to be sharpened up," he said to the Council on Foreign Relations, and this was the way to do it. As it stood, he told another audience, Washington's package was "a pretty drab affair" and needed "sex appeal" put into it "to make it exciting": his proposals would make it easier to rouse enthusiasm in the American public and Congress, and in Europe as well.[31]

For all of his clear and frequently discussed reservations about the evolving Marshall Plan, it must be emphasized that Dulles never really wavered from his basic *public* support. His qualms about the neglect of European unity and German integration were consistent with personal convictions of long standing and must have been deeply felt. Coupled with what might easily have been a degree of resentment at being left very much on the sidelines regarding design and strategy, he might have adopted a negative or at best indifferent posture. He did not. Dulles obviously persuaded himself that aid to Europe à la Truman and Marshall was better than no aid to Europe at all. As he put it to the Senate Foreign Relations Committee on January 20, "I say, first of all, that I am for the Plan. In certain respects I think the State Department proposal can be improved. . . .But this is not the time to be a perfectionist."[32]

With this kind of statement as a signpost to his basic position, Dulles showed himself ready to jump into the extensive public debate on the European Recovery Plan that extended from November 1947 through March 1948. Though he regularly discussed his proposals for alterations, he always did so in a broad supportive context—as in his testimony to the Senate Foreign Relations Committee. Occasionally, he even tucked his reservations totally out of sight and offered what he hoped would be dramatic and effective endorsements. One December statement to the press talked about the danger of "the economic sabotage of Western civilization" and the magnificent determination of the French, Italians, and others "to sacrifice that free institutions may survive." What was needed to help these valiant efforts, he urged, "is to translate European economic recovery from the realm of speculation into the realm of fact"—and it was up to Congress to make this possible. He was also ready, as in the past, to make a special effort to tap Protestant sentiment in the Untied States. By way of the Federal Council of Churches, he helped organize a series of early March meetings at which, as he put it, "the Christian citizens of this land will show their support of the European Recovery Plan."[33]

Dulles's work on behalf of E.R.P. legislation, even when backed up by organized Protestants, was only one small engine among the many which helped pull Congress and the man in the street into supportive moods. The Truman Administration itself spent months carefully coordinating elaborate public relations efforts, involving special committees, endorsements by hopefully prestigious leaders, and a degree of information and news management, among other things. In addition, many organizations, especially those with an "internationalist" focus or bias, made their support known and assisted in selling the Marshall Plan to their countrymen. Dulles, therefore, joined a broad-flanking campaign in late 1947 and early 1948.

The effort was successful, of course. A Senate vote in support of the Economic Cooperation Act came on March 13, and a House vote in favor on March 31. A disagreement on precise dollar amounts of aid was resolved in a conference report passed on April 2, and the first appropriations of $6 billion were forthcoming in June.[34]

14

Campaigns, Crises, and Limbo, 1948–1949

JUST DAYS BEFORE the initial congressional votes on the Marshall Plan, Dulles had news which could only have convinced him that he had been right to offer it support rather than critical opposition. Following on the heels of what he considered the stalemates and vagaries of 1947, a new series of meetings in London had yielded important breakthroughs on European and German problems. A March 6 communique announced that after weeks of consultation, U.S., British, French, and Benelux representatives had reached agreement on a number of approaches that Dulles had long been advocating. In broad terms, there was now accord on the logic of integrating the western zones of Germany into an evolving European community. More particularly, there was even reference made to the desirability of some form of international control of the Ruhr and the overall relevance of German resources to "the economic reconstruction of western Europe."

Dulles's old friend Ferdinand Mayer expressed great satisfaction that "things really seem to be moving along the lines of European development you and I have so often . . . hoped for many years past." After going over details of the preliminary agreements during a visit to Washington, Dulles confessed to pleasure too. Neither man was ready merely to bask in the warmth of accomplishment, however. If European affairs were "moving along," there was still a long road ahead, with many obstacles that the United States could play a role in overcoming. Mayer believed it was time to tackle the major problem of Britain's future economic relationship with the Continent and urged Dulles "to do the same great work for this second pillar of Hercules as you did for its twin, the internationalization of the Ruhr. . . ." In reply, Dulles mentioned his own concern over what decisions would be made about the political and economic structure of an emerging Western Germany, that is, whether "three or four autonomous states" or "a new Reich" would emerge—as well as fear of "the money problem," which could stymie reconstruction and integration.[1]

If John Foster Dulles had been able to follow personal intellectual inclinations in early 1948, it is easy to imagine him turning his energies toward these kinds of new Herculean problems. He did not do so, however. Though he and an old classmate could identify the logical next steps in shaping a malleable European situation that had long been a central preoccupation, Dulles at least was soon to find other matters distracting his attention. Some distractions were essentially forced on him: the formation of NATO, a crisis in Berlin, and major alterations of the situation in the Far East, among other things, grabbed headlines throughout 1948 and 1949 and helped channel the thoughts of all individuals concerned with international affairs. Dulles often felt such issues intruded on matters of more basic importance, but he never found a practical way of avoiding them. Other distractions were more of his own choosing, such as gearing up for extensive personal involvement in another presidential election campaign. In either case, the result was a shifting of concentration away from the particular kinds of European issues with which he had been involved in 1946 and 1947.

I

The first distraction from Dulles's ongoing concern for closer integration within the European political economy—and something explicitly recognized as a distraction—was the early maneuvering for what ultimately became the North Atlantic Treaty Organization.

A Treaty of Brussels had been signed by the British, French, and Benelux governments on March 17, 1948, pledging the participants to cooperation in the event of aggression by Germany, which was mentioned specifically, or the Soviet Union, which was presumably being eyed suspiciously. London immediately appealed to Washington for aid in fleshing out this skeletal security system for Western Europe, and U.S. policy makers began to weigh alternative methods of taking part. Not the least of the Truman Administration's concerns was the practical matter of dealing with a Congress controlled by Republicans: participation in formal transatlantic collective security arrangements would be a major departure from traditional American foreign policy and would likely be expensive at that. Using what was already a tried and true technique, the Administration moved behind the scenes to co-opt some of the opposition's key leaders. Under Secretary of State Robert Lovett moved in on Arthur Vandenberg, who was especially important, a delicate task undertaken at a series of informal meetings over drinks at the Senator's Wardman Park Hotel suite beginning in April. As anticipated, Vandenberg grabbed the ball and ran. He was soon busy planning the maneuvers that would yield a Senate resolution in favor of a North Atlantic pact under the umbrella of the U.N. Charter's Article 51.[2]

With the key Vandenberg pump primed, some effort was made to draw Dulles into the project as well. He was invited to a secret Blair House meeting with Secretary Marshall, Lovett, and Vandenberg on April 27. Though he eventually came around, Dulles acted at first as if he were going to be difficult to satisfy. Perhaps to the others' surprise, he expressed numerous reservations about evolving plans. He queried whether Article 51 was really an appropriate mechanism, given his own "recollection" that it "was intended to apply to distinctive associations of nations that had grown up like a family": to treat the North Atlantic community as such "for purposes of temporary expediency . . . might result in frustrating the United Nations." He questioned the formality of the method too. "I felt that we were dealing with a temporary and transitional situation, and that permanent long-term commitments would be out of place," he said. Most importantly, he worried about the psychological impact that such a pact would have on the Europeans. Would it be viewed by them, he asked, as a guarantee of "the status quo and make it less likely, rather than more likely, that the western European democracies would unite to create greater strength as between themselves?" Dulles certainly thought it would. He saw the easy possibility of a North Atlantic security pact becoming a comfortable screen to hide behind, and he argued it would thus distract attention from the reform of the continental political economy, which he continued to see as the key goal of U.S. policy in Europe. As he expressed it, he was afraid that "any firm commitment [by the U.S.], either military or economic, would be used by the governments of western Europe as an excuse to continue their own particular social and economic experiments, which required insulation from others. . . ." Obviously aware of the desire for some initiative in this area, Dulles did suggest an alternative to the pact approach:

> I expressed the view that what we were seeking was to guaranty the rebuilding of Europe against arson and that a *unilateral statement of our intentions, coupled with practical military cooperation* of the nature we now had with Canada, might be better than a formalized agreement. . . . There would be advantage in *keeping our policy in our own hands* as I did not see very well how it would be possible to draft a convention which would promote a growth and development rather than guaranty an existing status. [Emphasis added.]

But Dulles must quickly have realized that the Blair House meeting had been arranged more for the purpose of giving him information about an evolving program than seeking his counsel on its wisdom. Neither Marshall nor Lovett evidenced any readiness to reconsider their direction, confident no doubt of Vandenberg's support via pride of authorship. And when Dulles himself understood his friend's inclinations, which became obvious when Vandenberg failed to pick up on any questions and criticisms, he shifted away from a debate on basics. If the Senator was ready to go along with the Administration, it must not have seemed practical or advisable to disagree. Dulles did reiterate his fears, but finally joined in "further discussion as to how practically to proceed with Congress. . . ."[3]

The working out of NATO's details would take more than a year, but Dulles's role in the process was almost nonexistant until close to the end. In the meantime, other distractions emerged, which proved more demanding of his time and vested energy. The most important of these was the 1948 presidential campaign.

Though it might intrude on national and global concerns of great importance, politics had to be tended to as far as Dulles was concerned: if successfully handled, of course, it provided the foundation on which one could build a foreign policy of one's own choosing. Besides, in the past Dulles had enjoyed political chores. This was more than ever likely to be the case in 1948. Republicans in general were virtually straining at the bit in anticipation of the presidential election. Accumulated grievances among and against the long-entrenched Democrats coupled with the seemingly pedestrian and even inept performances of Harry Truman suggested that the door to the White House was wide open to the G.O.P. for the first time in two decades.

If Dulles shared the general Republican excitement of early 1948, his

close association with Tom Dewey would have provided a special anticipation. Dewey faced considerable opposition in his effort to gain the presidential nomination for a second time, given the optimism in his party's
ranks, but he triumphed over the field with relative ease. The one man he
would almost surely have failed to defeat, Dwight Eisenhower, made it
clear in January to Republicans and Democrats alike that he would not
run, and from that point on the rivals proved consistently weaker.
Douglas MacArthur dropped out of the race after poor showings in the
Wisconsin and Nebraska primaries, and Harold Stassen fumbled the
momentum gained with victories in those two states by losing to Dewey in
Oregon in mid-May. Robert Taft and Arthur Vandenberg tried playing
with delegations and party machines behind the scenes, both before and
at the opening of the Philadelphia convention in June, but Dewey's lead in
the delegate count and Stassen's obstinacy regarding release of his committed forces stymied the two Senators' efforts: the New York governor
was nominated unanimously on the third ballot.[4]

Dulles's role in Dewey's second presidential campaign by and large followed the pattern established in 1944. Day-to-day strategy and campaigning were still not his "cup of tea," and Dewey relied heavily on a team including Allen Dulles, Herbert Brownell, and Elliot Bell for advice and
management in these areas. When it came to broadly conceived deliberations and the delineation of the "Dewey Administration's" foreign policy,
however, Foster Dulles was the acknowledged senior adviser. His hand
was discernible in virtually all of the candidate's stands on the major
issues, and he was for all practical purposes the Secretary of State–desig-
nate in the event of a Republican victory. He helped draft, as in the past,
many of the candidate's major speeches dealing with foreign policy. He
served, as well, as the conduit through which those who wanted to consult with the presumed next President about international questions had
to go: it was Dulles rather than Dewey who met most regularly with key
party leaders such as Arthur Vandenberg; it was Dulles who traveled to
Washington for talks with representatives of numerous foreign governments in the closing weeks of the campaign or who traveled to foreign
capitals to gather impressions (e.g., a whirlwind tour of Scandinavia in
October.)

As to the overall foreign policy stance of the Republican candidate,
Dulles and Dewey's other advisers worked out a predictable package.
Most basically, they followed through on the thrust of the 1944 effort and
made Dewey's "internationalist" inclinations as clear as possible, accepting the inevitable alienation of a small minority of diehards within the
party. Most debates were really over the *extent* of U.S. global com-

mitments: participants quibbled over degrees, but a true isolationist was a rarity in the mainstream political arena. The foreign policy plank declared concern for "the stability, security and liberty of other independent peoples," endorsed "collective security" principles and a strengthening of the United Nations, and urged "progress toward unity in Western Europe," among other things. To underline the general outward-looking perspective of the platform, Dewey then went on to reject the suggestion that House Majority Leader Charles Halleck be his running mate. Halleck had been one of the leaders of last-minute congressional efforts to cut European Recovery Program funds, and his name on the ticket would have conjured up all of the old "isolationist" clichés about the G.O.P. Instead, Dewey settled on California governor Earl Warren, who, though he did not have a particularly high profile on foreign affairs, was quickly touted as a favorite of the internationalists. [5]

On the bedrock of general "internationalism," which was evident in every statement Dewey made about foreign affairs, Dulles helped to construct other major themes of the campaign. In June, Dulles tried to help the party and Dewey project what he hoped would be accepted as two logically connected points. On the one hand, he wanted to join Arthur Vandenberg in emphasizing the way "Republicans have demonstrated their complete competence and dependability in dealing with the critical international crisis which is the over-riding hazard of the moment [the Cold War clash with the Soviet Union]." On the other hand, he wanted to slash away at what he was ready to denounce as the tragic, almost criminal record of the Democrats.

As for "competence," Dulles and others felt it was absolutely essential to point to four years of "bipartisan" cooperation. As a counter to any lingering images of the 1920s, he was ready to flash what he believed were impressive new G.O.P. credentials: strong support for U.S. involvement in the United Nations, consistent cooperation with respect to major foreign aid proposals (including Vandenberg's key role in the passage of the Marshall Plan enabling legislation), and a willingness to take the public lead in historically significant new collective security arrangements (including Vandenberg's close identification with the Rio Pact and his more recent May 1948 resolution paving the way for the North Atlantic Treaty Organization). Dulles and Vandenberg were particularly anxious to point to the performance of the Republican-*controlled* 80th Congress. As the latter put it in one letter, "the record of the Senate Foreign Relations Committee" alone "clearly makes this Congress . . . the *best* Congress in history. There is nothing remotely like it in the whole Congressional story for more than 150 years." Although they had not occupied the White House for four terms, Dulles and others were ready to argue that Republicans had demonstrated a clear capacity to guide the United States to responsible behavior in the international arena.[6]

Democrats, on the contrary, were to be pictured as dangerously inept. One of Dulles's earliest drafts for the 1948 foreign policy plank argued that the Roosevelt–Truman Administrations had bequeathed a "heritage of *appeasement* and . . . inability to find clarity, competence or consistency"; they had "often made our nation appear *uncertain, inefficient, vacillating* and *unreliable*. The result is that our national prestige has waned and those who openly work against us have been expanding their influence and power in the world" (emphasis added). Other paragraphs in other Dulles drafts indicate that he was preparing a broad critical base from which Dewey could hurl bricks at supposed Democratic failures in Eastern Europe and China. Mercifully, Dulles would then go on to argue, Republicans had been vigilant and had forestalled an even worse series of disasters from befalling the United States and the rest of the world.

> We were ever alert to the deadly danger of Soviet communism and saw that its antidote was not weakness, but strength in the right. We checked a trend toward appeasement which already has cost our nation dearly and which, but for Republican intervention, would have left our nation dangerously isolated and encircled in the world.

The punch line of this kind of attack in one Dulles draft was that Republicans "have been able to prevent disaster; but we have not been able to provide success. That will come when the Republican Party has the initiative which the Constitution confides to the Presidency."[7]

The double-barreled tactic of proclaiming Republican expertise in foreign policy while vigorously denouncing Democratic failures had its share of unsavory features, of course, though this hardly distinguished it from many another American election strategy. None of the G.O.P. planners, from Dewey, Dulles, and Vandenberg down, seemed phased by the inconsistency of trying to have it both ways at the same time on the subject of "bipartisanship." If Republicans were going to argue that they had proven their mettle by supporting such policies as U.S. involvement in the United Nations and the Marshall Plan, were they not essentially offering praise to the Roosevelt–Truman Administrations which had conceived of these initiatives in the first place? Granting the possibility of claiming credit for *improving* original proposals, the contention that all positive developments had been the G.O.P.'s doing and all negative ones the Democrats' strains credulity. The idea of "bipartisan" involvement, in other words, was a sword that cut two ways as far as Republican–Democratic performance was concerned, and it is hard to imagine a member of the Dewey entourage being able to walk its fine edge with any respectable conviction. Aside from inconsistency, and a rather typical dollop of dishonesty, Dulles's June platform drafts contained proposed attacks on Democratic failures in Eastern Europe and the Far East that glossed over the fact that neither Dewey nor Dulles had, even to that moment, developed any alternative proposals for dealing with past or current issues in these areas. This whole ploy would simply have been an extension of 1944's last-ditch efforts to capitalize on problems in Poland, public positions that actually contradicted Dulles's personal assessments.

Whatever the strengths or weaknesses of this kind of strategy may have been, Dewey was ready to charge into the campaign with it as his guide. He confined himself to a vague, innocuous acceptance speech at the Philadelphia convention, but he was soon firing a few exploratory rounds. At a special press conference on July 1, in particular, he seemed ready to open the box of G.O.P. explosives. He was planning to direct "major criticism" at those Truman foreign policies which had not been formulated with due regard to bipartisan cooperation, he told reporters, and went on to list the Potsdam Conference, relations with Greece and Turkey, the "entire China policy or lack of policy" and Palestine as likely possibilities for his attention.[8]

Then, with the lid of the box loosened, Dewey essentially slammed it shut again. Though there would be scattered shots heard later in the fall, the basic concept of scathing attack on the Democrats was rather quickly shelved by the Dewey team during the early summer doldrums of their second presidential campaign. In a move that dramatically affected the overall tone and subject matter of interparty debate on foreign policy, they opted instead for a cooler, deliberately more "statesmanlike" approach.

Why the shift? Among other causes was the clear determination of Arthur Vandenberg to rise above street-scrapping techniques in the 1948 campaign. On one occasion after another, with respect to one issue after another, he utilized his very considerable influence to steer Dewey away from the tantalizing political gutter. He had several reasons for doing this. First, he believed that a more dignified campaign would project a better image for the Republican Party. Lashing out at the Democrats might be seen as irresponsible politicking and might weaken the sense of competence that bipartisan efforts had created. "From the standpoint of sheer politics," he wrote Dulles during one debate about a policy commitment, "I respectfully submit that we can *prove* from the *record* that Republicans can be *wholly* trusted with these foreign policy responsibilities. I respectfully submit that our only political danger is to *unprove* it." Or, as he put it to Herbert Brownell, "I am completely convinced that nothing can lick us except our own mistakes. . . ." The air of confidence in the latter comment links up with a second reason for Vandenberg's choice of strategy in 1948. Concluding very early, like so many, that victory was a virtual certainty in November, the Senator was inclined to maneuver in a way that would pay practical dividends after Dewey's inauguration. No one should doubt, he wrote Dulles at the very start of the campaign, "that the next Republican Secretary of State is going to need Democratic votes in the Senate just as badly as the present Administration has needed Republican votes. . . . It is peculiarly *our* job—yours and mine—to see that bipartisan liaison in the next Congress does not become impossible. Otherwise, November will represent a pyrrhic victory." He made the same point in a later statement about his personal part in the campaign: "I am anxious to do anything I can for November so long as none of us forget the difficult role I shall be expected to fill, come January 20th."[9]

Aside from practical matters inherent in shaping and implementing foreign policy, Vandenberg's concern about inauguration as well as election day also owed something to an increasingly strong attachment to the whole concept of a "bipartisan" foreign policy. Though he was capable of being snappish about the limits of Democratic readiness to share information and program development, he argued more and more regularly that something very vital and significant had been created since 1945. Interparty cooperation beyond "the water's edge" had yielded strength in a time of global crisis and was too important to sacrifice for temporary partisan advantage, he argued in 1948. The "record of constructive . . . cooperation" in the 80th Congress had been "amazing" he told Dulles in one letter—"and I think it is largely responsible for the country's substantial unity in its foreign policy voice (*a 'unity' which may spell the difference between peace and war*)" (emphasis added).[10] One might argue that Vandenberg's ego was caught up with the principle of "bipartisanship" as much as his concern for unity and peace, given the special role the Truman Administration had encouraged him to play, but if this is true it would only have reinforced his determination to rise above playing politics with foreign policy in the 1948 campaign.

Vandenberg was so influential a figure within the Republican Party that he might have forced a change of campaign strategy almost single-handedly. As it turned out, a test of wills never really took place. After briefly flirting with knockabout tactics in June, Dewey himself, as well as Dulles and other members of the team, were easily persuaded of the essential wisdom of the Senator's advice. From mid-July on, there were regular public and private expressions of concern about maintaining national unity in a time of high global tension. Dewey's nomination had come only days before the onset of the potentially explosive crisis over Berlin (to be discussed more fully below) and this, in particular, created a mood of genuine caution among Republican strategists. The candidate's initial comments on the Berlin situation were totally noncommital in spite of some suggestions that he cite Democratic ineptitude at past negotiations as the cause of problems, and when he spoke more fully on July 24 it was to express full support for the Truman Administration's current policy. In a statement worked out with Dulles and Vandenberg, he said that while better arrangements should have been negotiated, "the present duty of Americans is not to be divided by past lapses but to unite to surmount present dangers. We shall not allow domestic partisan irritation to divert us from this indispensable unity." Similar words were forthcoming throughout the succeeding months of the campaign, most often as part of further comments on the Berlin crisis. The G.O.P. "campaign will not create division among our people," Dewey told an audience in September. "Instead this campaign will unite us as we have never been united before. It will unite us so strongly that no force will again attack us and we will labor unceasingly and with unity to find common grounds of firm and peaceful agreement with all the nations of the earth."

Dulles too voiced his own similar concerns, but usually with reference to a more general context. He referred in a number of confidential communiques to Dewey to the way in which suspicions of sharp divisions within the U.S. might weaken the resolve of America's Allies to hold fast against the broad-flanking communist onslaught. While attending General Assembly meetings in Paris during September and October, Dulles sensed real "nervousness" about U.S. resolve. In one of many ironic communications with Dewey, he wrote that immediately after election day concerted efforts should be made to persuade the Allies that Republicans would make no drastic alterations of policy in January: this was "important from the standpoint of preventing collapse in the morale of friendly countries."

> During the five weeks I have been in Paris I have had private talks with the Foreign Ministers of the following countries, among others: England, France, Belgium, Holland, Austria, Greece, Turkey, Iran, China, Korea, Argentina, Brazil, Chile, etc. I have, by going to Berlin, evidenced support of the airlift. Unless Republicans carry on in that role, there is grave risk that, in the next months, the anti-Soviet governments in Europe and the Far East will largely collapse, and Latin America become distrustful.[11]

Other facets of the evolving campaign began to complement Dewey's and Dulles's reading of the need for unity via an emphasis on bipartisanship and made them even more inclined to adopt the cool and statesmanlike stance that Vandenberg had proposed. In Dulles's case, the Democrats in Washington brilliantly co-opted him back into policy making in the very midst of the campaign. Whether Truman and his advisers were acting because of their own genuine concern for keeping politics from spreading beyond the water's edge or some more Machiavellian campaign strategy is not clear, but whatever their motives, they accorded Dewey's principal adviser considerable status and reinforced in him something of the same vested interest in bipartisanship that had long affected Arthur Vandenberg. In the first days following the Republican convention, Under Secretary of State Robert Lovett was given the responsibility of keeping Dulles informed about important matters under consideration in his department. In mid-July, Dulles was invited to attend special meetings in which policy on Berlin was being debated. At the first of these, George Marshall told him that he wanted to tap his thoughts as "an intelligent observer who had only publicly available information"; the Secretary and Lovett then went on to give him the fuller inside story and asked him to share in deliberation on alternative courses of action with Charles Bohlen, George Kennan, and other department officers. And as a capstone to these kinds of developments, Dulles was asked to join the U.S. delegation to the U.N. General Assembly meeting which was scheduled to begin in Paris in late September and continue until well after the election. At the beginning of the Democratic wooing, Dulles may have been somewhat skeptical. He complained angrily to Robert Lovett on July 19 about the partisan tone of the Democratic platform on foreign policy and pointedly asked George Marshall if he were planning to take an active part in the upcoming campaign. "Thank goodness I expect to keep out of that," Marshall said, to which Dulles replied that he "was glad to know that because if it were otherwise I might have to change my plans," From this point on, however, Dulles rarely expressed doubts about dropping harsh partisan tactics. [12]

Nor did Dewey strain in any dramatic way under the more temperate bridle. Washington attention to Dulles was, of course, essentially a function of deference to the Republican candidate himself, and this alone would have given a more attractive glow to bipartisanship. Dewey could only have been pleased at the elaborate arrangements made for him to carry on regular consultation with Dulles during the Paris General Assembly sessions: he was provided with a confidential, around-the-clock teletype line, including placement of a receiving machine in his car. As

Dulles put it, this was "comparable to the facilities which Secretary Marshall will have to President Truman." Newsmen drew their own conclusions. One said that "this arrangement doesn't just put the Governor in the State Department, it puts him in the White House"; another argued that it created a situation in which the U.S. would "actually have two secretaries of state"—which prompted a classically coy rejoinder from Dulles that "you will have to draw your own inference." When, in the bargain, this kind of special treatment was coupled with the notorious avalanche of polls predicting an overwhelming Republican victory, it should not be surprising that Dewey found the role of "statesman" somewhat prematurely satisfying. It certainly became an oft-noted ingredient in his campaign style. As *Time* put if after a major speech by Dewey in Salt Lake City, he "seemed less like a candidate bidding for votes and more like a statesman speaking not only for his party but for his country."[13]

Confident of victory at home and concerned about Allied morale abroad, Dewey, Dulles, and the Republican team ended up dealing with foreign policy in a way quite different from what would have been expected on the basis of early indications. Their less bellicose approach was both negative and positive: on certain "issues," the Republicans consciously avoided mounting the attacks they had contemplated in earlier months; on other "issues," they went out of their way to endorse the policies that had been declared by the Truman Administration. Taken together, their positions essentially turned foreign policy into a non-issue during the presidential campaign.

The subjects the Republicans chose to side-track included the Soviet "satellites", Palestine, China, and the internal subversion or "spy" question that was already becoming so prominent. Almost incredibly, the Republicans made no systematic effort to cultivate ethnic groups generally seen as politically potent. Though the Democrats, rightly or wrongly, would have been highly vulnerable to criticism about "concessions" to Soviet imperialism in Eastern Europe, they were not thrown regularly on the defensive. Except for a few very random comments in the closing days of the campaign, Dewey never followed through on his July 1 warning that he would prepare a damning brief regarding developments in Poland, Hungary, and other countries.

Nor did the G.O.P. prove adept at appealing to Jewish voters. Though Truman had played to the political grandstands in May and offered immediate recognition of the new state of Israel, Dewey made no moves to top this Democratic coup in succeeding months. He applauded the *de facto* recognition of Israel and approved the Republican platform pledge of support for "boundaries as sanctioned by the United Nations and in developing its economy," but this was too vague and chronologically open-ended to do much good. On any number of issues of great importance to Zionists, he shied away from specific comments week after week as the campaign evolved: on the questions of *de jure* recognition, the lifting of an arms embargo, and the extension of major loans to the new country, among others. Even George Marshall's September 26 endorsement of the controversial Bernadotte Report did not lead to a Dewey initiative. Zionists were enraged by the U.N. mediator's proposals for altering earlier plans for partition of Palestinian territory, in particular the idea of taking the Negev from Israel in return for western Galilee. When Truman bowed to his Secretary of State's inclinations and refused to criticize the report, to the deep chagrin of his political advisers, a superb opportunity was opened up for Dewey. He did not take it. Dulles informed Marshall that the Republicans would no longer consider Palestine a subject on which bipartisan cooperation existed and privately informed Zionist leaders of this move, but neither he nor Dewey felt prepared to go any further. As Dulles put it in a letter to Vandenberg, "it is not practical for me to study the matter sufficiently to have any opinion as to the merit of the recommendation." And as Dewey explained to Rabbi Abba Hillel Silver, "constant travel and campaigning were keeping him from getting full information and so he could not make any statement for publication."

For an amazingly long time Truman ducked issues concerning Israel and took advantage of the lee in the political winds which the Republicans had helped build by doing likewise. It is impossible to say whether he would have continued to back away from questions of importance to Jewish voters until after election day. He was under constant pressure to take the initiative by Democratic politicians and Zionist leaders and friends. But ultimately it was Dewey who opened the way for partisan maneuvering, making it easier for Truman to barrel ahead with blatant last-minute appeals. In a move that might be seen as twice stupid, Dewey decided to make a statement on "Palestine" in late October, only to allow his initiative to fade away in some classic vagaries. Responding publicly to a request for clarification of his views from the American Christian Palestine Committee, Dewey reaffirmed his support of earlier U.N. proposals for Israeli boundaries, thus coming close to rejection of the recent Bernadotte recommendations. He also emphasized his own consistency on this issue, leading some to comment that he had implied that Truman had backed away from a previous commitment more in Israel's favor. Having gone this far, he stopped, leaving the boundary question not very precisely addressed and loans and arms questions quite untouched. The President then unleashed his political advisers and cooperated almost to their heart's content in the closing days of the campaign. With a self-righteousness that is hard to take at face value, he proceeded to act as if Dewey had leveled some major attack on his honesty which required a more elaborate outline of his policies toward Israel. On October 24, he promised both financial aid and *de jure* recognition immediately after the Israeli elections scheduled for early November; he also started backing away from the Bernadotte plan, indicating a willingness to negotiate about boundaries but a preference for earlier proposals. By October 28, in a major Madison Square Garden address, he was brandishing the Palestine issue with great gusto—pointing to his early recognition decision and demanding an Israel "large enough, free enough and strong enough to make its people self-supporting and secure." Such strong appeals far outmatched the hedging words Dewey was willing to use and resulted in clear reinforcement of the advantage that Truman and the Democrats probably had with Jewish voters in any event. [14]

There were other issues Dewey chose to sidestep through virtually all of the campaign as well, some even more surprising than Eastern Europe and Palestine. In spite of deep concern within his own party, the Republican candidate kept his comments on China thoroughly nonpartisan. Where one might have expected angry assertions about Democratic culpability in the rapidly declining fortunes of Chiang Kai-shek—assertions that could have bounced off the daily news reports of the disasters befalling the Nationalists, including the fall of Mukden just days before the election—Dewey allowed the already vague words of the June platform to stand without elaboration. "We will foster and cherish our historic policy of friendship with China and assert our deep interest in the maintenance of its integrity and freedom," that document had declared, and Dewey added nothing with a tougher bite. There was an interesting parallel to the candidate's behavior in his adviser's conduct in Paris as well. In spite of pressure from the Chinese Minister of Foreign Affairs regarding aid that might be forthcoming from a Dewey Administration, Dulles remained totally noncommital: he passed the arguments and memo's of Chiang's representative along, but indicated neither interest in dealing with them before the election nor any sign of how he would want to deal with them once the election was won. [15]

The same paucity of driving Republican attacks characterized the "spy" issue. The summer and fall of 1948 would have been a thoroughly propitious time for charges of Democratic negligence regarding the appointment of subversives to government positions. Controversy over the disloyalty or espionage activities of executive branch officials had been slowly mounting for years, but reached a new and explosive stage when

Elizabeth Bentley and Whitaker Chambers offered their notorious testi-
monies to a special Senate subcommittee. [16] Widely credited allegations,
particularly those concerning former State Department officer Alger
Hiss, might well have seemed valuable ammunition for the G.O.P. Dewey
chose not to pound away at an ostensibly vulnerable opponent, however.
Instead, the sparks this issue had sometimes produced were smothered by
the stateman's determination to rise above mud-slinging.

Though it meshed with his general campaign strategy, it should be indicated that Dewey had a strong additional reason for ducking the espionage imbroglio. One of his own senior advisors was not invulnerable to
attack on this issue. When the uproar over Whitaker Chambers's accusations began in the summer of 1948, Alger Hiss was serving as President of
the Carnegie Endowment for International Peace, a post that John Foster
Dulles had helped secure for him. His role in Hiss's appointment to the
Carnegie Endowment and the relationship it implied was to be a source of
nagging annoyance for Dulles for several years. He usually succeeded in
keeping his name out of the glaring public spotlight that hit others connected with the case, but he was often just on the edge of the controversy
nonetheless.

Dulles had come to know Hiss during the San Francisco Conference in
1945 and seems to have shared in the general praise for the administrative
skills Hiss had demonstrated there. Later in the year, after Dulles had
become "prospective" Chairman of the Board of Trustees of the Carnegie
Endowment, he was drawn into the search for a new President for the organization. Hiss's name was one of many suggested for consideration,
along with others such as Adlai Stevenson and William Fulbright. After
months of deliberations, three men were approached and declined, and as
Dulles later expressed it, "It then seemed that Mr. Hiss was the next most
available person." "Uniformly laudatory" reports had been coming in
from the State Department and the various law firms that Hiss had been
connected with, and there was general agreement to make him an offer.
Negotiations about departure dates took place between Secretary of State
Byrnes and the candidate, and he was formally elected President at a
board meeting in December 1946. [17]

Aside from the basic fact of Hiss's connection with the Endowment,
Dulles and his associates found themselves particularly vulnerable to
criticism because of charges that they had been careless in heeding early
warnings about him. There had, in fact, been some. As early as two weeks
after Hiss's election, Dulles began hearing from several sources that the
successful candidate had a "provable Communist record." Dulles later
wrote that these reports "were similar to rumors then prevalent regarding
several highly placed persons and it did not seem that they justified

credence as against the overwhelming verdict by those who had known Hiss, as to his loyalty to American tradition." Nevertheless, he took steps to investigate the matter. On January 2, 1947, he held a meeting with Alfred Kohlberg, one of those who had first contacted him about Hiss's purportedly subversive past. Kohlberg was an importer-exporter of Chinese textiles who had become an important propagandist concerning "communist subversion" in the United States. He wrote hundreds of letters to government officials and newspapers and even financed the publication of a magazine called *Plain Talk*, which often focussed on the subject. Dulles asked Kohlberg if he had "any actual proof of Mr. Hiss's communist affiliations" and was told that it existed and that efforts would be made to secure it. Two months later, however, Kohlberg wrote that though he was convinced his Washington informants were correct in their charges about Hiss, hard evidence was available only in secret F.B.I. files: "In view of the fact that these files are not available for reference, I could not, and I do not believe that you, could accept the available evidence uncorroborated as definitive. I am therefore dropping the matter." While waiting for Kohlberg's evidence, Dulles also discussed the problem with Alger Hiss himself. He "denied in the most categorical terms that he was or ever had been a communist or 'fellow traveler' and went on to indicate that F.B.I. investigations had cleared him to the government's satisfaction."[18]

Following Kohlerg's retreat and Hiss's denials, Dulles let the matter rest for almost a year—or was at least allowed to let it rest. He seems to have kept his ears tuned for further information about the Endowment President's past, but was apparently ready to dismiss the accusations as malicious and unfounded. In early 1948, however, Dulles and an increasing number of political leaders in Washington began hearing accusatory reports again; Chambers had been telling his story to more and more people, and some of them had passed it along to create an ever-widening rumor circuit. During February, Hiss himself was called to testify before a Federal Grand Jury looking into communist subversion. At this point, Dulles seems to have felt forced to pick up the trail once again. He contacted Representative Walter Judd, a long-time acquaintance and a man who had worked closely with Kohlberg, asking him if he had heard of any new hard evidence damaging to Hiss's reputation. Judd responded with the disturbing news that he was convinced the stories were true, that the evidence was in F.B.I. hands, and that John Puerifoy, Assistant Secretary of State for Administration, had essentially admitted this to him! No doubt worried, Dulles met with Hiss himself the same day he heard from Judd. Though he "questioned him searchingly," Hiss reasserted his total lack of communist affiliations: the closest he could come to any basis for concern was that early in his career, "when he was practicing law and when he was in the Department of Agriculture, he was thrown into casual association with some persons who had communist sympathies." Shortly after this meeting, Dulles phoned John Puerifoy at the State Department—and received some welcome reassurance.

> Puerifoy indicated that while he thought Hiss might be mentioned in some of the F. B. I. files, he, himself, was absolutely satisfied as to the complete loyalty of Hiss, and that he knew of no evidence of any kind which cast any doubt on the matter. He said that in the Department Hiss had been looked upon as rather to the "right" and more conservative than many in the Department.

This was enough for Dulles, at least for the time being. He wrote to Judd about Puerifoy's information and added his own bit of assessment concerning the importance of Hiss's clear public support for the Marshall Plan ("the phase of our foreign policy which the Communists are fighting most bitterly," he said.) "I shall keep alert," he concluded, "but so far have not changed my judgment."[19]

There matters stood until all hell broke loose four months later, in the middle of the presidential campaign. Whitaker Chambers gave his formal testimony before the House Un-American Activities Committee on August 3. Hiss was given the opportunity to speak on August 5—and a now-public problem reared its ugly head before Dulles once again.

According to Hiss himself, Dulles's initial response was to try to placate the whirlwind. When he asked the Chairman of the Endowment's trustees for advice on dealing with Chambers's public accusations, Hiss later said, he was told that "caution" would be wise: Dulles "reminded him that many people of Hiss's generation had been rather radical when they were young, and probably got mixed up with Communists whether they realized it or not, and nobody would hold anything against Hiss if he said something like that had happened to him too, and that now he was older and wiser he knew better and wouldn't have anything to do with Communists."[20] If Hiss's recollections are accurate and Dulles really hoped that this kind of sop to the House Un-American Activities Committee and the media would be sufficient, he was of course greatly underestimating the situation. Neither congressional spy-sniffers such as Richard Nixon nor naturally eager reporters were ready to accept such an explanation. Nor was Hiss himself, for that matter. He voluntarily appeared before H.U.A.C. on August 5, thus beginning a process of public battle with his accusers that quickly escalated beyond anyone's control.

Within days he and his wife had been drawn into more exhaustive testimony, and Chambers had taken his earliest charges and offered a variety of elaborations. Within weeks, Hiss was goaded by his accusers to file suit for libel. A series of formal and notorious court proceedings that would unwind over many months then began.

Although Hiss immediately rejected Dulles's August 3 counsel of "caution," Dulles was apparently inclined to stick by him. "I am not quite clear in my mind as to what, if any, action the Trustees should take," he wrote Philip Jessup, "and it seems to me better to defer decision until after the present hearings have been concluded." Though this hardly bespeaks vigorous support to begin with, it was soon seriously weakened. On August 11, H.U.A.C. member Richard Nixon asked for a meeting with fellow Republican Dulles in order to inform the Dewey inner circle of the seriousness of the Hiss situation. That night, at campaign headquarters in New York's Roosevelt Hotel, Dulles and his brother Allen heard Nixon out and read some of Chambers' testimony. As Nixon recalled the scene:

> When they had finished reading, Foster Dulles paced the floor, his hands crossed behind him. . . . He stopped finally and said, "There's no question about it. It's almost impossible to believe, but Chambers knows Hiss."
>
> . . . I asked Foster Dulles whether he thought I was justified in going ahead with the investigation. He replied without hesitation, "In view of the facts Chambers has testified to, you'd be derelict in your duty as a Congressman if you did not see the case through to a conclusion."

The meeting with Nixon was the turning point in Dulles's relationship with Alger Hiss. From that day on, he sought to distance himself from the Endowment President he had himself helped to select. There is nothing in his words to Nixon to indicate any clear presumption of Hiss's "guilt," but at the least he seems to have decided that the man had become too controversial for comfort.

Dulles made his first move on August 18. Asking Hiss to come see him in the hope of settling the problem, he "told him that while he was confident that the Trustees would not themselves want to take action that might imply judgment against him or be prejudicial to him in relation to disputed facts, he thought that Mr. Hiss, out of consideration for the Endowment, should voluntarily resign and relieve the Endowment of embarrassment." Hiss was not to be moved so easily, however, and indicated a desire to wait until the H.U.A.C. hearings were completed before considering departure. Dulles then tried to work around Hiss as much as possible. He created something of an administrative cocoon for him by having James Shotwell take over administrative duties for the Carnegie

Endowment on September 1. He also talked to fellow trustees about a more permanent solution: "it would be precipitate to take any action at the present time," he wrote one of them on September 7, "but I am inclined to think that some positive course should be taken as soon as we feel we have all the facts and can arrange for an adequately prepared and attended meeting of the Trustees." Before anything could come of this, he went off to Paris for the General Assembly meeting and left the problem in the hands of John W. Davis, Vice Chairman of the Endowment's Trustees. Communications from his colleagues in ensuing weeks indicate that most of them were adamant about avoiding any action which might prejudice Hiss's case in advance, but there is no indication of Dulles's reaction to this strategy of postponement.[21] Perhaps he was simply relieved to have gotten somewhat away from the Hiss problem during the closing weeks of the presidential campaign.

Fears of guilt or at least suspicion by association with Alger Hiss certainly would have contributed to Dulles's and Dewey's decision to sidestep the "spies and subversives" issue in the fall of 1948. However, this decision also meshed with the general campaign strategy of avoiding virtually all hot issues while opting for a demonstration of "statesmanship" and national unity. Hiss's ties to Dulles did not really keep the Republican candidate from throwing any punches he would have wanted to throw.

There were only occasional doubts about the wisdom of a temperate campaign. Dulles grew somewhat annoyed in August, when Arthur Vandenberg complained about the divisive impact of a Dewey suggestion to give Italy U.N. trusteeship responsibility for some of its former colonies. This was classic maneuvering for advantage with an important ethnic group, Dulles felt, and the Senator was probably exaggerating its importance. He wrote a soothing letter to his friend, but concluded by asking him to "be tolerant of the exigencies of the campaign and of political influence from which certainly Mr. Truman does not divorce himself and from which the Governor cannot *wholly* divorce *himself*." He also wrote to his old confidante Ferdinand Mayer: "The policy to follow in foreign affairs is difficult because Vandenberg is particularly anxious to avoid anything in the nature of an attack. . . . I think that not being a candidate for office himself he is a little too dispassionate, but his point of view cannot be ignored as there must not be any 'break' between him and Dewey . . . ." Such doubts were not expressed with any regularity, however, and never led to a real change in campaign strategy. There were scatter-shot charges made in the closing days of the campaign—"Millions upon millions of people have been delivered into Soviet slavery while our administration has tried appeasement one day and blustered the next," Dewey told one audience—but these were little more than tit for tat for the last-minute flares emanating from the Truman camp. As Dulles put it at one point, "It was inevitable that one side or another would feel that there was a little 'cheating' for political advantage," but he did not think this would "disrupt unity with respect to the critical and vital issues, particularly involving current issues with the Soviet Union." Besides, as Robert Divine has concluded in his study of the 1948 election, such charges were too random and delayed to qualify as meaningful debate on foreign policy.[22]

II

Dewey's and Dulles's determination to avoid real debate on foreign affairs was nowhere more clearly evident than in their approach to the Berlin crisis. It was on June 24 that the Soviets stopped all land and water traffic into the German capital and the repercussions of that action dominated the news for months afterwards. In spite of this, the Republican team consistently shied away from turning Berlin into a major issue in the presidential campaign.

Though Westerners have tended to be struck by the suddenness of the Soviet move, any observer sensitive to Moscow's behavior and to unfolding developments in Germany should have been able to anticipate the emergence of some kind of crisis by late June or July, 1948. The United States, Great Britain, and France had agreed on major new German initiatives by that time, and it would have been extraordinary only if the Soviets had *not* responded in some significant fashion. Extended negotiations among the three western nations had begun in February, prompted by dismay at continued stalemate in yet another session of the Council of Foreign Ministers, and had produced a series of "London Recommendations" on June 2: a call for closer economic coordination in the three Western occupation zones, for a full West German role in the European Recovery Plan, for an international authority to control the Ruhr, and for preparatory work on the constitution of a new and independent German Federal Republic. This was a package of nightmares as far as the Soviets were concerned, promising a truncated but presumably potent Germany allied with an increasingly hostile Western coalition. And if circumstances could grow any worse, they did so on June 18. As the first fruit of the commitment to fuller coordination, Washington, London, and Paris agreed to "reform" the currency in their occupation zones, both in West Germany and Berlin: the Soviets quite accurately presumed the latter move would wreak havoc with their own currency reform plans for the city and create a constant irritant deep within their occupation zone. A response to the immediate predicament in Berlin certainly seemed called for, and the "blockade" begun on June 24 was designed to forestall the Western currency program. Though it is impossible to gauge their strategy or motives with real precision, first and subsequent Soviet moves suggest that they hoped a sudden crisis would bring at least a delay in implementation of the American–British–French plan—and perhaps even a reassessment of their program for Western Germany as a whole.[23]

John Foster Dulles played no role in determining the initial U.S. response to the Soviet blockade, though he was kept informed of some facets of Washington's deliberations by Arthur Vandenberg. There is, in fact, no evidence of his personal reactions to the first moves decided on by the Truman Administration: to the clear decision to remain in Berlin in spite of formidable obstacles and pressure; the almost immediate resort to the air corridors as a means of transporting food and other material to the city, the shifting of two squadrons of B-29's, potentially capable of delivering atomic bombs, to Germany; the July 6 diplomatic protest to Moscow, which called the blockade "a clear violation of existing agreements concerning the administration of Berlin," but which offered renewed negotiations concerning overall German issues if the blockade were ended. Only in mid-July did the State Department seek to bring Dulles into the bipartisan fold as far as Berlin was concerned. On July 14, the Soviets had formally rejected the arguments and proposals for negotiations put to them by the United States. The problem in Berlin had arisen because of violations of agreements on four-power control of Germany by the U.S., Great Britain, and France, the Soviets had insisted, violations inherent in three-power moves toward "separate currency reform" and "the dismemberment of Germany". The Soviet Union did desire negotiations concerning these German problems, they went on, but could not accept any call for pre-conditions such as an end to the blockade.[24] The collapse of their original démarche forced American policy makers to reassess the Berlin situation and to weigh alternative courses of action. It was in the course of these deliberations that Dulles was consulted.

First conversations took place at the State Department on July 19. Secretary of State Marshall indicated initially that he wanted "the reaction of an intelligent observer who had only publicly available information." An hour later he asked Dulles to meet with the "department working group" on Berlin "and go into the facts in detail": as Dulles put it afterwards, Marshall "said he was talking with me as one who had had much experience with the Russians in relation to Germany and whose personal judgment he wanted." A long meeting then took place that same day, with Under Secretary of State Robert Lovett, Charles Bohlen, George Kennan, Dean Rusk, and others; this was followed by telephone conversations with Lovett during the next few days.

Throughout these consultations, Dulles revealed clear reservations about the direction U.S. policy had taken to that point as well as quite specific thoughts about what should happen next. His immediate response to Marshall's first request for an outsider's opinion was that "I had had some doubts about note sent to Moscow":

> It seemed to me that Soviet prestige was deeply engaged, particularly in view of set-backs in Finland and Holland elections, the Tito quarrel and unrest in Czechoslovakia, and that they could hardly afford a public diplomatic back-down about Berlin, and there was danger that diplomatic argument might force them to crystalize publicly a stronger position than they had yet taken and one which would preclude their backing down in fact at the working level. I observed that even their reply note had referred to their obstructive measures as "temporary."

(At another point, he expanded on the question of prestige by arguing that "in Soviet circles it was not merely a question of *national* prestige, but of the *individual* standing of members of the Politburo for whom failure in policy they espoused was almost literally fatal.") As to alternatives to public posturing, Dulles had clearly thought the matter through and offered the State "working group" a precise agenda. He was convinced, he said, that "(1) the Soviet leaders did not want war but (2) their prestige was so engaged that they could not retreat unless we eased it." Therefore, he urged a step by step "diplomatic" procedure:

> . . . after clearance with Britain and France, private discussion with Molotov or, preferably, Stalin to say: (a) We will accept the Soviet proposal to negotiate not only about Berlin, but also about Germany as a whole, at a Four Power Conference to be held, preferably, at Berlin; (b) We will not demand, as conditions precedent, that the Soviet should formally lift the blockade or concede our rights; (c) We assume that the "temporary" difficulties will be quickly altered and we plan, accordingly, to resume land service by truck, train or both; (d) We would consider any forcible stoppage, under these circumstances, as creating a new situation which would have to be dealt with by the U.N.
>
> Following this diplomatic position, a formal note could be transmitted and if the Four Power Conference were agreed to, then the transport effort would be resumed by truck or railroad or both as technical factors dictated.

As he emphasized on several other occasions, Dulles thought this series of initiatives would make it possible to ascertain "whether, in fact, the Soviets are prepared actually to use force to stop us, even *under conditions which we design to make it easy for them* to relax the present blockade, without serious loss of prestige" (emphasis added).[25]

Dulles's emphasis on the Soviets' psychological problems and the need "to create new conditions" in which it would be easier for them to retreat clearly set him somewhat apart from the President and his State Department advisers. The Truman Administration had immediately moved to the public arena in dealing with the Berlin "crisis" and had shown no interest in the kind of private and informal talks with the Russians that Dulles was urging. Indeed, the only concrete new measure that Dulles was told was under consideration on July 19 would have yielded more of the same: following the Soviet rejection of Allied claims, the State working group told him, they were debating how best to bring the issue before the United Nations.

To go one important step further, this difference of opinion concerning methods seems to have been matched by, and perhaps caused by, a certain incompatibility of basic perspectives on the Berlin issue. Implicit in his recommendations and explicit in a number of comments made while presenting them is the fact that Dulles had a more limited sense of Berlin's importance than did the Administration's policy makers. As to the latter, their reading of the situation's strategic and psychological ramifications led them to posit their concern in sweeping terms. George Marshall told the President that "we had the alternative of following a firm policy in Berlin or accepting the consequences of *failure of the rest of our European policy*"; Truman wrote that "if we moved out of Berlin we would be *losing everything we were fighting for*"; and Robert Lovett warned Dulles that "weakness at Berlin would invite pressure at Vienna and so on through *all Western Europe*" (emphasis added). This kind of assessment within the Administration led to consideration of the full range of methods for dealing with the crisis, up to and including war. There was a clear desire to avoid armed conflict, of course, but it was never ruled out as a last resort for securing what seemed transcendent interests. Former O.S.S. chief William Donovan told reporters in Berlin on July 17 that the United States should simply send an armed convoy down the road to Berlin and deal with the consequences as they arose: "If the Russians are determined to have war we might as well have it here as 500 miles farther back." Donovan was a private citizen at this point and had not earned the nickname "Wild Bill" for nothing, but his words cannot be ignored on either count. He was close to General Clay and any number of Washington leaders as well, and his sentiments were shared by some of them. There was widespread consideration of the armed convoy idea within the Truman Administration throughout the first three weeks in July. Then too, Secretary of Defense Forrestal regularly pressed the President for a decision on whether atomic bombs would be used in the event of war in

Europe over Berlin. On one occasion Truman was quite explicit in response: "he prayed that he would never have to make such a decision, but that if it become necessary, no one need have a misgiving but that he would do so. . . ."[26]

This kind of talk and an apparent willingness to tolerate war as an ultimate tool was too much for Dulles. At no point in his July discussions with Marshall, Lovett, and others did he express agreement with their reading of Berlin's enormous importance or use similar phraseology himself. And what he did say had a very different thrust. There was no doubt that he wanted very much to try to secure a Western presence in Berlin, but the city did not seem to him to have sufficient intrinsic political or economic importance to justify major risks. While he was certainly ready to support efforts to remain there, he assumed they would be limited and was prepared to live with their ultimate failure. Speaking to Lovett on July 22, he said "We should not allow events to force an evacuating of Berlin or an abandoning of the Germans in our zones until exhausting every possibility of peaceful supply by land." Such words clearly implied a perspective that was capable of coping with evacuation when and if "peaceful supply" possibilities were exhausted. Special emphasis might well be placed on the word "peaceful" as well. When it came to choices of techniques for dealing with the crisis, Dulles explicitly precluded military steps and/or war. When Lovett asked "how much force would be used" in conjunction with the attempt to resume truck transport that Dulles had recommended, he was told he misunderstood the recommendation. Dulles envisioned no use of force at all, hoping instead that the right kind of behind-the-scenes diplomacy would lead the Soviets to grant access to Berlin to *unarmed* vehicles. He told Lovett that "the Soviet position would be tested *merely* to the point of seeing whether the Soviets would still block us by deed as distinct from word. Of course, I had no idea of our trying to shoot our way through. . . ." Carrying his thoughts to their logical conclusion, he then added that "indeed, he was *not* willing to envisage *the possibility of hostilities on account of the Berlin situation"* (emphasis added).[27] The same fundamental point was made in reacting to talk of bringing the issue to the United Nations. In practical terms, Dulles said, "it seems that at best the United Nations could give moral sanction to a large scale use of force which, however, is not what we want. We want peace, not a legal basis for war." Telescoping two months ahead, to the time when Dulles was involved with U.N. discussions on Berlin, this was an opinion he maintained. James Reston described the Republican adviser as "in an interesting and extremely difficult position" after meeting with him in Paris.

He does not agree with the present emphasis on the Berlin situation in the U.N. He foresees the day when he may very well have to assume responsibility for recommending that we get out. Yet, he cannot indicate strong opposition or allow the British or French to know that he sides with their moderate policies on Berlin rather than with Marshall's.[28]

Dulles's discussions with Administration leaders in mid-July, in other words, revealed some rather clear differences of perspective and policy. In comparison to the general homogeneity of positions on other international issues, it is tempting to say that there may have been more potential for a partisan clash in this area than in any other. Just how would one of the Republican Party's senior authorities on foreign affairs or the Republican presidential candidate himself have reacted if the Berlin situation had reached a point where American policy went beyond the bounds Dulles was indicating during his talks in Washington? What if a moment had come where the choice for the Truman Administration was to evacuate the city or to stay by resorting to other than "peaceful supply" techniques? Certainly, many policy makers in Western capitals would have found it easy to envision such a moment in the early weeks of the crisis. There was, in particular, a real sense that the airlift, which was allowing food and material to reach the beleaguered Berliners, could provide only a short-term mechanism for dealing with mind-boggling supply problems. As impressive as everyone found the early deliveries of the C-47 aircraft that began landing at Templehof airport on June 25, the overwhelming consensus was that the start of winter would create needs that could not be dealt with in this way: greater demands for food and especially coal would simply outmatch the airlift's capacity. If the Soviets had not altered their position by then, had not come around in four-power or U.N. negotiations, what then?

As it turned out, a crunch never came. Aside from the way in which Soviet motives and alternatives may have kept the situation from turning into a real crisis, it is also clear that the external pressure that might have been imposed by the calendar and the weather never became operative. It was a change in the capabilities of the airlift that made this possible, of course. Estimates of delivery capacity had steadily risen during July, especially after introduction of the larger C-54 cargo plane and construction of additional landing facilities in West Berlin. By July 22, Truman was able to conclude in a National Security Council meeting that the idea of sending an armed convoy toward the city should be shelved and primary reliance placed on a long-range airlift and negotiations.[29] What emerged from this point on was a very different kind of crisis, one that could be kept within manageable proportions because it had an essentially open-ended time frame. Issues might continue to boil, but they would do so as if in an uncovered pot; there was much less likelihood of an explosion in some pressure-cooker. Negotiations could go on indefinitely and in any variety of settings: if they succeeded, all well and good; if they failed, Berlin would continue to be supplied—and "held." Unless the Soviets altered their tactics in some significant way, there would be no need for the United States to resort to less "peaceful" methods.

Dulles would have been well aware of the varying implications of the airlift's capacity. On July 19, he was told by the State Department working group that substantial deliveries could be made to Berlin "until about October": "there must be some solution by October," the experts concluded, "or our position would be untenable and . . . we would then have to try large scale force under time pressures that might mean war." Three days later, however, in commenting on continuing deliberations in Washington, Lovett told Dulles that "there was one new important development namely that they had now developed the possibility of additional air lift . . . probably *making it possible to carry the situation through the winter*" (emphasis added).[30] This news and the associated, ongoing reliance on peaceful methods by the Administration made it very easy for Dulles, and Dewey, to fall in line with U.S. policy on Berlin. Prior to July 22, Dulles himself made no public comments on the German crisis and Dewey kept his statements completely vague and noncommital—the Dewey team as a whole had clearly not yet settled on a definable position. When a decision came, it emerged in a context in which information about the likely long-range utility of the airlift had become available. A long July 24 meeting between Dewey, Dulles, and Arthur Vandenberg seems to have been particularly crucial in tacking down a Republican line on Berlin. In a carefully drafted statement to the press, the G.O.P. candidate revealed a clear decision to opt for bipartisan support of the Truman Administration's policies. Though he began with a minor jab at past Democratic failure to negotiate adequate formal access rights, real emphasis came in the argument that "the present duty of Americans is not to be divided by past lapses but to unite to surmount present danger. We shall not allow domestic partisan irritations to divert us from this indispensable unity." And what was the point of this unity? To make sure that "in Berlin we must not surrender our rights under duress."[31]

From this point on, the public would have had no reason to doubt essential Democratic–Republican consensus on the Berlin crisis. Though neither Dewey nor Dulles made any public statements on the issue for more than six weeks, they were kept informed about general developments and would have had an initial opportunity to express reservations behind the scenes. Not surprisingly, none were expressed. Dulles, and Dewey by implication, would clearly have favored the negotiations in Moscow which the Truman Administration undertook along with the British and French at the end of July. When these seemed to produce some very general agreements on currency arrangements and a lifting of the blockade in late August, this could only have yielded a sense of rightness about the course that he had recommended earlier.[32] Even when matters threatened to go downhill once more, a real crack in bipartisanship never materialized. Charged with working out the details of the principles decided on in Moscow, zonal authorities in Berlin began lengthy meetings on August 24. For more than two weeks, resolution of the problem seemed tantalizingly close, but always just out of reach. Continuing difficulties about nuts and bolts arrangements and, to a degree, a continuing incompatibility of Western and Soviet visions of the city's future ultimately prevented a settlement. By September 7, Truman and the National Security Council decided to try one more appeal to Moscow and then bring the issue to the United Nations. The latter move emerged as official policy shortly thereafter, just as the General Assembly began its regularly scheduled meetings in Paris.

The impasse in the technical discussions in Germany led to a resumption of formal Republican comments on the Berlin situation. Coming just as the presidential campaign began to move into traditional high gear, it might hypothetically have provided an opportunity for reconsidering earlier support of Democratic policies. This never happened. Another Dewey–Dulles–Vandenberg meeting was held in New York on September 10, and when the Senator expressed joint sentiments to newsmen afterward, he was emphatic about a continuation of bipartisanship:

> Regardless of political differences at home, we are serving notice on the world that America is united to protect American rights everywhere. . . . We shall be in internal controversy regarding many phases of foreign policy. But we shall not be in controversy over the basic fact that America is united against aggression and against the foes of freedom.

When Dulles became "deeply engrossed" in shaping strategy at the United Nations ten days later as a member of the U.S. delegation in Paris, he had qualms about what emerged, but nothing weighty enough to crack this veneer of unity. He did not share the State Department's inclination to submit the question to the Security Council at that point; because he thought specific procedures there were likely to yield a resolution calling for " 'action' to compel lifting blockade." Though the Soviets were sure to veto any such resolution, this in itself could produce unfortunate results.

As Dulles explained it to Vandenberg, a Soviet veto "would afford ammunition to the two extremes of public opinion at home, i.e., those of isolationist disposition who would claim that this spectacular veto demonstrated once and for all the futility of the United Nations and those who would like a 'preventive' war who would claim that the Security Council resolution created a moral, if not legal, obligation, on the United States to use force to uphold the prestige of the United Nations." Again communicating with Vandenberg, Dulles wrote that "it seems to me particularly desirable that in the immediate pre-election period the possible choices should not be narrowed down to either a use of force by us or a retreat which might itself stimulate further Soviet aggression and consequent war." And in a cable to Dewey at this same time, he explained that "my concern has been that there should not be started a chain of events which might face you with necessity of going to war to vindicate Security Council decision or having to show such weakness as would itself invite further Soviet aggression." Dulles's own preference, and that of the British and French as it turned out, was for submission of the Berlin issue to the General Assembly if it were going to be submitted at all. The theory, he said at one point, was that the problem "is not 'action' but to educate and consolidate public opinion regarding Soviet methods," and this could be more adequately and safely dealt with in the "town meeting of the world" setting of the Assembly.[33]

Dulles's debate over methods with colleagues in Paris never produced a public separation from them. Within a few days, he expressed himself as ready to go along with the Administration on "the understanding that our initial submission would not call for any concrete action and that there would be a genuine effort to bring to bear within the Security Council the fresh minds of the members not actual parties to the dispute and that there would be time for consideration and discussion within the Security Council rather than an effort to push through quickly a pre-digested resolution." This was not a perfect course of action, Dulles felt, but it was reasonable. Its denouement would probably be manageable as well. Following debate and an anticipated Soviet veto of any resolution, for example, an "immediate crisis could be avoided by then referring the situation to Assembly as was done after action on Greece was vetoed by Soviet Union." "Prolonged debate" could be expected in the Assembly, which would make it "unlikely that crisis would arise until after November. . . ." Even then, Dulles felt, an Assembly resolution was likely only to condemn Soviet behavior rather than specify action to end the blockade.

Dulles's willingness to endorse the Truman Administration's strategy for the United Nations set the tone of Republican–Democratic collaboration on the Berlin issue for the balance of the campaign. In a campaign speech in Los Angeles on September 24, just after resolution of the U.S. delegation's internal discussions in Paris, Dewey used words that might just as easily have come from the most melodramatic Democrat:

> At this moment, planes built in the great aircraft factories of this West Coast are shuttling back and forth, day and night, in all kinds of weather to keep the torch of freedom lit in tense and explosive Berlin. . . . In Berlin, our planes and our men are giving the world fresh proof that America has what it takes. That's something we need to be very sure of right now. Today it is our way of life that is being challenged and threatened.

In time, Dulles too showed himself ready to speak with heightened rhetoric on this subject. Going beyond the temperate perspective of July, in public at least, he adopted the tone of the day during a weekend trip to Berlin midway in the U.N. meetings. "The Soviets," he told newsmen in the city on October 17, "started here a coercive operation doubtless hoping that privation would break men's resistance, drive the Western powers from their agreed positions and subject another $2\frac{1}{4}$ million people to Soviet rule." The Allies refused to retreat, however, and brought "into being an airlift so spectacular that all the world marvels;" Moscow now actually had to deal with a stronger rather than weaker Western morale. And lest anyone not appreciate Republican contributions to this situation, Dulles concluded by pointing out that "despite a national election, bi-partisan unity has been forged to meet external dangers." His trip to Berlin, in fact, was designed to shake Moscow policy makers out of any thoughts that a Republican President might alter U.S. policy; they should know that the anticipated "new administration is equally or more determined to sustain airlift and use it to build up morale of Western Europe and in that way turn Berlin blockade into Western Power asset rather than liability."[34]

III

As Dewey and Dulles tried to play statesman's roles in dealing with Berlin and any number of other foreign policy issues during the 1948 campaign, they did so with essentially unadulterated conviction. As suggested above, there were several mutually reinforcing perceptions behind this conviction. On the one hand, the Dewey team believed that a "unity" strategy was one that would not endanger the overall interests of the

United States in a time of international crisis—that friends and foes alike would realize that there was consensus on fundamentals between the two major political parties and determine their behavior accordingly. They were also convinced that emphasis on "bipartisanship" would pay dividends at home, by highlighting Dewey's trustworthiness and counteracting any lingering images of Republican "isolationism."

As to their presumption of election-day benefits, Dulles and his associates might well be forgiven their premature optimism. There were few, after all, who doubted that Dewey would indeed be the next President of the United States. All prominent pollsters predicted his victory by at least five percentage points. The *New York Times* national survey concluded that the Republicans "appear certain" to win, by an electoral college margin of 333 to 90! Even foreign diplomats pressed for the equivalent of an audience with Dulles at the General Assembly meetings going on in Paris during the last six weeks of the campaign, convinced that he would be the next American Secretary of State.[35]

So persuaded of their future were Dewey and his advisers that by mid-October they were beginning to engage in planning exercises concerning post election-day problems. As they did so, they came very close to allowing their heads to be turned in the most melodramatic fashion. They took off from the premise that the two and a half months separating the election and Dewey's "inauguration" cried out for special arrangements because of the uniquely troubled moment in which the United States and the rest of the world was enmeshed. In two cables to his brother on October 22 and 23, Allen Dulles reported on talks about post-election strategy at Dewey headquarters in New York: there was concern about the problems of timing and delay which inevitably plague a lame-duck Administration, he wrote; discussions were underway about the "puzzler" of what to do with respect to "the obviously critical situation" at the United Nations (concerning Berlin) and a host of other "pending matters crying for some settlement," such as Palestine and Greece. Picking up on the mood of his stateside colleagues, Dulles sent off a lengthy special memorandum from Paris two days later, detailing his own reading of the predicament and his ideas on how to deal with it. "The problem," he declared "is how to avoid in the period until January 20th such increased uncertainty as to the intentions and capacity to act of the United States as will increase to the danger point the already growing fear among our friends which the Soviet is spreading and increase the boldness of our potential enemies. Grave risk can only be avoided by well-calculated measures."[36]

To be fair to Dulles and Dewey's other advisers, it should be pointed out that they had plentiful encouragement to think about the future in such electric terms. In an extraordinary meeting in Paris on October 24, for example, George Marshall apparently initiated a lengthy discussion with Dulles of post-election problems: as the latter summarized it at least, the Secretary of State himself began by arguing that "the next few months may the be most critical in United States history from standpoint of foreign relations, and it is imperative that during this period there should be the possibility of conducting foreign affairs in a manner that will be effective, with ability to act promptly, decisively and with maximum authority."

As to ways of dealing with this "critical" period, there were both vague and precise suggestions. Intriguingly, George Marshall's seem to have been the most elaborately developed. In his "highly confidential" talk with Dulles, Marshall indicated that he had carefully thought out a range of possible approaches. His preference was for his own hasty resignation to be followed by the appointment of Dewey's nominee as his replacement. "It would be unusual to have a Secretary of State really representing a President-elect, rather than the President," he explained, "but the emergency character of the situation justifies unusual measures." If such a procedure proved undesirable or impractical, Marshall was ready to consider two alternatives. One was to tap the potential of the Under Secretary of State's position and arrange for a Dewey choice to be appointed to that post immediately after the election. The other, involving the least strain as far as tradition was concerned, was for "the President to name as Acting Chief of the U.S. Delegation at Paris—where much of the conduct of foreign policy is now centered—a Republican in whom the President-elect has confidence."[37]

The Dewey team's plans for the interregnum cannot be described precisely, but some of their broad outlines are apparent. One general sentiment was that, while the Democratic Secretary of State's ideas were pertinent, there were certain factors that suggested the desirability of moving somewhat more slowly. Even before Dulles had had a chance to comment on Marshall's thoughts, he had heard from his brother about some likely Dewey reservations. "I rather surmise," Allen wrote, "that after November 2 it will be the tendency of both Truman and Marshall to dump the difficult and contentious questions in the Governor's lap and more or less take the position they can no longer speak authoritatively unless they know what the Governor's views are." The following day he cabled a postscript: "I have a hunch that he [Dewey] thinks it wiser for George [Marshall] to carry on until he has the constitutional power and the team to carry out action." Whether Allen's hunch was correct or not, Foster certainly felt this way. In two memoranda on the meeting with Marshall, he expressed a number of reservations about the proposals. Most immediately, he too wondered about the essential legality of some of them. "The President, not the Secretary of State has, under the constitution, the ultimate responsibility for the conduct of foreign affairs," he wrote. "President Truman has virtually abdicated in this respect. Nevertheless, every effort should be made to avoid extra-Constitutional devices. . . ." There was also clear Dulles concern about allowing the public to get the impression that there was no meaningful difference at all between Democratic and Republican foreign policies. "I believe that a fresh approach on foreign affairs is imperative," he wrote on October 26; "it would be unfortunate to drift into such identification with *existing* policies as would make it embarrassing to change them."

Dulles's preference, which was apparently shared by advisers in Dewey headquarters at home, was to deal with the interregnum's potential dangers in more subtle ways at first and wait upon events. He hoped that both Marshall and Under Secretary of State Lovett would be willing to continue in their posts until January, because with them "bi-partisan cooperation could continue to make the U.S. effective internationally during the interim period." He believed that both men would be willing to treat "certain concrete situations" requiring speedy attention as "special cases" in which fuller discussions with G.O.P. figures would help shape immediate policies. Concerning "Palestine, Italian colonies, internationalization of the Ruhr and possible military commitments to Western Europe through an Atlantic Pact or otherwise," Dulles assumed that Marshall and Lovett would welcome "more affirmative Republican participation than has as yet been evidenced." Dulles had other recommendations as well. He urged that likely Dewey appointees to the State Department be identified behind the scenes as soon as possible. This would allow them "to familiarize themselves with the present international situation generally, so as to be able to move promptly after January 20th"; they might even "begin to work alongside of present incumbents." Dulles also wanted the designation of "some persons to whom representatives of foreign governments can talk with confidence that they have the ear of the incoming Administration." Citing his own role along these lines in Paris, he argued that this kind of activity was "important from the standpoint of gathering information, but even more important from the standpoint of preventing collapse in the morale of friendly countries." Finally, Dulles suggested that serious consideration be given to a Dewey trip to Europe after election day. This too could serve a dual purpose: it would provide "the President-elect with very useful background impressions" and "be of inestimable value in sustaining morale in Western Europe. . . ."[38]

Though Dulles preferred to think about moving slowly and unofficially after Novemeber 2, he was prepared to do otherwise under certain circumstances. His memoranda indicate that a tendency to melodramatic speculation existed just barely below the surface, in fact, as was the case with other Dewey advisers and even Secretary of State Marshall. His initial expression of concern about the constitutionality of Truman appointing a Dewey choice as Secretary of State had a rider attached to it: "extra-Constitutional devices" should be avoided, he wrote "if without them, *our national safety* can be secured" (emphasis added). Explaining himself more fully on another occasion, he pointed to the widespread doubt in other countries about whether the U.S. would be "capable of decisive action" between election day and the inauguration:

> . . . it must be recognized that there is great nervousness about this, and *events may become so critical* between now and January 20th that more affirmative Republican responsibility will be imperative as *a matter of national security*. If, therefore, general responsibility is initially avoided, which seems desirable, there should be readiness to meet the contingency that that attitude might have to be altered *to avert great national peril*. [Emphasis added.][39]

There is abundant irony in all the fretting about a potentially critical interregnum, of course. In an upset that has now become part of American political folklore, underdog Harry Truman took twenty-eight states on November 2 and defeated Thomas Dewey by two million votes. As Dulles put it in a letter to his brother, "The election was quite a bombshell. . . ."

Postmortems then and since have been unable to obscure the fact that the foreign policy debate contributed to Dewey's surprising loss. Though hindsight makes it clear that he was seriously hurt by domestic issues such as farm policy, international affairs played their part too. The Berlin confrontation was especially important. For all of Dewey's statesmanlike demeanor, many average citizens seem to have rallied round the President rather than the pretender at a time of apparent global crisis. Truman proved more than an accidental beneficiary in this situation as well, as he and his advisers played the tension for all it was worth. They shrewdly blended a base of Cold Warrior toughness with dollops of "peace" protestations, using the former to build up the President's prestige at Dewey's expense and the latter to gravely weaken Henry Wallace. Then too, the general G.O.P. emphasis on bipartisanship compounded the specific problems posed by Berlin. At a time when global anxiety was raising Truman's stock, many analysts concluded that the weakest approach Dewey's team could have developed was one of the "me too" variety.

Allen Dulles concluded that "the greatest mistake in Mr. Dewey's campaign strategy was the failure to attack the Democratic record more vigorously." Arthur Vandenberg saw the same problem, but expressed it more cooly, almost wistfully:

> . . . I am one of those who did *not* see this "accident" coming. I thought the Dewey campaign strategy was sound. It *would* have been sound if the polls had been correct because under such circumstances Dewey had only to keep from "rocking the boat" and to strive toward a new American unity behind his foreordained Administration. He did a grand job on that hypothesis. . . . I am sorry for Dewey. I am still more sorry for the country. In my opinion, our young friend would have made a *great* President.[40]

Though Dulles wrote to many friends in the immediate aftermath of the November 2 disaster, he never offered explicit personal assessments of the failings of the strategy he had helped design. He expressed shock and disappointment, even a spark of melodramatic suspicion: "I am rather frightened by the influences which prevented it [the campaign] from succeeding," he cabled Dewey—but nothing more specific.[41] His behavior in yet another election campaign four years later, however, suggests that his silence did not denote blindness to the political lessons of 1948.

IV

What would he do with himself after the unexpected results of November 2? John Foster Dulles has left no evidence of a systematic attack on this question, but he would have been less than human had it not figured significantly in his thoughts in the weeks following the election. Things had seemed so clearly laid out in the months before: a G.O.P. victory would be followed by his own appointment as Secretary of State, and a position toward which he had been moving for the better part of a decade would have been his for at least several years. With that scenario scrapped by the voters, what would take its place?

As it turned out, it was limbo that ensued. For more than a year, Dulles was unable to chart a clear course for himself, or powerless to arrange circumstances so that he could do what he wanted. He was sixty years old, and his actions demonstrated a clear ongoing preoccupation with political and diplomatic affairs and a concomitant hesitancy about returning to full-time work at Sullivan & Cromwell, but there was little that would be clear and predictable beyond this. For months he would scurry from chore to chore and appointment to appointment essentially subject to the pleasure of those with jobs to offer; he would look for, but only slowly find, what would be for him just the right issues, the right work, the right niche.

Harry Truman and George Marshall gave him a cushion to fall on immediately after election day. The re-elected President asked him to remain at the General Assembly meeting in Paris and serve as "Acting Chairman" of the U.S. delegation after the Secretary of State returned to Washington for consultation. Dulles acceded, but could hardly have found much satisfaction in the appointment. The aura that had surrounded him during preceding weeks in France, which had had the leaders of other delegations clamoring to see him and ignoring George Marshall, had vanished, and the contrast may have been ego-damaging. Then too, Paris was a very temporary haven. Within weeks the Assembly session had ended, and Dulles found himself at home with a glaringly open schedule in front of him.

One initial impulse during his first months back in New York was to consider reviving close ties with the Federal Council of Churches. His role as chairman of the Commission on a Just and Durable Peace had been an important part of his life during World War II, but he had sharply curtailed his work with it during 1946. Only occasional contacts with Protestant leaders had ensued, as politics and official appointments to various Council of Foreign Ministers and United Nations meetings ate into the time he was able to spend away from Sullivan & Cromwell. Now, with an uncertain future before him, the charms of church-related work beckoned again. He began attending a variety of Federal Council meetings dealing with international problems and the role to be played by American Protestants in dealing with them; he accepted a series of invitations for speaking engagements before church audiences or under church sponsorship, including several that were broadcast on national radio networks. His keynote address to a National Study Conference on the Churches and World Order, given in Cleveland on March 8, 1949, captured the thrust of his thoughts about this kind of work at this time. Church leaders could make two distinctive contributions to "world order," he argued. First, they could help persuade Americans that "the United States must accept the responsibility for constructive action commensurate with its power and opportunity." Second, they could encourage the exercise of that responsibility with due attention to "Christian principles" concerning "the nature of man, the moral law and the mission of men and nations." For all practical purposes, this amounted to dusting off some of the most elementary components of his earlier Commision on a Just and Durable Peace pronouncements.[42]

It is impossible to tell how a revived Dulles role within the Protestant

389

community might have evolved over time, because he never gave it a chance to take on real substance. Opportunities in diplomacy and politics quickly distracted him once again. By the time he spoke to the Cleveland conference, he already knew that he would be a member of the U.S. delegation at the session of the General Assembly which was to begin in New York several weeks later. Attractive in itself, the invitation to pick up work at the United Nations would have had clear implications for his government career in a general sense. Truman and his advisors were obviously not prepared to abandon "bipartisanship" in the wake of their surprising electoral victory nor prepared to put Dulles into some form of enemy camp: personal sentiments aside, John Foster Dulles was the second most important Republican leader in foreign affairs as far as the Truman team was concerned (Vandenberg was of surpassing first importance), and he would be drawn back into the policy-making fold.

Thus, aside from wanting him to attend General Assembly meetings, Washington was anxious to use Dulles in other ways. By mid-February, he was being invited to take part in discussions of unfolding plans for NATO, as well as the extensive public relations efforts that followed formal unveiling of the program in March. He helped to line up support or at least diminish opposition to the treaty within the Federal Council of Churches, delivered several speeches on its behalf, took part in a State Department–National Broadcasting Company radio program and gave widely praised testimony to both the Senate and House Foreign Relations Committees.

Dulles had had virtually nothing to do with work on an Atlantic regional security agreement after the idea had first been broached to him in April 1948. Then he had been skeptical and critical, but had gone along because of the obvious interest of Arthur Vandenberg. Now, a year later, he seemed more genuinely committed. He was ready to approach NATO as one more prescription for the European–American problems he had been discussing for years. He had worried previously about the way preoccupation with military matters would distract Europeans and Americans from crucial questions of economic integration, but progress on that front had been made. The London Recommendations announced in June, in particular, promised a close coordination of West Germany's and Western Europe's recovery and even moved toward creation of an international authority for the Ruhr. Military integration might now be seen as "a logical step" in overall continental unification. Indeed, it seemed by mid-1948 as if it might be a necessary precondition to further movement of any kind. *"Fear* is rampant in Western Europe," Dulles now argued, and because of its paralyzing presence "few have been concentrating on long-range creative effort." Unless a greater sense of security emerged, the vital push for unity would falter.[43]

As to the source of this fear, Dulles bowed in totally consistent fashion to his previous analyses of the transatlantic situation. As far as many colleagues and the media were concerned, his primary emphasis was on the culpability of the Soviet Union. This *was* a very real concern. Already during the fall 1948 meetings of the General Assembly in Paris, he had been struck by the way Moscow's igniting of a crisis over Berlin had spread alarm across the Continent. He regularly warned Dewey of the way his words on bipartisan cooperation could be "important from the standpoint of preventing collapse in the morale of friendly countries"; there was, in particular, "growing fear among our friends which the Soviet is spreading" about "the intentions and capacity to act of the United States. . . ." Anxiety about Soviet ambitions and likely American responses was still great in early 1949. How can Europeans "feel secure," Dulles asked in a State Department radio program "when in recent years they have seen ten of the thirty nations of Europe fall, one by one, under an alien despotism? How can the remainder help but be concerned lest a similar fate is waiting for them?" It was not that they believed that "Soviet leaders actually intended an armed invasion of Europe," he explained further to the Senate Foreign Relations Committee in May:

> But communists, in France for example, gain adherents by spreading rumors that the Red Army will soon march in. Premier Queiulle told me that he estimated that nearly half of the members of the large French Communist Party had joined up merely to gain security as against that risk.[44]

As with his earlier efforts on behalf of economic integration and the Marshall Plan, however, Dulles never made Moscow's behavior a solitary focus for his thoughts. In early 1949 as in the past, Germany was as much a part of the problem as the Soviet Union. "There are still 70,000,000 Germans possessed of great qualities of industriousness, discipline and ambition, painfully compressed in a strategic area between the East and West," he maintained. Europeans were afraid that this situation was fraught with danger, believing in particular that:

> Germans will be strongly tempted to develop a bargaining position between East and West and they might even come into a temporary alliance with the Soviet. It has much to offer the Germans at the expense of Poland, and the Soviets and the Germans in partnership, could readily dominate the continent.

It was clear to Dulles, as it had been for years, that Western European economic recovery and hence security could not be achieved without a significant German contribution—but fears of Germany were keeping Europeans from allowing the kind of reconstruction which would make it possible to take *from* Germany the vital resources she had to offer. The most concrete advantage of a North Atlantic regional security system for the Dulles of 1949 was that it would help overcome this core problem. In a memorandum summarizing his thoughts prior to a February meeting with Secretary of State Acheson, he wrote:

> What is required first of all is a rapid strengthening and unification of our Western European allies. So long as there is weakness and disunity . . . that requires them to seek the weakness and disunity of Germany. *Only within a framework of Western unity and strength can the German problem be solved* and peace reestablished on the Continent. [Emphasis added.]

The United States had the key role to play in this process. As he put it to the Senate Foreign Relations Committee:

> The statesmanlike course is to provide the Germans with a decent and hopeful future within the orbit of the West. But again the Germans would be too strong for the comfort and safety of our European allies, *unless the West is strengthened by the adhesion of the United States. Germans can be brought into the West if that West includes the United States. They cannot safely be brought into the West if the West does not inlcude the United States.* [Emphasis added.]

Dulles often tied this kind of logic into discussions of the Soviet threat, to be sure, but both the terms of analysis in 1949 and the deeper historical roots of his qualms over Germany indicate that this logic had an important life of its own as well. He made this quite clear when he told Dean Acheson that "the pressing and central problem was that of Germany. . . ."[45]

In addition to his conviction that NATO was a necessary step by early 1949, it is important to note that Dulles retained several qualms. They were not sufficient to block his basic public support, but they were nagging enough to require regular explication. From the beginning of new discussions with Administration leaders in February 1949, Dulles made it clear that he preferred a much more limited organization than was being contemplated. All would "be better off if the Atlantic Pact were originally confined to the five Brussels Pact Powers, plus Canada and the United States," he felt. He was disturbed by Washington's prodding of the Scandinavians, for instance. Given clear Swedish opposition, he preferred the encouragement of Scandinavian unity *outside* the Atlantic Pact: this would make for easier long-term relationships with the area as a whole and would also diminish any appearance of a threat to legitimate Russian security concerns by keeping the new organization some considerable distance from Soviet territory. He was also cool to talk of incorporating Italy in the new arrangements. This would distort their logic. Italy was "a non-Atlantic, ex-enemy, ex-fascist power" in a quite different category from the members Dulles envisioned. Where could one safely stop if Italy came in? What about "Greece, Turkey, Israel, Iran, etc. . . .?"

> If the Pact is looked upon as defining a strategic line that the United States is prepared to defend, *then it increases the peril of states beyond that line*. This is not the result if the Pact reflects a drawing together of nations that have . . . a "common heritage" in terms of "political liberty, constitutional traditions and the rule of law" and an established tradition of having come together in the past to defend that heritage. Italy [among others] does not share that common heritage and tradition. [Emphasis added.]

Drawing in states like Italy also seemed to pose problems for the United Nations as far as Dulles was concerned. If the U.S. went beyond a membership list that had some sort of historic legitimacy to it, the organization might "in fact mark the beginning of the end of the U.N. . . . by setting an example that might be followed by others, e.g. the Asiatic States, so that the U.N. is fragmentized."[46]

To repeat, however, Dulles's reservations about the Truman Administration's Atlantic Pact proposals were not strong enough to deflect his predominantly positive attitude. As with his doubts concerning the Marshall Plan in 1947–48, they were discussed in a spirit of constructive criticism, offered by a man pleased with the government's basic initiative but convinced improvement was possible. Hence the regular endorsements during speaking engagements and the supportive testimony to Congress.

In addition to attendance at the General Assembly and in the campaign for NATO, the Democrats were ready to tap Dulles for yet one more chore during the first half of 1949. He was asked to serve as an advisor at the Council of Foreign Ministers meeting that took place in Paris from May 23 to June 20. It was the fourth session of the Council to which he had been invited, and its focus was the German peace settlement that had so long been one of his foremost concerns.

The Paris meetings were predictably futile. Their origin was makeshift, and their potential almost nil. During secret spring negotiations concerning the Berlin crisis, Moscow had agreed to lift the blockade if the Western Allies threw themselves into a new round of four-power talks on the German problem as a whole. But there was no real point to the resumption of such talks. During the preceding two years, "Germany" had become more and more a divided country. Could that process be reversed? Certainly the Westerners showed no inclination to do this. Even before the blatant schism of the March 1947 Moscow Foreign Ministers meetings, U.S. policy makers had been pushing Great Britain and France to go along with a *de facto* division of the defeated enemy that would allow reconstruction and the integration of a Western Germany into a Western Europe. The move had gathered momentum in 1948, via the evolving European Recovery Program and the "London Recommendations," and a sense of confidence about its appropriateness had been reinforced by the Berlin imbroglio. (Dulles, of course, as has been seen, applauded the steps taken at Washington's initiative and urged yet faster movement.)[47] By late May 1949, Western leaders might still have spoken about the abstract desirability of a united Germany, but they were less ready than ever to take the concrete steps that would have altered their actual direction. They prepared for the Paris meetings as if they were a relatively pointless but unavoidable engagement—a diplomatic sop.[48] For their part, it is hard to imagine the Soviets seriously anticipating anything but such a sop, i.e., a Foreign Ministers gathering that would provide a face-saving exit from the increasingly unproductive Berlin blockade. They too would still have cited a single Germany as the ultimate goal, but had understood full well the thrust of developments in Western Germany in 1947–48 and also knew the direction of their own quite independent policies in Eastern Germany. Without major concessions, they could hardly have expected a reversal of the shift toward two increasingly defined and increasingly different Germanies.

There were no concessions. Soviet Minister of Foreign Affairs Andrei Vishinsky was the first to put forth developed proposals and urged resumption of four-power control of Germany via the Allied Control Council; he pointedly referred to the need for a Soviet share in control of the Ruhr as well. Secretary of State Dean Acheson told the press he was "chilled" by these ideas, and his rejection was solidly endorsed by French Foreign Minister Schuman and British Foreign Minister Bevin. Subsequent Soviet initiatives were also dismissed by the Western Allies as "futile, farcical and unworthy of discussion" according to one statement. Given progress toward unification in three zones, it was argued, why allow a shift backwards to four-power administration that was bound to be stymied by disagreements? The Americans, British, and French did indicate an interest in full German unity, but insisted that decisions within a four-power Control Council would have to be made by majority rather than unanimous vote. Moscow was certainly not prepared to sanction this. In the end, no agreement on Germany was reached: as Dulles put it in a press briefing on June 22, it became "apparent that nothing much could be accomplished with regard to Germany because the positions were too irreconcilable. . . ." There were signs of tighter coordination of policy by the Western powers (Dulles was impressed by the almost daily meetings of Acheson, Schuman, and Bevin at the Quai D'Orsay) and progress on a few technicalities concerning an Austrian peace treaty, but nothing more substantive.[49]

For almost eight months after Dewey's defeat, Dulles was dependent on the Democrats for any diplomatic or political responsibilities. It was their concern for maintaining a bipartisan foreign policy that brought him invitations to the General Assembly and the Council of Foreign Ministers and to participate in the NATO drive. In early July 1949, another fount of opportunity suddenly appeared. New York's Senator Robert Wagner announced his early retirement because of serious health problems. thus giving Governor Dewey the right to name the man who would serve out the remaining months of an unexpired term. Though it was not the plum of Secretary of State, Dewey offered the job to John Foster Dulles.

The Governor later recalled that his old friend had been "a little scandalized by the whole idea." One might easily understand why. Dulles had shown no interest at all in holding any elected office, and a move to the United States Senate, even a temporary one, involved a wild careen off the established routes of his life. Still, at a stage in his career when he was subject to the whims of others, it must not have seemed an unattractive possibility. He accepted immediately, on the understanding that he had no plans to run for a full term in November.[50]

He threw himself into Senate routines with a bravado that was a function of his rather special experience and status. Ignoring traditions that would have had him seen but not heard as a new, junior member of the chamber, he gave a long first speech to his colleagues four days after arrival. It was a rousing defense of the North Atlantic Treaty. He called NATO "a living instrument for righteousness and peace" and picked up all the themes of his spring efforts to explain why: the way in which it would foil Soviet maneuvers against "divided and distraught elements of the free world"; the way in which it would foster "great cooperative ventures" in Western Europe; the way it would deal with "the Problem of Germany."[51]

Dulles rushed to speak during the closing days of Senate deliberation on the North Atlantic Treaty, at a time when its proponents were feeling somewhat insecure about the extent of the opposition. As it turned out, they needn't have worried. A few days after Dulles's speech, the treaty was resoundingly approved by a vote of 82 to 13. No sooner was this accomplished, however, than a long second debate began on what everyone recognized as the price tag on NATO—a $1.4 billion dollar Military Assistance Program, which President Truman submitted to Congress on July 25. The financial obligations that would be incurred under the North Atlantic Treaty had already been a source of controversy for several months. Robert Taft and other critics had argued that only the United States could be expected to foot the bills for the "mutual" development of armed strength which the agreement called for, and they were convinced the costs would be staggering and damaging. Their arguments along these lines had not prevented the treaty's passage, but they were quite ready to resume attack when a specific money bill was presented.

Dulles's approach to the costs of NATO underwent some change during his early weeks in the Senate. His first tack, before passage of the treaty, was to take what he must have known was a misleading legalistic approach. It was "preposterous," he said on July 12, to argue that the new regional organization would give anyone "a blank check on the United States." There were no specific commitments to aid in the treaty and no way of knowing what would eventually be recommended. He surmised that the U.S. would probably not give arms aid to "most of the countries in the pact" and cited as an example of his reasoning a belief that "the best thing the U.S. might be able to do . . . for the security of France . . . was to hold an atomic bomb in readiness in this country." Critics argued that he was making "fine distinctions" or ignoring "moral" obligations, but Dulles insisted that in any event Congress would inevitably be involved in vetting whatever money proposals did materialize.

Such initial views suggest a man who was not particularly worried about the impact of NATO's costs on the United States, and this impression is confirmed by his behavior during the turmoil over the Military Assistance Program. Unable to dodge the arguments of the opposition with technical niceties once a hefty package was formally on the agenda, Dulles simply shifted gears. He tried to direct attention to the question of *how* it was to be spent. In the process, he joined the ranks of the Truman Administration's moderate critics. The thrust of his approach was the same as that he had already developed concerning the obviously more expensive Marshall Plan: funds provided by the United States should be used to foster greater unity—and should not be provided until signs of such unity were forthcoming. In a July 28 statement, he argued that "the chance to get real military unification as between the 12 Atlantic Pact powers depends on establishing the procedures for unification *before* we are committed to any *major* buildup of separate national military establishments" (Dulles's italics). A major buildup *per se* did not bother him, in others

words, as long as it took place in the integrating context he had emphasized so often before. And money, especially large amounts of money,
seemed a likely tool for creating such a context.

> Until the procedures and organs for collective defense have been
> worked out, probably our military aid should be on a modest interim
> basis. Otherwise, there is a good chance that a collective defense will never
> be established. There is a natural disposition on the part of each country
> to prefer, if it can, to build up its own independent, rounded military
> establishment. [52]

Dulles's concern for moving beyond "words of unity" to "deeds of
unity" was complemented by a variety of other Senate qualms about the
Military Assistance Program. Arthur Vandenberg worried that the bill
would turn Truman into "the number one war lord of the earth" by allowing him virtually unchecked power to lease or give away American
military hardware; William Knowland was scandalized by the absence of
military aid for Chiang Kai-shek. Together, the critics gave the administration a very hard time of it. Weeks of hearings and redrafts and
debates ensued in which the Truman team was forced into a number of
compromises in order to gain the money that was its key objective.
Vandenberg and Dulles jointly introduced several amendments that were
eventually accepted: one set up a more complex procedure for transfers of
U.S. military stocks; another stretched out the timetable for provision of
monetary aid so as to require the hastier adoption of "common defense
plans." All in all, the Senate in the summer of 1949 gave Dulles a rare setting in which he was able to go beyond his usually ineffective efforts to
force alterations in a Democratic policy initiative that had his basic but
not total support. [53]

The debates over NATO and Military Assistance occupied the lion's
share of Dulles's Senate tenure. He did dabble in other issues (a displaced
persons bill and the reappointment of a controversial candidate to the
Federal Power Commission, for example), and he was a member of the
District of Columbia and Post Office committees, but nothing came close
to piquing his interest in the way major foreign policy questions did. Of
course, there was the question of time as well. Just how much could a
Senate novice do in a term whose span was most logically measured in
weeks? He arrived in Washington in July to fill a seat whose long-range
fate would be decided by an election in November; as quickly as he
jumped into routines, he could never be far from the end of his stay.

He was pressed to consider and ultimately succumbed to the idea of
running in the forthcoming election. He never explained just why he decided to back away from his early opposition to becoming a candidate, but

the key factor was probably the heavy pressure placed on him by New York Republican leaders. The declared Democratic hopeful was the popular former Governor Herbert Lehman, and the G.O.P. went through most of the summer of 1949 without producing a challenger brave enough to take him on. Dulles was well-known and potentially viable, and he was appealed to by many as the only hope for the party.[54] It is not so unlikely that he also felt some interest in running on his own account. He had developed a relatively high profile in the Senate in a very short time; he had had some concrete impact on a major Truman Administration policy; and he had no particular opportunity beckoning to him from the other side of November. He might well have concluded that a Senator's role was a fitting one for him, after all. He announced his willingness to run on September 7 and was unanimously endorsed by a relieved Republican State Committee a week later.[55]

A year earlier, Dulles had allowed optimism about the presidential contest to lead him to favor a temperate, statesmanlike style of campaigning. This time he was himself the candidate, and he knew from the beginning that Lehman was an experienced and formidable foe with much the better chance of winning the election. Working with a team of advisers loaned to him by Governor Dewey, most of whom probably also felt they had learned lessons from the 1948 experience, he plotted a highly partisan and aggressive strategy. He would concentrate on vigorous attacks on Lehman and the Democrats in the upstate areas of New York in the hope of rousing voters there to go to the polls in particularly high numbers: in the ideal scenario, this would offset the great majority that Lehman was expected to win in the huge downstate metropolitan region.[56]

As for the subject matter of the attacks, Dulles developed two interrelated themes in the course of the campaign. One involved a concentration on domestic affairs (itself evidence of a turning away from his only interest in 1948) and the indictment of the Democratic Party's role in encouraging a "trend to Statism." As he put it in one speech, New Yorkers would be able to decide "whether you are going to have in the Senate someone pushing us down the road to Socialism or whether you are going to have someone there who is going to act as a check." Aiming particular fire at such Truman Administration projects as federal aid to education, medical insurance, and the Brannan Plan, Dulles insisted that talk of socialism involved no exaggeration: if such programs came into being they would do much to turn Americans into "a dependent people—on leash from birth to death to a Federal bureaucracy." He described himself as a man anxious to prevent such an eventuality, "now and here," and Lehman as a pushover for the Left.

There were numerous variations on the theme of the evils of "Welfare State" socialism. Some were pointed and pragmatic. The "price tag" on Truman's programs was described as staggering, likely to add $40 billion a year to the federal budget and a concomitant weight to the shoulders of already overburdened taxpayers. Others were more philosophical in tone, a hybrid product of older interests and newer public activities. Dulles made much of the way the trend to statism undercut honorable American individualism. Once government leaders begin to operate on the assumption that they are the special guardians of "the general welfare," he wrote for *The Daily Compass*, "they automatically take from the many both their independent means and their sense of personal responsibility. The result is that individuals degenerate, the society collapses and the promised 'welfare' vanishes." What else could be expected from a system that "dries up productive and creative effort, because very few people are willing to work hard to create wealth for others to spend?" Or "which seems to make it unnecessary for people to exercise self-restraint for themselves or generosity, for the State undertakes to provide for all." Inevitably, "moral fiber rots away."

The process of degeneration would likely be hastened, Dulles usually went on to argue, by the lust for power of those political leaders who identified themselves with socialist policies. Elaborate government programs concentrate "excessive power in the hands of a few," he maintained, "but that power is the kind that corrupts." Look at what happened in Russia, he told a radio audience at one point in his campaign:

> . . . Communist leaders . . . promised many alluring things to end "the exploitation of man by man" and "from each according to his ability, to each according to his need." But there was a catch. There usually is. To get all this, the leaders said, you must make us all-powerful. That will be all right for you, the working people, because we promise to use our power to destroy your class enemies. After that has been done, we will give up our power and our dictatorship will wither away.
>
> Well, after 32 years, the withering is not yet visible.

Dulles said that it was not inappropriate to compare the contemporary scene in the United States with the Soviet history of preceding decades. Fair Deal programs, endorsed by Lehman, "would involve a very serious loss of personal liberties. . . ." There was much to worry about with respect to federal aid to education, for example. Would this not open the door to thought control, to the "kind of schooling which the politicians in Washington decree. . .?" Could the government ultimately decide to encourage the teaching of "irreligion"? And what of medical insurance?

Ask your doctor what socialized medicine will do. He will tell you that instead of a great body of devoted men and women, loyal to their patients and generous to those who can't afford to pay, there will be substituted a lot of regimented doctors, dentists, nurses and surgeons—and a lot a regimented patients.

Dulles did occasionally seek to tone down the hyperbole of his campaign statements in order to appeal to moderate sentiments. "Modern society has complexities that require cooperative effort, and I would not undo most of what has been done," he said at one point. He felt age and unemployment insurance were sensible and desirable programs, and should actually be expanded. His real concern was to prevent too many *additional* accretions to the government's role in society: "there is a point where trends, which at the beginning were good, become dangerous and must be stopped." This kind of relative moderation, however, was easy to miss in the bulk of Dulles's campaign rhetoric. His strategy clearly concentrated on raising conservative hackles, not soothing liberal sensitivities, and he spent most of his time aiming more extreme appeals to the more extreme audience. It was far more common for him to talk of needing help to defeat Lehman in order to prevent "a new Dark Age." "There may be some few Americans who with their eyes open would choose a benevolent dictatorship," he concluded, but they could be overmatched by those still anxious to preserve admirable traditional values. "I do not believe that Americans are now ready to abdicate, to surrender their individuality. I believe the American citizen today wants something better for himself and his children than a code number in a Government index."[57]

If Dulles's quasi-philosophical oratory could reach melodramatic peaks, its tone was pallid compared to that which permeated the other principal theme of his aggressive campaign. In a carefully orchestrated counterpoint to diatribes against statism, he charged that Lehman was little more than a tool of the communists. Already in his acceptance speech, he said that "it is not going to be easy for the people of New York to turn back the Washington invasion. . . . The half million Communists and fellow travelers who last year voted for Henry Wallace, who will they vote for now? You know the answer." In case there was any doubt, he filled in the blanks in many succeeding remarks. When Lehman spurned communist support, Dulles issued a biting press release. Such a repudiation "was exactly as I expected; it was exactly what the Communists expected. It is the old New Deal political game of spanking the Commies and their fellow travelers in public and coddling them in private." He pointed to Lehman's past endorsements by the American Labor Party and said that "it's about time that the people of this State become fully acquainted with this little game of 'we don't like the Commies either, but we'll take their votes.'" The Republican State Chairman charged at one point that the Democrats and the communists were "in cahoots" and going "all out to beat Senator Dulles." A flier handed out before a Dulles speech in Geneseo had a headline that read "The Reds Will Register and Vote. Will You?" In contrast, Dulles polished his own anticommunist armor to a high shine:

> No un-Americans have picked me as a soft spot. None of them are getting into my corner. Mr. Vishinsky, the Soviet Minister of Foreign Affairs, has called the signals . . . he said that I ought to be thrown into chains. That is a tribute that I welcome.

During the last week of the campaign, he told one audience that "if I am defeated in this election, the greatest rejoicing will not be in New York or Washington but will be in Moscow." [58]

It should be added that what might have been seen as one spot of tarnish on Dulles had been removed by the time Alger Hiss went on trial for perjury several months earlier. Dulles had broken all ties with Hiss by then and had maneuvered for his resignation from the Carnegie Endowment. More, he had agreed to appear as a prosecution witness in order to recount the supposedly questionable stories the accused had told associates during the early stages of the uproar over his past. Before and during what became two trials, Dulles gave the appearance of having been chastened by the Hiss experience. At one point, he even attempted a rapprochement with Alfred Kohlberg, the red-hunter who had been so doubtful about Dulles himself in the past: "developments should convince even the most doubting that there has been highly organized and formidable Soviet communist penetration into the public and private affairs of our nation," Dulles wrote him. While Kohlberg was unmoved and remained poised to pounce on Dulles on any number of future occasions, others of his kind seemed happy enough to welcome the prominent Republican into the fold. Dulles went out of his way to respond in a complimentary fashion to letters from Richard Nixon, for example, and doubtless avoided potential problems from that quarter as a result. [59]

There had been flashes of Dulles's willingness to attack political opponents with hammer and sickle before, in particular during the two presidential elections in which he had worked with Tom Dewey, but Dulles pulled out all the stops in 1949. The environment of the day was becoming increasingly conducive to irrational descriptions of political positions even remotely left of center, and he produced his fair share of grotesqueries. As for many, the mood of an election battle was often a particularly relevant factor in triggering the salvos.

Lehman, it should be added, was capable of his own demagoguery.

The main thrust of his campaign in early weeks involved a calm restatement of New Deal—Fair Deal sentiments concerning social welfare programs: in spite of Dulles's denunciations, he refused to back away from strong support of federal aid to education. Dulles's jump for the jugular on the communist support question brought a speedy turn to dirty tricks by the Democrats. Lehman began lifting sentences from his opponent's statements and embroidering his own elaborate theories of extremism around them. At one point, Dulles speculated about the problems of future generations if statism was allowed to take hold: would they have to fight their way back to good old values through "bloody" revolution someday, he asked? It was a silly question and deserving of a silly response perhaps, but Lehman was quite ready to rant. This was the "immoral language of dictatorship, Communist and Fascist alike," he charged, "always extending a ready welcome to revolution . . . sinister and incendiary." On October 6, in a rambling discussion of the communists who lurked in New York City, Dulles told an upstate audience: "If you could see the kind of people in New York City making up this bloc that is voting for my opponent, if you could see them with your own eyes, I know you would be out, every last man and woman of you, on election day." Worse than silly, this was described as "diabolical" by Lehman. He extrapolated a theory of Dulles's anti-Semitism from it, arguing that the Republican candidate was really saying that upstaters would be able to see the Jewish features of many New York City voters—and drew parallels with Hitler and Nazi Germany. This was then broadened into an overall charge of bigotry. There was even speculation about a supposed rift between Dulles and his son Avery, who had left the Presbyterian Church to enter a Jesuit seminary.[60]

Dulles was self-righteously furious about the bigotry charges and scurried to gather countering statements from men like Bernard Baruch and James Rosenberg, head of the Human Rights Commission of the National Conference of Christians and Jews; he made special efforts to recount his support for the creation of the state of Israel as well. And to cover the Catholic front, he arranged a meeting with his son to which press photographers were cordially invited. He had asked for the problem in a number of ways, however. When he threw his own absurd bricks at a highly experienced New York politician, he should have anticipated a less than gentlemanly reaction. In addition, he had said some curious things which any opponent would have found it easy to exploit. As he himself later admitted, he was unused to off-the-cuff political oratory: "I didn't speak from a text at all, and, of course, you can't conduct a campaign where you're going around speaking ten or twelve times a day extemporaneously without risk of using at least one sentence which can be torn from its context. . . ."[61] Experienced lawyer though he may have been, he found that he had a tongue that could veer somewhat out of control under tense, particularly partisan circumstances. It was a problem that would rear its head several times during his term as Secretary of State.

Dulles's wild charges of communist associations and Lehman's howls about anti-Semitism each probably appealed to enough voters so as to cancel the other out. At all events, the final count that emerged on election day was not very different from what insecure Republicans would have predicted in August: the Democratic candidate won by 196,000 votes. Dulles ran well in the upstate areas, but no where near well enough to compensate for Lehman's tremendous strength in New York City. Trying to put the best face on the results, Dulles reminded friends that he had carried 57 out of 62 counties in the state and that "outside the three . . . counties embracing Brooklyn, Manhattan and the Bronx, I carried the state by 550,000 votes. Unhappily, those three counties are the tail that wags the dog."[62]

Aside from a sense of accomplishment regarding developments outside New York City, Dulles and his campaign associates emerged from the 1949 election with other positive afterthoughts. The general feeling seems to have been that they had done as well as could be expected under difficult circumstances. There was never any doubting of the appropriateness of the themes chosen for emphasis or of the highly aggressive style that was utilized. Old G.O.P. hands were quick to praise Dulles's personal campaign style, as well, especially a common touch which took many by surprise. He adapted comfortably to the extensive bus-touring of upstate towns and the working of the crowds at street rallies and in school halls. He was quite ready to fall in with tried and true methods of appealing to important ethnic groups and released "What I Have Done For . . ." memos concerning Israel, Poland, and Italy. Tom Dewey thought his longtime adviser had done "a glorious job. . . . He learned the trick—any hotel he went into, he left through the kitchen and shook hands with every waitress." And Arthur Vandenberg was especially enthusiastic about his friend's ability to politick. "I think your fighting speech was swell," he cabled at one point. "If you keep this up neither the voters of New York nor the Lord will permit a mistake next November. You amaze me with the facility with which you have shed the language of a million dollar lawyer and dropped into the lingo of Joe Doakes."[63]

But whatever compliments were floated after election day, the basic fact remained that Dulles in November 1949 was back in the same position as in November 1948. He was once more a man with a highly uncertain future. For a year, he had bounced from pillar to post in search of work that could fill in the vacuum left by Dewey's defeat. After another unsuccessful electoral campaign, it looked as if his days of limbo were going to continue.

15

Focus on the United Nations,
1945–1950

ONE OPTION DULLES MIGHT HAVE LOOKED FORWARD TO in the aftermath of the 1949 Senate race was the prospect of continuing work at the United Nations. His own and the Truman Administration's interest in bipartisanship had made it possible for him to attend the founding San Francisco Conference in 1945 and had led to his appointments as a member of the American delegation at the first session of the General Assembly in 1946 and at succeeding sessions in 1947, 1948, and the spring of 1949. Involvement on the two latter occasions had helped in a limited way to fill the vacuum that had opened before Dulles following Tom Dewey's defeat; future appointments might do the same now that he had suffered his own.

Dulles was concerned about the fate of the new international organization and the place of the United States within it. His personal involvement never became a crucial component of his day-to-day activities nor an overriding intellectual preoccupation, but it can be seen as an interesting minor theme in the overall course of his life after World War II. What he did at the General Assembly throws its own light on the way he viewed international affairs in these years and the kinds of foreign policies he wanted the United States to pursue.

I

Very soon after he began to think about the possibility of a successor to the League of Nations, Dulles concluded that there was nothing wrong with being both excited and pragmatic about the United Nations.

Throughout World War II, he left no doubt about his basic enthusiasm. His Commission on a Just and Durable Peace identified from the very beginning its "most important" task as the encouragement of American support for a new international organization. Countless pamphlets, radio broadcasts, and speeches held out the hope of "life and happiness, rather than death and destruction" if a reasonable "political framework" for ongoing global cooperation could be constructed. There were extensive discussions, as well, of the kind of "curative and creative" tasks that could be undertaken, with regular emphasis on economic cooperation, disarmament, human rights, and autonomy for subject peoples.

At the same time, Dulles almost invariably insisted that it would be foolish and probably dangerous to overestimate what would develop in the immediate future. He quite clearly believed that only "something very elemental" would actually emerge at first. Nations were like "savage chieftains" about to "gather around the campfire," he argued at one point: they wanted to talk, but were too suspicious to consider putting much faith in those around them. "Consultation" was probably the most that could initially be hoped for, because "no society moves at a single bound from the primitive stage of anarchy to a highly developed order." More might be desirable, he would have agreed, but why risk sacrificing something substantively good for something hypothetically ideal? Americans should be "realistic" and accept the need to "begin at the beginning," he warned; otherwise the disillusionment that had come in the wake of World War I would be repeated and wipe out even minimal progress. He was very critical of the "over-elaborate" plans which emerged from the Dumbarton Oaks Conference. In counterpoint to some of the glowing commentary of the day, he insisted that neither his own countrymen nor other peoples would accept the idea of a "super-state" armed with substantial military power.[1]

Dulles's personal experiences at the San Francisco Conference convinced him that he had been right to keep his sights low. It quickly became evident that the new "United Nations" was going to be an organization of limited powers. As he himself participated in extensive deliberations on subjects such as the veto, regional organizations, and "domestic jurisdiction," for that matter, he quite willingly advocated the establishment of fences that would protect the interests perceived by his own government. Since he had assumed that this would be the inevitable inclination of almost all delegates, it prompted no serious qualms, but neither did it allow anything beyond the "elemental" steps he had predicted.[2]

In the aftermath of the founding conference, Dulles usually held to the combination of enthusiasm and minimalism that he had developed in earlier days. He did occasionally review developments in rhapsodic terms, calling the Charter "a Magna Carta for the world" in one speech. More often he reiterated his plea for realistic expectations. He could not share the despair of some about the circumscribed power of the Security Council, for example. The existence of veto power over enforcement actions was simply necessary, he argued, "because in the present state of the world, with the distrusts that exist, it was not . . . practical to build a Security Council in the nature of a police force, which would function in the way in which a police force functions in our own society." The Charter as a whole, with all of its other limitations, was "an honest document" worthy of respect and support:

> The present Charter represents a conscientious and successful effort to create *the best world organization which the realities permit.* Of course, anyone who is free to disregard realities and to act only in the realm of theory can write a "better" Charter. A reasonably intelligent schoolboy could do that. The task of statesmanship, however, is to relate theory to reality. Political institutions ought to come as close to theoretical perfection as is consonant with their vigorous survival in the existing environment. Orchids may be the perfect flower. But it is a waste of time to plant orchids in Iceland.[3]

In the months prior to his attendance of the first session of the General Assembly, he paid particular attention to what he described as that body's enormous potential. The Assembly could halt "the normal trend toward disintegration" of the great wartime coalition, for example, by identifying "new enemies to fight together." It could "pick the social, the economic, the moral enemies of mankind and organize nations in campaigns against those enemies. Just as during the war, when we worked together . . . against the common enemies, out of that working together developed fellowship, friendship, and understanding—that process is to go on in peace in terms of working together against the great social enemies of mankind." Why not a broadflanking attack on cancer, for example, or multilateral programs to deal with access to vital food and raw materials supplies? Specific benefits from such "curative and creative" efforts would be tremendous. More importantly, perhaps, they would help develop an organizational and operational momentum that would carry the United Nations toward real growth:

> The theory of the General Assembly is that if the peoples of the world come to work together on great social and economic tasks for human betterment, in the process they will be drawn together in fellowship; they will come to know each other better; *come to trust each other more, and that will create the foundation upon which a more adequate political structure can be erected.* [Emphasis added.][4]

When the first session of the General Assembly opened in London in January 1946, Dulles was an alternate member of the U.S. delegation. His role in the weeks ahead would prove to be highly limited, involving only occasional contributions to behind-the-scenes deliberations among the Americans and an occasional speech. Nevertheless, he was present and able to observe the day-to-day activities of the new organization: this allowed an opportunity for fairly precise comparison of expectations and actual performance.

Dulles found much to disturb him in London. Like many of his colleagues, he was distressed by what he saw as the unreasonable behavior of the Soviet Union. As part of the audience during Security Council sessions, he witnessed the vituperative style of Andrei Vyshinsky and worried about the farflung targets at which it was aimed. Were attacks on British behavior in Greece and Indonesia merely a means of distracting attention from protests regarding Soviet troops in Iran? If so, this would be bad enough, but Dulles wondered whether Moscow might also be using the Council forum to encourage "violent independence movements which would weaken the colonial powers." And what of similar diatribes against France's role in Syria and Lebanon? He found it easy enough to speculate that Vyshinsky was "maneuvering to gain influence with the Arab League and to embarass the French Minister of Foreign Affairs, who heads the strongest anti-communistic party in France." In the General Assembly, the Soviets seemed equally inclined to be troublesome. Dulles was angered by the furor over the role of the World Federation of Trade Unions, for instance. He saw the W.F.T.U. as a left-wing coalition supported by governments "sympathetic to communism or subject to the political pressure of communist parties" and seemed convinced that if given the opportunity, as Moscow wished, "it could dominate the Assembly and its Economic and Social Council." He found Vyshinsky's attacks on a Refugee Resolution "rather frightening" too, involving as they did an apparently categorical resistance to political or ideological "tolerance."[5] Even on rudimentary administrative matters, Dulles saw the Soviets as deviously maneuvering for advantage. He himself was drawn into a heated struggle over the selection of the first Secretary General. He thought Moscow's preference for Trygve Lie was suspicious, and he backed up a firey Arthur Vandenberg when he insisted that "Mr. Lie, as a citizen of Norway located near the Soviet Union, could not be a free agent and would not dare to be a free agent. . . ." When pressed by Charles Bohlen, Dulles did agree that "Norway was not in the USSR zone and probably would not be penetrated." However, he went on, "Norway could be placed in an awkward position with sudden deterioration in her trade, finance, etcetera, whereas the USSR could not, for example, exert such serious influence on Canada or on the Netherlands." Dulles was quite annoyed, in fact, at the Truman Administration's readiness to offer only mild backing for the candidacy of Canada's Lester Pearson. Even months later, responding to a question about some action of Lie's which he did not like, he argued that the Secretary General may have "heard 'his master's voice'" from Moscow.[6]

Dulles did not allow his perceptions of Soviet behavior in London to produce either categorical Cold War denunciations or a disillusioned rejection of original hopes for the United Nations. As bitingly critical of Moscow as he was prepared to be, he insisted that bitter confrontation "was bound to happen. The First Session of the United Nations would inevitably reflect past discords and old habits." His earlier predictions of slow progress had been based on exactly this kind of expectation. "What we are seeing now," he told a U.S. audience on March 1, "is the kind of thing that generally went on, only in the past it went on under the surface." Dulles was even prepared to apportion the responsibility for discord. "At London the nations were up to the old game of maneuvering against each other," he said at one point, refusing to identify a single culprit. In an extended commentary on the frustrations of the Security Council, he was quite explicit: "the Soviet Union is not the only permanent member which is unwilling to subject its vital interests to the arbitrary disposition of the other members. . . . The Security Council is not, and cannot now be made a world government acting by majority vote. It is a tool, upon which *each great power* keeps a restraining hand" (emphasis added).[7]

"Like Pilgrim, we must stumble forward," Dulles had written about work on an international organization in 1943, and the thought was still very much with him in early 1946. If a perfect new world order could not be created in one fell swoop, that is, this was no reason not to make more limited moves toward it. As he surveyed the scene in London, he seems to have been convinced that a few valuable steps had been taken. Aside from maneuvering for position, he believed "a difficult job of organization was done in good spirit." Fairly well-balanced standing committees had been created, in which all had agreed to participate. Dulles was also impressed by the wide-ranging debate on the problems of refugees and believed that the eventual involvement of the Assembly's Economic and Social Council might yield the kind of cooperation on "curative and creative tasks" which he saw as so important to the U.N.'s future.[8] Most important to him as a portent was the one General Assembly undertaking in which he had had some personal role—the devising of international programs concerning dependent peoples. Following in Woodrow Wilson's footsteps, Dulles had spoken extensively about the relevance of colonial regions to the problems of war and peace as early as the 1930s. He thought it eminently desirable to include plans for encouraging some degree of international accountability concerning colonies within the United Nations Charter. Initial efforts might not yield a full opening up of the "vast underdeveloped areas" of the kind he had glowingly described a decade earlier, but they could only help to get the process started. This is exactly what he thought took place during his months of work on General Assembly Committee IV, charged with oversight of "Trusteeship Questions."

Article 77 of the Charter specified three types of territories that might ultimately come under the province of the United Nations: former mandates of the League of Nations, lands taken from the defeated enemies, and any or all other possessions of the colonial powers. Dulles, like many, believed it was logical to begin with the first and hoped even prior to meetings in London that the various mandatory states would quickly accede to "trusteeship agreements" with the new world organization. To his pleasant surprise, most of them quickly indicated a willingness to do so. Ernest Bevin announced his government's plans to grant independence to Transjordan, for example, and to assume trusteeship responsibilities for Tanganyika, the British Cameroons, and Togoland. Australia, New Zealand, and Belgium followed suit regarding all their mandates. France seemed hesitant, but generally willing, leaving only the Union of South Africa refusing to make any commitments regarding the disposition of South West Africa. Dulles was encouraged by this. With the backing of the U.S. delegation as a whole, he urged speedy progress on specific terms so that the Assembly could approve actual agreements during its fall session and bring a formal Trusteeship Council into existence. Having gotten this far, he also pushed for a broadly conceived commitment to extending United Nations attention to *all* non-self-governing territories. If former mandates were eventually transformed into trusteeships, he argued, "only about 15 million people" would be affected. Would the new world organization have nothing to do with the "hundreds of millions of people" who lived in colonies and dependencies beyond the mandates? This was "a large percentage of the population of the world," Dulles felt, among whom "unrest" was becoming increasingly prevalent: they "constituted a problem with which this Assembly should concern itself, as did the Charter."[9] His American colleagues were easily persuaded that since some progress had been made on the mandates question, virtually without trying, it made sense to push on a little further. As a result, the U.S. moved to expand the preamble of the Committee IV report to the General Assembly: they wanted it to include a statement that those attending were "keenly aware of the problems and aspirations of the peoples who are not directly represented here because they have not yet attained self-government" as well as a reference to the Charter clauses on trusteeship, which had clearly assumed the need to go beyond the mandates. Since this American proposal merely reiterated earlier abstract commitments and made no effort to identify mechanisms for fulfilling them, it was easy enough for all to accept.[10] For Dulles, it seemed valuable anyway. It put the first working session of the General Assembly on record concerning open-ended trusteeship objectives and inched it closer to the Wilsonian vision Dulles had so long shared.

II

In the immediate aftermath of the London General Assembly meetings, Dulles would have argued that the United Nations had gotten off to a satisfactory start. It was "not yet the 'harmonizing center' which is its charter goal," he admitted, recognizing the obvious hostilities that had flared in the Security Council. Nevertheless, problems had been inevitable, and certain rudimentary steps had been taken in spite of them. If a degree of cooperation on a variety of "curative and creative tasks" could be continued, enough "fellowship" might eventually develop to improve the overall workings of the new organization.

While hardly pulsing with excited anticipation, Dulles's early 1946 assessment of the United Nations proved to be the most positive he would muster from that time on. Never again would he see the world organization coming even this close to the kind of ideals he had developed through so many preceding years. Though his expectations had been so limited in comparison to those of many others and his patience regarding the pace of development so apparently open-ended, he soon found himself ready to admit that he had hoped for too much. Signs of change in his abstract vision of the United Nations began to appear before the end of 1946 and grew ever more obvious from 1947 on.

Dulles, like many, would have pointed to the Soviet Union as the spoiler of the promise of the new world organization. His own extensive reassessment of Moscow's behavior, undertaken during mid-1946, produced evaluations so harsh and dramatic that they convinced him that even the elementary possibilities he had envisioned were irrelevant to the particular atmosphere of the postwar world. Like the "tide of Islam" in the tenth century, he concluded, international communism was engaged in a virulent expansionist campaign. Faced with an evil combination of military assault, subversion, incitement, and propaganda, could those peoples who spurned communism hope for any kind of meaningful cooperation with the Soviets in the United Nations? By the end of 1946, Dulles thought not. If he had once pictured U.N. members as rival tribal chieftains gathered round a campfire to talk hesitantly about the possibility of future harmony, he came to see one of those chieftains as bent on destroying all the others: talk became irrelevant under such circumstances, even dangerous if it lulled any of those participating into a false sense of security.

Whatever a precise measurement of Soviet culpability in blocking United Nations progress might be, it is very clear that at best Dulles was developing a grossly oversimplified analysis. In earlier days, he himself had made much of the inevitable resistance of many governments to almost any kind of substantive surrender of sovereignty and had even explicitly exempted Moscow from charges of unique obstreperousness on a number of occasions. The melodramatic mood that began to take hold in mid-1946 saw a steady deterioration in the appreciation of the subtleties and complexities of international problems in general, and those of the new international organization never proved to be an exception. Even allowing for the degree of purposeful overstatement that became part of Dulles's approach to the Soviet "menace," his view of the United Nations grew steadily more simplistic.

Among the basic facts of U.N. life which Dulles generally chose to ignore after mid-1946 was the behavior of his own country. In several respects, it was Americans who played crucial roles in preventing the materialization of earlier expectations. It is evident that Washington was as capable as Moscow of resisting the creation of a genuinely potent international organization. Dulles certainly knew this on the evidence of his own experiences during the San Francisco Conference. Reluctantly in some cases, but with ultimate sureness in all, he had personally done battle to protect all kinds of U.S. interests and sensitivities. The most blatant examples concerned "regional organizations" and "domestic jurisdiction," where he recognized in the clearest terms that the perimeters of the new body were being considerably narrowed. He had a number of clear reminders of American desires for a limited United Nations during the 1946 General Assembly meetings as well. With Dulles as occasional spokesman, the United States delegation emerged with a trusteeship policy that was a good deal more suggestive than substantive. At the sessions held in London early in the year, as indicated, Dulles had helped push ostensibly impressive efforts: a speedy transfer of "mandates" to "trusteeship" status, creation of a Trusteeship Council, and a broad pronouncement expressing concern for the well-being of all non-self-governing peoples. When more specific actions were undertaken at the Assembly meetings in New York during the fall, however, it became apparent that these efforts were at least partially hollow. With respect to the "hundreds of millions of people" living in dependent status outside the mandates, the U.S. delegation neither urged nor supported concrete programs. One proposal authorizing the Economic and Social Council to arrange regional conferences of representatives of non-self-governing peoples was indeed described as unconstitutional by Dulles himself, on the grounds that the administration of territories such as Alaska and Hawaii "remains exclusively in the Government of the United States": "the United Nations has no authority to intervene in such territories." As to the much more limited realm of the mandates, the clear limits of U.S. policies were also shown. Dulles made and supported several statements on the specific terms of trusteeship agreements which were unappealing to more vigorous reformers: as at San Francisco, he advocated the identification of "self-government" instead of "independence" as a long-range goal; he accepted the principle of "single nation" as opposed to "United Nations" administration of trusteeships, and in spite of Soviet and other protests, he endorsed the right of such national administrators to construct such "naval, military and air bases" as they deemed necessary within their trust territories.[11]

Among other reasons for these policies was the fact that the United States intended to become the administrator of several former mandates itself and was determined to secure maximum latitude for its own future actions. The Marshall, Caroline, and Mariana islands, among others held as mandates by Japan, had been occupied by the United States at the end of World War II. Civilian and military leaders in Washington immediately assumed that the islands could serve as vital links in a postwar strategic network and made plans for the construction of bases and other facilities. There did emerge some debate, however, about reconciling these plans with wartime pledges such as the Atlantic Charter. When the War and Navy Departments, with some congressional support, advocated outright annexation of the territories, State Department figures took the lead in urging an approach that would bow in some minimal way to the new United Nations trusteeship system. Dulles, among others, argued that it was possible to secure all the U.S. wanted in these islands by placing them under "strategic trusteeship": the right to build bases, station troops, and administer in strictly unilateral fashion would be tempered only by such annual reports or inspection visits as Washington chose to allow as time went by. If the Security Council or Trusteeship Council would have no power to demand anything more than what they were voluntarily given, the argument ran, what was the harm in paying at least surface respect to the U.N. Charter's abstract ideals? President Truman brought skeptical military authorities into line and presented suitable accords to the Security Council in November 1946. By threatening to withdraw even this kind of "strategic trusteeship" plan, U.S. representative Warren Austin secured all terms desired—including a limitation on economic privileges in the islands for non-Americans that was a blatant counterpoint to the pressure Washington brought to bear on all other trusteeship powers for "open door" principles in their territories. All in all, the arrangements made for the former Japanese mandates provide interesting evidence of the way American practice could clash with American theory concerning the United Nations. In January 1946, the *New York Herald Tribune* had urged the Truman Administration to "import some reality into the idea of an international order" by giving meaningful backing to trusteeship arrangements, arguing that these should not be turned into "a lot of handsome window dressing covering our own relapse into as pure nationalistic power politics as any empire ever played." Though Dulles and most Americans seem to have persuaded themselves that they had accomplished the former by the end of the year, it was the latter eventuality that had actually come to pass.[12]

United States resistance to real limitations on its sovereignty and freedom of movement was one of the factors that prevented the emergence of a viable international organization after 1946. Though Dulles chose to ignore it while making his categorical denunciations of the Soviet Union, his own earlier observations and continuing experiences should have told him that it was so. There was another American contribution to the creation of an unbridged gap between his early expectations and the realities of the United Nations scene, the importance of which he also refused to recognize: his own and his government colleagues' increasing emphasis on turning the world body into a forum for propaganda and public relations efforts. The Soviets had rather routinely attempted this from the beginning, with stertorous blasts of many kinds, but their essential political weakness among the fifty-odd members of the Assembly gave their efforts little more than an eccentric, sometimes comical quality. When the Americans moved in the same direction, their tremendous power in the Western world, which dominated the United Nations in its early years, produced very different results.

By late 1946, Dulles had begun to move away from a belief that the United Nations could serve as the "harmonizing center" of a postwar international order. Rightly or wrongly, as suggested above, he believed that Soviet behavior had made this impossible. He had hoped, he said, for cooperative efforts against "the social, the economic, the moral enemies of mankind" in order to produce "fellowship, friendship, and understanding." The "seeds" that had been planted in San Francisco had actually produced "early sprouts" in London, he felt, but that was as far as the process had been allowed to go: constant communist venom and obstructionism had then produced a "poisonous atmosphere" which, in Dulles's words, made it "impossible for the United Nations to grow up as planned."[13]

What Dulles saw happening within the new international organization was, of course, only one component of what he and many were coming to perceive as a vicious global pattern: the "challenge" to "civilization" posed by a Moscow "bent on eradicating the non-Soviet type of society." As already indicated, he was soon proposing various means by which this overall challenge could be parried. Some of his recommendations were quite specific and involved policy objectives which he would have considered essential with or without a Soviet "menace," i.e., the economic integration of Europe and the rehabilitation of Western Germany. Others were of a more nebulous variety, with emphasis on the need for "moral" and "spiritual" crusades to counter the "ideological" thrust of communism. In thoughts about this latter category, Dulles quickly saw considerable potential in the United Nations.

The first clear indication of a new Dulles approach to the U.N. came in a February 1947 address to the Inland Daily Press Association in Chicago. "We should begin to *use the United Nations to mobilize world opinion against international injustices*," he said. Because the Security Council was constantly stymied by Soviet vetoes, this would have to be done in the

General Assembly; that body was one Dulles had preferred to emphasize (for different reasons) for a long time. On Arthur Vandenberg's midwestern territory, he recalled his friend's frequently uttered desire to create a "town meeting of the world" within the General Assembly, "where all nations, strong and weak, could speak freely and as equals; where the conscience of the world could make itself felt; and where justice could be sought."

It quickly became clear that the "injustices" that Dulles wanted to tackle in the General Assembly *qua* town meeting were all spin-offs of the "international communist conspiracy." With his eye very much on the session which could begin in New York in September, he spoke regularly through mid-1947 about this facet of his new strategy. In order to restore its "moral influence" and "moral leadership in the world," he told graduating students at Northwestern University, the United States must insure that "the moral issue be clarified." "That issue is not the issue of economic communism against capitalism or state socialism against free enterprise. It is not an issue of relative national power. . . . The moral issue is the issue of the free state as against the police state." If "we . . . use the United Nations" as one of various tools, he went on, success could be achieved:

> The efforts of Soviet leaders to spawn police states throughout the world would, if persisted in, lead to widespread violence, even war. . . . The future must not unfold in that way. It need not if, while most of the world is still free, the issue is clarified. Then there will develop a world opinion strong enough to stop a program which otherwise will be stopped by violence.

In a July 1 statement published by the Commission on a Just and Durable Peace, he made similar points. The United States should not ignore "the United Nations as a means for promoting the consolidation of moral force which is indispensable to peace," he wrote. The General Assembly, in particular, could help "focus the moral judgment of mankind so as to influence the policies of governments."

As to implementing this rather grandiose conception, Dulles had one straightforward mechanism in mind: the Charter provisions that allowed the General Assembly to "study" and make "recommendations" for the "peaceful solution" of threatening international problems. He saw no reason why the United States should not become much more vigorous in the submission of "proposals" or agenda items along these lines. As early as February, he cited "injustices like those occurring in Poland" as an example worthy of attention and argued that "the time has come for the

United States to ask the Assembly to concern itself with areas in Europe where purges and discrimination go on, despite international pledges, and where aspirations for self-government are suppressed." By mid-summer, he had added two more possibilities for early action: the problems in Greece that had spurred the "Truman Doctrine" and the presumed destruction of an even moderately democratic political system underway in Hungary at just that point. If "study" produced accepted solutions for any of these problems, he felt, the procedure would of course be justified; even if not, or if the Soviets and their "friends" blocked approval, it would still help "focus" world opinion and clarify issues. [14]

Until late August, Dulles geared up for the 1947 General Assembly session very much on his own, a bit annoyed in fact about the lack of policy consultation by the State Department. When he was finally made privy to Washington's plans, he must have found them intriguingly similar to his own in terms of background and tactical logic. Ready, as Dulles had been, to put great emphasis on Soviet obstructionism in the Security Council and perverse aggressiveness everywhere, Truman, Secretary of State Marshall, and others had decided in their own right that the General Assembly could be turned into a useful Cold War front. They knew that on most occasions involving Soviet–American disagreements in the 1946 sessions, final votes on resolutions had shown more than a four-fifths majority for the so-called "Free World" position: this promised a safe environment within which to do battle, at least with words and emotions.

The clearest indication of the way Administration and Dulles plans had come together was the identity of program concerning Greece, which emerged by late August 1947. On several occasions after the pronouncement of the "Truman Doctrine," Dulles had privately expressed his reservations about a dramatic unilateral commitment that could outrun U.S. capabilities: in a distant and heterogeneous region like the Balkans, he felt, the Soviets "with very little expense can bleed us badly. . . ." By July 1, he was suggesting as an alternative that Greece's problems be one of the issues which the American delegation would place before the upcoming General Assembly. By August 25, a day before participating in discussions with Administration leaders, he was saying that there were several opportunities for increasing the Assembly's potency, "but in no matter more significantly than the Greek affair." "Should we not ask for a considered judgment of the 55 nations as to how, under present circumstances, we and others can in this Greek matter best serve the United Nations and sustain its principles?" He then prepared a memorandum which, among other things, speculated about "what would be the principal American 'line' to appeal to public sentiment?" He urged "featuring human rights and freedoms as the foundation of free society . . . put in a way to appeal to the dependent peoples and counteract Soviet propaganda. . . ."[15]

Washington too had decided that an appeal to the General Assembly would be worth making, after failed efforts in the Security Council. Bitter exchanges concerning the relative culpability of Greece, Yugoslavia, Bulgaria, and Albania for virtual civil war along shared borders had led the Security Council to create a Commission of Investigation in December 1946. After several months of extensive travel and hearings, a report was issued in May: eight of the eleven members concluded that there were deep and complex roots to the problems of the moment, but that northern neighbors were in fact providing left-wing Greek guerillas with aid and comfort; the Polish and Soviet members placed blame on Athens for border incidents; and the French representative indicated a preference for emphasizing opportunities for solutions rather than condemnatory accusations regarding either side. Washington immediately moved to use the majority findings as the basis for a new Security Council resolution, urging in June that another U.N. commission be established to help resolve local disputes, negotiate new frontier agreements, and deal with the problems of refugees. Since Truman had announced his own Greek aid program three months before, this Security Council maneuver looked at best like an *ex post facto* effort to spread the weight of a burden the Americans had decided to carry whatever other nations thought. Alternatively, as some at the time surmised, it was designed merely to draw public attention to Greece and "to put the Russians on the defensive." Reasoning of the latter variety seemed particularly strong after a Soviet rejection of the United States' proposal on July 29. Declaring himself unwilling to attempt "to appease further a threatening veto," U.S. representative Herschel Johnson introduced a new resolution to "register for the whole world" the "facts" of the Greek situation: it called upon the Security Council to find Yugoslavia, Bulgaria, and Albania responsible for threats to the peace by virtue of their efforts to establish in Greece "a minority totalitarian government which would be subservient to the Communist-controlled countries." Even before the inevitable Soviet veto of this resolution, Johnson made it clear that the United States would probably take the matter to the General Assembly in September. The veto came in a vote on August 19, at just the point when Dulles began renewing his earlier suggestion: the result was a shared game plan for the upcoming meetings.[16]

Dulles did express some short-lived concern at the end of August that the State Department might have in mind an Assembly "mandate to send troops into Greece to patrol the northern boundaries" and he opposed that as "reckless" and unlikely to win the endorsement of European allies.[17] He soon found that, while the Administration did plan to utilize its own military devices (about which he had other doubts), its U.N. tack would be confined to the kind of "civilian commission" which he himself now supported. A resolution was introduced in late September and yielded weeks of extremely bitter debate in committee and plenary session. By October 21, after the elimination of phrasing that spotlighted the guilt of Greece's neighbors, it was passed by a vote of 41 to 6 (the negative votes cast by the Soviet Union, Byelorussia, the Ukraine, Poland, Czechoslovakia, and Yugoslavia, already referred to by many as the Soviet or "Slav" bloc.) Despite the almost universal assumption that it would be unable to function on non-Greek territory, a Special Committee on the Balkans was to be established in Macedonia in order to observe compliance with a United Nations order "to do nothing which could furnish aid and assistance to the . . . guerillas." A counter-resolution by the Soviets, ascribing guilt to Athens and ordering the evacuation of all foreign troops from Greece, was defeated by exactly the same count.[18]

In spite of his early interest in dealing with "the Greek affair" in the General Assembly, Dulles actually played only an obeserver's role once decisions on policy had been made in Washington. Secretary of State Marshall himself and Herschel Johnson, fresh from the Security Council front, handled all of the presentation and debating chores. Dulles did become more overtly involved with two other issues, however, each of which also demonstrated his own and his colleagues' determination to wage "moral" and propaganda battle with the Soviets in this global "town meeting": American proposals concerning Korea and the so-called "Little Assembly."

Korea had turned into an aggravating problem for the United States, and there was a desire to gain tangible or at least moral support from the General Assembly. A 1945 division of the peninsula for occupation purposes had proven difficult to heal in the hostile atmosphere of the postwar years. By mid-1947, Soviet forces were still in position north of the 38th parallel, providing backing to a communist government in Pyongyang, and U.S. forces were still in position south of the 38th parallel, providing support to a right-wing government in Seoul. Moscow and Washington had carried on more or less steady negotiations to devise a procedure by which the two Koreas could be reunited and an integrated, sovereign state created, but all had failed. The Koreans themselves were bitterly divided, with both northern and southern elements determined to unify their country on their own very different terms, and they drew sustaining support from their respective occupiers.

When George Marshall addressed the opening session of the General Assembly on September 17, he announced that his frustrated government wanted to place the Korean problem on the agenda, and an American resolution was shortly submitted. After minor alterations of phrasing and emphasis, it proposed in its final form that the Assembly recommend elections for a National Assembly by March 31, 1948; that a U.N. Commission be sent to observe these elections and consult with existing authorities about transition to a unified, independent government; and that the resulting government negotiate with the United States and the Soviet Union for the speedy withdrawal of all occupation forces. Ostensibly, these steps were designed to provide a multilateral solution to the problems bilateral efforts had failed to resolve. In fact, it is difficult to believe that any of the American delegates seriously anticipated such a solution. Given immediately preceding developments involving Greece, given their own obvious frustrations with one-on-one negotiations on Korea itself, there would have been no justification for doing so. Assembly involvement could offer only the more limited and particular goals that had been settled on with Greece: first, it could draw attention to the problem and provide a nebulous kind of international moral support for U.S. policies being pursued in any event; second, it could eventually create opportunities for highly visible attacks on what the Americans presumed were evil Soviet designs.[19]

Dulles was uninformed about Korean developments prior to September 1947, but fully endorsed the U.S. desire to bring them before the "town meeting of the world." He was particularly anxious to see the creation of a counterpart to the Special Committee on the Balkans: it would serve, he told the Australian Minister for External Affairs, as "an international eye backed by the prestige of the U.N. . . . ." He made a number of the principal American statements in both Committee I and plenary sessions and was involved in behind-the-scenes efforts to carefully line up support. When the Soviets introduced a counter-resolution calling for almost immediate withdrawal of all forces and the settlement of political questions by the Koreans themselves, Dulles presented the U.S. critique of this as well. His overall approach was to argue that the Soviet procedure "would leave Korea in a chaos amounting to civil war" and that "the Korean people deserve a better fate." The American proposal, on the contrary, would allow withdrawal of occupation forces to "be accomplished in an orderly manner after some machinery has been provided which will make possible the transition from two widely different types of government to a single united government which will be representative of the Korean people." The U.S. delegation in general avoided in the Korea debate the kind of melodramatic indictments that had become more common in discussions of Moscow's policies on other subjects. There were occasional flashes of Dulles acerbity, however, indicative of the tone that would become predominant a year later—after a Korean Commission had had the chance to accumulate the type of ammunition already gathered by the Balkan Commission. On November 4, he responded to an obviously exaggerated Soviet portrait of the advantages of life in North Korea:

> According to that picture there is a beautiful spectacle of a people who for forty years or more have not known or practiced self-government, but who, in two short years have adopted a complete and detailed system of government dealing with political organization, economic organization, agrarian reform and education. This whole elaborate pattern had been adopted, we are told, in this short time, by these inexperienced people with complete unanimity or at least 99.2%. This new pattern which so suddenly has been effected with complete unanimity is, strangely enough . . . by curious coincidence . . . precisely the pattern of . . . the Soviet Union.[20]

On the premise, espoused by Dulles, that the Assembly was a forum within which points could be scored in some "free world" vs. "police state" debate, this was a witty, well-aimed jab.

Another example of the American, and Dulles's, desire to approach the General Assembly as something less than the "harmonizing center" initially aimed for was the so-called "Little Assembly" proposal, also first put forward in September 1947. This urged the creation of an "Interim Committee" of the whole, which would stay in session constantly during the months between regular meetings of the General Assembly. In explaining the need for the Interim Committee, Dulles and the U.S. delegation argued that because of the ineffective operation of the Security Council, the workload on the Assembly agenda had become too great to handle during meetings of only a few months duration. A year-round subgrouping could help lighten the burden: it could engage in what Dulles called "preparatory functions," such as the gathering of information on questions scheduled for discussion at an upcoming session, thus allowing the most efficient use of time by the larger assemblage; it could discharge "follow through" duties, such as supervision of investigative committees; and it could "institute studies" designed to point the way to possible new programs for the Assembly.

Though there was a real desire to encourage smoother operations, Dulles and his colleagues might never have put forward the Interim Committee proposal if they had not seen it as a valuable mechanism for dealing with some of their Cold War concerns. Quite clearly, they assumed that a more efficient General Assembly would be able to spend that much more time "focussing" world opinion against the Soviet Union. There was no public discussion of this facet of the proposal, but it was often commented on in private. During one delegation meeting, Dean Rusk listed some of the "specific studies" an Interim Committee might undertake and included the "activities of the Comintern . . . Soviet pressure on Turkey and certain forms of Soviet economic penetration in the Balkans." Dulles understood and applauded this ingredient in the plan, though he knew caution would be required to put it across. As he put it in an early meeting, original phrasing concerning examination of "'acts designed to subvert the political independence and territorial integrity of a State'" should be dropped: "it was going too far to indicate that a principal purpose was policing the U.S.S.R. While, undoubtedly, the Committee would have to watch that sort of thing, it was not thought to be a good idea to specify it in the resolution."

With Dulles handling many of the American presentations, the Interim Committee worked its way through to an Assembly vote by November 13. Though few seemed enthusiastic about the proposal, fewer still were prepared to oppose it with any energy. The British did urge and achieve a provision requiring a two-thirds majority before the Committee could place items on the Assembly agenda or undertake investigations. Given U.S. confidence about voting trends up to that point, this seemed safe enough to accept. Indeed, when the vote on this proposal itself was tallied, it turned out to be the 41 to 6 that had become rather standard.[21]

III

The tough, Cold War style of the Americans must have been obvious to anyone participating in or observing the 1947 session of the General Assembly. At a private luncheon arranged to discuss the Interim Committee proposal, Dulles was treated to the agitated thoughts of Brazil's Oswaldo Aranha, President of the General Assembly:

> He asserted that the League of Nations died because both France and Great Britain used it as an instrument of their own national policies. The United States . . . is using the United Nations in the very same way. . . .
> Dr. Aranha stated that he was very much puzzled by United States

policy towards the United Nations, and United States policy towards the U.S.S.R. He wanted to know whether our intention is to drive Russia out of the United Nations. He wanted to know further whether our aim was to go to war against Russia. . . .

Dr. Aranha was critical of the fact that we were using the United Nations to air our conflicts with the U.S.S.R. . . .

(These were the words of a friendly critic, it should be emphasized. Aranha indicated that if the U.S. was indeed planning to go to war, "the Latins were with us, but all they wanted to know is if that was the case.")

Dulles tried to reassure the Brazilian, telling him that "the notion that we are using the United Nations as an instrument of our national policy is totally wrong and misleading." Such words were rather vague, however, and Dulles made no effort to deny the anti-Soviet element in U.S. thoughts about the General Assembly. [22] Nor did his subsequent behavior as an American delegate demonstrate any resistance to the strategy that had taken shape in 1947. At sessions in 1948, 1949, and 1950, he and his colleagues revealed a notable consistency: again and again, they approached the General Assembly as a forum whose primary function was the scoring of political or propaganda points against Moscow.

As Assembly meetings began in Paris in September 1948, Dulles was widely recognized as the likely Secretary of State-designate of the seemingly invincible Thomas Dewey. This put certain strains on his full participation in the international body's work at this particular session: time had to be found for almost daily communication with the Republican candidate and his stateside advisers, as well as constant meetings with foreign representatives anxious to make early contact with a man they assumed would be a crucial figure in Washington after election day. [23] Still, Dulles took part in General Assembly affairs with reasonable regularity during the three months he spent in Paris.

One of the issues with which he was most extensively involved was the ongoing problem of Greece and its neighbors. The United Nations Special Committee on the Balkans (UNSCOB), which had been created in late 1947, had conducted extensive travels and hearings in the Greek border region and had prepared reports that came before this next Assembly session for consideration. The reports contended that Greek guerrillas were in fact receiving extensive moral and material support from communist governments to the north and that forces were allowed to move freely back and forth across borders. Citing such outside aid as a threat to Greece's independence and world peace, UNSCOB urged continuation of its investigative activities and reaffirmation of its willingness to offer "good offices" during any negotiations among the Balkan states.

UNSCOB's work had been hedged in by two fundamental difficulties:

the refusal of Poland and the U.S.S.R. to assume two of the eleven seats on the investigative body and the total lack of cooperation by Albania, Bulgaria, and Yugoslavia with respect to access to their territories or provision of information. Reports, as a result, were obviously lopsided as far as their factual bases were concerned: what was included was not necessarily wrong, but certainly incomplete. This did not stop the U.S. delegation from vigorously endorsing the UNSCOB findings and urging extension of the group's mandate. Dulles's presentation of the American case, in particular, placed it carefully in line with the overall tack developed the previous year. Surveying the data being offered, his first statement in Committee I urged that:

> This violent effort to establish in Greece a government subservient to Soviet communism is but part of a general effort to extend the power of Soviet communism throughout the world. . . . Wherever one looks, whether it be to Europe, Africa, Asia or the Americas, there is apparent the same pattern of effort, namely, the use of coercion and force to achieve political objectives, the manifestations differing only as the efforts are adjusted to meet local situations.

It was necessary, he went on, to avoid cynicism about what the United Nations could accomplish in the face of such a communist menace, in Greece or anywhere else. Though the Security Council had been stymied by perverse use of the veto, the General Assembly could proceed as it had begun in 1947:

> The Assembly can *expose the facts* and by so doing can *build up a moral judgment so widespread and so weighty that no nation will ignore it.* Marshall Stalin said of the League of Nations that "despite its weakness the League might nevertheless serve as a place where aggressors can be exposed." He put his finger on a great power. . . . It does not work with precision or immediacy, but it is, in the long run, a power to which all are sensitive for history has proved that those who flout it pay, someday, a heavy penalty. [Emphasis added.]

As before, most other delegations were willing to go along with the American conception of the General Assembly's role in Greece. A resolution endorsing UNSCOB's conclusions and extending its mandate was passed in late November by a vote of 47 to 6.[24] As soon as this was accomplished, Dulles and his colleagues began to push for similar action with respect to Korea.

The Temporary Commission created in November 1947 had, like its Balkan counterpart, prepared reports and recommendations for this Assembly session. These cited partial success in early efforts and urged an ongoing U.N. commitment. The elections over which the Commission was supposed to have presided, for example, had taken place in May 1948. Predictably, however, they had been confined to the South and even there had been boycotted by a number of parties of various political complexions. It was clear that there was still a long road to a peaceful, unified Korea, and the U.S. urged that the Temporary Commission be given a longer lease on life: its efforts below the 38th parallel should be commended through recognition of the government in Seoul as a lawful government, and its earlier instructions to seek to remove political and other barriers between north and south should be reaffirmed. In presenting American arguments on behalf of these proposals, Dulles lost no opportunities to "expose" the same kind of Soviet perfidy he had just recently cited in the Balkans. "As in the case of Greece," he told Committee I on December 6, "communist elements seek, by violence, to impose their will, and there is danger that these efforts will be supported in one form or another by neighboring communist regimes." From "the darkness" of northern Korea, he charged, "acts of terrorism and cruelty that shock all decent people" had already been committed. Though not necessarily persuaded that the American view was correct in all details, the Assembly voted 48 to 6 to establish a new Commission on Korea along the lines suggested. [25]

Even when his own role was quite minimal in 1948, Dulles showed consistent inclinations regarding the desired role of the General Assembly. He spoke far less often than his colleagues about a debate on disarmament proposals, for example, but always shared two basic attitudes with them: one, that deliberations and resolutions would have no practical effect and two, that they could nevertheless be useful for pointing up the aggressive posture of the Soviet Union. [26] And if the Berlin crisis had come before the Assembly, he would have approached it in the same way. As indicated in Chapter 14, he had had serious doubts about initial Administration plans to submit the Berlin issue to the Security Council, fearing some effort to rally support for " 'action' to compel lifting the blockade." Operating with a more limited game plan, Dulles preferred "prolonged debate" in the Assembly, where a simple condemnation of the Soviets might be forthcoming. The problem "is not 'action,' " he explained to Arthur Vandenberg, "but to educate and consolidate public opinion regarding Soviet methods. . ." (emphasis added). [27]

By mid-December 1948, after twelve weeks of work, there were still many items on the agenda of the Third Session of the General Assembly. In order to give delegates a respite and an opportunity to consult with their governments, a temporary adjournment was arranged, to be followed by a shorter, concluding round of meetings in New York in April

1949. The only issue with which Dulles became substantively involved here was the disposition of former Italian colonies. The Council of Foreign Ministers had been unable to reach agreement on these African territories, and under the provisions of the ItalianPeace Treaty, ultimate decision-making power passed to the General Assembly. Though of relatively esoteric importance, Dulles's role meshed easily with what had become his standard position at the "town meeting of the world."

On one level, Dulles demonstrated again his own and his colleagues' generally minimalist ambitions concerning United Nations actions on matters other than denunciation of the Soviet Union. In spite of grand rhetoric in 1945, as suggested above, concrete trusteeship measures advocated by the Americans in 1946 and after had been of consistently limited dimensions. Now, in early 1949, they followed through on this with conservative proposals for Italy's former possessions in Africa. In a common front worked out with London and with general support from Paris and Rome, it was moved that Libya be granted independence in ten years, but that in the interim its three principal constituent parts be administered by Great Britain, France, and Italy; that a portion of Eritrea be absorbed by Ethiopia and the remainder by the Anglo–Egyptian Sudan; and that Somaliland be placed under Italian trusteeship. [28]

Dulles offered his regular support to this package plan. He did fret somewhat about the blatant continuation of a quasi-imperialistic European presence in northern Africa, particularly an Italian presence so soon after World War II. The reasoning behind his concern, however, was not necessarily of the variety common among more vigorous reformers. In a private conversation with French Foreign Minister Schuman, he explained:

> The Italian colonies must be looked on as part of the general problem of Europe and Africa. Tensions between the East and West and the iron curtain have largely interrupted East–West developments and require us to think in terms of North–South, i.e., Western Europe and Africa. There are in Africa vast resources which can be developed to the natural advantage of Africa and West Europe and more than make good the loss of access to the natural resources of eastern Europe and the loss of Asiatic colonies. This North–South development, however, requires friendly collaboration between the native peoples and the peoples of Europe. . . . If the Italian colonies were dealt with in a manner which excited a Moslem Holy War or a race war of black against white, then the foundation for North–South development would disappear. [29]

Dulles was clearly still being moved by the kind of Wilsonian logic that had prompted his interest in opening up the "vast, underdeveloped areas of the world" in the 1930s. How could these areas—be they in Eastern

Europe, Asia, Africa, or elsewhere—help solve the problems of more highly developed states? The "North–South" relationship envisaged by 1948 involved certain concessions to the sensitivities of the weak, but presumed an ongoing second-class economic position for them as producers of natural resources. Even in political terms, Dulles was prepared to hedge their futures. The problem he discussed with Schuman was not the avoidance of European governance in Africa, but the devising of means of allowing it which would be more acceptable to the "native peoples." In 1948, he was quite prepared to believe that the British and French at least could handle this and willingly served as supportive spokesman when resolutions were being debated in the General Assembly. He must surely have understood the likely long-range repercussions as well. As the French Foreign Minister put it with respect to Libya, for example, "the British if they were there for two or three years more, would never get out except perhaps as part of an independence scheme, like that of Trans-Jordan, which would give the British a continuing special position. . . . The British had a quality, for which he did not reproach them, of looking out for themselves. [30]

On another level, it is interesting to note the way in which Dulles and his colleagues blended anticommunism into any number of their statements on the Italian colonies. The Soviets, to be sure, made sharp commentary almost inevitable by hurling their own rather absurd and self-serving attacks, but the Americans were more than happy to respond. In one early statement, Dulles described the contrasting behavior of the Western Allies and Moscow with respect to conquered territories. "There is no area that the Soviet Union conquered in the world which has been brought in any aspect whatever before the United Nations for decision." He went on to comment on the fact that there might even be more members within the General Assembly if so many pre-war states "had not been swallowed up in the maw of the Soviet Union."

Though the U.S. delegation might have preferred to create the impression that it was perverse communist obstructionism that prevented a settlement of the Italian colonies issue, it quickly became clear that many states beyond the Soviet bloc had grave reservations about the tabled resolutions. For varying reasons, debate became angry and incredibly convoluted. Postponement until the next session of the Assembly ultimately proved necessary. [31]

Dulles did not return to the General Assembly until September 1950, at the opening of its Fifth Session. He had made his unsuccessful bid for a Senate seat in the fall of 1949 and had not attended the Fourth Session held in New York at that time. An absence of almost eighteen months made little difference in his approach, however. In May 1950, for example, knowing he would be participating in the next round of meetings, he delivered a national radio address in which he looked back over his earlier experiences:

> We who have served at the Assemblies of the United Nations have welcomed the change to meet face to face with those who differ from us and to present, so that all the world could hear, our different philosophies and our different ideas as to how to achieve peace. United Nations meetings give the representatives of free peoples *a chance to strip Communist propaganda of the veneer that makes it dangerous. It exposes the tactics and intolerant creed of Soviet Communism.* [Emphasis added.]

Two months later he was urging more emphasis on the use of U.N. observation commissions such as those sent to Korea and the Balkans. On the borders of Yugoslavia or "throughout the areas that abut on the Soviet perimeter," would not inspection of military preparations be tremendously beneficial? To allow inspection would offer "dramatic evidence to the world of peaceful intentions." And if there were refusal to allow it, this too, "could have *tremendous propaganda value as evidence of aggressive intentions*" (emphasis added.)[32]

As ever, Dulles found his U.S. delegation colleagues quite happy to go along with this kind of strategy. Indeed, as the September opening drew closer, the Truman Administration in general showed clear signs of wanting to go yet further: if the General Assembly had proven its worth as a forum within which world opinion could be cultivated and moral sanctions secured, had the time not come to seek more tangible, even miltary support for American policies?

Events in Korea prompted thought along these lines. Thanks to a coincidental boycott of meetings by the Soviet representative, the Security Council had been able to move with speed and ease to respond to Pyongyang's move into southern territory at the end of June. The creation of a United Nations army under Douglas MacArthur's command, even if overwhelmingly American in manpower, had provided the U.S. with a comforting sense of multilateral aid for actions that would have been taken in any event. It had demonstrated to many what Dulles called "the great possibilities of good inherent in the United Nations": but for "one malevolent vote in the Security Council," a similar "momentum of action" and "lift of spirit" might be achieved concerning many other global problems. Knowing that other opportunities for "action" would not develop often, if at all, in the Security Council, Dean Acheson in particular pushed for the devising of alternative mechanisms. He turned to the General Assembly, where the United States felt confident of overwhelming international support on most issues. After weeks of deliberation in Washington, the Secretary of State announced on September 20 that his government was tabling an omnibus "Uniting for Peace" resolution. It went through minor modifications during debate and voting procedures, but involved from the beginning a number of key ingredients: delineation of the General Assembly's right to take action, including the use of armed force, to deal with a breach of international peace when and if the Security Council was unable to act because of a veto; a request to all member states to have units of their armed forces available for use by the U.N. at short notice; the creation of a fourteen-nation Peace Observation Commission to investigate potentially explosive situations anywhere in the world; and the creation of a fourteen-nation Collective Measures Committee to study methods of securing global peace. Precise details aside, the Americans were proposing a dramatic end run around the Soviet veto in the Security Council via a significant addition of power to the arsenal of the General Assembly. That this development, particularly in its military components, clashed quite sharply with the Assembly role they themselves had envisioned in 1945 did not disturb them, as long as majority votes remained as easy to achieve as had thus far been the case. [33]

Dulles certainly should have been conscious of the way the "Uniting for Peace" resolution departed from his own earlier conceptions. He had shown himself willing to take one significant step away from 1945 thoughts when he grew excited about the propaganda potential of the "town meeting of the world" after early 1947. Now, some three years later, he took a further leap. The man who had criticized the Dumbarton Oaks Proposals for unrealistically and undesirably envisioning global armed forces under the aegis of the Security Council was ready to place them at the disposal of a majority of the General Assembly; the man who had argued that the primary value of the Assembly was in talk and the encouragement of cooperative work on social and economic problems was ready to concentrate efforts on political and military matters that would by their very nature heighten already bitter international relationships. He gave his full endorsement to the "Uniting for Peace" plan and regularly served as both behind-the-scenes advocate and public spokesman in its behalf. In one private meeting with members of the Israeli delegation, he elaborated on his convictions and some of the reasoning behind them. In the face of the Korean crisis, he said:

> The UN must be prepared to act in cases of aggression and the member states must have a real feeling of responsibility in connection with collective security. The real question was whether member states were con-

cerned with discharging these responsibilities, or whether they were merely "along for the ride" and expected the United States to come to their assistance if they were attacked. In the case of Korea, the United States, although not prepared, and although our action has meant a redirection of our national economy, undertook the principal burden, and public opinion in this country accepted that. However, in a future case of aggression, public opinion would hardly understand if other countries of the world would not take their full share in combating such agression.[34]

In public statements, not suprisingly, Dulles put primary emphasis on the need to develop more effective means of deterring virulent Soviet aggression. "The basic problem, as we see it, is to create enough collective strength to protect the freedom of those people who want to be free," he told a plenary session of the General Assembly when it began to debate the U.S. proposal. Citing Korea, Poland, and Czechoslovakia as examples of the problems he had in mind, he left no doubt about what he considered the source of dangers: "No people yet have come under the yoke represented by the Soviet brand of imperialist Communism except by violent coercion. . . . " What was required was a method for cutting "the noose of the veto that would strangle us" and prevent ameliorative action; this the U.S. proposals could allow the General Assembly to do.[35]

"Uniting for Peace" was adopted by an overwhelming majority, in spite of some reservations among even noncommunist states about the long-range problems that might arise concerning their own particular national interests. Given the membership of the Assembly and the Cold War environment of immediately succeeding years, it became an occasionally useful tool for the United States. It would, of course, be utilized selectively. As had been true in general in the past, the Americans would be anxious to encourage U.N. action when it served their interests—and to oppose it when it did not. At the 1950 session, for example, Dulles persuaded his colleagues to drop plans for a full-fledged Assembly discussion of Formosa when it seemed that this might cause difficulties not originally envisioned. There existed "great sensitiveness" among Republicans and others about any facet of the China problem, he argued, and suspicions would be easily aroused if it appeared that decision-making power was being transferred away from Americans themselves. In addition, obvious differences of opinion about Peking and the Nationalist Government had arisen among U.S. Allies, and the comfortable majorities that could usually be counted on might not materialize if any concrete proposals came to a vote. In contrast to action concerning Korea, it seemed safer to drop Formosa from the Assembly agenda and continue an essentially unilateral policy.[36] Similarly, Dulles and the Truman Administration in general opposed any involvement of the General Assembly or the Trusteeship Council in the problems of Indochina. Though he felt that support for France's efforts involved choosing "the lesser of two evils," Dulles concluded that it was "not practical" to seek a U.N. role.[37]

In view of Dulles's year-to-year contributions, it should be clear that the gaps that existed between early visions of the United Nations and the realities of the organization as it operated by late 1950 were not particularly disturbing to him. He had shown himself consistently ready to shelve some of his initial expectations and had proven as enthusiastic an advocate of the new-style General Assembly, in particular, as any American policy maker of the Truman period.

In view of Dulles's other year-to-year activities after 1945, it should also be clear that he would probably not have been greatly concerned about U.N. developments even if he had disapproved of the direction they were taking. Looking at his work and thoughts in the early postwar period as a whole, it is evident that the new international organization simply did not occupy a position of major importance in his ladder of priorities: what happened at the U.N. might be of some interest to him, but of limited interest relative to other matters.

Work and thought were closely intertwined in this respect. As to the former, the totality of Dulles's involvement suggests a spasmodic and relatively aloof role. He was, after all, a Republican, generally brought onto the Truman Administration's U.N. team just prior to Assembly sessions in order to strengthen bipartisan support: as he found in other areas, this kind of timing tended to keep his contribution to actual policy formation rather marginal or *ex post facto*. He almost invariably proved willing to go along with plans being formulated, which made him doubly attractive to the Democrats, but was often conscious of the way basics were being decided by others. In 1946, for example, he returned from the first General Assembly meetings in London urging Truman to appoint delegates to the next session more quickly: this would give them the opportunity to help shape policies, not just serve as spokesmen or tacticians. But by 1950 not much had changed. After a series of meandering delegation debates about how to handle the Formosa issue in the Assembly, Dulles told his colleagues that "it was hardly fair to ask the Assembly delegation to deal with Formosa as a separate matter." It was "interlocked with other matters in the Far East" about which those in New York were uninformed or over which they were powerless to act. Dulles also expressed chagrin midway in the 1950 meetings about lack of information and consultation concerning a controversy over Trygve Lie's continuation as Secretary General. [38]

Dulles found it easy enough to accept his usually random, frontman's role at the General Assembly. It could peeve him occasionally and keep him from finding deep satisfaction in this work generally, but it was unlikely that he would have wanted much more than this in any event. Intellectually, that is, Dulles's real priorities in the post–World War II period were not centered on the United Nations. At one point in early 1945, he had urged his countrymen to support a continually activist foreign policy, particularly with respect to certain areas: "Our government ought to participate actively in the decisions now being taken in Europe," he said, "decisions which, *more than any Security Organization*, will determine whether there is to be a Third World War" (emphasis added). [39] What happened in Europe and the way it affected the United States were the real foci of Dulles's attention and efforts. He could turn his mind to the problems of mandates and trusteeships for two months, but long before and after he would demonstrate deeper concern for the problems of Germany. He could turn his interest to the propaganda value of an investigative commission on Korea for several weeks, but long before and after he would demonstate his more basic preoccupation with the possibility of continental economic integration. By 1950, other issues *had* begun to challenge the primacy of European–American ties in Dulles's mind and to absorb the lion's share of his time as well—but those issues involved developments in East Asia and proved, as usual for him, only marginally connected with the United Nations.

16

Focus on Eastern Asia, 1950–1952: I

For JOHN FOSTER DULLES, 1949 had been a hectic year, but it had done nothing to ease the quandary he had been placed in by Dewey's defeat in the 1948 presidential election: with the door to the State Department closed at least temporarily and perhaps permanently, what was to be done with the kind of political and diplomatic ambitions that had been growing for almost a decade? Appointments to General Assembly delegations were only marginally satisfying; prospects for a Senate career were dashed in a bitter campaign and failure at the polls. Would there be an indefinite limbo for a non-office building, opposition expert on foreign affairs? For a while, it looked as if there would. Several months after Lehman's victory in the Senate race, Dulles was still adding patches to the crazy-quilt that had been his "career" for more than a year. Within months, however, his own efforts, the continuing strength of Arthur Vandenberg, and the needs of the Truman Administration brought him yet another government appointment. This evolved into his most important responsibility to date, the negotiation of the Japanese Peace Treaty.

I

The unsettled days of late 1949 and early 1950 found Dulles with one apparent preoccupation: building or finding a position that would give him continuing public visibility as far as political and international affairs were concerned. Having staved off oblivion in the aftermath of Dewey's defeat, he was no more anxious to fade from the scene after his own. At a minimum, Dulles seems to have been angling for additional diplomatic assignments from the Truman Administration. It is also likely that he was aware of the value of keeping his name alive in the public eye, so that he would not be forgotten when the Republicans had another crack at the White House in 1952.

As to the methods, he was willing to try diverse possibilities. Some were tried and true for him: he accepted a number of invitations to speak before Protestant church audiences, for example, and participated in functions sponsored by the Federal Council of Churches. Others were older practices adapted and/or expanded, such as the writing of his second book. Drafted in a few weeks of marathon dictation and typing sessions, *War or Peace* was a world apart from the treatise he had published in 1939 and offers ample testimony to the changes that a decade had wrought in Dulles's sense of his public and professional role. Where *War, Peace and Change* had been turgid and philosophical, this new volume used punched-up prose and a near-sensational style to appeal to a mass audience. Its outline was a survey of the major diplomatic events of the postwar era, with emphasis on those in which Dulles himself had played some role.[1]

In his concern for retaining public prominence, Dulles was also willing to consider avenues that would have been totally new to him. December 1949 found him considering apparent feelers concerning the presidencies of Columbia and Yale universities. Dulles's own specific reactions are unclear, but after consultation with his old friend Ferdinand Mayer, the latter wrote that if "that sort of platform" was desired, Columbia was likely to be "less parochial" and to "afford much more opportunity for the type of international interest which you have always had. . . ."[2]

Before seriously pursuing any academic opportunities, however, Dulles tried prodding the Truman Administration into calling on his services once more. The early months of 1950 seemed like an opportune time. The President and some of his key foreign policy advisers were besieged by critics on many fronts. Senators Taft and Knowland and others were offering scathing denunciations of what they saw as a disastrous American policy toward the Far East, zeroing in on the staggering "loss" of China to the communists. Joseph McCarthy was testing out the strategem of flaying the State Department as a haven for subversives and finding that, in the aftermath of Alger Hiss's conviction for perjury and the Soviet explosion of an atomic bomb, his colleagues and the media would actually listen. Dean Acheson later wrote that early 1950 saw the beginning of the "Attack of the Primitives" on the Administration and his own personal "immolation" in the Senate; Republicans were preparing a "veritable witches' brew" for public consumption, gearing up for a period of "partisan in-fighting as bloody as any in our history." In this kind of environment, Dulles may have thought he had much to offer the Democrats: along with Arthur Vandenberg, who was ill but still firmly committed to bipartisanship, he could provide concrete reassurance that there was still a wing of the G.O.P. that was amenable to cooperation.

Acheson seemed mildly interested in a new Dulles role even before the end of 1949. In a December 22 "chat," held while Dulles was in Washington to visit the recuperating Vandenberg, Acheson talked about the sorry state of bipartisanship at that particular moment, and expressed the desire "to be able to see me [Dulles] regularly so that we could talk things over together." Dulles seems to have taken this as a first step toward an invitation. He told the Secretary that he "would be happy" to meet with him in order to gain fuller information about "basic facts" and said this would help create the kind of "good will" needed for "agreement on policy." To reinforce further the seriousness of his interest, he undertook a number of speaking engagements and writing assignments in subsequent weeks, in each of which he put heavy emphasis on the importance of bipartisanship. The need for unity was a consistent theme in *War or Peace*, with Dulles arguing that no other course was defensible at a time when "the United States faces . . . the greatest danger that ever confronted it." If Americans bickered about their foreign policy instead of closing ranks, "the whole non-Communist world will crumble and we may crumble with it." He developed the same thought in a widely reported address in Chicago on March 10, 1950:

> To all intents and purposes we are being warred against by the most dangerous enemy we have ever had to face. . . . The United States is the only nation in the world which can provide effective leadership to meet the menace of communist encirclement. If we disqualify ourselves from that leadership because Democrats and Republicans in Washington think primarily in terms of domestic feuding, then there is little hope of stopping the process of slow strangulation of which there is such clear evidence as we look around the world today.

434

But Acheson was slow to follow through on the admittedly limited offer of December. By the end of March, Dulles had not even had appreciative comments on his public statements much less a formal invitation to return to Washington. Annoyed, but not ready to give up, he was willing to try one more blatant hint of his availability. In a letter to Acheson that was released to the press, he commended the appointment of Republican John Sherman Cooper as adviser to the American group that would soon be attending a round of European meetings. "I hope that this step toward restoring bipartisanship in foreign policy will be followed by others on both the Republican and Democratic side," he wrote, "so that we can get solid unity in the nation and in the Congress behind foreign policies adequate to meet the grave peril we face." He added that this would be a more positive approach than the "dissemination of rumors and suspicions" in which so many had been indulging.[3]

For all of his interest in getting back to Washington in early 1950, Dulles avoided signs of fawning or desperation. He was quite prepared to join his party colleagues in some of their criticisms, for example. "The policies of the Administration have collapsed conspicuously in the Far East," he told one audience, "where the Administration never did invite Republican cooperation." He was also ready to be somewhat biting about the Democrats' lack of appreciation for his own past services. On March 30, he was in Washington and stopped at the State Department to see Deputy Under Secretary Dean Rusk and Dean Acheson. To Rusk, he complained that "a grave blow had been struck to bipartisanship when the Democratic High Command during the Senatorial campaign had tried to smear me and to destroy public confidence in my qualifications for international work, and to belittle my contribution to bipartisan foreign policy. I, myself, had abstained carefully during the campaign from any criticism of the conduct of foreign policy. . . ." When Acheson thanked him for the letter about Cooper's appointment, Dulles snappishly responded that the "message had not been easy to send, for I was criticizing those who had been loyal to me at a time when I was being smeared as fascist, nazi and bigot by the Democratic political organization, when none of the Administration had publicly or privately said a word of protest." Dulles did make sure to underline his willingness to forgive and forget, however. He had written the letter about Cooper, and he now explicitly told Rusk and Acheson that he "would be disposed to respond to any offer of important responsibility. . . ."[4]

The Administration seems to have been favorably disposed toward Dulles at the time. Acheson did not like Dewey's adviser and thought him distastefully ambitious, but with great numbers of critics behaving like a "yelping pack at one's heels," to use the Secretary's words, he decided to take up one of the few offers of support that had come along. One final push to that decision came with a March 31 letter from the ailing Arthur Vandenberg. Bringing Dulles "back into active and important cooperation with the State Department" was "an indispensable necessity" if bipartisanship were to stand a chance for survival, the Senator told Acheson, and urged him to move "as soon as possible." Three days later, with Truman's approval, Acheson did just that. In a series of phone calls, he worked out the outlines of a new Dulles appointment as "adviser to the Secretary of State with reference to making and implementing our foreign policy." By April 6, Dulles was back in Washington.[5]

II

"This will be a general responsibility without geographical or topical limitations," Dulles told reporters the day his advisory appointment was announced. Though technically correct, such a job description was almost immediately misleading. Even while the maneuvering that yielded his reentry into the Truman Administration was going on, it was quite clear that there would be one overall area of concern to which he would be responding, and one major task that he would be assigned.

As a general focus of his new work, the Far East was almost inevitable. For more than a year, events in Asia had been stealing headlines from the European issues that had dominated media and public attention for so long. The penultimate working out of the Chinese Civil War, with Chiang Kai-shek's exile to Formosa and the arrival of the victorious communists in Peking had been especially mesmerizing for Americans. There had also been increasing interest in the faltering French effort to reassert authority in Indochina and the sparks emanating from an artificially and bitterly divided Korea. Some Americans had reacted with measured concern to such developments: they talked of a communist menace that had been such a preoccupation in Europe, yet revealed a certain puzzlement about the role and interests of the United States in this remoter area. Others were far more troubled and far less puzzled. The conservative wing of the Republican party, Senators Knowland, Taft, and McCarthy in particular, castigated Democratic policy makers as fools or traitors for allowing the "loss" of China and shrilly prophesied the demise of American civilization if something like a crusade was not mounted to right other Far Eastern problems.

Given tensions abroad and at home, the Truman Administration quite logically decided to draw Dulles into Asian policy making. He had made his commitment to bipartisanship abundantly clear and had stopped considerably short of the blasts being issued by some of his G.O.P. colleagues. To involve him in day-to-day decision making might help deflect at least some of the opposition's fire. He would bring the aura of unity that he and Vandenberg had helped create regarding Europe and the United Nations to an area in which it had never materialized, thus giving more moderate Republicans nad perhaps the public some pause to think.

Within the overall context of the Far East, one particular problem emerged as the focus of Dulles's appointment: the Japanese Peace Treaty. The new adviser had no familiarity with any of the complex early deliberations about an Asian peace settlement, but he quickly learned that it had become a major concern within the Administration and that he would be asked to deal with it. Deputy Under Secretary Rusk had mentioned this as a possibility on March 30, prior to Acheson's formal offer of renewed association; Dulles himself told reporters on April 6 that he would be studying the "status" of work on the Japanese Peace Treaty. Though he retained a somewhat open agenda for a while thereafter, allowing involvement in policy deliberations on Korea and Formosa among other things, it soon became clear that Japan would take the lion's share of his attention. By the end of May, he was beginning to draft memoranda on the problems associated with the negotiation of a Peace Treaty, and on June 14 he set off on a journey to Tokyo that would cement his role in the task.[6]

When the Truman Administration moved to draw Dulles into Japanese and general Asian policy making, they found a man quite willing to cooperate. In a strictly tactical sense, he sincerely believed that partisan sniping by some of his Republican colleagues had gone too far. As he had put it in a letter to Acheson on March 29, he was dismayed by the "public dissemination of rumors and suspicions which create unnecessary confusion and dismay. That result encourages our enemies and discourages our friends abroad by making them feel that our nation has not grown up to the responsibilities of leadership." In his first public statement as the secretary's "adviser" a week later, he reiterated this point and allowed reporters to apply it explicitly to Joseph McCarthy: though he too was deeply troubled by the loss of China, Dulles said, it was time to end "public attacks and recrimination" and shift attention from "mistakes of the past" to "the circumstances of the present." He was obviously speaking as a Republican who was prepared to do what he could to close ranks.[7]

In a larger sense, Dulles was also intellectually ready to concentrate on

Asian affairs. There had been signs of this for some time. During his regular intervals of work at the United Nations, he had developed some concern for two issues that were far from his usual sphere of interest. From the fall of 1947 on, he had been personally involved with United States maneuvers regarding Korea and had become steadily attentive to the situation there as a result. During the same period, though he had no particular role to play concerning it, he also seems to have been a close observer of the debate over the independence and future of the Dutch East Indies that boiled so regularly in the Security Council.

Dulles could hardly have avoided being drawn to the dramatic events taking place in China. The prevalence of media coverage aside, several factors would have pushed his thoughts in this direction. Family history encouraged a certain general curiosity: some of his ancestors had served as missionaries in China; grandfather Foster had had intimate business and diplomatic connections with Chinese leaders of his generation, and Dulles had met some of them during his childhood summers at the family compound on Lake Ontario. He had developed his own professional ties too, serving as counsel on a number of loan arrangements made with the Nationalist government in the 1930s and as a U.S. lawyer for that government during World War II. He had come to know several of the Soongs and had even met Chiang Kai-shek. And if these influences had not been present, the political currents of 1949 and 1950 likely would have carried Dulles across the Pacific all on their own. The American "mission" in China had been a preoccupation in some Republican quarters since the days of John Hay and Theodore Roosevelt (and John Watson Foster), and it mounted to a fever pitch in the late 1940s. Though Dulles found the extreme attacks of men like Senator Knowland distasteful and dangerous, he could not help but have his attention caught by them and could not hope to have continuing influence within the G.O.P. without confronting in some way the issues they raised. By January 1949, he was cogitating about a formal statement of party policy on China, which was never made but which shows he was willing to move toward the extremists. Recognition of Peking was not only "premature" at this time, he wrote, but "will continue, for an indefinite time, to be 'premature'. . . ." Further, Washington should actually work for the overthrow of "the Red regime"—short, at least, of military measures. "In China I would give moral and, where feasible, economic support to those Chinese who are naturally disposed to resist Red rule and who will surely do so if we give them hope and encouragement," he argued. The closest he came to defining this was to say that the Nationalists "should be allowed to be a government in exile" on Formosa and should be protected against Peking's assault, perhaps through transformation into a United Nations trusteeship. The island could then be developed in such a way as "to put on a demonstration there of how much better the people were under an administration that *we* supervised than were the Chinese on the mainland under Communist domination. . . . In that way I believed we could stimulate unrest within China . . . pin down the Communists to the mainland, create internal troubles which would prevent their further expansion and in the end lead to their internal collapse."[8]

It was his own accumulated concerns that brought Dulles to Asia as much as the needs of the Truman Administration. This interest led him to declare on April 6, 1950, that his appraisal of the global scene persuaded him that "the situation that is most acute at the moment is in the Far East." It should not be surprising that those accumulated concerns would continue to affect him once he entered the State Department. As he began to participate in shaping United States policy toward Japan, in fact, Dulles's mind was in no way like the proverbial blank page on which impressions and judgments had yet to be written. Several years of intense involvement would yield interesting new dimensions and subtleties in his views, but he never escaped or sought to escape from several basic preconceptions that were discernible well before mid-1950.

Most obviously, Dulles brought a sharply etched vision of the Soviet Union to analysis of the Asian scene. His sense of Moscow's ambitions, which had been an important stimulus to his concern for European problems throughout the later 1940s, was transferred to the other side of the globe and served as a backdrop to policy-making efforts in this new area from the beginning.

The shift of his Soviet-centered anxieties to a new locus had involved a slow, two-step intellectual process for Dulles: the continued elaboration of core conceptions and the development of certain variations that had been only implicit before 1949. The core was and remained his sense of a Moscow-based international communist conspiracy bent on world conquest. By 1949, he had not deviated at all from the early Cold War commentaries along these lines; he had worked and reworked his message many times, giving it a well-known melodramatic sheen, but he remained fully consistent in his conclusions. His first speech in the Senate in July 1949 used his by then traditional view as an initial base for explaining the logic of NATO: "The Soviet communists' purpose . . . was no less than world domination to be achieved by gaining political power successively in each of the many areas that had been afflicted by war so that in the end the United States, which was openly called the main enemy, would be isolated and closely encircled."

In the increasingly charged atmosphere of early 1950, he was ready to repeat this theme in an even more vibrant key: "there is loose in the world a great terror—the black plague of Soviet Communism. It is an aggressive force, operating ruthlessly in accordance with a carefully prepared and superbly implemented program which, in a single generation, has brought a small Communist group into control of over one-third of the world's population. That offensive is still in full swing." This conception also figured prominently in *War or Peace*. In the first pages of this book, published in April 1950, Dulles wrote:

> There exists a great power—Russia—under the control of a despotic group fanatical in their acceptance of a creed that teaches world domination and that would deny those personal freedoms which constitute our most cherished political and religious heritage. . . . The Soviet program is to encircle us and to isolate us. They want this, not in order that we may go on living our own lives in peaceful isolation, but in order that they may finish us off in quick order.

(Interestingly, *Life* magazine published a lengthy condensation of *War or Peace* at the time of its appearance: it was *Life* which, four years earlier, had published Dulles's first carefully written analysis of the sinister efforts to create a global *Pax Sovietica*.)[9]

The most important variation on this basic theme which Dulles developed by early 1950 was his much more specific emphasis on the way "world domination" involved Soviet activities beyond *Europe*. In abstract terms, he had long believed that Moscow's reach was unlimited. He had mentioned the Arab world, China, Korea, Latin America, and former colonial territories in Africa as targets in his first *Life* article. In practice, as has been shown, he had really spent almost all of his time from 1946 to 1949 concentrating on the one area he considered of surpassing importance: Europe, the "Inner Citadel."

Signs of his sharper attention to other horizons began to appear by mid-1949. In the aftermath of the Berlin blockade and the June Council of Foreign Ministers meeting, Dulles announced that Moscow had concluded there would be no easy additional progress toward dominating Europe and was shifting its attention to Asia. Dramatic U.S. programs like the Marshall Plan, NATO, and the airlift, had forced Soviet policy makers to "pass from the offensive to the defensive" and "may" have brought about "the end of the cold war in Europe." "Under present conditions," Dulles saw them concluding that "the going for them is not very good going, therefore, they're going to try to go elsewhere . . . where they can get more results for their efforts, perhaps in the Far East." Or, as he put it to newsmen on another occasion, "Soviet leaders may feel that their immediate problem in Europe is not to get more, but to keep what they have . . .their ambitions for the moment lie more in the Far East. . . ."

Events in China at just this point certainly contributed to the drift of Dulles's speculations. Like so many Americans, he seemed absolutely convinced that the Chinese communist armies successfully battering the Nationalists were essentially a pawn in Moscow's global game plan. In 1938 he had called Mao Tse-tung an "agrarian reformer," and during World War II he had dubbed Mao's followers "the so-called 'Red Army' faction," both terms implying some appreciation for the indigenous roots of the C.C.P. By 1949, however, he believed that Soviet leaders had, in typical fashion, subverted what may have begun as a genuine grassroots movement. Boring from within, they had taken control and created the mechanism for a puppet regime in Peking. "Thus," Dulles wrote in *War or Peace*, "the 450,000,000 people in China have fallen under leadership that is violently anti-American, and that takes its inspiration and guidance from Moscow. . . . Soviet Communist leadership has won a victory in China which surpassed what Japan was seeking and we risked war to avert."

Significant enough in itself, Moscow's victory in China was seen by Dulles as only the most blatant and immediate example of the international communist conspiracy's generally rising efforts in Asia and other underdeveloped areas. On numerous occasions in later 1949 and 1950, he offered a sweeping overview of Soviet objectives which made this clear. Recent Far Eastern developments, he said in Seattle in January 1950, were the fruits of policies laid down years before:

> Twenty five years ago Stalin, looking at the colonial situation, said that it offered the best chance of overthrowing the West. "The road to victory of the revolution in the West lies through the revolutionary alliance with the liberation movement of the colonies and dependent countries." He noted the economic value of colonies to the Western countries and saw that violent revolution would not only take away this economic value, but involve the colonial countries in costly and futile struggles that would exhaust them.

Moscow would find victory in China a valuable new tool for work along these lines, Dulles believed. "Most of China is under a Communist Government which today spearheads the Soviet Communist policy of inciting peoples of South Asia and the Pacific to violent revolution against their existing governments on the theory that these governments are merely the 'lackies' of the West." Referring specifically to Indochina, Burma, and Indonesia, he speculated on possible consequences before an audience in Chicago in March:

If that area is consolidated by Communism, there are plenty of prepared soft spots waiting in Latin America and in Africa. If these areas are taken, Communism will have completed its first phase of world conquest, the encirclement of the inner citadel of the West. Then the situation will be ripe for the second and final phase of assault unless, as Stalin has suggested, the Western people are then so weak that they will voluntarily surrender.[10]

Though he saw the Soviets shifting their attention from Europe to the Far East, Dulles did not see any dramatic alteration in their preferred method of operation: subversion. His 1946 *Life* articles had indicated his belief that Moscow would be consistently shy of direct military action or war. Conscious of inherent weakness vis à vis the United States, the Soviets would opt for indirect aggression and slower expansion in areas at any distance from Soviet borders. Developments in France, Italy, and Germany had provided Dulles with detailed examples during the years in which he had concentrated on Europe, leading to regular restatements of his general conviction: as he put in January 1948, the Soviet Union "has developed, to a high degree, the techniques of propaganda and penetration, of smear and strike and sabotage. Its schools turn out agitators trained as specialists to operate in each capitalistic society. In this field, they are supreme." By 1950, Dulles thought he had ample evidence of the application of these communist methods to the Third World as well, and he frequently commented on it. A commencement audience at Vanderbilt University received a particularly elaborate description:

> . . . Soviet Communists do not rely primarily on open military aggression as a means of world conquest. Their preferred method is so-called *indirect* aggression.
>
> The Soviet Communists stir up class war, civil war and guerrilla war wherever conditions seem propitious. They did that in Greece. They are doing it now in Indo-China, Burma, Malaya and the Philippines. They used the civil war method to put their followers into control of most of China.
>
> Where the situation is not ripe for large scale civil violence, the Soviet Communist Party introduces its agents into key positions in labor unions and political parties so as to be able to cause strikes, sabotage and parliamentary confusions. In that way Russian leaders make it hard for free governments to discharge their normal responsibilities and thus communists try to lay the foundation for civil unrest. You can see those methods being used in France and Italy.
>
> Throughout all the non-communist world they use propaganda to stir up discontent. They picture their own system as one that will give all the unsatisfied all that they want. They ruthlessly suppress all opponents who

fall under their power and thus strike terror into the hearts of many elsewhere who would otherwise be disposed to resist.

Those are the methods that Soviet Communists use. They have perfected them to a very high degree, and with them they have been extraordinarily successful. These are evil methods, diabolical methods. . . ."[11]

A perspective on Far Eastern affairs colored by alarmed reactions to an international communist conspiracy was quite consistent with earlier Dulles thoughts on the postwar European scene, of course. Significantly, consistency went further than this. Just as in 1945–1949 Dulles had taken off from a base of concerns that only partially attended to Soviet designs on Europe, so in 1950 he would have more to preoccupy him than Soviet designs on China, Korea, and Japan.

Most important, Dulles's new diplomatic assignment in the Far East would result in his appreciation for that region's role in breaking the cycle of economic crisis and war that had so long been at the center of his world view. In the 1930s, Japan had always been coupled with Germany and Italy in Dulles's discussions of the clashes between "dynamic" states and a rigid political economy. Though Japanese actions had often been reprehensible, he had insisted that defenders of the status quo such as the United States had to bear some of the responsibility for this. As he wrote to Lord Lothian in 1940:

> . . . I agree that the basic difficulty in Japan was the universal economic nationalism to which you refer. Except for that the Japanese probably would not have been greatly interested in China. They would doubtless have much preferred to get raw materials and find markets elsewhere. As, however, these possibilities gradually shrank, they then looked to China feeling that if the western white races put trade barriers up against them at least they should have a free hand with the adjoining yellow race.

If there was a certain logic behind Japanese behavior, however, it was a tragic logic, and Dulles always made it clear that he wanted to alter the circumstances that had caused problems rather than simply tolerate the consequences. He argued that there was every reason for the United States and other Western powers to resist Japan's campaign to dominate China—in order to prevent yet more international rigidity and an even greater risk of ultimate war. At the same time, Japanese needs and ambitions would have to be given alternative outlets in a more open global arena. This could be achieved by methods Dulles expounded on at great length throughout the decade: e.g., less restrictive trade and currency practices by the great powers and the "opening up" of the "vast" colonial regions, something of great potential relevance to Asia. Thus, Dulles could tell Wendell Wilkie in September 1949 that Washington should use its "influence toward creating a sound economic basis for peaceful Japanese policies and a China of greater political stability. . . ." And in his critical essay on the Atlantic Charter's status quo orientation, he cited Far Eastern conditions as among those which could benefit from significant change: "There should be adjustments which will assure to Japan effective access to markets and raw materials, so that she may raise the standard of living of her people. But China must be preserved from political domination by Japan or any other alien power."[12]

After American entrance into the Second World War, Japan and its environs remained objects of attention for Dulles. Though there was already some tendency to concentrate on the European scene, the Far East was still regularly seen as an integral part of the more peaceful and prosperous world order he hoped would emerge after victory. Continuing references to freer trade practices and the diminution of imperialistic controls (the second and fourth of the "Six Pillars of Peace"), for example, were always seen as relevant to this area. There was also periodic commentary on the kind of peace settlement that should eventually be developed in the Pacific. A statement on Japan, which he helped draft at the July 1943 Princeton Roundtable, reveals the essence of many Dulles perceptions on the Far East:

> Although the terms exacted from Japan will be severe, as Christians, we urge that they be just, constructive, and not retributive. . . .
>
> Because the restoration of territories now occupied by Japan, notably Formosa, Korea and Manchuria will inevitably deprive her of important features of the economy which she had built up before the war, steps must be taken (e.g. by providing access to markets for her exports and thus the means of obtaining foodstuffs and other vital materials, and by lending capital) to enable her to adjust her postwar economy to the legitimate welfare of her people without detriment to the economies of her neighbors.

The core nature of such attitudes is further demonstrated by the strikingly similar terminology that came out of the Cleveland National Study Conference of January 1945:

> As in the case of Germany, so with Japan, the power and will to make war must be removed. However, Japan's basic economic problems, aggravated by the war and by the expected loss of her colonial possessions must be met by "access, on equal terms to the trade and raw materials of the world" as pledged by the Atlantic Charter "to all States, great or small, victor or vanquished." Treatment of Japan by the United Nations should be favorable to constructive forces within Japanese society, and should aim to bring Japan at an early date into normal relations with the world community.[13]

Explicit references to Japan diminished during the first few postwar years, but Dulles's intense concentration on European affairs offered constant reinforcement for his general desire for politico-economic reforms. When circumstances eventually allowed or encouraged, therefore, he found it extremely easy to transfer judgments and proposals from the Atlantic to the Far Eastern theater. Strong interest in European economic integration was a major but not unique means of creating freer commercial and financial relations among nations in general—and the basic continuing goal could and would be applied to Japan and its neighbors again as time went on. Even more obviously, the kind of peace that Dulles came to urge for Germany had an applicability to Japan that would eventually extend to very detailed ingredients. The "lessons of Versailles," which led him to oppose a heavy reparations burden or severe economic restrictions, were not confined to the European environment, nor was the Wilsonian conception of a liberal peace settlement, which would allow the integration of a reformed enemy into a reformed world order.

His attitudes toward the Soviet Union, forged during the mid-1940s, and his desires for international reforms, which were the product of his entire adult life, would both affect Dulles's views on Far Eastern problems after April 1950. They would be joined by a third preconception as well: his vision of the special role and responsibilities of the United States in the global arena.

It has already been shown that what began as Dulles's youthful enthusiasm for Woodrow Wilson's Great War crusade slowly developed into his near-millennial statements of the Second World War. The economic, military, and spiritual powers of the United States were badges of an exceptional destiny, Dulles believed by the 1940s: Americans, and seemingly only Americans, could break the shackles of conflict and misery that had imprisoned mankind for so long and lead the world to a future of peace and prosperity. During the early days of the Cold War, this exhilirating prospect remained undimmed. War-ravaged Europe continued to be seen as the key laboratory for the working out of Wilsonian conceptions; and if perverse communists created obstacles on the road to a better world order, then both the burden and concomitant glory of overcoming them could be seen as that much greater for the United States.[14]

Though Dulles began to shift his concentration away from Europe in 1949 and 1950, he did not alter the thrust of his commentary on the American mission. He clearly saw it as equally relevant to the Far East and to the "inner citadel." In the "struggle to determine whether ways of peace or ways of violence are to prevail, the United States is called upon to play *the* decisive role," he told an audience at the University of Pennsylvania:

> . . . If the United States does not assume the leadership now freely offered us, then the non-communist world will quickly succumb in a panic of fear. *Resistance cannot be organized except around the United States. . . .*
>
> The stakes are the greatest that were *ever* in jeopardy. They represent nothing less than the sum total of what devout and enterprising men have been able to accomplish throughout the world during the last several centuries. [Emphasis added.]

In June 1950, three weeks before the outbreak of war in Korea, he spoke similarly:

> The peaceful road has become a rough and narrow path and *humanity* will hardly travel it safely *except under the leadership of the United States.* We have that responsibilty not because we want or ask for it, but because we are the most powerful nation on earth, and as such we cannot escape responsibility. Only as we lead the way with wisdom, courage and confidence can mankind escape the abysses that lie on either side—on one side the abyss of war, on the other side the abyss of human servitude. [Emphasis added.][15]

As those statements make clear, Dulles had not dropped the melodramatic tone that had more and more regularly permeated his words in the 1940s. It is arguable, in fact, that the volatile atmosphere of 1949 and 1950 actually encouraged such strong language. Religious imagery, which had been a feature of Dulles's hyperbole for a decade to some degree, seemed to crop up more regularly than at any time since the decline of the Commission on a Just and Durable Peace. One audience was told:

> We have grown mighty and our fame has spread throughout the earth. Hundreds of millions of human beings look now to us. They live in fear, yet they still hope. They are despairing, but still they have faith. . . . they want leadership that would mean fellowship in a great task of *salvation* that would bring them peace. [Emphasis added.]

The Biblical tones and terminology evident here emerged in particular in a whole new round of exhortations to spiritual dynamism. Americans should not rely only on military hardware and economic strength to foil communism and create a better world order, Dulles maintained: as in the past, they should add the special fire of religious faith to their arsenal. Throughout the early months of 1950, he fretted about the way the "free world" was growing "lackadaisical" and the way "our people no longer feel the old sense of mission and of destiny in the world." Though he never really explained why he had reached this conclusion, he did insist it would be suicidal to allow the trend to continue. "Our greatest need is to regain confidence in our spiritual heritage," he wrote in *War or Peace*. "Religious belief in the moral nature and possibilities of man is, and must be, relevant to every kind of society, throughout the ages past and those to come." A few paragraphs later he quoted some of the last words written by Woodrow Wilson: "The sum of the whole matter is this, that our civilization cannot survive materially unless it be redeemed spiritually." In a January speech in Seattle, he surveyed what he described as the great "moral power" of the United States throughout most of its history and concluded with a plea for stoking the fires:

> I am convinced that we need a strong military force and that we should give economic aid within our means. But it is fatal to consider that our objectives must be trimmed and that our policies must be bounded by the reach of our physical fist. . . .
>
> It is up to the churches to shake the American people out of their present suicidal materialistic mood. . . . "Not by might, not by power, but by my spirit, saith the Lord of Hosts."[16]

Dulles's particular approach to the interplay of religion and American foreign policy would eventually become a major source of annoyance for his critics, and it is easy to see how statements like those of 1949 and 1950 could be found grating. They exuded arrogance and self-righteousness, which are doubly unattractive because they masquerade as humble, almost reluctant obedience to divine will. It might be added that spiritual presumptions could also produce near-incredible distortions. An example that emerged at just this time and that has some relevance for Dulles's perception of the American role in the Far East is his explanation of the way Christianity had softened the horrors of imperialism. At a time when communists were tapping reservoirs of anti-Western sentiment in Asia and elsewhere, Dulles tried to persuade colonials and former colonials that they should not exaggerate the problems they had experienced. During the centuries in which "10% of the world's people came to have political dominance over seven or eight times their own number," he argued, "it was Christianity . . . that had made tolerable the world-wide political mastery of the West and that now makes it possible to have a peaceful transition from that mastery to freedom." Missionaries, in particular, had "curbed and offset" the disposition of Europeans and Americans to assume attitudes of racial superiority or to engage in exploitation of subject peoples. "Wherever a soldier or a trader went, a missionary went too," and with him or her "the Christian conception of a universal God who had endowed every person with the right to develop in accordance with the dictates of his individual reason and conscience." Ultimately, Dulles also maintained, "tolerable" Western imperialism was made even better by its "self-liquidating" nature!

> Within the last three years alone, over 500 million people who formerly were in colonial status have become independent and self-governing and another 500 million people have been freed of political shackles with the West. This great transformation, which is the most spectacular in history, is the kind of thing which in the past used to ruin great empires. Now it is taking place on the whole, peacefully, with little violence between East and West, because the peoples of the East feel a sense of fellowship with the West, largely because of what Christianity has done for them . . . the peoples of the West have been taught the Christian view of freedom and equal opportunity for all men, so we see what is now going on as a natural fulfillment of a Christian view of the world and not as a disaster to be formally resisted.

Even allowing for the dollop of overstatement that was usually added to his church-oriented pronouncements, it is not hard to see how such views, voiced regularly in 1949 and 1950, would create a lack of understanding between Dulles and some of the Asian leaders he had come to see as so important to the United States.[17]

III

If Dulles brought an accumulation of preconceptions to his work on the Japanese Peace Treaty, he was joining a Truman team whose attitudes could hardly be described as unformed or open-minded. In some quarters of the Administration, views on the basic nature of the peace settlement and even many of its details had been developed and refined over a long period of time. Dulles was actually to be a relative newcomer in intensively worked territory.

As with Germany, the views of many Washington policy makers regarding Japan had gone through a noticeable cycle by the spring of 1950. Early U.S. plans for the defeated Pacific enemy involved relatively harsh terms: there was a clear presumption of Japanese guilt for causing the Far Eastern War; a clear acceptance of the logic of stripping away conquered territories, suppressing future military strength, imposing punitive reparations burdens; and a clear willingness to create formal agencies that would carry out deep reforms within Japanese society and guarantee obedience to dictated terms for a quarter-century or more. By 1947, a number of factors began to produce significant alterations in this agenda. Congress's concern about the mounting costs of U.S. duties in Germany were easily transferred to the other side of the globe, and both military and civilian authorities became increasingly aware of legislators' chagrin at a bill that had reached $1 million a day for Japan. Within the State Department and some offices of General MacArthur's headquarters in Tokyo, this particular budgetary issue was seen as symptomatic of a larger problem as well. Could a reformed, restructured Japan, working under considerable economic burdens and restrictions, ever produce a stable, relatively prosperous society? Many began to doubt the possibility. Speculation mounted about the threat that ongoing economic weakness posed to the internal stability of the islands; events in China also helped to produce classic Cold War nightmares about the appeal and susceptibility of Japan to the global communist conspiracy. As a result, initial policy inclinations were steadily modified from 1947 on. Occupation authorities essentially reversed the deconcentration program, which had broken up the giant cartels (zaibatsu); plans for extensive reparations were put in low gear, and more than $150 million in aid was provided for industrial rehabilitation. By the fall of 1949 at the latest, some American policy makers had followed the German example to its logical conclusion in the Pacific: Japan too should be reintegrated into the international community on terms that were liberal enough to allow the evolution of a stable society that would be amicably disposed toward the "Free World."

Strongest support for the general idea of a lenient reintegrationist policy came from the State Department and Douglas MacArthur. Appropriate treaty drafts began to take shape between October 1949 and March 1950, the last of which Dulles found waiting for him when he returned to Washington. There was no likelihood of speedy movement, however. Within the Truman Administration as a whole, there had emerged a series of contentious disagreements about particular facets of a peace settlement. There was delaying debate concerning proper negotiating tactics: should the U.S. utilize the Council of Foreign Ministers and risk Soviet obstructionism? Should there be one peace conference or two or none, and when? More significantly, there was determined foot-dragging at the Pentagon about all security aspects of a treaty. As one State memo put it, "Uncertainties in the Far East in the face of a growing Soviet–Communist menace" had created a situation in "which the U.S. military does not want any change in the situation that might increase U.S. security risks"; this meant opposition to any terms that did not guarantee open-ended American base and maneuver rights throughout Japan. Others, including MacArthur, believed this would be a compromise on sovereignty that would plague long-range prospects for cordial cooperation between the sensitive Japanese and the United States. Beyond administration in-fighting, which was serious enough to stymie progress all by itself, there were major problems involving the Allies who would be asked to sign a peace treaty. If American opinions had changed after 1947, the same could not be said for British, Australian, New Zealander, Phillipine, and Indian opinions, among others. Outside the United States, in fact, there was still quite general and sometimes passionate support for an old-fashioned treaty of vengeance and repression. The State Department knew at every stage of its own evolution that it was moving in directions which other governments found alarming, and it rightly anticipated hard, comlex negotiations on reparations, economic restrictions, and Japanese rearmament and security arrangements.[18]

Dulles stepped into the jumble of internal disagreements among the Allies in early April and gave himself two months of briefings and study to sort out the details of his own position: it was one thing to have thought about a peace settlement in the Far East in general terms, quite another to get down to the brass tacks of specific arrangements and clauses. By the first week in June he had begun to piece together what others in Washington might have considered a somewhat eclectic approach.

In crucial basic terms, Dulles predictably endorsed the State Department line. Japan's sovereignty should be restored in a fashion conducive to amicable relations with the U.S. and the Free World: the role of the Occupation should be steadily reduced, "post-treaty control machinery" should be avoided, and plans for Japan's prompt admission to the United Nations should be laid. As the Director of the Office of Northeast Asian Affairs put it, Dulles was "particularly interested" in the economic prerequisites for a friendly, reintegrated Japan. This interest produced precise proposals at a very early date: he argued that the Peace Treaty should "provide full opportunity for peaceful economic development without reparation and with a minimum of, or no, special economic restrictions." He speculated about ship-building capacity and likely raw materials supplies and urged the avoidance of "discriminatory trade provisions against Japan by the Pacific and Southeast Asian countries."

Dulles was dubious, however, about the State Department security proposals that had been developed by the time of his arrival in Washington. Concerned about Pentagon and Allied qualms and responsive to any number of their own concerns, Secretary of State Acheson and his associates had drawn blueprints for an ambitious "Pacific Pact"—a multilateral agreement that would complement a speedily negotiated and lenient Peace Treaty. Similar to NATO, the Pact would pledge signatories to consider an armed attack against Japan as an attack against all, calling for assistance even to the point of using armed forces; in addition, an attack *by* Japan on any signatory was to be considered an attack on all and would yield the same full joint response.

Dulles had analytical and tactical problems with this. His own long-established views on Germany's place in a suspicious European community engendered complete understanding of the need to reassure friends such as Australia and the Philippines, but he thought the type of "Pacific Pact" envisaged by the State Department a poor mechanism. Where would the line be drawn as far as membership was concerned, he asked, recalling his discomfort about suggesting that some European nations were outside U.S. concern when NATO was being designed? Was the Senate likely to accept so grandiose a project for an area that was not part of the "inner citadel," he queried as well? He believed "that the one-for-all and all-for-one commitment of the Atlantic Pact was regarded in the Senate as indicative of a very intimate relation among the nations involved," and he "doubted that the Senate would be willing to have the United States engage in a similar 'brotherhood' undertaking with respect to Japan." More fundamentally, was a major "Pacific Pact" really necessary? He could see some of the strategic implications of the Cold War context in which discussions of Japan had been placed. ("Since Japan from a geographical standpoint is closely encircled [North, West and South] by areas controlled by Communists of dynamic and aggressive tendencies, can Japan be saved from Communism?" as he asked in his first memorandum to Dean Acheson.) Faithful to frequently articulated convictions, however, he insisted that the actual dangers in the foreseeable future involved subversion from *within* a potentially unstable Japan rather than some massive assault from without. As he put it, "He did not anticipate such an attack so long as the USSR continued to be so eminently successful in achieving its objectives by means of indirect aggression." Under the circumstances, a great military alliance seemed an inappropriate response. It would be more logical to concentrate on fostering Japan's internal strength, by means of economic recovery and an expanded "police force, constabulary and coast-guard." If it was felt that more was needed, as salve for the Allies or a warning to Moscow, then limited strategic arrangements could be made to suffice. There might be an agreement among interested Pacific nations simply to declare their concern for Japan's security, in phrasing that should be borrowed from the United Nations Covenant; such an accord could put "greater emphasis on consultation" than existing plans and "make the commitment to use armed force less automatic."[19]

Disapproval of State Department security plans did not make Dulles an ally of the Pentagon, of course: the particulars of respective critiques varied considerably. From his side, at least, it took Dulles several months to figure out just what military leaders wanted with respect to Japan. Told of their concern for bases, his first reaction was to describe himself as "skeptical about the future utility of small bases scattered around the world"; in any event, he considered the arrangement of bases "a technical military problem" which should not delay a Peace Treaty. Weeks later, he seemed to have been persuaded that the Pentagon saw the matter otherwise, but he remained unsure about reasons. Do the Joint Chiefs of Staff "want to use Japan generally as a major advanced *offensive* air base," he asked in June, or did they have in mind some *"defensive"* system "stiffened by a continuing presence of some skeleton U.S. force?" He requested "further clarification of the views of the Defense Department" (Dulles's italics).[20]

Whatever he may have anticipated regarding problems over strategic dispositions from the State Department or the military, Dulles was quickly convinced that there was both sufficient justification and agreement to move ahead rapidly on a Peace Treaty. By June 4, he was publicly citing the need "to act decisively . . . and creatively" in Japan. On June 6, he sent Acheson a lengthy memorandum outlining his views on the key logical ingredients of a treaty and plotting a negotiating schedule that would begin with a Preliminary Peace Conference in Hawaii during the late summer. And on June 14, he set off for Tokyo in order to gather first-hand impressions of the situation there.[21]

After a few days in Seoul, a stopover arranged out of curiosity because of his long association with the Korean issue at the United Nations, Dulles settled down to two weeks of constant meetings in Japan. He was convinced that Douglas MacArthur would be a crucial figure in any initiatives for the foreseeable future and made sure to have several sessions with him: they discussed the overall need for a Peace Treaty and undertook some particular speculation about security arrangements that might satisfy the General's more skeptical colleagues in Washington. To the pleasure of leaders from the Emperor down, Dulles went beyond the Supreme Commander's headquarters and sought out numerous Japanese as well. He consulted with Prime Minister Yoshida and his advisers, the President of the House of Councilors, representatives of organized labor, and leaders of the opposition Socialist and Democratic parties, among many others.

Midway in his schedule, on June 25, Dulles had his attention wrenched away from Tokyo by the dramatic North Korean invasion across the 38th parallel. Only days before, he had been in Korea. He had met with Syngman Rhee, spoken to the National Assembly, and toured the North–South border. Though a correspondent-friend in his party had expressed the conviction that a conflict was brewing in the tense area, primarily because of Rhee's evolving military plans to move north, Dulles and most others were shocked by the apparent suddenness of Pyongyang's move. In an atmosphere of mounting alarm, there were hasty deliberations about the nature of an appropriate response, and it took weeks before anyone was ready to give a Japanese Peace Treaty full attention once more.

Dulles could not but have felt an integral part of the U.S. policy-making community as it gathered momentum during the early stages of the Korean crisis. Except for one tactical disagreement that would gnaw at him occasionally over the months, his views and policy proposals meshed easily with those of his colleagues in Tokyo and Washington. In basic analytical terms, he was as inclined as Truman Administration leaders in general to place this new conflict into a melodramatic Cold War context. In his June 19 address to the National Assembly in Seoul, he had described "the constant struggle between good and evil" in which Koreans were being forced to participate, and he had praised the South's resistance to Soviet expansionism "on the front line of freedom." The North's invasion became a new maneuver in "the world strategy of international communism" being masterminded in Moscow. As to what the maneuver was supposed to accomplish, Dulles suggested at least three possibilities. Korea itself may have been the primary target. "The open military assault . . . occurred because the Republic of Korea was too good a society to be tolerated on the otherwise communist dominated mainland of North Asia," he told one audience on July 7. The South "was growing in such a healthy way that its presence on the Continent of Asia was an embarrassment to the communist areas," was how he put it in a national radio broadcast: the communist aggression was designed to crush "a happy, wholesome society." (Such overviews of the South Korean scene were intriguing new examples of Dulles's occasional penchant for wild hyperbole in public statements. Behind the scenes, in contrast, he could talk in much more ambiguous terms: in one memorandum to Dean Rusk, he urged against any tendency "to ditch Syngman Rhee" by saying that "he is far from perfect but he is a great patriot and anticommunist and organized his country so that they put up a good fight, and he is not as bad as Communist smear portrays him.") Or perhaps Japan was the key object of attention. In part, at least, Dulles could see the Soviets moved by:

. . . the desire to embarrass our plans for putting Japan more and more onto a peace basis, with increasing self-government in the Japanese people themselves. . . .

The Communists must have feared the positive and constructive steps which we were considering in regard to Japan. They probably felt that if they could capture all of Korea this would throw a roadblock in the path of Japan's future development. The Russians already hold the island of Sakhalin, just to the north of Japan, and Korea is close to the south of Japan. Thus . . . Japan would be between the upper and lower jaws of the Russian Bear. That obviously would make it more difficult to provide the Japanese people with security as self-governing, unarmed members of the free world.

Finally, the United States itself might be the ultimate goal. Referring back to his frequently elaborated theory of long-range Stalinist goals in Asia, Dulles believed that "the communists doubtless calculated that if the attack failed through the use of United States force . . . the process would bog down the West in the mire of anti-colonialism. . . ." Moscow would find it valuable to have Americans on the wrong side of "an all-Asia struggle of the 'masses' against the 'colonial imperialists' and their 'lackeys.' "[22]

Dulles's scenarios matched those developed by many Washington figures in mid-1950. So did his conclusion that if Korea, Japan, and/or the United States were experiencing a new and dramatic attack by the international communist conspiracy, then a counterattack was required. Only hours after news of the North Korean move had reached Tokyo, Dulles fired off a cable urging action on Secretary of State Acheson. If the Republic of Korea could not repel the attack, he said, "US force should be used even though this risks Russian counter moves. To sit by while Korea is overrun by unprovoked armed attack would start disastrous chain of events leading most probably to world war." In the days and weeks ahead, he offered regular reiteration of this advice and vigorous public support for the Administration's efforts. There was a manifest need for a policy of "firmness and resolution," he concluded; Truman was responding with "statesmanship of a very high order."[23]

Having joined the chorus calling for a strong response, Dulles went on to endorse most of the particular techniques that were forthcoming under this banner. He had himself immediately suggested utilization of the United Nations and was particularly pleased by Truman's steady reliance on the organization: the U.S. and other members were "waging peace," he said at one point, making it clear "that aggressors cannot now act with impunity." He also had praise for the refusal of his fellow policy makers to "become mere battle-watchers" and their sensitivity to "vital political objectives" beyond the hills of Korea. Truman Administration initiatives regarding Formosa, Indochina, and the Philippines thus received Dulles's solid backing.

Only one tactical move made Dulles uncomfortable—the decision to utilize extensive numbers of American ground forces in Korea. As early as July 1, he was told at a meeting with Acheson, Secretary of the Army Pace, and others that serious thought was being given to sending two U.S. divisions to Korea from Japan. He expressed strong immediate reservations:

> I said that this was a very serious decision because the North Korean army could not be treated as a limited force with a specific number of planes, tanks and troops. It was subject to maintenance and expansion out of the virtually unlimited resources controlled by the Soviet Union in East Asia, including Communist China. In that part of the world we could be a sea and land power but it was hazardous for us to challenge communist power on the mainland.

He proceeded to interrogate Pace, in particular about "Defense Establishment" estimates concerning probable results of ground force operations. Could the communists be defeated "without such a concentration there of United States power as would dangerously expose us elsewhere?" Would a hasty commitment "lead to a Dunkirk?" He also mentioned his last conversation with MacArthur in Tokyo, a few days earlier, in which the General had said "that anyone who advocated commitment of U.S. troops . . . ought to have his head examined."

The Secretary of the Army evidenced some qualms of his own in responding to Dulles and admitted that there was no "reliable estimate of the results which might flow from a land operation in Korea." He quite explicitly said that the sending of divisions would not take place "because of *their* desire to do so, but because they thought it necessary to support the political policies of the government." This was hardly comforting for Dulles. He reaffirmed his opposition to the transfer of troops and urged design of "a political policy which would be adequately sustained by the use of sea and air power in relation to Korea." Such a policy "would be awkward," he admitted, "but it would be better than a Dunkirk or fatal exposure elsewhere. . . ."

Dulles's concerns were not shared by Truman's principal counselors, and before this July 1 meeting was completed the decision to commit U.S. troops was approved. Indeed, Dulles later said that it was his "impression that the divisions were already *en route* and that the discussion was academic." For not the first time, he found himself a Republican adviser who was in general but not full agreement with an evolving Democratic policy. And, for not the first time, he learned to live with it. Periodically in the months ahead, he would express continuing qualms about military tactics. Weighing alternatives that included "economic sanctions, blockade [and] air cover to the Republic of Korea's army," he told Walter Lippmann he had "doubts as to the wisdom of engaging our land forces on the Continent of Asia as against an enemy army that could be nourished from the vast reservoirs of the U.S.S.R." But the "doubts" never became particularly intimidating. What voice Dulles gave to them remained soft and always private, in contrast to his more forceful and fully public disagreements with the Administration's design of the details of the Marshall Plan. More to the point perhaps, discussion of his reservations even with friends or confidential correspondents seemed to be prodded only by the occasional military crises encountered in Korea: when the course of battle was going well or tolerably for the United States, Dulles was inclined to note only his overall agreement with Democratic policies.[24]

It deserves emphasis that Dulles's feelings, such as they were, about the use of American ground forces were not evidence of some basically temperate approach to the Korean conflict. They were part of a very specific tactical debate that never translated into disagreement about the overall direction and goals of U.S. policy. This was true at the beginning, when he endorsed action within hours. It remained true even as the nature of the crisis changed or was changed. In July and August 1950, Truman and his advisers transformed an initially defensive response into a more aggressive and long-range tactic: it was decided, in particular, that as the communists were pushed back, MacArthur's forces would move north of the 38th parallel and undertake a formal reunification of Korea under United Nations' supervision. In the heated emotional atmosphere of that summer, Dulles was as ready as most other U.S. policy makers to give strong support to this alteration of objectives. In a memorandum for Paul Nitze and the Policy Planning Staff, he offered numerous justifications. Most importantly, he saw no reason to allow the 38th parallel to demark an "asylum" for "the aggressor." It would be "folly" to allow North Korean forces to regroup in a privileged sanctuary only to "attack again the now ravaged and weakened Republic of Korea." Rather than expose the South to "ever-present danger of new war . . . the North Korean Army should be destroyed . . . even if this requires pursuit. . . . That is the only way to remove the menace." Besides, Dulles argued, "Neither equity nor good sense dictates that an unprovoked act of aggression should occur without risk of loss to the aggressor. . . . There must be a penalty to such wrong-doing unless we want to encourage its repetition." He did offer two caveats. First, military leaders would have to be confident of carrying the operation through to a conclusion. "In my opinion, there is every reason to go beyond the 38th Parallel except *possibly* one," he told Nitze in August *"and that is our incapacity to do so* and the fact that the attempt might involve us much more deeply in a struggle on the Asiatic mainland with Soviet and Chinese Communist manpower. . . " (emphasis added). Second, even a successful resolution would have to have narrower parameters than some might imagine. "I think we must recognize that the portions of North Korea which are close to Vladivostok and Port Arthur are particularly sensitive areas from the standpoint of the Soviet Union," he wrote; therefore, "I would not suppose that a united Korea would necessarily include the North Hamgyong Province . . . or the North Heian Province. . . ." Since his first condition seemed to be met by the circumstances of the fall and early winter of 1950 and his second was irrelevant to immediate moves, there was ample room for Dulles's enthusiasm concerning the evolving U.S. policy in Korea.[25]

As a highly visible representative of bipartisanship in foreign policy, Dulles could hardly have avoided involvement in the policy deliberations spurred by the Korean explosion. Nor would he have wanted to, given his experiences in Far Eastern affairs in general. At no point, however, did Dulles evidence any desire to extend involvement into preoccupation. Immediately after his return to Washington on June 29, he made it clear that crises in Korea notwithstanding, he was anxious to proceed with the matter that had engaged his attention in April—a Japanese Peace Treaty. Indeed, as he argued on any number of occasions, "the Korean attack makes it more important, rather than less important, to act" on Japan. He saw practical reasons for this, such as the obvious desirability of lifting occupational and policy responsibilities from now heavily burdened American shoulders. He also saw a more fundamental logic. "The very fact that the attack in Korea may be aimed at Japan and designed to check positive and constructive action there shows how important it is to take such action," he maintained. Communist plans should be foiled by a U.S. policy designed to stabilize and strengthen Japan and to integrate it into the Free World. "If matters drift because of total preoccupation with the Korean war," he warned Acheson, *"we may lose in Japan more than we can gain in Korea"* (emphasis added).[26]

Neither Acheson nor other State Department leaders really needed convincing. By July 21, the Secretary of State had agreed to follow a Dulles suggestion to go to the President for uneqivocal authorization to proceed with the negotiation of a treaty and on July 24, Truman gave it.

With the go-ahead from the White House, Dulles faced an obvious first task: the clarification of a basic United States position regarding the nature of a Japanese settlement. He spent the better part of the next two months accomplishing this, preparatory to undertaking negotiations with American Allies. On most questions, ingredients fell into place quite easily. There had been broad agreement among many policy makers for some time about the desirability of lenient terms, which would allow the integration of a prosperous, friendly Japan into a peaceful Free World community: earlier proposals concerning full sovereignty, opposition to reparations, minimal economic restrictions, and United Nations membership, for example, were thus resurrected in the drafting efforts now overseen by Dulles.

Only one issue threatened to bog the new treaty effort down. Throughout 1949 and early 1950, State Department and Pentagon officials had testily argued about the kind of security arrangements that might be imposed on defeated Japan. Would Dulles be able to work out a policy on bases, facilities, and troops that would be accepted by all of his own Washington colleagues, much less the leaders of other governments he had yet to encounter? Yes, as it turned out, and more easily than might have been anticipated. The debate within the Administration had actually been more tactical than substantive all along. Careful reading of earlier State Department proposals makes it clear that there was no lack of concern in that quarter for the long-range security of Japan and the utility of the former enemy to anticommunist efforts in the Pacific. Problems really stemmed from disagreements about *how* such goals could be achieved. Where Defense favored an indefinite prolongation of an Occupation that gave the U.S. all it needed, State insisted that substitute arrangements would have to be worked out in order to avoid resentment against continuing control and that those arrangements would have to be of such a form as to encourage willing support from the sensitive Japanese. Dulles's first reactions to the treaty debate, it should be added, revealed views like those of the department he had joined. He indicated on April 7 that he knew of and had no doubts about the logic of a U.S. base on Okinawa. As to bases elsewhere in Japan, he was uninformed and a bit dubious, but not opposed: it was really "a technical military problem," he concluded, and the only warning he offered was that "bases in a hostile country would be useless and the Japanese must be willing . . . to request the United States to establish bases. . . ." Dulles did emphasize his own heightened concern about "internal" order in the aftermath of a Peace Treaty, but this only made him more rather than less attentive to the need for adequate security arrangements.[27]

His June visit to Japan and the outbreak of war in Korea gave Dulles, and perhaps other State Department figures, a reinforced sense of overall strategic objectives. He was dismayed by the "confused and uncertain" atmosphere of Tokyo, by the lack of "evidence that the Japanese had thought through the significance of their position in the world of today." Prime Minister Yoshida was "vague" about security arrangements and inclined to rely on naive talk of other nations' respect for his country's disarmament and constitutional renunciation of war. Worse, as far as Dulles was concerned, there was almost universal recognition of the inadequacy of measures to deal with "peace and order within Japan. . . ." Using sketchy data supplied by the State Department and Occupation authorities about left-wing activities, Dulles concluded that "the Japanese police was not strong and unified enough to cope adequately with any Communist agitation which might arise. . . ." He did believe the Korean crisis would have a valuable salutary effect on leaders in Tokyo. "With the North Korean attack and successes and the consequent increasing Communist menace," he reported, "the Japanese began to see that there is no simple solution of their security problem." At a diplomatic reception held June 26, he found "more open admission than had previously been obtained of the continuing need of United States military forces' remaining in Korea." And when he prodded Dean Acheson on July 19, he specifically referred to this as one of the reasons to move ahead rapidly: "The Japanese people have been in somewhat of a postwar stupor. The Korean attack is awakening them and I think that their mood for a long time may be determined by whether we take advantage of this awakening to bring them an insight into the possibilities of the free world and their responsibility as a member of it."[28]

With heightened concerns of his own and a sense that the Japanese would be more malleable than before, Dulles was quite ready to aim at security arrangements that would satisfy Pentagon as well as State Department policymakers. During July and August he and his associates carried out studies and discussions dealing with the acquisition of bases, arrangements for full military maneuverability throughout the islands, the recentralization and supplying of the Japanese police and coast guard, and the creation of an FBI-like "investigative and surveillance agency," among other things. The proposals that emerged, as Dulles himself described them, "gave the United States the right to maintain in Japan as much force as we wanted, anywhere we wanted, for as long as we wanted. . . ." Even at this, there were a few tricky moments with the Pentagon. Defense Secretary Louis Johnson proved personally irritable and uncooperative at many points (Acheson believed he was mentally unstable), and there was an abiding skepticism about the State Department's desire for speed. Truman's adamant stand seemed to help with the former and a significant concession finally overcame the latter in early September. In a virtual mini-treaty signed by Acheson and Johnson it was agreed that "the Treaty shall not become.effective until such time as the interests of the United States dictate and in no event until after favorable resolution of the present United States military situation in Korea."[29] Dulles and others would shortly start an end run around this clause, but for the time being it cleared the Washington decks and allowed substantive negotiations with the Allies.

17

Focus on Eastern Asia, 1950–1952: II

I

STATE DEPARTMENT SPECULATION about treaty making procedures had followed traditional lines prior to Dulles's appointment. It was generally assumed that there were two options: that the Council of Foreign Ministers, which had thus far dealt with the European treaties, could serve as the venue for negotiations; or that the delineation of desired policies in Washington would be followed by American invitations to one or more peace conferences at which negotiations on the details of a Japanese settlement would take place. Neither alternative seemed attractive. There was particularly extensive speculation about the possibility of obstreperous behavior by the Soviets in both settings, the assumption being that Moscow would try to prevent repetition of the West German pattern of integrating a defeated enemy into the "Free World." Truman and the National Security Council had decided in December 1949 that a Japanese Peace Treaty lacking Moscow's final approval was a perfectly viable objective for the United States, but this was only likely to increase Moscow's determination to disrupt any kind of international gathering dealing with Japan.[1]

When a uniform U.S. position began to take shape in August, Dulles suggested another method for proceeding: bilateral talks with each of the Allies and Japan in turn. He held open the possibility of "a preliminary and/or final 'Peace Conference'" somewhere down the road, but also emphasized that "it might be decided to proceed by diplomatic channels" right up to the end of the Peace Treaty process. Both Acheson and Truman quickly approved this strategy, noting no doubt several potential benefits. Aside from minimizing opportunities for Soviet obstructionism and grandstanding, bilateral negotiations offered a way around what had become a thorny China problem for the United States. Great Britain and other important Allies had recognized the communist government in Peking by mid-1950 and were assuming that it would represent "China" in any negotiations concerning Japan. Initially, the State Department seemed at least partially open to this possibility. When Dulles first speculated on procedure in June, he envisioned a conference to which "both the Nationalist and Communist Regimes were to be invited, with one vote each when they disagree, and a single vote when they agree. . . ." During the summer, however, particularly after the outbreak of war in Korea, opinion on formal or even tacit recognition of Peking hardened, and Washington opted for exclusive loyalty to Chiang Kai-shek. Dulles found it easy enough to live with this, mindful if nothing else of the concerns of some of his Republican associates, and he specifically urged bilateral talks on Japan as a way of getting around some Allied qualms. Since it would be up to the American negotiators to choose the governments they would consult, they could decide unilaterally to meet only with Nationalist representatives and simply, in Dulles's words, "avoid the problem of Chinese participation in a Peace Conference."[2] Though it is hard to say whether they anticipated it in advance, Dulles and others in Washington also found that a one-on-one strategy would make it easier to deal with ostensibly friendly Allies: something of a "divide and conquer" concept emerged in which concerted resistance to American policies on subjects such as reparations seemed less likely.

The first step in the bilateral process was a simple one to arrange, involving no more than the trip back to New York, which Dulles had already been planning for the opening of the fifth session of the General Assembly. With so many high-ranking representatives of other governments likely to be present at some point during the several months the session would last, it seemed to offer a fortuitous setting for what were dubbed "informal discussions." Dulles would meet Allied leaders during breaks in the United Nations routine and use rather low-key conversations to start building momentum for the complex negotiations that were bound to come.

Though a formal "draft treaty" prepared under Dulles's supervision was available, more casual initial discussions were encouraged when only an outline of American "principles" was given to representatives of Australia, Burma, Canada, the Nationalist Chinese Government on Taiwan, France, India, Indonesia, the Netherlands, New Zealand, Pakistan, the Philippines, the Soviet Union, and the United Kingdom. A state of war with Japan should come to an end, it was proposed, and the defeated enemy should be welcomed as a sovereign "equal" into "the society of free peoples." Territorial terms should conform with assumptions that virtually all had accepted since 1945, meaning the surrender of Tokyo's control over numerous possessions: Korea would become independent; the U.S. would undertake trusteeship over the Ryukyu and Bonin Islands; and Formosa, the Pescadores, South Sakhalin, and the Kuriles would have their specific fates negotiated by the victors (or pending failure to reach agreement, by the General Assembly.) The economic settlement should be lenient enough to allow healthy recovery from the damages of war. In the American definition, this would translate as a waiving of virtually all claims to reparations and acceptance of the idea that Japan and the victors would establish the same kind of nonrestrictive commercial and financial relationships that the United States was encouraging among all nations. As for Japan's long-range safety and the question of the Allies' future protection vis-à-vis Japan, Washington proposed that pending the creation of an effective United Nations security system, "there would be continuing cooperative responsibility between Japanese facilities and U.S. and perhaps other forces for the maintenance of international peace and security in the Japan area."[3]

Between mid-September and mid-November, Dulles had numerous opportunities to delineate the reactions of other governments to these American "principles." Both personal meetings and the formal written responses that sometimes followed revealed precisely the kind of problems he and others would have anticipated. He heard predictable disagreements about the possibility of eliminating reparations, for example, from the representatives of Australia, Burma, New Zealand, the Philippines, and Taiwan. All of these but the latter also expressed grave concern about "the absence of military restrictions" on the defeated enemy: Australian Prime Minister Spender spoke of needing "firm guarantees against Japanese aggression" and New Zealand's Foreign Minister made it clear that his country had to evaluate potential treaty terms "from the standpoint of her own 'precarious' security position." The British were in relative accord, but Dulles found some considerable concern about the prospect of a "resurgence" of Japanese "commercial competition during the post-Treaty period" if no restrictions were imposed on industrial capacity or trading privileges.

As far as Dulles was concerned, however, none of these reactions created insurmountable obstacles to pushing ahead with a Japanese Peace Treaty. He believed most Allied leaders "realize they are up against a practical impossibility" as far as reparations were concerned. They seemed to be going through the motions of protest in order to satisfy voters at home and would fall into line if Washington stuck to its position. Concerns about security against a revived Japan went much deeper, Dulles felt, but the State Department had long before concluded that some form of long-range American commitment to the region could be used to assuage understandable fears. As he put it in mid-November, "I think Australia and New Zealand will give way if we can find some formula for assuring them of U.S. protection in the event of attack. . . . It ought to be possible to find a formula—perhaps a Presidential Declaration—which would . . . clear the way. . . ." As for British anxieties, Dulles and his colleagues seem to have believed that London could be brought around through toughness and persuasion: one instruction to the U.S. Ambassador in the United Kingdom said that "the British must face the realities of the situation and be prepared to meet Japanese competition if Japan is to be kept oriented toward the West and free from Communist pressures."[4]

Not even a critical Soviet response to the broad American proposals of September 1950 seemed to Dulles to stand in the way of speedy progress on a Peace Treaty. The Soviets criticized plans for U.S. trusteeship of the Ryukyus, site of the major Okinawa military base; they also questioned the prospect of Japanese rearmament and drew attention to Washington's attempt to ignore Peking in the discussions being held. But neither Dulles nor any of his colleagues really cared what Moscow thought about these subjects. Given the previous consensus that a treaty lacking Soviet approval was likely to be the only kind of treaty acceptable to the United States, Dulles was able to be quite blunt in his conversation with Jacob Malik, Moscow's Security Council representative: "It was our hope that the treaty would be signed by all the nations represented on the Far Eastern Commission [the occupation advisory body on which all of the principal victors sat]," Dulles told Malik, "but . . . if any failed to participate it was our intention to proceed anyway. . . ." Dulles did make what he doubtless considered an effort at meaningful dialogue, but both the premise from which he was operating and the thrust of his reasoning made the effort gratuitous. The Soviets should adopt "a realistic view towards this treaty," he advised Malik:

> We had been unable to agree on a treaty for Germany and Austria to date largely because each of the four powers was afraid that it would lose a position of strength in those areas which it now held. In Japan the Soviet Union had no such position and would lose nothing by adhering to the type of treaty suggested, and if it took a realistic attitude, it could make a real contribution towards the relaxation of tensions without sacrificing anything of importance.

(Malik responded that "the realistic approach should be mutual. Ever since the end of the war, United States military power had flowed into areas which the war had left in a state of political or military vacuum until the Soviet Union was now surrounded by United States military bases. The United States had a base on Okinawa but the Soviet Union had none in the Caribbean.")[5]

Convinced that friendly governments could be dealt with and the Soviets ignored, Dulles was ready by mid-November to accelerate the Peace Treaty negotiations. He saw no reason to delay a visit to Tokyo for detailed discussions with Japanese leaders and speculated about how to follow this up with negotiations on precise treaty terms with the Allies. Then, beginning on November 26, massive numbers of Communist Chinese troops crossed the Yalu River to fight in Northern Korea and pushed United States forces back below the 38th parallel within three dizzying weeks. Nothing on the Asian horizon looked quite so simple after this.

Dulles and other American policy makers were stunned by the basic fact of Chinese intervention in Korea and then devastated by its scale and success. After months of MacArthur's progress and assurances, after even more months of planning regarding the future of the East Asian region in general, it seemed as if the bottom had dropped out and catastrophes of many kinds were threatening. "The situation is indeed desperate, almost numbing," Dulles wrote his ailing friend Arthur Vandenberg on November 30. "We were on the way out in Korea," he told the American delegation at the United Nations; what was happening was nothing short of "a major disaster." There would be awful reverberations elsewhere too. It might prove impossible to keep Indochina from falling to the communists because Peking's now obvious readiness to marshal armed strength could produce "a hopeless military situation" he told Senator

Taft. He worried about the "grave psychological repercussions" of Chinese victories as well: given severe American reversals in Korea, what would happen to the will to resist among the Japanese, who were in so delicate a position already; among the Indonesians and Filipinos; even, or perhaps especially, among Western Europeans?[6]

Visions of cataclysm were striking, but intriguingly short-lived for Dulles and most others in the Truman Administration. Late November and early December 1950 proved to be a trying period that yielded a renewed sense of direction. A whole cluster of interrelated Asian and European issues was reappraised in the harsh light of retreat and though a convincing sense of confidence would only slowly return, an agenda for action rather than surrender quickly emerged.

In Dulles's case, "numbing" despair turned into outrage and determination within a week. He was soon ready to support the proposals forthcoming from Truman's principal advisers and was pushing some of his own ideas as well. Regarding Korea itself, he offered loyal support to Administration efforts—in spite of what may have been contrary temptations. He had had doubts about the extent of U.S. ambitions in North Korea all along and had criticized easy assumptions about moving to the Yalu on several occasions. When he saw Robert Taft a few days after the Chinese move, he said that "through underestimating the risks, we may have been sucked into a major military disaster in Korea. . . ." Disaster in an absolute sense did not descend, however, as MacArthur's forces regrouped and began a move back toward the 38th parallel early in the new year. Dulles found such developments tolerable and kept his grievances private. As in the past, he even endorsed continued military action and United Nations maneuvers. He was not sure how much could be done at first: "it is important to hold at least a sizeable beachhead in south Korea," was the limited goal he set in a November 30 memorandum—but he believed the effort should be made.[7]

With respect to the Chinese who had seemingly caused the new crisis in Korea, Dulles was angered enough to give his already hard position an even more aggressive thrust. "What has happened shows that our policies have been sound in so far as they have recognized the impossibility of separating the Chinese and Soviet communist, at least for the predictable future," he told Acheson on November 30. "The mistake has been inadequate appraisal of the danger that resulted from the hostile alliance." If Peking was going to do Moscow's bidding in Asia, in spite of its internal problems and limited resources, then the United States would have to proceed with more vigorous policies.

This conclusion involved some change of direction for Dulles. After a

466

fairly typical hard-nosed Republican reaction to the Chinese developments of 1949, his enthusiasm for action was cooled by Peking's low profile and problems elsewhere. By mid-1950, he was even considering the
possibility of cutting free from the Nationalists. In one conversation with
a high-ranking representative from Formosa, he said "that I had in all
frankness to say to him that there had been both in official quarters and in
American public opinion a very complete loss of confidence in the will of
the Nationalist forces to fight." He remained opposed to recognition of
Peking and committed to the possibility of U.N. protection for Formosa,
but he had become dubious about the latter's potential in a long-range
propaganda struggle with the mainland: he speculated that Chiang's
followers "had not developed the type of national and spiritual loyalties
such as prevailed in the Western countries. If that were the case, there was
nothing to be done about it." During fall meetings at the General Assembly, where the future of Formosa was expected to come up for discussion late in the proceedings, he became a regular advocate of devising
some kind of procedure to "neutralize the island."

Events in Korea pushed Dulles back to his earlier position regarding
the "Red regime" in Peking, in the sense that he came once more to favor a
policy more dynamic than "watchful waiting." "We can not safely go on
playing a purely defensive role," he insisted. To Taft, Vandenberg,
Acheson, and others, he urged using Formosa "as a base for *covert and perhaps open Chinese activities against the mainland.* . . . Consideration should
be given to the possibility of *stimulating guerrilla and insurrectional activities
in China against the Communist government.* We presently have good will
and friends, but this will not be indefinitely available in the face of propaganda and purge" (emphasis added). He did assume there were Chinese
who could be stimulated in these directions and that they would carry the
lion's share of day-to-day efforts: he was willing to conceive of U.S. air and
naval power protecting Formosa, but remained as convinced as ever that
"the United States should not engage itself in mainland operations." Still,
even with these caveats, Dulles had clearly become more aggressively inclined toward Peking then he had yet been.[8]

Determined new actions in Korea and China were means of dealing
with the critical problems of late 1950 for Dulles, but rapid progress on a
Japanese Peace Treaty was even more important. "Japan is, with Germany, one of the two great assets that the Soviet power seeks for exploitation in aid of its aggressive policies," he wrote on December 8: it was the
element of the East Asian equation whose loss would be the most
dangerous. Six months earlier he had warned Acheson that too much
concentration on the mainland war was risky for this reason—"we may

lose in Japan more than we can gain in Korea"—and he repeated that warning now. Washington's earlier commitment to establish a sovereign, stable, and secure Japan was as logical as it had ever been, and nothing should be allowed to divert efforts in this direction. Indeed, "time is of the essence" he advised the Secretary of State. The prospect of a "Korean defeat" was creating "disquiet in Japan" and "increasing doubt on the part of the Japanese leaders as to the wisdom of any definitive commital to our cause." If Washington did not move quickly, it was easy to imagine a point of no return, where "delay will be fatal to our hopes as regards Japan." Speedy action might save the situation, however: "there is probably more chance of mobilizing Japanese public opinion and getting a Japanese commitment now than in a month or two."[9]

The operative ingredient in Dulles's injunctions was a request for authorization to go to Tokyo in order to undertake concrete negotiations with the Japanese. He urged speed, but waited almost six weeks for high-level clearance. A strongly supportive Acheson found obstacles that took time to overcome. The Secretary himself was almost unavoidably preoccupied with immediately critical developments in Korea. More importantly, the Pentagon's initial reservations about a transformation of the U.S. position in Japan were dramatically reinforced by the dismaying military reverses being experienced. Still, Truman had overruled the military doubters in September, and when the early weeks of the new year suggested that a complete collapse in Korea had been avoided, he gave Dulles the go-ahead. On January 10, he appointed him "Special Representative of the President, with the personal rank of Ambassador" and authorized a visit to Japan and any other countries that seemed "necessary to bring a Japanese Peace Settlement to a satisfactory conclusion."[10]

II

Dulles arrived in Tokyo on January 25 and spent the next two and a half weeks engaged in what he considered the most crucial remaining work of the peacemaking process. Friendly Allies would fall into line behind the essentials of an American treaty, he had concluded in November, but what about the Japanese? With memories of Versailles and the 1930s still sharp in his mind, he was convinced that genuine acquiescence in peace terms by the defeated enemy itself was a fundamental necessity for long-range success. "The United States and its Pacific friends have not the power to continue indefinitely to exert the necessary force to keep Japan restrained under the terms of a punitive or restrictive treaty," Dulles had told the Philippine Foreign Minister in September, anymore than the victors of World War I had been able to repress Germany for any length of time. "Our aim, therefore, must be to take a calculated risk and produce such a treaty as will encourage Japan of her own free will to cast her lot with us. . . ." It was time to find out from the Japanese just what kind of treaty they could accept with sincere conviction. [11]

The particular circumstances of early 1951 made negotiations with the Japanese very delicate as far as Dulles was concerned. Reverses in Korea had had "grave psychological repercussions. . . ." Could the United States and the other victors persuade the Japanese to go along with them in spite of this? Immediately after Chinese intervention in Korea, Dulles had seemed dubious about the prospect. Strong doubts permeated a December 8 explanation of the need for a trip to Tokyo, for example: "*if Japan is willing on certain terms to accept commitment to our cause, then these terms should be ascertained to see whether the price is practical and worth paying*"; a mission "bearing in mind U.S. capabilities and objectives, legal, economic, and military, would ascertain *what, if any, arrangement were feasible*" (emphasis added). A month later he had become somewhat more confident, but still clearly anticipated hard tasks. Conscious of their region's problems and their own greater value accordingly, the Japanese were likely to have substantive prerequisites for genuine cooperation with the "Free World"—a price tag on which conditions and demands would be entered. Dulles put it quite bluntly to the Senate Foreign Relations Committee a few days before going to Tokyo: "the real purpose of his trip," he said, "was to find out how dependable a commitment could be obtained from the Japanese Government to align itself with the nations of the free world against Communist imperialism, and *what the cost to the United States would be*" (emphasis added). It might prove difficult and annoying for Americans and other victors to have to pay these costs. Dulles himself seemed to find it frustrating that under existing pressures certain U.S. desires "now become matters to be negotiated for and obtained as fully as possible, rather than conditions which in September it seemed that we could obtain unconditionally merely by stipulating them." Nevertheless, whatever his own or Allied qualms might prove to be, negotiations with the Japanese were a fundamental necessity; there was no alternative but to deal with them as essentially equals even before a Peace Treaty officially recognized them as such. As he put it upon arrival in Tokyo, "We look upon Japan as a party to be consulted and not as a vanquished nation to be dictated to by the victors." [12]

Before leaving for Tokyo, Dulles logically tried to estimate some of the particulars of Japanese concerns. His best guess was that there would be a package of political, economic, and strategic expectations. As he summed them up for Acheson, the Japanese would almost surely want "a basic decision by the U.S. to seek to maintain and defend the island chain of Japan, Ryukyus, Formosa, and the Philippines and, in particular, a certain commitment to Japan in terms of sea and air power; certain economic assurances and a prompt restoration of Japanese sovereignty. . . ." He proved close to the mark in his identification of subjects that came up for discussion, though he seems to have anticipated a good deal more trouble than actually emerged concerning some of them. In his numerous meetings with Prime Minister Yoshida and other government officials, leaders of the major opposition parties, and representatives of business groups, universities, and labor unions, he discovered a broad consensus on the fundamentals of U.S. policy. Where problems arose at all, it was because of the complexity of working out detailed arrangements rather than any substantive discord.

Concerning political arrangements, it is hard to imagine how the Japanese could have had difficulties with the approach Dulles presented to them. From the beginning of his work on a Peace Treaty, he had known the State Department's approach presumed "a very complete restoration of sovereignty of Japan free of onerous restrictions." This was made abundantly clear to Prime Minister Yoshida and his associates as outlines and drafts of treaty terms were presented to them, and they never, understandably, raised questions about it. Economic questions were somewhat more complicated, but equally easy to resolve. For reasons that were only partially connected with Japanese sensitivities, Dulles and virtually all policy makers in Washington had long since concluded that the imposition of a heavy reparations burden on the defeated enemy would be unwise. It was proposed, therefore, that a treaty clause specify that "all parties would waive claims arising out of acts taken during the war. . . ." There would be two exceptions granted to the victors, allowing retention of some Japanese property within their own territories and the restoration of Allied properties within Japan, but these were quite minor items in relative terms and Yoshida made no effort to resist them. The American position on other kinds of economic impositions was almost identically lenient. All suggestions from the Allies (e.g., limits on shipbuilding capacity urged by the British) were disregarded. In keeping with Dulles's and general American policy on nonrestrictive trade practices, it was specified that Japan should extend "most-favored-nation" treatment to all of the treaty's signatories, yet even here Tokyo was to be allowed to back off in individual cases if they were not granted equivalent treatment. Only in one instance did anything like an economic restriction on Japan emerge. After prodding, Yoshida "voluntarily" agreed to undertake negotiations with interested states about his country's long-controversial fishing practices and to respect the limits observed by others in a number of "conserved fisheries" around the Pacific and Indian Oceans. These were actions to be undertaken outside the purview of a formal peace settlement, but the assumption of Dulles and the Japanese was that it would help defuse some of the Allied pressure for harsher economic treaty terms in general. [13]

As significant as the avoidance of heavy reparations burdens and commercial restrictions in the Peace Treaty was to Dulles, it should be added that he wanted to go considerably beyond this in dealing with economic questions. He had believed for many years that an economically healthy Japan (or Germany) would be a more temperate and cooperative member of the international community. Now, in the aftermath of World War and the Chinese Civil War, he found his basic concerns compounded by what he perceived as an international communist menace. Could the Japanese cope with "the loss of the normal trading areas of China and Manchuria and the threatened loss of Southeast Asia with its ricebowl and other raw materials," he asked? Or would economic deprivation produce such severe internal strains as to cause either revolution or a slower-paced accommodation with the communists who were now so powerful in the East Asian area? Because he wanted neither to return to the dangerous atmosphere of the 1930s nor surrender to the pressures of the present, Dulles urged a full-scale American commitment to Japanese economic health. As with his thinking about Germany, he envisioned clear and positive efforts that would go beyond merely avoiding the inclusion of stumbling blocks in a Peace Treaty. When he briefed House and Senate leaders prior to his departure for Tokyo, he cited his two chief concerns as "the future security and the economic stability of Japan." If necessary, he told the Congressmen, the United States would have to assume the financial burden of tiding the defeated enemy over its "precarious" economic situation. He specifically mentioned the possible need for an additional $250 million a year in aid. A few days later he consulted the Director of the Office of Defense Mobilization about prospects for increased allocations of scarce raw materials for Japan. "If Japan is to be on the side of the free world," he told Charles Wilson, "it will be necessary to assure that its industry can keep running and that it will receive sufficient quantities of the necessary raw materials, particularly coking coal and iron ore. . . . If the United States were to use all of these materials for its own industry and not be willing to make reasonable quantities available to the

Japanese, it would be futile to expect the Japanese to keep away from Communism." With these kinds of concerns evident prior to negotiations in Tokyo, it is not suprising that Dulles tried to communicate to Japanese leaders some sense of his genuine interest in their economic future. As he put it at one point, the United States wanted to create circumstances that would guarantee "the ability of the Japanese nation to maintain a reasonable rising standard of living for their people. . . ." Discussions with Yoshida and his advisers revolved primarily around treaty terms of necessity, but Dulles indicated a readiness to move on to such broader subjects as the encouragement of American investments in Japan and the revenues obtainable from offshore procurement of military supplies for use in the Korean conflict. In addition, he went out of his way to arrange meetings with business and labor leaders. All in all, his interest could only have increased the pleasure that the Japanese must have taken in U.S. plans for an economic settlement. [14]

The ease with which political and economic issues were settled with the Japanese was not quite matched in discussions of security provisions. Dulles's and the State Department's own concerns had been strongly reinforced by varying pressures from the Pentagon and the Allies, with the result that Japan's future safety had become a question of major significance: in Washington, Tokyo, and other capitals, it actually came to absorb more time than any other facet of the Peace Treaty. As far as bilateral discussions between Dulles and the Japanese were concerned, however, it cannot be said that serious problems emerged. Even before the Tokyo talks, it had become relatively clear that there was an identity of conviction on the basic need to provide for the defeated enemy's security and even shared assumptions about the logical methods for doing so. The only real difficulty Dulles encountered was the inevitable one of moving beyond abstract discussions to the delineation of precise arrangements and treaty terms.

At the heart of American policy was the presumption that the defeated enemy would "invite" the United States to station troops on Japanese territory after restoration of sovereignty and that those troops, supported by air and naval power, would have all the facilities and rights of movement they might require to carry out their defensive tasks. This arrangement was to be couched in language about global security borrowed from the United Nations Charter and was to hold open the possibility of transferring responsibility to the international organization at some appropriate future opportunity, but no one expected such window dressing to interfere with the basic power scheme behind it. Douglas MacArthur had regularly insisted that the Japanese would be completely willing to go along with this plan, and amenable to providing necessary facilities, but Dulles saw the definition of terms as one of his major tasks in Tokyo. "Do we get the right to station as many troops as we want where we want and for as long as we want or do we not? That is the principal question," he said at the meeting he held with his aides after arrival. [15]

His first conversation with Yoshida left him quite worried. The Prime Minister proved as vague as he had been during talks the previous summer: though "the idea of some form of collective security arrangement to which Japan could contribute seemed to appeal to him . . . it appeared that Mr. Yoshida did not wish at this time to be definitely committed in any manner." Dulles disgustedly reported that he had been treated to "a puff-ball performance." Still, matters soon fell into place. Yoshida's hesitancy seems to have stemmed from his own more slowly paced negotiating style and a certain desire to hold off until the last possible moment on commitments that the opposition political parties might denounce as denigrations of Japanese honor. The U.S. plan was very attractive as far as his government was concerned, however, in offering substantial security at limited cost, and acceptance of terms was quickly indicated. As early as February 3, agreement had been reached on all but minor details of what became a three-tiered package: a brief Peace Treaty clause involving no more than a formal statement of Japan's "inherent right of individual or collective self-defense" (i.e., the U.N. Charter phrasing, which Dulles had helped draft in San Francisco); a separate bilateral accord that would be signed simultaneously with the Peace Treaty, in which the United States agreed to meet Tokyo's request for stationing "land, air and sea forces in and about Japan"; and a series of bilateral "administrative agreements" in which the "conditions which shall govern the stationing of armed forces" would be arranged. [16]

In addition to the fundamental conception of a U.S. defense role in Japan, there were three other security-related issues that came up for discussion between Dulles and the Yoshida government. One stemmed from Dulles's continuing attention to a problem he had first identified the previous April: granting the necessity of defending the former enemy against Soviet attack, what could be done about *internal* subversion and security? Dulles's assessment of the "international communist conspiracy" persuaded him that the latter was more likely to arise as a danger than the former, and he pressed throughout the summer and fall for steps to deal with it. He and his aides carried on detailed discussions about ways in which Occupation authorities could begin strengthening, equipping, and centralizing the Japanese National Police Reserve, in particular. In Tokyo in the new year, he found Japanese authorities quite interested in the possibility of ongoing U.S. assistance in maintaining domestic order. Yoshida and his colleagues quickly accepted a treaty caveat that specified "assistance given at the express request of the Japanese Government to put down large-scale internal riots and disturbances in Japan would not be deemed intervention in the internal affairs of Japan."[17]

There were more complicated negotiations about Japanese rearmament. Though the core agreement on creating an American defense force in Japan might have implied to some an indefinite prolongation of the defeated enemy's disarmament, Dulles and other Truman Administration leaders had begun to assess the desirability of encouraging some independent defense capacity almost immediately after the outbreak of war in Korea. Previous concerns for the financial burdens of maintaining armed forces in Asia were doubled under combat circumstances and reinforced even further by some practical strategic problems—e.g., was there really enough U.S. manpower and material to wage war and defend sizeable populations and territories at one and the same time? By the time President Truman authorized Dulles's January visit to Tokyo, official U.S. policy had come to the point of urging "that Japan should increasingly acquire the ability to defend itself. . . ." When transmitting advance information on the visit to Occupation headquarters, one State Department official wrote that while, "Mr. Dulles has attempted to play down the idea that we are going out on a mission to rearm Japan . . . we have not shrunk from stating that in our opinion Japan will sooner or later have to assume at least part of the burden of its own defense. . . ."

There might have been formidable obstacles to gaining Japanese agreement to the general concept of gradual rearmament. The Japanese Constitution drafted under MacArthur's supervision contained a formal renunciation of war, which many in Washington believed was a reflection of genuine grassroots sentiment in the country. Having gone through the devastation and atomic destruction of World War II, would the Japanese be willing to recreate a military arm and establishment? In his first meeting with Dulles, Yoshida cited his fear of bringing "back the Japanese militarists who had now gone 'underground' and might expose the State to the danger of again being dominated by the military." Yoshida also admitted an additional reason for hesitancy about rearmament, one that later U.S. policy makers found increasingly difficult to deal with: "the creation of a military force just at the time when Japan was beginning to get on its feet financially," he argued, "would be a severe strain and probably result in a lower standard of living." Still, given the lengths to which the United States was prepared to go regarding economic and security terms as a whole, the Prime Minister did not feel he could completely spurn the American desires. From the first discussions, he argued only against "precipitate rearmament." Ideally, he and his associates suggested on February 3, the treaty and bilateral agreement between the United States and Japan would remain silent on the question in order to avoid additional complications with the Allies and opposition groups within Japan itself. Lest this suggestion be misunderstood, Dulles was presented with an outline of the steps Tokyo would take to begin rearmament under its own volition. [18]

As Dulles and Yoshida both fully understood, any plans for developing Japanese military capability would necessitate special procedures for insecure Allies, and the nature of those procedures became a final subject touched on during the Tokyo meetings. In Dulles's words, "the problem was to devise some arrangement which would protect Japan from outside aggression and at the same time re-assure to the greatest extent possible Japan's former enemies that Japan would never again be a threat to them." Detailed discussions were to be held shortly in the Allied capitals, and Dulles simply informed the Japanese that something like the "Pacific Pact" on which speculation had long been circulating would probably be forthcoming. [19]

It is obvious that all of the consultations Dulles held with Prime Minister Yoshida went more smoothly than he had been able to imagine in the tense Washington atmosphere from which he had come. Feeling plagued by reverses in Korea, he had worried about being able to pay the kind of price the defeated enemy would expect for its cooperation. He found that what he and the Truman Administration were prepared to offer would do very nicely. Whether the subject was political, economic, or security arrangements, Tokyo proved perfectly amenable. Dulles even found satisfying evidence of support for an American-style Peace Treaty beyond the Prime Minister's coterie. He had worried as early as the previous summer about the danger of repeating the post-1919 experience of Germany and argued now that the "Versailles Treaty stigmatized the socialist government which signed it and provided the reactionaries with a platform on which they were able to climb to power." In Japan, he told his State Department associates, "We do not want to crucify the party that makes the treaty." During meetings with Yoshida, Dulles emphasized "the importance he attached to a broad basis of political support for the understandings achieved" and asked how the endorsements of opposition parties could be worked out in advance. Yoshida immediately insisted there was no problem: "there would be no real difficulty in obtaining approval by the Diet of any treaty and informed Mr. Dulles that there was a secret agreement between the Liberal and the People's Democratic Parties . . . which would assure approval." Dulles went out of his way to consult opposition leaders, nonetheless; he found a certain readiness to politick, but it was so minor as to lay his fears to rest. [20]

There were varying explanations for the ease with which U.S.-Japanese agreement on treaty terms was reached in early 1951. Dulles himself often ascribed the results to a genuine readiness on the part of "the Japanese people" to have their nation become "a sustaining member of the free world." Douglas MacArthur, who had been consulted early, insisted as he had for months that the Japanese had behaved in predictable fashion: the Occupation had done a splendid job of reforming the defeated enemy, and reasonable cooperative behavior was one of the inevitable rewards. Prime Minister Yoshida seemed to see the situation with a mixture of cynicism and realism which may have been closer to the mark. In one of his first conversations with Dulles, he "gave the impression that the Japanese were so eager for a treaty that they would be willing to approve almost anything." [21] As it turned out, of course, the package Dulles had helped prepare with at least one eye on Japanese sensibilities was attractive enough to qualify as a good deal better than "almost anything." The terms were obviously more lenient than those which would have been imposed by the other victors, and a defeated enemy even less "eager" than the Japanese of 1951 might well have found them easy to accept.

But what about the Allies? Even before Dulles's involvement with Peace Treaty negotiations, it had been understood in Washington that there would be many objections to American plans from Australia, New Zealand, Great Britain, and the Philippines, among others. High expectations of reparations payments and punitive conceptions of commercial and industrial restrictions were to be found in many quarters outside the United States and would make agreement on an economic settlement difficult. There were yet greater concerns about hedging Japan's potential military strength in order to prevent future aggression. The basic U.S. desire to avoid post-treaty controls alone had frightened Japan's former victims; when the prospect of allowing or even encouraging rearmament materialized, the alarms grew louder yet.

Dulles had learned of Allied sensibilities shortly after reentering the State Department and had received personal confirmation of them during his informal conversations at the General Assembly session in New York. By mid-November 1950, he had settled on his own preferred strategy for dealing with them: he was ready to listen sympathetically to Allied leaders and entertain suggestions for minor changes in American treaty drafts, but that was all. With the exception of the multilateral security arrangements Washington had already recognized as desirable for a variety of reasons, he did not believe the rewards of Allied support would justify the risks of significantly altering the U.S. agenda for Japan. Nor did he think significant changes would really be necessary. Virtually all of the Allies had recognized U.S. supremacy in Japanese affairs even before the end of World War II and had accepted the institutionalization of this in the almost untouchable independence of the American Occupation. Whatever their preferences to the contrary might be, could they realistically expect to overturn the hierarchy of power at this late date? Dulles did not think so. As he wrote to Douglas MacArthur, "If we can get as a fixed and solid point, U.S.–Japanese agreement, then I think that the others, except for the Soviet Union and Communist China, will come into line if we *combine firmness with some placating modifications which will be of form rather than of substance*" (emphasis added). Both the toughness and optimism inherent in this strategy carried over into early 1951. Unchecked by any alternative approaches within the Truman Administration, Dulles prepared to deal with the Allies in exactly this frame of mind after his departure from Tokyo. On January 27, he restated his case in person to MacArthur when outlining the schedule of the near future: he would discuss treaty terms with Allies, but would make it "clear . . . that the United States intended to go ahead whether or not the others joined it. It was his belief that if the United States left no doubt of its determination to proceed alone if necessary the Allies would follow."[22]

Dulles was right, though it took about four months for him to work out the details with the followers. He personally undertook visits to Manila, Canberra, Wellington, London, and Paris to lend credence to the idea of genuine interest in Allied thoughts on the Peace Treaty; he spent countless hours in Washington consulting with other governments' representatives or poring over *aides-mémoires* from many capitals on the precise delineation of clauses. By mid-June, all the holding firm and placating were done, and Dulles had a treaty that was faithful in every essential respect to the blueprint with which he had begun. Any number of the Allies made it clear that they had nagging doubts about the treaty—one British minister said London would support it "little as one feels enthusiasm for it"—but very few were prepared to carry disagreement beyond the coupling of "for the record" oral statements with their final signatures.

The Pacific Allies were the first to "come into line," after more or less successful resolution of their varying anxieties. General chagrin at the virtual elimination of reparations was talked about at great length and

ultimately ignored. Even with the Philippines, where he found reparations on "the mind of everyone to the exclusion of almost anything else,"
Dulles remained basically adamant. He could not accept what MacArthur had called "skin them alive" proposals:

> . . . I emphasized that we recognized and sympathized with the justice of
> reparation claims of the Philippines but that past experience with Ger-
> many and the most exhaustive examination of every possible procedure
> had led us to the inevitable conclusion that the extraction of reparations
> from a naturally poor country like Japan was impossible except at the ex-
> pense of the American taxpayer, or at the expense of such low living stan-
> dards as would bring in communism.

He did make one concession, but it proved to be a minor one in the
aftermath and was designed with at least as much emphasis on Japanese as
Allied needs. Final treaty terms on "claims," at Dulles's suggestion, required Japan to process at no charge certain quantities of raw materials
provided by interested victors. This would give those who participated
something they could label "reparations," Dulles argued; more importantly, it "might help to reopen channels of trade with the Philippines,
Malaya, Burma and other reparations claimant countries" and thereby
ease Japan's economic rehabilitation. "If . . . Japan does a portion of its
business with these countries for a limited period on a reparations basis,
and raw materials start flowing into Japan from the reparations claimant
countries and manufactures out once more, the result may be an overall
advantage to Japan." This cycle, in other words, seemed likely to have
relevance for broad economic problems that had been of concern to
Dulles regarding Japan even prior to World War II.

The Allies responded with varying grace to the American position on
reparations, and Dulles apportioned his own reactions accordingly. The
Australians and New Zealanders earned his respect for their honest
statement of their interests, but they earned his gratitude for their realism
in dealing with them in a "more or less perfunctory" fashion. The passion
in the Philippines annoyed him, in contrast. Claiming $8 billion in
damages, "President Quirino seemed to realize the impossibility of
extracting such a sum from Japan and suggested, therefore, that the
reparations bill be guaranteed by the United States!" The government in
Manila was in an "embarrassed financial condition" and lacking in
"courage" and "stability," he concluded. [23]

In November, Dulles had called Australia and New Zealand "the only
two dependable countries in the Pacific area" and next to Japan itself, he
seemed to see them as the countries most important to a satisfactory Peace
Treaty. When both matched their flexibility on reparations with what he

saw as cooperative behavior on other outstanding issues, therefore, his appreciation grew stronger and stronger. On other economic matters, he found no real difficulties. Canberra and Wellington did urge the desirability of restrictions on armaments manufacture and ship-building and expressed the desire to do something about Japan's prewar tendency to utilize "unfair trade practices" like "dumping." They pressed neither the first nor second of these, however, confining themselves to what Dulles described as "for the record" statements. On the last, Dulles helped devise a satifactory "Preamble" to the Peace Treaty in which Japan simply declared its intention to observe "internationally accepted fair practices" in commerce, leaving definitions and enforcement in limbo. [24]

Australia's and New Zealand's willingness to live with an American-style Peace Treaty quite different from one they would have designed themselves stemmed primarily from Washington's willingness to satisfy their anxieties about long-range safety. Those anxieties had existed for many months, but had been exacerbated by the prevailing interpretation of the Korean conflict as a new example of communist aggression in Asia. There was now an obvious willingness, acknowledged by all, to "trade" lenient political and economic terms for some form of mutual security agreement among the victors. Already in October 1950, New Zealand's Foreign Minister had told Dulles that "before accepting the principle of no military restrictions on Japan," his government "would want to ascertain the United States attitude towards a Pacific Pact or other form of security guarantee." Australia's Minister of External Affairs had likewise "expressed the intent of his Government to hold out for a Pacific Pact as the price for a liberal treaty with Japan." Truman certainly recognized the bargain being contemplated in the instructions he approved for Dulles prior to the latter's trips to Japan and other Pacific countries. Clearing the way for discussions of "a mutual assistance arrangement," he specified that the U.S. "should agree to this course of action only as the other nations accept the general basis on which the United States is prepared to conclude a peace settlement with Japan." And when Dulles left Canberra on February 18, he left behind letters indicating his understanding "that there is an interdependence between the contemplated Japanese peace treaty . . . and the contemplated security treaty in the sense that neither of us would be obligated to accept one without the other." [25]

It should be added that Dulles personally favored some form of multilateral security arrangement for reasons beyond satisfying Allied qualms. As with his evolving conception of Europe's postwar order, he genuinely believed that any rebuilding of a former enemy should take place in a context that could provide natural, ongoing constraints. In

Europe, this had meant providing an integrated continental economy within which Germany's industrial recovery would be safe and broadly beneficial and a North Atlantic Treaty Organization within which even German rearmament could prove tolerable. In the case of Japan, he was explicitly conscious of the related benefits of what was loosely referred to as a Pacific Pact. As he put it to General MacArthur in December 1950, "this would provide a framework within which a Japanese force, if developed, could have an international status rather than a purely national status. . . ." Or, as he phrased it after all of the details had been worked out, the series of security agreements the United States was entering "will effectively assure that there will be no *unbridled rearmament* which could become an offensive threat."[26]

Agreement on the basic premise of a peace treaty–security system combination left two specific issues in need of clarification. First, what countries would be involved in the latter? By the time of his February 1951 visits to some of the Allies, Dulles was operating under guidelines that envisioned five or six participants: Australia, New Zealand, the Philippines, Japan, perhaps Indonesia, and the U.S. itself. Others had been eliminated for a variety of reasons. Because of the impracticality of spreading American military responsibility too thinly, it had been decided to concentrate on the "island nations." Over the next several months, changes in this conception proved necessary. The governments in Canberra and Wellington felt their constituents would "recoil" from the idea of committing themselves to the defense of Japan so soon after the end of the war and urged Washington to rely on its own bilateral arrangements with the defeated enemy for the time being. London, already miffed at being left out of a system involving two important Commonwealth partners, expressed grave reservations about membership for the Philippines; the inclusion of only one among all of the Southeast Asian countries would invite angry invidious comparisons, it was argued. Finally, the government of Indonesia made it clear that it would not consider participation. Dulles and other policy makers in Washington were somewhat annoyed by the varying Allied demands and reactions, but opted for a flexibility that might pay dividends in terms of freedom of movement over time. It was decided to accept the suggestion of utilizing bilateral arrangements between the U.S. and Japan and to apply the same logic to a U.S.–Philippine agreement. This would then clear the way for a trilateral U.S.–Australia–New Zealand accord. All in all, the Peace Treaty with Japan would be coupled with a series of mutual security arrangements in which the United States would find itself serving as an interlocking common denominator.[27]

The second issue requiring clarification concerned the precise nature of the security obligations into which the various governments were entering. As early as the previous April, Dulles had been dismayed by the prospect of a NATO-like system in which attack on a member would require immediate military response by all: he seemed to view the Pacific situation as less strategically crucial than the "inner citadel" and had doubts about the Senate's willingness to endorse an elaborate new program as well. By late 1950, he and Douglas MacArthur were urging the Truman Administration to rely on a "Presidential Declaration" of U.S. concern for the security of countries such as Australia and New Zealand, leaving to time and events an exact delineation of the substance of responses to aggression. The State Department was not wedded to its earlier proposals, which it had felt pushed into by Pentagon pressures in any event, but concluded that something as informal as "an announcement like the Truman Doctrine" would not satisfy Allied needs. After complex internal deliberations, which grew easier when Japan separated from the pack, it was finally decided to return to a proposal Dulles had made at the very beginning of his involvement with the problem. The Australia–New Zealand–U.S. accord would enjoin the signatories to "consult together whenever in the opinion of any of them the territorial integrity, political independence or security of any of the Parties is threatened in the Pacific"; further, in the event of "armed attack," each would "act to meet the common danger in accordance with its constitutional processes." Similar phrasing was to be utilized in the U.S.–Philippine agreement. Dulles preferred the less-demanding emphasis on consultation and felt that even the injunction on armed attack would leave Washington ample flexibility regarding where and how to "meet the common danger." Meanwhile, the general principle of American involvement in their security was satisfying enough to those Pacific Allies involved as to relieve any doubts about the relative imprecision of that involvement.[28]

By early April, Dulles believed almost all obstacles to a final peace settlement had been cleared away. Besides minor details over words and terminology still being thrashed out with Canberra and Wellington, there were only some final problems with the British requiring resolution. These did not seem sufficient to alter what had become hopes for formal treaty signing during the upcoming summer.

Once before Dulles had felt poised on the threshhold of a key breakthrough regarding Japan and had been knocked temporarily off balance by Chinese entry into the Korean War. Now, on April 11, he experienced another blow: Harry S. Truman's relief of General Douglas MacArthur for his public and essentially insubordinate questionning of Washington's policies regarding the war in Korea. Though the President's action and the uproar that followed did not interfere with a Peace Treaty as much as Dulles initially feared, he himself deserved some of the credit for this. There were potential complications in both Tokyo and Congress, in particular, and he took the time and care that Truman and his other advisers might not have to deal with them effectively.

Acheson had dragged him out of bed at 11 P.M. on April 10 to tell him of Truman's action, and Dulles expressed the kind of shock and dismay that would become commonplace over the next few weeks. In his particular case, there were a number of intertwining reasons for these emotions. He was, for example, more than peeved about his total lack of involvement in the decision: he would have agreed with the words of Senator Milliken that "it was an outrage that, in view of the importance of the Japanese situation and my responsibility in regard to it, action gravely jeopardizing the desired result had been taken without any prior consultation with me." Dulles was also angered by the loss of a man he saw as a great military leader. He admitted to Acheson that he could see that "the present strains and lack of confidence made the action inevitable," but he bluntly added "that the responsibility for bringing this situation to pass lay very largely with the Administration and particularly with the Joint Chiefs. . . ." The General had not been consulted regularly or seriously enough and had been forced to conclude "that the only way to make his thinking an element in policy making was through indirect channels." More sensitivity in Washington could have avoided the whole problem: Dulles, in a fascinating thumbnail sketch, told Senators Taft and Smith that Truman and the Joint Chiefs did not seem to have the capacity "to work with a high-strung person of great moral stature and sense of the dramatic . . . and I felt this was the root of the trouble."[29]

The single most disturbing facet of the Truman–MacArthur imbroglio, as far as Dulles was concerned, was its potential impact on his nearly completed Peace Treaty. "The situation created by the MacArthur action was very precarious," he felt; it "would undoubtedly have a very serious effect upon Japanese public opinion. . . ." One U.S. official in Tokyo had immediately cabled about a "visibly shaken" Yoshida and the "tremendous shock" that many had received. Dulles wondered what effect this would have on "the major objective which I had been seeking, namely the commital of the Japanese nation to the cause of the free world." Would the defeated enemy conclude that the United States was an unstable, unreliable ally for the difficult days inevitably ahead in Asia?

Dulles had assumed from the very beginning that MacArthur's support would be crucial in the accomplishment of the kind of Peace Treaty the United States desired. He saw the General's stature and prestige as of inestimable value in persuading the Japanese to go along: as he put it to MacArthur at the beginning of the Tokyo consultations in January, he considered his "assistance and support indispensable to the success of his mission." He also appreciated the General's clout with Republicans back at home: "General MacArthur must be one hundred percent behind the treaty," he told his aides at one point. "If he were to indicate that it did not exactly reflect his thinking or that he had been left out the treaty would be attacked by the Hearst–McCormick press and might be defeated in the Senate." Thus convinced, it should be added, Dulles tried to take MacArthur's "high strung" and "dramatic" personality into account. He consistently appealed to him for guidance, paid "tribute" to his leadership in virtually every public statement made during the treaty negotiations, and kept him fully informed about developments as they proceeded. A man of lesser ego might have found some of Dulles's efforts cloying. "Your own position is central, dominating and indispensable," he told him at one point. Conscious of the role MacArthur could play in encouraging Japanese support, Dulles warned that he "did not propose to let General MacArthur off the hook." He neither intended to let himself move away from General MacArthur nor to let General MacArthur get away from him.[30]

Whatever his abstract reactions to MacArthur's dismissal, April 11 found Dulles in the kind of predicament that had come his way before: disturbed by an action of the Truman Administration, was his disturbance great enough to cause a break? On this as on every other occasion, it was not. His clearly genuine convictions persuaded him that the U.S.–Japanese relationship was more important than any one man, and his own ego convinced him that he was the person who should try to secure that relationship.

The possibility of action immediately presented itself at Dulles's midnight meeting with Acheson. The Secretary asked him to go to Tokyo to "reassure Japanese leaders of our intentions" and inform the new Supreme Commander about the Peace Treaty situation. Before Dulles agreed, he sought reassurances of his own. Was it "the determination of the Administration to proceed with the Japanese Peace and related matters vigorously and strongly along the lines already shaped in consultation with General MacArthur," he wanted to know first? He did not want to be a "fall guy" if basic policy was in some process of transition. Both Acheson and Truman emphatically reaffirmed previous commitments, arguing that this was precisely the reason they wanted him to go to Japan. A second concern could have been trickier to assuage. Anticipating as well he might have the explosion of Republican anger about the President's action, he wanted some sign of ongoing support for Japanese policies from his party colleagues. More precisely, would they share his conviction that the treaty was a crucial enough objective to warrant his continuing to work within an increasingly mistrusted Administration? It was Thomas Dewey who gave Dulles the best handle on this predicament, in a telephone conversation just hours after word of the crisis was received. "I was the only person who could perhaps salvage the situation in Japan," the Governor said, "and . . . this was of such paramount importance that I should make the effort even though there might not be a very good chance of success." Dulles used this line of reasoning in hastily arranged meetings with Senators Milliken, Smith, Taft, and Wiley and was told by all that partisan considerations should not stand in the way. (Milliken did speculate that "the situation permitted . . . a dramatic move which would be greatly to the advantage of the Republican Party.")[31]

Within a week Dulles was on his way across the Pacific, his plane literally passing MacArthur's going in the opposite direction. In Tokyo, he made all the appropriate gestures. There were meetings with Prime Minister Yoshida and other officials, speeches and news conferences, all built around the same message: as the minutes of a Dulles staff meeting put it, "that U.S. policies toward Japan have firm bipartisan support and are unchanged." Indeed, as Dulles phrased it for Yoshida, U.S. policy, "like the house which had withstood the earthquake, could now be considered firmer than ever." It quickly became apparent that these assurances had produced their desired efffect—or had not been necessary in the first place. At the several meetings with the Prime Minister, in particular, there were no indications of aftershock. On the contrary, there was every indication of readiness to get on with work on the few outstanding problems like British reservations and the details of an anticipated final peace conference. Dulles later said he had purposely initiated the discussions of details "to get things back on a matter-of-fact basis," but there was no discernible Japanese hesitation to indicate that such a ploy had been necessary.[32] In terms of substantive Peace Treaty issues, MacArthur's departure turned out to have literally no effect.

With renewed confidence regarding the situation in Tokyo, Dulles returned to Washington at the end of April to jump the last remaining hurdles to a Japanese Peace Treaty. Almost all of them involved Great Britain. It had long been evident that London did not completely accept the U.S. vision of a Pacific settlement. During mid and late 1950, Dulles himself had had regular reminders of the particularly strong discrepancies on economic terms: the tougher British position on reparations, involving interest in Japanese gold reserves, or the insistence on imposing limits on the former enemy's ship-building capacity. For several months after Dulles's February 1951 travels, as well, the British had dragged their feet on approving the Australia–New Zealand–U.S. security agreement, which was becoming an increasingly important element in overall arrangements. Dulles and others appreciated the psychological problems the British were having with Canberra's and Wellington's pivot toward Washington and also understood some of the politicking going on regarding elections in Australia. Still, he found the lack of forthright support "worrying" and sometimes annoying.

Dulles had combined sympathetic attention, minor concessions, and firmness to bring most other disagreeing Allies into line. Though it took a little longer to work, he now used the same combination on the British. The attention came in the form of steady effort between early April and mid-June. Dulles began by meeting with the British Ambassador in Washington for conversation and the exchange of *aide-mémoires*. He then sent one of his key deputies to London and immediately thereafter welcomed a British delegation to Washington for almost two weeks of constant negotiations. Finally, after further routine diplomatic communication, he went to London himself on June 4.

As to concessions, there were quite a few. Some were very specific, such as the U.S. agreement to require Japanese renunciation of prewar commercial rights under the Congo Basin Treaties, desired by the British in order to limit competition in one particular cheap textiles market. Others were of a more general nature and demonstrated shrewd psychology on Dulles's part. In mid-April, he indicated a willingness to blend a lengthy British draft of Japanese liability clauses with the very brief American text. He had assumed that detailed explanation of the limited claims the U.S. was willing to tolerate would be unnecessary and would better be left to Tokyo to elaborate on its own, but he was willing to use British wording if this would yield some useful pride of authorship: "he had never expected that the final treaty would be as short as our original proposal and that, desirable as a short and general draft was, we would not want to sacrifice agreement with the British and others on a treaty simply to preserve a literary and artistic triumph." Dulles carried this logic to a grander conclusion in June and asked the British to serve as "cosponsor" of the Peace Treaty and the conference that would soon be arranged. Resentments over lost glory and lost clauses might be somewhat assuaged by a boost in diplomatic dignity.[33]

Concessions and stroking probably played some role in British acquiescence to American views, but so did the proverbial fist in the velvet glove. Dulles made it clear that he was as ready to be firm with London as with lesser powers. On claims, for example, his willingness to utilize British drafts was tempered by insistence that they deal only with provisions "to which the Japanese and the U.S. do not have substantive objections. . . ." On ship-building restrictions, Dulles simply refused to move until the British gave up "vigorous effort to overcome our adamant position. . . ." And on Tokyo's gold reserves, he finally told the British Foreign Minister in early June that "we have the gold and he doesn't" and that was that. In broader strokes, Dulles even held out the possibility of going ahead with a treaty that did not have London's support. His words to the British Ambassador at one point contained an only thinly veiled threat: "he hoped a situation would not arise where the U.S. would have to choose between dealing with Japan without awaiting a common position with the U.K., or incurring such a delay . . . as would involve grave risk that Japan would be lost to the free world."[34]

On only one issue did the British force a change of some significance in the U.S. approach to the Japanese Peace Treaty. After months of intimations, which Washington had essentially ignored, London formally proposed on March 30 that Peking "be invited to participate in any negotiations for the conclusion of a peace treaty" and that final terms should recognize the cession of Formosa to the mainland government. There were plentiful reasons why such representations were likely to cause chagrin among American policy makers. As to dealing with Peking, there had been a studied determination from mid-1950 on to devise a bilateral negotiating strategy that would make it possible to do exactly the opposite. Further, it had been only months since Chinese entrance into the Korean War, and the furor of Americans had hardly had a chance to wane given the fact that bloody combat was still very much in progress. As to the ceding of Formosa, Washington had been gradually shaping plans to involve the United Nations in determining the island's future, presuming that full control by the communists could somehow be avoided. It wanted the Japanese treaty to do no more than recognize the surrender of Tokyo's title to Formosa, explicitly leaving the issue to be resolved later.

Dulles bluntly told the British that the United States could not consider negotiations with Peking and periodically offered explanations that were an admixture of firmness and condescension. Peking's reaction to U.S. proposals for a Japanese Peace Treaty was "a parrot-like echo of what the Soviet Union has said," so what would be accomplished by negotiating with the Chinese? Besides, he argued on another occasion, "we can look after the interests of Communist China a lot better than Mao Tse-tung can [!] because he's looking out for the interests of Russia and we really are concerned with the interests of China. We've been friends of China for a hundred and fifty years and Mao Tse-tung is nothing but a puppet. . . ."[35]

Whatever Dulles's assumptions about Peking, however, London's push brought to a head the almost inevitable realization that some alteration of the original U.S. plans would be necessary. If the United States refused to consider a Communist Chinese signature on a Japanese Peace Treaty, as it continued to do, it would not be able to carry its resistance to the point of allowing the withered Nationalist Government to sign instead. Aside from tangible doubts of their own about the viability of the exiles on Formosa, the Americans found they would be almost totally isolated if they tried to push for the latter. As Dulles cabled a U.S. official in Tokyo, it "wld be seriously objected to by probably all Commonwealth and Western Eur countries, and India, Burma and Indonesia. Even Canada, Aus, NZ which continue recognize Natl regime consider its present lack of governmental relationship to great bulk of Chi people on mainland renders it unqualified to bind them for all time in matter as important as China-Jap peace treaty."

When the British agreed to drop their proposal for pinpointing the disposition of Formosa in the Peace Treaty, Washington began to move toward compromise on the Peking involvement issue. By mid-May, Dulles was reasserting his position that "Signature by Commie regime . . . is absolutely out," but was suggesting that the Nationalist government enter into the Peace Treaty at some time separate from and after the other Allies. London saw this, for good reason, as too patent a dodge and held out for more. In June, Dulles then went as far as he felt he safely could, given the political climate in the United States. He worked out an agreement which specified that after all other interested Allies had signed the Peace Treaty, it would be up to the Japanese themselves to decide which "China" they would relate to: in the exercise of their essentially sovereign rights, they could choose to enter into a related, but bilateral Peace Treaty with either or neither or both of the rival governments.[36]

The British reluctantly accepted this Dulles proposal in order to allow the dragging treaty negotiations to reach a conclusion. If they took comfort in the implicit possibility of Japanese recognition of Peking, however, they should not have. Dulles and the Truman Administration in general had become too vehemently antagonistic to "the Red regime" to tolerate such an eventuality. Prior to cementing arrangements with London, Dulles made sure to check on the likely predispositions of Yoshida and his associates—what would they do if given the right to move on this issue on their own? The Prime Minister's circle had reservations of its own about immediate relations with the communists on the mainland and recognized in any event the surpassing importance of pleasing the United States rather than Great Britain. As a result, Dulles was told on several occasions that "Japanese Govt under no circumstances desires signature by Chi Commie regime." Dulles admitted out of British earshot that such "assurances . . . were what made the present formula acceptable to us."[37] After the formal signing of the Peace Treaty, furthermore, Senate qualms led Dulles to seek even more definite pledges from the government in Tokyo. Under the circumstances of 1951 and the foreseeable future, at least, the British underestimated the kind of pressures that Washington could bring to bear on a hypothetically sovereign Japan.[38]

III

The end of the Peace Treaty process was in sight once Dulles returned from London in mid-June. There were almost two months of attention to last-minute formalities and an elaborate "signing conference" before him, but neither posed problems of any real significance.

The formalities concerned preparation of a final treaty text acceptable to the largest possible number of these states which had declared war against Japan. A first Anglo–American draft was circulated on July 3, with an invitation to submit proposals for specific alterations or clarifications. Enough suggestions materialized over the next two weeks to warrant distribution of a revised draft on July 20. Following yet further submissions, a definitive text was published on August 13. While thirty changes were ultimately made in the original joint draft, no substantive alterations were allowed., Dulles admitted that some of those agreed to were of "considerable significance to one or more countries," but concluded that "none of them [are] in our opinion of a major character." His line-by-line description of the revisions for newsmen found constant repetition of words like "slight" and "inconsequential," and a comparison of texts demonstrates the appropriateness of such terminology. The clause on reparations in the form of free processing of raw materials, for example, had originally included a reference to "the skills and industry" of Japan. A number of Asian governments saw invidious comparisons here—the implication that the Japanese "had skills and had more industry than some other countries"—and suggested the alternative phrase "services and production." In another case, an original reference to "Spratly Island" was changed to "Spratly Islands" because geographers had concluded "there were several rocks instead of just one."[39]

With a technically much-altered treaty in hand, Great Britain and the United States invited more than forty governments to send delegations to San Francisco in September for a "signing conference." The designation was emphatic. This was "an invitation to conclude peace 'on the terms' of the present text," Dulles told a national radio audience, not to debate yet further amendments or alterations to those terms. Through extensive travel and consultations in Washington, he had conducted "an eleven months' peace conference"; avoiding traditional great power exclusivity such as that he had witnessed himself in 1919, he argued, this alternative method had produced "the most broadly based peace treaty in all history." Why, therefore, reopen discussions? "There come times when to seek the perfect is to lose the good," he eventually told a plenary session of the conference. "This is such a time."[40]

Most of the Allies were prepared to accept these perimeters. Coming to terms with American principles and American demands *had* taken place over the preceding eleven months, and there was no reason to imagine that some last-ditch effort would alter the obvious realities. As a result, the vast majority of delegates arriving in San Francisco during the first week in September looked upon the conference about to begin as an essentially ceremonial occasion. There would be days filled with uninterrupted speeches and nights of formal diplomatic dinners and receptions; there would be an elaborate treaty-signing ritual—and that was all. If there was to be any practical significance to the proceedings, it would be with respect to the domestic political circumstances some of the representatives would have to face after returning home. The ceremonial speeches, that is, could go beyond congratulatory words and optimistic prophecies to express the understandings of respective governments concerning the nature of the peace settlement and its evolution. It was a procedure consciously designed to allow rhetorical variations of emphasis: "for the record" statements might prove psychologically satisfying and politically protective without interfering with the ultimate approval of the Anglo–American treaty.

Of the fifty-two countries represented in San Francisco, only the Soviet Union, Poland, and Czechoslovakia sought to break through the fences constructed by the United States. For much of 1951, Washington had assumed that Moscow would simply boycott a U.S.-style treaty, and there was considerable surprise when it was announced in August that Moscow would send a delegation to the peace conference. It was and still is difficult to understand just what the Soviets thought they might accomplish. Dulles publicly warned them that there would be no tolerance for "wrecking crew" tactics, and unless they greatly overestimated the restlessness of American Allies, simple arithmetic should have told them that they would be outvoted on every maneuver they might attempt. That is certainly what happened. When Andrei Gromyko rose at the first plenary session to urge that Peking be invited to send a delegation forthwith, presiding officer Dean Acheson ruled him out of order because an Anglo–American motion on procedural rules was already on the floor; after adoption of the previous motion, Gromyko tried again, but was now told that he was out of order because his proposal was not allowable under the rules just approved: it was an absurd Catch-22 which the vast majority of delegations endorsed when an appeal was made to overturn the ruling of the chair. Toward the end of the conference, the Soviets tried to introduce "amendments" that would have struck out provisions of basic significance to the United States. They were told that amendments could not be entertained, and found themselves outvoted 46 to 3 when they appealed for a counter-ruling by the delegates.[41]

Dulles and the other Americans active in San Francisco emerged from the conference with a particularly heightened sense of exhiliration thanks to the Soviets. Inevitable pleasure in the conclusion of the lengthy Peace Treaty undertaking was doubled by what Dulles called the "great moral defeat" inflicted on Moscow, "the most ignominious defeat in conference history." In memoirs written almost two decades later, Secretary of State Acheson could still recall the intense excitement of sinking Soviet schemes with his parliamentary torpedoes—and being able to do so in full view of a national television audience created by the first transcontinental network hookup ever arranged. The proceedings of the peace conference in general became far more newsworthy than they would ever have been without the Soviet presence, and the public and media interest helped create a conducive environment for the task of gaining Senate approval.[42]

"In John Foster Dulles we had a negotiator domestically acceptable to both Administration and opposition," Dean Acheson once wrote, recalling an obvious factor behind the Republican's reentry into the Truman Administration in April 1950. Almost a year and a half later, with a Japanese Peace Treaty signed by forty-nine nations in hand, the

Democrats were in no hurry to forget the potentially ongoing relevance of that factor. The President arranged to see Dulles on October 3 and immediately asked him if he would serve as Ambassador to Japan. With a presidential election on the horizon, Truman had suspected that this offer would be unappealing. When this quickly became apparent, the conversation moved on to what may have been its purpose in the first place: would Dulles be willing to "assume responsibility for handling the case for ratification" of the Peace Treaty before the Senate?[43]

Given the general climate of congressional–White House relations in 1951, affected as it was by the fallout from Senator McCarthy's blasts and the Truman–MacArthur explosion, Administration leaders may have long assumed that Dulles was the logical man to coordinate efforts for ratification. The Japanese Peace Treaty and related security agreements seemed to be obvious candidates for broad, nonpartisan support, but it could not hurt to have a leading Republican ride herd on some of his colleagues during such a volatile period. And as it turned out, there was specific reinforcement for this logic before the end of the San Francisco conference. Fifty-six Senators, including leaders of both parties, sent a letter to Truman on September 13 indicating that as they evaluated the Peace Treaty they would be concerned about the apparent uncertainty of Tokyo's attitude toward Peking. Anglo–American understandings seemed to hold open the possibility of "the recognition of Communist China by Japan or the negotiating of a bilateral treaty with the Communist Chinese regime," and the Senators wished "to make it clear" that they would consider any such moves "to be adverse to the best interests of the people of both Japan and the United States." More than half of the Senate's members were in effect warning that they had doubts about the Administration's devotion to national needs and were not simply going to rubber stamp the package sent to them by the President.[44]

Dulles agreed to take on ratification chores. His only real condition was that Truman push for action as soon as the Senate reconvened in January, in order to clear the decks for the upcoming election.[45] Like other steps in the treaty process, the work proved more difficult in anticipation than execution. Even the potentially thorny China question required no more than a few fancy public relations maneuvers.

Dulles had, in fact, carefully prepared the way for relatively easy Senate approval of the Japanese Peace Treaty. His memories of the Treaty of Versailles had affected him in many ways in 1950–51, one of them being to prod him toward regular attention to congressional sensitivities. Every three to four months at the least, from July 1950 on, he met with key Senate and sometimes House leaders to review progress on negotiations and answer questions: he never asked for formal endorsement of policies or tactics, but no doubt correctly assumed that serious problems would have bubbled to the surface. None did. At sessions prior to his January 1951 departure for the key Tokyo consultations, for example, "there was definite approval of the approach being made."

Conscious of his special bipartisan role, Dulles took particular pains to tend his Republican fences. Senators Vandenberg, Taft, Milliken, Wiley, Smith, and Hickenlooper were conscientiously consulted and regularly asked for renewed expressions of confidence, both in the logic of the evolving treaty and the role that Dulles was playing in bringing it about. As a way around knee-jerk antagonism toward Administration policies, Dulles consciously tried to deal with Japanese policy as a distinct entity, something worthy of G.O.P. support in spite of many other problems. He never hid the fact that he had been highly critical of China policies before returning to Washington. He also carefully separated himself from Truman's firing of MacArthur: he explicitly shared his own anger at the action with Republican colleagues and communicated the same to the President; he then went out of his way to make laudatory comments about the General's accomplishments in Japan long after MacArthur's official role had come to an end. There was almost complete willingness to go along with Dulles's effort to create a Japanese lee in the partisan hurricane raging in Washington. Taft seems to have felt as if he were being backed into a corner at times—immediately after the MacArthur dismissal for example—but clearly never felt as if he could refuse to go along with either the treaty or his colleagues once explicitly put on the spot.[46]

As testimony to Dulles's effectiveness in his own party perhaps, the only problem involving the treaty that required careful attention was the China issue, which was of concern to Senate Democrats as well. Dulles himself had no doubts about Tokyo's inclinations for the immediate future, having secured indications of a desire to spurn ties with Peking from Yoshida before agreeing to rule out Nationalist participation in San Francisco. Some Congressmen saw the situation as too ambiguous, however, particularly after the Prime Minister made a number of statements in the Diet in October which seemed to have loopholes as far as relations with the mainland were concerned. Dulles decided to deal with this potential problem before the treaty came up for formal consideration in the Senate and took the extraordinary step of arranging a visit to Tokyo for John J. Sparkman and H. Alexander Smith, ranking members of the Far Eastern Subcommittee of the Foreign Relations Committee. At a meeting with Yoshida on December 18, the three Americans made it clear that without "an early resolution on the part of Japan of the China problem . . . it would probably be impossible to obtain ratification of the Treaty." There was, of course, a specific "resolution" which they had in mind. Yoshida was handed a letter which he was urged to send to Dulles, who would hold it until a suitable opportunity for publication during or just prior to Senate debate. The letter indicated Yoshida's presumable desire to establish normal relations with the Nationalist government through negotiation of a bilateral peace treaty; the terms of that treaty would "be applicable as regards *the territories now or hereafter under the actual control* of the Japanese and Chinese National governments." Of equal importance, the letter concluded with an indictment of the Peking government "condemned by the United Nations" and the assurance that "the Japanese Government has no intention to conclude a bilateral treaty with the Communist regime. . . ." Yoshida indicated a certain amount of discomfort about the prospect of jumping into what would obviously become a breach between Washington and London, but seems to have appreciated the fact that Parliament had by then ratified the Peace Treaty while the U.S. Senate had not even begun formal consideration. He signed the letter on December 24 and approved its release on January 16. It performed its role nicely, allowing just the kind of emphatic Senate endorsement of the Peace Treaty and security agreements which Dulles had been so anxious to arrange.[47]

Though it meant little, the British were predictably angry. Beyond complicated questions about the etiquette and timing of the Yoshida letter's release, they were probably most upset by being outmaneuvered. The British Ambassador in Tokyo had been trying through low-key representations to prepare Yoshida for some eventual coming to terms with Peking, only to find the Americans wheeling in very big guns to do just the opposite. If London felt that Washington had not been faithful to the terms of agreement of the preceding June, imagining that the Japanese would be left alone to make their own decision, Dulles would have quite explicitly disagreed. "It was from the beginning recognized by the British Cabinet that the formula proposed as regards China would almost inevitably lead Japan to align herself with United States policy," he explained to Acheson. "The comments of the British press at the time, particularly the Labor press, shows that there was no doubt in their minds as to what the result of this formula would be." Dulles had refrained from drawing attention to this point prior to the peace conference, but was essentially right: the merits of U.S. policy toward China notwithstanding, the British should hardly have expected that the Japanese would be allowed to make their decision in a vacuum devoid of American pressures.[48]

The Japanese Peace Treaty is justifiably seen as a major landmark in the diplomatic history of the post–World War II era and earlier studies of John Foster Dulles have generally made much of his "accomplishment" in connection with it. Even those critical of other aspects of his previous and subsequent record seem to see the successful negotiation of the treaty as a well-deserved highpoint in his career. There is reason to be on guard against overstating the case, however.

As "Advisor" and "Ambassador" between April 1950 and January 1952, Dulles reached a governmental level higher than any he had attained in his life. It offered the opportunity for influence and the exercise of responsibility. Nevertheless, in the day-to-day conduct of this work, he was always an individual within a larger whole: above him were Dean Acheson and Harry Truman, beside him were assistant and under secretaries of state, below him were numerous lower-level members of the State Department. This was a context of substantive and circumscribing significance. Most routinely, Dulles was subject to the normal inhibitions of a chain of command. State Department records indicate the regularity with which he received instructions, submitted reports, sought clarification or expansion of orders: he was not allowed to play a lone hand. More importantly, Dulles was subject to the basic policy commitments of the Truman Administration. With respect to Japan—or China or Korea— Washington did not wait until his arrival to identify problems and formulate responses. As he found in a four-hour briefing the day after the announcement of his appointment, there were elaborate State Department plans for the defeated enemy and its neighbors already in existence when he turned his attention to the subject. In basic terms, these plans served as the blueprint from which Dulles would work for the next year and a half. Though he oversaw any number of alterations in the original design (e.g., the devising of security arrangements quite different from the grand "Pacific Pact" first described to him), he remained completely faithful to the fundamentals agreed on before his arrival. A close Japanese– American relationship, the restoration of full sovereignty, lenient economic arrangements, adequate strategic precautions, among other things, had all evolved as basic State Department and White House commitments prior to April 1950. Dulles had no trouble living with such policies, of course, given the fact that he had developed thoughts along the same lines for more than a decade with respect to both Europe and Asia. What must be realized, however, is that his enthusiastic work on their behalf, albeit born of genuine conviction, gave him no claim to special accomplishment as far as conceptualization is concerned. Though he might have been if Dewey had won the 1948 election, Dulles was not the "architect" of the Japanese Peace Treaty. Given the time frame and government structure within which he was operating, he was at most something like a supervisor of construction.

Which is not to say that his role was unimportant or that he did not fulfill it in a distinguished fashion. He brought a real flair to the task of breathing life into paper plans. Within the United States government, his outsider's identity and his lawyer's experience made it possible for him to close gaps between the State Department, the Pentagon and MacArthur that others had found intimidating. Truman's vehemence might have eventually created the same unity in some other fashion, but the fact remains that this had not happened before the summer of 1950 and that it was Dulles who took particular responsibility for unity then. In creating broad Allied support for Washington's treaty plans, he was even more impressive. To obvious American power, admittedly crucial, he added a measure of diplomatic skill which brought more nations more quickly "into line" than others might have managed. It was one thing to assume that a combination of "firmness" and minor "placating modifications" would turn the trick, quite another to actually make it happen. Dulles seems to have had at least two skills that made the latter possible for him. First, he was able to listen with what others took to be sympathetic interest. With the Filipinos, the Australians, and the New Zealanders, among others, he helped dilute major doubts by taking the time to pay attention and make soothing noises: he traveled more than 100,000 miles while negotiating the Peace Treaty, a demonstration of his readiness to make respectful gestures toward Allied sensibilities. An ultimate refusal to go along on proposals for reparations, for example, may have been easier to digest because of his willingness to express, in person, clear agreement with the abstract justice of the numerous claims. Second, Dulles clearly possessed enough diplomatic or legal agility to devise the kind of modifications of U.S. terms that would make them at least minimally acceptable to most of the Allies. This was a talent already evident at the Paris Peace Conference in 1919 and utilized on countless occasions for corporate and banking clients over the intervening years. "Concessions of detail," as he described them, may often have appeared to give more than they did or to have been offered with a certain smugness as to ultimate dispositions, but they *were* forthcoming. And sometimes, changes produced by flexibility and imagination did offer something meaningful to the other side, e.g., the multitiered collective security arrangements which proved more satisfying to London, Canberra and Wellington than the original Pacific Pact plans.

If Dulles had some significance in the evolution of the Japanese Peace Treaty, the developments of 1950–51 had significance for him in turn. In terms of life experience alone, his role within the Truman Administration provided him with a bridge across what had become a frustrating gap. His government ambitions, which had risen in the earlier 1940s, had been blocked by Dewey's defeat in 1948. The familiar satisfactions of Sullivan & Cromwell, the Federal Council of Churches, and the United Nations had been available in the aftermath, but seemed insufficient; a wild stab at an independent political position, by way of the 1949 Senate race in New York, had failed. It was Truman and Acheson who, bowing somewhat reluctantly to the political realities surrounding them, offered Dulles egress from the awkward limbo into which he had slid. The position they tendered in April 1950 was substantial enough to be genuinely satisfying and sustaining enough to tide him over until the new opportunities of 1952 began to materialize.

Work on the Japanese Peace Treaty had a deeper intellectual significance for Dulles as well. It provided new opportunities for action based on the abstract perceptions developed during years of thought.

As with the German and European problems of the postwar years, Dulles's approach to Japan reveals a combination of assumptions and goals. Most striking is his obvious preoccupation with the "international communist conspiracy" in the Asian context. If Soviet expansionists had plotted to move westward toward the Atlantic, he argued again and again, they were equally attracted to eastern targets like Japan and its neighbors. "Two principal postwar goals of the Soviet communists are Japan and Germany," he said in one speech, and it was frightening to think of what might happen if either were achieved. If Russia's rulers could exploit the industrial and human potential of either Japan or Germany, it would be a sad day for peace. That would involve such a shift in the balance of world power that these new imperialists might calculate that they could start a general war with good prospect of success." This was a message which Dulles reiterated with considerable emphasis at every step of the treaty-making process. "Tsarist Russia was the historic enemy of Japan and the Soviet Communists have enthusiastically taken over that role," he told the Senate at the end, during ratification hearings in January 1952. "They have closed in on Japan, seizing its northern islands and seeking by conquest of Korea, to complete Japan's encirclement."[49]

Though Dulles spoke so often and so colorfully about the need to block some presumed Soviet reach toward Japan, it is clear that his policy commitments had other sources as well. In dealing with European problems after World War II, he had never been stirred by blatant Cold War concerns alone. This was equally true with respect to Asia.

In the most fundamental terms, Dulles was always conscious of the way settlement with Japan would affect the grand-scale politico-economic problems he had so often grappled with over the years. "The Treaty before us is a step toward breaking the vicious cycle of war—victory—peace—war," he told the delegates at the San Francisco Conference, precisely adapting half a lifetime's concerns to this particular situation.[50] He had become preoccupied with that cycle in the 1930s, when events led him to see the failures inherent in the design and execution of the Treaty of Versailles, and had urged the need to learn the "lessons of Versailles" throughout the 1940s. His attention had been focused primarily on the preparation of a superior European peace settlement, but he had never doubted the applicability of his general conceptions to Eastern Asia.

Dulles believed that two interrelated elements were crucial for promising postwar arrangements in any region. First, essentially lenient terms would have to be offered to the defeated enemy in order to convince it that the victors were genuinely anxious to share a friendly, cooperative relationship in the future. Any attempt at punishment or insistence on grabbing for spoils of war would induce suspicion and an inevitable yearning for revenge: "a treaty warped by passion often becomes a boomerang which, thrown against an enemy returns to strike its authors," Dulles said at one point. And any attempt at "compulsion" could have only short-term effectiveness, for, as he put it with respect to Japan, "eighty million people cannot be compelled from without. . . ." Better to aim for "a non-punitive, non-discriminatory treaty, which will restore Japan to dignity, equality and opportunity in the family of nations."[51]

Second, Dulles had a particularly heightened concern for what he considered the economic prerequisites of a lasting peace. Here he built on logic already clear in 1919, repeated with great emphasis in the 1930s, and consistently applied to Germany and Europe in the 1940s. In an interview with a Japanese journalist, he said "one of the things we must try to do is to help create in that part of the world, Asia and the Pacific, *economic health*. . . . A greater degree of economic health . . . is *a thing which is perhaps most of all wanted* in that part of the world" (emphasis added.) There were numerous specific facets to this overall goal as well, many of which occupied him throughout the 1950–1951 negotiations: reparations, commercial restrictions, shipbuilding capacity, textile and general industrial productivity, trade opportunities in China and Southeast Asia, and dollar resources via U.S. military expenditures in Japan, among others. Japanese leaders, it should be reemphasized, fully appreciated the economic aspect of Dulles's approach to their future and often consulted with him about it. In a letter written in July 1951, Prime Minister Yoshida jumped from profuse thanks for Dulles's role in producing a final treaty draft to a plea for help in encouraging a flow of "American capital" into hydroelectric development projects.[52]

The combination of broadly lenient treaty terms with particular attention to Japan's economic health, Dulles believed, held out the promise of a truly lasting peace in the Pacific. It could "mark the beginning of a new relationship" between former enemies and, in conjunction with similar steps in Europe, allow the emrgence of "a world-wide commonwealth of peace."[53] As such, the kind of Japanese Peace Treaty he desired could help move the international order toward goals that had been crucial to Dulles for many years. The Cold War tensions of the post–World War II era had complicated the path to those goals and had affected the process of reaching them in significant ways, but Dulles, at least, would have moved in the same direction in any event.

Conclusion

WHEN DULLES TURNED DOWN Harry Truman's invitation to become Ambassador to Tokyo, he said "there was no point in being at the end of a transmission line if the power house itself was not functioning. . . ." It was a waspish sort of remark to make to the President who had given him an important government position a year and a half earlier, but it revealed the rather cocky mood in which Dulles completed work on the Pacific peace settlement. He was very conscious of the presidential election that loomed on the horizon, and he was optimistic about what it held in store for him.[1] In spite of uncertainties in the aftermath of the 1948 defeat, he had remained a key G.O.P. spokesman on foreign affairs. Indeed, his high-profile work on the Japanese Peace Treaty may have engendered greater visibility than ever. Odds seemed good that he would play a role of some importance in the campaign ahead. And, considering his extensive party and international activism throughout the 1940s, it was not at all unlikely that any of a number of potential Republican Presidents would ask him to serve as Secretary of State.

It could have turned out otherwise, of course, but any personal ex-hiliration that Dulles may have felt in early 1952 proved justified. He was at the threshhold of the opportunity he had looked forward to for years.

Dulles was sixty-four years old in 1952. It was inevitable that both his behavior and thoughts as the next American Secretary of State would be profoundly affected by all the accumulated experiences he brought with him to this last role. Childhood in a Watertown parsonage and a Wash-ington townhouse; schooling at Princeton and the Sorbonne; early undertakings on Wall Street, at the War Trade Board, and the Paris Peace Conference; partnership in Sullivan & Cromwell, deeply immersed in the billowing waters of international finance and commerce; "philoso-phizing" in the 1930s; church-related activities during World War II; Republican politicking throughout the 1940s; and wide-ranging diplo-matic assignments within the Truman Administration: he had lived through all of these times and activities and preoccupations by 1952.

What was their cumulative impact? What kind of a man, what kind of a mind had they produced? There are a number of basic characteristics that stand out.

He had become, for one, an individual of considerable breadth. The four decades that followed his move to New York City in 1911 saw regu-lar, significant shifts in the apportionment of his time and concern: from law to government in 1917, or from business to politics and churches dur-ing World War II. Even during periods when one particular kind of activ-ity was predominant, he usually varied his pace to some degree: while he continued to put most of his time into Sullivan & Cromwell during the 1930s, he dabbled in the work of internationalist organizations and turned his hand to writing, with a degree of success. There were always im-portant links—intellectual ones in particular—between Dulles's changing activities, but the fact that he actively sought out multiple arenas and mul-tiple roles shows at least a degree of openness to varieties of experience.

If there was breadth, there was more notable depth as well. Occa-sionally during World War I and the 1920s and then in earnest after the mid-1930s, Dulles demonstrated a genuine concern for issues of fun-damental significance to American society and international affairs. He also developed a sometimes impressive capacity to articulate these issues. While Dulles's great success at Sullivan & Cromwell testifies to the fact that he never neglected the nuts and bolts of world-wide investments and trade, his work over time makes it clear that he always went on to use his legal experience in the construction of a larger intellectual whole.

Most basically, his involvement with international banks and corporations helped prompt continual awareness of the world beyond his own country's borders and the way global developments intertwined with American interests. Time and again, in fact, he set himself the task of demonstrating this to some of his less well-informed countrymen. We live in a close-knit world, he told them: the United States could not hope to cut itself off from the economic problems of a devastated Germany after the Great War, the strains of a world Depression, the political and military clashes of the 1930s, or the profound dislocations of World War II and its aftermath.

There is a rather elementary cast to this kind of reasoning, to be sure, though it is evident enough that many Americans of Dulles's time had not reached the same conclusions, or were often inclined to pay them little more than lip service if they had. In any event, his interest in international affairs never stopped with the abstract concept of an interdependent globe. Rather, he used it as an analytical base for many explorations.

He was most interested in what he justifiably saw as two of the fundamental, interrelated problems confronting his twentieth century world. War and economic crises were almost constant preoccupations for him. With a feeling of continual foreboding, he put great energy into trying to understand just what led governments and societies to opt for armed conflict with each other. Some of his speculation was a fairly common reading of unfolding events, e.g., that if defeat in one war was followed by harsh punishment, it would simply produce a thirst for revenge and another war. Some was far more grandly conceived, e.g., the theory of immemorial struggles between "static" and "dynamic" forces with which he was so taken during the 1930s. Though this latter approach, reaching its apogee in *War, Peace and Change*, could be turgidly abstract, it did allow Dulles to say some interesting things about the interwar period. In particular, it gave him greater appreciation for the complex background of the Second World War than many of his more stridently chauvinistic contemporaries.

Dulles was probably at his analytical best when tracing the economic roots of conflict. His professional activities provided him with ample practical experience, and he chose to apply it freely. German reparations in 1919, American investments in Europe in the 1920s, tariffs and currency regulations and access to raw materials in the 1930s, and economic integration in the 1940s: he had a sharp and constant sensitivity to the core significance of such matters and some of the political, military, social, ideological, and psychological sparks which could be thrown off by them.

He was also impressive, for a while, in his ability to integrate the various problems that concerned him. During the late 1930s and World

War II, in particular, he offered insightful and sometimes eloquent commentary on the way various particular developments were symptomatic of a deep-seated global crisis—or, as he more often spoke of it, a cycle of crises. He concluded that the existing world order, relatively stable through most of the nineteenth century, had been teetering on the verge of collapse during the first three decades of the twentieth. The great Depression, war in Europe and the Pacific, unrest in the colonial regions and spiritual malaise in many quarters had knocked it over. "The old politico-economic order has failed," he wrote in 1942, "and all the King's horses and all the King's men cannot put it together again."[2] To his credit, Dulles had enough perceptivity to go beyond preoccupation with immediate problems. The patterns that he conceptualized and articulated in the process suggest a far from pedestrian mind grappling with the historical currents whirling around him.

The clear strengths of Dulles's intellect deserve recognition. So do the weaknesses. If there was some breadth of experience and vision, if there was capacity for percipient analysis of significant issues, there were also serious limitations. They were in evidence at all stages of his adult life, but took their toll increasingly as time went on.

Dulles's limits become obvious when his movement across the line separating speculation from action is examined. Given his notable sensitivity to the complex global problems of his time, what was to be done about them? How was the vicious cycle of war and depression to be broken? His responses to such questions ultimately proved so confounded by backtracking and dubious loopholes as to overshadow the more positive intellectual understanding that had led him to ask them.

It is clear that Dulles often focused on rather narrow programs as likely solutions to fundamental problems. His life-long belief in the need for tariff reduction and stable currency exchangeability, most obviously, always seemed to him to be the overriding requirement for a peaceful international environment. He could speak or write at great length about the need for a "dilution of sovereignty" in an "interdependent world," about the global relevance of federalist principles, but when he reached the bottom line of any agenda for action, it was his specific desire for easing commercial and financial transactions which was given pride of place. Even at his most grandiloquent, in the early years of work with the Commission on a Just and Durable Peace, this kind of reductionism was his standard pattern: while there were some doubtlessly well-intended vagaries about things such as "religious and intellectual liberty" and disarmament, the most concrete and frequently cited examples of what Dulles meant by "a moral way of international living" emerged from the list of economic desiderata he had clutched for many years.

With his attention directed toward only certain trees, much of the forest simply remained unnoticed as far as Dulles was concerned. If freer "interstate commerce" was the key to peace and prosperity, many institutions and traditional behavior patterns would be safe from questioning or attack. Capitalism as an economic system is a primary example. Indeed, so persuaded of the merits of "free enterprise" was he that Dulles periodically and emphatically argued that economic problems tended to reach crisis proportions only when "politicians" began to meddle. Though some challenge to capitalism would have been wildly improbable in a man of Dulles's vocation, the very predictability of his views here makes them that much more basic an indication of his intellectual identity.

Nor was Dulles inclined to question the *internal* orders of his own and other societies. He appreciated, certainly, the way local developments could contribute to the cycle of crises that so preoccupied him. In the immediate aftermath of World War I, he worried about the reverberations that might be produced if some restoration of economic and political stability did not ease the pains for farmers, workers, and manufacturers—in Germany or France or the United States. In the 1930s, he recognized the kind of urge toward aggression that could be born in a distraught domestic environment. In the 1940s, he speculated about the dangers of postwar devastation and disequilibirum in countries such as France and Italy and particularly within Germany and Japan. When it came to devising *remedies* for war, depression, and instability, however, Dulles concentrated solely on reforms in the international arena. Changes in the way nations related to each other in economic transactions or the way a group in one nation related to a group in another, he concluded, would rectify the problems.

As his very occasional but stridently conservative attacks on New Deal and Fair Deal "statism" make clear, he saw no reason to question the existing order of things *within* the United States. Similarly, all of his elaborate prognostications regarding the creation of a new-style Germany and Japan revolved around the way cooperative relationships could be established with other nations or regions. With neither of the defeated enemies did he express interest in educational developments, land reform, or deconcentration of cartels or *zaibatsu*, subjects which for a while at least received a good deal of attention from American Occupation authorities. In both cases, indeed, he reveals far stronger concern about guaranteeing adequate resources for the control of internal "unrest."

There were other problem areas that Dulles did notice, and even question, but was prepared to leave untouched: he made any number of significant compromises with the status quo. As his behavior at the United Nations and within the Truman Administration indicates, he had no difficulty in accepting the ongoing potency of the nation-state system. He had urged dilution of sovereign controls over foreign economic policy, but was obviously resigned to very slow progress. Aside from this, there were no other substantive limitations that he seems to have considered seriously. Similarly, his resolution of questions about the nature of imperialism was more impressive rhetorically than practically. The "new deal" for colonies he spoke of during World War II turned out to be more a new deal for the colonial *powers* than anything else. He did want to see a shift away from formal political control of Africans and Asians, but his primary emphasis was on opening up the economic resources of colonial regions in order to eliminate a primary cause of conflict among highly developed states. On regular occasions after World War II, Dulles commented on the way African resources could make a key contribution to the development of a prosperous and cooperative Western Europe, and Southeast Asian resources could do the same for a revitalized but peaceful Japan. While easier access to raw materials, markets, and investment opportunities might be conducive to more rational great-power relationships, Dulles simply ignored the fact that his priorities had little to recommend them to those whose resources were being tapped: their place in a hierarchy of relationships remained low, and he certainly did not suggest any ways in which their exploitation by several more powerful states would be an improvement over exploitation by one. At best, one is left to imagine something like a Hamiltonian "trickle down" theory, writ large on a global scale—if peace and prosperity were achieved by the great powers, benefits would somehow flow outward to all members of the world community.

The intrinsic shallowness of Dulles's programs for dealing with the global crises of the twentieth century suggests a mind of ultimately conservative character. Dulles always thought of himself as a "reformer," of course. His Wilsonian enthusiasm in early life, his "philosophizing" in the 1930s, his vibrant injunctions regarding a "new world order" during World War II, his postwar ideas on continental integration, Germany and Japan: all involved commentary on the inevitability of change and emphasis on the need for reforms of traditional global routines. While Dulles's self-perception may mesh with his rhetoric, however, it clashes with his behavior. Having sensed and articulated profound dislocations in the international order of his time, he stopped far short of advocating profound alterations to right them. There was a persistent lack of proportion between the essentially primordial problems he described and his handful of measures regarding trade and currency, for example. His disregard of domestic opportunities for change and his regular compromises with key facets of the existing order are crucial gauges as well: they reveal pretensions that were spurious or conceptions of "reform" that were strikingly narrow. In the end, Dulles emerges as a man who was far more comfortable with the status quo than he may have been willing to admit.

This conservative substratum of his policy proposals, it should be added, helps to explain the fragility of Dulles's "reform" identity. Compounded by the pressure of events, its veneer cracked regularly. Whenever a challenge to the existing order more profound than his own emerged, or seemed to emerge as far as his sensibilities were concerned, he regrouped quite solidly behind those anxious to resist assault. This was demonstrated first during World War I, when he followed Wilson's reformist inclinations to one of their logical conclusions: a bitter, active antagonism toward Bolshevism that revealed greater tolerance for the prewar European order than his earlier rhetoric had suggested. There were mounting numbers of examples after World War II. Abstract statements regarding moves away from imperialism could be transformed into acceptance of actions that were hardly conducive. Though Dulles explicitly saw French efforts to regain authority in Indochina as the lesser of two evils, he was prepared to go along rather than to consider accommodation with the deeper, apparently "communist" challenge represented by Ho Chi Minh. And while his attention to developments in China was minimal until late 1948, he showed no propensity to adopt an even remotely open-minded attitude toward the Chinese Communist Party: here again he was aware of the deep failures of the Nationalists, but favored basic support for them when confronted by the "Red Regime."

Even the *prospect* of a more radical program than his own was enough to send Dulles scurrying for the lee of the status quo by the post–World War II period. His approach to developments in Japan, for example, involved regular attention to the potential for "instability." He found it easy to work with Prime Minister Yoshida's government and was anxious to arrange economic and political conditions so as to keep its conservative hold secure. If left-wing disenchantment or "subversion" threatened this, furthermore, he had made sure to arrange appropriate mechanisms, such as a strengthened Japanese national police force and on-the-scene U. S. troops.

Another weakness of the Dulles vision and its followup was his increasing tendency to fall prey to the classic trap of confusing national interests with universally desirable goals. Over and again after the onset of the Depression, in particular, Dulles presumed that developments which he thought would be beneficial to the United States would be equally salutary for the rest of the world. With good reason, few non-Americans ever consistently bought his reasoning. Given American economic strengths in the 1930s and 1940s, to cite a very basic example, it was difficult to find enthusiasm elsewhere for his emphasis on open and peaceful economic competition. If your competition is likely to outbid or undersell you, where is the appeal? Far better to rely on hypothetically artificial advantages like colonies, tariffs, or currency regulations. A competitor's insistence that "open door" practices would make possible a more peaceful and prosperous world could be dismissed as naive—or as a highsounding rationalization for policies that were really designed to benefit ones own farmers and manufacturers. Dulles, and the Truman Administration in general, confronted parallel problems in devising long-range policies for defeated Germany and Japan. The French, Russians, and others in Europe or the Australians, Filipinos, and others in the Pacific, never came comfortably to terms with the lenient, "liberal" approach. They generally accepted it, but out of obedience to the circumstances created by U.S. power: it involved a set of policies designed to serve American interests, they quite rightly believed, and claims to universal rewards could be viewed with skepticism.

Dulles developed two other tendencies that significantly compounded this element in his policy proposals. First, he added a heavy dollop of religiosity. His leadership of the Commission on a Just and Durable Peace after 1941, in particular, involved a steady process of placing Christian imprimaturs on certain plans for the postwar world. Those so blessed proved to be precisely the ones he had supported prior to his church involvement; once pragmatically desirable, they were now "moral" as well. Though his formal Protestant ties dwindled after 1946, it is well known that highflying rhetoric regarding divine approval did not.

Second, in a related way, he convinced himself and tried to convince others that the United States had a unique role to play in the twentieth century world. Americans needed a firey "faith" to fulfill their special "mission," he preached again and again during World War II—to teach others how to create a better world order. Concerning issue after issue, problem after problem, he came to argue that if his countrymen did not take the lead, failures and disasters would ensue regarding the creation and early functioning of a new international organization, the reconstruction of devastated Europe in other than "firetrap" fashion, the rehabilitation of Germany and Japan so as to avoid old patterns of punishment and revenge, among others. The ultimate challenge was seen in the indispensable U.S. contribution to the Manichean struggle with the "black plague" of Soviet communism.

Dulles was less and less able to understand the problems which others might have with such patterns of analysis and planning. Well before 1952, he had ceased to appreciate the potential for cynicism about an approach to international politico-economic relations that revolved around his country's remarkably fortuitous ability to serve both its own and everyone else's interests at one and the same time. At some earlier stages of his life, he would not only have understood cynicism, but shared it. During the 1920s, he prided himself with some justification on hard-headed analysis. "Our national policy, dictated by our national self-interest, calls for the economic rehabilitation of Europe," he wrote at one point, in partial summary of his own deep desires:

> Generally speaking, we want the rest of the world to grow rich—so that we may get some of its wealth.
>
> I doubt if there is anything particularly moral about our position. It is true that our program does involve an improvement in conditions in other nations, but our interest in this improvement is not so much altruistic as due to the fact that they are at once our customers and our debtors. . . .

He was even more emphatic on another occasion, when warning his countrymen not to carry irritation with a number of annoying French policies too far. It would be foolish to assume "that any difference between ourselves and a foreign nation is due to the inherent righteousness of our own cause and the inherent perverseness of our neighbor. Moral distinctions, though pleasing to those who draw them, are hard to sustain in fact, and I know of no historic reasons to justify our approaching these problems of international relations with the complacent assumption that we are a party to a clashing of the forces of good and evil. . . ."[3] During the 1930s, he was on fairly steady guard against the most blatant kinds of pretensions. A regular theme of his quasi-philosophical writings was the role of the United States as a typical "static" power. This led to some biting criticisms and, of relevance here, implicitly argued against any notion of American uniqueness.

There was no intrinsic reason why such objectivity could not have continued to strengthen Dulles's analysis of international affairs. Certainly his day-to-day experiences back in the realm of diplomacy after 1945 should have offered plentiful reinforcing evidence: e.g., the strong determination of his own delegation to protect American interests during the San Francisco founding of the United Nations; the steady questioning by many, who could not be dismissed as perverse communists, about his own and Truman Administration plans for Germany and Japan. But the evidence was not read in this way. After his involvement with the churches and the waxing of vigorous nationalist energies during World War II, most importantly, much of the subtlety and sophistication of vision that Dulles had possessed was lost. At one point in 1950, he quoted the perceptive comment made by John Quincy Adams when spurning American involvement in the Holy Alliance: referring to Alexander I's leadership, the Secretary of State had said he was dubious about the way the czar "finds a happy coincidence between the dictates of his conscience and the needs of his Empire."[4] Unfortunately, Dulles used Adams' words only to attack a Soviet propaganda ploy—and failed to see their ongoing relevance to his own and his country's behavior as well.

What Dulles's behavior before 1952 suggests in the end is something that might be called "intellectual brinksmanship." He went to the edge of an understanding of some of the most profound problems of the twenti-eth-century world—and then either stopped or turned back. War, economic crises, and colonial unrest in particular, he saw, were threatening institutions and patterns that had been predominant for centuries. But when it came to working for, or adjusting to, some new global order, he proved less enthusiastic than he had been perceptive. He fell back on a very traditional pursuit of national interest, with strong emphasis on the economic facets with which he had had such extensive experience. He increasingly camouflaged this pursuit with a series of facile assumptions about the profundity of his proposals, the benefits that would prevail for mankind, and the divine approval which seemed manifest.

Many of his concerns and presumptions are part of American tradition, of course, or part of a tradition shaped by the policy makers of many great powers over centuries. It is even tempting to see the Dulles who was about to become Secretary of State in 1952 as an essentially *typical* figure—an interchangeable digit on some time line of American diplomacy. An examination of the way he played his roles in the Truman Administration suggests this. There were some subtle differences of opinion over tactics (the proper approach to the problem of Rumania at the London Council of Foreign Ministers meeting in 1945, the timing and parameters of NATO); there were even occasional splits regarding more basic perceptions (the nature of the Berlin Crisis). While interesting, however, these were simply not substantial enough to suggest any basic Dulles incompatibility with his surroundings, not the least because he himself was usually willing to fall into line once having simply expressed some idiosyncratic view.

Still, to label Dulles "typical" is to focus only on the lowest common denominator. While he was certainly not unique among those who have played a significant role in shaping United States foreign policy, he was part of a more unusual strain within the tradition. Like an Alexander Hamilton or John Quincy Adams in earlier American history, like a Theodore Roosevelt or Woodrow Wilson in more recent times, he stands out, though not apart, in interesting ways. With them, he shared a capacity for vision that was broader and deeper than that of many in similar positions: the ability and the desire, at times, to go beyond the narrow particulars of issues facing their country; the ability and the desire to discern the general patterns or fundamental problems of relationships within the global arena.

Unfortunately, sharper perceptions do not automatically yield more impressive or admirable actions. Theodore Roosevelt's occasional insights into the irrationality of great-power conflicts at the turn of this century did not prevent heavy-handed moves in Panama or Rough Rider bellicosity after the outbreak of war in Europe in 1914. Wilson's often shrewd and eloquent analysis of a disturbed world order existed alongside his dismal performance regarding Mexico, Russia, and the U.S. Senate. Ironically, failures or even pedestrian performance under such circumstances are doubly disappointing, in proportion perhaps to higher expectations concerning what might have been or almost was; there is likely to be more intense criticism than would be directed toward some hypothetically "typical" policy maker, as well. So too with John Foster Dulles. Though much that would demonstrate this most clearly—or most unfortunately—was yet to come, the signs were already plentiful by 1952.

Notes

CHAPTER 1

1. Emmet J. Hughes, *The Ordeal of Power: A Political Memoir of the Eisenhower Years* (New York: Atheneum, 1963), 50–52.

2. Edith Foster Dulles, *The Story of My Life* (privately printed, 1934), *passim.* This is an autobiography written by Dulles's mother for her grandchildren: a copy is available in The Personal Papers of John Foster Dulles, Princeton University Library, Princeton, New Jersey. (The Personal Papers of John Foster Dulles will hereafter be cited as DP.)

3. Eleanor Lansing Dulles, *John Foster Dulles: The Last Year* (New York: Harcourt, Brace & World, 1963), 158–161 (hereafter cited as Eleanor Dulles, *The Last Year*). Transcript of interview with Margaret Dulles Edwards, Dulles Oral History Project, Princeton University Library, Princeton, N.J. (The Dulles Oral History Project will hereafter be cited as DOHP.)

4. Eleanor Dulles, *The Last Year*, 61, 126–127.

5. Transcripts of interviews with Margaret Dulles Edwards and Nataline Dulles Seymour, DOHP. Eleanor Dulles, *The Last Year*, 126, 128–129, 160–161, 199.

6. Dulles album, 1888–1895, DP.

7. Eleanor Dulles, *The Last Year*, 126. Transcript of interview with Margaret Dulles Edwards, DOHP.

8. Edith Dulles, *The Story of My Life, passim*, DP. *Who's Who in America*, 1918–1919 (Chicago: A. N. Marquis & Co., 1918).

9. John Watson Foster, *Diplomatic Memoirs* (Boston: Houghton Mifflin Co., 1909), II, 156–157, 281–302 and *passim*. William R. Castle, Jr., "John Watson Foster," in *The American Secretaries of State and Their Diplomacy* (New York: Alfred A. Knopf, 1928), VIII, 187–227.

10. Foster, *Diplomatic Memoirs*, 281–302 and *passim*.

11. Edith Dulles, *The Story of My Life, passim*, DP.

12. Ibid. Eleanor Dulles, *The Last Year*, 63, 159–161.

13. Ibid.

14. Dulles album, 1888–1895, DP. Transcript of interview with Margaret Dulles Edwards, DOHP. Eleanor Dulles, *The Last Year*, 61–62, 167–168.

15. Scholastic records of John Foster Dulles, 1904–1908, Princeton University Archives, Princeton, N.J. *Catalogue of Princeton University, 1907–1908* (Princeton University, 1908), 360. Transcript of interview with Margaret Dulles Edwards, DOHP. Eleanor Dulles, *The Last Year*, 125–126.

16. See below, pp. 172–177.

17. Henry Wilkinson Bragdon, *Woodrow Wilson: The Academic Years* (Cambridge, Mass.: The Belknap Press of Harvard University Press, 1967), 207, 219.

18. Arthur Dean, "John Foster Dulles: An Appreciation," reprinted from Memorial Book of the Association of the Bar of the City of New York, DP.

19. Arthur Dean, "John Foster Dulles," DP. Transcripts of interview with Margaret Dulles Edwards and Henry Van Dusen, DOHP. Eleanor Dulles, *The Last Year*, 127–128.

20. Dulles diary, 1907; "Remarks introducing Mr. Huber at a Bar Association luncheon," June 3, 1931, DP.

21. See below, pp. 178–217.

22. Dulles notebook, 1909–1911; Edith Dulles, *The Story of My Life, passim*; Arthur Dean, "John Foster Dulles," DP.

23. Dulles notebook, 1909–1911, DP. Eleanor Dulles, *The Last Year*, 128.

24. Transcript of interview with Margaret Dulles Edwards, DOHP.

25. Eleanor Dulles, *The Last Year*, 159.

CHAPTER 2

1. Transcript of interview with Margaret Dulles Edwards, DOHP.

2. John Watson Foster to A. S. Sullivan, February 15, 1911, DP

3. *Who's Who in America, 1936–1937* (Chicago: A. N. Marquis Co., 1936); Dwight Carrol Miner, *The Fight for the Panama Route: The Story of the Spooner Act and the Hay–Herran Treaty* (New York: Columbia University Press, 1940), 80.

4. Miner, *The Fight for the Panama Route, passim*; Gerstle Mack, *The Land Divided: A History of the Panama Canal and Other Isthmian Canal Projects* (New York: Alfred A. Knopf, 1944), 417–500.

5. Dulles to John Watson Foster, August 18, 1911; John Watson Foster to Dulles, August 20, 1911, DP.

6. John Watson Foster to Dulles, November 11, 1911; Dulles to St. Joseph's Nurseries, Trinidad, September 18, 1912, DP.

7. Dulles memorandum, "For Personal File—1918"; Dulles to Robert Lansing, February 14, 1913; John Watson to Dulles, April 9, 1914, DP.

8. Dulles memorandum, "For Personal File—1918"; Dulles to Robert Lansing, April 2, 1915, DP. Dulles to Foreign Trade Adviser, March 13, 1915, March 19, 1915, March 29, 1915, October 16, 1915, State Department files 611.519/50, 361.11/420, 361.11/455, 611.629/175, National Archives, Washington D.C. (hereafter cited as NA)

9. See below, chapters 4 and 6.

10. Dulles to F. H. Covington, February 24, 1913, and general correspondence for 1913; James Brown Scott to Dulles, March 17, 1913; Dulles to *American Journal of International Law*, June 26, 1913; James Brown Scott to Dulles, October 6, 1915, DP.

11. At one point during his brief tenure as Secretary of State, Foster said: "Whatever difference of opinion exists among American citizens respecting the policy of territorial expansion, all seem to be agreed upon the desirability of commericial expansion. In fact it has become a necessity to find new and enlarged markets for our agricultural and manufactured products." Quoted in William Appleman Williams, ed., *From Colony to Empire: Essays in the History of American Foreign Relations* (New York: John Wiley & Sons, 1972), 198.

12. Dulles to Henry Van Dyke, April 18, 1915; Robert Lansing to Dulles, February 16, 1916; Dulles to the Reform Club, February 15, 1916, DP.

13. John Watson Foster to Dulles, November 11, 1911, and August 30, 1912; Dulles to John Watson Foster, April 2, 1915, DP.

14. Robert Lansing to Dulles, January 29, 1913; Dulles to Robert Lansing, January 31, 1913, February 14, 1913, August 8, 1914, November 13, 1914, April 2, 1915; Albert Strauss to Dulles, October 20, 1916, DP.

15. Emiliano Chamorro to Dulles, June 27, 1916, September 4, 1916; Dulles to Emiliano Chamorro, July 28, 1916; Dulles cable to Emiliano Chamorro, October 3, 1916; Dulles to Robert Lansing, October 20, 1916; Lansing to Dulles, July 29, 1916, DP. Dana G. Munro, *The Five Republics of Central*

America: The Poltical and Economic Development and Their Relations with the United States (New York: Oxford University Press, 1918), 249–252.

16. Among the corporations represented by Sullivan & Cromwell were the Cuban Cane Sugar Corp., with investments of $60 million, and the Manati Sugar Co., with investments of $10 million. All of the firm's clients together held more than $170 million in Cuban investments: Dulles to Secretary of State, February 14, 1917, and March 1, 1917, State Department files 337.11/162 and 337.11/241, NA.

17. Dulles memorandum, "Activities Relating to Cuban Affairs, February 13 to February 20, 1917," DP. Secretary of the Navy Josephus Daniels to Secretary of State Robert Lansing, February 25, 1917, *Papers Relating to the Foreign Relations of the United States, 1917* (Washington: Government Printing Office, 1926), 360. Russel H. Fitzgibbon, *Cuba and the United States, 1900–1935* (Menasha, Wisconsin: Collegiate Press, 1935), 156–159.

18. Robert Lansing to Dulles, cable, March 28, 1917; Dulles to Helen Bramble, October 24, 1928, DP. Robert Lansing, *The War Memoirs of Robert Lansing* (New York: Bobbs-Merrill Co., 1935), 314.

19. Dulles cable to Robert Lansing, May 18, 1917; Dulles memorandum, "Political and Economic Conditions in Costa Rica as Bearing on the Question of Recognizing the Government of General Tinoco—Confidential Report of Mr. John Foster Dulles to the Secretary of State," May 21, 1917; J. A. Urtecho to Dulles, May 20, 1917; memorandum, "Notes on Nicaragua," May 23, 1917; memorandum, "For Personal File—1918," DP.

20. Dulles to Emiliano Chamorro, May 26, 1917; memorandum, "For Personal File—1918," DP. It is tempting to look on Dulles's first official assignment as a foretaste of United States policy toward Latin America in the 1950s. The big brother behavior, the concern for "better" classes and economic matters, the willingness to let European or other "crises" shape Latin American policy: these are interesting hints of later tendencies. Of course, Dulles was a very minor cog in 1917—and the characteristics of U.S. policy toward Latin America evident at that time were hardly absent in the years that intervened between his special mission and his appointment as Secretary of State.

21. Dulles memorandum, August 1917, DP.

22. Dulles memorandum, August 29, 1917, State Department file 838.51/880, NA.

23. Dulles to Chief of Staff, July 23, 1918, DP.

24. Dulles to Chief of Staff, August 14, 1918, DP. *Report of the War Trade Board* (Washington, D.C.: Government Printing Office, 1920), 5.

25. *Report of the War Trade Board*, 20–21. Dulles to Chief of Staff, August 14, 1918; draft statements of March 21, 1918, and April 13, 1918; "Eleven Documents Relating to Work with the War Trade Board, 1918–1919," DP.

26. William Appleman Williams, *American–Russian Relations, 1781–1947* (New York: Rinehart & Co., 1952), 101–130; N. Gordon Levin, Jr., *Woodrow*

Wilson and World Politics: America's Response to War and Revolution (New York: Oxford University Press, 1968), 50–73.

27. Williams, *American–Russian Relations*, 94–95, 149, 153; George F. Kennan, *The Decision to Intervene* (New York: Atheneum, 1967), 359. Dulles, T. L. Chadbourne and C. M. Wooley to the War Trade Board, memorandum, June 5, 1918, DP.

28. Kennan, *The Decision to Intervene*, 385.

29. Williams, *American–Russian Relations*, 151–157; Levin, *Wilson and World Politics*, 221–236; Kennan, *The Decision to Intervene*, 381–404.

30. Item from summer 1918, "Eleven Documents relating to Work with the War Trade Board, 1917–1918," DP.

31. Dulles and others to Woodrow Wilson, October 1, 1918; mimeographed announcement, November 30, 1918, in ibid.

32. Williams, *Amiercan–Russian Relations*, 153.

33. See below, p. 53.

CHAPTER 3

1. Woodrow Wilson memorandum, December 2, 1918, DP.

2. Edward Mandell House and Charles Seymour, eds., *What Really Happened at Paris: The Story of the Peace Conference, 1918–1919* (New York: Charles Scribners' Sons, 1921), 1; James T. Shotwell, *At the Paris Peace Conference* (New York: Macmillan Co., 1937), 3–15.

3. Edwin F. Gay to Dulles, December 19, 1918; Dulles to Edwin F. Gay, January 24, 1919, DP. Laurence E. Gelfand, *The Inquiry: American Preparations for Peace, 1917–1919* (New Haven: Yale University Press, 1963), 177–178.

4. Dulles to Edwin F. Gay, January 24, 1919, DP.

5. Charles Seymour, ed., *The Intimate Papers of Colonel House* (Boston: Houghton Mifflin Co., 1928), IV, 268.

6. Philip Mason Burnett, *Reparation at the Paris Peace Conference: From the Standpoint of the American Delegation* (New York: Columbia University Press, 1940), I, 17–19, 445–467, 500–502. Burnett's work is invaluable for a study of reparations negotiations in 1919. His two volumes are almost entirely made up of *verbatim* documents from various private and government sources. One major source, and Burnett admitted to a great debt in 1940, was the materials loaned to him by John Foster Dulles. Dulles had saved a small mountain of documents from the Paris Peace Conference. These are now available in the Dulles Papers, but Burnett's volumes provide a readily available version of a major number of items. Hereafter, the work will be cited as: Burnett, *Reparation*.

7. Burnett, *Reparation*, I, 53–59, 62–75, 600–609, 656–679, 781, 811–817, 872–876, 908–913, 936–941, 1041–1044, 1077–1103, 1112–1113, 1129–1130; II, 119–120, 125–128, 157–161, *passim*.

8. Ibid., II, 105, 107–128, 157–161.

9. Ibid., 275–351 provides abstracts of relevant documents dealing with Austria, Hungary, Bulgaria, Turkey.

10. Dulles to Joseph C. Grew, July 25, 1919; Dulles memorandum, undated but included in 1913–1925 file, DP.

11. Bernard Baruch, *The Making of the Reparation and Economic Sections of the Treaty* (New York: Harper & Bros., 1920), 45. This book is a deceptively important source for studying Dulles's role at the Paris Peace Conference. Despite Baruch's nominal role as "author," the book was actually a joint project of several men who had been in Paris in 1919. The section on reparations was written by Dulles. See Dulles's secretary to Dulles, April 27, 1920, and Dulles to Bernard Baruch, May 22, 1920, DP. Thomas Lamont, "Reparations," in House and Seymour, eds., *What Really Happened at Paris*, 259.

12. Burnett, *Reparation*, I, 3–157; Seth P. Tillman, *Anglo–American Relation at the Paris Peace Conference of 1919* (Princeton: Princeton University Press, 1961), 229–259; Arno Mayer, *Politics and Diplomacy of Peacemaking: Containment and Counterrevolution at Versailles, 1918–1919* (New York: Alfred A. Knopf, 1967), 152–158, 623–652; Thomas A. Bailey, *Woodrow Wilson and The Lost Peace* (New York: Quadrangle Books, 1963), 238–251.

13. Plenary Commission on Reparation of Damage, Minutes of Fourth Meeting, February 10, 1919, in Burnett, *Reparation*, II, 294–307.

14. Seymour, *Intimate Papers of Colonel House*, IV, 343–344, and a selection from the House Diary, Yale University Library, included in Burnett, *Reparation*, I, 600.

15. Dulles, address on "Principles of Reparations," in Commission on Reparation of Damage, February 7, 1919: Burnett, *Reparation*, I, 536–543.

16. House and Seymour, eds., *What Really Happened at Paris*, 269–270.

17. Burnett, *Reparation*, I, 25–26; II, 317–323.

18. Ibid., I, 27, 613–614.

19. Paul Mantoux, ed., *Paris Peace Conference, 1919: Proceedings of the Council of Four (March 24–April 18)* (Geneva: Librairie Droz, 1964), 57.

20. Dulles drafts of February 21, 22, 24, 25, 26, and March 6, 7, 8, 12, 13, for example, are in Burnett, *Reparation*, I, 600–609, 619–620, 627–631, 656–657, 662–668, 671–679; see also 51–52.

21. Ibid., 600–604.

22. Extract from diary of David Hunter Miller, February 24, 1919, ibid., 618.

23. Lloyd George draft, March 29, 1919, ibid., 754–756; see also 66–70.

24. Minutes of the Experts' meeting, April 1, 1919, ibid., 781–784.

25. Second American Proposed Preamble Clause, April 2, 1919, ibid., 785.

26. It might be mentioned that long after the Peace Conference, Dulles and others were arguing that what became Article 231 of the Peace Treaty was *not* meant to saddle Germany with a grievous weight of moral guilt. While recognizing the problems caused by the clause, Dulles always maintained that it was nothing more than a device to compromise the divergent Allied and American approaches to the theoretical financial responsibility of Germany. It was, he believed, a question of money and not morality. As proof, he suggested that neither the Council of Four nor the officially established Commission on Responsibilities would have allowed the reparations negotiators to deal with so basic and sweeping an issue as Germany's moral guilt for the Great War. For an example of Dulles's later thinking on the "war guilt" clause, see the "Foreword" to Burnett, *Reparation*, I, v–xiv. For all of his emphasis on the financial focus of the clause, however, there is really no reason to doubt that the reparations experts in 1919 would have been willing to pronounce a sweeping moral denunciation against the defeated enemy. See, for example, the comments by Norman Davis in Mantoux, *Proceedings of the Council of Four*, 117.

27. Seymour, *Intimate Papers of Colonel House*, IV, 343–344; Burnett, *Reparation*, I, 35–36.

28. Ibid., 600–604.

29. Mantoux, *Proceedings of the Council of Four*, 11–17. Among other evidence indicating that the initial inspiration for the Reparation Commission came from Dulles is Colonel House's attribution in Seymour, *Intimate Papers of Colonel House*, IV, 381.

30. Memorandum of Lord Sumner, March 27, 1919, Burnett, *Reparations*, I, 719–725. "Pensions," of course, were defined as payment to wounded or maimed war veterans and payments to the orphans or widows of soldiers killed in the war; "separation allowances" were those payments made by governments to the families of men who were called to military service to compensate those families for the income they would be deprived of for the length of service.

31. Wilson's comments reported in a letter by Thomas W. Lamont, cited in ibid., I, 63; Dulles's memorandum, March 29, 1919, ibid., 758–762.

32. Smuts memorandum of April 1, 1919, ibid., 773–775.

33. Dulles and Lamont memoranda of April 1, 1919, ibid., 775–777.

34. Ibid., 51–60, 78; Seymour, *Intimate Papers of Colonel House*, IV, 398–399.

35. Burnett, *Reparation*, I, 77–78.

36. Seymour, *Intimate Papers of Colonel House*, IV, 399–405; Mantoux, *Proceedings of the Council of Four*, 116–128; Baruch, *The Making of the Reparation and Economic Sections of the Treaty*, 29, 129–130; Burnett, *Reparation*, I, 51–60, 77–78, 788–800.

37. Burnett, *Reparation*, I, 106–108.

38. Ibid., 78–83, 126–130.

39. Ibid., II, 1–2, 6–9, 31–35, 52–78.

40. Mayer, *Politics and Diplomacy of Peacemaking*, 795–804; Burnett, *Reparation*, II, 101–105.

41. Burnett, *Reparation*, II, 107–109, 125–128, 148–154, 161–166, 170, 191–202.

42. Ibid., 109–118, 167–168, 191–202.

43. Ibid., 167–168, 191–202.

44. There were any number of minor factors that contributed to the shaping of the U.S. position as well. Perusal of the day-to-day records of delegation meetings makes it clear that the Americans, as well as the Allies in general, were fearful of treating Germany too harshly lest she refuse to sign the Peace Treaty and thereby open a pandora's box of occupation and reprisal problems. Yet it is equally apparent that this fear was only occasionally voiced and was not among the most important of determining factors. A similar secondary importance can be attached to American and occasional British concern for the effect of reparations on Germany's future status as an economic competitor and customer. Might not the German economy burgeon as it was forced to work harder in order to pay extensive damages to the victors, and might not that economy become enormously powerful on the world scene once reparation payments were completed? Or, in a related scenario, might not Germany's heavy debt make it impossible for her to import as extensively from the Allies as she had in the prewar years? On these and other factors, see Baruch, *The Making of the Reparation and Economic Sections of the Treaty*, 49; Burnett, *Reparation*, I, 460, 687–689; Mantoux, *Proceedings of the Council of Four*, 3, 14–15.

45. Among the best surveys of the reactions of the Wilson Administration to the Bolshevik Revolution are George F. Kennan, *The Decision to Intervene* (New York: Atheneum, 1967); N. Gordon Levin, *Woodrow Wilson and World Politics: America's Response to War and Revolution* (New York: Oxford University Press, 1968); Arno J. Mayer, *Politics and Diplomacy of Peacemaking* and *Political Origins of the New Diplomacy* (New Haven: Yale University Press, 1959); William Appleman Williams, *American–Russian Relations, 1781–1947* (New York, Rinehart & Co., 1952), 105–156.

46. See, for example, Mayer, *Politics and Diplomacy of Peacemaking*, 368, 716, 732–733, 744 and *passim*.

47. Quoted in Levin, *Wilson and World Politics*, 131, 133–135.

48. Mantoux, *Proceedings of the Council of Four*, 14–15.

49. Quoted in Levin, *Wilson and World Politics*, 137–138.

50. Burnett, *Reparation*, I, 460; II, 101–104.

51. Seymour, *Intimate Papers of Colonel House*, IV, 325; Robert Lansing, *The Peace Negotiations: A Personal Narrative* (Boston: Houghton Mifflin Co., 1921), 210.

52. House and Seymour, *What Really Happened at Paris,* 263.

53. Burnett, *Reparation,* II, 103–104.

54. Ray S. Baker and William E. Dodd, eds., *The Public Papers of Woodrow Wilson* (New York: Harper & Bros., 1925–1927), V, 168–174; Burnett, *Reparation,* II, 115–116.

55. Seymour, *The Intimate Papers of Colonel House,* IV, 391.

56. House and Seymour, *What Really Happened at Paris,* 285–286, 289.

57. Quoted in Levin, *Wilson and World Politics,* 138.

58. Baker and Dodd, *Public Papers of Woodrow Wilson,* V, 586–589.

59. Ibid., 624–625.

60. Dulles to Edwin F. Gay, January 29, 1919, DP.

61. Dulles memoranda of June 1, 2, 3, 1919: Burnett, *Reparation,* II, 105, 107–109.

62. Dulles diary and notes, March 29, July 7, 11, 15, 1919, DP.

63. Dulles memoranda, August 8, 1919, DP.

64. Baker and Dodd, *Public Papers of Woodrow Wilson,* V, 382–383, 559–560, 637.

65. Dulles memorandum, August 1917, DP.

66. See Levin, *Woodrow Wilson and World Politics, passim*; Mayer, *Politics and Diplomacy of Peacemaking, passim.*

CHAPTER 4

1. Within the United States, friendships established during government service in the Great War included those with Herbert Hoover; Norman Davis; Thomas W. Lamont, of J. P. Morgan & Co.; Richard Crane, Minister to Czechoslovakia in the early 1920s; William Wilson Cumberland, a trade and finance adviser for the Department of State during the 1920s and 1930s; Ellis Dresel, American Commissioner to Germany and Chargé d'Affaires in Berlin during the 1920s; Christian Herter, Assistant to the Secretary of Commerce; Arthur Young, Economic Adviser in the Department of State; Frank L. Polk, Acting Secretary of State during the Paris Peace Conference and then a Director of the Chase National Bank; and Bernard Baruch. Across the Atlantic, Dulles's contacts in government and business circles were also extensive. In Great Britain, he maintained friendships with John Maynard Keynes; Lionel Curtis, of the Royal Institute of International Affairs; Lord Sumner; and the Lord Lothian who would be Ambassador to the United States. In France, he was particularly close to Louis Loucheur and Georges Jouasset, both active in French business and banking and both likewise regular members of French cabinets after 1919. Georges Theunis, who would serve as Prime Minister of Belgium in the mid-1920s, saw Dulles regularly in Brussels. And with Eduard Beneš, one of the foremost leaders of Czechoslovakia following the Great War, Dulles also maintained regular contact. Mention might also be made of Manley O. Hudson, a good friend at the League of Nations Secretariat in Geneva. For examples of Dulles's extensive correspondence with these men and others, see DP *passim*.

2. *The New York World*, August 14, 1919, for example, DP.

3. Dulles memorandum to the Senate Foreign Relations Committee, Fall 1919; Dulles to Robert Lansing, cable, August 6, 1919, DP.

4. Diary entry, March 10, 1919; Dulles to William Nelson Cromwell, June 28, 1919; Dulles to Joseph C. Grew, July 4, 1919, DP.

5. Herbert Hoover to W. B. Ryan, American Legation, Prague, January 28, 1920; Dulles to John S. Drum, November 12, 1920, DP.

6. Dulles to Allen W. Dulles, December 4, 1919; Dulles to John S. Drum, November 12, 1920, DP.

7. James W. Gantenbein, *Financial Questions in United States Foreign Policy* (New York: Columbia University Press, 1939), 226; Cleona Lewis, *America's Stake in International Investments* (Washington, D.C.: Brookings Institution, 1938), 198; Woodbury Willoughby, *The Capital Issues Committee and the War Finance Corporation* (Baltimore: Johns Hopkins Press, 1934), 85–116. Dulles to Louis Loucheur, December 18, 1919, DP.

8. Dulles calendars, 1926–1941, DP. John Moody, *Moody's Analysis of Investments and Security Rating Books, 1926* (New York: Moody's Investment Service, 1926), 1.

9. Dulles calendars, 1920–1941, DP. *Moody's Manual of Railroads and Corporation Securities, 1920* (New York: Poor's Publishing Co., 1920), 2143–2145.

10. Dulles calendars, 1920–1924, DP. *Moody's Manual of Railroads and Corporation Securities, 1920*, 41–45.

11. Dulles caldendars, 1921–1924, DP. *Moody's Manual of Railroads and Corporation Securities, 1920*, 2175–2176.

12. Dulles calendars, 1923–1941, DP. *Moody's Manual of Investments: American and Foreign Industrial Securities, 1933* (New York: Moody's Investors Service, 1933), 93.

13. Allen Dulles to Department of State, January 9, 1928, State Department file 821.6363 Barco/67, National Archives, Washington, D.C. (National Archives will be identified as NA hereafter.)

14. Dulles calendars, 1922–1923, DP.

15. Dulles calendars, 1920–1921, DP. *Moody's Manual of Railroads and Corporation Securities, 1921* (New York: Poor's Publishing Co., 1921), I, 446–448.

16. Dulles calendars, 1920–1926, DP.

17. Dulles calendars, 1923–1936, DP. John Moody, *Moody's Analysis of Investments and Security Rating Books, 1924* (New York: Moody's Investment Service, 1924), 2027.

18. Dulles calendars, 1920–1941, DP. *Moody's Manual of Railroads and Corporation Securities, 1920,* 2693–2695; John Moody, *Moody's Analysis of Investment and Security Rating Books, 1926,* 2121. Also, see below, pp. 127–128.

19. Dulles calendars, 1924–1941, DP. John Moody, *Moody's Analysis of Investment and Security Rating Books, 1924,* 2118–2119.

20. Dulles to Department of State, October 12, 1928, State Department file 838.77/358 F. W., NA.

21. Dulles to Secretary of State, November 28, 1923; Department of State to Dulles, November 20, 1923; Dulles to Secretary of State, December 3, 1923; Department of State to Dulles, February 19, 1924; Department of State to American Chargé in Warsaw, April 2, 1924: State Department file 360c.1153 Ov2, NA.

22. Dulles to Department of State, September 2, 1922, State Department file 332.15 P83, NA.

23. Dulles calendars, 1920–1933, DP. *Moody's Manual of Railroads and Corporation Securities, 1920,* 1611.

24. Dulles calendars, 1928–1934, DP.

25. Dulles calendars, 1924–1927, DP.

26. State Department files 462.11D88/1, 462.11D955, NA.

27. Dulles to Secretary of State, January 7, 1920; Dulles to Secretary of State, November 14, 1921; Dulles to Secretary of State, December 9, 1921; Dulles to Russian Division, Department of State, January 29, 1927: State Department files 860c.5064/L, 463.11/2, 463.11Eq52/, 116.3/1150½, NA. The New York Times, August 20, 1931, p. 7. Dulles to Dr. Hans Heymann, December 30, 1943; "P.L.M." to Dulles, December 29, 1943, DP.

28. Dulles to Secretary of State, July 2, 1920; Dulles to Department of State, April 25, 1924; Division of Mexican Affairs Memorandum, May 7, 1924; Dulles to Department of State, December 27, 1924: State Department files 814.6463Em7/25, 814.6463Em7/99, 812.6363/B2, 819.6463/4, NA. Dulles calendars, 1921–1931, DP.

29. John Kenneth Galbraith, *The Great Crash: 1929* (Boston: Houghton Mifflin Co., 1954), 36, 67–69, 117, 129, 147, 187.

30. See above, pp. 5–6.

31. George Soule, *Prosperity Decade: From War to Depression, 1917–1929* (New York: Harper Torchbooks, 1947), 252–272.

32. For surveys of the attitudes of American businessmen at the end of the Great War, with particular reference to the international scene, see Carl P. Parini, *Heir to Empire: United States Economic Diplomacy, 1916–1923* (Pittsburgh: University of Pittsburgh Press, 1969) and Joan Hoff Wilson, *American Business and Foreign Policy, 1920–1933* (Lexington: University Press of Kentucky, 1971).

33. Dulles to Allen W. Dulles, December 4, 1919; Dulles to Louis Loucheur,

December 18, 1919; Dulles to John S. Drum, November 12, 1920, DP. See also Parini, *Heir to Empire*, 72–100. Dulles's work in this area was concomitant with his services to the War Finance Corporation, a government agency designed to provide interim assistance in the area of foreign trade financing; see above, p. 61.

34. Lewis, *America's Stake in International Investments*, 351–397.
35. Dulles calendar, 1923, DP.
36. Dulles calendar, 1924, DP.
37. State Department file 825.51 H15, NA.
38. State Department file 821.51Ag8/4, NA.
39. State Department file 821.51H14, NA.
40. State Department file 839.51/2881, NA.
41. State Department file 825.51Sa61/7, NA.
42. State Department file 824.51/394, NA.
43. State Department file 835.51 B861/27, NA.
44. State Department file 832.51Sa61/7, NA.
45. State Department file 821.51/365, NA.
46. State Department file 832.51M66/10, NA.
47. State Department file 821.51/393, NA.
48. State Department file 835.51 C81/8, NA.
49. State Department file 821. 51B 22/6, NA.
50. State Department file 832.51 R471/18, NA.
51. State Department file 835.51 B861/39, NA.
52. Dulles calendars, 1920 and 1922, DP. State Department file 893.51/4541 and State Department file 893.51/2655, NA.
53. State Department file 867.6020t81/394, NA.
54. State Department file 860F51/87, NA.
55. State Department file 859.51 B92/ , NA.
56. State Department file 859.51 C79, NA.
57. State Department file 860d.51 H36/1, NA.
58. State Department file 859. 51 As7/13, NA.
59. State Department file 841.51 C91, NA.
60. State Department file 859.51 F22/ , NA.
61. State Department file 865.51 G28/1, NA.
62. State Department file 865.51 R66/1, NA.
63. State Department file 865.51 T27/2, NA.
64. State Department file 859.51 C791/4, NA.
65. State Department file 859.51 R81/5, NA.
66. State Department file 863. 51 C86, NA.

67. Dulles, "Polish Stabilization Plan," 1927 pamphlet, DP. State Department file 860c.51 P751/ , NA.

68. State Department file 857.51 Brown Bros. & Co./1, NA.

69. State Department file 859.51/157, NA.

70. State Department file 857.51 Akershus/1, NA.

71. State Department file 867.51 Glommens & Laagens/1, NA.

72. State Department file 855.51 City of Antwerp/2, NA.

73. State Department file 863.51 Upper Austria/1, NA.

74. Dulles calendar, 1929, DP.

75. Robert R. Kuczynski, *Bankers' Profits from German Loans* (Washington, D.C.: Brookings Institution, 1932), 5–11.

76. Dulles to Helen Bramble, October 24, 1928, DP. Kuczynski, *Bankers' Profits from German Loans*, 182.

77. Dulles calendar, 1925, DP. Kuczynski, *Bankers' Profits from German Loans*, 183.

78. State Department file 862.51 EL2, NA.

79. State Department file 862.51 D48, NA.

80. State Department file 862.51 L55, NA.

81. State Department file 862.51 Sa91, NA.

82. Dulles to Horace G. Reed, October 21, 1925, DP. Kuczynski, *Bankers' Profits from German Loans*, 194.

83. State Department file 862.51 Un31, NA.

84. State Department file 862.51 M312, NA.

85. State Department file 862.51 W52/6, NA.

86. State Department file 862.51B452/4, NA.

87. State Department files 862.51B32/23, 862.51B32/25, NA.

88. State Department file 862.51 H/173, NA.

89. State Department file 862.51 B751/9, NA.

90. State Department file 862.51 N18, NA.

91. State Department file 862.51 F85/12, NA.

92. Dulles to Leon Fraser, January 21, 1927, DP. Kuczynski, *Bankers' Profits from German Loans*, 190. State Department file 862.51P95/40, NA.

93. State Department file 862.51 Sa94/1, NA.

94. Dulles to Stimming, July 20, 1926, DP. Kuczynski, *Bankers' Profits from German Loans*, 190.

95. State Department file 862.51 Hamburg Street Railways/1, NA.

96. State Department file 862.51 B45/37, NA.

97. State Department file 862.51 Gewerkschaft/1, NA.

98. State Department file 862.51 Thueringer Gas Gesellschaft/3, NA.

99. State Department file 862.51 H19/7, NA.

100. Dulles to H. F. Albert, December 27, 1935, DP. Kuczynski, *Bankers' Profits from German Loans*, 201.

101. Dulles to Edward S. Greenbaum, February 5, 1931, DP. Kuczynski, *Bankers' Profits from German Loans*, 202–203.

102. Lewis, *America's Stake in International Investments*, 376–423.

103. Parini, *Heir to Empire*, 212–247; Soule, *Prosperity Decade*, 264–272; Wilson, *American Business and Foreign Policy*, 65–100.

104. *Fortune*, III:1, January 1931, p. 62.

105. Dulles addresses, "The Power of International Finance," March 24, 1928, and the address to the International Chamber of Commerce, April 29, 1929, DP.

106. Dulles, "Polish Stabilization Plan," 1927 pamphlet, DP.

107. See below, pp. 94–96, 98–100.

108. Joseph Brandes, *Herbert Hoover and Economic Diplomacy: Department of Commerce Policy, 1921–1928* (Pittsburgh: University of Pittsburgh Press, 1962), 180–188; Kuczynski, *Bankers' Profits from German Loans*, 7–11. Dulles to Robert E. Olds, December 22, 1925; Robert E. Olds to Dulles, February 17, 1926; Robert E. Olds to Dulles, February 20, 1926; Dulles to Robert E. Olds, February 24, 1926; Frank Altschul to Dulles, February 19, 1926, DP. Dulles, "Our Foreign Loan Policy," *Foreign Affairs*, 5:1 (October 1926), 33–48.

109. For another example of Dulles's protective attitude toward his banker clients see his address, "German Securities as Affected by Germany's Financial Obligations Under the Treaty of Versailles and Dawes Plan," printed in *The International Bankers Association of America Bulletin*, December 30, 1926, DP.

CHAPTER 5

1. Dulles to James Brown Scott, March 19, 1921, DP.

2. Nicholas Murray Butler to Dulles, April 19, 1932, for example, DP.

3. J. W. Beatson to Dulles, August 22, 1923, DP.

4. Dulles to John J. Esch, June 6, 1930, DP.

5. A. H. Froendt to Dulles, March 2, 1922, DP.

6. Charles Strong to Dulles, July 22, 1925, DP.

7. Dulles to American Arbitration Association, February 26, 1927, DP.

8. Dulles to Joseph Schain, May 5, 1938, DP.

9. Frederick J. Libby to Dulles, January 30, 1939, DP.

10. Dulles to Esther Evereth Lape, December 30, 1926, DP. For extensive background information on these and other internationalist organizations

in the United States during the interwar years, see Robert H. Ferrell, *Peace in Their Time: the Origins of the Kellogg–Briand Pact* (New Haven: Yale University Press, 1952).

11. Dulles and/or his secretary kept an excellent set of desk calendars during the 1920s, which provide an interesting source of information about the business, social, and leisure side of his life. Though sketchy to be sure, there are plentiful references to daily office appointments as well as theater and opera dates and dinner engagements. The calendars are in DP.

12. Dulles to Bernard Baruch, 1919 memorandum; Dulles to John W. Davis, January 13, 1920; Dulles to Herbert Hoover, April 5, 1921; Herbert Hoover to Dulles, April 6, 1921; Herbert Hoover to Dulles, April 7, 1921; Christian Herter to Dulles, April 14, 1921; Dulles to Herbert Hoover, April 16, 1921; Dulles to Allen W. Dulles, June 3, 1921; Dulles to Ruel Smith, *The World*, March 11, 1927; "A Reply to Mr. Keynes," February 16, 1920, clipping from *London Times*; "Ray Stannard Baker's *Woodrow Wilson and World Settlement*," 1923 book review, DP.

13. A. H. Froendt to Dulles, March 2, 1922; Dulles to Van S. Merle–Smith, February 28, 1922; H. G. Mendenthal to Dulles, April 17, 1924; Dulles to Harold A. Hatch, June 5, 1924; Dulles memorandum on "War," 1923, DP. Ferrell, *Peace in Their Time*, 13–30; Merlo J. Pusey, *Charles Evans Hughes* (New York: Macmillan Co., 1951), II, 466–506.

14. Dulles to James G. MacDonald, February 1, 1923; Dulles to Charles Evans Hughes, February 10, 1923; Dulles to Manley O. Hudson, February 13, 1923; Manley O. Hudson to Dulles, February 15, 1923; William B. Hale to Dulles, May 16, 1925; Dulles to R. Allen Stephens, June 11, 1925; "An Opinion with Respect to Adherence by the United States to the Permanent Court of International Justice," February 1923; Address before the Illinois Bar Association, May 29, 1925, DP. Denna Frank Fleming, *The United States and World Organization, 1920–1933* (New York: Columbia University Press, 1938), 254–259; Pusey, *Charles Evans Hughes*, II, 599–602.

15. Dulles to Henry Goddard Leach, September 27, 1923; "The Renunciation of War," 1928, DP.

16. Dulles to John W. Davis, June 3, 1920, July 14, 1920; Dulles to Louis Loucheur, January 17, 1921; Dulles to Eduard Beneš, September 27, 1920, DP. The New York Times, October 15, 1920, p. 2.

17. Dulles to Bernard Baruch, February 4, 1924; Dulles to John W. Davis, July 18, 1924 and undated memorandum; *New York Journal of Commerce*, July 18, 1924, clipping, DP.

18. Theodore E. Burton to Dulles, March 10, 1928; Dulles to Theodore E. Burton, March 12, 1928; Herbert Hoover to Dulles, March 12, 1928; May 31, 1928; Dulles to Herbert Hoover, March 21, 1928; Dulles to Franklin D. Roosevelt, September 17, 1928; *New York Herald Tribune*, September 20, 1928, clipping, DP.

19. See, for example, Wilson, *American Business and Foreign Policy*, 31–64.

20. By 1931, Dulles was looking back at the great effort to outlaw war and musing that "the cause of peace is not served by erecting scarecrows." "Economic Sanctions: Remarks by John Foster Dulles," January 1932, DP.

21. Robert Lansing to Albert Rathbone, cable, February 7, 1920; Dulles to Albert Rathbone, February 22, 1920; W. W. Cumberland to Dulles, December 16, 1920; Arthur N. Young to Dulles, February 21, 1922; Edwin S. Parker to Dulles, April 9, 1925, DP.

22. See above, pp. 60–72.

23. Dulles to Norman Davis, April 1, 1920, DP.

24. Dulles to Allen Dulles, August 9, 1921; Memorandum on trip to Berlin, July 1921, DP.

25. Dulles memorandum concerning 1923 European Conferences with reference to Ruhr occupation; Max Warburg to Dulles, manuscript draft enclosure, 1942; Dulles to Max Warburg, November 30, 1942; Dulles memorandum, January 9, 1956, DP.

26. Charles Seymour, ed., *The Intimate Papers of Colonel House* (Boston: Houghton Mifflin Co., 1928), IV, 488–489.

27. Dulles memorandum, 1919, DP.

28. "A Reply to Mr. Keynes," clipping from *London Times*, February 16, 1920, DP. Bernard Baruch, *The Making of the Reparation and Economic Sections of the Treaty* (New York: Harper & Bros., 1920), 130, 158–160.

29. John Maynard Keynes to Dulles, March 2, 1920, DP.

30. Dulles to Norman Davis, April 1, 1920, DP.

31. Dulles, "The Reparation Problem," *The Bulletin of the Foreign Policy Association*, II (June 1921), 1–3. Dulles address, "The Allied Debts," March 1922; Dulles memorandum concerning 1923 European Conferences with reference to Ruhr occupation, DP.

32. Wilson, *American Business and Foreign Policy*, 123–156.

33. See above, pp. 51–53. Dulles memorandum, 1919; "Memorandum on the Importance to the United States of the Economic Provisions of the Treaty of Versailles," April 5, 1921; Dulles to John W. Davis, June 3, 1924, July 14, 1924, DP.

34. Dulles paper, August 12, 1922; Dulles to John W. Davis, June 3, 1924, July 14, 1924, DP.

35. Dulles memorandum, 1919; Dulles to Louis Loucheur, January 17, 1921; "Ray Stannard Baker's *Woodrow Wilson and World Settlement*," 1923; Dulles to John W. Davis, July 18, 1924, DP.

36. Address to the Foreign Policy Association, December 19, 1922; Undated address, probably 1924, "The Relation of France to a Program of World Reconstruction," DP. Dulles, "The Reparation Problem." This difference in kind, Dulles often went on, came to involve particular difficulties in arrang-

ing repayment of these debts. The only way in which Germany or the Allies could accumulate enough money for repayment of debts was to sell products or services abroad, he argued. Yet, realizing this, the U.S. and the Allies made no strong efforts to assist their respective debtors. Fearing competition for their own industries and workers, trade restrictions were imposed in a way that limited Allied sales in the U.S. and German sales everywhere. Under such circumstances, Dulles did not see how the debts could possibly be cleared.

37. See, for example, Dulles's address, "The Relation of France to a Program of World Reconstruction," undated but probably 1924, and Dulles to John W. Davis, July 18, 1924, DP.

38. Dulles to Louis Loucheur, January 17, 1921; memorandum of a conference with Louis Loucheur, July 21, 1923, DP. For another of Dulles's suggestions, see his address to the Foreign Policy Association, December 19, 1922, DP.

39. Dulles to Mrs. A. J. Boulton, December 5, 1923, DP.

40. Dulles to Louis Loucheur, January 17, 1921; "The Allied Debts," March 1922, DP.

41. George P. Auld, "The Dawes and Young Loans: Then and Now," *Foreign Affairs*, XIII (October 1934), 11–12; Rufus C. Dawes, *The Dawes Plan In the Making* (Indianapolis: Bobbs-Merrill Co., 1925), 285–286; Pusey, *Charles Evans Hughes*, II, 581–582.

42. Dulles to Christian Herter, April 1924; "Charles Dawes' *Journal of Reparations*," 1926 book review, DP.

43. Wilson, *American Business and Foreign Policy*, 123–156.

44. George Soule, *Prosperity Decade: From War to Depression, 1917–1929* (New York: Harper Torchbooks, 1947), 254–273 *passim*.

45. Dulles address, "America's Part in an Economic Conference," January 19, 1922, DP.

46. Ibid.

47. Ibid.; Dulles article for *New York Evening Post*, October 7, 1921; Dulles article, August 12, 1922, DP.

48. Dulles address, "America's Part in an Economic Conference," January 19, 1922, DP.

49. Ibid.

50. Ibid.; "The Allied Debts," March 1922, DP.

51. "The Allied Debts," March 1922; Dulles address, "The Relation of France to a Program of World Reconstruction," undated but probably 1924, DP.

52. Dulles address, "America's Part in an Economic Conference," January 19, 1922, DP.

53. Ibid.

54. Dulles to Louis Loucheur, January 17, 1921; Memorandum of a conference with Louis Loucheur, July 21, 1923; Dulles to Van S. Merle–Smith, February

28, 1922; Dulles to Harold A. Hatch, June 5, 1923; Dulles memorandum on "War," 1924, DP.

55. Dulles address, "The Power of International Finance," March 24, 1928, DP.

56. Dulles to Norman Davis, April 1, 1920, DP.

57. Cleona Lewis, *America's Stake in International Investments* (Washington: Brookings Institution, 1938), 376–397.

58. Dulles address, "The Power of International Finance," March 24, 1928, DP. In an address the following year, Dulles reached the same conclusion. Speaking to the International Chamber of Commerce, he praised the work of American bankers and the Federal Reserve Board. Their ability to create suitable money conditions in the United States had been "an amazing achievement and one to which our present prosperity is largely ascribable." Address to the International Chamber of Commerce, April 29, 1929, DP.

59. Dulles memorandum concerning 1923 European conferences with reference to Ruhr occupation; Dulles to Christian Herter, April 1924, DP.

60. Dulles to Frederic R. Dolbeare, February 2, 1922; Dulles memorandum, October 30, 1925, DP.

61. Dulles address to Conference on the Cause and Cure of War, 1924, DP.

62. Dulles address, "The Power of International Finance," March 24, 1928, DP.

63. Dulles address to the International Chamber of Commerce, April 29, 1929, DP.

64. Dulles, "Our Foreign Loan Policy," *Foreign Affairs*, V:1 (October 1926), 33–48. Dulles, "German Securities as Affected by Germany's Financial Obligations Under the Treaty of Versailles and the Dawes Plan," December 30, 1926, DP.

65. Dulles, "The Reparation Problem," *New Republic*, XXVI:330 (March 30, 1921), 133

66. Dulles to Norman Davis, April 1, 1920, DP.

67. See above, pp. 23–24.

68. Dulles address, "America's Part in an Economic Conference, January 19, 1922, DP.

69. Wilson, *American Business and Foreign Policy*, 3.

70. Dulles address, "The Relation of France to a Program of World Reconstruction," undated, but probably 1924, DP.

71. See, for example, Dulles address to the Foreign Policy Association, 1922; Dulles address, "The Power of International Finance, March 24, 1928; Dulles address to the International Chamber of Commerce, April 29, 1929, DP. Also, Dulles, "The Allied Debts," *Foreign Affairs*, I:1 (September 15, 1922), 115–132; "Allied Indebtedness to the United States," *Annals of the American Academy of Political and Social Science*, XCVI (July 1921), 173–177; "The Reparation Problem," *New Republic*, XXVI:330 (March 30, 1921), 133–135.

CHAPTER 6

1. Broadus Mitchell, *Depression Decade: From New Era Through New Deal, 1929-1941* (New York: Harper & Row, 1947), *passim.*

2. Transcript of interview with Eustace Seligman, Dulles Oral History Project (hereafter referred to as DOHP.) Mitchell, *Depression Decade,* 233; John Brooks, *Once in Golconda* (New York: Harper & Row, 1969), 211-212.

3. Mitchell, *Depression Decade,* 67, 268.

4. Stephen V. O. Clarke, *Central Bank Cooperation: 1924-1931* (New York: Federal Reserve Bank of New York, 1967), 144-160; Laurence Lafore, *The End of Glory: An Interpretation of the Origins of World War II* (Philadelphia: J. B. Lippincott Co., 1970), 78-120.

5. Clarke, *Central Bank Cooperation,* 160-219. Notes on Conversations Concerning Moratorium and Memorandum Left with President, June 1931, DP.

6. Robert E. Olds to Dulles, July 3, 1931; Robert E. Olds to Dulles, July 17, 1931: Dulles to Robert E. Olds, August 4, 1931, DP.

7. Clarke, *Central Bank Cooperation,* 182-194.

8. Transcripts of interviews with George Murnane and Eustace Seligman, DOHP. Dulles to D. C. Poole, May 1, 1936, DP.

9. Cleona Lewis, *America's Stake in International Investments* (Washington: Brookings Institution, 1938), 398-403, 412.

10. Herbert Feis to Henry L. Stimson, December 31, 1931, with enclosure of Dulles memorandum, December 16, 1931, State Department file 810.51/1349, NA.

11. James W. Gantenbein, *Financial Questions in United States Foreign Policy* (New York: Columbia Univeristy Press, 1939), 172-177.

12. Ibid., 159-160; Lewis, *America's Stake in International Investments,* 414. Dulles to Henry L. Stimson, February 16, 1932; Harvey H. Bundy to Nicholas Roosevelt, American Minister, Budapest, February 29, 1932; Harvey H. Bundy to Dulles, February 20, 1932; and Henry L. Stimson to American Legation, Budapest, February 25, 1932, State Department file 864.51/684, NA.

13. Dulles to Cordell Hull, June 6, 1933, DP.

14. Ibid. Lewis, *America's Stake in International Investments,* 401.

15. Dulles to Cordell Hull, June 6, 1933; Dulles to Eleanor Dulles, June 16, 1933, DP.

16. Lloyd Gardner, *Economic Aspects of New Deal Diplomacy* (Boston: Beacon Press, 1964),

17. Report of John Foster Dulles on Berlin Debt Discussions, December 1933, DP.

18. Ibid.

19. Report of John Foster Dulles and Laird Bell to American Banking Houses, January 1934, DP. William E. Dodd to Cordell Hull, with enclosures, December 1933, State Department file 862.51/3733, NA.

20. Lewis, *America's Stake in International Investments*, 414–416.

21. The New York Times, March 13, 1932, pp. 1, 22; April 6, 1932, pp. 1, 10; April 7, 1936, p. 37.

22. The New York Times, April 6, 1932, pp. 1, 10.

23. The New York Times, January 4, 1933, p. 25. Transcript of interview with George C. Sharpe, DOHP.

24. *The New York Times*, August 5, 1932, p. 21; September 1, 1932, p. 19; February 1, 1933, p. 24.

25. Transcript of interview with George C. Sharpe, DOHP. The New York Times, August 6, 1932, p. 17; September 22, 1933, p. 27; January 7, 1933, II, p. 7; March 2, 1934, p. 16; March 3, 1934, p. 3; March 10, 1934, p. 3; October 30, 1934, p. 35; October 31, 1934, p. 27; November 11, 1934, II, p. 11; May 11, 1935, p. 23; July 2, 1935, p. 37; August 4, 1935, p. 27; July 3, 1936, p. 23.

26. Transcript of interview with George C. Sharpe, DOHP. Candler Cobb to Dulles, September 1, 1936; Candler Cobb to Baldwin Maull, September 4, 1936, September 28, 1936 (2); Candler Cobb to Dulles, September 28, 1936, October 17, 1936, DP. Dulles to Wallace Murray, Chief, Division of Near Eastern Affairs, Department of State, July 16, 1940; Wallace Murray to Dulles, July 20, 1940, State Department file 868.51/1604, NA. *The New York Times*, March 16, 1936, p. 31; April 7, 1936, p. 37; September 4, 1936, p. 27; September 28, 1936, p. 32; October 28, 1936, p. 37; October 30, 1936, p. 35; August 25, 1937, p. 29.

27. Transcript of interview with George C. Sharpe, DOHP.

28. William O. Douglas, *Go East Young Man* (New York: Random House, 1974), 261–263.

29. Dulles to William Nelson, October 16, 1934; Cromwell to Dulles, October 18, 1934, DP.

30. See above, pp. 61–64.

31. Dulles appointment calendars, 1930–1939, DP. *Poor's Register of Directors of the United States and Canada, 1934*, 7th annual edition (New York: Poor's Publishing Co., 1934), 531–532.

32. Dulles to Emma Lansing, November 21, 1935; Dulles to George S. Brown, Special Committee to Investigate Lobbying Activities, January 29, 1936; Dulles to Silas H. Strawn, March 18, 1936; Silas H. Strawn to Dulles, March 24, 1936, DP. Douglas, *Go East Young Man*, 276–278.

33. Dulles to Secretary of State Henry L. Stimson, June 6, 1930, State Department file 860c.6463—Harriman and Company 1./17, NA. Transcript of interview with Averill H. Harriman, DOHP.

34. Dulles to Allen Dulles, March 19, 1930, DP.

35. See above, pp. 63–64. *The New York Times,* August 20, 1931; p. 7. Dulles to Dr. Hans Heymann, December 30, 1943; "P.L.M." to Dulles, December 29, 1943, DP.

36. Dulles to Reichsbank President Hjalmar Schacht, October 12, 1933; Dulles to H. F. Albert, December 27, 1935, DP.

37. Dulles to Allen Dulles, April 7, 1933, DP. *The Stock Exchange Official Yearbook, 1936* (London: Thomas Skinner & Co., 1936).

38. Dulles appointment calendars, 1930–1939; Dulles to Hans Petschek, July 1, 1930, DP.

39. See below, p. 320.

40. John Foster Dulles, Inzer B. Wyatt, Richard G. Pettingill, Memorandum on Behalf of Plaintiff, Banco de Espana Sigmund Solomon, L71/239, etc., June 2, 1938, United States District Court for the Southern District of New York; Dulles to Henry L. Stimson, January 26, 1939, DP.

41. Dulles to Luman J. Shafer, September 16, 1944, DP. *Christian Century,* LXI:43 (October 25, 1944), 1224–1225.

42. Transcript of broadcast, Berlin, January 22, 1947; transcript of J. Raymond Walsh broadcast, February 26, 1947; Dulles to George C. Marshall, March 10, 1948, DP. It might be mentioned that the spirit of such charges has been carried on since the 1940s by journalist I. F. Stone. "A lifelong servant of the most materialistic forces in our society," Stone has written of Dulles, "a Big Lawyer for the Big Money, a pre-War apologist for Japanese aggression and Nazi expansion, an exponent of Machiavellianism so long as the Axis was winning, an advocate of a Christian peace as soon as its defeat was foreseen. . . ." The traditional charges of ties with German industry, banking, and cartels have generally been made by Stone, while sentences have been lifted from late 1930s addresses and writings to demonstrate isolationism and the lack of moral outrage against fascism. See; for example, I. F. Stone, *The Haunted Fifties* (New York: Vintage Books, 1969), 12–16, 262–263.

43. Dulles to Luman J. Shafer, September 16, 1944, October 2, 1944; Dulles to I. J. Bookbinder, July 17, 1947, August 21, 1947; Dulles to George C. Marshall, March 10, 1948, DP.

44. Transcripts of interviews with Allen W. Dulles and Eustace Seligman, DOHP: Mr. Seligman has stated that "we closed that office in Berlin when it became apparent that Mr. Hitler was going to take over the government. We got out somewhat in advance. . . . Mr. Dulles was very active in that." See also *Christian Century,* LXI:43 (October 25, 1944), 1224–1225.

45. Dulles to William Nelson Cromwell, February 19, 1934; Hjalmar Schacht to Dulles, September 27, 1935; Dulles to H. F. Albert, December 27, 1935; Dulles to George S. Brown, January 29, 1936; Dulles to Hjalmar Schacht, June 15, 1937; Dulles to H. F. Albert, June 15, 1939, DP.

46. See, for example, the research material collection in *"Christian Century editorial"* file, *DP*.

47. George W. Stocking and Myron W. Watkins, *Cartels in Action: Case Studies in International Business Diplomacy* (New York: Twentieth Century Fund, 1946), 3–14; Wendell Berge, *Cartels: Challenge to a Free World* (Washington, D.C.: Public Affairs Press, 1946), 1–18; George W. Stocking and Myron Watkins, *Cartels or Competition? The Economics of International Controls by Business and Government* (New York: Twentieth Century Fund, 1948), 3–5, 408–421.

48. United Nations, Department of Economic Affairs, *International Cartels: A League of Nations Memorandum* (New York: 1947), 2; Stocking and Watkins, *Cartels in Action*, 4–5.

49. United States vs. International Nickel Co., Ltd. of Canada and International Nickel Co., in U.S. District Court for the Southern District of New York (Civil Action 36–31), May 16, 1946. (The records of the U.S. District Court for the Southern District of New York are located in the Federal Records Center, New York City. Court records include full documentation of the government case, all evidence and arguments presented by the defendants, and verdicts or final judgments.)

50. Ibid.

51. Stocking and Watkins, *Cartels in Action*, 363–429.

52. Ibid., 430–438; United States vs. Imperial Chemical Industries, Ltd., et al., in the U.S. District Court for the Southern District of New York (Civil Action 24–13), January 6, 1944; United States vs. United States Alkali Export Association, Inc., in the U.S. District Court for the Southern District of New York (Civil Action 24–464), March 16, 1944; United States vs. Allied Chemical and Dye Corp., et al., in the U.S. District Court for the Southern District of New York (Civil Action 14–320), Complaint and Consent Decree, May 29, 1941; United States vs. Allied Chemical & Dye Corp., et al., in United States District Court for the District of New Jersey (Criminal Action No. 753c), Indictment, May 14, 1952.

53. *Moody's Manual of Investments, American and Foreign: Industrial Securities 1933* (New York: Moody's Investors Service, 1933), 3176; *The New York Times*, June 2, 1933, p. 27.

54. *The New York Times*, June 2, 1933, p. 27; June 7, 1933, p. 31; June 10, 1933, p. 19; June 15, 1933, p. 25; June 17, 1933, p. 17; June 21, 1933, p. 29; June 23, 1933, p. 27; June 25, 1933, II, p. 9; June 26, 1933, p. 27; June 27, 1933, p. 23; June 28, 1933, p. 35; June 30, 1933, p. 28; July 1, 1933, p. 19; July 10, 1933, p. 22.

55 Dulles's appointment calendars are very helpful in plotting his continuing connection to the Solvay American–Allied Chemical relationship. From 1933 on, entries indicate a regular round of meetings with various directors of Solvay–American and *gérants* (owner-directors) of Solvay & Cie. itself. In

1935, 1936, and 1937, entries indicate regular meetings with George Murnane and H. F. Atherton, as well. See also *Moody's Manual of Investments, American and Foreign, Industrial Securities, 1936* (New York: Moody's Investors Service); Stocking and Watkins, *Cartels in Action*, 435–436, 478.

56. *Poor's Register of Directors of the United States and Canada, 1934* (New York: Poor's Publishing Co., 1934), 531–532; *The New York Times*, March 19, 1934, p. 12.

57. Ervin Hexner, *The International Steel Cartel* (Chapel Hill, N.C.: University of North Carolina Press, 1943), 92–109.

58. See *Trials of War Criminals Before the Nuernberg Military Tribunals and Control Council Law No. 10, Nuernberg, October 1946–April 1949*, Volume VI (Washington, D.C.: U.S. Government Printing Office, 1952).

59. Gabriel Kolko, "American Business and Germany, 1930–1941," *The Western Political Quarterly*, XV (December 1962, 713–728.

CHAPTER 7

1. See above, pp. 94–96.

2. Dulles address, April 29, 1929; Dulles to Fred M. Boyer, May 2, 1929, DP.

3. Dulles to Fred Dolbeare, November 1, 1929, DP. John Kenneth Galbraith, *The Great Crash: 1929* (Boston: Houghton Mifflin Co., 1954), 116–117.

4. Dulles address, February 13, 1930, DP.

5. Dulles "Remarks," October 20, 1939, DP.

6. Broadus Mitchell, *Depression Decade: From New Era Through New Deal, 1929–1941* (New York: Harper & Row, 1947), 60–61; Arthur M. Schlesinger, Jr., *The Crisis of the Old Order, 1919–1933* (Boston: Houghton Mifflin Co., 1957), 162–164.

7. An excellent survey of major world economic developments in this period can be found in Charles P. Kindleberger, *The World in Depression, 1929–1939* (Berkeley: University of California Press, 1973), particularly chapter 6.

8. Notes on conversations concerning moratorium and memorandum left with President, June 1931, DP.

9. Kindleberger, op. cit., chapters 7–8; Mitchell, op. cit., 444.

10. Confidential Report to the Federal Reserve Board, November 26, 1931, DP.

11. Memorandum Concerning the Central European Situation, November 1932, DP.

12. Dulles, "The Securities Act and Foreign Lending, *Foreign Affairs*, XII (October 1933), 33–45.

13. Memorandum on "The New Deal," 1934, DP.

14. See below, chapter 8.

15. Dulles to Fred Dolbeare, November 1, 1929; Dulles addresses, April 29, 1929, February 13, 1930, DP.

16. Notes on conversations concerning moratorium and memorandum left with President, June 1931, DP.

17. Robert E. Olds to Dulles, July 3, 1931, July 17, 1931; Dulles to Robert E. Olds, August 4, 1931, DP.

18. Confidential Report to the Federal Reserve Board, November 26, 1931, DP.

19. Dulles to *The New York Times*, March 8, 1933, DP.

20. Memorandum on "The New Deal," 1934, DP.

21. Memorandum Concerning the Central European Situation, November 1932, DP.

22. Allen Dulles to Dulles, November 14, 1932, DP.

23. See below, chapter 10

24. Dulles to Cordell Hull, June 6, 1933; Report on Berlin Debt Discussions of December 1933; Report of Laird Bell and John Foster Dulles on Berlin Debt Discussions of January 1934, DP.

25. Mitchell, op. cit., 14.

26. See, for example, Dulles memorandum, August 14, 1944, DP.

CHAPTER 8

1. Dulles to *The New York Times*, March 12, 1933, DP.

2. Dulles, "The Road to Peace," *Atlantic Monthly*, 156 (October 1935), 492.

3. Ibid.

4. There were several key items in the progression toward *War, Peace and Change* (New York: Harper & Bros., 1939): beginning with "The Road to Peace" and including "Peaceful Change Within the Society of Nations," a lecture delivered at Princeton University, March 19, 1936 and a short manuscript entitled "The Problem of Peace in a Dynamic World," dated November 9, 1936, DP.

5. *War, Peace and Change*, 1–5.

6. Ibid., 6–8; "The Road to Peace," 493.

7. *War, Peace and Change*, 1–5.

8. Ibid., 30–37.

9. Ibid., 137–149.

10. "The Problem of Peace in a Dynamic World," *passim*.

11. *War, Peace and Change*, 9.

12. Ibid., 11–16.

13. "The Road to Peace," 495–498.

14. Ibid., 495–498.

15. Ibid.

16. *War, Peace and Change*, 101.

17. "The Road to Peace," 495–498.

18. *War, Peace and Change*, 115–120.

19. Ibid., 137–138; "The Road to Peace," 497.

20. "The Road to Peace," 497–499.

21. "The Problem of Peace in a Dynamic World," *passim.*

22. Ibid.; *War, Peace and Change*, 124–132.

23. "Peaceful Change Within the Society of Nations," *passim.*

24. "The Problem of Peace in a Dynamic World;" *War, Peace and Change,* 127–133.

25. Ibid.

26. "A North American Contribution to World Order," June 1939; Dulles to Henry Stimson, January 10, 1939; "Statement of an American Foreign Policy," June 1940, DP.

27. "Peaceful Change Within the Society of Nations," March 19, 1936; "The Problem of Peace in a Dynamic World," DP.

28. *"War, Peace and Change"* file, DP.

29. "The Road to Peace" 492.

30. Dulles address, April 26, 1937; Dulles to Lord Lothian, January 3, 1940, DP.

31. Dulles address, April 26, 1937, DP.

32. See, for example, *War, Peace and Change*, 120–133.

33. Dulles to John Pelenyi, April 4, 1936, DP.

34. Dulles address, April 26, 1937; *War, Peace and Change*, 122–123, 132.

35. Dulles to Lord McGowan, September 5 or 15, 1943, DP.

36. See above, pp. 24, 44–57.

37. See, for example, the interesting discussion of Kautsky's perspective in N. Gordon Levin, *Woodrow Wilson and World Politics: America's Response to War and Revolution* (New York: Oxford University Press, 1968), 28–31.

38. Dulles to Francis B. Sayre, March 20, 1936, DP. On the strategy and style of the Roosevelt Administration during the 1930s, see Lloyd C. Gardner, *Economic Aspects of New Deal Diplomacy*, (Boston: Beacon Press, 1971), *passim.*

39. "The Road to Peace" 492; Dulles "Remarks," July 3, 1937, DP.

40. "The Road to Peace," *passim;* "Peaceful Change Within the Society of Nations;" "The Problem of Peace in a Dynamic World;" DP. *War, Peace and Change,* 166.

41. "The Problem of Peace in a Dynamic World," DP.

42. Ibid.; "Peaceful Change Within the Society of Nations," DP.

43. *War, Peace and Change*, 120–133.

CHAPTER 9

1. Dulles addresses, March 18, 1939, March 22, 1939, DP.
2. Dulles address, "America's Role in World Affairs," October 28, 1939, DP.
3. Ibid.; see also another Dulles address, "The Church's Contribution Toward a Warless World," October 11, 1939, DP.
4. Dulles address, March 22, 1939, DP.
5. See above, pp. 123–126.
6. Dulles address, "America's Role in World Affairs," October 28, 1939, DP.
7. Dulles to Tertius VanDyke, October 8, 1935; Dulles address, March 18, 1939, DP. Dulles, *War, Peace and Change* (New York: Harper & Bros., 1939), 148.
8. Dulles address, March 22, 1939, DP.
9. Henry L. Stimson to Dulles, May 1, 1936, January 5, 1939, DP.
10. See above, pp. 127–131.
11. See above, pp. 123–126.
12. Dulles address, March 22, 1939; Dulles to William E. Borah, April 3, 1939, DP.
13. See, for example, Dulles address, March 22, 1939, DP.
14. "Commission to Study the Organization of Peace" folder; Dulles memorandum "The Aftermath of the World War," February 1940; Hamilton Fish Armstrong to M. E. Denner (carbon), February 16, 1940; Whitney H. Shepardson to Lionel Curtis (carbon), February 21, 1940; Frederick J. Libby to Dulles, June 22, 1939, DP.
15. Dulles to Clarence Streit, January 23, 1939; Dulles to Hugh Wilson, June 13, 1941; "Clarence Streit–Union Now" folder, DP.
16. Tertius VanDyke to Dulles, March 6, 1922; Samuel McCrea Cavert to Dulles, December 29, 1922; Sidney L. Gulick to Dulles, November 30, 1925; Mrs. A. M. Dulles to Dulles, May 21, 1937; "Presbyterian General Assembly Correspondence" file; Dulles article, "As Seen by a Layman," *Religion in Life*, (winter 1938), reprint, DP. Transcripts of interviews with Roswell P. Barnes, John Coleman Bennett, Samuel McCrea Cavert, Margaret Dulles Edwards, Henry Van Dusen, DOHP. *The Message and Decisions of Oxford on Church, Community and State.* (New York: Universal Christian Council, 1937), 3–7, 31–53, 76–88 and *passim.*
17. Federal Council of the Churches of Christ in America, *Biennial Report, 1939* (New York: 1939), 47–51.
18. Dulles address, July 1939; Dulles to Lionel Curtis, July 19, 1939; Dulles address, "The Churches and the International Situation," February 1940, DP.
19. Roswell Barnes to Dulles, January 5, 1939, DP.
20. Henry VanDusen to Dulles, with enclosure, January 11, 1940, DP.

21. Dulles to Henry VanDusen, March 18, 1940, DP.

22. Henry Sloane Coffin to Dulles, with enclosure, May 18, 1940; Dulles to Henry Sloane Coffin, May 20, 1940, DP.

23. Walter VanKirk to Dulles, May 15, 1940; Roswell Barnes to Dulles, May 28, 1940; Harry Emerson Fosdick to Dulles, May 25, 1940; William Adams Brown to Dulles, May 24, 1940; George Butterick to Dulles, June 6, 1940, DP.

24. William Adams Brown to Dulles, May 24, 1940; Dulles to William Adams Brown, June 3, 1940; Dulles to Walter VanKirk, June 13, 1940, DP. Transcript of interview with Henry P. VanDusen, DOHP. "A Statement on the Present Opportunity and Duty of Christians," in Federal Council of the Churches of Christ in America, *Biennial Report, 1940*, 182–184.

25. Dulles address, December 10, 1940, DP. Transcripts of interviews with Roswell Barnes and Henry P. VanDusen, DOHP. Federal Council of the Churches of Christ in America, *Biennial Report, 1940*, 214.

26. Transcripts of interviews with Roswell Barnes and Henry VanDusen, DOHP.

27. "A Just and Durable Peace: Memorandum of preliminary views on certain basic questions of the Committee of Direction of the Commission to Study the Bases of a Just and Durable Peace," undated but May 1941, DP. (The full name of the group was shortened very quickly to the "Commission on a Just and Durable Peace.")

28. Dulles to Arthur H. Sulzberger, May 21, 1941; "The American Churches and the International Situation," December 1940; Dulles memorandum, "Long-Range Peace Objectives," September 18, 1941, DP. Dulles, "Peace without Platitudes," *Fortune*, XXV (January 1942), 42–43, 87–88, 90.

29. "Long Range Peace Objectives," September 18, 1941; Dulles address, "Toward World Order," March 5, 1942, DP. "Peace Without Platitudes," *Fortune*.

30. See, for example, ibid. and "Statement of Guiding Principles," March 1942, DP.

31. Dulles to John Bassett Moore, January 21, 1941; "Memorandum of preliminary views. . . ."; "A Just and Durable Peace" handbook, 1941, DP.

32. See, for example, the "Commission on a Just and Durable Peace—1943" file, containing extensive information on media and publicity efforts connected with the launching of the "Six Pillars of Peace," DP.

33. "Long Range Peace Objectives," September 18, 1941, DP. "Peace Without Platitudes," *Fortune*.

34. "Analyses of Moscow Declarations in the Light of 'Six Pillars of Peace,'" November 1943; "The Churches and the Dumbarton Oaks Proposals," November 1944; "A Personal Appraisal of the Crimea Conference," February 26, 1945, DP.

35. *Time*, XXXIX (March 16, 1942), 44–45; "Statement of Guiding Principles," March 1942, DP.

36. Dulles to members of the Commission on a Just and Durable Peace, January 6, 1943, February 9, 1943; Dulles address, March 18, 1943, DP.

37. Dulles to John D. Rockefeller, Jr., March 3, 1943; "A Just and Durable Peace: Discussion of Political Propositions (Six Pillars of Peace)," March 1943, DP.

38. Dulles to Arthur Ballantine, September 22, 1943; Dulles to Wendell Willkie, September 28, 1943; Dulles to Herbert Hoover, October 5, 1943; Dulles to Sumner Welles, October 26, 1943; Dulles to Walter Yust, December 27, 1943, DP.

39. Dulles to Sumner Welles, August 19, 1942; Dulles to Sumner Welles, October 30, 1942; Sumner Welles to Dulles, November 19, 1942, DP.

40. Memorandum of conversation with Sumner Welles, March 4, 1943; "Confidential Memorandum of Conference with the President," March 26, 1943, DP.

41. Dulles to Henry VanDusen, December 23, 1943, DP.

42. "Notes taken by Bob as Foster recounted to the family his trip to England, July 1942"; "Confidential Memorandum Prepared by John Foster Dulles and Walter Van Kirk on Their Recent Visit to England," summer 1942; "A Christian Basis for Reconstruction," August 1943, DP.

43. Dulles to Sumner Welles, May 6, 1943, DP.

44. "Purposes, Agenda, Personnel of the International Round Table of Christian Leaders, Princeton, July 1943"; "A Christian Message on World Order, from the International Round Table of Christian Leaders," July 1943, DP.

45. Dulles address, December 10, 1940; Dulles address, "Christianity in This Hour," April 21, 1941, DP.

46. Dulles, "As Seen by A Layman," *Religion in Life*, Winter 1938, reprint; "A Just and Durable Peace: Memorandum of Preliminary Views. . . .", May 1941, DP.

47. "Statement of Guiding Principles," March 1942; Dulles to Sumner Welles, August 19, 1942, DP.

48. "A Righteous Faith for a Just and Durable Peace," October 1942, DP.

49. "Christian Message Address," delivered in Newark (November 4, 1943), Macon (November 8, 1943), Birmingham (November 9, 1943), and Mobile (November 10, 1943), DP.

50. Dulles address, March 18, 1943; "Analyses of Moscow Declarations. . . .", November 1943, DP.

51. Dulles to Luman Shafer, December 7, 1943, December 21, 1943, DP.

52. Ibid.; "A New Year's Statement to Public Leaders and Our People," January 1944; "Memorandum of Meeting with the President," February 15, 1944, DP.

53. Ibid.; Dulles address, "The Churches and World Order," May 16, 1944, DP.

54. Dulles to Lionel Curtis, September 19, 1944; Dulles to Brooks Emeny, October 15, 1944; Dulles address, November 28, 1944, DP.

55. Dulles address, January 16, 1945, DP.

56. "A Message to the Churches," January 1945, DP.

57. Dulles addresses, March 26, 1945, April 22, 1945, DP.

58. See below, pp. 226–234.

59. "Statement of Guiding Principles," March 1942; "Memorandum of Preliminary Views. . . .", May 1941, DP.

60. See below, pp. 169–174.

61. Dulles to Arthur Sulzberger, May 21, 1941, DP.

62. "Peace without Platitudes," *Fortune*, XXV (January 1942), 42–43, 87–88, 90; Dulles address, "Christianity in this Hour," April 21, 1941, DP.

63. "Memorandum of Preliminary Views. . . .", May 1941, DP.

64. "Long Range Peace Objectives," September 18, 1941; "Toward World Order," March 5, 1942, DP.

65. See above, pp. 98–100.

66. "Toward World Order," March 5, 1942; Dulles to Hugh Wilson, June 13, 1941, DP.

67. "Long Range Peace Objectives," September 18, 1941, DP.

68. "A Righteous Faith for a Just and Durable Peace," October 1942; "Christian Message Address," November 1943, DP.

69. See above, pp. 100–103.

70. "A Righteous Faith for a Just and Durable Peace," October 1942; Dulles address, March 18, 1943, DP.

71. Dulles to John McNeill, October 1, 1941, DP.

72. "Notes taken by Bob as Foster recounted to the family his trip to England—July 1942"; "Confidential Memorandum Prepared by John Foster Dulles and Walter W. VanKirk on Their Recent Visit to England," summer 1942, DP.

73. Dulles address, January 16, 1945; Dulles address, "Appraisal of United States' Foreign Policy," February 5, 1945, DP.

74. See below, pp. 235–252.

75. See above, pp. 56–57.

76. Dulles to Henry Van Dusen, January 18, 1944, DP.

77. "Memorandum of meeting with the president," February 15, 1944, DP.

78. See above, pp. 102–103.

79. See above, pp. 168–169.

80. Dulles address, "Toward World Order," March 18, 1942; "The Churches and the Dumbarton Oaks Proposals," October 1944; Dulles to Walter VanKirk, December 21, 1944, DP.

81. See below, pp. 254–258.

82. N. Gordon Levin, *Woodrow Wilson and World Politics: America's Response to War and Revolution* (New York: Oxford University Press, 1968), 18, 35.

83. Dulles address, May 20, 1937, DP.

CHAPTER 10

1. *Poor's Register of Directors and Executives, 1942* (New York: Standard & Poor's Corp., 1942), 1663.

2. Dulles to Sumner Welles, June 2, 1942; Dulles to Zygmunt Kerpinski, June 30, 1944; Dulles to Luman J. Shafer, with enclosure, October 2, 1944; Dulles to Robert Y. Johnson, with enclosure, October 8, 1946, DP.

3. Transcript of interview with Margaret Dulles Edwards, DOHP.

4. See above p. 78. See also, for example, Dulles to William Nelson Cromwell, June 2, 1936; Dulles to Frank O. Lowden, October 26, 1936, DP.

5. Transcripts of interview with Thomas E. Dewey, DOHP.

6. Transcripts of interviews with Herbert Brownell, Thomas E. Dewey and James Hagerty, DOHP.

7. Donald Bruce Johnson, *The Republican Party and Wendell Willkie* (Urbana, Ill.: University of Illinois Press, 1960), 108. Wendell Willkie to Dulles, cable, July 8, 1940; Dulles to Wendell Willkie, August 2, 1940; "Statement of an American Foreign Policy," September 6, 1940; Dulles to William Nelson Cromwell, September 6, 1940, DP.

8. Johnson, *Republican Party and Wendell Willkie*, 125–135.

9. For interesting highlights of Dulles's gradually expanding political contacts, see Dulles's correspondence with Ruth Simms, in the "Political Data, 1939–1944" file, DP. For examples of his efforts to develop contacts with major newspapers and periodicals, see Dulles to David Lawrence, *U.S. News*, January 20, 1944; Dulles to Thomas E. Dewey, March 30, 1944; Ferdinand Lathrop Mayer to Dulles, October 20, 1941; Dulles to Ferdinand Lathrop Mayer, October 21, 1941; "Elliot," *New York Times*, to Dulles, October 20, 1941, DP. Dulles's closest personal associates and advisers were Ferdinand Lathrop Mayer, a Princeton classmate who went on to diplomatic posts in Peking, Tokyo, and Berlin and service at the Washington Conference of 1921-1922 and the Geneva Disarmament Conference of 1932; Hugh Wilson, a retired Foreign Service officer with experience in Switzerland and as Ambassador to Germany in 1938 and 1939; and "Mott" Belin, a Dupont vice president who undertook diplomatic posts in China, Turkey, and Poland. An early example of their systematized efforts to analyze American foreign policy can be traced in Dulles's memorandum to Hugh Wilson, Mott Belin, and Ferdinand Mayer, September 15, 1941, DP.

10. Johnson, *The Republican Party and Wendell Willkie*, 69–86 and *passim*; A. H. Vandenberg, Jr., ed., *The Private Papers of Senator Vandenberg* (Boston: Houghton Mifflin Co., 1952), 21–89; Robert A. Divine, *Second Chance: The*

Triumph of Internationalism in America During World War II (New York: Atheneum, 1967), *passim*; Joseph Martin, *My First Fifty Years in Politics* (New York: Doubleday, 1960), *passim*.

11. H. Alexander Smith to Dulles, August 7, 1943; Dulles to H. Alexander Smith, August 10, 1943, DP.

12. Dulles to Ruth Simms, September 15, 1943, DP.

13. *Private Papers of Senator Vandenberg*, 30; Arthur Vandenberg to Dulles, November 11, 1944, DP.

14. Arthur Vandenberg to Thomas Dewey, May 22, 1944; Dulles platform draft, May 26, 1944; Dulles to Arthur Vandenberg, May 27, 1944; Arthur Vandenberg to Dulles, May 29, 1944, June 2, 1944, June 10, 1944; Dulles to Arthur Vandenberg, June 12, 1944, DP.

15. Dulles to Sophia Dulles, August 10, 1943; Dulles to Lord McGowan, September 5 or 15, 1943; Dulles to Henry VanDusen, December 23, 1943, DP.

16. Robert A. Divine, *Foreign Policy and U.S. Presidential Elections, 1940–1948* (New York: New Viewpoints, 1974), 121–122.

17. Dulles, *War or Peace* (New York: Macmillan Co., 1948), 34–35, 123–126; Cordell Hull, *The Memoirs of Cordell Hull* (New York: Macmillan Co., 1948), 2 volumes, II, 1689–1695, 1708.

18. Divine, *Foreign Policy*, 117, 131. See for example, Dulles to Thomas Dewey, January 26, 1944, and October 17, 1944, with enclosure, DP.

19. Divine, *Foreign Policy* 136.

20. Ibid., 121–125; Dulles to Hugh Wilson, September 22, 1944, September 25, 1944; Hugh Wilson to Dulles, November 8, 1944, September 30, 1944; Dulles to Thomas Dewey, October 5, 1944, DP.

21. Divine, *Foreign Policy*, 147–153.

22. Ibid., 145–147.

23. Ibid., 138–143; John L. Gaddis, *The United States and the Origins of the Cold War, 1941–1947* (New York: Columbia University Press, 1972), 146–147.

24. Dulles to Thomas Dewey, October 17, 1944, with enclosure, DP.

25. Ibid.; Dulles–Dewey press conference transcripts, August 19, 20, 1944, DP.

26. Dulles to Laird Bell, November 21, 1944; Arthur Vandenberg to Dulles, November 11, 1944, DP.

27. Arthur Vandenberg to Dulles, June 2, 1944; November 11, 1944; Dulles to Arthur Vandenberg, November 10, 1944, DP.

28. "Carnegie Endowment for International Peace" and "Rockefeller Foundation" files; Philip Keebler to Dulles, August 14, 1944, DP.

29. Dulles, "A Righteous Faith," *Life*, XIII (December 28, 1942), 49–50; Joseph Chamberlain, "John Foster Dulles," *Life*, XVII (August 21, 1944), 84–86.

30. Divine, *Second Chance*, *passim*. See above, pp. 227–229.

31. Arthur Vandenberg to Dulles, February 17, 1945, February 22, 1945, March

21, 1945; Dulles to Arthur Vandenberg, February 21, 1945, March 20, 1945; Edward Stettinius to Dulles, March 31, 1945, DP. *Private Papers of Senator Vandenberg,* 157.

32. Dulles address, November 28, 1944, DP. Walter Millis, ed., *The Forrestal Diaries* (New York: Viking Press, 1951), 41–42.

33. See above, pp. 202–203.

34. Dulles to Bishop Oxnam, November 8, 1944; Dulles address, November 24, 1944, DP.

35. Dulles to Arthur Vandenberg, February 21, 1945; Dulles to Walter Lippmann, March 15, 1945; Dulles address, March 17, 1945, DP. *Private Papers of Senator Vandenberg,* 146–166.

36. Ruth B. Russell, *A History of the United Nations Charter: The Role of the United States, 1940–1945* (Washington, D.C.: Brookings Insitution, 1958), chapter XXVII (hereafter referred to as "Russell").

37. *Foreign Relations of the United States: Diplomatic Papers, 1945,* Volume I, General: The United Nations (Washington, D.C.: Government Printing Office, 1967), 1319. (Hereafter referred to as "FR, 1945, I.")

38. Russell, chapter XXVIII.

39. Ibid., chapters XXIX, XXX, XXXI.

40. A list of all delegation discussions in which Dulles participated would be too lengthy to include here. Important yet representative examples would include meetings on the regional question: FR, 1945, I, 591–596, 617–628, 644, 648–649, 651–658, 676; and the "domestic jurisdiction" question, ibid., 893, 945–948. Dulles's memoranda for the delegation include those of May 8 and 11 on regional organizations, May 7 on withdrawal, May 25 and June 6 on the Security Council veto and June 20 on the right of discussion in the General Assembly, all in DP.

41. FR, 1945, I, 870–871. Dulles memorandum, May 28, 1945, DP.

42. FR, 1945, I, 931–932, 1095–1098, 1272–1273.

43. Transcript of interview with Douglas Mode, DOHP. San Francisco Diary of Janet Avery Dulles, DP.

44. FR, 1945, I, 640, 660, 698–704, 705, 922.

45. Dulles memoranda, May 8, 1945 (#19), May 11, 1945, DP. FR, 1945, I, 596.

46. Dulles memoranda, May 8, 1945 (#17), May 11, 1945, DP. FR, 1945, I, 637.

47. FR., 1945, I, 590, 620–621. See below pp. 312–321, for more information on the emerging Dulles tendency to draw distinctions between an American role in Eastern as opposed to Western Europe.

48. FR, 1945, I, 676, 678.

49. Ibid., 644.

50. Ibid., 705; Russell, 693–712.

51. FR, 1945, I, 648–649. Dulles memorandum, May 8, 1945 (#17), DP.

52. Introductory overview, Dulles file on San Francisco Conference, undated; Dulles memorandum, May 25, 1945, DP. *FR*, 1945, I, 883.

53. *FR*, 1945, I, 771, 873, 1090. Dulles memoranda, May 25, 1945, June 8, 1945, DP. *Private Papers of Senator Vandenberg*, 203, 207.

54. For example, Dulles to Brooks Emeny, October 15, 1944, DP. See above, pp. 191, 207–209.

55. *FR*, 1945, I, 308–309.

56. Ibid., 332–333, 765, 850–851, 980. Dulles memoranda, May 4, May 23, May 24, June 11, June 12, June 14 (2), 1945, DP.

57. *FR*, 1945, I, 308–309.

58. Ibid., 320, 1417–1420.

59. Ibid., 247–248, 780–781, 1286–1287. Dulles memorandum, May 17, 1945, DP.

60. Florence Snell to Reuben Crispell, May 29, 1945; Clement Eaton to Dulles, June 23, 1945, DP.

61. Dulles to Allen Dulles, December 8, 1945; Dulles to Arthur Vandenberg, February 21, 1945, March 20, 1945, DP.

62. Dulles remarks, June 26, 1945; Dulles testimony, July 13, 1945; Dulles to Phillip Brown, July 18, 1945, DP.

63. Frederick Libby to Dulles, December 20, 1945; Dulles to Frederick Libby, December 24, 1945, DP.

64. See above, pp. 101–103. Dulles to William Adams Brown, May 1940, DP.

CHAPTER 11

1. Dulles address, February 5, 1945; "New Year's Statement," January 22, 1944, DP.

2. "Christian Action on Four Fronts for Peace," November 1945, DP. Dulles, "Thoughts on Soviet Foreign Policy and What to Do About It," *Life*, June 3, 1946, 124.

3. Dulles's activities and thoughts on these various positions are detailed in chapters 12–17, below.

4. Dulles to Dewitt Wallace, May 22, 1946, DP. Dulles, "Thoughts on Soviet Foreign Policy. . .," *Life*, June 3, 1946, 112–126; June 10, 1946, 119–130.

5. George Kennan, *Memoirs, 1925–1950* (New York: Bantam Books, 1969), 309.

6. Dulles to Roswell P. Barnes, May 8, 1946, DP.

7. See above, pp. 25–28.

8. Dulles to John W. Davis, July 18, 1924 and undated memorandum, DP. See above, pp. 63–64.

9. Dulles to Arthur Sulzberger, May 21, 1941; Dulles to Lammot Dupont, December 30, 1941; Dulles addresses, October 11, 1939, October 28, 1939, DP.

10. Dulles to S. L. W. Mellen, January 6, 1942; Dulles to Thomas E. Dewey, January 26, 1944, DP.

11. Dulles to William A. Irwin, November 17, 1941; Dulles to Lewis Brown, March 22, 1943; Dulles to Nelson Gaskill, March 8, 1944; Dulles to J. H. Oldham, September 13, 1944, DP.

12. "Confidential Memorandum Prepared by John Foster Dulles and Walter W. VanKirk on Their Recent Visit to England," summer 1942; Dulles to Lord Astor, February 18, 1943, DP.

13. Dulles to Lord Astor, February 18, 1943, DP.

14. Dulles to Herbert Brownell, October 18, 1944, DP.

15. Dulles to Thomas E. Dewey, January 26, 1944; Dulles addresses, November 24, 1944, January 16, 1945; "A Christian Message on World Order from the International Round Table of Christian Leaders," July 1943, DP.

16. Dulles to Henry Luce, September 29, 1943; Dulles to Marquis Childs, February 29, 1944; Dulles address, March 26, 1945; "A Personal Appraisal of the Crimea Conference," February 26, 1945, DP.

17. Dulles to Lord Astor, February 18, 1943; "Confidential Memorandum of conference with the President," March 26, 1943, DP.

18. "A Personal Appraisal of the Crimea Conference," February 26, 1945, DP.

19. Dulles address, February 5, 1945, DP.

20. Dulles to Thomas E. Dewey, October 9, 1944, October 29, 1944; Dulles to Walter Lippman, October 22, 1944, DP.

21. Dulles to John Higgins, December 4, 1945; Dulles address, February 28, 1946; Dulles address and interview, March 1, 1946; Dulles memoranda, May 17, 1945, June 6, 1945, San Francisco Conference file, DP. Dulles, "Thoughts on Soviet Foreign Policy. . .," *Life*, June 3, 1946, p. 113. *Foreign Relations of the United States: Diplomatic Papers, 1945*, Volume I: General, The United Nations (Washington: Government Printing Office, 1967), 641–650. (This volume of *Foreign Relations* will hereafter be referred to as *FR*, 1945, I.)

22. Dulles address, June 29, 1945; Dulles memorandum, May 17, 1945, San Francisco Conference file, DP.

23. *FR*, 1945, I, 644.

24. Dulles memorandum, undated, London Council of Foreign Ministers papers, Volume II, Part I, 232.

25. Dulles memorandum, September 27, 1945, London Council of Foreign Ministers papers, Volume II, Part II, 297–298.

26. Dulles address, October 6, 1945, DP. John Lewis Gaddis, *The United States and the Origins of the Cold War, 1941–1947* (New York: Columbia University Press, 1972), 290–291.

27. Dulles address, March 1, 1946; "Christian Action on Four Fronts for Peace," November 1945; "The Churches and World Order," March 1946, DP.

28. Arthur Vandenberg to Dulles, April 7, 1946, May 13, 1946; Allen W. Dulles to Dulles, May 14, 1946; Dulles to Roswell Barnes, May 8, 1946; Henry Luce to Dulles, June 16, 1946, DP.

29. A. J. Muste to Dulles, June 10, 1946, July 1, 1946; Dulles to A. J. Muste, June 17, 1946; H. M. Robins to Dulles, September 11, 1946; Dulles to H. M. Robins, September 17, 1946, DP.

30. Dulles address, September 8, 1941, DP.

31. Dulles to Irving Fisher, September 23, 1946, DP.

32. See above, pp. 195–196, 200–203.

33. Dulles addresses, November 15, 1945, February 22, 1946; "Christian Action of Four Fronts for Peace," November 1945; "The Churches and World Order," March 1946, DP.

34. See, for example, Dulles address, September 8, 1946, DP.

35. Dulles addresses, October 6, November 15, December 7, 1945, DP.

36. Allen W. Dulles to Dulles, May 14, 1946; Arthur Vandenberg to Dulles, April 7, May 13, 1946, DP.

37. See above, pp. 200–203.

38. See above, pp. 254–258.

39. Dulles to Dewitt Wallace, May 22, 1946; Dulles to Walter Lippmann, June 4, 1946, February 11, 1948; Dulles to James P. Warburg, September 16, 1946; Dulles address, September 8, 1946, DP.

40. Dulles to Arthur Vandenberg, September 4, 1945, DP.

41. For discussions of the utilization of anticommunism by other U.S. policy makers, see Richard M. Freeland, *The Truman Doctrine and the Origins of McCarthyism: Foreign Policy, Domestic Politics and Internal Security, 1946–1948* (New York: Schocken Books, 1974); Lloyd C. Gardner, *Architects of Illusion: Men and Ideas in American Foreign Policy* (Chicago: Quandrangle Books, 1970); and Joyce and Gabriel Kolko, *The Limits of Power: The World and United States Foreign Policy, 1945–1954* (New York: Harper & Row, 1972).

CHAPTER 12

1. Dulles to Chandler Smith, November 11, 1945; Dulles address, September 8, 1946, DP.

2. Dulles addresses, December 7, 1945, February 22, 1946, DP.

3. Dulles addresses, March 18, 1943, November 15, 1945, February 22, 1946; Dulles testimony, July 13, 1945; "Christian Action on Four Fronts for Peace" statement, November 1945, DP.

4. Dulles to Arthur Vandenberg, September 12, 1946; Dulles address and interview, March 1, 1946; "Crossroads of American Foreign Policy" statement, July 1, 1947, DP.

5. Dulles statement for *Look*, December 10, 1945; Dulles statement for *New York Times*, June 10, 1946, DP. Dulles, "Thoughts on Soviet Foreign Policy and What to Do About It," *Life*, June 10, 1946, p. 122.

6. Dulles addresses, January 17, 1947, June 18, 1947; "Soviet–American Relations" statement, October 1946; "Crossroads" statement, July 1, 1947, DP.

7. Dulles address, February 10, 1947; "Soviet–American Relations" statement, October 1946, DP. Dulles, "Thoughts on Soviet Foreign Policy," *Life*, June 10, 1946, p. 122.

8. Dulles address, January 17, 1947; "Crossroads" statement, July 1, 1947, DP. Dulles, "Thoughts on Soviet Foreign Policy." *Life*, June 10, 1946, pp. 122, 124.

9. Dulles address, February 10, 1947, DP. Dulles, "Thoughts on Soviet Foreign Policy," *Life*, June 10, 1946, p. 119.

10. Dulles addresses, January 17, 1947, June 18, 1947; "The Churches and World Order" statement, March 1946, DP. Dulles, "Thoughts on Soviet Foreign Policy," *Life*, June 10, 1946, pp. 120, 122, 130.

11. Dulles address, February 10, 1947, DP. Dulles, "Thoughts on Soviet Foreign Policy," *Life*, June 10, 1946, pp. 119–121.

12. Arthur Vandenberg to Dulles, April 7, 1946, May 13, 1946, DP.

13. Arthur Vandenberg to Dulles, May 13, 1946, DP.

14. Dulles memorandum, September 6, 1940; Dulles address, June 1939, DP.

15. Dulles to Thomas E. Dewey, October 9, 1941; Dulles addresses, March 5, 1942, January 16, 1945; "Long Range Peace Objectives" statement, September 1941, DP.

16. Dulles to Whitney Shepardson, April 28, 1942; Dulles to Lord McGowan, September 5, 1943; Dulles to David Lawrence, October 6, 1944; Dulles address, March 5, 1942, DP.

17. Dulles interview, December 19, 1944; Dulles press conference, August 19, 1944, DP.

18. Dulles to Thomas Lamont, October 1, 1941; "A Christian Message on World Order, from the International Round Table of Christian Leaders," July 1943; minutes of March 7, 1944 meeting, Commission on a Just and Durable Peace file, DP.

19. Dulles to Frederick Stern, November 20, 1942; Dulles to Raymond Buell, September 5, 1944; "A Message from the Cleveland Study Conference," statement January 1945; notes on trip to England, July 1942; minutes of March 7, 1944 meeting, Commission on a Just and Durable Peace file, DP.

20. Notes on trip to England, July 1942, DP. See above, pp. 202–203.

21. Notes on trip to England, July 1942, DP.

22. Memorandum on meeting with President Roosevelt, March 1943, DP.

23. Ibid. Dulles to Sumner Welles, May 6, 1943; Dulles address, January 16, 1945; memorandum on Yalta Conference, February 26, 1945, DP.

24. Dulles memoranda, May 24, 1945, June 20, 1945, San Francisco Conference file; London Council of Foreign Ministers files, DP. Dulles, "Thoughts on Soviet Foreign Policy," *Life,* June 3, 1946, pp. 114–116.

25. See above, p. 211.

26. Dulles memoranda, May 11, 1945, May 17, 1945, San Francisco Conference file; London Council of Foreign Ministers files, Volume II, Part I, p. 232 and Volume II, Part II, p. 480; "Christian Action on Four Fronts for Peace" statement, November 1945, DP. *Foreign Relations of the United States: Diplomatic Papers, 1945,* Volume I: General, The United Nations (Washington: Government Printing Office, 1967), p. 644.

27. Dulles to Laurence A. Steinhardt, June 10, 1947, September 11, 1947, December 11, 1947, May 6, 1948, June 15, 1948; Laurence A. Steinhardt to Allen W. Dulles, August 4, 1948, Laurence A. Steinhardt Papers, Library of Congress, Washington, D.C.

28. Dulles to Thomas E. Dewey, October 9, 1944, October 22, 1944; Dulles memorandum, May 16, 1944, DP. Robert A. Divine, *Foreign Policy and U.S. Presidential Elections, 1940–1948* (New York: New Viewpoints, 1974), pp. 140–141. See above, pp. 231–232.

29. See below, pp. 360–362.

30. Allen Dulles to Dulles, February 6, 1945, DP.

31. Dulles to Charles Halleck, November 19, 1945; Dulles to Arthur Vandenberg, December 17, 1945; Dulles to Ivor Thomas, August 22, 1947; Dulles addresses, December 7, 1945, March 1, 1946; "Christian Action on Four Fronts for Peace," November 1945, DP.

32. Arthur Vandenberg to Dulles, December 19, 1945, DP.

33. Arthur Vandenberg to Dulles, December 19, 1945; Dulles to Arthur Vandenberg, April 26, 1946; Dulles to Clement Eaton, July 15, 1946; Dulles address, February 28, 1946; "Faith and Works" statement, March 1946, DP.

34. Dulles to Ferdinand Mayer, July 15, 1946, September 24, 1946; Dulles to Arthur Vandenberg, September 12, 1946; Dulles to James Warburg, September 16, 1946, DP.

35. Dulles address, January 17, 1947, DP.

36. Dulles to Ivor Thomas, February 5, 1947; Dulles to Geoffrey Parsons, February 6, 1947; Bernard Baruch to Dulles, February 8, 1947; Dulles to Arthur Vandenberg, February 9, 1947, March 3, 1947; Dulles addresses, January 25, 1947, February 10, 1947; Dulles press conference, February 10, 1947; Dulles press clippings, January 17, 1947, January 21, 1947, DP.

37. John Gimble, *The Origins of the Marshall Plan* (Stanford: Stanford University Press, 1976), 53–175. Joyce and Gabriel Kolko, *The Limits of Power: The World and United States Foreign Policy, 1945-1954* (New York: Harper & Row, 1972), 121, 137, 139, 166, 167, and 111–175 *passim*.

38. Ibid.

39. Walter Lippmann editorial, in Dulles press clippings, January 21, 1947, DP.

40. Dulles to George C. Marshall, February 9, 1947; Dulles memorandum, February 26, 1947, DP.

CHAPTER 13

1. Dulles address, February 28, 1946, DP. See above, pp. 291–292, 303–307.

2. Dulles address, January 17, 1947, DP.

3. Dulles addresses, January 17, 1947, January 25, 1947; Dulles memorandum, February 26, 1947, DP.

4. Dulles addresses, December 7, 1945, January 17, 1947, January 25, 1947, DP. See above, pp. 324–328.

5. Dulles address, January 17, 1947, DP.

6. Dulles addresses, January 17, 1947, January 25, 1947, DP.

7. Dulles address and press conference, February 10, 1947, DP.

8. Dulles address, December 7, 1945, DP. See above, pp. 163–168, 206–209.

9. Dulles address, March 11, 1948, DP.

10. Dulles memorandum, February 26, 1947, DP. John Gimbel, *The Origins of the Marshall Plan* (Stanford: Stanford University Press, 1976), 179–186. Joyce and Gabriel Kolko, *The Limits of Power: The World and United States Foreign Policy, 1945-1954* (New York: Harper & Row, 1972), 350–351.

11. See, for example, Marshall's statement of March 17, 1947, in Volume II, Part I of Dulles's collected papers from the Moscow Council of Foreign Ministers meetings, DP. (Dulles's collection will hereafter be cited as MCFM, with appropriate volume and item indicated.)

12. Gimble, *The Origins of the Marshall Plan*, 124–126, 188, 229–233.

13. Ibid., 186–193.

14. Dulles address, January 17, 1947, DP.

15. Dulles to Arthur Vandenberg, March 22, 1947; Dulles addresses, April 29, 1947; Dulles memorandum, March 30, 1947, MCFM, I, DP.

16. Dulles addresses, April 29, 1947, June 6, 1947; Dulles memorandum, March 7, 1947, MCFM, I, DP.

17. Ibid.

18. *Foreign Relations of the United States: Diplomatic Papers, 1947*, Volume II: Council of Foreign Ministers; Germany and Austria (Washington, D.C.: Government Printing Office, 1972), 220–221, 324, 339. (Hereafter cited as FR, 1947, II.)

19. Dulles address, April 29, 1947; Dulles memorandum, March 7, 1947, MCFM, I, DP.

20. Dulles to Arthur Vandenberg, March 22, 1947; undated Dulles memorandum, approximately April 7, 1947, item 12, MCFM, I, DP. *FR, 1947*, II, 323–328.

21. Undated George Marshall note to Dulles and Dulles note to George Marshall, item 11, MCFM, I, DP. Gimbel, *The Origins of the Marshall Plan*, 198–199.

22. Dulles address, April 29, 1947, DP.

23. Dulles press clipping, April 29, 1947, DP. Joyce and Gabriel Kolko, *The Limits of Power*, 141.

24. Dulles to Arthur Vandenberg, March 29, 1947; Dulles address, January 17, 1947; Dulles press conference, February 10, 1947; Dulles memorandum, March 21, 1947, MCFM, I, DP.

25. Dulles to Homer Ferguson, May 23, 1947; Dulles addresses, April 29, 1947, June 6, 1947, DP.

26. Dulles to Arthur Vandenberg, April 10, 1947, July 21, 1947; Dulles to Paul Hutchinson, June 24, 1947, DP.

27. Dulles to Benjamin Cohen, June 23, 1947; Dulles to Paul Hutchinson, June 24, 1947; Dulles to Leroy Foster, June 25, 1947; Dulles memorandum, July 1, 1947, DP.

28. Dulles to Arthur Vandenberg, July 21, 1947; Dulles addresses, November 14, 1947, January 17, 1948, February 2, 1948; Dulles testimony to Senate Foreign Relations Committee, January 20, 1948, DP.

29. Dulles to Thomas E. Dewey, January 30, 1948; Dulles testimoney to Senate Foreign Relations Committee, January 20, 1948, DP.

30. Dulles address, February 2, 1948; Dulles testimony to Senate Foreign Relations Committee, January 20, 1948, DP.

31. Dulles addresses, December 11, 1947, January 17, 1948, February 2, 1948; Dulles memorandum, December 16, 1947; Dulles testimony to Senate Foreign Relations Committee, January 20, 1948, DP.

32. Dulles testimony to Senate Foreign Relations Committee, January 20, 1948, DP.

33. Dulles address, March 11, 1948; Dulles statement, December 24, 1947, DP.

34. Richard M. Freeland, *The Truman Doctrine and the Origins of McCarthyism: Foreign Policy, Domestic Politics, and Internal Security, 1946–1948* (New York: Schocken Books, 1974), 246–292.

CHAPTER 14

1. Ferdinand L. Mayer to Dulles, March 19, 1948; Dulles to Ferdinand L. Mayer, March 22, 1948, DP.

2. Walter LaFeber, *America, Russia and the Cold War, 1945–1975*, 3rd ed. (New York: John Wiley and Sons, 1976), 75–76. Arthur H. Vandenberg, Jr., ed., *The Private Papers of Senator Vandenberg* (Boston: Houghton Mifflin, 1952), 399–407.

3. Dulles Memorandum, April 27, 1948, DP.

4. Robert A. Divine, *Foreign Policy and U.S. Presidential Elections, 1940–1948* (New York: New Viewpoints, 1974), 167–171, 188–196, 210–214. *The Private Papers of Senator Vandenberg*, 421–445.

5. See above, p. 225. Divine, *Foreign Policy and U.S. Presidential Elections*, 213–214. Donald Bruce Johnson, comp., *Naitonal Party Platforms*, 2 vols. (Urbana: University of Illinois Press, 1978), I, 453–454.

6. Arthur Vandenberg to Dulles, August 9, 1948; Dulles to Arthur Vandenberg, August 31, 1948; Dulles platform draft, June 1, 1948, DP.

7. Dulles platform drafts, June 1, 1948, June 8, 1948, DP.

8. Divine, *Foreign Policy and U.S. Presidential Elections*, 223–224. *New York Times*, July 2, 1948.

9. Arthur Vandenberg to Dulles, July 2, 1948, August 21, 1948; Arthur Vandenberg to Herbert Brownell, September 23, 1948, Arthur Vandenberg Papers, William L. Clements Library, University of Michigan, Ann Arbor, Michigan. (The Vandenberg Papers will hereafter be cited as VP.)

10. Arthur Vandenberg to Dulles, July 2, 1948, August 9, 1948, VP.

11. Dulles cable to Thomas E. Dewey, October 22, 1948, October 30, 1948; Dulles memorandum, October 26, 1948, DP. Divine, *Foreign Policy and U.S. Presidential Elections*, 224, 243–244.

12. Dulles memorandum, July 20, 1948, DP.

13. Dulles–Thomas E. Dewey press conference, September 17, 1948, DP. Divine, *Foreign Policy and U.S. Presidential Elections*, 245.

14. Dulles to Arthur Vandenberg, September 20, 1948; Dulles cables to Thomas E. Dewey, September 27, 1948, September 28, 1948, October 23, 1948, DP. Divine, *Foreign Policy and U.S. Presidential Elections*, 250–254, 262–266. Johnson, *National Party Platforms*, 453.

15. Dulles cables to Thomas E. Dewey, October 21, 1948, October 25, 1948, DP. Johnson, *National Party Platforms*, 453.

16. Earl Latham, *The Communist Controversy in Washington: From the New Deal to McCarthy* (Cambridge: Harvard University Press, 1966), 184–194. John Chabot Smith, *Alger Hiss: The True Story* (New York: Holt, Rinehart & Winston, 1976).

17. Dulles memorandum, December 30, 1948; Carnegie Endowment file, 1944–1946, DP.

18. Larry S. Davidow to Dulles, December 23, 1946; Dulles to Larry S. Davidow, undated but December 1946 or January 1947; Alfred Kohlberg to Dulles, February 24, 1947; Dulles memorandum, December 30, 1948, DP.

19. Dulles to Walter Judd, March 22, 1948; Allen W. Dulles to Malcolm Muir, May 4, 1950; Dulles memoranda, December 30, 1948, March 18, 1948, DP.

20. Smith, *Alger Hiss*, 160–161.

21. Dulles to Philip Jessup, August 9, 1948; Dulles to Eliot Wadsworth, September 7, 1948; Allen W. Dulles to Malcolm Muir, May 4, 1950; Dulles memoranda, March 18, 1948, December 30, 1948, DP. Richard Nixon, *Six Crises* (London: W. H. Allen, 1962), 21. Smith, *Alger Hiss*, 160–234.

22. Dulles to Ferdinand L. Mayer, September 7, 1948; Dulles memorandum, August 20, 1948, DP. Dulles to Arthur Vandenberg, August 20, 1948, VP. Divine, *Foreign Policy and U.S Presidential Elections*, 269.

23. A good overview of the background to and early stages of the Berlin Crisis can be found in W. Phillips Davison, *The Berlin Blockade: A Study in Cold War Politics* (Princeton: Princeton University Press, 1958), 3–151.

24. Davison, *The Berlin Blockade*, 123–124, 128.

25. Dulles memoranda, July 19, 1948, July 22, 1948, DP.

26. Dulles memoranda, July 19, 1948, July 22, 1948, DP. Divine, *Foreign Policy and U.S. Presidential Elections*, 222. Walter Millis, ed., *The Forrestal Diaries* (New York: Viking Press, 1951), 459. Harry S. Truman, *Memoirs, Volume II: Years of Trial and Hope* (New York: Signet Books, 1965), 151.

27. Dulles memoranda, July 19, 1948, July 22, 1948, DP.

28. James Reston to Arthur Krock, September 28, 1948, Arthur Krock Papers, Princeton University Library, Princeton, New Jersey.

29. Truman, *Memoirs*, II, 149–151.

30. Dulles memoranda, July 19, 1948, July 22, 1948, DP.

31. Dulles cable to Thomas E. Dewey, October 22, 1948, DP. Divine, *Foreign Policy and U.S. Presidential Elections*, 223–225.

32. Dulles to Arthur Vandenberg, August 17, 1948; Dulles memorandum, August 20, 1948, DP.

33. Dulles to Arthur Vandenberg, September 22, 1948, September 28, 1948; Dulles cables to Thomas E. Dewey, September 22, 1948, September 24, 1948; Arthur Vandenberg statement, September 10, 1948, DP. Davison, *The Berlin Blockade*, 237–253.

34. Dulles cables to Thomas E. Dewey, September 24, 1948, September 28, 1948, October 21, 1948, October 22, 1948; Dulles statement, October 17, 1948, DP. *New York Times*, October 6, 1948.

35. Dulles memorandum, October 26, 1948, DP. Divine, *Foreign Policy and U.S. Presidential Elections*, 267–268.

36. Dulles memorandum, October 26, 1948, DP.

37. Dulles memorandum, October 25, 1948, DP.

38. Dulles cables to Thomas E Dewey, October 22, 1948, October 23, 1948, October 25, 1948; Dulles memoranda, October 25, 1948, October 26, 1948, DP.

39. Dulles memoranda, October 25, 1948, October 26, 1948, DP.

40. Dulles to Allen W. Dulles, November 4, 1948; Arthur Vandenberg to Dulles, November 13, 1948, DP. Divine, *Foreign Policy and U.S. Presidential Elections*, 271–276 and 167–270 *passim*.

41. Dulles cable to Thomas E. Dewey, November 3, 1948, DP.

42. Dulles to Harold Dodds, February 21, 1949; Dulles addresses, March 6, 1949, March 8, 1949, April 25, 1949, for example, DP.

43. Commission on a Just and Durable Peace to all United States Senators, April 22, 1949; Dulles address, March 18, 1948; Dulles testimony, May 4, 1949, DP. See below, pp. 426–430.

44. Dulles memorandum, October 26, 1948; Dulles address, March 18, 1949; Dulles testimony, May 4, 1949, DP.

45. Dulles memoranda, February 11, 1949, February 14, 1949; Dulles address, July 12, 1949; Dulles testimony, May 4, 1949, DP.

46. Dulles to Arthur Vandenberg, March 29, 1949; Dulles memoranda, February 5, 1949, February 8, 1949, February 11, 1949, February 12, 1949, February 14, 1949; Dulles testimony, May 4, 1949, DP.

47. See above, Chapter 13.

48. Dean Acheson, *Present at the Creation: My Years in the State Department* (New York: W. W. Norton, 1969), Chapters 30, 32 *passim*.

49. Dulles press conference, June 22, 1949, DP. Acheson, *Present at the Creation*, 291–301. *New York Times*, May 25, 1949, June 12, 1949.

50. Transcript of interview with Thomas E. Dewey, Dulles Oral History Project, Princeton University Library, Princeton, New Jersey.

51. Dulles address, July 11, 1949, DP.

52. Dulles statements, July 22, 1949, July 28, 1949, DP. *New York Times*, July 13, 1949.

53. Dulles statement, July 22, 1949, DP. Acheson, *Present at the Creation*, 309–313.

54. Dulles interview, November 8, 1949, DP. Transcript of interview with R. O'Connor, Dulles Oral History Project, Princeton University Library, Princeton, New Jersey.

55. *New York Times*, September 8, 1949, September 16, 1949.

56. Dulles interview, November 8, 1949, DP. *New York Times*, September 16, 1949.

57. Dulles address, October 25, 1949; Dulles interview, November 8, 1949; Dulles article for *Daily Compass*, September 1949, DP. *New York Times*, September 8, 1949, September 16, 1949, September 29, 1949, October 14, 1949, October 16, 1949.

58. Dulles memorandum, September 1949, Senate campaign file, DP. *New York Times*, September 16, 1949, October 5, 1949, October 14, 1949, October 16, 1949, October 29, 1949.

59. Dulles to Alfred Kohlberg, December 30, 1948; Alfred Kohlberg to Dulles, March 3, 1949; Dulles to Richard Nixon, February 10, 1950, DP. Smith, *Alger Hiss*, 585.

60. Dulles to Jacob Potofsky, undated, Senate campaign file, DP. New York Times, October 6, 1949, October 27, 1949. John Robinson Beal, *John Foster Dulles: A Biography* (New York: Harper, 1957), 113–114.

61. Dulles interview, November 8, 1949, DP. *New York Times*, October 19, 1949, October 26, 1949, October 27, 1949.

62. Dulles to Robert Murphy, December 19, 1949; Dulles memorandum, November 1949, Senate campaign file, DP.

63. Arthur Vandenberg to Dulles, September 16, 1949, DP. Transcript of interview with Thomas E. Dewey, Dulles Oral History Project, Princeton University Library, Princeton, New Jersey.

CHAPTER 15

1. See above, pp. 237–238.

2. See above, pp. 238–252.

3. Dulles address, December 14, 1945, DP. Dulles, "The General Assembly," *Foreign Affairs*, XXIV:1 (1945), 1–11.

4. Ibid.; "Christian Action on Four Fronts for Peace," November 1945, DP.

5. Dulles address and interview, March 1, 1946, DP.

6. Dulles to Arthur Vandenberg, September 12, 1946, DP. *Foreign Relations of the United States: Diplomatic Papers, 1946*, Volume I: General; The United Nations (Washington, D.C.: Government Printing Office, 1972), 172–182.

7. Dulles address, February 22, 1946; Dulles address and interview, March 1, 1946, DP.

8. Dulles address, March 1, 1946, DP.

9. Dulles statements, February 4, 1946, February 9, 1946, DP. *Foreign Relations of the United States, 1946*, I, 559.

10. Ibid.

11. Dulles address, December 14, 1946; Dulles statements, November 22, 1946, November 27, 1946, DP. See above, pp. 238–252.

12. Dulles memorandum, October 9 1946, DP. John C. Campbell, *The United States in World Affairs, 1945–1947* (New York: Published for the Council on Foreign Relations by Harper & Bros., 1947), 82 and 79–83 *passim*.

13. Dulles address, October 21, 1946, DP.

14. Dulles addresses, February 10, 1947, June 18, 1947, August 6, 1947; "Crossroads of American Foreign Policy" statement, July 1, 1947, DP. See above, pp. 285–287.

15. Dulles to Arthur Vandenberg, July 21, 1947; Dulles to Robert Lovett, August, 25, 1947; Dulles memorandum, August 26, 1947; "Crossroads of American Foreign Policy Statement," July 1, 1947, DP.

16. Stephen Xydis, *Greece and the Great Powers: Prelude to the Truman Doctrine* (Thessaloniki: Institute for Balkan Studies, 1963) provides basic information about the situation in the Balkans. A chronology of developments at the United Nations can be found in John C. Campbell, *The United States in World Affairs, 1947–1948* (New York: Published for the Council on Foreign Relations by Harper & Bros., 1948), 386–394.

17. Dulles to Arthur Vandenberg, August 28, 1947, DP.

18. Campbell, *United States in World Affairs, 1947–1948*, 399.

19. Leon Gordenker, *The United Nations and the Peaceful Unification of Korea: The Politics of Field Operations, 1947–1950* (The Hague: Martinus Nijhoff, 1959), 1–25. Campbell, *The United States in World Affairs 1947–1948*, 167–181.

20. John Allison to Dulles, September 15, 1947; Dulles interview, October 29, 1947; Dulles statements, October 25, 1947, November 4, 1947, DP. *Foreign Relations of the United States: Diplomatic Papers, 1947*, Volume VI: The Far East (Washington, D.C.: Government Printing Office, 1972), 553.

21. Dulles statement, October 9, 1947, DP. *Foreign Relations of the United States: Diplomatic Papers, 1947*, Volume I: General; The United Nations (Washington, D.C.: Government Printing Office, 1973), 177, 197, 213. Campbell, *The United States in World Affairs, 1947–1948*, 400–401.

22. *Foreign Relations of the United States, 1947*, I, 81–83.

23. See above, pp. 358–374.

24. Dulles statements, October 26, 1948, November 4, 1948, November 27, 1948, DP.

25. Dulles statement, October 26, 1948, DP. John C. Campbell, *The United States in World Affairs, 1948–1949* (New York: Published for the Council on Foreign Relations by Harper & Bros., 1949), 309.

26. *Foreign Relations of the United States: Diplomatic Papers, 1948*, Volume I: General; The United Nations (Washington, D.C.: Government Printing Office, 1975–1976), 392, 394, 441–442, 444, 448, 454–456, 462–472, 475–478, 482, 486, 490–491, 503.

27. See above, pp. 374–379.

28. Richard P. Stebbins, *The United States in World Affairs, 1949* (New York: Published for the Council on Foreign Relations by Harper & Bros., 1950), 360–361.

29. Dulles statements, April 6, 1949, April 23, 1949, May 3, 1949, DP. *Foreign Relations of the United States: Diplomatic Papers, 1949*, Volume IV: Western Europe (Washington, D.C.: Government Printing Office, 1975), 544–551.

30. *Foreign Relations of the United States, 1949*, IV, 545.

31. Dulles statement, April 23, 1949, DP. Richard P. Stebbins, *The United States in World Affairs, 1949*, 355–366.

32. Dulles address, May 18, 1951; Dulles memorandum, July 26, 1950, DP.

33. Dulles address, July 31, 1950, DP. Richard P. Stebbins, *The United States in World Affairs, 1950* (New York: Published for the Council on Foreign Relations, by Harper & Bros., 1951), 367–377.

34. *Foreign Relations of the United States: Diplomatic Papers, 1950*, Volume II: The United Nations; The Western Hemisphere (Washington, D.C.: Government Printing Office, 1976), 365–366.

35. Dulles address, October 13, 1950; Dulles statement, October 31, 1950, DP.

36. *Foreign Relations of the United States: Diplomatic Papers, 1950*, Volume VI: Asia and the Pacific (Washington, D.C.: Government Printing Office, 1977), 572–573.

37. Dulles to Frank Laubach, October 31, 1950, DP.

38. Dulles address, March 1, 1946; Dulles memorandum, March 16, 1946, DP. *Foreign Relations of the United States, 1950*, II, 132–134, 172. *Foreign Relations of the United States, 1950*, VI, 571.

39. Dulles address, January 16, 1945, DP.

CHAPTER 16

1. Dulles addresses, January 9, 1950, February 12, 1950, DP. Dulles, *War or Peace* (New York: Macmillan, 1950).

2. Ferdinand L. Mayer to Dulles, December 7, 1949, DP.

3. Dulles to Dean Acheson, March 29, 1950; Dulles address, March 10, 1950; Dulles memorandum, December 29, 1949, DP. Dulles, *War or Peace*, 180–181. Dean Acheson, *Present at the Creation: My Years at the State Department* (New York: W. W. Norton, 1969), 344–345, 354, 775.

4. Dulles address, March 10, 1950; Dulles memorandum, March 30, 1950, DP.

5. Arthur Vandenberg to Dean Acheson, March 31, 1950; Dulles memorandum, March 30, 1950; Dulles statement, April 6, 1950, DP. Acheson, *Present at the Creation*, p. 359.

6. Dulles statement, April 6, 1950, DP. Acheson, *Present at the Creation*, 432. *Foreign Relations of the United States: Diplomatic Papers, 1950*, Volume VI:

East Asia and the Pacific (Washington, D.C.: Government Printing Office, 1976), 1160–1161. (Hereafter referred to as *FR,50*, VI.)

7. Dulles to Dean Acheson, March 29, 1950; Dulles statement, April 6, 1950, DP.

8. For Dulles's early interest in China see, for example, his diary of a trip to the Far East, 1938, and cables to Thomas E. Dewey, October 1, 1948, October 21, 1948, October 25, 1948, DP. For late 1949 and early 1950, see Dulles memorandum, December 22, 1949; Dulles draft memorandum, January 8, 1950, DP.

9. Dulles addresses, July 11, 1949, April 27, 1950; Dulles statement, April 6, 1950, DP. Dulles, *War or Peace*, 2, 17.

10. Dulles addresses, January 9, 1950, March 10, 1950, April 27, 1950; Dulles interview, June 29, 1949; Dulles press conference, June 22, 1949, DP. Transcript of interview with Richard Rovere, Dulles Oral History Project, Princeton University Library, Princeton, New Jersey. Dulles, *War or Peace*, 147.

11. Dulles addresses, January 17, 1948, March 10, 1950, April 27, 1950, DP.

12. Dulles to Lord Lothian, January 3, 1940; Dulles memorandum, September 6, 1940; "Long Range Peace Objectives," September 18, 1941, DP.

13. "A Christian Message on World Order, from the International Round Table of Christian Leaders," July 1943; "Message from the Cleveland Conference" January 1945, DP.

14. See above, pp. 209–210, 291–293.

15. Dulles addresses, February 2, 1949, June 4, 1950, DP.

16. Dulles addresses, February 12, 1949, January 9, 1950, May 16, 1950, DP. Dulles, *War or Peace*, 261, 253–261 *passim*.

17. Dulles addresses, March 6, 1949, January 9, 1950, DP. Dulles, *War or Peace*, 74–75 and 74–87 *passim*.

18. Frederick S. Dunn, *Peace-making and the Settlement with Japan* (Princeton: Princeton University Press, 1963), 39–40, 58–59. FR, *50*, VI, 1110–1111, 1127.

19. *FR, 50*, VI, 1161–1166, 1207–1214, 1222–1223.

20. *FR, 50*, VI, 1162, 1211, 1222–1223.

21. Dulles address, June 4, 1950; Dulles memorandum, May 24, 1950, DP. *FR, 50*, VI, 1207–1212.

22. Dulles addresses, June 19, 1950, July 1, 1950, July 7, 1950, July 31, 1950, DP. William R. Matthews memoranda to Dulles, June–July 1950, William R. Matthews Papers, University of Pennsylvania Library, Philadelphia, Pennsylvania. *FR, 50*, VI, 1230–1237. *Foreign Relations of the United States: Diplomatic Papers, 1950*, Volume VII: Korea (Washington, D.C.: Government Printing Office, 1976), 237–238. (Hereafter referred to as *FR, 50*, VII.)

23. Dulles statements, June 30, 1950, July 4, 1950, July 19, 1950, DP. *FR, 50,* VII, 140, 238.

24. Dulles to Walter Lippmann, July 13, 1950; Dulles addresses, July 1, 1950, July 31, 1950; Dulles memorandum, July 1, 1950, DP. See below, pp. 465–467.

25. Dulles to William Matthews, July 24, 1950, DP. *FR. 50,* VII, 386–387, 514.

26. Dulles address, July 31, 1950; Dulles memorandum, July 6, 1950, DP. *FR, 50,* VI, 1243–1244.

27. *FR, 50,* VI, 1140–1147, 1162.

28. Ibid., 1230–1235, 1243.

29. Ibid., 1230, 1242–1248, 1265. Acheson, *Present at the Creation,* 430.

CHAPTER 17

1. *Foreign Relations of the United States: Diplomatic Papers, 1950,* Volume VI: East Asia and the Pacific (Washington, D.C.: Government Printing Office, 1976), 1131, 1272. (Hereafter referred to as *FR, 50,* VI.)

2. Ibid., 1211, 1272.

3. Ibid., 1296–1297.

4. Dulles to Douglas MacArthur, November 15, 1950, DP. *FR, 50,* VI, 1306–1310, 1320–1336, 1344, 1348–1349, 1352–1354.

5. *FR, 50,* VI, 1332–1336.

6. Dulles to Douglas MacArthur, November 15, 1950; Dulles to Arthur Vandenberg, November 30, 1950; Dulles memorandum, November 30, 1950, DP. *FR, 50,* VI, 162. *Foreign Relations of the United States: Diplomatic Papers, 1950,* Volume VII: Korea (Washington, D.C.: Government Printing Office, 1976), 1286. (Hereafter referred to as *FR, 50,* VII.)

7. Dulles memorandum, November 30, 1950, DP.

8. Ibid. *FR, 50,* VI, 162–164, 343–344, 543, 560.

9. *FR, 50,* VI, 1359. *Foreign Relations of the United States; Diplomatic Papers, 1951,* Volume VI: Asia and the Pacific (Washington, D.C: Government Printing Office, 1977), 781–783. (Hereafter referred to as *FR, 51,* VI.)

10. *FR, 50,* VI, 1385–1392, for example, *FR, 51,* VI, 788–790.

11. *FR, 50,* IV, 1308–1311.

12. Dulles statement, January 25, 1951, DP. *FR, 50,* VI, 1359. *FR, 51,* VI, 781–783.

13. *FR, 50,* VI, 1359. *FR, 51,* VI, 852–853. Frederick S. Dunn, *Peace-making and the Settlement with Japan* (Princeton: Princeton University Press, 1963), 166–170.

14. *FR, 51,* VI, 790–791, 804–805, 827–830, 863–870.

15. *FR, 51*, VI, 811–815.

16. Ibid., 849–851.

17. Ibid., 849–852.

18. Ibid., 171, 789, 807, 829, 849.

19. Ibid., 790.

20. Ibid., 812–813, 828.

21. Dulles statement, February 10, 1951, DP. *FR, 51*, VI, 818–819, 828.

22. Dulles to Douglas MacArthur, November 15, 1950, DP. *FR, 51*, VI, 819.

23. *FR, 50*, VII, 955. *FR, 51*, 880–883, 885–887, 900–901, 981. Dean Acheson, *Present at the Creation: My Years at the State Department* (New York: W.W. Norton, 1969), 541.

24. *FR, 50*, VI, 163. *FR, 51*, VI, 902. Dunn, *Peace-making and the Settlement with Japan*, 166 for example.

25. *FR, 50*, VI, 1308, 1322. *FR, 51*, VI, 170, 175, 789.

26. Dulles address, March 31, 1950, DP. *FR,50*, VI, 1364.

27. *FR, 51*, VI, 164–222, 789.

28. Dulles to Douglas MacArthur, November 15, 1950, DP. *FR, 50*, VI, 1361–1363. *FR, 50*, VII, 956. *FR, 51*, VI, 172–173, for example.

29. *FR,51*, VI, 970–974.

30. Dulles to Arthur Vandenberg, May 24, 1950, DP. *FR, 51*, VI, 818, 823, 903, 931, 972–973.

31. *FR, 51*, VI, 973–975.

32. Dulles address, May 25, 1951, DP. *FR, 51*, VI, 981, 982, 984.

33. *FR, 51*, VI, 931, 964–967, 981, 1118. Dunn, *Peace-making and the Settlement with Japan*, 160–161.

34. *FR, 51*, VI, 981, 1108.

35. Dulles interview, May 15, 1951, DP. *FR, 51*, VI, 953, 977.

36. *FR, 51*, VI, 1044–1045, 1105–1110.

37. *FR, 51*, VI, 1050.

38. See below, pp. 492–493.

39. Dulles press conference, August 15, 1951, DP.

40. Dulles addresses, August 15, 1951, September 9, 1951, DP.

41. Dulles address, August 15, 1951, DP. Dunn, *Peace-making and the Settlement with Japan*, 172–186.

42. Dulles interview, September 12, 1951, DP. Acheson, *Present at the Creation*, 539–550.

43. Dulles memorandum, October 3, 1951, DP. Acheson, *Present at the Creation*, 539.

44. Acheson, *Present at the Creation*, 603. *New York Times*, September 14, 1951.

45. Dulles memorandum, October 22, 1951, DP.

46. Dulles testimony to Senate Foreign Relations Committee, January 21, 1952; Dulles memorandum, April 1951, DP.

47. *FR, 51,* VI, 1443–1445, 1466–1467.

48. Dulles memoranda, January 9, 1952, March 6, 1952, DP. *FR, 51,* VI, 1467–1470.

49. Dulles address, March 31, 1951; Dulles testimony to Senate Foreign Relations Committee, January 21, 1952, DP.

50. Dulles address, September 5, 1951, DP.

51. Dulles addresses, August 15, 1951, September 5, 1951, DP.

52. Shigeru Yoshida to Dulles, July 2, 1951; Dulles address, May 25, 1951; Dulles interview, September 12, 1951, DP.

53. Dulles to Shigeru Yoshida, September 27, 1951; Dulles address, September 5, 1951, DP.

CONCLUSION

1. Dulles memorandum, October 3, 1951, DP.

2. Dulles, "Peace Without Platitudes," *Fortune,* XXV (January 1942).

3. See above, pp. 101–103.

4. Dulles address, May 18, 1950, DP.

Selected,
Annotated Bibliography

Most biographies of public figures walk a tightrope as far as background information is concerned, trying to offer enough to make sense of the thoughts and actions of their subject without falling over into extended histories of certain eras.
For those who would like more information about the times and events through
which Dulles lived before his appointment as Secretary of State, the following can
be highly recommended.

ACHESON, DEAN. *Present at the Creation: My Years in the State Department* (New
York: W. W. Norton, 1969). Acheson's advertisements for himself. Though considerably more than a pinch of salt needs to be taken to counteract the very self-
conscious and distorting wit, this is an autobiography that still offers much interesting information on important events in which its author—and John Foster
Dulles—participated.

BEALE, HOWARD K. *Theodore Roosevelt and the Rise of America to World Power*
(New York: Collier Books, 1962). In spite of a studied determination to avoid recognizing the significance of economic concerns among American foreign policy
makers, Beale's work is a superb portrait of Theodore Roosevelt and many of his

contemporaries at the turn of the century: it captures beautifully the mood of excitement—and arrogance—in which some Americans of Dulles's youth contemplated the global arena.

BRANDES, JOSEPH. *Herbert Hoover and Economic Diplomacy: Department of Commerce Policy, 1921–1928* (Pittsburgh: University of Pittsburgh Press, 1962). A good study of a key figure of the 1920s. Department of Commerce activities in the international arena suggest the vacuity of "isolationist" images of this period and indicate something of the business–government milieu in which Dulles was so active.

DIVINE, ROBERT A. *Foreign Policy and U.S. Presidential Elections, 1940–1948* (New York: New Viewpoints, 1974) and *Second Chance: The Triumph of Internationalism During World War II* (New York: Atheneum, 1967). Two extremely useful studies offering background for understanding Dulles and information on the general American scene of the 1940s. The strongest point of each is probably Divine's ability to take enormous quantities of disparate information and emerge with clear, reasonable overviews.

GARDNER, LLOYD. *Economic Aspects of New Deal Diplomacy* (Boston: Beacon Press, 1964). An essential study of the Depression's influence on American foreign policy during and after the 1930s.

GIMBEL, JOHN. *The Origins of the Marshall Plan* (Stanford: Stanford University Press, 1976). Some would argue that Gimbel has overstated the importance of a French connection for U.S. policy makers, but that potential problem aside, this book offers the clearest and most detailed information available on a key facet of post–World War II American foreign policy. It is especially relevant to John Foster Dulles, given his intense interest in Germany and European economic integration.

KOLKO, JOYCE AND GABRIEL. *The Limits of Power: The World and United States Foreign Policy, 1945–1954* (New York: Harper & Row, 1972) and GABRIEL KOLKO, *The Politics of War: The World and United States Foreign Policy, 1943–1945* (New York: Vintage Books, 1968). The two most important studies of American foreign policy in the early Cold War years, each of which combines deep research with broad vision and percipient analysis.

LAFEBER, WALTER. *America, Russia and the Cold War, 1945–1975*, 3rd. ed. (New York: John Wiley and Sons, 1976). The best brief overview of post–World War II American foreign policy and international affairs.———.*The New Empire: An Interpretation of American Expansion, 1860–1898* (Ithaca: Cornell University Press, 1963). An excellent picture of late nineteenth-century American attitudes toward world affairs and opportunities. It says much about the environment in which Dulles's grandfather worked and in which Dulles himself spent his early life.

LEVIN, N. GORDON, JR. *Woodrow Wilson and World Politics: America's Response to War and Revolution* (New York: Oxford University Press, 1968). Levin persuasively posits a Wilson who combined idealism and pragmatism—and who did it easily if not well. This study offers basic information about a President who had great influence on the young John Foster Dulles and about the milieu in which Dulles was personally active from 1917 to 1919.

MAYER, ARNO J. *Politics and Diplomacy of Peacemaking: Containment and Counter-revolution at Versailles, 1918–1919* (New York: Alfred A. Knopf, 1967) and *Wilson vs. Lenin: Political Origins of the New Diplomacy. 1917–1918* (Cleveland: World Publishing, 1964). Grand-scale studies of the international order before and immediately after World War I. Mayer's discussions of Wilson and other Americans who sought to "reform" traditional institutions and international behavior patterns offer numerous insights into both the thoughts and behavior of John Foster Dulles.

OFFNER, ARNOLD. *The Origins of the Second World War: American Foreign Policy and World Politics, 1917–1941* (New York: Praeger Publishers, 1975). The best brief overview of interwar American foreign policy.

PATERSON, THOMAS G. *Soviet-American Confrontation: Postwar Reconstruction and the Origins of the Cold War* (Baltimore: Johns Hopkins University Press, 1973). A solidly researched and precisely written study. It offers excellent background information on a subject which became of major significance to Dulles.

VANDENBERG, ARTHUR H., JR., ED. *The Private Papers of Senator Vandenberg* (Boston: Houghton Mifflin, 1952). An inimitable source: selections from Vandenberg's diaries, speeches, and letters are frequently valuable for an understanding of a friend and colleague such as Dulles of and American foreign policy in the 1940s.

WILKINS, MIRA. *The Emergence of Multinational Enterprise: American Business Abroad from the Colonial Era to 1914* (Cambridge: Harvard University Press, 1970) and *The Maturing of Multinational Enterprise: American Business Abroad From 1914 to 1970* (Cambridge: Harvard University Press, 1974). Two valuable surveys that detail the long and intense involvement of American individuals and firms in the global economy. The volume dealing with the more recent period offers particularly useful information about the business environment in which Dulles functioned for almost four decades.

WILLIAMS, WILLIAM APPLEMAN. *The Tragedy of American Diplomacy* (New York: Delta Books, Dell, 1962). The seminal revisionist work on U.S. foreign policy since the late nineteenth century: it has encouraged countless new studies of familiar subjects and still offers sensitive, insightful analysis on a wide range of issues and problems.

WILSON, JOAN HOFF. *American Business and Foreign Policy, 1920–1933* (Boston: Beacon Press, 1973). An excellent overview of business attitudes on international affairs that suggests the limitations of *Babbitt* clichés. Dulles did not always share the opinions of the corporate and banking leaders he worked with in these years, but Wilson's book offers valuable information on his environment nonetheless.

YERGIN, DANIEL. *Shattered Peace: The Origins of the Cold War and the National Security State* (Boston: Houghton Mifflin, 1977). Though there is some tendency to try too hard to squeeze policy makers into neat analytical compartments in this book, Yergin offers frequently interesting commentary on the thoughts of influential figures in the Roosevelt and Truman Administrations: their perceptions of global problems, the Soviet Union, and U.S. needs provide valuable comparisons with John Foster Dulles in these years.

Index

Pruessen, Ronald W.

John Foster Dulles